HISTORIC HOUSES
CASTLES & GARDENS

Open to the public

1992
EDITION
Completely Revised

Editor: Sheila Alcock

Published by British Leisure Publications, Windsor Court,
East Grinstead House, East Grinstead, West Sussex RH19 1XA
Telephone: (0342) 326972   Fax: (0342) 315130   Telex: 95127 INFSER G

BRITISH
Leisure
PUBLICATIONS

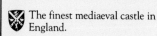

HISTORIC HOUSES CASTLES & GARDENS
in Great Britain & Ireland

INTRODUCTION

This Guide to Historic Houses, Castles and Gardens open to the public has been published annually since 1954, and this edition will be printed in full colour throughout the book for the first time.

The introductory article is by Angus Stirling, Director-General of the National Trust, and discusses the work of the National Trust in conserving the great house, its contents and its surrounding parkland.

Parham was the winner of the Historic Houses Association/Christie's Garden of the Year Award, and is featured on our title page. More information about Parham can be found on page 188.

Gardens open by courtesy of the owners in aid of the National Gardens Scheme or the Gardeners' charities, are included where these gardens are open on several occasions during the summer months.

Photographs illustrating properties administered by English Heritage were supplied by English Heritage, and those illustrating National Trust properties were supplied by the National Trust. The symbols shown against the property names denotes the administrative body, and details of these symbols are shown on page 27.

All admission charges quoted are subject to change without notice. All dates are inclusive, i.e. May to September, Weds, means first Wednesday in May to last Wednesday in September. **Opening times and dates apply to 1992 only**.

CONTENTS

Cover picture: Audley End House.

Title Page picture: Parham
winner – Christie's/HHA Garden of the Year Award.

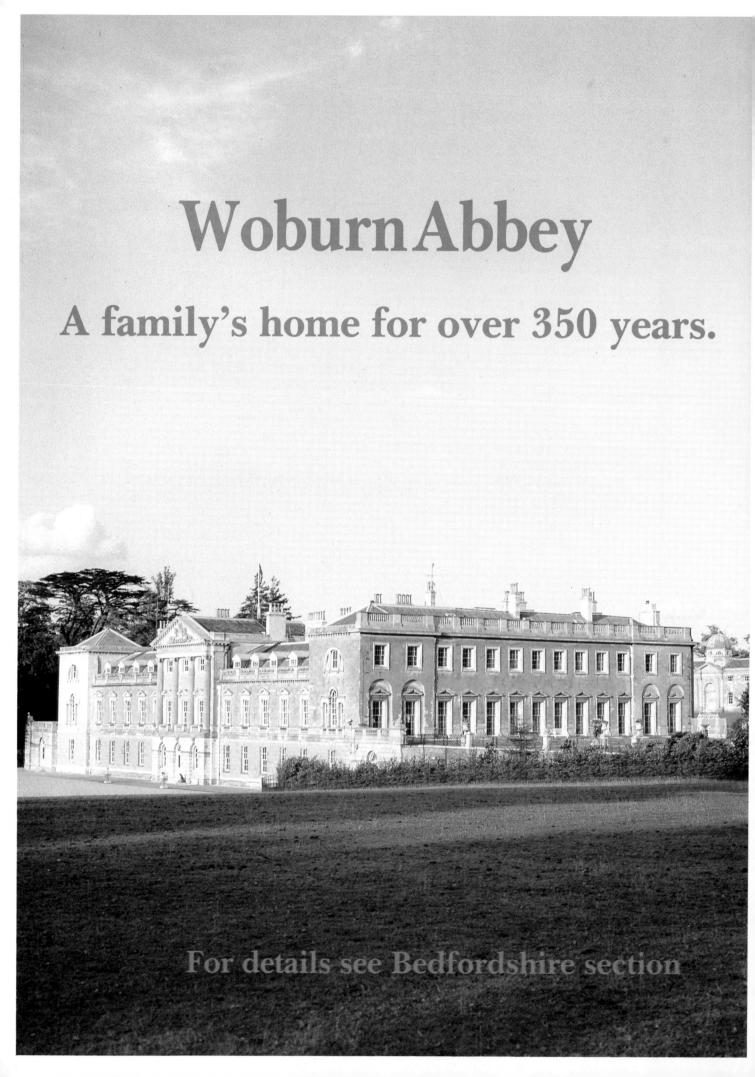

Woburn Abbey

A family's home for over 350 years.

For details see Bedfordshire section

Landscape and the Country House

by
Angus Stirling, Director-General of the National Trust

National Trust Photographic Library – Nick Meers.

Blickling Hall, distant view across the reeds and grasses of the lake bank.

The View from the Window

How often does the visitor turn from enjoying the splendour of a great room, like the Stone Hall at Houghton or the Dining Room at Kedleston, to take in the view from the window? For many, I suspect, those glimpses of park or of walled garden give as much pleasure as the fine plasterwork on the ceiling or the Old Master paintings on the walls. From the Cistercian monks of Fountains Abbey in the twelfth century to Winston Churchill at Chartwell in the 1920s, the British have always been interested in shaping the landscape that surrounds their homes. If we are no longer a nation of shopkeepers, we are assuredly a nation of gardeners. Indeed, some consider the landscape garden to be Britain's greatest single contribution to the visual arts. You can test the truth of this claim by visiting the many great gardens featured in the following pages, such as Stowe in Buckinghamshire and Stourhead in Wiltshire, which are now in the care of the National Trust; or Rousham in Oxfordshire and Levens Hall in Cumbria, happily still flourishing in private hands.

Because Britain is blessed with such a diversity of countryside, it is not surprising that it should have produced some of the world's best landscape painters. When their work still hangs in the places that inspired it, then both are enhanced. Petworth in Sussex would be impoverished without the views of the park that Turner painted for the 3rd Earl of Egremont. Yet close comparison of Turner's vision and the park today reveals how much even such created and maintained landscapes can change in a century and a half. We may attempt to mould nature, but we cannot entirely tame it. In the 1970s Dutch Elm disease cut a swathe through the English countryside, wiping out the great South Avenue at Wimpole in Cambridgeshire and leaving many parts of the country looking like a tree cemetery. Plantations which have taken generations to reach maturity can be swept away in a single night by a great storm. It will be decades before Petworth, Polesden Lacey, Knole and many other parks and gardens in southern England recover fully from the hurricane of October 1987. Comparable devastation was wrought in the South-West by

5

National Trust Photographic Library – Joe Cornish.

The red-brown slopes of Cat Bells with Derwent Water beyond and distant snow-capped mountains of Skiddaw, Lonsdale Fell and Blencathra.

the winter storms of 1990. Recovery does not, however, always mean copying what went before. What may at first appear as a catastrophe can lead to unforeseen opportunities for new creation, and can inspire in today's Reptons and Capability Browns plans which will ultimately bring greater pleasure to the eye.

An English Arcadia

Disease and tempest are merely the most dramatic of the forces of change that affect the landscape, and the people who work in it. To highlight some of these issues, the National Trust has decided to designate 1992 Landscape Year. By the end of the year we hope that everyone who loves the British countryside will have a better understanding of the work the Trust is doing to conserve the varied landscapes in its care and to provide enjoyment to those who visit them. The Trust is also organising an exhibition entitled *An English Arcadia,* which celebrates three centuries of landscape gardening at its properties. The exhibition will open at Hazlitt, Gooden & Fox Ltd in London in September 1992 and is accompanied by a comprehensive catalogue prepared by Gervase Jackson-Stops.

The Private Owner

The parks surrounding Britain's greatest country houses have usually been but one element in a much larger estate, from which, in the past, the status and economic power of their owners derived. Many of the private houses featured in this guide still lie at the centre of just such a thriving estate, and long may they continue to do so. The Trust is sometimes portrayed as a somewhat acquisitive creature, ever ready to gobble up country houses that fall on hard times. This is far from the truth. In the Trust's opinion historic houses are generally best owned and cared for by the families who have lived in them for generations. The Trust is a reluctant bride for them, unless and until it becomes clear that no other *appropriate* solution is available which would safeguard the integrity of a historic and beautiful house with its chattels and works of art intact.

The Trust supports the efforts of the HHA to secure fiscal conditions which, in today's demanding circumstances, are essential if private owners are to meet the relentless, high costs of maintenance. The private owner nowadays is in every sense a trustee of historic property for the nation, and should be treated as such by Government.

When a great country house comes to the National Trust, it has always been its policy to encourage the donor and the family to continue to live at the property whenever it is

practicable to do so. Naturally circumstances vary; such an arrangement is not always feasible, but the relationship between the Trust and its donor families reflecting the generosity so often displayed by the latter, is one which is greatly valued not only by the Trust, but also by the public. It was, for example, through the extraordinary generosity of the Acland and Bankes families that the Trust acquired respectively the entire estate at Killerton in Devon and of Kingston Lacy in Dorset. It is thus responsible not only for a great house and its collections, but also for farms and woods, lakes and villages. At Clumber Park in Nottinghamshire, the seat of the Dukes of Newcastle was demolished in the 1930s. When the surviving estate was offered to the Trust in 1945, it was recognised to be of such importance that a 50th anniversary appeal was launched to preserve it. Under the Trust's management the Clumber estate has now taken on a successful life of its own, drawing over a million visitors a year to enjoy the renowned parkland, lakes and woods.

The Great House and its Estate

The Trust has always sought to explain how a great house and its estate relate to one another. Wherever possible, visitors are encouraged to explore the park and surrounding landscape. When the Trust acquired Erddig in Clwyd in 1973, the customary order of the visitor route was reversed, so that the estate yard is seen first, with its sawmill, smithy and joiner's

National Trust Photographic Library

Speke Hall.

shop, and the house is entered through the servants' quarters. At Cragside in Northumberland the Victorian industrialist and inventor, William Armstrong, used hydro-electric power generated on the estate to light his drawing-room and turn the spits in his kitchen. With the help of sponsorship and funds raised by appeal, the Trust has restored many of Armstrong's pioneering machines. In many cases estate buildings are of outstanding architectural importance. Sir John Soane's late eighteenth-century Home Farm at Wimpole is as impressive in its way as his dramatic remodelling of the house. The Home Farm has now become a popular centre for displaying rare breeds of farm animal and traditional farm machinery, drawing as many visitors as the house itself.

The connection between house and landscape is more than one of academic interest; it has a significance beyond that of giving pleasure to thousands of visitors. Through the management of an estate such as Wallington in Northumbria or Blickling in Norfolk, the Trust assumes its own share of the responsibility for maintaining an economically viable rural community. As everyone knows, rental from farms is a declining source of income in many parts of the country. The changes in agriculture represent great difficulties for the Trust's farm tenants in many areas, especially in the uplands;

at the same time we seek to harness these changes to introduce less intensive agricultural practice and, in partnership with our tenants, more positive conservation measures for the protection of wildlife and traditional features in the landscape. The costs of such a policy are formidable, and the Trust will continue to urge that the principle of public subsidies for farm conservation schemes should be extended and more widely applied.

The Local Community

There are other ways, too, of maintaining rural life. In many places the old pattern has been reversed. Where once the estate provided the wherewithal to build a great house, now the house, through the visitors it attracts, is coming to the aid of the estate. Bed-and-breakfasting holidaymakers can provide an important boost to farm incomes. Disused field barns have been converted into 'stone tents' for campers, following the example pioneered in Derbyshire by the Duchess of Devonshire, who has written so entertainingly and thoughtfully about life on the Chatsworth estate today. Cleaners keep the state rooms in good order; gardeners tend the grounds; foresters provide fence posts for the park; carpenters and electricians, plumbers and plasterers look after all the innumerable small repairs that any old house demands, most of which can only be done when the visitors have gone and the house has been 'put to bed'. Many are carrying on the work their parents and grandparents did, albeit with more modern machinery and scientific know-how. These are local people, living in their own district for twelve months of the year and not just in the high season. They send their children to the local school, buy goods at the local shops and pay their phone bills at the local post office, and so help to make the phrase 'local community' more than an overused platitude.

At Wallington a party is regularly held in the house for all those who work in the house and on the estate, for the family of the donors, who still live nearby, and for the staff from the Trust's regional office. I like to think that this not only continues an enjoyable tradition from the days of the Trevelyans, but also symbolises the interdependence of the house, the estate and all who work to preserve them.

Bird's eye view of Dunham Massey from the North, c.1750, by John Harris.

KNEBWORTH HOUSE
HERTFORDSHIRE
HISTORIC HOME OF THE LYTTON FAMILY SINCE 1490

For details see Hertfordshire section

HERITAGE EDUCATION TRUST

DORSET'S JEWEL – EDUCATION AT KINGSTON LACY
Important National Trust Regional Development

At Kingston Lacy, Sandford Award 1990, words like 'flagship' and 'jewel in the crown' inevitably spring to mind. They are not inappropriate but there is no sense of exclusivity in the attitude of the Administrator, Howard Webber, or his staff. The welcome and the feeling of co-operation are almost palpable, and nowhere more so than the reception and arrangements made for schools conducting educational visits to this superb property.

Special Problems

Education is the responsibility of Barbara Webber, wife of the Administrator, and she is the first to acknowledge that it derives much of its strength from the enthusiasm and support which is evident in so many of the staff at the house, including the voluntary members. The house itself presents special problems because of the fragile and precious nature of the unique and original collections which it houses. It is impossible to give total freedom of access to school groups where activity and handling artefacts are a central part of the visit. Barbara Webber's solution is quite simply brilliant. Three less vulnerable areas of the house are freely used for group work and activity together with outbuildings and yards. In these surroundings there is virtually no limit to the children's properly organised and supervised freedom of expression and activity.

Within these constraints the education staff have devised a splendid house-based project inspired by events which occurred there and all now recorded by Pamela Watkin in 'A Kingston Lacy Childhood, Reminiscences of Viola Bankes' and published by Dovecote Press, £5.95. The project selects a visit by King Edward VII to plant a Cedar of Lebanon at Kingston Lacy in 1905 which is inter-woven with the death from an unnoticed appendicitis of Alice Maud Baker a nursery maid for the Bankes family at the time. The story is simple, absorbing and moving and was devised in conjunction with the Bournemouth Centre for Community Arts. The children are all given roles to play and spend the day experiencing the preparations which would have gone on for a royal visit – and of course the King arrives to plant his tree and in a wholly permissible anachronism goes walk-about among the excited children. Then when it is all over there are specially devised tours of the house to put the project in its wider

Talbot Combined School Studying "Homes" – The Victorian Period.

setting. This is where more co-operation is in evidence: Pat Rex, Mary and James Farmer were initially room stewards. They now bring their detailed knowledge of the house and enthusiasm for education to bear in acting as Educational Volunteers and one of their tasks is to lead the children's tours.

Co-operation a Keynote

The spirit of co-operation extends beyond the four walls of the house into the surrounding estate, and beyond

"The loveliest Castle in the whole world."

LORD CONWAY

LEEDS CASTLE, KENT

Open every day from mid-March to
October; at weekends in winter; plus "Christmas Week"

'A' Level Art Studies from Queen Elizabeth's School.

Frizzell, has formed HEAR – Heritage in the Environment for the Active and Retired. Its members work on the Kingston Lacy estate in all sorts of ways: one is to produce historic costumes and patterns which can be used either on-site or borrowed by schools for classroom work. Frizzell has also presented a computer compatible with the Acorn Archimedes which are in all Dorset Schools. Kingston Lacy is now working on putting its education packs on computer which will provide teachers wishing to use the educational opportunities at Kingston Lacy with a huge new resource.

The Shape of Things to Come

All this is good news for education in Dorset. But the really good news is that what is going on at Kingston Lacy is a sign of things to come for education in the National Trust. Barbara Webber has just been made the first Regional Education Officer for the Trust whose policy is, over the years, to appoint such an Officer in all of its Regions. At the moment that responsibility is one of many carried by one of the Trust's administrative officers in each Region. As the new policy gathers momentum the unique advantages of Heritage Education will become available nationwide. For the sake of the children it is to be hoped that both schools and Local

the boundary of the estate into the local Dorset community. On the estate itself the Warden, David Smith, enthusiastically promotes a bewildering array of educational initiatives comprising a medieval moot on its original site in the grounds, conservation initiatives which include children planting, managing and learning from a new wood, and an archaeological handling collection covering the period from neolithic to medieval times. He also oversees a residential centre built originally for Young National Trust workers but now increasingly rented to distant schools wanting to use Kingston Lacy as a field-work base, disabled parties and inner-city groups.

Education at Kingston Lacy owes a lot to many outside agencies. The Chief Education Officer for Dorset, Peter Gedling, supports the concept of Heritage Education wholeheartedly. As a result LEA advisory help is never far away and has resulted in some first class teacher packs. One of these was devised by the Dorset Mathematics Advisory Team, led by Fran Ashworth. A series of well produced cards assumes that the children can 'do sums' and carries the process of mathematical education forward into observation, deduction and problem solving, coupling these challenges with the important practical skill of accurate recording. The building and its contents provide stimuli more varied and more exciting than would be possible to find within a classroom and at the same time relate mathematical activity to a whole range of other educational influences.

Other outside help has come from commercial sponsors: the Ford Motor Company has presented a Dis-A-Loo – a toilet for the disabled. In an exceptionally imaginative move the Poole based Insurance Group,

Edward VII plants a tree.

Authorities, house Administrators, Regional Directors of the Trust and commercial interests follow the Dorset example. Barbara Webber's words indicate why they should: 'I feel a great sense of excitement in the beauty of the house, its history and what it has to give everyone. We have a desire and a duty to share it.'

MARTYN DYER
Heritage Education Trust

Blenheim Palace

Home of the 11th Duke of Marlborough, birthplace of Sir Winston Churchill.

Open daily 10.30am–5.30pm (last admission 4.45pm) mid March to 31st October 1992.
A visit to Blenheim is a wonderful way to spend a day. An inclusive ticket covers the Palace tour, Park and Gardens, Butterfly House, Motor Launch, Train, Adventure Play Area and Nature Trail. Optional are the new Marlborough Maze and Rowing Boat Hire on Queen Pool. Car parking is free for Palace visitors and there are Shops, Cafeterias and a Garden Centre. Events for 1992 include the Annual Grand Charity Cricket Match, in aid of the Oxfordshire Association of Boys Clubs, between a Lords Taverners XI and an Oxford University XI on 24th May and The Blenheim Audi International Horse Trials take place on 3rd, 4th, 5th and 6th September. Further details from The Administrator, Blenheim Palace, Woodstock, Oxon OX20 1PX. Telephone: 0993-811091.

The right to close the Palace or Park without notice is reserved.

THE GARDENS AT
HATFIELD HOUSE Hertfordshire

"There are nearly 14 acres of formal and informal gardens dating back to the late 15th century. From 1609 to 1611 John Tradescant the Elder laid out and planted the gardens for Robert Cecil, the builder of the House. Today the gardens, much embellished in the last years, contain many of the same plants growing in knot gardens typical of the period, arranged in the court of the 15th century Palace where Queen Elizabeth I spent much of her childhood. There are herb and sweet gardens, a parterre of herbaceous plants and roses, fountains, statuary and a foot maze or labyrinth, the whole enclosed in ancient rose-brick walls, topiaried yews, holly and pleached limes.

A wilderness garden, planted with forest and ornamental trees, blossoms in the spring with crabs, cherries, magnolias and rhododendrons underplanted with many flowers and bulbs, the whole providing colour and interest (for there are many rare and unusual plants) for all seasons."
"Photographs by Mick Hales, Garry Rogers and Jeremy Whitaker."

"I feel at home here as I gaze down and respond to the feeling of total delight which it gives me . . ."   Sir Roy Strong

"Hatfield's gardens are the most completely beautiful and fit for their purpose of any great house in England."   "Tradescant" of the RHS Journal.

FOR DETAILS SEE HERTFORDSHIRE SECTION

Come and enjoy two outstanding examples of 18th century genius near Ripon, North Yorkshire

Newby Hall

Newby Hall, the lived-in home of the Compton family contains wonderful and rare treasures. The glorious gardens cover some twenty-five acres and in 1986 received the Christies/Historic Houses Association "Garden of the Year" Award.

Fountains Abbey

and Gardens

The magnificent views of Fountains Abbey provide the dramatic focal point of the eighteenth century landscape garden at Studley Royal. Famous for its water gardens, ornamental buildings and vistas, this National Trust property has been awarded World Heritage Status.

& Studley Royal

For opening times see North Yorkshire section.

Sandford Award Winners

Complete List, 1978–1991

The following properties received Sandford Awards in the years in brackets after their names in recognition of the excellence of their educational services and facilities and their outstanding contribution to Heritage Education. Two or more dates indicate that the property has been reviewed and received further recognition under the system of Quinquennial Review introduced by the Heritage Education Trust in 1986.

Any property which wishes to retain its listing must apply for review of its educational services and facilities five years after the date of its last award.

The closing date for initial applications and quinquennial review is 31st March.

AVONCROFT MUSEUM OF BUILDINGS, Bromsgrove, Worcs (**1988**)

*BASS MUSEUM, VISITOR CENTRE AND SHIRE HORSE STABLES, Burton on Trent, Staffs (**1990**)

BEAULIEU ABBEY, Nr. Lyndhurst, Hampshire (**1978**) (**1986**) (**1991**)

*BEDE MONASTERY MUSEUM, Jarrow, Tyne and Wear (**1988**)

BICKLEIGH CASTLE, Nr. Tiverton, Devon (**1983**) (**1988**)

BLENHEIM PALACE, Woodstock, Oxfordshire (**1982**) (**1987**)

*BOLLING HALL, Bradford, West Yorkshire (**1978**) (**1987**)

*THE BOAT MUSEUM, Ellesmere Port, South Wirral (**1986**)

BOUGHTON HOUSE, Kettering, Northants (**1988**)

BUCKFAST ABBEY, Buckfastleigh, Devon (**1985**) (**1990**)

CANTERBURY CATHEDRAL, Canterbury, Kent (**1988**)

CASTLE MUSEUM, York (**1987**)

CASTLE WARD, County Down, Northern Ireland (**1980**) (**1987**)

CATHEDRAL & ABBEY CHURCH OF ST. ALBAN, St. Albans, Herts (**1986**) (**1991**)

*THE CECIL HIGGINS ART GALLERY AND MUSEUM & THE BEDFORD MUSEUM, Bedford (**1989**)

*CHATTERLEY WHITFIELD MINING MUSEUM, Tunstall, Stoke on Trent (**1988**)

*COLDHARBOUR MILL, Working Wool Museum, Cullompton, Devon (**1989**)

COMBE SYDENHAM, Nr. Taunton, Somerset (**1984**) (**1989**)

CROXTETH HALL and COUNTRY PARK, Liverpool, Merseyside (**1980**) (**1989**)

CULZEAN CASTLE and COUNTRY PARK, Ayrshire, Scotland (**1984**) (**1989**)

DODDINGTON HALL, Doddington, Lincolnshire (**1978**) (**1986**)

*DOVE COTTAGE and THE WORDSWORTH MUSEUM, Grasmere, Cumbria (**1990**)

DRUMLANRIG CASTLE and COUNTRY PARK, Dumfriesshire, Scotland (**1989**)

DULWICH PICTURE GALLERY, London (**1990**)

ERDDIG HALL, Nr. Wrexham, Clwyd (**1991**)

GAINSBOROUGH OLD HALL, Gainsborough, Lincolnshire (**1988**)

GEORGIAN HOUSE, Edinburgh, Lothian Region (**1978**)

HAREWOOD HOUSE, Leeds, West Yorkshire (**1979**) (**1989**)

HELMSHORE TEXTILE MUSEUM, Lancashire (**1990**)

HOLDENBY HOUSE, Northampton, Northamptonshire (**1985**) (**1991**)

HOLKER HALL, Cark in Cartmel, Cumbria (**1982**) (**1988**)

HOPETOUN HOUSE, South Queensferry, Lothian Region (**1983**) (**1991**)

*HORNSEA MUSEUM, North Humberside (**1987**)

KINGSTON LACY HOUSE, Wimborne, Dorset (**1990**)

LEIGHTON HALL, Carnforth, Lancashire (**1982**)

LICHFIELD CATHEDRAL AND VISITORS' STUDY CENTRE, Lichfield, Staffordshire (**1991**)

MACCLESFIELD MUSEUMS, Macclesfield (**1988**)

MOSELEY OLD HALL, Wolverhampton, West Midlands (**1983**) (**1989**)

NATIONAL WATERWAYS MUSEUM, Gloucester (**1991**)

*OAKWELL HALL COUNTRY PARK, Birstall, West Yorkshire (**1988**)

PENHOW CASTLE, Nr. Newport, Gwent (**1980**) (**1986**)

QUARRY BANK MILL, Styal, Cheshire (**1987**)

RANGER'S HOUSE, Blackheath, London (**1979**) (**1987**)

ROCKINGHAM CASTLE, Nr. Corby, Northamptonshire (**1980**) (**1987**)

THE SHUGBOROUGH ESTATE, Stafford (**1987**)

TATTON PARK, Knutsford, Cheshire (**1979**) (**1986**) (**1991**)

*TOWER OF LONDON, Tower Bridge, London (**1978**) (**1986**) (**1991**)

*WIGAN PIER, Lancashire (**1987**)

WIGHTWICK MANOR, Wolverhampton, West Midlands (**1986**) (**1991**)

WIMPOLE HALL, Nr. Cambridge (**1988**)

*WILBERFORCE HOUSE and the GEORGIAN HOUSES, Hull (**1990**)

YORK MINSTER, York (**1984**) (**1989**)

1991 RESULTS
Full Sandford Awards

ERDDIG HALL
LICHFIELD CATHEDRAL AND VISITORS' STUDY CENTRE
NATIONAL WATERWAYS MUSEUM

Highly Commended

THE QUEENS HOUSE

Quinquennial Review

At quinquennial review a successful applicant will receive either a second Sandford Award indicating that educational services and facilities have been developed and improved since the date of the last award, or continued listing indicating that the educational services have maintained their original level of excellence.

BEAULIEU	**Sandford Award**
CATHEDRAL & ABBEY OF ST. ALBAN	**Sandford Award**
HOPETOUN HOUSE	**Sandford Award**
TATTON PARK	**Sandford Award**
TOWER OF LONDON	**Sandford Award**
WIGHTWICK MANOR	**Sandford Award**

Full details of the Sandford Award and the work of the **Heritage Education Trust** from: **Martyn Dyer, Chief Executive, Heritage Education Trust, St. Mary's College, Strawberry Hill, TW1 4SX. Tel: 081-892 0051 ext 202.**

*For details of museums shown in the above list with a star, please refer to **Museums and Galleries in Great Britain and Ireland, 1992 edition.**

Belvoir Castle

HOME OF THE DUKE AND DUCHESS OF RUTLAND

A CASTLE IN THE GRAND STYLE commanding a magnificent view over the Vale of Belvoir ("beautiful view").
The name dates back to the famous Norman Castle that stood on this same site.
The Castle was rebuilt in 1816 after a catastrophic fire and owes much to the inspiration of Elizabeth the 5th
Duchess of Rutland. There are many notable art treasures and interesting military relics.

THE GARDENS

The Statue gardens contain many beautiful 17th Century
sculptures. There are flowers in bloom throughout most of
the season.

MEDIEVAL JOUSTING

The world famous Medieval Jousting Tournaments on the
Castle terrace attract 25,000 visitors annually.
These exciting professionally staged tournaments are a must
for overseas visitors.
50p extra admission charged on Jousting days.

JOUSTING DATES 1992

Sunday and Monday May 24th and 25th
Sunday June 28th
Sunday July 26th
Sunday and Monday August 30th and 31st
Sunday September 13th

SCHOOL VISITS

Guided tours, talks and special projects are all devised to
capture a child's imagination.

CONFERENCE/FILMING

A magnificent backdrop for conferences, banquets, film and
TV location.

PARKING FREE

The Castle makes no additional charges of admission to
special events excluding the Medieval Jousting Tournaments,
when a 50p supplement is added to all admissions.

ADMISSION PRICES 1992

£3.20 Adults £2.20 Children/OAP's.
Group rates: 30+ adults £2.50. School parties £1.80.
All coach tours and excursions £2.50.

PRIVATE PARTIES

Can be arranged by appointment when the Castle is
otherwise closed.
For opening details, please see under Belvoir Castle,
Leicestershire.
For Free Colour Leaflet with all opening hours, group rates,
catering tariffs and any other information—please contact:
The Controller, The Estate Office, Belvoir
Castle, FREEPOST, Grantham, Lincs. NG31 6BR (no stamp
needed) or telephone Grantham 0476 870262.

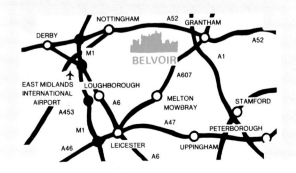

On Gardens Great and Small

by
Lynn Curtis

If England could export her gardens, the balance of payments problems would disappear overnight! The English Style of gardening is recognised and admired worldwide, the glorious product of our temperate – if rain-sodden – climate, and centuries of plant collecting and horticultural study.

In the blistering summer of 1990, professional tour guides Rosemary Ewing-Gay and Diana Black realised that London's tourists and residents alike were missing out on one of the chief glories of an English summer – its gardens. "We felt that people were getting an un-balanced view of England," says Rosemary. "It's not just towns and cities and ancient monuments. Tour Planners started to show them England's great tradition of gardening."

London, for instance, is more than the Tower, Madame Tussaud's and Nelson's Column. There's a green heart to the city with its royal parks, ancient remnants of the monastic tradition of herbalism, and the strict classi-fication of botanical species between the redbrick walls of the picturesque Chelsea Physic Garden. Added to this there are fascinating curiosities such as Hampstead's hidden garden and the flamingoes amid the whimsical roof top greenery above the old Derry and Toms building in Kensington High Street.

Lunch in the Garden of Prue Leith.

From introducing people to the delights of London's green corners, it was only a short step to extending their tours to cover notable gardens in nearby Kent, Hertfordshire and the Cotswolds. Each of the country garden tours includes a famous English garden as its highlight: the romantic splendour of Vita Sackville-West's incomparable Sissinghurst with its famous White Garden and mediaeval tower; the Old English knots of Hatfield House; and present day garden doyenne Rosemary Verey's inspirational ornamental garden and *jardin potager* at her seventeenth-century Cotswolds home, Barnsley House.

Tour Planners visit such famous gardens as Hidcote and Sezincote with its practically unaltered Repton Garden; or Cliveden with its Nancy Astor associations – a tour that includes Rousham, famous for its archi-tectural splendour or perhaps a day in Essex to include Beth Chatto's wonderful nursery which specialises in water plants, to mention just a few of their days.

Diana explains that Tour Planners also like to offer a change of pace and scale on their country tours. "Three Sissinghursts in one day would be too much for even the most dedicated garden visitor," she says. "We like to offer a contrast by incorporating among the three

Oxford Botanical Gardens in April.

Windsor Castle

For over 900 years, Windsor Castle has served as residence and fortress for the British Monarchy, acting as a spectacular backdrop for the important Ceremonies of State, including the gatherings of The Knights of The Garter.

See Berkshire section for further details.

gardens visited in a day perhaps a smaller private garden, or a specialist centre for perhaps roses or rhododendrons in season." A herb garden and a horticultural college where a variety of garden styles are demonstrated are other popular destinations.

Besides their regular country garden tours on Wednesdays, Thursdays and Sundays there is an opportunity, on certain of these days for a Tour of London's wonderful gardens to see the Capital through a green and therapeutic light. Tour Planners occasionally offer special one-off garden days. A visit to Prue Leith's Oxfordshire gardens complete with the man-made lake and Chinese style pagoda and bridge, a visit to Miriam Rothschild's Fields of wild flowers, an 'Edwardian Day' visiting Goddards the famous Lutyens house. Hidcote, the grandest and most influential of twentieth-century English gardens. Even Vita Sackville-West admired it, and Tour Planners' visitors are spellbound. For some from overseas the day in the heart of the English countryside, seeing three beautiful and contrasting gardens is the highpoint of their stay.

Tour Planners offer their customers a chance to sit back, relax, and enjoy the scents, sounds and spectacle of English gardens at their best. At only £38 for a full day's outing, they offer a treat for the wallet too.

Walking in the wild part of Prue Leith's Garden.

The James A. de Rothschild Collection
WADDESDON MANOR
The National Trust
Buckinghamshire

**The Grounds, Aviary, Shop, and Tearoom will be open during 1992
but the House will be closed for essential repairs until 1993.
For details see Buckinghamshire section.**

English Heritage.
The Best Days Out in the Country.

Audley End 1788-89 by William Tompkins

THE ENGLISH COUNTRY-side is rich in buildings and antiquities that form the vast pattern of our heritage.

Castles and country houses, abbeys and stone circles; plotting the story of England from enigmatic pre-history through medieval pageants to the twentieth century.

Many of these properties are in the care of English Heritage, preserved for you to enjoy today on days out in the country.

Days in the South in coastal forts like Dover and Portchester. Days in the North visiting abbeys like Rievaulx or Whitby. Or walking the Roman wall of Emperor Hadrian.

A day out full of surprises in Essex at Audley End, pictured here in 1789, or full of mystery in Wiltshire at Stonehenge or Avebury.

This book will give you many ideas for days out in every county, particularly in this 350th anniversary year of the English Civil War. Days full of the experience, education and enjoyment that is English Heritage.

English Heritage

Palace of Holyroodhouse
Edinburgh

The ridge, known as the Royal Mile, that slopes downwards from Edinburgh Castle, comes to a majestic conclusion at Holyroodhouse where Palace and Abbey stand against the spectacular backdrop of Salisbury Crags.

See Lothian Section for further details.

ARUNDEL CASTLE
Family home of the Dukes of Norfolk
For details see West Sussex section

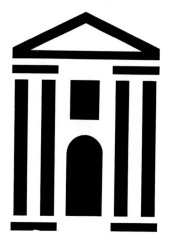

Become a Friend of the Historic Houses Association

over 270
Houses & Gardens
to
Visit Free

What is the HHA?

The Historic Houses Association was formed in 1973 by owners of some of Britain's best known Heritage properties. It has grown to represent over 1,400 owners and guardians of historic houses, parks and gardens in private ownership in the United Kingdom. The owners are responsible for looking after and financing their own properties. The HHA exists to provide practical advice and professional services to the owners and to represent them as a group. Private ownership is now widely recognised as the best way to preserve the Nation's great country houses, interiors and gardens and to maintain their atmosphere and sense of continuity.

Who are the Friends?

Friends are a small but important group of people who are interested in the heritage and enjoy visiting country houses. They can visit 280 HHA members' properties free of charge and become involved in the HHA's work at a regional level. They pay a subscription to the Association on an annual basis.

Please ask for information and subscription rates:
Mrs. Rachel Oakley,
Historic Houses Association, Membership Department
PO Box 21, Unit 7, Campus 5, The Business Park, Letchworth, Herts. SG6 2JF.
Tel: (0462) 675848

Historic Houses Castles & Gardens

in Great Britain and Ireland

△ Denotes guided tours of the House

&. Denotes the major part of the property is suitable for wheelchairs

Ⓔ Denotes educational services recognised by the Heritage Education Trust

Ⓢ Denotes that all property is a recipient of the Sandford Award

Denotes properties in the care of The National Trust

Denotes properties in the care of The National Trust for Scotland

Denotes properties in the care of English Heritage

Denotes property owned and administered by a member of HHA

Denotes property in the care of CADW

AVON

ALGARS MANOR

Iron Acton, Bristol   map G4
Telephone: (0454) 228372
(Dr & Mrs J. M. Naish)

3 acre woodland garden beside River Frome; mill-stream; native plants mixed with azaleas, rhododendrons, camellias, magnolias, eucalyptus.

Location: 3 m W of Yate Sodbury. Turn S off Iron Acton bypass B4059, past village green, 200 yds, then over level crossing (Station Road).
Opening Times: For *National Gardens Scheme* Suns, Mons April 19, 20; May 24, 25, 2–6. Also by appointment.
Refreshments: Teas.

BARSTAPLE HOUSE (TRINITY ALMSHOUSES)

Bristol   map G4
Telephone: Bristol (0272) 265777 (Warden)
(Bristol Municipal Charities)

Victorian almshouse with garden courtyard.

Location: Old Market Street, Bristol; ½ m from City centre on A420.
Station: Bristol Temple Meads (³/₄ m).
Opening Times: GARDEN & EXTERIOR OF BUILDINGS ONLY, now extensively renovated. All the year—Week-days 10–4. Adm free. *The Almshouse is occupied mainly by elderly residents & their rights for privacy should be respected.*

BECKFORD'S TOWER

Bath   map G4
Telephone: Bath (0225) 312917
(The Beckford Tower Trust)

Built 1827 by William Beckford of Fonthill. A small museum (first floor) illustrating Beckford's life; fine views from Belvedere (156 steps).

Location: 2 m from Bath Spa Station via Lansdown Road.
Station: Bath Spa (2 m).
Opening Times: Apr 4 to end Oct—Sats, Suns & Bank Hol Mons 2–5. Adm £1p, Chd & OAPs 50p. *Parties other days by arrangement.*

BLAISE CASTLE HOUSE MUSEUM

Henbury   map G4
Telephone: Bristol (0272) 506789
(City of Bristol)

18th century house set in landscaped park; containing collections illustrating every-day life of the last 300 years.

Location: 4 m NW of central Bristol.
Station: Sea Mills (2 m).
Opening Times: All the year—Sats to Weds 10–1, 2–5. *Closed* Thurs & Fris; Christmas Day, Boxing Day, New Year's Day & Good Friday. Adm free.

CLAVERTON MANOR

nr Bath   map G4   △
Telephone: Bath (0225) 460503
(The American Museum in Britain)

A Greek Revival house high above the valley of the Avon. Completely furnished rooms, 17th, 18th and 19th century brought from the U.S.A.

Location: 2½ m from Bath Station via Bathwick Hill; 3¾ m SE of Bath via Warminster Road (A36) & Claverton village.
Station: Bath Spa (2½ m).
Opening Times: Mar 28–Nov 1 Daily (except Mons) 2–5; Bank Hols Sun and Mon 11–5. *Mornings and winter months on application only.* School parties by previous arrangement, except Jan. Educational Tel 463538. Adm House & Grounds £4.50, Chd £2.50, and Senior Citizens £4. Grounds and new Galleries £1.50, Chd £1. Parties of children not admitted during normal opening hours. *Pre-arranged parties over 30 at reduced rate.* Gardens open throughout the season (*except Mon*) 1–6.
Refreshments: Tea with American cookies (*Gingerbread cooked in 18th century oven*).

CLEVEDON COURT, The National Trust

nr Clevedon   map F4
Telephone: (0272) 872257

A 14th century manor house incorporating a 12th century tower and a 13th century hall with terraced 18th century garden; rare shrubs and plants. The home of the Elton family. Important collections of Nailsea glass and Eltonware.

Location: 1½ m E of Clevedon on the Bristol Road B3130.
Station: Yatton (3 m).
Opening Times: Apr 1 to Sept 30—Weds, Thurs & Suns, also Bank Hol Mons 2.30– 5.30 (last adm 5). Adm £2.80, Chd £1.40 (children under 17 must be accompanied by an adult). No dogs. Unsuitable for wheelchairs. Coaches by appointment.
Refreshments: Tearoom in old kitchen open 2.30–5 (not NT).

NUMBER ONE, ROYAL CRESCENT

Bath map G4
Telephone: Bath (0225) 428126
(Bath Preservation Trust)

A Georgian Town House at the eastern end of Bath's most magnificent crescent; redecorated and furnished to show the visitor how it might have appeared in the late 18th century.
Location: Bath.
Opening Times: Mar 1 to Mar 31 and Oct 1 to Dec 13, Tues to Sun 11–4, (*Closed* Mon). Apr 1 to Sept 30: open every day 11–5 (*Closed* Good Fri), Last adm half an hour before closing. Special tours by arrangement with Administrator. Adm £3, Chd/Students, Senior Citizens, Adult groups £2. Museum. Shop.

DYRHAM PARK, The National Trust

nr Bristol and Bath map G4
Telephone: 027582 2501

Late 17th century house in a splendid deer park. The Blathwayt furniture and Dutch paintings in a fine series of panelled rooms.
Location: 12 m E of Bristol approach from Bath/Stroud Road (A46), 2 m S of Tormarton interchange with M4, 8 m N of Bath.
Opening Times: Park—Daily 12–5.30 (or dusk if earlier), last adm 5. *Closed* Christmas Day. House & Garden: Apr 1 to Nov 1—Daily (except Thurs & Fris) 12–5.30. Last adm 5, or dusk if earlier.
Adm House, Gardens & Park £4.40, Chd £2.20. *Parties must book.* Park only: £1.40, Chd 70p. Dog walking area provided but no dogs in deer park. Wheelchairs provided. Braille guide.
Refreshments: In the Orangery.

HORTON COURT, The National Trust

Horton map G4

A Cotswold manor house restored and altered in the 19th century. 12th century hall and late Perpendicular ambulatory in garden only shown.
Location: 3 m NE of Chipping Sodbury, ¼ m N of Horton, 1 m W of Bath/Stroud Road (A46).
Opening Times: HALL & AMBULATORY ONLY: Apr 1 to Oct 31—Weds & Sats 2–6 (or sunset if earlier). *Other times by written appointment with the tenant.* Adm £1.40, Chd 70p. *No reduction for parties.* No dogs. Unsuitable for coaches. Wheelchairs—ambulatory only. No WCs.

THE MANOR HOUSE

Walton-in-Gordano map F4
Telephone: Clevedon (0275) 872067
(Mr & Mrs Simon Wills)

Four acres—mainly shrubs and fine trees, bulbs, alpines and herbaceous plants, mostly labelled.
Location: W of Bristol; via B3124 from Clevedon to Portishead; driveway on left before 1st houses in Walton-in-Gordano.
Station: Yatton (6 m).
Opening Times: GARDEN ONLY: Weds & Thurs Apr 8 to Sept 17; also Oct 21, 22, 28, 29 and Nov 4, 5, 10–4. Suns May 3, 24, Aug 30. Mons Apr 20, May 4, 25, Aug 31, 2–6. Open by appointment all year. Adm £1, accompanied Chd free. Plants for sale. No dogs. Coaches by appointment only. *In aid of National Gardens Scheme and St. Peter's Hospice.*

NUMBER ONE, ROYAL CRESCENT – *See above*

ORCHARD HOUSE

Claverton map G4
(Rear Adm & Mrs Hugh Tracy)

Plantsman's garden of 2½ acres in which owners have tried to combine botanical interest with attractive and informal layout. Collections of foliage plants, herbs, alpines, ground-cover and silver plants; rock gardens, herbaceous borders, lawns, shrubs, views.
Location: 3½ m from centre of Bath via A36 (Warminster) road; turn off at signpost for American museum: or ½ m down hill from American Museum, Claverton.
Station: Bath Spa (3½ m).
Opening Times: GARDEN ONLY. Weds 2–6, May 6, 13, 20, 27; June 3; July 1. 8. Adm £1, Chd free. Groups welcome on other dates by appointment. *In aid of National Gardens Scheme & Abbeyfield Cirencester Society.* No dogs. Plants for sale. Small nursery.

SHERBORNE GARDEN (PEAR TREE HOUSE)

Litton BA3 4PP map G4
Telephone: (0761) 241220
(Mr & Mrs John Southwell)

3½ acres landscaped into several gardens of distinctive character. Cottage garden, rock garden, large ponds with moisture gardens, pinetum, mixed wood. Collections of acers, birches, species roses, clematis. Special collection of hollies (over 180 varieties). Featured on 'Gardeners World'. Picnic area. Permanent exhibition of watercolours.
Location: Litton, 8 miles N of Wells on B3114 off A39.
Opening Times: Apr 19, 20; June 13, 14. Oct 10, 11; *for National Gardens Scheme;* also Sat, Sun and Mon from June 15 to Sep 7, 11–6.30. Other times by appointment. Adm £1, Chd free. Parties by arrangement. Free car parking. Suitable for the disabled. Dogs on leads allowed.
Refreshments: Home-made teas on National Gardens Scheme days (except in Apr) and for parties; at other times tea/coffee available.

VINE HOUSE

Henbury, Bristol   map G4
Telephone: Bristol (0272) 503573
(Professor & Mrs T. F. Hewer)

Two acres. Trees, shrubs, small water garden; bulbs; naturalised garden landscape.

Location: 4 m NW of Bristol centre next to 'Salutation' Bus stop.
Stations: Bristol Parkway; Bristol Temple Meads each about 4 m from Henbury.
Opening Times: GARDENS ONLY. Suns & Mons Apr 19, 20, May 24, 25. 2–7. Also open by appointment throughout the year. Adm £1, Chd & OAPs 50p. Dogs on leads. *In aid of National Gardens Scheme & 'Friends of Blaise'.*

BEDFORDSHIRE

BUSHMEAD PRIORY ⌗

map K6
Telephone: (023 062) 614

The priory was a small house for Augustinian canons and founded in about 1195. The remains consist of the 13th century canon's refectory occupying one side of the former cloister. The timber-framed roof is a rare example of an almost complete crown-post construction of about 1250. The refectory contains wall-paintings and interesting stained glass.

Location: 4 m west of A1 at St Neots. OS map ref TL115607.
Opening Times: Good Friday or Apr 1 (whichever is earlier) to Sept 30: Daily 10–6; Winter: Oct 1 to Maundy Thurs or Mar 31 (whichever is earlier) Tues to Sun 10–4. Adm £1.10, Concessions 85p, Chd 55p.

CECIL HIGGINS ART GALLERY & MUSEUM

Castle Close, Bedford MK40 3NY   map J6   &
Telephone: Bedford (0234) 211222
(Gallery jointly owned and administered by the North Bedfordshire Borough Council and the Trustees of the Cecil Higgins Art Gallery)

Award-winning re-created Victorian Mansion, original home of Cecil Higgins. Rooms displayed to give 'lived-in' atmosphere, including bedroom with furniture designed by William Burges (1827–1881). Adjoining gallery with outstanding collections of ceramics, glass and watercolours. Situated in gardens leading down to the river embankment.

Location: Centre of Bedford, just off The Embankment.
Station: Bedford Midland (1 m).
Bus Station: (¹/₂ m).
Opening Times: Tues–Fri 12.30–5, Sat 11–5, Sun 2–5. *Closed* Mons (except Bank Hol Mons), Christmas Day, Boxing Day, Good Fri.
Adm free. Group bookings and refreshments by prior arrangement. Facilities for the disabled.
Trains from London (St. Pancras), and King's Cross Thameslink – fast trains 36 mins.
United Counties ×4 Bedford/Milton Keynes – Buckingham – Bicester – Oxford; ×3 Northampton – Bedford – Cambridge; Coach link from London Marylebone Station.

CHICKSANDS PRIORY

Shefford   map K5
Telephone: (02302) 4195
(Ministry of Defence Property Administered by RAF Commander. Friends of Priory licensed to open Priory to public and redecorate interior)

Photograph P. Wood.

Chicksands Priory was founded by Payne De Beauchamp and his wife Countess Rohese for Nuns and Canons of the English Order of Gilbertines c 1150. Dissolved and surrendered 1538, it was sold by Henry VIII for £810 11s 8d to the Snowe family 1540. Acquired by the Osborne family in 1576, it so remained their family home until sold to The Crown, 1936. 13th and 15th century monastic remains survive with architectural work by Isaac Ware (1740) and James Wyatt (1813). Stained glass, Chinese wallpaper, Coade statuary have been uncovered since the Anglo-American Group of Friends opened the building to the public, 1975. The 18th century Venetian Prayer Book purchased by Sir Danvers Osborn, 3rd Baronet, is shown in the refurbished Private Chapel. Ghosts of former inhabitants are said to haunt the building; a plaque boasts of a walled up Nun within the cloisters and remains of monastic residents are buried in the still landscaped gardens. Game larder, Orangery and grapevines are on show exclusive of guided tour of the interior, which takes approximately 45 minutes. Past visitors to Chicksands include St Thomas Becket, King James I, HRH Princess Alice, Duchess of Gloucester, the Duke of Bedford, Terence, Cardinal Cooke. Following intensive external restoration by the Ministry of Defence, The Friends are decorating and restoring the interior.

Location: In RAF Chicksands 1¼ miles from Shefford. Entrances on A507 Shefford to Ampthill Road and on A600 Shefford to Bedford Road.
Opening Times: 1st & 3rd Suns of Month Apr to Oct 2–5; last tour 4.30. Guided tours only. No adm charge – donations for interior decoration requested, suggested donation £1 per adult. Parties by appointment only. Car Parking. Unsuitable for wheelchairs.
Refreshments: Light refreshments at Priory. Nearest hotels at Biggleswade, Bedford & Hitchin, all being 7 miles from Chicksands.

LUTON HOO – *See page 30*

THE SWISS GARDEN

Old Warden, nr Biggleswade   map K5   &
Telephone: Bedford (0234) 228330
(Bedfordshire County Council)

A unique Romantic landscaped garden dating from the early 19th century containing the Swiss Cottage, splendid Fernery and Grotto, other original buildings, bridges and unusual iron artefacts. The complex landscape design includes a wide variety of plants and trees, some of great size and rarity. Resident pea fowl. Attractive lakeside picnic area in adjoining woodlands. Sales point where publications, gifts and souvenirs can be purchased.

Location: 2½ m W of Biggleswade, adjoining Biggleswade/Old Warden Road; approximately 2 m W of A1. Adjacent to Shuttleworth Museum of Historic Aircraft and approximately 1m from the picturesque 'Swiss' style village Old Warden.
Station: Biggleswade (3 m).
Opening Times: Apr to Oct – Weds to Suns & Bank Holidays. Mons 1.30–6 (last admission 5.15). Adm (1991 rates) £1.10, Chd (5–16) and OAPS 50p. Special rates for guided tours. School parties & group visits by prior arrangement. Wheelchair access, wheelchairs available on free loan. Lakeside picnic area and woodland walk open at all times. Public lavatory (facilities for disabled).
Refreshments: Cafeteria at adjoining Shuttleworth Aeroplane Collection.

LUTON HOO

Luton   map K5
Telephone: Luton (0582) 22955
(The Wernher Family)

Exterior commenced by Robert Adam, 1767. Interior remodelled in the French style early in this century. Magnificent art collection includes Fabergé jewels, paintings, tapestries, porcelain and Medieval Ivories. Park landscaped by 'Capability' Brown.

Location: Entrance at Park Street Gates Luton 30 m N of London via M1 (exit 10, junction A1081 – formerly A6). Railway & Bus Stations 3 m.
Station: Luton (2½ m).
Opening Times: HOUSE & GARDENS. Apr 14 to Oct 18, 1992. Open daily 1.30–5.45. *Closed* Mons except Bank Hols; last adm 5; £4.30, Senior Citizen £3.70, Chd £1.75. Reduced rates for parties by prior arrangement (minimum 25 adults). No dogs admitted to House or Gardens. (Guide dogs excepted.)

Lancelot 'Capability' Brown

Born 1716 in Northumberland, Capability Brown began work at the age of 16 in the vegetable gardens of Sir William and Lady Loraine at Kirharle Tower. He left Northumberland in 1739, and records show that he worked at Stowe until 1749. It was at Stowe that Brown began to study architecture, and to submit his own plans. It was also at Stowe that he devised a new method of moving and replanting mature trees.

Brown married Bridget Wayet in 1744 and began work on the estate at Warwick Castle in 1749. He was appointed Master Gardener at Hampton Court in 1764, and planted the Great Vine at Hampton Court in 1768. Blenheim Palace designs are considered amongst Brown's finest work, and the technical achievements were outstanding even for the present day.

Capability Brown died in February 1783 of a massive heart attack. A monument beside the lake at Croome Court was erected which reads "To the memory of Lancelot Brown, who by the powers of his inimitable and creative genius formed this garden scene out of a morass". There is also a portrait of Brown at Burghley.

Capability Brown was involved in the design of grounds at the following properties included in Historic Houses Castles and Gardens:

Luton Hoo	*Corsham Court*	*Stowe*	*Burton Constable*
Bowood	*Fawley Court*	*Weston Park*	*Sledmere House*
Burghley House	*Longleat*	*Wotton House*	*Syon House*
Chilham Castle (reputed)	*Moccas Court*	*Wrest Park*	*Warwick Castle.*
Claremont	*Nuneham Park*	*Broadlands*	
Chillington Hall	*Petworth*	*Berrington Hall*	

WOBURN ABBEY

Woburn   map J5
Telephone: Woburn (0525) 290666; Catering (0525) 290662; Antiques Centre (0525) 290350
(The Marquess of Tavistock and Trustees of the Bedford Estates)

Home of the Dukes of Bedford for over 350 years, the Abbey contains one of the most important private art collections in the world, including paintings by Canaletto, Van Dyck, Cuyp, Teniers, Rembrandt, Gainsborough, Reynolds, Velazques and many other famous artists. French and English 18th century furniture, silver and the fabulous Sevres dinner service presented to the 4th Duke by Louis XV of France. The 3,000 acre Deer Park has lots of wild life, including nine species of deer, roaming freely. One of these, the Pere David, descended from the Imperial Herd of China, was saved from extinction at Woburn and is now the largest breeding herd of this specie in the world. In 1985 twenty two Pere David were given by the Family to the People's Republic of China with the hope that the specie may become re-established in its natural habitat. The Marquess of Tavistock visited Beijing (Peking) to release the herd at Nan Haizi, the former Imperial hunting ground outside Beijing (Peking). The tour of the Abbey covers three floors including the Crypt. It is regretted that wheelchairs can only be accommodated in the House by prior arrangement with the Administrator but unfortunately the Crypt area is not accessible. The 40 shop Antiques Centre is probably the most unusual such centre outside London – the shop fronts having been rescued from demolition sites in various parts of Britain. Shipping can be arranged on a world wide basis. All catering is operated by ourselves with banqueting, conferences, receptions and company days out our speciality, in the beautiful setting of the Sculpture Gallery, overlooking the private gardens. There is a Pottery and summer weekend events are arranged. Extensive picnic areas with ample coach and car parking. Gift shops, Pottery and Camping Equipment Centre.

Location: In Woburn 8½ m NW of Dunstable on A4012. 42 m from London off M1 at junctions 12 or 13.
Stations: Leighton Buzzard and Bletchley (Euston) and Flitwick (Kings Cross Thameslink). The three local stations are between 6 and 7 miles from Woburn village, which is 1½ m from the Abbey.
Opening Times: HOUSE AND GARDENS. Dec 28 to Mar 28 – Sats & Suns only. House 11–4.45; Park 10.30–3.45. Mar 29 to Nov 1 – Daily. House: Weekdays 11–5.45; Suns 11–6.15. Park: Weekdays 10–4.45; Suns 10–5.45. Last adm to House 45 mins before closing time every day. House Adm £5.50, Chd (7–16) £2, OAPs £4.
Party rates are available.
Free car park.
Refreshments: Flying Duchess Pavilion Coffee Shop, Restaurants for pre-booked parties.

WREST PARK HOUSE AND GARDENS

Silsoe   map J5
Telephone: (0525) 60718
(English Heritage)

Here is a history of English gardening in the grand manner from 1700–1850, which would not, of course, be complete without some designs by 'Capability' Brown. Every whim of fashion is represented, whether it be for a Chinese bridge, artificial lake, classical temple or rustic ruin. The present house was built about 1839 by the Earl de Grey, whose family had lorded over the Manor of Wrest for 600 years. The State Rooms and gardens are open to the public.

Location: ¾ m (1 km) east of Silsoe.
Opening Times: Good Friday or Apr 1 (whichever is earlier) to Sept 30, weekends and Bank Hols only 10–6. Adm £1.50, Concessions £1.10, Chd 75p. Refreshments available.

Thomas Gainsborough (1727–1787)

His paintings can be seen at the following properties included in Historic Houses Castles and Gardens:

> *Althorp*
> *Arundel Castle*
> *Christchurch Manor*
> *Gainsborough's House*
> *Kenwood*
> *Shalom Hall*
> *Weston Park*

BERKSHIRE

BASILDON PARK, The National Trust

nr Pangbourne map J4
Telephone: Pangbourne (0734) 843040

Classical house built 1776. Unusual Octagon room; fine plasterwork; important paintings and furniture, Garden and woodland walks.

Location: 7 m NW of Reading between Pangbourne and Streatley on A329. Leave M4 at junction 12.
Stations: Pangbourne (2¹/₂ m); Goring and Streatley (3 m).
Opening Times: Apr to end Oct — Weds to Sats 2–6; Suns & Bank Hol Mons 12–6. Last adm to house half-hour before closing. Adm House & Grounds £3. Grounds only £2, Chd half price. Reductions (except Suns and Bank Hol Mons) to House & Grounds for parties of 15 or more (Booking essential). *Closed* Mons (except Bank Hols), Tues & Weds following Bank Hols and Good Friday. Shop. Dogs in grounds only on leads. House unsuitable for wheelchairs.
Refreshments: Tea room in house accessible to wheelchairs.

FROGMORE GARDENS

Windsor map J4
(Her Majesty The Queen)

Beautifully landscaped gardens with trees, shrubs and lake.

Location: Entrance to garden through Long Walk Gate. *(Visitors are requested kindly to refrain from entering grounds of the Home Park).*
Stations: Windsor & Eton Central; Windsor & Eton Riverside (both 20 mins walk).
Opening Times: GARDEN ONLY. Open on Wed May 6 & Thurs May 7: 10.30–7 (last adm 6.30). Adm £1.50, accompanied Chd free. No dogs. Free car park. Coaches by appointment only (apply to National Gardens Scheme, Hatchlands Park, East Clandon, Guildford, Surrey GU4 7RT. Tel: (0483) 211535, stating whether am or pm pass is required). The Royal Mausoleum also open on above 2 days, adm free. (In addition Mausoleum open Wed May 20: 11–4, but *not* the gardens).
Refreshments: Tent at car park – May 6 & 7.

FROGMORE HOUSE

Windsor map J4
Telephone: (0753) 831118

One of the least known royal residences Frogmore House is situated within the private Home Park at Windsor Castle. Built in the late 17th century the house is particularly associated with Queen Charlotte and with the Duchess of Kent, Queen Victoria's mother. The house has been extensively restored and is furnished with many of its original contents reflecting the taste and interests of former residents.

Opening Times: Early August to late September. Telephone (0753) 831118 for details.

MAPLEDURHAM HOUSE – SEE UNDER OXFORDSHIRE

THE OLD RECTORY

Burghfield map J4
(Mr & Mrs R. R. Merton)

Garden of horticultural interest; roses, hellebores, lilies, many rare and unusual plants from China and Japan; old-fashioned cottage plants; autumn colour.

Location: 5½ m SW of Reading, between M4 junctions 11 & 12.
Stations: Reading and Mortimer (3¹/₂ m).
Opening Times: GARDEN ONLY. Last Wed of every month except Nov, Dec, Jan, (11–4.) Adm 50p, Chd 10p. *In aid of National Gardens Scheme.* (Share to Save the Children and NCCPG). Plants & produce for sale. No dogs.

SAVILL GARDEN – *See page 33*

SWALLOWFIELD PARK

Swallowfield map J4
(Country Houses Association Ltd)

Built by the Second Earl of Clarendon in 1678.

Location: In the village of Swallowfield 6 m SE of Reading.
Opening Times: May to September — Weds & Thurs 2–5. Last entry 4.30. Adm £1.50, Chd 50p. Free car park. No dogs admitted.

VALLEY GARDENS

Windsor Great Park map J4
(Crown Property)
Telephone: (0753) 860222

Extensive woodland gardens of 400 acres which include a large heather garden offering beauty and charm at all seasons of the year.

Location: To be approached from Wick Road off A30 (1 m walk).
Station: Egham (3 m).
Opening Times: Open daily from sunrise to sunset. Adm free to pedestrians. Car park adjoining gardens. £2 per car.

WELFORD PARK

nr Newbury map H4
Telephone: Boxford (048838) 203
(Mrs. A. C. Puxley)

Queen Anne house with later additions. Attractive gardens and grounds.

Location: 6 m NW of Newbury and 1 m N of Wickham village off B4000.
Opening Times: Spring and Summer Bank Hols and June 1–26 inclusive from 2.30–5. Interior by prior appointment only. Adm £2, OAP's and under 16's £1.50.

WINDSOR CASTLE

Windsor map J4
Telephone: Windsor (0753) 868286
(Official residence of H.M. The Queen)

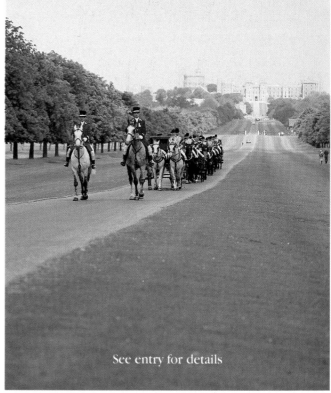

Windsor Castle

See entry for details

Perhaps the largest fortress of its kind in the world, Windsor Castle has belonged to the Sovereigns of England for over 900 years, and is by far, the oldest residence still in regular use. The Castle has the following areas open to the public:–
State Apartments (except when HM The Queen in official residence).

WINDSOR CASTLE – *continued*

Queen Mary's Dolls' House.
Exhibition of The Queen's Presents and Royal Carriages.

Location: 3m off J6 of M4.
Opening Times: Open all year (State apartments closed when Her Majesty The Queen is in official residence). **Group Discounts:** Special group rates on application. This applies to the following: The State Apartments, Exhibition of The Queen's Presents and Royal Carriages, Queen Mary's Dolls' House.

Whilst there is every intention to adhere to the above schedule this cannot be guaranteed as Windsor Castle is always subject to closure, sometimes at short notice. Enquiries: Castle (0753) 831118; St. George's Chapel (0753) 865538.
Refreshments: Castle Hotel (opposite).

SAVILL GARDEN

Windsor Great Park   map J4
(Crown Property)
Telephone: (0753) 860222

World renowned woodland garden of 35 acres with adjoining area of herbaceous borders, rose gardens, alpine raised beds and an extensive dry garden. The whole garden offering much of great interest and beauty at all seasons.

Location: To be approached from A30 via Wick Road & Wick Lane, Englefield Green.
Station: Egham (3 m).
Opening Times: Open daily 10–6. *Closed* for a short period at Christmas. Adm £2.50, OAPs £2.30. Parties of 20 and over £2.30, accompanied Chd (under 16) free.

BUCKINGHAMSHIRE

CHICHELEY HALL 🏛

Newport Pagnell   map J5
Telephone: North Crawley (023 065) 252
(Trustees of the Hon Nicholas Beatty)

Chicheley Hall, home of the Hon. Nicholas Beatty, is an exceptionally fine early Georgian House built 1719-1723 by Francis Smith of Warwick. Here is some of the most notable brickwork to be found in any house of the period, with the four sides of the house displaying a carefully graduated crescendo of architecural effect. The interior has a striking Palladian Hall designed by Flitcroft and beautiful panelled rooms including Sir John Chester's ingenious hidden library. The rooms are furnished with fine period furniture and pictures. The BEATTY NAVAL MUSEUM at Chicheley contains many mementoes of Admiral Earl Beatty and World War I at sea. The gardens contain a formal three-sided canal designed in 1700 by George London who also worked at Hampton Court. Recently renovated 18th century dovecote. Tea Rooms and Gift Shop.

Location: 2 m E of Newport Pagnell; 11 m W of Bedford on A422.
Opening Times: Apr 19 to May 31, and Aug: every Sun. Also Bank Hol Mons 2.30–6. Last tour 5. Day or evening parties, with or without meals, by appointment at any time throughout the summer. Adm £3, Chd £1.50, parties (over 20) £2.50.
Refreshments: Tea room.

ASCOTT, The National Trust

Wing   map J5   △
Telephone: Aylesbury (0296) 688242

Anthony de Rothschild collection of fine pictures. French and English furniture, exceptional Oriental porcelain containing examples of the Ming, K'ang Hsi and Chun. ware of the Sung dynasty. Gardens contain unusual trees, flower borders, topiary sundial, naturalised bulbs and water lilies.

Location: ½ m E of Wing; 2 m SW of Leighton Buzzard, on the S side of Aylesbury/Leighton Buzzard Road (A418).
Station: Leighton Buzzard (2 m).
Opening Times: HOUSE & GARDENS. Apr 14–May 17; Sept 1–29, Tues to Suns 2–6. Bank Hol Mon, Apr 20 & May 4, 2–6 (but closed Apr 21 & May 5). Garden only: May 20–Aug 31 and every Wed and last Sun in each month and Bank Hol Mons May 25, Aug 31 2–6. Last adm 5. Adm House & Gardens £4, Chd £2; Gardens only £2.50, Chd £1.25. *No reduction for parties.* Dogs on leads, in car park only. Wheelchair access to ground floor and part of garden only. Enquiries: Estate Manager.
NB Owing to large number of visitors, entry is by timed ticket. Occasionally there will be considerable delays in gaining admission to the House.

CHENIES MANOR HOUSE 🏠

Chenies   map J5
Telephone: Little Chalfont 2888
(Lt Col & Mrs MacLeod Matthews)

Photograph Clive Nicholls Photography.

15/16th century Manor House with fortified tower. Original home of the Earls of Bedford, visited by Henry VIII and Elizabeth I. Home of the MacLeod Matthews family. Contains contemporary tapestries and furniture. Hiding places, 'secret' passages, collection of antique dolls; medieval undercroft and well. Surrounded by beautiful gardens which have featured in many publications – a Tudor sunken garden, a white garden, herbaceous borders, a fountain court, a physic garden containing a very wide selection of medical and culinary herbs, and a pentitential maze. The kitchen garden is in the Victorian style with unusual vegetables and fruit. Special exhibitions throughout open period. Flower drying and arrangements.

Location: Off A404 between Amersham & Rickmansworth (M25 – junction 18).
Station: Chorleywood (1½ m).
Opening Times: First week in April to end of Oct Weds and Thurs 2–5. Also open Bank Hol Mons May 25 & Aug 31, 2–6. Adm £3, GARDENS ONLY £1.50, Chd (under 14) half-price. Parties throughout the year by prior arrangement – min charge £50. Free parking. No dogs.
Refreshments: Home-made teas.

CHICHELEY HALL – *See page 33*

CHILTERN OPEN AIR MUSEUM

Newland Park, Gorelands Lane, Chalfont St Giles   map J4
Telephone: Chalfont St Giles (024 07) 71117
(Chiltern Open Air Museum Ltd)

A museum of historic buildings, rescued from demolition, and which reflect the vernacular heritage of the Chilterns region. You can explore barns, granaries, cartsheds and stables, a blacksmith's forge, a toll house and a vicarage room – and the collection is growing all the time. Several of the buildings incorporate displays illustrating their original use, or house exhibitions on Chiltern life and landscape. The Museum occupies 45 acres of parkland and woodland which has an attractive Nature Trail running through it.

Location: At Newland Park, Chalfont St Giles; 4½ m Amersham, 8 m Watford, 6 m Beaconsfield; 2 m A413 at Chalfont St Peter, 4 m from junction 17 on the M25 via Maple Cross and the Chalfonts.
Station: Chorleywood.
Opening Times: Apr to Oct – Weds to Suns & Bank Hols 2–6. Parties & School parties by arrangement weekdays all year round. Adm £2.50, OAPs £2, Chd under 16yrs £2, under 5 free. Family ticket (2 adults 2 chd £8).
Refreshments: Home-made teas.

CLAYDON HOUSE, The National Trust

Middle Claydon, nr Winslow   map J5   ♿
Telephone: Steeple Claydon (0296) 730349/730693

Built mid 18th century as an addition to an earlier house. The stone-faced West front contains a series of magnificent and unique rococo state-rooms, also Florence Nightingale Museum, her bedroom and sitting room.

Location: In the village of Middle Claydon, 13m NW of Aylesbury, 3½ m SW of Winslow. Signposted from A413, A421 and A41.
Opening Times: Apr to end Oct – Sat to Wed 1–5, Bank Hol Mons 1–5. Last adm 4.30. *Closed Thurs & Fris (inc Good Friday).* Adm £3, Chd £1.50. Parties write to Custodian. Dogs in park on leads only. Wheelchairs provided (access to ground floor only, half price adm).
Refreshments: Available at house.

CLIVEDEN, The National Trust

Maidenhead (1851)   map J4   △
Telephone: Burnham (0628) 605069

Gardens contain temples by Giacomo Leoni. Box parterre, fountain, formal walks; amphitheatre, water garden, rose garden, herbaceous borders. Views of Thames.

Location: 3 m upstream from Maidenhead; 2 m N of Taplow on Hedsor Road. Main entrance opposite Feathers Inn.
Stations: Taplow (2¹/₂ m) (not Suns); Maidenhead (4¹/₄ m).
Opening Times: GROUNDS: Mar to end Oct—Daily 11–6 or sunset if earlier. Nov and Dec: daily 11–4. *Closed* Jan & Feb. HOUSE: Apr to Oct, Thurs & Suns 3–6 (last adm 5.30). Adm Grounds £3. House £1 extra (timed ticket), Chd half price. *Parties must book. No dogs in House or in gardens, in specified woodlands only on lead.* Wheelchairs available. Shop: Apr to end Oct, Weds to Suns (incl Good Friday) & Bank Hol Mons 1–5.30. Also pre-Christmas (s.a.e. for details).
Refreshments: Light lunches, coffee, teas in Conservatory Restaurant Apr to end Oct (Weds to Suns & Bank Hol Mons 11–5).

COWPER & NEWTON MUSEUM

Olney   map J6
Telephone: Bedford (0234) 711516

Personal belongings of William Cowper and Rev. John Newton. Bobbin lace and items of local interest.

Location: Market Place, Olney; N of Newport Pagnell via A509.

DORNEY COURT 

nr Windsor   map J4
Telephone: Burnham (0628) 604638
(Mr & Mrs Peregrine Palmer)

"One of the finest Tudor Manor Houses in England" Country Life. A visit to Dorney is a most welcome, refreshing and fascinating experience. Built about 1440 and lived in by the present family for over 400 years, this enchanting, many gabled pink brick and timber house is a joy to behold. The rooms are full of the continuing atmosphere of history: early 15th and 16th century oak, beautiful 17th century lacquer furniture, 18th and 19th century tables, 400 years of family portraits and stained glass and needlework. Charles II came here to seek the charms of Barbara Palmer, Countess of Castlemaine – 'the most intelligent beautiful and influential of ladies'. The 14th century church of St. James next door, is a lovely, cool, cheerful and very English Church.

Location: 2 m W of Eton & Windsor in village of Dorney on B3026. Signposted from M4, exit 7.
Station: Burnham (2 m).
Opening Times: Easter weekend Fri to Mon; May Suns & Bank Hol Mons; also Sun, Mon & Tues in June, July, Aug & Sept; 2–5.30. Adm £3, Chd over 9 £1.50. 10% discount for National Trust and NADFAS members and OAPs. Parties at other times by arrangement. Last admission and last orders for teas at 5.
Refreshments: Home-made cream teas.

HUGHENDEN MANOR, The National Trust   ❧

High Wycombe   map J4   ♿
Telephone: High Wycombe (0494) 532580

Home of Benjamin Disraeli, Earl of Beaconsfield (1847-1881). Small formal garden.

Location: 1½ m N of High Wycombe on W side Gt Missenden Road (A4128).
Station: High Wycombe (2 m).
Opening Times: HOUSE & GARDEN. Mar – Sats & Suns only 2–6 (or sunset if earlier), Apr to end of Oct—Weds to Sats 2–6; Suns & Bank Hol Mons 12–6. *Closed* Good Friday. Adm £3, Chd half price. Shop open as House and pre-Christmas Nov to Dec 13 Wed to Sun, 12–4. *Parties must book in advance.* Dogs in Park & car park only. Wheelchair provided. Parties Weds to Fris only if booked in advance.

MILTON'S COTTAGE

Chalfont St Giles map J5 ♿
Telephone: Chalfont St Giles 2313
(Milton Cottage Trust)

The Cottage where John Milton completed 'Paradise Lost' and began 'Paradise Regained', contains many Milton relics and a library including first and early editions and many translations into other languages. Preserved as it was in 1665. Two museum rooms and charming cottage garden open to the public.

Location: ½ m W of A413; on road to Seer Green and Beaconsfield.
Station: Gerrards Cross L.T. to Amersham or Chalfont and Latimer.
Opening Times: Mar to Oct—Tues to Sats 10–1, 2–6; Suns 2–6. Spring & Summer Bank Hol Mons 10–1, 2–6. *Closed* Mons (except Bank Hols) & Jan, Feb, Nov & Dec. Adm £1.50, Chd (under 15) 60p, Parties of 20 or more £1.20. Car park for visitors.

NETHER WINCHENDON HOUSE

Aylesbury map J5 △ ♿
Telephone: Haddenham 290101
(Trustees of Will Trust of J. G. C. Spencer Bernard Dec'd)
Correspondence to Administrator, R. V. Spencer Bernard Esq.

Tudor manor house with 18th century additions. Home of Sir Francis Bernard, Governor of New Jersey and Massachusetts, 1760.

Location: 1 m N of A418 Aylesbury/Thame Road, nr village of Lower Winchendon, 6 m SW Aylesbury.
Station: Aylesbury (7½ m).
Opening Times: May 4 to May 31; Aug 30 & 31. 2.30–5.30. Last party each day at 4.45. Parties at any time of year by written appointment. Adm £1.75, Chd (under 12) £1.25; OAPs £1.25 (not weekends or Bank Hols).

PRINCES RISBOROUGH MANOR HOUSE, The National Trust

Princes Risborough map J5 ♿

17th century red-brick house with Jacobean oak staircase.

Location: Opposite church off market square in town centre.
Station: Princes Risborough (1 m).
Opening Times: Open by written arrangement only—Weds 2.30–4.30. Last adm 4. Principal rooms and staircase shown. Adm £1, Chd 50p. No reductions for parties. No dogs. Wheelchair access.

STOWE LANDSCAPE GARDENS, The National Trust

nr Buckingham *map J5*
Telephone: (0280) 822850

Splendid landscape gardens with buildings and temples by Vanbrugh, Kent and Gibbs. One of the supreme creations of the Georgian era. (N.B. the main house is in the ownership of Stowe School.)

Location: 3 m NW of Buckingham, via Stowe Avenue off the A422 Buckingham/Banbury Road.
Opening Times: Mar 28 to Apr 20 (Easter Bank Hol Mon), June 28 to Sept 6, Oct 24 to Nov 1, Dec 19–24 and Dec 27–31, Jan 1–10, 1993, and Mar 27 to Apr 18, 1993: daily 10–6 or dusk if earlier. Also Apr 22 to June 26, Sept 7 to Oct 23: Mon, Wed & Fri 10–5 or dusk if earlier. Last adm 1 hour before closing. *Closed* Good Friday, Dec 25 and 26. Entry to Gardens £3. The main house belongs to Stowe School and may be open during Stowe School holidays at an additional charge of £2 (inc NT members). Dogs on lead only. Batricar available for disabled visitors, telephone Administrator for details.
Refreshments: Light refreshments and teas as above 12–5 (12–4 during Dec and Jan).

STOWE (Stowe School)

Buckingham map J5

Famous 18th century house formerly the home of the Duke of Buckingham. Superb landscaped gardens with largest collection of garden buildings in England by Bridgeman, Kent, Gibbs, Vanburgh and 'Capability' Brown.

Location: 4 m N of Buckingham town.
Opening Times: HOUSE ONLY: Apr 1–14; July 6 to Sept 6: 11–5. Adm £2, Chd £1. **Please note** it may be necessary to close the house for private functions. Please check before visiting. Tel: (0280) 813650.
Refreshments: Pre-booked only. Guide books, postcards, souvenirs and prints available from the Stowe Bookshop.

THE THATCHED COTTAGE

Duck Lane, Ludgershall, Nr. Aylesbury, Buckinghamshire
Telephone: (0844) 237415
(Mr & Mrs D. A. Tolman)

An enchanting cottage garden crammed with rare and old fashioned plants, surrounding a pretty thatched hovel, a type of building almost extinct. The diminutive cottage is lived in by the owners and is too small to admit visitors inside but they are welcome to look in through the windows. The garden contains many rare plants including old fashioned pinks, violets, primulas, foxgloves and geraniums; roses, clematis and unusual shrubs and herbs. Many interesting features including topiary, gnarled oak structures and stone paths, all neatly fitted into half an acre. Plants are labelled.

Location: Ludgershall is 2m S of the A41 between Bicester and Aylesbury (Bicester 6m; Aylesbury 13m).
Opening Times: Suns May 17, 24, June 28 and July 5, 2–6. Also by appointment if arranged in advance. Adm £1 in aid of National Gardens Scheme, Chd free. Parties by appointment in advance. No coaches, parking available nearby. Not suitable for disabled visitors.
Refreshments: Teas are available at the owners' nearby nursery. See Nursery entry for Plants From A Country Garden, Ludgershall, Bucks.

WADDESDON MANOR, The National Trust ❦

nr Aylesbury   map J5   △   ♿
Telephone: Aylesbury (0296) 651211

In 1874 Baron Ferdinand de Rothschild acquired the Buckinghamshire hilltop which became the site for the Destailleur designed château, around which is set one of the finest late Victorian formal gardens and parks designed by Lainé. Restoration plans for the gardens include shrubberies and additional bedding to the fountain terrace. The elegant cast iron rococo style aviary, built in 1889, contains mainly softbill birds and some parrots.
House closed for refurbishment during 1992. Open again in 1993.
Grounds, aviary, gift shop and tea room remain open during 1992.
Location: At W end of Waddesdon village: 6 m NW of Aylesbury on Bicester Road (A41). *Station: Aylesbury (6 m).*
Buses: Red Rover 1, 15, 16, from Aylesbury. (Tel: Aylesbury 28686.)
Opening Times: GROUNDS & AVIARY ONLY Mar 18 to Dec 22—Wed to Fri 12–5, weekends and Bank Hol Mons 12–6. Adm £3, Chd (5–17) £1.50, Chd under 5 free.
Free guided tours of the grounds and aviary (to include information about refurbishment) will be available to visitors, weather permitting. Free parking near stables. Play area for young children. Dogs not admitted except guide dogs. Free entry to stables for gift shop and tea room.
Shops: Gift shop, which includes Christmas shopping, open as grounds.
Refreshments: Light lunches and teas in tearoom, open as grounds.

WEST WYCOMBE PARK (1750), The National Trust ❦

West Wycombe   map J4   △
Telephone: High Wycombe (0494) 524411

Palladian house with frescoes and painted ceilings. 18th century landscape garden with lake and various classical temples.
Location: At W end of West Wycombe, S of Oxford Road (A40), 2½ m W High Wycombe.
Station: High Wycombe (2½ m).

Opening Times: GROUNDS ONLY. Apr & May Suns & Weds 2–6, and Easter, May Day and Spring Bank Hols. Sun & Mon 2–6. *Closed* Good Friday. HOUSE & GROUNDS: June, July & Aug, Suns to Thurs inc Summer Bank Hol Mon 2–6 (last adm 5.15). Entry to house by timed tickets on weekdays. Adm House & Grounds £4; Grounds only £2.50, Chd half price. *No reduction for parties.* Dogs in car park only. House unsuitable for wheelchairs.

WINSLOW HALL

Winslow   map J5   △
Telephone: (0296) 712323
(Sir Edward & Lady Tomkins)

Built 1698–1702. Almost certainly designed by Sir Christopher Wren. Has survived without major structural alteration and retains most of its original features. Modernized and redecorated by the present owners. Good eighteenth century furniture, mostly English. Some fine pictures, clocks and carpets. Several examples of Chinese art, notably of the Tang period. Beautiful gardens with many unusual trees and shrubs.
Location: At entrance to Winslow on the Aylesbury road (A413).
Opening Times: Open all Bank Holiday weekends except Christmas 2–5. July and Aug: Wed and Thurs 2.30–5.30 or by appointment throughout the year. Adm £3, Chd free.
Refreshments: Catering by arrangement.

WOTTON HOUSE 🏛

nr Aylesbury   map J5
(Administrator Mrs Patrick Brunner)

Built 1704, on the same plan as Buckingham House, which later became Buckingham Palace. Interior remodelled by Sir John Soane 1820. Wrought iron by Tijou and Thomas Robinson. 'Capability' Brown landscape 1757-1760.
Location: In Wotton Underwood 2 m S of A41 midway between Aylesbury and Bicester.
Opening Times: Aug to end of Sept—Weds. Tours 2 and 3.15 (last tour).

CAMBRIDGESHIRE

ANGLESEY ABBEY, The National Trust ❦

nr Cambridge   map K6   ♿
Telephone: Cambridge (0223) 811200

The Abbey, founded in the reign of Henry I, was later converted to an Elizabethan manor. Contains Fairhaven collection of art treasures. About 100 acres of garden including flower borders, trees, avenues, unique garden statuary and a working water mill that grinds corn.
Location: In village of Lode 6 m NE of Cambridge on B1102, signposted off A45.
Station: Cambridge (6 m).
Opening Times: HOUSE. Mar 28 to Oct 18—Wed to Sat 1.30–5.30; *closed* Good Fri. Sun & Bank Hol Mons 1–5.30. Adm House and Garden £4.50, Sun & Bank Hol Mon £5.50. Pre-booked parties of 15 or more £3.50 (Weds, Thurs, Fris and Sats only). GARDEN. Mar 28 to July 12—Wed to Sun & Bank Hol Mons 11–5.30; July 13 to Sept 8 daily 11–5.30. Sept 12 to Oct 18—Sat to Wed 11–5.30. Adm £2,25, Sun & Bank Hol Mon £2.50, Chd (with adult) half price. No dogs. Wheelchair access (house difficult); chairs provided. Free car park & picnic area.
Lode Mill: Mar 28 to Oct 18—Sat, Suns & Bank Hol Mons 1.30–5.30.
Refreshments: Restaurant open same days as House 11–5, lunches and teas. Table licence. Kiosk service only Mon & Tues, July 15 to Sept 10.

DENNY ABBEY

map K6
Telephone: (0223) 860489

After a brief life as a Benedictine priory, the abbey passed to the Knights Templar who used it as a hospital for their sick and aged members. In 1308 the Order was suppressed and the inmates arrested. The abbey remained empty until 1339 when the widowed Countess of Pembroke acquired it and moved the Franciscan nuns from her Abbey at Waterbeach to Denny. Most of the monastic buildings were demolished in the 16th century, but there are remnants of the 12th century church and 14th century additions.

Location: 6 m (9.7 km) north of Cambridge on A10. OS map ref TL495684.
Opening Times: Good Friday or Apr 1 (whichever is earlier) to Sept 30: Open Daily 10–6. Oct 1 to Maundy Thursday or Mar 31 (whichever is earlier): Open Suns only 10–4. *Closed* Dec 24–26, Jan 1. Adm £1.10, Concessions 85p, Chd 55p.

DOCWRA'S MANOR

Shepreth   map K6
Telephone: (0763) 261473, 261557 or 260235
(Mrs John Raven)

Two acres of choice plants in a series of enclosed gardens.

Location: Opposite War Memorial in centre of Shepreth village; ½ m W of Cambridge to Royston Rd (A10) bus stops at gate.
Station: Shepreth.
Opening Times: GARDEN ONLY. All year Mon, Wed, Fri 10–5. Suns Apr 5, May 3, June 7, July 5, Aug 2, (2–6), also Bank Holiday Mons (10–5); Adm £1, accompanied Chd free. Proceeds for garden upkeep. Also Suns May 10, Sept 6 (2–7) £1.50 *in aid of National Gardens Scheme.* Also open by appointment. No dogs. Small nursery for hardy plants.
Refreshments: Teas Suns May 10, Sept 6. Proceeds shared with Shepreth Church Funds.

ELTON HALL

nr Peterborough   map J6
(Mr & Mrs William Proby)
Telephone: (0832) 280 468

Spanning five centuries, this romantic and gracious house has been the home of the Proby family for over 300 years. The house, with its mixture of medieaval, gothic and classical styles, reflects the family's passion for collecting, and this is shown in the remarkable contents to be seen today – excellent furniture outstanding paintings by Gainsborough, Reynolds, Constable, Alma Tadema, Millais and other fine arts.

There are over 12,000 books, including Henry VIII's prayer book. Attractive gardens, including restored Rose Garden, new herbaceous borders and recently planted Arboretum.

Location: On A605, 5 m W of Peterborough.
Opening Times: Easter Sun, Mon 2–5; Bank Hols during May and Aug, Sun, Mon 2–5; July–Weds & Suns 2–5; Aug–Weds, Thurs, Suns 2–5. Adm £3, Chd £1.50. Private parties by arrangement with House Manager, prices on application. Free parking. Shop.
Refreshments: Home-made teas. Lunches by arrangement.

ISLAND HALL

Godmanchester   map K6
(Mr Christopher & The Hon Mrs Vane Percy)

An important mid 18th century mansion of great charm owned and being restored by an award winning Interior Designer. Lovely rooms with fine period detail and interesting possessions relating to the owners' ancestors since their first occupation of the house in 1800. Tranquil riverside setting with ornamental island forming part of the grounds.

Location: In centre of Godmanchester next to the car park. 1 m S of Huntingdon (A1); 15 m NW of Cambridge (A604).
Station: Huntingdon (1 m).
Opening Times: June 14 to Sept 6 Suns only 2.30–5. Parties particularly welcome May to Sept by appointment. Party rate £1.50 groups over 40. Adm House and Grounds £2, Chd £1 (grounds only). Grounds only £1.
Refreshments: Teas.

KIMBOLTON CASTLE

Kimbolton   map K6
(Governors of Kimbolton School)

Tudor manor house associated with Katherine of Aragon, completely remodelled by Vanbrugh (1708-20); courtyard c. 1694. Fine murals by Pellegrini in chapel, boudoir and on staircase. Gatehouse by Robert Adam. Parkland.

Location: 8 m NW of St Neots on A45; 14 m N of Bedford.
Station: St Neots (9 m).
Opening Times: Easter Sun & Mon; Spring Bank Hol Sun & Mon; Summer Bank Hol Sun & Mon also Suns only late July and Aug: 2–6. Adm 75p Chd & OAPs 50p.

LONGTHORPE TOWER ⚏

map K6
Telephone: (0733) 268482

This three-storey tower, added to an existing fortified manor house about 1300, is remarkable for the richness and completeness of its early 14th century wall-paintings. These were discovered less than 40 years ago under layers of limewash and distemper, and depict scenes from the Bible and of life in the East Anglian countryside; the most complete set of such paintings of the period in Northern Europe.

Location: 2 m (3.2 km) west of Peterborough on A47. OS map ref TL163983.
Opening Times: Good Friday or Apr 1 (whichever is earlier) to Sept 30: Open Daily 10−6. Oct 1 to Maundy Thursday or Mar 31 (whichever is earlier): Open Weds 10−4. *Closed* Dec 24 −26, Jan 1. Adm £1.10, Concessions 85p, Chd 55p.

OLIVER CROMWELL'S HOUSE

Ely   map K6
Telephone: Ely (0353) 662062

The historic home of Cromwell and his family, beautifully restored to recreate a 17th century atmosphere. An audio visual presentation on Cromwell, and life size animated models are both informative and entertaining.

Location: 29 St Mary's Street, Ely.
Station: Ely (1 m).
Opening Times: Oct 1 to Apr 1: Mon−Sat 10−5.15; May 1 to Sept 30: daily, including Sun and Bank Hols 10−6. Adm charge. Party rates available and guided tours by arrangement.

PECKOVER HOUSE AND GARDEN, The National Trust ❧

Wisbech   map K7   △   ᨒ
Telephone: Wisbech (0945) 583463

Important example of early 18th century domestic architecture. Fine rococo decoration. Interesting Victorian garden contains rare trees, flower borders, roses. Under glass are orange trees. Georgian stables.

Location: Centre of Wisbech town on N bank of River Nene (B1441).
Station: March (9½ m).
Opening Times: HOUSE & GARDENS: Mar 28 to Nov 1, Sun, Wed & Bank Hol Mon. 2−5.30. Garden also open Mon, Tues, Sat. Adm £2.20, Chld £1.10. Party rate £1.60. Garden only days, adm £1. No dogs. Wheelchairs garden only.

PRIOR CRAUDEN'S CHAPEL

The College, Ely   map K6
Telephone: (0353) 662837
(The Bursar, The King's School)

Built as a private chapel in 1324/1325 for Prior Crauden, the Prior of the Mediaeval Benedictine Monastery from 1321 to 1341. Recently restored to show glimpses of coloured walls, painted glass and wall paintings. In 1649 Cromwell's Commissioners planned to destroy the Chapel, but it was saved by being turned into a dwelling house for two hundred years, until a restoration in 1850. Now on view to the public and used for services by the King's School, Ely.

Location: In the precincts of Ely Cathedral.
Opening Times: Mon to Fri 9−5, excluding statutory and Bank Hols. Key available from Chapter Office in Firmary Lane. Adm free. Parking in Cathedral Car Park. Not suitable for disabled visitors.
Refreshments: Lamb Hotel, and restaurants in City of Ely.

WIMPOLE HALL, The National Trust ❧

nr Cambridge   map K5   Ⓢ
Telephone: Cambridge (0223) 207257

An architecturally refined house of aristocratic proportions, sumptuous 18th and 19th century staterooms, set in a beautifully undulating park devised by the best of the landscape architects. Exhibition at Stable Block.

Location: 8 m SW of Cambridge; signposted off A603 at New Wimpole.
Stations: Shepreth (5 m) (not Suns); Royston (7 m).
Opening Times: HOUSE, GARDEN & PARK. Mar 28 to Nov 1, Tues, Weds, Thurs, Sat, Sun 1−5, Bank Hol Sun & Mon 11−5 also Fris July 24 to Aug 21. Adm: £4.40, Chd £2. Pre-booked parties of 15 or more £3.40 (Tues to Thurs only). Joint ticket Hall & Farm £6. Picnic area. Shop. Dogs allowed in park only on leads. Wheelchair access, 3 chairs provided.
Refreshments: Lunches & teas in the Dining Room 12−5. Table licence. Light refreshments at stable block 10.30−5.

WIMPOLE HOME FARM, The National Trust ❧

nr Cambridge   map K5

An historic farm, faithfully restored by the National Trust, set in 350 acres of beautiful parkland. Approved Rare Breeds Centre. Children's corner. Agricultural museum. Adventure playground. Shop. Film loft.

Location: 8 m S of Cambridge; signposted off A603 at New Wimpole.
Stations: Shepreth (5 m); Royston (7 m).
Opening Times: Mar 28 to Nov 1: Tues, Wed, Thurs, Sat, Sun & Bank Hol Mon, 10.30−5. Also open Fris July 24 to Aug 21. Adm £3.40, NT members £1.50, Chd over 3 £1.50, parties (pre-booked) £2.40. Joint ticket for Hall and Farm £5.
Refreshments: Lunches & teas at Wimpole Hall. Snacks at Home Farm.

CHESHIRE

ADLINGTON HALL 🏛

Macclesfield   map G8
Telephone: Prestbury 829206
(Charles Legh, Esq.)

ADLINGTON HALL – *continued*

Adlington Hall is a Cheshire Manor and has been the home of the Leghs since 1315. The Great Hall was built between 1450 and 1505, the Elizabethan 'Black and White' in 1581 and the Georgian South Front in 1757. The Bernard Smith Organ was installed c 1670. A 'Shell Cottage', Yew Walk and Lime Avenue are features of the gardens.

Location: 5 m N of Macclesfield on the Stockport/Macclesfield Road (A523).
Station: Adlington (¹/₂ m).
Opening Times: Good Friday to Oct 4 – Suns & Bank Hols: 2–5.30. Adm HALL AND GARDENS £2.50, Chd £1. GARDENS ONLY £1, Chd 50p. *Special parties by arrangement other days (over 25 people £1.90).* Gift shop. Car park free.
Refreshments: At the Hall.

ARLEY HALL AND GARDENS 👁

nr Great Budworth and midway between Warrington and Northwich   map G8
Telephone: Arley (0565) 777353, Fax: (0565) 777465
(The Hon M. L. W. Flower)

ARLEY HALL AND GARDENS
Near Great Budworth, Northwich, Cheshire
(Between Warrington and Northwich)

the home of the Hon. Michael and Mrs Flower

Arley Hall is still owned by the family after 500 years, and the present Victorian country house contains fine plaster work, oak panelling, paintings, family furniture and other artefacts. Private chapel, 12 acres of Gardens, woodland walk, 15th century tithe barn and picnic area. Frequently used for TV, filming, functions and events. Guided tours and parties by arrangement. For other details see editorial reference or phone (0565) 777353.

Victorian country house and private Chapel (c 1840). Gardens with magnificent displays throughout the open season and elegant woodland walk. Special features include award-winning herbaceous border, Ilex avenue, topiary, herb garden, fine yew hedges, walled gardens, azaleas.

Location: 5 m N of Northwich; 6 m W of Knutsford; 7 m S of Warrington; 5 m off M6 at junctions 19 & 20; 5 m off M56 at junctions 9 & 10. Nearest main roads A49 and A50.
Opening Times: Mar 29 to Oct 4 – Tues to Suns & Bank Hol Mons 12–5, extended hours for group and party bookings. Adm GARDENS £2.50, HALL £1.50.
Refreshments: Lunches and other refreshments in converted Tudor barn. Shop, and plant sales. Craft workers and farm for children nearby. Facilities for disabled visitors.

BEESTON CASTLE ✣

map F8
Telephone: (0829) 260464
(English Heritage)

Built on an isolated crag, Beeston Castle is visible for miles around. The view across the Cheshire plain extends to the Pennines in the east and westwards to Wales. Begun about 1220 by Ranulf de Blundeville, the castle was further fortified by Edward I. The ditch alone can have been no small task, as it is hewn from the solid rock. There is an exhibition on the history of the castle in the museum.

Location: 2 m (3.2 km) west of Bunbury. 11m (18 km) south east of Chester. OS map ref SJ537593.
Opening Times: Good Friday or Apr 1 (whichever is earlier) to Sept 30: daily 10–6. Oct 1 to Maundy Thursday or Mar 31 (whichever is earlier) Tues to Sun 10–4. *Closed* Dec 24–26, Jan 1. Adm £1.80, Concessions £1.40, Chd 90p.

CAPESTHORNE – *See page 41*

CHOLMONDELEY CASTLE GARDENS – *See page 42*

DORFOLD HALL 👁

Nantwich   map G7   △
Telephone: Nantwich (0270) 625245
(R. C. Roundell, Esq.)

Jacobean country house built 1616. Beautiful plaster ceilings and panelling. Attractive gardens. Guided tours.

Location: 1 m W of Nantwich on A534 Nantwich/Wrexham Road.
Station: Nantwich (1¹/₂ m).
Opening Times: Apr to Oct – Tues & Bank Hol Mons 2–5. Adm £2.50, Chd £1.50. *At other times by appointment only.*

DUNHAM MASSEY, The National Trust 🌿

Altrincham   map G8
Telephone: 061-941 1025

Fine 18th century house with Georgian and Edwardian interiors. Huguenot silver collection, fine furniture and family portraits. Large garden, extensively replanted with shade loving and waterside plants, with attractive woodland. Deer park and water mill.

Location: 3 m SW of Altrincham off A56; junction 19 off M6; junction 7 off M56.
Opening Times: Apr 1 to Nov 1: House: Sat to Thur 1–5 (Sun and Bank Hol Mons 12–5); Garden open daily 12–5.30 (Suns & Bank Hol Mons 11–5.30). Last adm 4.30. Guided evening tours by arrangement at an extra charge. Shop: open same days as house 12–5.30 (Sun & Bank Hol Mons 11–5.30). Also open Nov 5 to Dec 13: Thurs to Sun 12–4; June 9 to Mar 28, 1993: Sat, Sun 12–4. Park only £1.50 per car (NT Members free). Coaches free. Adm: House and Garden £4, Chd £2. Garden only £2. Family ticket £10. Reduced rates for pre-booked parties. Dogs in park only on lead. Wheelchairs provided – access to shop, garden and park. Limited access to house. Information from the Administrator, Dunham Massey Hall, Altrincham, Cheshire. WA14 4SJ.
Refreshments: Licensed self-service restaurant for lunches & teas open as shop. Also open for booked parties, functions etc – by arrangement. Tel: 061-941 2815.

CAPESTHORNE

Macclesfield   map G8
Telephone: Chelford (0625) 861221, 861779   Fax: 861439
(Mr and Mrs William Bromley-Davenport)

CAPESTHORNE

near MACCLESFIELD, CHESHIRE

Capesthorne is the home of the Bromley-Davenport family where they and their ancestors, the Capesthornes and Wards have lived since Domesday times. Adjoining the house is a beautiful Georgian Chapel where services are still held. Tea rooms overlook the gardens and lakes. An unusual feature is the family theatre situated in the east wing and used for plays, recitals etc.

The extensive grounds include an Arboretum, nature trail and delightful woodland walk.

Other amenities include a Touring Caravan Park, Fishing and children's play area, Craft and souvenir shops.

Capesthorne is available for Corporate Entertaining and a brochure outlining the many advantages of using the hall and grounds is available on request.

Enquiries to:-
Commander J. D. Hegarty R.N., Administrator, Capesthorne Hall, Macclesfield, Cheshire SK11 9JY.   Tel: (0625) 861221/861779   Fax: (0625) 861439.

ADMISSION – SEE EDITORIAL REFERENCE

Capesthorne has been the home of the Bromley-Davenport family and their ancestors the Capesthornes and Wards since Domesday times. The family were originally Chief Foresters responsible for the law and order in the King's Forests of Macclesfield and Leek. The family crest, a felon's head with a halter of gold around his neck, denoted the power of life and death without trial or appeal. Later members of this same family were to serve as Speakers to the House of Commons and in the last and present centuries, as Members of Parliament. Recent research has revealed that Francis and William Smith of Warwick were almost certainly the original architects of this Jacobean style house built in 1722. Later alterations were made by Blore and Salvin. Pictures, furniture, Capesthorne collection of vases, family muniments and Americana. The extensive grounds include an arboretum, nature trail and delightful woodland walk. Other amenities include a Touring Caravan Park, fishing and children's play area, craft and souvenir shops. Capesthorne is available for Corporate entertaining and a brochure outlining the many advantages of using the hall and grounds is available on request. Enquiries to: Commander J.D. Hegarty RN, Administrator, Capesthorne Hall, Macclesfield, Cheshire SK11 9JY. Telephone: (0625) 861221/861779. Fax: (0625) 861439.

Location: 7 m S of Wilmslow, on Manchester/London Road (A34); 6½ m N of Congleton, Junction 18 (M6).
Station: Chelford (3 m).
Opening Times: PARK, GARDENS AND CHAPEL 12–6, HALL 2–4. April—Suns only; May: Suns & Weds; June/July: Tues, Weds, Thurs & Suns. Aug/Sept: Wed and Sun. *Open* Good Fri and all Bank Hols. Caravan Park open Mar to Oct inc. Adm PARK, GARDENS & CHAPEL £1.75, Chd (5–16 years) 50p, OAP £1.50. PARK, GARDENS, CHAPEL & HALL £3.50, OAP £3, Chd £1. Budget Family ticket £7.50. Visitors to Gardens, Caravanners etc, may visit the Hall by paying the excess of £1.75, Chd 50p, at the desk in the Hall entrance. Chd under 5 years accompanied by an adult free. Coach and Car Park free. Dogs (exempt from government control regulations) are permitted in the Park area only. Organised parties are welcome on any open day plus Tues, Thur, May to Aug inc. by appointment (please send for booking form and coloured brochure). Special reductions for parties of 20 or more at £2.50 per person to Hall, Park, Gardens & Chapel. Evening parties are also welcome on any open day except Sun, May to Aug (by appointment). Evening party rate £3 per person, minimum number 20.
Refreshments: Garden Restaurant & Bromley room.

CHOLMONDELEY CASTLE GARDENS

Malpas   map F7
Telephone: Cholmondeley (0829) 720383 or 720203
(The Marquess of Cholmondeley)

Extensive pleasure gardens dominated by romantic Gothic Castle built in 1801 of local sandstone. Imaginatively laid out with fine trees and water gardens, it has been extensively replanted from the 1960's with rhododendrons, azaleas, cornus, acer and many other acid loving plants. As well as the beautiful water garden, there is a rose and lavender garden and herbaceous borders. Lakeside picnic area, rare breeds of farm animals. Ancient private chapel in park.

Location: Off A41 Chester/Whitchurch Road and A49 Whitchurch/Tarporley Road.
Opening Times: GARDENS & FARM ONLY. Easter Sun to Sept 27—Suns & Bank Hols only 12—5.30. Adm £2.50, OAPs £1.50, Chd 75p. Weekday visits accepted by prior arrangement. Enquiries to: The Secretary, Cholmondeley Castle, Malpas, Cheshire. Gift Shop, Plants for sale. (House not open to public.)
Refreshments: Tea room.

GAWSWORTH HALL

Macclesfield   map G8
Telephone: North Rode (0260) 223456
(Mr & Mrs Timothy Richards)

Tudor half-timbered manor house with tilting ground. Former home of Mary Fitton, Maid of Honour at the Court of Queen Elizabeth I, and the supposed 'dark lady' of Shakespeare's sonnets. Pictures, sculpture and furniture. Open air theatre with covered grand stand – June/July/August. Situated half-way between Macclesfield and Congleton in an idyllic setting close to the lovely medieval church. Open Air Theatre – Taming of The Shrew – June 19 to 27; Gilbert and Sullivan – HMS Pinafore – July 2 to 11; Heroic Brass Band Evenings July 16 to 18; Comedies July 22 to Aug 1. Audience seated in covered stand. Tel: (0260) 223456.

Location: 3 m S of Macclesfield on the Congleton/Macclesfield Road (A536).
Opening Times: Apr 11 to Oct 4 – Daily 2–5.30. Evening parties by arrangement. Adm £3, Chd £1.50. Party rates on application.
Refreshments: In the Pavilion

HANDFORTH HALL

Handforth, nr Wilmslow   map G8
(Dr J. C. Douglas)

Small 16th century half-timbered manor house. Fine Jacobean staircase. Collection of oak furniture. Formal gardens.

Location: ½ m E of Handforth on B5358.
Opening Times: June to Sept by written appointment only.

HARE HILL GARDEN, The National Trust

Over Alderley, nr Macclesfield   map G8

Walled garden with pergola, rhododendrons and azaleas; parkland.

Location: Between Alderley Edge and Prestbury off B5087 at Greyhound Road. Link path to Alderley Edge 2 m in each direction. Free parking at Alderley Edge.
Stations: Alderley Edge (3½ m); Prestbury (2½ m).
Opening Times: Apr 1 to Oct 25 — Weds, Thurs, Sats, Suns and Bank Hol Mons 10–5.30. Special opening for rhododendrons and azaleas May 18 to June 5, daily 10–5.30. Oct 31 to end Mar 1993: Sat & Sun 10–5.30. Adm £1.50. Entrance per car £1, refundable on entry to the garden. Parties by appointment in writing to the Head Gardener, Garden Lodge, Oak Road, Over Alderley, Macclesfield SK10 4QB. Unsuitable for school parties. Wheelchair access – some assistance needed. Wheelchair available.

LITTLE MORETON HALL, The National Trust

Congleton CW12 4SD   map G7
Telephone: Congleton (0260) 272018

Begun in the 15th century, one of the most perfect examples of a timber-framed moated manor house in the country. Remarkable carved gables. Restored 16th century wall paintings are on view. Attractive knot garden.

Location: 4 m SW of Congleton off Newcastle-under-Lyme/Congleton Road (A34).
Opening Times: Apr 1 to Sept 30: Wed to Sun 12–5.30. Bank Hol Mon 11–5.30; last adm 5. *Closed* Good Fri. Oct: Wed, Sat, Sun 12–5.30. School parties: Apr to end Sept: Wed to Fri mornings only by prior arrangement with Administrator (sae please). Optional guided tours most afternoons. Adm weekends & Bank Hols £3; weekdays £2.50; Family ticket £7.50. Pre-booked parties by arrangement. Dogs in car park and grass area in front of Hall only. Wheelchairs provided. Shop.
Refreshments: Light lunches and home made teas. Limited seating.
NB: The South Range was extensively restored in 1991 and new timbers have not yet weathered to blend in with the front of the building.

LYME PARK, The National Trust
(Financed and Managed by Stockport Metropolitan Borough Council)

Disley, Stockport   map G8   △
Telephone: Disley (0663) 762023

An Elizabethan House with 18th and 19th century alterations, particularly by Giacomo Leoni in the 1730's. A lively visitor centre evokes the atmosphere of Edwardian times which carries through into the Hall with the guides as costumed servants of 1910. Formal gardens, including a spectacular Dutch Garden. Over 1377 acres of designated Country Park with breathtaking views of Peak District and Cheshire Plain. The Park contains Red and Fallow deer herds and Countryside Centre. The Hall, park and gardens, are available for filming, promotional use, functions or entertaining.

Opening Times: Hall: Good Friday Apr 17 – Sun Oct 4. *Closed* Mon and Fris except Bank Hols. Freeflow May 23 to June 13 and July 18 to Sept 3 and all Suns 2–5. Last adm 4.15. Otherwise Guided Tours. Also Special Christmas Opening. Please telephone for details. Hall: £1.95, Chd £1 and concessions, £4.95 party ticket (5 people any age). Park & Gardens: Pedestrians free, car/minibus (up to 12 seats) £3 (N.T. members incl.) Motorcycle £2 (incl. riders). Coach passengers £1.50 (N.T. members incl.) for Hall, Park and Gardens. Garden: All year daily except Dec 25, 26. Summer (Apr 17 to Oct 4) 11–5, Winter (Oct 5 to Good Fri '92) 11–4. Other Activities: Pitch & Putt Course, Adventure playground, Orienteering, Nature Trails, Fishing and Horse riding permits. Extensive Events Programme – ask for leaflet. Guided walks and Chapel Services throughout the year. For further information contact: The Marketing & Events Manager, Lyme Park, Disley, Stockport, SK12 2NX – Telephone (0663) 762023.

NESS GARDENS

Wirral map F8 ♿
Telephone: 051-336 7769/8733
(Liverpool University Botanic Gardens)

Finest collection of rhododendrons and azaleas in the NW. Extensive gardens with sweeping lawns and fine specimen trees and shrubs, including some original specimens introduced by George Forrest. Rock, water, heather and terrace Gardens. Herbaceous borders. Rose collection and Herb Garden. Views across the Dee Estuary to the Clwyd Hills. Visitor Centre with slide show, indoor exhibitions and restaurant, Picnic area, children's play adventure playground and gift shop with plant sales area.

Location: Between Neston and Burton; NW of Chester off A540. (5 m from western end of M56).
Station: Neston (1½ m).
Opening Times: Nov to Feb 9.30–4. Closed Christmas day. Mar to Oct 9.30 to dusk. Adm £2.80, Chd (10–18) and OAPs £1.80. Family ticket £7.
Refreshments: Restaurant and tea room Mar to Oct. Tea room Oct to Mar (weather permitting). No dogs.

NETHER ALDERLEY MILL, The National Trust ❖

Nether Alderley map G8
Telephone: Wilmslow (0625) 523012

15th century corn-mill in use until 1939 and now restored; tandem overshot water wheels. Flour ground occasionally for demonstration.

Location: 1½ m S of Alderley Edge on E side of A34.
Station: Alderley Edge (2 m).
Opening Times: Apr 1 to end June & Oct—Weds, Suns & Bank Hol Mons 2–5.30. July, Aug & Sept— Daily (except Mons but open Bank Hol Mons) 2–5.30. Adm £1.50, Chd 75p. No dogs. Unsuitable for disabled or visually handicapped. Parties (maximum 20) by prior arrangement with Mrs Pamela Ferguson, 7 Oak Cottages, Styal, Wilmslow, SK9 4QJ.

NORTON PRIORY MUSEUM

Runcorn map F8
Telephone: Runcorn (0928) 569895
(Norton Priory Museum Trust)

The beautiful woodland gardens covering 30 acres contain the 12th century undercroft and excavated remains of the Priory. Displays of mediaeval tiles, stonework, ceramics etc. Shop, picnic area, refreshments. Two and a half acre award-winning walled garden.

Location: From M56 (junction 11) turn towards Warrington and follow Norton Priory Road signs.
Opening Times: Open daily all year. Apr to Oct—Sats, Suns & Bank Hols 12–6; Mons to Fris 12–5. Nov to Mar—Daily 12–4. Walled Garden open Mar to Oct. *Closed* Dec 24, 25 & 26, Jan 1. Special arrangements for groups. Adm all in ticket £2.20 (£1.10 concession).

PEOVER HALL – *See page 45*

QUARRY BANK MILL – *See page 45*

RODE HALL

Scholar Green, Stoke-on-Trent map G7
Telephone: Alsager (0270) 873237
(Sir Richard Baker Wilbraham Bt.)

18th century country house with Georgian stable block. Later alterations by L. Wyatt and Darcy Braddell.

Location: 5 m SW of Congleton between A34 & A50.
Station: Alsager (2¼ m).
Opening Times: Apr 8 to Sept 30: Weds and Bank Hols 2–5. Adm £2.50.
Refreshments: Bleeding Wolf Restaurant, Scholar Green.

TABLEY HOUSE COLLECTION

Tabley House, Knutsford map G8
Telephone: (0565) 750151
(Tabley House Collection Trust)

Fine Palladian mansion, designed in 1761 by John Carr of York for Sir Peter Byrne Leicester, Bt., and in part remodelled by his son, Sir John Leicester Bt (1st Lord de Tabley), to provide the handsome Regency picture gallery. The splendid series of English paintings, including *Tabley: Windy Day*, by J. M. W. Turner (1808) is part of the great collection assembled by Sir John Leicester during the first quarter of the 19th century, ultimately with the intention of establishing a National Gallery of British Art.

Location: 2 m W of Knutsford, entrance on A5033 (M6 Junction 19, A556).
Opening Times: Apr to Oct: Thurs, Fri, Sat, Sun and Bank Hols 2–5. Adm £2.50, OAP £1.50, Chd £1. Free car park. Main rooms suitable for disabled, but not the Chapel.
Refreshments: Tea room facilities. All enquiries to The Administrator.

PEOVER HALL

Over Peover, Knutsford map G8
(Randle Brooks)

An Elizabethan House dating from 1585. Fine Caroline stables. Mainwaring Chapel. 18th century landscaped park. Large garden with Topiary work, also Walled and Herb gardens.

Location: 4 m S of Knutsford off A50 at Whipping Stocks Inn.
Opening Times: Beginning of May to end of Sept (except Bank Holidays). House, Stables & Gardens—Mons 2.30–4.30. Adm £2, Chd £1. Thurs Stables & Gardens Only 2–5. Adm £1.
Enquiries: J. Stocks (0565) 72 2656.
Refreshments: Teas in the Stables on Mons.

WOODHEY CHAPEL

Faddiley, nr Nantwich map G7
Telephone: Faddiley (027 074) 215
(The Trustees of Woodhey Chapel)

'The Chapel in the Fields.' A small private chapel, recently restored, dating from 1699.

Location: 1 m SW of Faddiley off A534 Nantwich/Wrexham Road.
Opening Times: Apr to Oct—Sats & Bank Hol Mons 2–5. Adm 50p, Chd 25p. At other times by appointment.

QUARRY BANK MILL,
The National Trust & Quarry Bank Mill Trust Ltd

Styal map G8 Ⓢ
Telephone: Wilmslow (0625) 527468

Award-winning museum of the cotton textile industry, set in rural parkland, with England's largest working waterwheel, producing cloth on historic looms. The Apprentice House recreates the 1830's, when it was home to pauper child millworkers, and its unique garden grows rare, historic fruits, vegetables and herbs. Large shop selling goods made from mill-woven cloth and National Trust gifts and books. Licensed restaurant with excellent homecooked menu, also catering for private and business functions. Open all year: 2 miles from Manchester Airport: full details under listing.
Enquiries: (0625) 527468

Quarry Bank Mill A National Trust property. *Kitchen in Apprentice House*

Award-winning working museum of the cotton industry housed in a 200-year-old spinning mill. Skilled demonstrators operate vintage machinery showing cotton processes from carding and spinning to weaving on Lancashire looms. Displays on water power, the lifestyle of the mill-owning Greg family plus the millworkers' world at home and at work in the 19th century. Giant 1850 waterwheel restored to working order. Renovated Apprentice House. The millworkers' village of Styal and the mill are set in the 250 acre Styal County Park. Museum of the Year 1984. A winner of the Sandford Award for Heritage Education 1987.

Location: 1½ m N of Wilmslow off B5166. 1 m from M56 exit 5. 10 m S of Manchester (log: SJ 35835).
Stations: Styal (¹/₃ m); Wilmslow (2 m).
Opening Times: Mill: All year. Apr to Sept daily 11–5; Oct to Mar—Tues to Sun 11–4. Open all Bank Hols. Pre-booked parties from 9.30 throughout the year (not Sun or Bank Hols) and specified evenings May to Sept. APPRENTICE HOUSE AND GARDEN: Mon *closed* except Bank Hol Mons. Tues to Fri: as Mill opening times during school holidays. Wed, Thurs, Fri: 2pm to Mill closing time during term time. Sat, Sun: as Mill opening times. Please note that due to fire and safety regulations a maximum of 30 people can be accommodated in the house at one time. Admission is by timed ticket ONLY available from Mill Reception. Members wishing to avoid crowds are advised not to visit on Bank Hols and Sun afternoons in spring and summer. Adm charges not available at time of going to press. No dogs. Advance booking essential for all groups of 10 or more, one in 20 free, but not in June or July; please apply for booking form at least 3 weeks in advance. Guides, fee per guide per 20 persons, may be booked at same time. Shop, newly sited and refurbished, open as Mill. Stocks goods made from cloth woven in Mill. Disabled access: Exterior and special route through part of interior using step-lift. Please telephone for access details and leaflet. Cars may set down passengers in Mill yard. Disabled lavatory by Styal Workshop. Mill unsuitable for guide dogs.
Refreshments: Available during all Mill opening hours, licensed tearoom/refreshment for morning coffee, home-made soup, hot meals, regional dishes, vegetarian food and teas.

CLEVELAND

THE CASTLE, Castle Eden

Hartlepool, Cleveland   map H11

A Grade II listed Manor House principally dating from 1757, with 19th century additions.

Location: In the village of Castle Eden, Peterlee (2 m) Durham City (10 m).
Opening Times: May 15 to Aug 31 — Wed & Thurs 2–5. Spring & Summer Bank Hol Mons 2–5.

GISBOROUGH PRIORY ⊞

map H11
Telephone: (0287) 38301
Founded in the 12th century for Augustinian canons by Robert de Brus, the priory was among the richest and most magnificent in the north. The remains include an impressive gatehouse, and the wonderful east wall, an important example of early Gothic architecture.

Location: Guisborough, next to the parish church. OS map ref NZ618163.
Opening Times: Good Friday or Apr 1 (whichever is earlier) to Sept 30: Open Daily 10–6. Oct 1 to Maundy Thursday or Mar 31 (whichever is earlier): Open Tues to Sun 10–4. *Closed* Dec 24–26, Jan 1. Adm 75p, Concessions 55p, Chd 40p.

ORMESBY HALL, The National Trust 🌿

nr Middlesbrough   map H11   △
Telephone: Middlesbrough (0642) 324188

Mid-18th century house. Contemporary plasterwork. Small garden.

Location: 3 m SE of Middlesbrough.
Station: Marton (1½ m) (not Suns April, Sept & Oct).
Opening Times: Apr 4 to Nov 1. Apr: weekends and 18–20 incl. May to Sept: Wed, Thurs, Sat, Sun & Bank Hol Mons 2–5.30. Last adm 5. Adm: HOUSE & GARDENS £1.80, Chd 90p. Adult party £1.50, Chd party 80p. GARDEN: 70p, Chd 30p. No dogs (except guide dogs). Wheelchair access to ground floor only. Shop and tearoom open as house and some weekends in Nov & Dec.
Refreshments: Afternoon teas.

CORNWALL

ANTONY, The National Trust 🌿

Torpoint   map E2   △
Telephone: Plymouth (0752) 812191

The home of Mr. Richard Carew Pole. Built for Sir William Carew 1718-1729. Unaltered early 18th century house, panelled rooms. Fine furniture. Extensive garden.

Location: 5 m W of Plymouth via Torpoint car ferry. 2 m NW of Torpoint, N of A374.
Opening Times: Apr 1 to end of Oct — Tues, Weds & Thurs; also Bank Hol Mons and Suns in June, July and Aug 1.30–5.30 (last adm 5). Adm £3.20, Chd £1.60. Pre-arranged parties £2.40, Chd £1.20. No dogs. Unsuitable for wheelchairs. Shop. Guided tours.

ANTONY WOODLAND GARDEN AND NATURAL WOODS

Torpoint   map E2   △
(Carew Pole Garden Trust)

A woodland garden and natural woods extending to 100 acres in an area designated as one of Natural Beauty and a Site of Special Scientific Interest. The Woodland Garden established in the late 18th century with the assistance of Humphrey Repton features over 300 types of Camellias and a wide variety of Magnolias, Rhododendrons, Hydrangeas, Azaleas and other flowering shrubs together with many fine species of indigenous and exotic hardwood and softwood trees. Adjoining and contrasting with this long established woodland garden an additional 50 acres of natural woods bordering the River Lynher, featuring a "Fishful" Pond, many wild flower species and birds make this an area to delight botanists, ornithologists, or those who merely enjoy peaceful woodland walks.
Location: 5 m W of Plymouth via Torpoint Car Ferry. 2 m NW of Torpoint off A374.
Opening Times: ANTONY WOODLAND GARDENS and WOODLAND WALK: Mar 15 to Oct 31. Mon–Sat 11–5.30. Suns 2.30–5.30. Special openings in aid of Charities by arrangement. Adm £1, Chd 50p. Car parking available. No dogs allowed.

BOSVIGO HOUSE (GARDENS)

Bosvigo Lane, Truro TR1 3NH   map C1
Telephone: Truro (0872) 75774
(Wendy and Michael Perry)

A series of enclosed and walled gardens, still being developed, around Georgian house (not open). Mainly herbacious plants used for colour and foliage effect. Woodland Walk and Victorian Conservatory. Nursery open daily selling rare and unusual plants – see listing under the Garden Specialists Section.
Location: ¾ m from city centre. Take A390 towards Redruth. At Highertown turn right by Shell garage and drive 400 yards down Dobbs Lane.
Opening Times: GARDEN ONLY. June to end Sept — daily 11–6. Adm £1, Chd 25p. Parties by appointment. Sorry, no dogs.

CHYSAUSTER ANCIENT VILLAGE ⊞

map C1
Telephone: (0736) 61889

Halfway up a hillside, through a stone passage, lie the stone houses erected by our prehistoric ancestors. By the time the Romans came the village had already existed for two centuries. Each house, built around a courtyard, had its own terrace. Were these the earliest gardens?

Location: 2½ m (3.5 km) north west of Gulval, near Penzance. OS map ref SW473350.
Opening Times: Good Friday or Apr 1 (whichever is earlier) to Sept 30: Open Daily 10–6. Oct 1 to Maundy Thursday or Mar 31 (whichever is earlier): Open Tues to Sun 10–4. *Closed* Dec 24–26, Jan 1. Adm £1.20, Concessions 90p, Chd 60p.

COTEHELE, The National Trust 🌿

St. Dominick   map E2   ♿
Telephone: Liskeard 50434. Restaurant 50652.

Fine mediaeval house, the former home of Earls of Mount Edgcumbe. Armour, furniture, tapestries. Terrace garden falling to the sheltered valley, ponds, stream, unusual shrubs. Watermill and Cotehele Quay museum.

Location: On W bank of the Tamar, 1 m W of Calstock by footpath, (6 m by road). 8 m SW of Tavistock; 14 m from Plymouth via Saltash Bridge.
Station: Calstock (1½ m).
Opening Times: Apr 1 to Nov 1 — Garden, Mill and Quay every day, House every day *except Friday,* but open Good Friday 11–5.30, 11–5 in Oct. Closes dusk if earlier. Last adm ½ hr before closing. Nov to Mar — Garden open daily during daylight. Adm House, Gardens, Cotehele Mill and Quay £4.80, Chd £2.40. Gardens, Cotehele Mill and Quay £2.40 Chd £1.20. *Reduced fee of £4, Chd £2 for pre-booked coach parties. Organisers should book visits & arrange for meals beforehand with the Administrator.* DOGS IN WOODS ONLY – on lead. Wheelchairs provided; house only accessible. Shop.
Refreshments: Coffee, lunch and tea in Barn (*closed* Fri) and on Quay (open Fri) during season.

GODOLPHIN HOUSE 🏛

Helston map C1
(Mrs. Schofield)

A Former home of the Earls of Godolphin and the birthplace of Queen Anne's famous Lord High Treasurer – Sidney, first Earl of Godolphin. Parts of the house are of early Tudor date and additions were made in Elizabethan and Carolean times. The unique front was completed shortly before the Civil War and rests on massive columns of local granite. The fine 'Kings Room' is traditionally said to have been occupied by Charles II (then Prince of Wales) at the time of his escape from Pendennis Castle to the Scilly Islands. Pictures include 'The Godolphin Arabian' by John Wootton. Display of Farm Waggons and Civil War Exhibition on show in the old stables.

Location: 5 m NW of Helston; between villages of Townshend and Godolphin Cross.
Opening Times: Bank Hol Mons; May & June—Thurs 2–5. July & Sept—Tues 2–5, Thurs 2–5, Aug—Tues 2–5, Thurs 10–1, 2–5. Adm £2, Chd £1. Open at other times for pre-booked parties & all year round for arranged parties.

GLENDURGAN GARDEN, The National Trust 🌿

Mawnan Smith map C1

A valley garden of great beauty with fine trees and shrubs, overlooking Helford River. Giant's Stride and maze much enjoyed by children.

Location: 4 m SW of Falmouth ½ m SW of Mawnan Smith on road to Helford Passage.
Opening Times: Mar 1 to end of Oct—Tues–Sat incl (except Good Friday) but open Bank Hol Mons. 10.30–5.30 (last adm 5). Adm £2.50, Chd £1.25. *No reduction for parties.* No dogs. Unsuitable for wheelchairs.

GODOLPHIN HOUSE – *See above*

LANHYDROCK, The National Trust 🌿

nr Bodmin map D2 ♿
Telephone: Bodmin 73320. Restaurant 74331.

The great house of Cornwall, with 42 rooms open to the public. 17th century long gallery. Fine plaster ceilings. Family portraits 17th to 20th centuries. The extensive kitchen and servants' quarters (1883) are also shown. Formal garden with clipped yews, and parterre, laid out in 1857. Rhododendrons, magnolias, rare trees and shrubs. Woodland garden and parkland setting.

Location: 2½ m SE of Bodmin on Bodmin/Lostwithiel Road (B3268).
Station: Bodmin Parkway (1¾ m by signposted carriage-drive to house; 3 m by road).
Opening Times: House, Garden and Grounds – Apr 1 to Nov 1—Daily except Mon when House only is closed (*open* Bank Holiday Mons) 11–5.30 (last adm 5) 11–5 in Oct. Last adm ½ hr before closing. Nov to end of Mar—Garden and Grounds – open daily during daylight hours. Adm £4.80, Chd £2.40; Garden only £2.40, Chd £1.20. Pre-booked parties £3.80, Chd £1.90. *Organisers should book visits & arrange for meals beforehand with The Administrator.* Dogs in park only on leads. Wheelchairs provided. Shop (also open Nov & Dec).
Refreshments: Lunches and teas in restaurant at House; snacks in stable block (last adm 5).

LAUNCESTON CASTLE ⚌

map D2
Telephone: (0566) 772365

The impressive round keep stands high on its grassy mound within a circular wall. Inside, a tall cylindrical tower soars from the centre. The space between tower and keep was roofed. Like Launceston itself, the castle was important in the Middle Ages. Small site museum.

Location: Launceston. OS map ref SX330846.
Opening Times: Good Friday or Apr 1 (whichever is earlier) to Sept 30: Open Daily 10–6. Oct 1 to Maundy Thursday or Mar 31 (whichever is earlier): Open Tues to Sun 10–4. *Closed* Dec 24–26, Jan 1. Adm £1.10, Concessions 85p, Chd 55p.

Grinling Gibbons (1648–1721)

Sculptor and wood carver. His work can be seen at the following properties included in Historic Houses Castles and Gardens:

Fawley Court Historic House and Museum
Kentchurch Court
Lyme Park
Somerleyton Hall
Sudbury Hall

MOUNT EDGCUMBE HOUSE & COUNTRY PARK

nr Plymouth map E2
Telephone: Plymouth (0752) 822236
(City of Plymouth & Cornwall County Council)

"This Mount of all the Mounts of Great Britain surpasses. 'Tis the Haunt of the Muses, the Mount of Parnassus."
David Garrick (1717–1779).

Stretching along 10 miles of spectacular coastline from Plymouth to Whitsand Bay, the Park contains one of only three Grade I Historic Gardens in Cornwall. The earliest landscape park in Cornwall, it was designed 240 years ago with wonderful woodland walks and views and includes a deer park and Formal Gardens in the Italian, French and English styles. Two new gardens have been established, a New Zealand Garden and American Plantation, reflecting family associations with these countries. It is the site for the collection of the International Camellia Society. Mount Edgcumbe House, a restored Tudor mansion with the Earls Garden including the newly restored Victorian flower beds surrounding it, was the home of the Edgcumbe family for 400 years and has recently been refurbished and redecorated to reflect the late 18th century.

Location: On Rame Peninsula, 12 m from Torpoint or from Trerulefoot roundabout (A38) via A374 to Antony or Crafthole, and B3247 to Mount Edgcumbe, or by Cremyll (pedestrian) Ferry from Plymouth (Stonehouse) to Park entrance.
Opening Times: COUNTRY PARK, including LANDSCAPED PARK and FORMAL GARDENS open every day, all year round, Free. House and Earls Garden open Apr 1 to Oct 31 11–5.30 Wed to Sun and Bank Hol Mons. Adm £2.80 adult, Chd £1.55, concessions £2.05. Group rates – bonus discounts. Any booking made in advance with a value of £30 or more attracts a discount of 20%, which can be passed on to the booking agent (coach operator, driver, club secretary, group leader, etc.) to be used at their discretion. Visitor Centre and Shop selling guides and souvenirs open Apr 1 to Oct 31 every day. Gifts produced in Devon and Cornwall a speciality.
Refreshments: Lunches, teas and light refreshments available in the Orangery Restaurant/ Cafe, Apr 1 to Oct 31 daily. Reservations and enquiries telephone Plymouth (0752) 822586.

PENCARROW HOUSE AND GARDEN

Bodmin map D2 &
Telephone: St Mabyn (020 884) 369
(The Molesworth – St Aubyn Family)

Georgian house and listed gardens, still owned and lived in by the family. A superb collection of 18th century pictures, furniture and china. Mile long drive and Ancient British Encampment. Marked walks through beautiful woodland gardens, past the great granite Victorian Rockery, Italian and American gardens, Lake and Ice House. Approx 50 acres in all. Over 600 different species and hybrid rhododendrons and also an internationally known specimen conifer collection.

Location: 4 m NW of Bodmin off A389 & B3266 at Washaway.
Opening Times: House, Tearooms and Craft Centre Easter to Oct 15 – Every day *(except Fri and Sat)* 1.30–5 (Bank Hol Mon and from June 1 to Sept 10 from 11). GARDENS open daily. Adm (1991 rates) HOUSE AND GARDENS: £3, Chd £1.50. GARDENS ONLY: £1, Chd (over 5 yrs) 50p. Coaches £2.50. Guided tours. Car park and toilet facilities for disabled. Dogs very welcome in grounds. Plant shop. Picnic area. Small children's play area, and pets corner. Self pick soft fruit in season.
Refreshments: Light lunches and cream teas.

PENDENNIS CASTLE

Falmouth map C1
Telephone: (0326) 316594
(Cornwall English Heritage)

Henry VIII's reply to the Pope's crusade against him was to fortify his coastline. Two castles guarded the Fal Estuary, Pendennis and St Mawes. Built high on a promontory, Pendennis saw action in the Civil War when 'Jack-for-the-King' Arundell held the castle for five terrible months. It continued in military use until 1946. 1588 Gundeck tableau, exhibition, views and refreshments.

Location: Pendennis Head 1 m (1.6 km) south east of Falmouth.
Opening Times: Good Friday or Apr 1 (whichever is earlier) to Sept 30, daily 10–6. Oct 1 to Maundy Thursday or Mar 31 (whichever is earlier) Tues to Sun 10–4. *Closed* Dec 24–26, Jan 1. Adm £1.60, Concessions £1.20, Chd 80p.

PRIDEAUX PLACE

Padstow map D2
Telephone: (0841) 532411 and 532945
(The Prideaux-Brune family)

An Elizabethan Mansion House set in extensive grounds above the fishing port of Padstow. 20 acres of deer park. Guided tours through this family home include a visit to the Great Chamber with its interesting embossed plaster ceiling dating from 1585, dining room, morning room, drawing room, reading room and library. Newly restored Italian formal garden.

Location: 7 m from Wadebridge, 14 m from Newquay.
Opening Times: HOUSE, SHOP, TEAROOM — Easter Sat for two weeks then Spring Bank Hol to end of Sept, Sun to Thurs inclusive, 1.30–5. Spring and Aug Bank Hol Mon from 11. Adm HOUSE & GROUNDS £3.50. GROUNDS ONLY £1.50. Chd half price. Special party rates. Open all the year round by appointment. Large public car park on A389 nearby. Enquiries to the Administrator, Prideaux Place, Padstow PL28 8RP. Tel: (0841) 532945 or 532411.

RESTORMEL CASTLE

map D2
Telephone: (0208) 872687

Crowning a hill overlooking the River Fowey, the castle rises steeply above a dry but deep, wide moat. The outer 12th century wall is a perfect circle. Domestic buildings were later added inside and a rectangular chapel outside.

Location: 1½ m (2.4 km) north of Lostwithiel. OS map ref SX104614.
Opening Times: Good Friday or Apr 1 (whichever is earlier) to Sept 30. Open Daily 10–6. Adm £1.10, Concessions 85p, Chd 55p.

ST MAWES CASTLE

map C1
Telephone: (0326) 270526

Shaped like a clover leaf, this small 16th century castle, still intact, nestles among rock plants and tropical shrubs. During the Civil War the Governor capitulated without gunfire or bloodshed, unlike Pendennis on the opposite shore.

Location: St Mawes. OS map ref SW842328.
Opening Times: Good Friday or Apr 1 (whichever is earlier) to Sept 30: Open Daily 10–6. Oct 1 to Maundy Thursday or Mar 31 (whichever is earlier): Open Tues to Sun 10–4. *Closed* Dec 24–26, Jan 1. Adm £1.20, Concessions 90p, Chd 60p.

ST MICHAEL'S MOUNT, The National Trust

Marazion, nr Penzance map C1 △
Telephone: Penzance 710507

Home of Lord St Levan. Mediaeval and early 17th century with considerable alterations and additions in 18th and 19th century.

Location: ½ m from the shore at Marazion (A394), connected by causeway. 3 m E Penzance.
Opening Times: Apr 1 to end of Oct: Mons to Fri 10.30–5.45 (last adm 4.45). Nov to end of Mar: Guided tours as tide, weather and circumstances permit. *(NB: ferry boats do not operate a regular service during this period)*. Adm £2.90, Chd £1.45, Family ticket £8. Shop and restaurant — Apr 1 to end of Oct, daily. No dogs. Unsuitable for wheelchairs. NB: Access to The Mount and opening arrangements are liable to interruption in foul weather.

TINTAGEL CASTLE

map D2
Telephone: (0840) 770328
(English Heritage)

Amazing that anything has survived on this wild, windswept coast. Yet fragments of Earl Reginald's great hall, built about 1145, and Earl Richard's 13th century wall and iron gate still stand in this incomparable landscape. No wonder that King Arthur and his Knights were thought to have dwelt here. Site exhibition.

Location: ½ m (0.8 km) north west of Tintagel. OS map ref SX048891.
Opening Times: Good Friday or Apr 1 (whichever is earlier) to Sept 30 daily 10–6. Oct 1 to Maundy Thursday or Mar 31 (whichever is earlier) Tues to Sun 10–4. *Closed* Dec 24–26, Jan 1. Adm £1.80, Concessions £1.40, Chd 90p.

TINTAGEL — THE OLD POST OFFICE, The National Trust

Tintagel map D2 &

A miniature 14th century manor house with large hall.

Location: Nos 3 & 4 in the centre of Tintagel.
Opening Times: Apr 1 to Nov 1 — Daily 11–5.30 (or sunset if earlier), (11–5 in Oct). Last adm ½ hr before closing. Adm £1.80, Chd 90p. *No reduction for parties*. No dogs. Wheelchair access. Shop.

TREGREHAN

map D2
Telephone: (0726) 814389 or (0726) 812438
(Mr T. C. Hudson)

Woodland garden created since early 19th century by Carlyon family concentrating on species from warm-temperate regions. Fine glasshouse range in walled garden. Small nursery, also open by appointment, specialising in wild source material, and camellias bred by the late owner.

Location: 2 m E of St Austell on A390. 1 m W of St. Blazey on A390.
Opening Times: Mid Mar to end of June and Sept: Wed to Sun 10.30–5. Adm £2, Chd 75p. Guided tours for parties by prior arrangement. Parking for cars and coaches. Access for disabled to half garden only. No dogs.

TRELISSICK GARDEN, The National Trust

nr Truro map C1 &
Telephone: Truro 862090; Restaurant 863486

Large shrub garden. Beautiful wooded park overlooking the river Fal. Woodland walks. Particularly rich in rhododendrons, camellias and hydrangeas.

Location: 5 m S of Truro on both sides of B3289 overlooking King Harry Ferry.
Opening Times: GARDENS ONLY: Mar 1 to Christmas — Mons to Sats 10.30–5.30 (or sunset if earlier), Suns 1–5.30 (or sunset if earlier), 10.30–5 in Mar and Oct, 11–4 Nov and Dec. Last adm ½ hr before closing. Entrance on road to King Harry Passage. Adm £2.80, Chd £1.40. *No reduction for parties.* Shop, with special plants section. Art and Craft gallery. Dogs in woodland walk and park only, on leads. Wheelchairs provided.
Refreshments: In the barn Mon–Sat 10.30–5.30; Sun 12–5.30. (Closed 5 in Mar and Oct).

TRELOWARREN HOUSE & CHAPEL

Mawgan-in-Meneage, Helston   map C1   △
Telephone: Mawgan (032 622) 366
(Sir John Vyvyan, Bt.)

Home of the Vyvyan family since 1427 part of the house dates from early Tudor times. The Chapel, part of which is pre-Reformation, and the 17th century part of the house are leased to the Trelowarren Fellowship, an Ecumenical Christian Charity. The Chapel and main rooms containing family portraits are open to the public with guided tours. Concerts take place, and Sunday Services are held in the Chapel during the holiday season. Exhibitions of paintings.

Location: 6 m S of Helston off B3293 to St Keverne.

Opening Times: HOUSE & CHAPEL. Open from Apr 20 to Oct 7 — Weds & Bank Hol Mons. Always 2.30–5. Conducted tours. Adm £1, Chd 50p (under 12 years free), includes entry to various exhibitions of paintings. Concerts are held in Chapel and Chapel Services every Sun during the holiday season. Organised tours by arrangement. Ground floor only suitable for disabled.

TRENGWAINTON GARDEN, The National Trust

Penzance   map C1   &

Large shrub and woodland garden. Fine views. A series of walled gardens contain rare sub-tropical plants.

Location: 2 m NW of Penzance ½ m W of Heamoor on Morvah Road (B3312).
Station: Penzance (2 m).
Opening Times: Mar 1 to end Oct — Weds, Thurs, Fris, Sats & Bank Hol Mons 10.30–5.30, 10.30–5 in Mar and Oct. Last adm ½ hr before closing. Adm £2.20, Chd £1.10. *No reduction for parties.* No dogs. Wheelchair access.

TRERICE, The National Trust

nr. Newquay   map C2   &
Telephone: Newquay 875404; Restaurant 879434

A small Elizabethan house, fine furniture, plaster ceilings and fireplaces, in a recently planted garden. A small museum in the Barn traces the development of the lawn mower.

Location: 3 m SE of Newquay A392 & A3058 (turn right at Kestle Mill).
Station: Quintrel Downs (1½ m).
Opening Times: Apr 1 to Nov 1 — Daily (*except* Tues) 11–5.30, 10.30–5 in Oct. Last adm ½ hr before closing. Adm £3.40, Chd £1.70. *Reduced rate of £2.80, Chd £1.40 for pre-booked parties.* No dogs. Wheelchairs available; access to house only. Shop.
Refreshments: In the barn, opening times as for House. *Parties must book.*

TREWITHEN HOUSE AND GARDENS

Probus, nr Truro   map D1
Telephone: St Austell (0726) 882763/882764 (nurseries), 883794 (Garden Shop)

'Trewithen' means 'House of the Trees' which truly describes this exceptionally fine early Georgian house in its magnificent setting of wood and parkland. The origins of the house go back to the 17th century but it was the Architect Sir Robert Taylor, aided by Thomas Edwards of Greenwich, who were responsible for the splendid building and interiors we see today. Philip Hawkins bought the property in 1715 and began extensive rebuilding. The house has been lived in and cared for by the same family since that date. The magnificent landscaped gardens have an outstanding collection of magnolias, rhododendron and azaleas which are well known throughout the world. The gardens are particularly spectacular between March and the end of June and again in Autumn, although there is much to see throughout the year. A wide variety of shrubs and plants from the famous nurseries are always on sale. Other attractions include a children's playground and a 25-minute video of the house and gardens. The gardens are one of only two in this county to be awarded 3 stars by the Michelin Guide to the South West.

Location: On A390 between Probus and Grampound, adjoining County Demonstration Gardens.
Opening Times: GARDENS: Open Mar 1 to Sept 30, Mon to Sat 10–4.30. *Closed* Sun. Plants for sale. Dogs on leads. Adm Gardens: Mar–June £2, Chd (under 15) £1; July to Sept £1.75, Chd (under 15) £1. HOUSE: Guided tours Mon and Tues only Apr to July and Aug Bank Hol Mon (2–4.30). £2.80. Parties by arrangement please. Nurseries: Open throughout the year 9–4.30.

Sir John Van Brugh (1664–1726)

Architect. His work can be seen at the following properties included in Historic Houses Castles and Gardens:

Blenheim Palace
Castle Howard
Claremont
Grimsthorpe Castle

CUMBRIA

ABBOT HALL ART GALLERY
& MUSEUM OF LAKELAND LIFE & INDUSTRY

Kirkland, Kendal   map F10   &
Telephone: Kendal (0539) 722464
(Lake District Art Gallery & Museum Trust)

Impressive Georgian House; comprehensive collections of portraits by George Romney and Daniel Gardner, Lake District landscapes and furniture by Gillows of Lancaster displayed in elegant 18th century. rooms; lively temporary exhibition programme; craft shop selling work by leading artist-craftsmen. Adjacent Museum of Lakeland Life & Industry recaptures unique flavour of everyday life in Lake District: everything from hip baths to sheep dips; Arthur Ransome room; first Museum of the Year. Also visit award winning Kendal Museum of Natural History & Archaeology, Station Road.

Location: Off Kirkland nr Kendal Parish Church. From M6 exit 36.
Station: Oxenholme (1½m); Kendal (¾m).
Opening Times: All the year – daily except Dec 25, 26 and Jan 1. Mon–Fri 10.30–5, Sat & Sun 2–5, (Spring Bank Holiday – Oct 31; Sat 10.30–5). **Reduced hours during winter possible** – check before visit. Adm charge; concessions for OAPs, Chd, Students and families. Lift for disabled (Mon–Fri only).

ACORN BANK GARDEN, The National Trust 🌿

Temple Sowerby, Penrith   map F11

This 2½ acre garden is protected by fine oaks under which grow a vast display of daffodils. Inside walls are two orchards with medlar, mulberry, cherries, quince and apples. Surrounding the orchards are mixed borders with herbaceous plants and many flowering shrubs and climbing roses. The adjacent herb garden has the largest collection of culinary, medicinal and narcotic herbs in the north. The red sandstone house is let to the Sue Ryder Foundation and is open on application.

Location: Just N of Temple Sowerby, 6 m E of Penrith on A66.
Opening Times: GARDEN ONLY. Apr 1 to Nov 1 – Daily 10–6. Adm £1.40, Chd 70p. Reduction for pre- arranged parties. No dogs. Wheelchair access to parts of garden only. Small shop. Plant sales.

BRANTWOOD – *See page 53*

BROUGH CASTLE 🏰

map G11
Telephone: (0930) 42191

The importance of Brough-under-Stainmore, lying between Carlisle and York, did not escape the Romans. So it is hardly surprising that the Normans built a stronghold on the site of that derelict Roman fort. The Scots destroyed it in 1174 and the present castle is a product of the rebuilding that followed. Until 1204 Brough was a royal castle; then King John granted it to Robert de Vipont, ancestor of the Lords Clifford. Part of the 11th century wall remains and much of the 17th century repair work carried out by that energetic restorer of castles, Lady Anne Clifford.

Location: 8 m (13 km) south east of Appleby. OS map ref NY791141.
Opening Times: Good Friday or Apr 1 (whichever is earlier) to Sept 30: Open Daily 10–6. Oct 1 to Maundy Thursday or Mar 31 (whichever is earlier): Open Wed to Sun 10–4. *Closed* Dec 24–26, Jan 1. Adm 75p, Concessions 55p, Chd 40p.

BROUGHAM CASTLE 🏰

map F11
Telephone: (0768) 62488

The oldest part of the surviving building, the keep, was constructed in Henry II's reign after the Scots had relinquished their hold on the north west of England. The keep, later heightened, and its gatehouses formed an impregnable fortress, while also providing a lordly residence of spacious proportions. The castle was restored by Lady Anne Clifford in the 17th century.

Location: 1½ m (2.4 km) east of Penrith. OS map ref NY537290.
Opening Times: Good Friday or Apr 1 (whichever is earlier) to Sept 30: Open Daily 10–6. Oct 1 to Maundy Thursday or Mar 31 (whichever is earlier): Open Wed to Sun 10–4. *Closed* Dec 24–26, Jan 1. Adm £1.10, Concessions 85p, Chd 55p.

CARLISLE CASTLE 🏰

Carlisle   map F11
Telephone: (0228) 31777
(English Heritage)

Twenty-six years after the Battle of Hastings. Carlisle remained unconquered. In 1092 William II marched north, took the city and ordered the building of a stronghold above the River Eden. Since William's time the castle has survived 800 years of fierce and bloody attacks, extensive rebuilding and continuous military occupation. A massive Norman keep contains an exhibition on the history of the castle. D'Ireby Tower now open to the public, containing furnishings to authentic medieval design, an exhibition and shop. Guided tours are given by a local group of volunteers.

Location: North of town centre. OS map ref NY 397563
Open: Good Friday or Apr 1 (whichever is earlier) to Sept 30 daily 10–6. Oct 1 to Maundy Thursday or Mar 31 (whichever is earlier) daily 10–4. *Closed* Dec 24–26, Jan 1. Adm £1.80, Concessions £1.40, Chd 90p.

CASTLETOWN HOUSE

Rockcliffe, Carlisle   map F11
Telephone: Rockcliffe (0228 74) 205
(Giles Mounsey-Heysham, Esq.)

Georgian Country House set in attractive gardens and grounds. Fine ceilings. Naval pictures, furnishings and model engines.

Location: 5 m NW of Carlisle on Solway coast, 1 m W of Rockcliffe village and 2 m W of A74.
Opening Times: HOUSE ONLY. By appointment **only**.

DALEMAIN

nr Penrith map F11
Telephone: (07684) 86450
(Mr & Mrs Bryce McCosh)

Mediaeval, Tudor and early Georgian house and gardens lived in by the same family for over 300 years. Fine furniture and portraits. Countryside museum and picnic areas, Agricultural Museum, Westmorland and Cumberland Yeomanry Museum and Adventure Playground, Fell Pony Museum. Interesting garden as featured on BBC and in various publications. Plant Centre. Gift shop.

Location: 3 m from Penrith on A592. Turn off M6 exit 40 onto A66 (A592) to Ullswater.
Opening Times: Easter Sun to Oct 4 — daily except Fris and Sats, 11.15–5. Adm charged. Entry to car park, picnic area, shop and restaurant free.
Refreshments: Coffee from 11.15. Bar lunches 12–2.30. Home made teas from 2.30. High teas by arrangement. No dogs please.

FURNESS ABBEY

map F10
Telephone: (0229) 23420

At the time of its suppression in 1537, the abbey was one of the wealthiest monasteries in the land. Founded in 1124 by King Stephen, the abbey, set in a beautiful valley, belonged to the first Order of Savigny, then to the Cistercians. Ruined buildings of red sandstone evoke a vision of past splendour. Magnificent still are the canopied seats in the presbytery and the Chapter House. Exhibition in the museum at the entrance.

Location: 1½ m (2.4 km) north of Barrow-in-Furness. OS map ref SD218717.
Opening Times: Good Friday or Apr 1 (whichever is earlier) to Sept 30: Open Daily 10–6. Oct 1 to Maundy Thursday or Mar 31 (whichever is earlier): Open Tues to Sun 10–4. *Closed* Dec 24–26, Jan 1. Adm £1.80, Concessions £1.40, Chd 90p. Adm price includes a free Personal Stereo Guided Tour.

HADRIAN'S WALL

map G12

Snaking across the north of England, from Bowness to Wallsend, is Hadrian's remarkable wall, built between AD125–130 to demarcate the frontier of Britain and the northernmost limit of the Roman Empire at the time. With true Roman precision, a milecastle was constructed at every mile and two observation turrets between each milecastle, many sections have withstood the ravages of time. At strategic points great forts were built to garrison 500 or 1000 men. English Heritage has a well-preserved milecastle at Harrow's Scar, near Gilsland, and several turrets in the Brampton area, the best at Banks East.

(See also Northumberland Section)

HOLKER HALL

Cark-in-Cartmel, nr Grange-over-Sands
map F10   △   &   Ⓢ
Telephone: Flookburgh (05395) 58328
(Lord and Lady Cavendish)

25 acres of magnificent formal and woodland gardens with water features. (World Class Good Gardens Guide '91.) Zanussi Victorian and wartime kitchen exhibition, patchwork/quilting displays; exhibitions; adventure playground, deer park. Former home of the Dukes of Devonshire and still lived in by members of the family.

Location: ½ m N of Cark-in-Cartmel on B5278 from Haverthwaite; 4 m W Grange-over-Sands.
Opening Times: HOUSE, GARDENS & MOTOR MUSEUM. Apr 1 to Oct 31 — Daily (ex Sat) 10.30–4.30. Park open until 6. Group rates for parties of 20 or more. Free Coach and Car Park. Gift Shop.
Refreshments: Clock Tower Cafe serving salads, sandwiches, home made cakes and pastries, beverages including wine and beer. *Group catering by prior arrangement.*

BRANTWOOD

Coniston map F10
Telephone: (05394) 41396
(Brantwood Educational Trust)

BRANTWOOD, CONISTON

The home of John Ruskin 1872-1900

The most beautifully situated house in the Lake District, with the finest lake and mountain views in England. Splendid displays of Ruskin watercolours. Delightful nature walks. Excellent tea room, bookshop, video programme & craft gallery. Regular boat service to Brantwood from Coniston Pier.

OPEN ALL YEAR
Daily Mid-March to Mid Nov
Winter Season Wed-Sun
or Tel: Coniston (05394) 41396

The home of John Ruskin from 1872–1900. Large collection of pictures by Ruskin and his associates. Ruskin's coach, boat, furniture and other associated items. Ruskin's woodland gardens are currently being restored. There is a delightful nature walk around the 250 acre estate.

Location: 2½ m from Coniston. Historic House signs at Coniston, Head of Coniston Water & Hawkshead.
Opening Times: Open all year. Mid-Mar to mid-Nov – Daily 11–5.30. Winter season – Weds to Suns 11–4. Adm House, Exhibitions & Nature Walks £2.80, Chd free. Nature trails only £1 (including guide) Chd free. Steam Yacht Gondola sails regularly from Coniston Pier. Free car park Parking for disabled near house. Toilets (incl for disabled). Craft Gallery and shop.
Refreshments: Licensed restaurant/tea room/coffee; light meals available.

HUTTON-IN-THE-FOREST

Penrith map F11
Telephone: Skelton (085 34) 449
(Lord and Lady Inglewood)

One of the ancient manors in the Forest of Inglewood, and the home of Lord Inglewood's family since the beginning of the 17th century. Built around a medieval pele tower with 18th and 19th century additions. Fine English furniture and pictures, ceramics and tapestries. Outstanding gardens and grounds with terraces, walled garden, dovecote, lake and woodland walk through magnificent specimen trees.

Location: 6 m NW of Penrith on B5305 Wigton Road (from M6 exit 41).
Opening Times: All Bank Hol Suns & Mons from Easter; also Thurs, Fris and Suns from May 28 to Sept 27, 1–4. GROUNDS open every day (*except* Sat) 11–5. Private parties by arrangement any day from Apr 1.
Refreshments: Fresh home-made teas available in the cloisters when house open. Lunch and supper menus available on request.

19/20 IRISH STREET

Whitehaven map E11
Telephone: Whitehaven (0946) 693111 Ext 285
(Copeland Borough Council)

1840–50 Italianate design, possibly by S. Smirke. Stuccoed 3-storey building now occupied by the Council Offices.

Location: In town centre
Station: Whitehaven.
Opening Times: All the year during office hours. For details and appointments telephone Mr J. A. Pomfret. Ground floor only suitable for disabled.
Refreshments: Hotels and restaurants in town centre.

THE LAKE DISTRICT NATIONAL PARK CENTRE

Brockhole, Windermere, Cumbria map F10
Telephone: (05394) 46601

Photograph Andrew Morris.

Brockhole provides the ideal introduction to the Lake District. Exhibitions, slide shows, activity trails, varied events programmes, restaurant and tea rooms, gardens lakeshore grounds, plus an exciting adventure playground combine to make Brockhole 'The Key to the Lakes' for all ages.

Opening Times: Apr 5 to Nov 1, 10–5 daily (8 in high summer). Adm free. Car park charge £2 per car, £6 per coach.

LANERCOST PRIORY ⊞

map F11
Telephone: (06977) 3030

Just south of Hadrian's Wall, in the wooded valley of the River Irthing, stands this noble Augustinian priory founded by Robert de Vaux in the 12th century. Centrepiece is the priory church, 800 years old, and the nave is still a parish church. English Heritage cares for the area around the cloisters and the ruined East End of the church.

Location: 2 m (3.2 km) north east of Brampton. OS map ref NY556637.
Opening Times: Good Friday or Apr 1 (whichever is earlier) to Sept 30: Open Daily 10–6. Adm 75p, Concessions 55p, Chd 40p.

LEVENS HALL – *See page 55*

MIREHOUSE 🏛

Keswick map F11 ♿
Telephone: Keswick (076 87) 72287
(Mr & Mrs Spedding)

Seventeenth century Manor House with 19th century additions. Portraits and manuscripts of Francis Bacon and many literary friends of the Spedding family including Tennyson, Wordsworth, Southey. Children welcome. French, German and Spanish spoken. Walk through grounds to Bassenthwaite Lake. Adventure Playgrounds. Norman Lakeside Church of St. Bega.

Location: 4½ m N of Keswick on A591 (Keswick to Carlisle Road).
Opening Times: Apr to Oct – Lakeside Walk, Adventure Playgrounds – Daily 10.30–5.30. House – Suns, Weds & Bank Hol Mons 2–5. Parties welcome by appointment.
Refreshments: Old Sawmill Tearoom open daily 10.30–5.30; salads & sandwiches made to order, home baking. Parties please book (Tel: Keswick (07687) 74317).

MUNCASTER CASTLE – *See page 56*

NAWORTH CASTLE 🏛

Brampton map F11
Telephone: Brampton (069 77) 3666
(The Earl of Carlisle MC)

Historic border fortress, built by the Dacres in 1335, acquired and renovated by the Howard Family in 1602, the Castle is currently the home of the Earl and Countess of Carlisle. A stronghold for the Wardens of the West March in the 16th century, an impressive residence for the powerful Earls of Carlisle in the 17th century, and an artistic centre for the pre-Raphaelites in the late 19th century, the Castle features: the Great Hall with Gobelin Tapestries and Heraldic Beasts, Lord William's Tower, the Long Gallery, the Library designed by Philip Webb & Burne-Jones, and the original 14th century dungeons.

Location: 12 m E of Carlisle, near Brampton, off the A69 to Newcastle.
Opening Times: Easter Weekend to Sept 30 12–5, Weds, Suns and Bank Hols; five days/week Wed to Sun in Aug only. Adm £2, OAPs, Chd £1, Family ticket £5. Special parties by arrangement. Free car and coach park.
Refreshments: Tea room and visitors' shop on premises.

RYDAL MOUNT

Ambleside map F10
Telephone: Ambleside (05394) 33002
(Mrs Mary Henderson – nee Wordsworth)

Wordsworth home from 1813–1850. Family portraits and furniture, many of the poet's personal possessions, and first editions of his works. The garden which was designed by Wordsworth has been described as one of the most interesting small gardens to be found anywhere in England. Two long terraces, many rare trees and shrubs. Extends to 4½ acres.

Location: Off A591, 1½ m from Ambleside, 2 m from Grasmere.
Opening Times: Mar 1 to Oct 31 – Daily 9.30–5. Nov 1 to Mar 1 – 10–4 (*Closed* Tues in winter). Adm House & Gardens £2, Chd 80p, Parties, £1.70. See Lake District National Park Visitor Centre for out of season package.

SIZERGH CASTLE AND GARDEN, The National Trust 🌿

Kendal map F10
Telephone: Sedgwick (05395) 60070

The 14th century Pele tower (the oldest part of the castle) rises to 60 feet, contains some original windows, floors and fireplaces; 15th century Great Hall, extended in later centuries; 16th century wings; fine panelling and ceilings; contents include French and English furniture, china, family portraits. Extensive garden includes ²/₃ acre limestone rock garden, the largest owned by the Trust with large collection of Japanese maples, dwarf conifers, hardy ferns and many perennials and bulbs; water garden; herbaceous borders; wild flower banks; fine autumn colour.

Location: 3½ m S of Kendal NW of interchange A590/A591 interchange; 2 m from Levens Hall.
Opening Times: CASTLE & GARDEN: Apr 1 to Oct 29 — Suns, Mons, Tues, Weds & Thurs; 1.30–5.30 (last admission 5). Garden & Shop open from 12.30 same days. Adm £3.10 (House and Garden), Chd half-price. GARDEN ONLY: £1.60, Chld 80p. Parties by arrangement with The Administrator, Sizergh Castle, Tel: Sedgwick 60070. Please send sae. Shop. No dogs. Wheelchairs (one provided) in garden only.

STOTT PARK BOBBIN MILL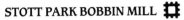

map F10
Telephone: (0448) 31087

The Victorian mill buildings forming Stott Park are virtually the same today as they were 150 years ago. The bobbin mill developed from man's ability to harness the power of the fast-flowing Lakeland streams to run machinery and also from the abundance of local coppice wood. Restored as a working industrial monument, much of the machinery still remains, including a turbine and steam engine.

Location: On unclassified road north of the village of Finsthwaite, 2 m (3.2 km) north of A590 Kendal/Barrow-in-Furness Road at Newby Bridge (near east bank of Lake Windermere). OS map ref SD373883.
Opening Times: Good Friday or Apr 1 (whichever is earlier) to Sept 30: Open Daily 10–6 (or dusk if earlier). Adm £1.80, Concessions £1.40, Chd 90p. Guided tours are available.

TOWNEND, The National Trust

Troutbeck   map F10
Telephone: Ambleside (05394) 32628

17th century Lakeland farmhouse with original furnishings including much wood-carving in traditional style. Home of the Browne family for 300 years, and last remaining glimpse into the old farming way of life.

Location: At S end of Troutbeck village, 3 m SE of Ambleside.
Opening Times: Apr 1 to Nov 1. Daily (except Mons & Sats but open Bank Hol Mons) 1–5 or dusk if earlier. Last adm 4.30. Adm £2.30, Chd £1.20. No reductions for parties. No dogs. No coaches. Unsuitable for wheelchairs.

WORDSWORTH HOUSE, The National Trust

Cockermouth   map F11   △
Telephone: Cockermouth (0900) 824805

North country Georgian House built in 1745, birthplace of the poet Wordsworth, furnished in the style of his time, with some of his belongings. The pleasant garden is referred to in his 'Prelude'. Video displays.

Location: In Main Street.
Opening Times: Apr 1 to Nov 1 — Mons to Sats (except Thurs) 11–5; Suns 2–5 (last admission 4.30). Adm £2.30, Chd £1.20. Reductions for pre-booked parties except on Suns. No dogs. Shop open winter: as summer but closed Sun and week after Christmas. Unsuitable for wheelchairs.
Refreshments: Light refreshments & lunches in the old kitchen (licensed).

LEVENS HALL

Kendal   map F10   &
Telephone: Sedgwick (05395) 60321
(C. H. Bagot, Esq.)

This magnificent Elizabethan home of the Bagot family, with its famous topiary garden (c.1692) is a must for visitors to the Lake District. The garden is unique in age and appearance, beautifully maintained in its original design with colourful bedding and herbaceous borders. The house contains a superb collection of Jacobean furniture, fine plaster ceilings, panelling, paintings and needlework, including the earliest English patchwork (c.1708). A collection of working model steam engines shows the development of steam power from 1820 to 1920, with full-sized traction engines in steam on Sundays and Bank Holiday Mondays.

Location: 5 m S of Kendal on the Milnthorpe Road (A6); Exit 36 from M6.
Opening Times: Easter Sunday to Sept 30. House, Garden, Gift Shop, Tearooms, Plants for sale, Play Area and Picnic Area. Suns, Mons, Tues, Weds & Thurs 11–5. Steam Collection 2–5. Closed Fris & Sats. Adm charge. Group rates for 20 or more. Regret house not suitable for wheelchairs.
Refreshments: Home-made light Lunches and teas.

MUNCASTER CASTLE 🏚

Ravenglass   map F10   △
(Mrs P. Gordon-Duff-Pennington)

Seat of the Pennington family since the 13th century, this magnificent castle with its famous rhododendron gardens and superb views of Eskdale dates from early 14th century, although the Pele tower is built on Roman foundations. There is an excellent collection of family portraits, tapestry and porcelain, but its outstanding feature is the large collection of 16th and 17th century furniture in beautiful condition. The octagonal library is one of Salvin's finest works and contains over 6,000 books. It is a very special family home. The gardens offer a variety of walks which can all offer some of the finest views in England, including those over the Esk Valley (Ruskin's Gateway to Paradise).

Location: 1 m SE of Ravenglass village on A595 (entrance ½ m W of Church).
Station: Ravenglass (1 m).
Opening Times: Gardens and Owl Centre daily throughout the year 11–5 (daily talk and display in the Owl Centre at 2.30). Castle: Mar 29 to Nov 1 Tues to Sun 1–4. Open all Bank Holiday Mons. Adm Gardens and Owl Centre £2.80, Chd £1.50. Castle, Gardens and Owl Centre: £4.50, Chd £2.50, Family tickets (2 + 2) Gardens and Owl Centre £7.50, Castle, Gardens and Owl Centre £12. Special Party Rates available. Write or telephone for Party Bookings and details of events during the season to: Muncaster Castle, Ravenglass, Cumbria. Telephone Ravenglass (0229) 717614 or 717203; Fax: (0229) 717010.

DERBYSHIRE

BOLSOVER CASTLE ⚜

map H8
Telephone: (0246) 823349
(English Heritage)

Castle in name only, the present mansion was built during the 17th century by Sir Charles Cavendish and his son William on the site of a 12th century castle. The Little Castle, separate and self-contained, is a delightful romantic Jacobean folly.

Location: Bolsover 6 m east of Chesterfield on A632. OS map ref SK471707.
Opening Times: Good Friday or Apr 1 (whichever is earlier) to Sept 30 daily 10–6. Oct 1 to Maundy Thursday or Mar 31 (whichever is earlier) Tues to Sun 10–4. *Closed* Dec 24–26, Jan 1. Adm £1.80, Concessions £1.40, Chd 90p.

CALKE ABBEY AND PARK – *See page 58*

CHATSWORTH – *See page 58*

EYAM HALL – *See page 58*

·HADDON HALL·

Estate Office, Haddon Hall, Bakewell, Derbyshire DE4 1LA Telephone: Bakewell (0629) 812855 Fax: (0629) 814379

The Derbyshire seat of the Duke of Rutland

HADDON HALL

Bakewell map H8
Telephone: Bakewell (0629) 812855
(His Grace the Duke of Rutland)

One of our few remaining 12th century manor houses, perfectly preserved. Noted for its tapestries, wood carvings and wall paintings. Standing on a wooded hill overlooking the fast flowing River Wye, Haddon is totally unspoiled. The beautiful terraced gardens dating from the middle ages are famous for roses, old fashioned flowers and herbs. Banqueting, conference and clay pigeon facilities available in Hall and Park. The House is extremely difficult for disabled visitors.

Location: 2 m SE Bakewell & 6½ m N of Matlock on Buxton/Matlock Road (A6).
Opening Times: Apr 1 to Sept 30 — Tues–Sun, 11–6. *Closed* Mons except Bank Hols, also closed Suns in July and Aug except Bank Hol weekends. Adm £3.20, Chd £1.90; Party rate £2.60, OAPs £2.60.
Refreshments: Morning coffee, lunches, afternoon teas at Stables Restaurant.

CALKE ABBEY AND PARK, The National Trust 💥

nr Derby　map H7
Telephone: Melbourne (0332) 863822 – recorded information 864444

Baroque mansion built 1701–3. House virtually unaltered since death of last baronet in 1924. Unique Caricature Room, gold and white drawing room, early 18th century Chinese silk state bed. Carriage display in Stable Block. Calke Park is a fine landscaped setting (approx. 750 acres). Park accessible via Ticknall entrance only. (One-way system in operation).

Location: 9 m S of Derby on A514 at Ticknall between Swadlincote and Melbourne.
Opening Times: Apr 1 to end Oct: Sat–Wed including Bank Holiday Mon. *Closed* Good Friday. 1–5.30 (last adm 5). Adm by timed ticket only. Ticket office open at 11 am. Visitors are advised that on busy days admission may not be possible. Long distance travellers are advised to contact the Calke office before setting out. Parties **must** book in advance with the Administrator. Adm £4, Chd £2.

CHATSWORTH

Bakewell　map H8
Telephone: Baslow (0246) 582204
(Chatsworth House Trust)

Built by Talman for 1st Duke of Devonshire between 1687 and 1707. Splendid collection of pictures, drawings, books and furniture. Garden with elaborate water-works surrounded by a great park. **Regret House impossible for wheelchairs, but they are most welcome in the garden.**

Location: ½ m E of village of Edensor on A623, 4 m E of Bakewell, 16 m from junction 29, M1. Signposted via Chesterfield.
Opening Times: HOUSE & GARDEN. Mar 29 to Nov 1—Daily 11–4.30. FARMYARD & ADVENTURE PLAYGROUND. Mar 29 to Oct 4—Daily 10.30–4.30. Adm charges not available at time of going to press. Gift shops. Baby Room. All details subject to confirmation.
Refreshments: Home-made refreshments. Coach Drivers' Rest Room.

EYAM HALL

Eyam　map H8
Telephone: 0433 31976
(R. H. V. Wright)

Seventeenth century manor house situated in the famous plague village of Eyam. Built and still occupied by the Wright family. A glimpse of three centuries through the eyes of one family. Family portraits and tapestries.

Location: 100 yds W of church. Eyam is off A623, 12 m W of Chesterfield, 15 m SW of Sheffield. Parking in village car park.
Opening Times: Mar 29 to Oct 25: Weds, Thurs, & Suns plus Bank Hols 11–4.30. Adm: £2.75, Chd £1.50, over 60s £2, family ticket £7. Advance booking essential for parties, reductions available. Tearooms and gift shop opening during 1992.

HADDON HALL – *See page 57*

HARDWICK HALL, The National Trust 💥

Nr Chesterfield　map H8
Telephone: Chesterfield (0246) 850430

Built 1591–1597 by 'Bess of Hardwick'. Notable furniture, needlework, tapestries. Gardens with yew hedges and borders of shrubs and flowers. Extensive collection of herbs. Information Centre in Country Park.

Location: 2 m S of Chesterfield/Mansfield Road (A617) 6½ m NW of Mansfield and 9½ m SE of Chesterfield. Approach from M1 exit 29.
Opening Times: HOUSE & GARDEN. Apr 1 to end Oct. HOUSE—Weds, Thurs, Sats, Suns & Bank Hol Mons 12.30–5 (or sunset if earlier). Last adm 4.30. Garden open daily to end Oct, 12–5.30. *Closed* Good Friday, Adm: House & Garden £5, Chd £2.50; Garden only £2, Chd £1. *No reduction for parties (including schools). School parties must book.* Car park (gates close 6). Dogs in park only, on leads. Wheelchairs in garden only. *Enquiries to The National Trust, Hardwick Hall, Doe Lea, nr Chesterfield, Derbys. Access to Hall may be limited at peak periods.*
Refreshments: In the Great Kitchen of Hall 2.30–4.45. Lunches 12–1.45 (last orders 15 mins before closing) on days when hall is open.

KEDLESTON HALL, The National Trust 💥

Derby　map H7
Telephone: Derby (0332) 842191

One of the best examples of neo-classical architecture in the country. Robert Adam designed the late 18th century house for Sir Nathaniel Curzon. Fine collection of furniture, tapestries and portraits. Landscaped park includes further examples of Adam's work.

Location: 4 m NW of Derby on Derby/Hulland Road via the Derby Ring Road Queensway.
Opening Times: HOUSE, PARK AND GARDENS: Apr 1 to end Oct, Sats to Wed including Bank Holiday Mons. PARK AND GARDENS: 11–6. Tea room: 12–5. House and Shop: 1–5.30 (last adm 5). £3.75, Chld £1.80. Coach parties welcome on days when the property is open, but **must** book well in advance in writing to the Administrator. 1992 events–details from Administrator.

LOSEHILL HALL

Castleton　map H8
Telephone: Hope Valley (0433) 620373
(Peak National Park Centre)

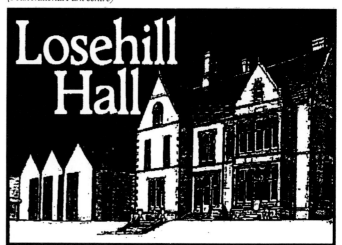

A residential study centre which organises holiday weeks and special interest weekends – 1992 programme includes Great Houses and Gardens, Historic Houses and Gardens, Derbyshire Villages and their People and Exploring the Peak District for the Over 50's. Other courses include Rambling, Photography, Painting and Natural History.

Location: ½ m E of Castleton Village on A625 towards Hope. Turn left after leaving Castleton before Caravan Site.
Station: Hope (2 m).
Opening Times: The hall is only open to guests on courses or to private groups who wish to book the facilities – special programmes can be arranged on request. Facilities include fully equipped lecture rooms and single or twin bedrooms, many en-suite. Prices on application.
Refreshments: Teas for booked parties. Full accommodation for holidays.

MELBOURNE HALL AND GARDENS 🏛

Melbourne　map H7
Telephone: (0332) 862502
(Lord Ralph Kerr)

This beautiful house of history is the home of Lord and Lady Ralph Kerr. In its picturesque poolside setting, Melbourne Hall was once the Home of Victorian Prime Minister William Lamb who as 2nd Viscount Melbourne gave his name to the famous city in Australia. This delightful family home contains an important collection of

So much to do at Chatsworth
for full details see under Derbyshire

MELBOURNE HALL AND GARDENS – *continued*

pictures and antique furniture. One of the most famous formal gardens in Britain featuring Robert Bakewell's wrought iron 'Birdcage'.

Location: 9 m S of Derby off the A453 in village of Melbourne.
Opening Times: HOUSE open every day of Aug only (except first 3 Mons) 2–5. Garden open: Apr to Sept: Weds, Sats, Suns, Bank Hol Mons 2–6. Garden adm £2, OAPs £1. Pre-booked parties in House – Aug only. Car parking limited – none reserved. Suitable for disabled persons.
Refreshments: Melbourne Hall Tearooms – open throughout the year Tel: (0332) 864224/ 863469. Craft Centre & Gift Shop open at various times throughout the year.

OLD HOUSE MUSEUM

Bakewell map H8
(Bakewell & District Historical Society)

An early Tudor house with original wattle & daub screen and open chamber. Costumes and Victorian kitchen, children's toys, craftsmen's tools and lacework.

Location: Above the church in Bakewell. ¼ m from centre.
Opening Times: HOUSE ONLY. Apr 1 to Oct 31 – Daily 2–5. Parties in morning or evening by appointment (Telephone Bakewell (0629) 813647). Adm £1, Chd 50p.

PEVERIL CASTLE ⚙

map H8
Telephone: (0433) 20613

The castle was built to control Peak Forest, where lead had been mined since prehistoric times. William the Conqueror thought so highly of this metal – and of the silver that could be extracted from it – that he entrusted the forest to one of his most esteemed knights, William Peveril.

Location: In Castleton on A625, 15 m west of Sheffield. OS map ref SK150827.
Opening Times: Good Friday or Apr 1 (whichever is earlier) to Sept 30: Open Daily 10–6. Oct 1 to Maundy Thursday or Mar 31 (whichever is earlier): Open Tues to Sun 10–4. *Closed* Dec 24–26, Jan 1. Adm £1.10, Concessions 85p, Chd 55p.

SUDBURY HALL, The National Trust ✹

nr Derby map H7 Ⓢ
Telephone: Burton on Trent (0283) 585305

A 17th century brick built house. Contains plasterwork ceilings. Laguerre murals staircase carved by Pierce and overmantel by Grinling Gibbons. Museum of Childhood.

Location: At Sudbury, 6 m E of Uttoxeter off A50 Road.
Opening Times: Apr 1 to end of Oct – Sat to Wed and Bank Holiday Mons 1–5.30 (last adm 5). Adm £3, Chd £1.50. Pre-booked parties special rates. Museum £2. Shop. Dogs in grounds only, on lead. Wheelchairs in garden only. 1992 events – details from the Administrator.
Refreshments: Light lunches & teas in Coach House, same open days as property, 12.30–5.30.

WINSTER MARKET HOUSE, The National Trust ✹

nr Matlock map H8
Telephone: Thorpe Cloud (033 529) 245

A stone market house of the late 17th or early 18th century in main street of Winster.

Location: 4 m W of Matlock on S side of B5057.
Opening Times: Weekends between Easter and end Oct and daily during July and Aug 10–4. Adm free. Information Room. No dogs. Unsuitable for wheelchairs.

DEVON

ARLINGTON COURT, The National Trust ✹

Barnstaple map E3 &
Telephone: Barnstaple (0271) 850296

Regency house furnished with the collections of the late Miss Rosalie Chichester; including shells, pewter and model ships. Display of horse-drawn vehicles in the stables. Good trees. Victorian formal garden.

Location: 8 m NE of Barnstaple on E side of A39
Opening Times: Footpaths through park open all year daily during daylight hours. House, Victorian garden, Carriage Collection, Stables, Shop: Apr 1 to Nov 1 – Daily (except Sats but open Sats of Bank Hol Weekends) 11–5.30. (Last adm ½ hour before closing.) Adm: House & Carriage Collection £4.40, Chd half-price. Gardens, Ground & Stables £2.20, Chd half-price. *Reduced fee of £3.30 for parties of 15 or more on application to the Administrator. Parties who do not pre-book will be charged full rate.* Shop. Dogs in park only, on leads. Wheelchairs provided. Carriage rides.
Refreshments: Licensed restaurant at the House: Apr 1 to Nov 1 – days and times as for House.

AVENUE COTTAGE GARDENS

Ashprington, Totnes map E2
Telephone: (0803) 732 769
(R. J. Pitts Esq, R. C. H. Soans Esq)

11 acres of garden and woodland walks. Part of 18th century landscape garden under going recreation by Designers/Plantsmen.

Location: 3 m SE of Totnes 300 yds beyond Ashprington Church (Sharpham Drive).
Opening Times: Apr 1 to Sept 30, Tues to Sat inclusive 11–5. Adm by donation. Parties by arrangement. No coaches. Limited access for disabled persons. No Wheelchairs available. Dogs on leads only. Plants for sale when available.

BICKLEIGH CASTLE – *See page 61*

BICKLEIGH CASTLE – *See page 61*

BRADLEY MANOR, The National Trust ✹

Newton Abbot map E2

Small, roughcast 15th century manor house set in woodland and meadows.

Location: W end of town, 7½ m NW of Torquay. On W side of A381.
Opening Times: Apr to Oct 1 – Weds 2–5; also Thurs, Apr 2 & 9, Sept 24 and Oct 1. Adm £2.40, Chd half-price. *No reduction for parties.* Parties of 15 or more must book in writing. No indoor photography. No access for coaches – Lodge gates too narrow. No dogs. Unsuitable for disabled or visually handicapped.

BICKLEIGH CASTLE

nr Tiverton   map E3   △   &.   Ⓢ
Telephone: Bickleigh (0884) 855 363
(Mr O. N. Boxall)

BICKLEIGH CASTLE A Royalist stronghold; 900 years of history and architecture.

Museum of 19th century domestic and agricultural objects and toys. Maritime history, including the Mary Rose and the Titanic. World War II original spy and escape gadgets.

The home of Alward mentioned in Domesday, the sons of the Earls of Devon in the 15th century and the Carews during the Civil War, the intriguing history of Bickleigh Castle spans nine centuries. The 11th century Chapel, the Armoury containing Cromwellian arms and armour, the Guard Room with Tudor furniture and pictures, the Great Hall, Elizabethan bedroom, and the 17th century farmhouse are all shown. The 'spooky' tower can be climbed for extensive views of the wooded Exe Valley and the attractive gardens are moated. Museum of 19th century domestic and agricultural objects and toys. Children may ride the period Rocking Horses. Exhibition showing Bickleigh Castle's connection with Maritime history, including the 'Mary Rose' and the 'Titanic'. World War II original spy and escape gadgets, M16, SOE, SAS. Heritage Education Trust award winner 1983 and 1988. A Royalist stronghold with 900 years of history and architecture, full of interest for all the family.

Location: 4 m S of Tiverton A396. At Bickleigh Bridge take A3072 and follow signs.
Opening Times: Easter Week (Good Fri to Fri) then Weds, Suns & Bank Hol Mons to late Spring Bank Hol; then to early Oct—Daily (except Sats) 2−5. *Parties of 20 or more by prior appointment only (preferably at times other than above) at reduced rates.* Adm £2.80, Chd half-price. Free coach & car park. Souvenir shops. Popular for Wedding Receptions etc.
Refreshments: Devonshire Cream Teas in the thatched Barn.

BUCKLAND ABBEY, The National Trust jointly managed with Plymouth City Council ✹

Yelverton   map E2
Telephone: Yelverton (0822) 853607

13th century Cistercian monastery bought by Sir Richard Grenville in 1541, altered by his grandson Sir Richard Grenville, of the 'Revenge', in 1576. Home of Drake from 1581 and still contains many relics of the great seaman, including Drake's drum. Exhibition to illustrate the Abbey's history. Restored buildings, including the monk's guesthouse and 18th century farm buildings. Great Barn. Craft workshops.

Location: 11 m N of Plymouth 6 m S of Tavistock between the Tavistock/Plymouth Road (A386) & River Tavy.
Opening Times: Apr 1 to Nov 1: daily (except Thurs) 10.30−5.30. Last admissions 45 mins before closing time. Nov to Mar 1993: Weds, Sats and Suns 2−5 (Wed pre-booked parties only). Adm £3.80, GROUNDS, including Great Barn and Craft workshops £1.80. Chd half price. Reduced rate for parties £3. Parties who do not pre-book will be charged at full rate. Dogs in designated areas only, on leads. Shop.
Refreshments: Licensed Restaurant serving home-made lunches, teas and coffee. Apr 1 to Nov 1: 11 to ½ hour before closing; Nov−Mar 1993 12−5.

CADHAY

Ottery St Mary   map F2   △
Telephone: Ottery St Mary 2432
(Lady William-Powlett)

Cadhay is approached by an avenue of lime-trees, and stands in a pleasant listed garden, with herbaceous borders and yew hedges, with excellent views over the original mediaeval fish ponds. Cadhay is first mentioned in the reign of Edward I, and was held by a de Cadehaye. The main part of the house was built about 1550 by John Haydon who had married the de Cadhay heiress. He retained the Great Hall of an earlier house, of which the fine timber roof (about 1420) can be seen. An Elizabethan Long Gallery was added by John's successor at the end of the 16th century, thereby forming a unique and lovely courtyard. Some Georgian alterations were made in the mid 18th century. The house is viewed by conducted tour. Photography is permitted outside.

Location: 1 m NW of Ottery St Mary on B3176.
Station: Feniton (2½ m) (not Suns).
Opening Times: Spring (May 24 & 25) & Summer (Aug 30 & 31) Bank Hol Suns & Mons; also Tues, Weds & Thurs in July & Aug: 2−6 (last adm 5.30). Adm £2.50, Chd £1. *Parties by arrangement.*

CASTLE DROGO, The National Trust 🌿

nr Chagford map E2 &
Telephone: Chagford (064 743) 3306

Granite castle designed by Sir Edwin Lutyens, standing at over 900ft overlooking the wooded gorge of the River Teign. Terraced garden and miles of splendid walks.

Location: 4 m NE of Chagford; 6 m S of A30.
Opening Times: Apr 1 to Nov 1 —Daily (except Fri, *Garden daily*) 11—5.30 (last adm ½ hour before closing). Adm £4.40; Grounds only £2. Chd half-price. *Reduced rates for parties (£3.40) on application to the Administrator. Parties who do not pre-book will be charged at full rate.* No dogs except guide dogs. Wheelchairs provided. Shop and Plant Centre. The restored croquet lawn is open. Equipment for hire from the shop.
Refreshments: Coffee, light lunches (licensed) & teas at the castle 11—½ hour before closing.

COLETON FISHACRE GARDEN, The National Trust 🌿

Coleton map E2 &
Telephone: Kingswear (080 425) 466

18 acre garden in a stream-fed valley. Garden created by Lady Dorothy D'Oyly Carte between 1925 and 1940; planted with wide variety of uncommon trees and exotic shrubs.

Location: 2 m from Kingswear; take Lower Ferry Road, turn off at tollhouse & follow 'Garden Open' signs.
Opening Times: Mar 1—29 inc—Suns 2—5; to Nov 1—Weds, Thurs, Fris & Suns 10.30—5.30. Adm £2.40, Chd half price. Pre-booked parties £1.80. Limited wheelchair access.

COMPTON CASTLE, The National Trust 🌿

nr Paignton map E2
Telephone: Paignton (0803) 872112

Fortified manor house. Great Hall (restored), Solar, Kitchen, Chapel and rose garden.

Location: 1 m N of Marldon off A381.
Opening Times: Apr to Nov 1—Mons, Weds & Thurs 10—12.15, 2—5 (last adm 30 mins before closing). Adm £2.40, Chd half-price. Parties £1.80—*organisers should please notify the Secretary.* No dogs except guide dogs. Additional parking and refreshments at Castle Barton, opposite entrance.

DARTMOUTH CASTLE ✠

Dartmouth map E2
Telephone: (0803) 833588
(English Heritage)

Boldly guarding the narrow entrance to the Dart Estuary this castle was among the first in England to be built for artillery. Construction began in 1481 on the site of an earlier castle which was altered and added to over the following centuries. Victorian coastal defence battery with fully equipped guns, a site exhibition and magnificent views can all be seen at the castle.

Location: 1 m (1.6 km) south east of Dartmouth.
Opening Times: Good Friday or Apr 1 (whichever is earlier) to Sept 30 daily 10—6. Oct 1 to Maundy Thursday or Mar 31 (whichever is earlier) Tues to Sun 10—4. *Closed Dec 24—26, Jan 1.* Adm £1.50, Concessions £1.10, Chd 75p.

ENDSLEIGH HOUSE

Milton Abbot, Nr Tavistock map E2
Telephone: (0822) 87 248
(The Endsleigh Charitable Trust)

Arboretum, Shell House, Flowering Shrubs, Rock Garden.

Location: 4 m W of Tavistock on A386.
Opening Times: House and Gardens: Apr to Sept: weekends 12—4; Tues and Fris by appointment 12—4; Bank Hols 12—4. Adm Honesty Box in Aid of Trust. Limited car parking. Not suitable for disabled. No wheelchairs.
Refreshments: Lunches and teas at Endsleigh House by appointment. No dogs. No coaches.

FLETE

Ermington, Ivybridge map E2
(Country Houses Association Ltd)

Built around an Elizabethan manor with alterations in 1879 by Norman Shaw.

Location: 11 m E of Plymouth at junction of A379 and B3210.
Stations: Plymouth (12m), Totnes (14m). Bus Route: No 93 Plymouth—Dartmouth.
Opening Times: May to Sept—Weds & Thurs, 2—5. Last entry 4.30. Adm £1.50, Chd 50p. Free car park. No dogs admitted.

FURSDON 🏛

Cadbury, Thorverton map E3 △
Telephone: Exeter (0392) 860860
(E. D. Fursdon, Esq)

Fursdon is set in a beautiful rural landscape and the Fursdon family have lived here for over 700 years. It remains primarily a family home. There is a Regency library, a recently discovered oak screen from the mediaeval hall, family portraits and annual displays from the family costume collection including some fine 18th century examples. Attractive developing garden.

Location: 9 m N of Exeter, 6 m SW of Tiverton; ¾ m off A3072.
Opening Times: Easter Mon to end Sept: Thurs and Bank Hol Mon only 2—4.30 (last adm 4). Parties over 20 by arrangement please. Adm House & Grounds £2.30. Reductions for children; under 10 years, free.
Refreshments: Home made teas in Coach Hall on open days.

HARTLAND ABBEY 🏛

Bideford, North Devon map D3
Telephone: Hartland (0237) 41264
(Sir Hugh Stucley, Bt.)

Abbey founded in 1157. Dissolved in 1539 and descended to the present day through a series of marriages. Major architectural alterations in 1705 and in 1779. Unique document exhibition dating from 1160 AD. Pictures, furniture and porcelain collected over many generations. Victorian & Edwardian photographic exhibition. Shrub gardens of rhododendrons, azaleas and camellias. Magnificent woodland walk to a remote atlantic cove with spectacular cliff scenery. Set in a designated area of outstanding natural beauty.

Location: NW Devon (Hartland Point); 15 m from Bideford; 5 m approx from A39.
Opening Times: May to Sept incl—Weds 2—5.30. Sun 2—5.30 in July & Aug, and first 2 Suns in Sept. Bank Hols (Easter to Summer) Suns & Mons 2—5.30. Adm £2.50, Chd £1.50. Parties welcomed £2. Shrub garden and grounds only: £1. Ample car parking close to house.
Refreshments: Cream teas provided at house.

HEMERDON HOUSE

Plympton, Plymouth map E2 &
Telephone: Plymouth (0752) 223816 (Office hours); 337350 (weekend & evenings)
(J. H. G. Woollcombe, Esq)

Regency house containing West country paintings and prints, with appropriate furniture and a Library.

Location: 2 m from Plympton.
Opening Times: May — 22 days including Bank Holidays and Aug — 8 days including Bank Holiday 2—5.30. For opening dates please contact the Administrator. Adm £2.

KILLERTON, The National Trust 🌿

nr Exeter map F2 &
Telephone: Exeter (0392) 881345

Late 18th century house in a beautiful setting containing the Paulise de Bush Collection of Costume. Lovely throughout the year, with flowers from early spring, and splendid late autumn colours. 19th century Chapel and Ice House. Estate exhibition in Stables. Paths lead up the hill to the Dolbury, an isolated hill with an Iron Age hill fort site.

Location: 7 m NE of Exeter on W side of Exeter Cullompton (B3181—formerly A38); from M5 s'bound exit 28/B3181; from M5 n'bound exit 30 via Broadclyst & B3181.
Opening Times: House: Apr 1 to Nov 1—Daily (except Tues) 11—5.30 (last adm ½ hour before closing). Park: All the year during daylight hours. Adm. House and Garden £4.20 (tickets available at Stable Block), Chd half-price; Garden only £2.40. *Reduced rates for parties (£3.20) on application to the Administrator. Parties who do not pre-book will be charged at full rate.* The Conference Room may be booked for meetings, etc. Applications (in writing) to: The Administrator, Killerton House, Broadclyst, Exeter, Devon. Shop and plant centre in Stables. Dogs in Park only. Wheelchairs provided. Motorised buggy for disabled visitors to tour the garden.
Refreshments: Licensed restaurant at House, entrance from garden—tickets necessary, available in Stables. Light refreshments and ice cream in Coach House, home baked bread and pastries for sale and to take away.

KNIGHTSHAYES COURT, The National Trust 🌿

nr Tiverton map E3 &
Telephone: Tiverton (0884) 254665

One of the finest gardens in Devon with specimen trees, rare shrubs, spring bulbs, summer flowering borders; of interest at all seasons. House by William Burges, begun in 1869, decorated by J D Crace.

Location: 2 m N of Tiverton; turn off A396 (Bampton/Tiverton Road) at Bolham.
Opening Times: Apr 1 to Nov 1—Garden daily 10.30—5.30. House—daily except Fri (but open Good Friday) 1.30—5.30 (last adm ½ hour before closing). *Nov and Dec: Sun 2—4; pre-arranged parties only.* Adm £4.60, Chd half-price. Garden & Grounds only £2.60. *Reduced rates for parties (£3.60) on application to the Administrator. Parties who do not pre-book will be charged at full rate.* Shop. Plants available at garden shop. Dogs in park only on leads. Wheelchairs provided.
Refreshments: Licensed restaurant for coffee, lunches and teas 11—½ hour before closing, daily. Picnic area in car park.

MARWOOD HILL

nr Barnstaple map E3
(Dr J. A. Smart)

Extensive collection of camellias under glass and in the open, daffodils, rhododendrons, rare flowering shrubs: rock and alpine garden, waterside planting. Bog garden. 18 acre garden with 3 small lakes. Many eucalyptus and NCCPG National Collection of astilbes and iris ensata (kaempferi).

Location: 4 m N of Barnstaple; opposite church in Marwood. Signs from A361 Barnstaple–Braunton Road.
Opening Times: GARDENS ONLY. All the year—Daily (except Christmas Day) dawn to dusk. Adm £1, Chd 10p. *In aid of National Gardens Scheme.* Plants for sale. Dogs allowed, on leads only.
Refreshments: Teas. Apr to Sept, Suns & Bank Hols, or by prior arrangement for parties.

OKEHAMPTON CASTLE

map E2
Telephone: (0837) 522844

Rebellion broke out in the south west after the Battle of Hastings and a stronghold was built here to subdue it. The castle passed from Baldwin FitzGilbert to Robert de Courtenay in 1172 and remained with this family, off and on, for 3½ centuries. The last Courtenay to own it, the Marquis of Exeter, was beheaded in 1538 and the castle dismantled.
Location: 1 m (1.6 km) south west of Okehampton. OS map ref SX584942.
Opening Times: Good Friday or Apr 1 (whichever is earlier) to Sept 30: Open Daily 10–6. Oct 1 to Maundy Thursday or Mar 31 (whichever is earlier): Open Tues to Sun 10–4. *Closed Dec 24–26, Jan 1.* Adm £1.50, Concessions £1.10, Chd 75p. Admission price includes a Personal Stereo Guided Tour.

OVERBECKS MUSEUM & GARDEN, The National Trust

Sharpitor, Salcombe   map E2
Telephone: Salcombe (054 884) 2893

6 acres of garden with rare and tender plants and beautiful views eastwards over Salcombe Bay. Part of house forms museum of local interest and of particular interest to children.
Location: 1½ m SW of Salcombe signposted from Malborough & Salcombe.
Opening Times: GARDEN: All the year—Daily 10–8, or sunset if earlier. Museum: Apr 1 to Nov 1—Daily except Sat 11–5.30. Last adm ½ hour before closing. Adm MUSEUM & GARDEN £3, Chd half-price. Garden only £2. *No reduction for parties.* No dogs except Guide dogs. Shop. Picnicking allowed in gardens. Not suitable for coaches.

POWDERHAM CASTLE

nr Exeter   map F2
(Lord and Lady Courtenay)

Medieval castle built c 1390 by Sir Philip Courtenay, ancestor of the present Earl of Devon. Damaged in the Civil War and restored and altered in 18th and 19th centuries. Music Room by Wyatt. Park stocked with deer. A family home.
Location: 8 m S of Exeter off A379 to Dawlish.
Station: Starcross 1½ m.
Opening Times: May 17 to Oct 1—Suns–Thurs 11–6 (last adm 5.30). Closed Fris & Sats but available for functions, conferences and receptions. For information please contact: The Administrator Tel. (0626) 890 243/252. Good free parking. Dogs admitted to shaded car park only.
Refreshments: Lunches, teas. Souvenirs.

ROSEMOOR GARDEN

Great Torrington   map E3
(The Royal Horticultural Society)

Important and internationally famous plantsmans' garden of 8 acres which is being expanded by the Royal Horticultural Society to 40 acres. New features include 2000 roses in 200 different varieties, colour theme gardens, herb garden and potager, stream and bog gardens, and herbaceous borders. New Visitors Centre with restaurant, shop and plant sales centre with many rare plants. Coaches welcome by appointment. Guide dogs only.
Location: 1 m SE of Great Torrington on B3220 to Exeter.
Opening Times: Garden open all year. Visitors Centre open from Mar 1 to Oct 31 10–6. Adm £2.25, Chd 50p. Parties of over 20 persons £1.75 each.
Refreshments: Refreshments, light lunches and Devon cream teas available in new restaurant.

SALTRAM HOUSE, The National Trust

Plymouth   map E2
Telephone: Plymouth (0752) 336546

A George II house, built around and incorporating remnants of a late Tudor mansion, in a landscaped park. Two exceptional rooms by Robert Adam. Furniture, pictures, fine plasterwork and woodwork. Great Kitchen. Beautiful garden with Orangery. Octagonal summer-house, rare shrubs and trees. Shop in stables.
Location: 2 m W of Plympton 3½ m E of Plymouth city centre, between A38 & A379 main roads.
Opening Times: HOUSE: Apr 1 to Nov 1. Suns–Thurs. House: 12.30–5.30. Garden, Kitchen, Shop & Art Gallery 10.30–5.30, Last adm ½ hour before closing. Adm £4.80, Chd half-price; Garden only £2. *Reductions for parties (£4) at certain times of day by prior arrangement for visits/meals with the Administrator.* The Chapel may be booked for meetings, etc. Applications (in writing) to: The Administrator, Saltram House, Plympton, Plymouth. Dogs in park only. Wheelchairs provided.
Refreshments: Licensed restaurant in House (entrance from Garden); Suns–Thurs 11–5.30 (last adm ½ hour before closing). Light refreshments at Coach House near car park during peak periods.

SAND

Sidbury, nr Sidmouth   map F2
(Lt Col P. V. Huyshe)

Lived in Manor house owned by Huyshe family since 1560, rebuilt 1592–4, situated in unspoilt valley. Screens passage, panelling, family documents, heraldry. Also **Sand Lodge** roof structure of late 15th century Hall House.
Location: ¾ m NE of Sidbury; 400 yds from A375, Grid ref 146925.
Opening Times: Suns & Mons—Apr 19, 20; May 24, 25; July 26, 27; Aug 30, 31; 2–5.30. Last tour 4.45. Adm £2, Chd & Students 40p. Sand Lodge and outside of Sand by written appointment, £1.
Refreshments: Light teas in house, cream teas in Sidbury (free car parking).

SHUTE BARTON, The National Trust

Shute, Nr Axminster EX13 7PT
Telephone: Axminster (0297) 34692

Remains of a manor house, built over three centuries and completed in late 16th century; grey stone with battlemented tower and late Gothic windows; gatehouse. Exterior may be viewed during daylight hours. The house is tenanted; there is access to parts of interior: April to Nov 1: Wed & Sat 2–5.30. Adm £1.40, pre-booked parties £1, Chd half price. No dogs except guide dogs. No refreshments available. Unsuitable for disabled or visually handicapped.
Location: 3 m SW of Axminster, 2 m N of Colyton on Honiton-Colyton road (B3161) [177(193): SY253974].
Station: Axminster 3 m.

TIVERTON CASTLE

Tiverton　map E3
Telephone: (0884) 253200 or 071-727 4854
(Mr and Mrs A. K. Gordon)

Historically important mediaeval castle commissioned by Henry I in 1106; magnificent mediaeval gatehouse and tower containing important Civil War armoury, notable clock collection, fine furniture and pictures, New World Tapestry.

Location: Next to St. Peter's Church. The Castle is well signposted in Tiverton.
Opening Times: Good Friday to last Sun in Sept—Suns to Thurs 2.30–5.30. Adm £2.50, Chd under 7 free, 7–16 £1.50. Party bookings at special rates. Free parking inside. Coach parties by appointment only.
Refreshments: Devon cream teas during Summer. Light lunches, evening parties by prior arrangement.

TORRE ABBEY

Torquay　map E2
Telephone: Torquay (0803) 293593
(Torbay Borough Council)

12th century monastery converted into a private residence after the Dissolution in 1539. Extensively remodelled in the early 18th century and currently undergoing complete renovation and restoration. Contains furnished period rooms, family chapel, extensive collection of paintings and other works of art, and the Dame Agatha Christie memorial room, containing many mementos of the Torquay born authoress. Over 25 rooms now open to the public including those in the newly restored South-West wing. Ruins of medieval Abbey also on show, including the remains of the Abbey Church, excavated in 1987/9. Formal gardens containing tropical palm house, summer bedding, rockeries and spring bulbs. Special exhibitions throughout the summer.

Location: On Torquay Sea front.
Station: Torquay (¹/₄ m).
Opening Times: HOUSE: Apr to Oct—Daily. Other times by appointment. Adm (1991 rates) £2, Chd/ Senior Citizens £1. Family ticket £4.50 (2 adults and up to 3 children). GARDENS: All the year—Daily. Adm free.

TOTNES CASTLE ✦

map E2
Telephone: (0803) 864406

The Normans also built a stronghold here to overawe the townspeople. But they surrendered without a blow, as they did again in the Civil War. The remains date largely from the 14th century, although the huge earth mound on which the castle rests is Norman.

Location: Totnes. OS map ref SX800605.
Opening Times: Good Friday or Apr 1 (whichever is earlier) to Sept 30: Open Daily 10–6. Oct 1 to Maundy Thursday or Mar 31 (whichever is earlier): Open Tues to Sun 10–4. *Closed* Dec 24–26, Jan 1. Adm £1.20, Concessions 90p, Chd 60p.

UGBROOKE HOUSE

Chudleigh　map E2
Telephone: Chudleigh (0626) 852179

Set in beautiful scenery and quiet parkland in the heart of Devon. The original House and Church built about 1200, redesigned by Robert Adam. Home of the Cliffords of Chudleigh, Ugbrooke contains fine furniture, paintings, beautiful embroideries, needlework and porcelain. Capability Brown landscaped Park with lakes, majestic trees, terraced gardens and scenic views to Dartmoor. Guided tours relate stories of Clifford Castles, Shakespeare's 'Black Clifford', Henry II's 'Fair Rosamund' Lady Anne Clifford who defied Cromwell, The Secret Treaty, the Cardinal's daughter, Charles II's Lord High Treasurer Clifford of the CABAL, and many more tales of intrigue, espionage and bravery.

Location: Chudleigh
Opening Times: May 23 to Aug 31 (except June 20, 21), Sat, Sun and Bank Hols **only**. GROUNDS – 1 –5. Guided tours of House at 2.15 and 3.45. Adm £3.40, Chd (5–16) £1.70, Groups (over 20) £3. Private tours/functions by appointment.
Refreshments: Snacks & afternoon teas at the Wyvern Café, 2–5.

WOODSIDE

Barnstaple　map E3
Telephone: Barnstaple (0271) 43095
(Mr & Mrs Mervyn Feesey)

2 acre plantsman's garden, south sloping, raised beds. Collection of ornamental grasses, bamboos, sedges and other monocots; unusual and rare dwarf shrubs and plants; troughs; variegated and peat-loving shrubs and conifers; New Zealand collection.

Location: N outskirts of Barnstaple; off A39 to Lynton (400 yds. beyond Fire Station).
Station: Barnstaple Junction (1 m).
Opening Times: GARDEN ONLY. Suns May 12, June 23, July 21; (2–6). Adm 75p, Chd 25p. *In aid of National Gardens Scheme.* Other days by appointment.

YARDE

Malborough, nr Kingsbridge
Telephone: 054 884 2367
(John and Marilyn Ayre)

An outstanding example of the Devon farmstead with a Tudor Bakehouse, Elizabethan Farmhouse and Queen Anne Mansion under restoration. Still a family farm.

Location: On A381 ½ m E of Malborough. 4 m S of Kingsbridge.
Opening Times: Easter to Oct 31: Suns, Weds, Bank Hol Mons 2–5.
Refreshments: Cream teas. Coaches by appointment.

DORSET

ATHELHAMPTON

Athelhampton   map G2   △   &
Telephone: Puddletown (0305) 848363
(Lady Du Cann)

One of the finest mediaeval houses in England. Five centuries of history in a family house built in 1485 on the site of King Athelstan's Palace. Great Hall with unique roof, oriel window, heraldic glass and linenfold panelling. Fine furniture in the Tudor Great Chamber. 18th century Dining Room, State Bedroom, Wine Cellar and exhibition room. 12 architectural and water gardens with rate plants and trees in 10 acres, encircled by the River Piddle. 15th century dovecote.

Location: 1 m E of Puddletown on Dorchester/Bournemouth Road (A35); 5 m NE of Dorchester.
Opening Times: Easter to end Oct, 2–6 on Weds, Thurs & Suns; Good Fri & Bank Hols; also Mons & Tues in Aug and Tues in May, June, July & Sept, also open Fris in July and Aug: 2–6. Entrance and Garden: £1.60, House £1.60 extra. (Chd free of charge in gardens). Special rate for pre-booked parties £2.70 incl. Dogs admitted only to shaded car park.
Refreshments: Tea at the House.

CHETTLE HOUSE

Chettle, Blandford   map G3
Telephone: Chettle (0258 89) 209
(J. P. C. Bourke)

One of the finest examples of a Queen Anne House in the English Baroque style by Thomas Archer. Set in 5 acres of garden with many unusual herbaceous plants and shrubs. Fine Art Gallery and vineyard.

Location: 6 m NE of Blandford on A354 & 1 mile W.
Opening Times: Adm £1.50. Car and Coach park. Apr–Oct daily (except Tues) 11–5. Plant Centre with unusual herbaceous plants. No dogs.
Refreshments: Many pubs within 2 miles. Picnic area available, teas usually.

CLOUDS HILL, The National Trust

nr Wool   map G2

The cottage home of T. E. Lawrence (Lawrence of Arabia) after the first World War; contains his furniture and other relics.

Location: 1 m N of Bovington Camp, ½ m E of Waddock crossroads (B3390), 9 m E of Dorchester.
Opening Times: Apr 1 to Nov 1—Weds, Thurs, Fris, Suns & Bank Hol Mons 2–5. Nov 8 to end Mar 1993—Suns only 1–4 (no electric lighting available, *closed* dusk if earlier). Adm £2.20. *No reduction for children or parties.* No photography. No dogs. Unsuitable for wheelchairs & coaches. No WCs.

CORFE CASTLE, The National Trust

nr Wareham   map G2
Telephone: Corfe Castle (0929) 481294

Ruins of former royal castle, sieged and 'slighted' by Parliamentary forces in 1646.

Location: In the village of Corfe Castle: on A351 Wareham-Swanage road.
Opening Times: Feb 9 to end Oct daily 10–5.30pm or dusk if earlier, open Good Friday. Nov to Feb 1993; Sat and Sun 12–3.30. Adm: £2.50, Chd £1.30, parties (15 or more) £2, Chd £1. Not suitable for wheelchairs. N.T. Shop and refreshments.

CRANBORNE MANOR GARDENS

map H3
Telephone: Cranborne 248
(The Viscount and Viscountess Cranborne)

Walled gardens, yew hedges and lawns; wild garden with spring bulbs, herb garden, Jacobean mount garden, flowering cherries and collection of old-fashioned and specie roses. Beautiful and historic gardens laid out in the 17th century by John Tradescant and much embellished and enlarged in the 20th century.

Location: 18 m N of Bournemouth, B3078; 16 m S of Salisbury, A354, B3081.
Opening Times: GARDEN CENTRE open Tues–Sats 9–5, Suns 10–5 (not Jan & Feb). *Closed* Mons except Bank Holidays. Something for every gardener, but specialising in old-fashioned and specie roses, herbs, ornamental pots and Italian statuary and garden furniture. GARDENS ONLY, Mar to Sept–Wed 9–5. Free car park.

DAWNAY HOUSE

Puddletown, nr Dorchester   map G2
Telephone: 0305 269741

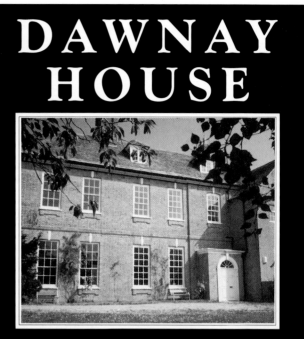
This attractive, lived in, early Georgian country house was built about 1725 for the Hon. Henry Dawnay. The house, built of local red brick is thought to be the finest example of the Blandford style in Dorset. Sir John Betjeman included it amongst his favourite Dorset houses. Although Georgian in date, Dawnay House is mainly Queen Anne architecturally. The lofty rooms, stately in nature, are unusual in a country house of this style. Most of the original features survive unaltered, including the splendid early Georgian oak staircase, surrounded as it is by elegant arched niches and archways. Some rooms are furnished in a style contemporary to Dawnay, whilst others are tastefully furnished with fine furniture of other styles including elegant Chinoiserie. Each room has a theme, including local subjects such as Thomas Hardy. The house contains collections of antiques, antiquities and oriental art. The unique Japanese garden creates its own special atmosphere which culminates in the Pavilion of Tranquillity.

Location: Puddletown 5 m E of Dorchester on A35, in square opposite church.
Opening Times: HOUSE AND GARDEN: Good Friday, Easter Sun and Mon; May to end Sept, Wed, Fri, Sun plus Bank Hols 1.30–5.30. Adm charge. Reduced rates for parties on request. Group visits on these and other days must be booked in advance. Parking in village. Access for disabled in gardens and ground floor of house.
Refreshments: Attic Tea Rooms in the house. Prince of Wales and Blue Vinny pubs in village. The Junction, The Kings Arms and The Wessex Royale hotels in Dorchester.

DEANS COURT 🏛

Wimborne   map H3   ♿
(Sir Michael & Lady Hanham)

Thirteen acres of partly wild garden, in a peaceful setting on the River Allen. Specimen trees, monastery fishpond with peacocks. Herb garden with over 100 varieties. Organically grown herb plants for sale.

Location: 2 m walk South from Wimborne Minster & Square; nr free car parks in town.
Opening Times: GARDEN. Apr: Sun 19 2–6, Mon 20 10–6; May: Sun 3, 24 2–6, Mon 4, 25 10–6; June: Thur 4, 25, Sun 7, 28 2–6; July: Thur 2, Sun 5 2–6; Aug: Sun 30 2–6, Mon 31 10–6; Sept: Thurs 3, 24, Sun 6, 27 2–6. Snowdrop Sun: Feb; Daffodil Sun: Mar. Dates and times to be arranged. Contact Wimborne Tourist Information Office, Wimborne (0202) 886116 for details. HOUSE. Open by prior written appointment only (not on garden open days).
Refreshments: Wholefood teas on all open days. Coffee on Bank Hol mornings. Some refreshments may be available on the Snowdrop and Daffodil Suns.

EDMONDSHAM HOUSE AND GARDENS

Cranborne, nr Wimborne   map H3
Telephone: Cranborne (072 54) 207
(Mrs J. E. Smith)

A family home since the 16th century, and a fine blend of Tudor and Georgian architecture, with a Victorian stable block and dairy, interesting furniture, lace and other exhibits. The Gardens include an old-fashioned walled garden, cultivated organically, with an excellent display of spring bulbs, shrubs, lawns and herbaceous border.

Location: Between Cranborne and Verwood, off the B3081.
Opening Times: HOUSE AND GARDENS: Easter Sun, all Bank Hol Mons, all Weds in Apr and Oct, 2–5. Groups by arrangement at other times. Adm £2, Chd £1. GARDENS: Apr, May, June and Oct: Wed–Sat incl. 10–12, and at other times when the owner is at home. Adm £1, Chd 50p.

FORDE ABBEY AND GARDENS 🏛

nr Chard   map F3   △
Telephone: (0460) 20231
(Trustees of Forde Abbey)

Cistercian monastery, founded 1140. Converted to private house mid 17th c. and unaltered since. Thirty acres of outstanding gardens—trees and shrubs, herbaceous borders, rock garden, bog garden and kitchen garden. Plants on sale.

Location: 1 m E of Chard Junction, 4 m SE of Chard signposted off A30.
Opening Times: GARDENS AND NURSERY: open daily throughout the year 10–4.30; HOUSE: April to end Oct. Suns, Weds & Bank Hol, 1–4.30. Our charges for 1992 are not yet finally decided.
Refreshments: Undercroft open for light lunches and teas mid-day to 4.45 daily during summer months.

HARDY'S COTTAGE, The National Trust 🌿

Higher Bockhampton   map G2   ♿
Telephone: Dorchester (0305) 262366

Birthplace of Thomas Hardy 1840–1928. A thatched cottage, built by his grandfather; little altered.

Location: 3 m NE of Dorchester; ½ m S of Blandford Road (A35).
Opening Times: Interior: by prior appointment with the custodian. Adm to interior £2.30. Garden: daily (except Thurs) from 11–6 or dusk if earlier. Exterior and garden free. Approached by 10 mins walk from car park via woods. No dogs. Wheelchairs, garden only. No WCs.

HIGHBURY

West Moors   map H3
Telephone: Ferndown 874372
(Mr & Mrs Stanley Cherry)

Half acre garden in mature setting; many rare and unusual plants and shrubs. Specialist collections. Botanical and horticultural interest with everything labelled.

Location: In Woodside Road off B3072 (last road N end of village).
Opening Times: GARDEN ONLY. Please see NGS yellow book for details. Adm 65p, Chd 25p, OAPs and parties 45p. *In aid of National Gardens Scheme.* No dogs.
Refreshments: Teas in the orchard when fine.

HORN PARK

Beaminster
Telephone: (0308) 862212
(Mr & Mrs John Kirkpatrick)

Magnificent view. Rhododendrons, azaleas, camellias, bulbs, rock and water gardens, herbaceous and unusual plants. Woodland walk in Spring.

Location: 1½ m N. of Beaminster on A3066.
Opening Times: Apr 1 to Oct 1 every Tues and Thur 1st and 3rd Sun each month, Bank Hol Mons. Adm £2 under 16 free.

ILSINGTON 🏛

Puddletown, Dorchester   map G2
Telephone: (0305) 848454
(Mr & Mrs P. Duff)

A family home. A classical William and Mary mansion built by the 7th Earl of Huntingdon. Home of George III's illegitimate grandson, born to HRH Princess Sophia in 1800, kept a secret until the Royal Scandal of 1826. Ilsington was visited by many members of the Royal Family during George III's reign. Fine furniture and present owners' private collection of pictures and sculpture. 11 acres of formal and landscape gardens with probably the longest haha in Dorset. New gardens being constantly redesigned and created.

Location: 4 m from Dorchester on the A35.
Opening Times: May 3 to Oct 4, Wed, Thurs and Sun 2–6. Plus Bank Hol Mons. HOUSE & GARDENS £3. Parties by special arrangement. Free car parking. Not suitable for disabled persons.
Refreshments: Lunch or tea for parties by arrangement in the House, teas available in the village.

KINGSTON LACY, The National Trust

nr Wimborne Minster   map G3   Ⓢ
Telephone: Wimborne (0202) 883402

17th century House designed by Sir Roger Pratt but with considerable alterations by Sir Charles Barry in the 19th century. Important Italian and English paintings collected by W. J. Bankes. Set in 250 acres of wooded park.

Location: on B3082 – Wimborne – Blandford Road, 1½ m W of Wimborne.
Opening Times: Apr 1 to Nov 1 daily except Thurs & Frid. HOUSE: 12 – 5.30 (last adm 4.30). PARK: 11.30 – 6. Adm: HOUSE: £4.80, Chd £2.40. PARK AND GARDEN: £1.70, Chd 80p. Parties by prior appointment with administrator. House not suitable for wheelchairs. One wheelchair available for use in Garden. Guide dogs admitted to grounds. Parties by arrangement **only**.
Refreshments: Lunches and cream teas. National Trust Shop.

MACPENNY'S

Bransgore, nr Christchurch   map H3
Telephone: Bransgore (0425) 72348
(Tim Lowndes, Esq)

Large woodland garden. Nurseries, camellias, rhododendrons, azaleas, heathers, herbaceous.

Location: 4 m NE of Christchurch; 1½ m W of A35.
Opening Times: Garden and nurseries open all year daily (except Christmas Hols and New Year). Mons to Sats 9 – 5; Suns 2 – 5. *Collecting box in aid of National Gardens Scheme.*

MAPPERTON

Beaminster   map G3
Telephone: (0308) 862645
(Montagu family)

Terraced and hillside gardens with topiary, formal borders and specimen shrubs and trees. Modern orangery in classical style, 17th century stone fish ponds and summer house. Tudor manor house, enlarged 1660. Magnificent walks and views.

Location: 1 m off B3163, 2 m off B3066.
Opening Times: Mar to Oct, daily 2 – 6. Adm £2.50, under 18 £1.50, under 5 free. House also open to group tours by appointment, adm £2.50.

MILTON ABBEY

Milton Abbas, nr Blandford   map G3
(The Council of Milton Abbey School Ltd)

A fine Abbey Church (Salisbury Diocese) partially completed 15th century on site of 10th century Abbey. The magnificent Abbot's Hall, completed 1498, with fine hammerbeam roof and carved screen, is incorporated in the Georgian Gothic mansion (now Milton Abbey School). Architect Sir William Chambers with ceilings and decorations by James Wyatt. The ancient St. Catherine's Chapel looks down on this unique group set in secluded valley seven miles SW of Blandford. The little town of Milton, swept away in the late 18th century by the imperious owner of the house, in order to improve his park, was rebuilt as a charming model village nearby.

Location: 7 m SW of Blandford, just N of A354 from Winterborne Whitechurch or Milborne St Andrew.
Opening Times: HOUSE & GROUNDS. Apr 11 to Apr 20 and July 6 to Aug 31 incl. – Daily 10 – 6.30. Adm £1, Chd free. ABBEY CHURCH: Throughout the year. Free except for above dates.
Refreshments: Available when House is open in summer only.

MINTERNE

Dorchester   map G3
Telephone: Cerne Abbas (0300) 341370
(The Lord Digby)

Important rhododendron and shrub garden, many fine and rare trees, landscaped in the 18th century with lakes, cascades and streams.

Location: On A352 2 m N of Cerne Abbas; 10 m N of Dorchester, 9 m S of Sherborne.
Opening Times: Apr 1 to Oct 31 – Daily 10 – 7. Adm £2, accom chd free. Free car park.

PARNHAM – *See page 69*

PORTLAND CASTLE

map G2
Telephone: (0305) 820539

Built in the middle of the 16th century on the northern shore of the Isle of Portland, the castle was part of Henry VIII's coastal defences and is little altered. Unusually shaped, like a segment of a circle, it was seized by Royalists in the Civil War, changing hands twice before yielding to Parliament in 1646.

Location: Overlooking Portland Harbour, adjacent to RN helicopter base. OS map ref. SY684743.
Opening Times: Good Friday or Apr 1 (whichever is earlier) to Sept 30: Open Daily 10 – 6. Adm £1.10, Concessions 85p, Chd 55p.

PRIEST'S HOUSE MUSEUM AND GARDEN

23 High Street, Wimborne Minster   map H3
Telephone: Wimborne (0202) 882533
(Mr Stephen Price, Curator)

A recently restored town house of medieval origin with many Tudor and Georgian features. Set in exquisite walled garden with new displays including reconstructed 1920's ironmonger's shop, working forge and Victorian kitchen plus regular special exhibitions. Tea room and museum gift shop.

Location: Centre of Wimborne Minster.
Opening Times: Easter – Oct: every day. Nov: Christmas weekends plus special Christmas season. Mon to Sat 10.30 – 4.30; Sun 2 – 4.30. Adm includes entrance to garden. Group bookings welcome.

PURSE CAUNDLE MANOR

nr Sherborne   map G3
Telephone: Milborne Port 250400
(Michael de Pelet, Esq)

Interesting 15th/16th century Manor House. Lived in as a family home. Great Hall with minstrel gallery; Winter Parlour; Solar with oriel; bedchambers; garden. Not commercialised! Come and visit us.

Location: 4 m E of Sherborne; ¼ m S of A30.
Opening Times: Easter Mon to Sept 26, Thurs, Suns & Bank Hols, 2 – 5, showing every half hour. Coaches welcomed by appointment. Adm £1.75, Chd 50p. Free car park.
Refreshments: Home-made cream teas by prior arrangement at £2 each.

SANDFORD ORCAS MANOR HOUSE

Sandford Orcas, Sherborne   map G3
Telephone: Corton Denham (096 322) 206
(Sir Mervyn Medlycott, Bt)

Tudor Manor House with gatehouse, fine panelling. furniture, pictures. Terraced gardens, with topiary, and herb garden. Personal conducted tour by owner.

Location: 2½ m N of Sherborne, ent. next to Church.
Opening Times: Easter Mon 10 – 6 then May to Sept – Suns 2 – 6 & Mons 10 – 6. Adm £1.60, Chd 80p. Pre-booked parties (of 10 or more) at reduced rates on other days if preferred.

SHAFTESBURY ABBEY RUINS AND MUSEUM

Shaftesbury   map G3
Telephone: Shaftesbury (0747) 52910
(Shaftesbury Abbey and Museum Preservation Trust Company Ltd)

Ruins of 9th century Abbey founded by Alfred the Great set in an attractive and peaceful garden. Museum displays finds from the site.

Location: 100 metres West of Shaftesbury Town Centre.
Opening Times: Easter to Oct, daily 10 – 5.30. Adm 80p, Concessions 50p, Chd 25p.

SHERBORNE CASTLE

Sherborne   map G3
Telephone: Sherborne (0935) 813182
(Simon Wingfield Digby, Esq)

Built by Sir Walter Raleigh in 1594 and enlarged in 1625 by Sir John Digby, 1st Earl of Bristol. Home of the Digby family since 1617, the house contains fine furniture, porcelain and pictures by Vandyck, Gainsborough, Reynolds, Lely, Kneller and other famous artists. Twenty acres of lawns and pleasure grounds planned by 'Capability Brown' around the 50 acre lake are open to the public.

Location: 5 m E of Yeovil off A30 to S.
Station: *Sherborne (few mins walk).*
Opening Times: Easter Sat to end of Sept – Thurs, Sats, Suns & Bank Hol Mons 2 – 5.30. Grounds open 12 noon Thurs, Sats, Suns and Bank Hol Mons. Adm charges available on request by telephone. *Special terms & days for parties by arrangement.* Gift shop.
Refreshments: Tea at the house.

PARNHAM

Beaminster   map G3
Telephone: Beaminster (0308) 862204
(Mr & Mrs John Makepeace)

PARNHAM
Celebrating the Living Arts!

Furniture by John Makepeace
Evocative Architecture and Interiors
Romantic Terraces and Topiary

Inspiring 20th-century craftmanship displayed in the home of John and Jennie Makepeace, who have restored and enlivened this fascinating historic house. Exhibitions of exciting contemporary paintings and work in glass, wood, textiles and ceramics.

Licensed Buttery   Shop   Furniture Workshop

Open: 10-5 on Suns., Weds. and Bank Hols.; April to October
Admission: £3.00; Children (10-15) £1.50; Under 10-Free
PARNHAM   BEAMINSTER   DORSET
On A3066, five miles north of Bridport

An Elizabethan manor, restored by Nash and surrounded by gardens landscaped by Inigo Thomas, extensively replanted over recent years by Jennie Makepeace. In the workshop, furniture designed by John Makepeace is made for public and private collections.

Location: On A3066, 1 m S of Beaminster; 5 m N of Bridport.
Opening Times: Apr 1 to Oct 28—Weds, Suns & Bank Hols 10–5. Group visits on these and other days by prior arrangement only. Adm Principal rooms, gardens, workshops, car parks, picnic areas: £3, Chd (10–15) £1.50; under 10, free.
Refreshments: Light lunches, teas etc in licensed 17th century buttery.

SHERBORNE OLD CASTLE

map G3
Telephone: (093581) 2730

The powerful and wealthy Bishop Roger de Caen built the castle in the early 12th century, but by 1135 it had been seized by the Crown. In 1592 the castle passed to Sir Walter Raleigh who built Sherborne Lodge in the grounds. The buildings were largely demolished after the Civil War, but a gatehouse, some graceful arcading and decorative windows survive.

Location: ½ m (0.8 km) east of Sherborne. OS map ref ST647167.
Opening Times: Good Friday or Apr 1 (whichever is earlier) to Sept 30: Open Daily 10–6. Oct 1 to Maundy Thursday or Mar 31 (whichever is earlier): Open Tues to Sun 10–4. *Closed* Dec 24–26, Jan 1. Adm £1.10, Concessions 85p, Chd 55p.

SMEDMORE

Kimmeridge   map G2   &
Telephone: Corfe Castle 480719
(Dr. Philip Mansel)

17th/18th century manor house, still lived in by the family who built it. Plenty to see including 18th century marquetry furniture, Dresden china, antique dolls, Nelson letters. Walled gardens, interesting shrubs, fuchsias and hydrangeas.

Location: 7 m S of Wareham.
Opening Times: Organised parties only for both House & Gardens by prior arrangement with Curator (0929) 480719, in the summer.

WOLFETON HOUSE

Dorchester   map G2
Telephone: (0305) 263500
(Capt. N. T. L. Thimbleby)

Outstanding medieval and Elizabethan manor house with magnificent wood and stone work, fireplaces and plaster ceilings; Great Hall and stairs; parlour, dining room, Chapel and Cider House. The medieval gatehouse, French in appearance, has two unmatched and far older towers.

Location: 1½ m from Dorchester on Yeovil road (A37); indicated by Historic House signs.
Stations: Dorchester South and West 1¾ m.
Opening Times: May to Sept—Tues, Fri and Bank Hol Mons 2–6. At other times throughout the year, parties by arrangement. Adm charges not available at time of going to press.
Refreshments: Ploughman's lunches, teas and evening meals for parties, by prior arrangement.
Cider for sale.

DURHAM

AUCKLAND CASTLE – *See page 71*

BARNARD CASTLE – *See page 71*

BOTANIC GARDEN, UNIVERSITY OF DURHAM – *See page 71*

DURHAM CASTLE

Durham   map H11   △
(The University of Durham)

The Norman castle of the prince bishops has been used by Durham University since 1832.

Location: In the centre of the city (adjoining Cathedral).
Station: Durham (¹/₂ m).
Opening Times: Guided tours: July to Sept inclusive, 10–12. 2–4. Oct to June 2–4 Mon, Wed, Sat. Adm £1.30, Chd 80p, Family ticket £3.

RABY CASTLE 🏛

Staindrop, Darlington   map G11   &
Telephone: Staindrop (0833) 60202
(The Lord Barnard, T.D.)

Principally 14th century, alterations made 1765 and mid-19th century. The Castle is one of the largest 14th century castles in Britain and was built by the Nevills although one of the towers probably dates back to the 11th century. Interior mainly 18th and 19th century; medieval kitchen and Servants' Hall. Fine pictures of the English, Dutch and Flemish Schools and good period furniture. Collection of horse-drawn carriages and fire engines. Large walled Gardens.

Location: 1 m N of Staindrop village, on the Barnard Castle/Bishop Auckland Road (A688).
Opening Times: Easter weekend (Sat–Wed) *closed* remainder of April, then May 3 to June 30, Weds & Suns; July 1 to Sept 30, daily (except Sats); May, Spring and Aug Bank Hols, Sat–Tues; CASTLE 1–5; PARK & GARDENS 11–5.30. Adm: CASTLE, PARK AND GARDENS: £2.75; Senior Citizens £2.25; Chd £1.30. PARK AND GARDENS ONLY: £1, Senior Citizens and Chd 75p. Separate adm charge for Bulmer's Tower when open. Rates may vary when charity events are held. Special terms for parties over 25 on above by arrangement (Tel Curator). Picnic area.
Refreshments: Tea at the Stables.

AUCKLAND CASTLE

Bishop Auckland   map H11
Telephone: Bishop Auckland (0388) 601627
(The Church Commissioners)

Historic home of the Bishops of Durham with parts dating from 12th century. Very fine private Chapel remodelled by Bishop Cosin from 1660. Fourteenth century Hall, gothicised by James Wyatt in 1795. State Rooms include a Gothic Throne Room lined with portraits of past bishops. Also large public park and unusual 18th century deerhouse.

Location: In Bishop Auckland, at the end of Market Place.
Station: Bishop Auckland.
Opening Times: CASTLE AND CHAPEL: Bank Hol Mons 2–5. May 3 to Sept 20: Tues 10–12. Suns, Wed and Thurs 2–5. Sats in Aug 2–5. Please ring warden for opening times and adm charges. Park: Daylight hours throughout the year.

BARNARD CASTLE 🔲

map G11
Telephone: (0833) 38212

Named after its founder, Bernard de Baliol, the castle overlooks the River Tees from a craggy cliff-top. Its ownership was disputed by the Bishops of Durham, one of whom seized it in 1296. He added a magnificent hall and refortified the castle. Part of the castle has recently been excavated to discover more of its complex building history.

Location: In Barnard Castle. OS map ref NZ049165.
Opening Times: Good Friday or Apr 1 (whichever is earlier) to Sept 30: Open Daily 10–6. Oct 1 to Maundy Thursday or Mar 31 (whichever is earlier): Open Tues to Sun 10–4. *Closed* Dec 24–26, Jan 1. Adm £1.10, Concessions 85p, Chd 55p.

BOTANIC GARDEN, UNIVERSITY OF DURHAM

Durham   map H11
Telephone: (091) 3742671
(University of Durham)

18 acres of trees and shrubs, set in mature woodland.

Location: Take the Durham turn off at A167 at Cock o' the North Roundabout. 1 m from Durham, along Hollingside Lane.
Opening Times: All year including Bank Holidays 10–4.30. Parties welcome, guided tours charged. Attractive Visitor Centre. Free parking.

DURHAM CASTLE — *See page 70*

RABY CASTLE — *See page 70*

ROKEBY PARK 🏛

nr Barnard Castle

Palladian House built by Sir Thomas Robinson in 1735. Fine rooms, furniture and pictures (including exceptional collection of 18th century needlework pictures by Anne Morritt).

Opening Times: May 4, then each Mon & Tues from May 25 to Tues Sept 8, 2–5 (last adm 4.30). Parties of 25 or more will also be admitted on other days if a written appointment is made with the Curator.

ESSEX

AUDLEY END HOUSE AND PARK 🔲

map K5
Telephone: (0799) 522399
(English Heritage)

AUDLEY END HOUSE AND PARK – *continued*

James I is said to have remarked that Audley End was too large for a king but not for his Lord Treasurer, Sir Thomas Howard, who built it. The house was so large in fact that early in the 18th century about half of it was demolished as being unmanageable, but this still leaves a very substantial mansion. The interior contains rooms decorated by Robert Adam, a magnificent Jacobean Great Hall, a picturesque 'Gothick' chapel and a suite of rooms decorated in the revived Jacobean style of the early 19th century.

Location: ¾ m (1 km) west of Saffron Walden off B1383. OS map ref TL525382.
Opening Times: Good Friday or Apr 1 (whichever is earlier) to Sept 30, Tues to Sun (except Bank Hols) 1–6. Park and Garden open 12 noon. Last admission 1 hr before closing. Adm £4.50, Concessions £3.40, Chd £2.30.

BELCHAMP HALL

Belchamp Walter, Sudbury   map L5
Telephone: Sudbury (0787) 72744
(M. M. J. Raymond, Esq)

Queen Anne period house with period furniture and 17th and 18th century family portraits. Gardens.

Location: 5 m SW of Sudbury.
Opening Times: By appointment only. May to Sept – Tues & Thurs and Easter, Spring & Summer Bank Hol Mons 2.30–6. Adm £2.50, Chd £1.25. Reduction for parties.
Refreshments: Ploughman's lunches, teas, by arrangement.

BETH CHATTO GARDENS

Elmstead Market   map L5
(Mrs Beth Chatto)

5-acre garden, attractively landscaped with many unusual plants in wide range of conditions.

Location: 4 m E of Colchester on A133 Colchester/Clacton Road.
Station: Colchester.
Opening Times: GARDEN ONLY. All the year – Mons to Sats 9–5 Mar to Oct. Mon–Fri 9–4 Nov to Feb. *Closed* Suns & Bank Hols also Sats Nov 1 to end of Feb. Adm £1, Chd free. *In aid of National Gardens Scheme.* Adjacent nursery also open. *Parties by arrangement.* No dogs please.

CASTLE HOUSE

Dedham   map L5   ♿
Telephone: (0206) 322127

Home of the late Sir Alfred Munnings. KCVO, President of the Royal Academy 1944-1949. Exhibitions of paintings, drawings, sketches and other works by this famous East Anglian artist in the house and studios.

Location: ¾ m Dedham village, 7 m NE Colchester 2 m E of Ipswich Road (A12).
Opening Times: May 3 to Oct 4 – Weds, Suns & Bank Hol Mons, also Thurs & Sats in Aug, 2–5. Adm £2, Chd 25p, OAPs £1. Private parties by arrangement. Free car park.

GOSFIELD HALL

Halstead   map L5
(Country Houses Association Ltd).

Very fine Tudor gallery.

Location: 2½ m SW of Halstead on Braintree/Haverhill Road (A1017).
Station: Braintree. Bus route 310 Braintree–Halstead.
Opening Times: May to Sept – Weds & Thurs 2–5. Last entry 4.30. Adm £1.50, Chd 50p. Free car park. No dogs admitted.

HEDINGHAM CASTLE

Castle Hedingham, nr Halstead   map L5
Telephone: Hedingham (0787) 60261
(The Hon Thomas & Mrs Lindsay)

A wonderfully preserved example of Norman architecture overlooking the beautiful village of Castle Hedingham. Home of the famous mediaeval family the de Veres, Earls of Oxford. Visit one of England's finest Keeps. Garrison Chamber, Banqueting Hall and Minstrels' Gallery. Approached over a splendid Tudor bridge. Set in peaceful surroundings of woods and lakeside walks. Ideal for family picnics. Within easy reach of M11 and A12. Close to Constable country.

Location: On B1058 4 m N of Halstead, turn off A604; 9 m N of Braintree; 30 m SE of Cambridge.
Opening Times: Easter Weekend to Oct 31. Parties and Schools especially welcome all year by appointment. Adm £2.50, Chd £1.50. Family ticket £7.
Refreshments: Light refreshments.

HYDE HALL

Rettendon   map L5
Telephone: (0245) 400256
(Hyde Hall Garden Trust)

Woodland garden, spring bulbs, rose garden, ornamental ponds, flowering shrubs and trees, herbaceous borders, glasshouses, fine views. National collection of Malus and Viburnum.

Location: 7 m SE of Chelmsford (off A130).
Opening Times: GARDEN ONLY. Suns, Weds, Sats and Bank Holidays 11–6 from Mar 25 to Oct 28. Adm £1.50, OAPs £1, Chd free. *In aid of National Gardens Scheme & other charities.* Plants for sale. Dogs on leads allowed.
Refreshments: Light refreshments available.

ST. OSYTH PRIORY 🏛

St. Osyth   map L5
Telephone: (0255) 820492
(Somerset de Chair)

The Great gatehouse c 1475, ("unexcelled in any monastic remains in the country", *Country Life*), was built 20 years before Christopher Columbus sailed. A unique group of buildings dating from the 13th, 15th 16th, 18th and 19th centuries, surrounding a wide quadrangle like an Oxford or Cambridge college. Gardens include Rose garden, Topiary garden, Water Garden etc. Peacocks. Art collection in Georgian wing includes world-famous paintings George Stubbs ARA.

Location: 65 miles from London via A12, A120; A133 12 miles from Colchester; 8 miles from Frinton.
Opening Times: Easter weekend. Then May 1 – Sept 30. Gardens and Ancient Monuments open 10–5. Art Collection 10.30–12.30, 2.30–4.30. Adm £3, Chld 75p, OAPs £1.50. Buildings and art collection *closed* Sat, although the gardens will remain open. Parties by arrangement. Free car parking. Gardens suitable for disabled persons. Gardens overlook but do not include deer park on the estuary of the River Colne. Contact Mrs Colby tel (0255) 820242 (9–10 am).
Refreshments: In village 100 yards from entrance.

LAYER MARNEY TOWER 🏛

nr Colchester   map L5
Telephone: Colchester (0206) 330784
(Mr Nicholas Charrington)

Lord Marney's 1520 masterpiece. The tallest Tudor gatehouse in the country, with exceptional terracotta work. Set in 120 acres, visitors can climb the tower for excellent views of the Essex countryside and the Blackwater estuary, Explore the formal gardens, Long Gallery and the adjoining Church with the 3 effigy tombs of the Marney's and the original St. Christopher wallpainting. See the rare breed farm animals and deer. A Farm Trail starts from the Medieval Barn. The family house is open to private visits, by arrangement (minimum number: 25 people). The Long Gallery and Carpenters Shop can be hired for Receptions, Banquets and Concerts.

Location: 6 m S of Colchester. Signpost off the B1022 Colchester/Maldon Road.
Opening Times: Apr 1 to June 30 & Sept, Sun & Thurs 2–6. July and Aug, Sun to Fri 2–6. Bank Hols 11–6. Parties other days by prior arrangement.

THE MAGNOLIAS

18, St John's Avenue, Brentwood CM14 5DF   map L4
Telephone: Brentwood 220019
(Mr & Mrs R. A. Hammond)

A plantsman's back garden. The ground is intensively planted with trees, shrubs, climbers, herbaceous groundcover and bulbs, good collections of acer, magnolia, rhododendron, camellia and pieris, plus the N.C.C.P.G. National Collection of arisaema. There are seven ponds including one in a green house, some with Koi Carp.

Location: 1 m from Brentwood High Street (A1023). At Wilsons Corner turn S down A128; after 300 yds turn right at traffic lights; over railway bridge: St. John's Ave 3rd on right.
Opening Times: Suns Apr 5, 19; May 3, 17, 24; June 7, 21; July 19; Aug 9, 30; Sept 20; Oct 18 10–5. Adm 70p, Chd 30p. *In aid of National Gardens Scheme.* Parties by appointment. Not suitable for disabled.
Refreshments: Teas.

OLIVERS

Olivers Lane, Colchester   map L5
Telephone: (0206) 330575
(Mr & Mrs D. Edwards)

Twenty acres of landscaped gardens slope down from redbrick, mainly Georgian house (not open). Fine trees and shrubs including rhododendrons and azaleas, underplanted with Spring bulbs. Three lakes and stream with bluebells and primulas. Yew hedges back mixed shrub and herbaceous borders with a wide variety of planting. Shrub roses. Eighteenth century dovecote.

Location: 3 m SW of Colchester between B1022 and B1026. Olivers Lane is a turning off Gosbeck's Road.
Opening Times: Sat & Sun May 9 & 10; Sun June 21 (2–6). All Weds in May, June and July (10–5). Adm £1, Chd free. *In aid of National Gardens Scheme.* Parties by appointment any time of year. Ample car parking. Suitable for disabled, no wheelchairs available. Plants for sale.
Refreshments: Teas at weekends.

PARK FARM (GARDEN)

Great Waltham   map L5
Telephone: (0245) 360871
(Mrs Jill Cowley & Mr Derek Bracey)

Young garden on farmyard site. Two acres of bulbs, herbaceous plants and especially roses planted in separate rooms formed by new hedges. There is also a newly-constructed pond garden.

Location: Take B1008 from Chelmsford: on Little Waltham Bypass turn W to Chatham Hall Lane: Park Farm ½ m on left hand side.
Opening Times: Every other Sun & Mon from Easter 2–6; Apr 19, 20; May 3, 4, 17, 18, 31; June 1, 14, 15, 28, 29; July 12, 13. Adm 75p, Chd 30p. *In aid of National Gardens Scheme.* Parties by arrangement. Not suitable for disabled.
Refreshments: Teas.

PAYCOCKE'S, The National Trust 🍃

Coggeshall (1500)   map L5
Telephone: Coggeshall (0376) 561305

Richly ornamented merchant's house, dating from about 1500. Special display of local lace. Delightful garden leading down to small river.

Location: On A120; S side of West St. Coggeshall next to Fleece Inn; 5½ m E of Braintree. *Station: Kelvedon (2½ m).*
Opening Times: Mar 29 to Oct 4 – Tues, Thurs, Suns and Bank Hol Mons 2–5.30. Adm £1.40, Chd (accompanied) half-price. *Parties exceeding six should make prior arrangements with the tenant.* No reduction for parties. No dogs.

ST. OSYTH PRIORY – *See page 73*

SALING HALL

Great Saling, nr Braintree   map L5
(Mr & Mrs Hugh Johnson)

12 acre garden; walled garden dated 1698; small park with fine trees, extensive new collection of unusual plants with emphasis on trees; water gardens.

Location: 6 m NW of Braintree; mid-way between Braintree & Dunmow (A120); turn off N at Saling Oak Inn.
Opening Times: GARDEN ONLY. Weds in May, June & July 2–5. Sun July 5 2–6. *Parties other days by arrangement.* Adm £1.50, accompanied Chd free. No dogs please. *In aid of National Gardens Scheme & Village Church Fund.*

SHALOM HALL

Layer Breton, nr Colchester   map L5
(Lady Phoebe Hillingdon)

19th century house containing a collection of 17th and 18th century French furniture and porcelain and portraits by famous English artists including Thomas Gainsborough, Sir Joshua Reynolds etc.

Location: 7 m SW of Colchester; 2 m from A12.
Opening Times: Aug – Mon to Fri 10–1, 2.30–5.30. Adm free.

TILBURY FORT ⚜

map L4
Telephone: (0375) 858489

After an audacious raid up the Thames by the Dutch in 1667, Charles II commissioned plans for a defensive fort at Tilbury, on the site of Henry VIII's smaller fortification. It took 13 years to build but never saw the action for which it was designed. In the First World War a German Zeppelin was gunned down from the parade ground. Entry is now from the landward side across two restored bridges. Admission price includes a Personal Stereo Guided Tour.

Location: ½ m (0.8 km) south east of Tilbury. OS map ref TQ651754.
Opening Times: Good Friday or Apr 1 (whichever is earlier) to Sept 30: Open Daily 10–6. Oct 1 to Maundy Thursday or Mar 31 (whichever is earlier): Open Tues to Sun 10–4. *Closed* Dec 24–26, Jan 1. Adm £1.50, Concessions £1.10, Chd 75p.

GLOUCESTERSHIRE

BARNSLEY HOUSE GARDEN 🏛

Barnsley, nr Cirencester   map H5   &
Telephone: Bibury 281
(Rosemary Verey)

Garden laid out 1770, trees planted 1840. Re-planned 1960. Many spring bulbs. Laburnum avenue (early June). Lime walk, herbaceous and shrub borders. Ground cover. Knot garden. Autumn colour. Gothic summerhouse 1770. Classical temple 1780. House 1697 (not open). Vegetable garden laid out as decorative potager.

Location: 4 m NE of Cirencester on Cirencester to Bibury and Burford Road (B4425).
Opening Times: GARDEN ONLY. All the year—Mon, Wed, Thurs, Sat 10–6 (or dusk if earlier); Adm (Mar to Nov inc) £2, OAPs £1. Season tickets £4. Guided Parties entrance + £25. Dec to Feb free. Plants for sale.
Refreshments: Morning coffee, lunch and supper – The Village Pub, Barnsley. Tea – Bibury & Cirencester.

BATSFORD ARBORETUM 🏛

Moreton-in-Marsh   map H5
Telephone: Blockley (0386) 700409 or Moreton (0608) 50722.
(The Batsford Foundation)

Over 1000 species of different trees set in fifty acres of delightful Cotswold countryside overlooking the Vale of Evenlode, with a unique collection of exotic shrubs and bronze statues from the Orient.

Location: 1½ m NW of Moreton-in-Marsh on A44 to Evesham. Turn right into Park drive prior to Bourton-on-the-Hill.
Station: Moreton-in-Marsh (2½ m).
Opening Times: GARDEN ONLY: Mar to mid-Nov—every day 10–5. Adm £2, Chd & OAPs £1 (1991 prices). Parties by arrangement. Free parking. Garden Centre open all year round (10–5).
Refreshments: Tea room for coffee, light lunches and teas (Apr to Oct except Mons). Picnic area.

BERKELEY CASTLE 🏛

nr Bristol   map G4   △
Telephone: Dursley (0453) 810332
(Mr & Mrs R. J. Berkeley)

BERKELEY CASTLE
Gloucestershire

England's most Historic Home and Oldest Inhabited Castle

Completed in 1153 by Lord Maurice Berkeley at the command of
Henry II and for nearly 850 years the home of the Berkeley family. 24
generations have gradually transformed a savage Norman fortress into
a truly stately home.

The castle is a home and not a museum. Enjoy the castle at leisure or
join one of the regular one-hour guided tours covering the dungeon,
the cell where Edward II was murdered, the medieval kitchens, the
magnificent Great Hall and the State Apartments with their fine
collections of pictures by primarily English and Dutch masters,
tapestries, furniture of an interesting diversity, silver and porcelain.

Splendid Elizabethan Terraced Gardens and sweeping lawns
surround the castle. Tropical Butterfly House with hundreds of exotic
butterflies in free flight – an oasis of colour and tranquility.

Facilities include free coach and car parks, picnic area and two gift
shops, Tea rooms for refreshments, light lunches and afternoon teas.

Opening times and admission charges–see editorial reference. Evening
parties by arrangement. Further information from the Custodian,
Berkeley Castle, Glos. GL13 9BQ. Telephone: 0453-810 332

Location: Midway between Bristol and Gloucester, just off A38. M5 junctions 13 or 14.
Opening Times: Apr – Daily (exc Mons) 2 – 5, May to Sept – Tues to Sats 11 – 5, Suns 2 – 5;
closed Mons. Oct – Suns only 2 – 4.30, also Bank Hol Mons 11 – 5. Grounds open same day as
House, until 6 pm (5.30 in Oct). Adm £3.40, Chd £1.60, OAPs £2.80; Group rate (parties of
25 or over) £3, Chd £1.50, OAP £2.50. Evening parties by arrangement. Further information
from the Custodian.
Refreshments: Light lunches (May to Sept) and teas at Castle.

BOURTON HOUSE GARDEN

Bourton-on-the-Hill GL56 9AE   map H5
Telephone: Blockley (0386) 700121, Fax: (0386) 701081
(Mr & Mrs R. Paice)

A fine early 18th century mansion set in a delightful and evolving three acre garden.
Of interest to all plantsmen is the wide range of unusual plants in herbaceous, mixed
and colour borders. There is a small fountain garden with more water planned for the
early 90's. Great use is made of tender perennials in the inventive planting of
numerous troughs, lead cisterns and terracotta pots. Also, a grand 16th century tithe
barn in an orchard setting.
Location: Bourton-on-the-Hill, 2 m W of Moreton-in-Marsh on the A44.
Opening Times: GARDEN ONLY for the *National Gardens Scheme* Bank Hol Suns: May 24 &
Aug 30, 1 – 6. In conjunction with Bourton-on-the-Hill village gardens. Adm £2.50. Children
free. Also for *National Gardens Scheme* last Thurs of every month May to Sept 12 – 5. Every
Thursday from May 28 to Sept 24 (12 – 5). Adm £2, Chd free.
Refreshments: Teas in the Old School at Bourton-on-the-Hill on Bank Hol Suns only.

CHAVENAGE 🏛

Tetbury   map G4
Telephone: Tetbury (0666) 502329
(David Lowsley-Williams, Esq)

Elizabethan House (1576) with Cromwellian associations. 16th and 17th century
furniture and tapestries. Family Chapel and medieval barn. Personally conducted
tours.
Location: 2 m N of Tetbury signposted off A46 B4014.
Opening Times: Easter Sun & Mon then May to Sept – Thurs, Suns & Bank Hols 2 – 5. Adm
£2.50, Chd half-price. Parties by appointment as above and also on other dates and times.

CHEDWORTH ROMAN VILLA, The National Trust 🦋

Yanworth, nr Cheltenham. map H5   ♿
Telephone: Withington 256

The best exposed Romano-British villa in Britain. It was built about AD120 and
extended and occupied until about AD400. There are good fourth century mosaics in
the bath suits and triclinium (dining room). The villa was excavated in 1864, and a
museum has a good range of household objects.

Location: 3 m NW of Fossebridge on Cirencester – Northleach road (A429).
Opening Times: Feb: Parties by prior arrangement. Mar to end Oct: Tues to Sun & Bank Hol
Mon 10 – 5.30. Last admissions 5. *Closed* Good Friday. Nov to Dec 6: Wed to Sun 11 – 4, also
Dec 12, 13. Adm £2.40, Chd £1.10. Family ticket £6.60. Parties by prior written arrangement
only. Disabled – all parts accessible but some with difficulty. Disabled WC. Shop open on site
– introductory film.

HAILES ABBEY ⬛

map G5
Telephone: (0242) 602398

His life in danger at sea, Richard, Earl of Cornwall, vowed he would found a religious
house if he lived. In 1245 his brother, King Henry III, gave him the manor of Hailes so
that he could keep his pledge. After its establishment Richard's son, Edmund,
presented the Cistercian monks of the abbey with a phial said to contain the Blood of
Christ and from then until the Dissolution Hailes became a magnet for pilgrims.
Extensive ruins survive and there is an excellent museum.

Location: 2 m (3.2 km) north east of Winchcombe. OS map ref SP050300.
Opening Times: Good Friday or Apr 1 (whichever is earlier) to Sept 30: Open Daily 10 – 6.
Oct 1 to Maundy Thursday or Mar 31 (whichever is earlier): Open Daily 10 – 4. *Closed* Dec
24 – 26, Jan 1. Adm £1.60, Concessions £1.20, Chd 80p.

HARDWICKE COURT

nr Gloucester   map G5
Telephone: (0452) 720212
(C.G.M. Lloyd-Baker)

Late Georgian house designed by Robert Smirke, built 1816 – 1817. Entrance hall,
drawing room, library and dining room open. Gardens under course of restoration.

Location: 5 m S of Gloucester on A38 (between M5 access 12 S only and 13).
Opening Times: Easter Mon to End Sept – Mons only 2 – 4. Other times by prior written
appointment. Adm £1. Parking for cars only. Not suitable for disabled.

HIDCOTE MANOR GARDEN, The National Trust 🦋

Hidcote Bartrim, nr Chipping Campden   map H5   ♿
Telephone: Mickleton 438333

One of the most beautiful English gardens.

Location: 4 m NE of Chipping Campden, 1 m E of A46 (re-designated B4632) off B4081.
Opening Times: Apr to end of Oct – Daily (except Tues & Fris) 11 – 7 (last adm 6 or one hour
before sunset). Adm £4.20, Chd £2.10. Family ticket £11.60. *Parties by prior written
arrangement only.* No dogs. No picnicking. Liable to serious overcrowding on Bank Holiday
Weekends and fine Sundays. Wheelchair access to part of garden only, wheelchairs available.
Refreshments: Coffee, light lunches & cream teas 11 – 5.

KIFTSGATE COURT

nr Chipping Campden   map H5
(Mr & Mrs J. G. Chambers)

Garden with many unusual shrubs and plants including tree paeonies, abutilons etc, specie and old fashioned roses.

Location: 3 m NE of Chipping Campden 1 m E of A46 and B4081.
Opening Times: GARDENS ONLY. Apr 1 to Sept 30 – Weds, Thurs & Suns 2 – 6 also Sats in June and July, Bank Hols 2 – 6. Adm £2.20, Chd 80p. Open in aid of *National Gardens Scheme* Sat May 16, June 20 and Aug 22 2 – 6. Coaches by appointment only. *Unusual plants for sale on open days.*
Refreshments: Whit Sun to Sept 1.

LITTLE DEAN HALL

Littledean   map G5
Telephone: (0594) 824213
(D. M. Macer-Wright, Esq.)

The Hall reflects 900 years of architectural history with interesting external elevations, 17th century interiors, Civil War connections, displays of archaeological finds and the remains of an ancient hall believed to be Saxon. In the grounds are restored Roman remains identified as a 2nd–3rd c. water shrine, also trees of an exceptional age, an informal water garden.

Location: 12 W of Gloucester; 2 m E of Cinderford; 400 yds from A4151 on Littledean/Newnham-on-Severn Road, turn at King's Head.
Opening Times: GARDENS & HOUSE. Apr 1 to Oct 31, daily 2 – 5.30. *Closed* Sats. Adm charges not available at time of going to press.
There are ongoing repairs and improvements which may cause changes in advertised details.

LYDNEY PARK

Lydney   map G5
Telephone: (Office) Dean (0594 842844)
(Viscount Bledisloe)

Extensive Woodland Garden with lakes and a wide selection of fine shrubs and trees. Museums and Roman Temple Site. Deer Park (picnics). Country shop.

Location: ½ m W of Lydney on A48 (Gloucester to Chepstow).
Opening Times: Easter Sun and Mon; every Sun, Wed and Bank Hol from Apr 5 to June 7, but every day from Sun May 24 to May 31, 11 – 6. Car park and accompanied chd free. Dogs on lead. **Coaches and parties** on Open Days and on other days by appointment (minimum 25). Easter to mid June; thereafter to end Sept for Temple Site and Museum only.
Refreshments: Teas in house (house not otherwise open).

MISARDEN PARK GARDENS

Miserden, Stroud   map G5
Telephone: Miserden (0285) 821309
(Major M T N H Wills)

The garden has a timeless quality of a typically English Garden. A particular feature is the extensive yew topiary. To the south of the house is a wide Terrace laid with York paving. Sir Edward Lutyens Wing contains a Loggia overhung with Wisteria and on a lower terrace against the wing is a magnificent Magnolia 'Soulangeana'. On the south lawn are two flights of finely detailed grass steps. West of the main lawn are a series of terraced lawns leading to the Nurseries. To the east of these lawns is a broad grass walk lined by two substantial and very colourful herbaceous borders and beyond this is a traditional rose garden (many new introductions and features added in 1990). There are many fine specimen trees throughout the garden and the bulbs in variety and blossom in the Spring are other particular features. The garden stands high overlooking the wooded 'Golden Valley'.

Location: Miserden 7 m from Gloucester, Cheltenham, Stroud & Cirencester; 3 m off A417 (signed).
Opening Times: Every Wed & Thurs from Apr 1 to Sept 30, 10 – 4.30. Adm £1.50 (includes leaflet), Chd (accompanied) free. Reductions for parties by appointment. Car parking provided. Suitable for disabled. No wheelchairs available. Nurseries adjacent to garden open from Apr 1 to June 14 on Weds and Suns, thereafter Weds and Thurs only to end Sept. *In aid of National Gardens Scheme* Suns Apr 5, July 5, 2 – 6.

NEWARK PARK, The National Trust

Wotton under Edge   map G4
Telephone: Dursley 842644

Elizabethan Hunting Lodge built on cliff edge, modified in 1790's by James Wyatt and rehabilitated by present tenant. Woodland garden.

Location: 1½ m E of Wotton under Edge, 1½ m S of junction of A4135 and B4058.
Opening Times: Apr, May, Aug & Sept; Weds & Thurs 2–5, guided tours every half hour. Adm £1.50, Chd 75p. Parties by prior written arrangement only. No reductions. Not suitable for coaches or wheelchairs. No dogs.

PAINSWICK ROCOCO GARDEN 👤

Painswick   map G5
Telephone: Painswick 813204
(Lord & Lady Dickinson)

This beautiful six acre garden, set in a hidden combe, is a rare and complete survivor of the brief eighteenth century taste for the Rococo in garden design. A restoration programme was begun in October 1984, based on a Thomas Robins painting of 1784, and this is now largely completed.
Location: ½ m from Painswick on B4073.
Opening Times: GARDEN ONLY: Feb 1 to mid Dec: Wed to Sun incl Bank Hols, 11–5. Groups by appointment. Adult £2.40, OAP £2, Chd £1.20.
Refreshments: In licensed restaurant, morning coffees and home made light lunches and afternoon teas. Present Collection shop.

RYELANDS HOUSE

Taynton   map G5
(Captain & Mrs Eldred Wilson)

Fascinating sunken garden of 1½ acres with great variety of plants, many rare and unusual, in beautiful unspoilt country setting. Country walk to see abundance of wild flowers and spectacular views; landscaped lake in woodlands.
Location: 8 m NW of Gloucester; on B4216 halfway between Huntley (A40) & Newent (B4215).
Opening Times: Suns Apr 5, 12, 19, 26; May Sun 3, Mon Apr 20, Mon May 4; Suns June 21, 28; July 5, 12. Adm £1.50, Chd and parking free. All dates 2–6. Parties by appointment. *In aid of National Gardens Scheme.* Dogs welcome on walk. Plants for sale.
Refreshments: Home made teas Suns and Bank Hol Mons.

SEZINCOTE 👤

Moreton-in-Marsh   map H5
(Mr & Mrs D. Peake)

Oriental water garden by Repton and Daniell with trees of unusual size. House in 'Indian' style inspiration of Royal Pavilion, Brighton.

Location: 1½ m W of Moreton-in-Marsh on A44 to Evesham; turn left by lodge before Bourton-on-the-Hill.
Opening Times: GARDEN. Thurs, Fris & Bank Hol Mons 2–6 (or dusk if earlier) throughout year, except Dec. Adm £2.50 (garden only), Chd £1. No dogs. HOUSE May, June, July & Sept, Thurs & Fris 2.30–6. Parties by appointment. Adm House & Garden £3.50. Open in aid of *National Gardens Scheme* Sun July 12, 2–6.
Refreshments: Hotels & restaurant in Moreton-in-Marsh.

SNOWSHILL MANOR, The National Trust 🦋

nr Broadway   map H5   ♿
Telephone: Broadway 852410

A Tudor house with c1700 facade; 21 rooms containing interesting collection of craftsmanship, including musical instruments, clocks, toys, bicycles and Japanese armour, with small formal garden.

Location: 3 m SW of Broadway off A44.
Opening Times: Apr & Oct: Sat & Sun 11–1, 2–5. Easter Sat to Mon 11–1, 2–6. May to end Sept: Wed to Sun & Bank Hol Mon 11–1, 2–6. Last admissions to house ½ hour before closing. Adm £3.80, Chd £1.90. Family ticket £10.40. Parties by prior written arrangement only. No coaches. No dogs. Liable to serious overcrowding on Suns & Bank Holiday weekends. Disabled – limited access to house (ground floor) and part of garden.

STANWAY HOUSE 👤

nr Broadway   map H5
Telephone: Stanton 469
(Lord Neidpath)

This jewel of Cotswold Manor houses is very much a home rather than a museum and the centre of a working landed estate which has changed hands once in 1275 years. The mellow Jacobean architecture, the typical squire's family portraits, the exquisite Gatehouse, the old Brewery, mediaeval Tithe Barn, the extensive gardens, arboretum pleasure grounds and formal landscape contribute to the timeless charm of what Arthur Negus considered one of the most beautiful and romantic houses in England.

Location: 1 m off B4632 Cheltenham/Broadway road; on B4077 Toddington/Stow-on-the-Wold road; M5 junction 9.
Opening Times: June, July and Aug—Tues and Thurs 2–5. Adm £2, OAPs £1.75, Chd £1.
Refreshments: Teas in Old Bakehouse in village (Stanton 204).

SUDELEY CASTLE 🏛

Winchcombe map G5 △
Telephone: Cheltenham (0242) 602308
(Lord and Lady Ashcombe)

Charming 12th century Cotswold home of Queen Katherine Parr, extremely rich in history. Art treasures include works by Turner, Rubens and Van Dyck. Magnificent gardens with award winning Tudor Rose Garden as their centrepiece. Also for visitors: Adventure Playground, Craft workshops, Sudeley Castle Roses, a plant centre specialising in old fashioned roses.

Location: 6 m NE of Cheltenham on B4632. Access A40, A438, M5 (junction 9, Tewkesbury turn off).
Opening Times: Apr 1 to Oct 31: daily (inc. Bank Hols). Grounds open: 11–5; Castle Apartments 12–5; Sudeley Castle Roses 10–5.30. All inclusive adm: £4.75; Chd £2.50. Ground adm: £3.10, Chd £1.40. Special rates for parties of 20 persons or more. Free car parking. Private Guided Tours available throughout season for parties by prior arrangement. Educational material available for school parties relating to Civil War and The Tudors.
Refreshments: The Old Kitchen Restaurant is open daily 10–5 for coffee, buffet lunches and afternoon tea.

WESTBURY COURT GARDEN, The National Trust 🌿

Westbury-on-Severn map G5 ♿
Telephone: Westbury-on-Severn (045 276) 461

A formal Dutch water-garden with canals and yew hedges, laid out between 1696 and 1705; the earliest of its kind remaining in England.

Location: 9 m SW of Gloucester on A48.
Opening Times: Apr to end Oct – Weds to Suns & Bank Hol Mons 11–6. *Closed* Good Friday. Adm £1.80, Chd 90p. Parties by prior written arrangement only. Picnic area. No dogs. Wheelchairs provided.

WHITTINGTON COURT 🏛

Whittington, nr Cheltenham Gl54 4HF map G5
Telephone: (0242) 820218.
(Mrs R. J. Charleston)

Small Elizabethan stone-built manor house with family possessions.

Location: 4½ m E of Cheltenham on A40.
Opening Times: Apr 18 to May 3. Aug 15–31. Daily 2–5. Adm £2, OAPs £1.50, Chd £1. Open to parties by arrangement.

GREATER MANCHESTER

Dunham Massey, Altrincham — See Cheshire.

HALL I' TH' WOOD

Bolton map G9
Telephone: Bolton (0204) 51159
(Bolton Metropolitan Borough)

Dating from latter half of the 15th century and furnished throughout in the appropriate period. The Hall, built in the post and plaster style, dates from 1483, a further extension was added in 1591, the last addition being made in 1648. Home of Samuel Crompton in 1779 when he invented the Spinning Mule. House contains Crompton relics.

Location: In Green Way, off Crompton Way; 2 m NE of town centre off A58 (Crompton Way); signposted. Hall i' th' Wood (½ m).
Station: Bolton (2½ m); Bromley Cross (1¼ m). Hall i' th' Wood (½ m).
Opening Times: Apr to Sept: Tues to Sat 11–5; Sun 2–5. *Closed* Mons except Bank Holidays. Oct to Mar: *Closed* to general public. Open to pre-booked parties and evening party tours.

SMITHILLS HALL

Bolton map G8
Telephone: Bolton (0204) 41265
(Bolton Metropolitan Borough)

One of the oldest manor houses in Lancashire, a house has stood on this site since the 14th century. The oldest part of Smithills, the Great Hall, has an open timber roof. Smithills has grown piece by piece over the centuries and such irregularly planned buildings, with the cluster of gables at the west end, gives the hall its present day picturesque effect. Furnished in the styles of the 16th and 17th centuries. Withdrawing room contains linenfold panelling. Grounds contain a nature trail and trailside museum which is open to the public between Easter and October.

Location: Off Smithills Dean Road; 1½ m NW of town centre off A58 (Moss Bank Way); signposted.
Station: Bolton.
Opening Times: Apr to Sept: Tues to Sat 11–5, Sun 2–5. *Closed* Mons except Bank Holidays. Oct to Mar: *Closed* to general public. Open to pre-booked educational parties and to evening party tours.

HAMPSHIRE

ALRESFORD HOUSE 🏛

Alresford map J3
Telephone: (0962) 735218 or 732843
(Mr & Mrs P Constable Maxwell)

Georgian country house built by Admiral Lord Rodney 1750.

Location: 8 m E of Winchester off A31 Winchester/Alton Road.
Opening Times: By appointment only. Please telephone.

AVINGTON PARK – *See page 81*

BASING HOUSE

Basingstoke SU6 5SE map J4
Telephone: (0256) 467294
(Hampshire County Council)

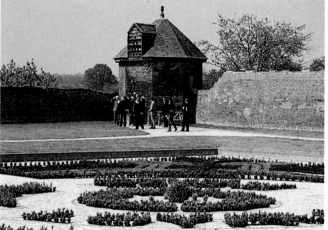

Basing House ruins were once the country's largest private house, the palace of William Paulet, 1st Marquess of Winchester who was Lord Treasurer of England under three Tudor monarchs. The Civil War brought disaster to Basing which fell to Oliver Cromwell in person after 2½ years of siege in 1645. The ruins, which cover about 10 acres, contain Norman earthworks, the remains of Tudor kitchens, cellars, towers, a 300 foot long tunnel, a spectacular barn, Civil War defences designed by Inigo Jones and a recently re-created 16/17th century formal garden. Special events in 1992 to commemorate 350th anniversary of the English Civil War.

Location: 2 m from Basingstoke Town Centre & 2 m from Junction 6 of M3.
Opening Times: Apr 1 to 27 Sept: Wed to Sun and Bank Hols 2–6 Adm £1.10, Children & Senior Citizens 60p. Parties any time by prior arrangement. Car parking. Suitable for disabled persons.
Refreshments: Meals can be obtained at two public houses near main entrance. Tea shop usually open on site most Suns.

BEAULIEU – *See page 81*

BISHOP'S WALTHAM PALACE ⚙

map J3
Telephone: (0489) 892460
(English Heritage)

The Bishops of Winchester held Waltham since Saxon times, but they did not build here until about 1135. Heavily fortified, this was more castle than palace, and was dismantled by Henry II. Most of the present remains are from the spacious 15th century palace with its walled garden, all within this vast moated site. Forfeited by the bishops at the Reformation, the palace was reduced to a ruin in the Civil War, when it was held for the King against Parliament. The Dower House or Farmhouse was the medieval lodging of the Palace. It now houses an exhibition, carved stone display, and the downstairs rooms are furnished in the style of a 19th c Farmhouse.

Location: Bishop's Waltham. OS map ref SU552173.
Opening Times: Good Friday or Apr 1 (whichever is earlier) to Sept 30 daily 10–6. Oct 1 to Maundy Thursday or Mar 31 (whichever is earlier) Tues to Sun 10–4. *Closed* Dec 24–26, Jan 1. Adm £1.50, Concessions £1.10, Chd 75p.

AVINGTON PARK

Winchester   map H3
Telephone: 0962-78 260
(Mr and Mrs J B Hickson)

William Cobbett wrote of Avington that it was 'one of the prettiest places in the County' and indeed it is true today. Avington Park, where Charles II and George IV both stayed at various times, is an old house enlarged in 1670 by the addition of two wings and a classical Portico surmounted by three Statues. The State Rooms on view include the Ballroom with its magnificent ceiling, the Red Drawing Room, Library etc. Avington Church, one of the most perfect Georgian Churches in Hampshire, is in the grounds close by and may be visited.
The facilities are available for filming or still photography.
The Library is also available for Wedding Receptions, Conferences etc.

Location: 4 m NE of Winchester, just S of B3047 in Itchen Abbas.
Opening Times: May to Sept—Suns & Bank Hols 2.30–5.30 (last tour begins 5). Adm on gate. *Other times for large parties by prior arrangement.*
Refreshments: Tea at the House during opening times.

BEAULIEU

Beaulieu   map H3
Telephone: Beaulieu (0590) 612345
(The Lord Montagu of Beaulieu)

Palace House & Gardens Abbey & Exhibition

National Motor Museum and `Wheels´

BEAULIEU, offers a day filled with variety and enjoyment for everyone, encompassing *three* major attractions.

Palace House has been the home of Lord Montagu's family since 1538. Today's visitors particularly enjoy its warm, friendly, "lived in" atmosphere.

Beaulieu Abbey, largely destroyed 450 years ago, has been conserved with sensitivity. The cloisters in particular are beautiful and tranquil, while the Lay Brothers quarters house a fascinating display on the daily life of the monks.

The National Motor Museum is one of the finest transport museums in the world. Here, over 250 vehicles and other exhibits tell the story of motoring in Britain. Within the Museum is "Wheels", a spectacular display celebrating 100 years of motoring, through which visitors are transported in moving "pods".

Additional attractions to complete a great day out include a Monorail, a Veteran Bus, Miniature Cars and Bikes and many other features. Full catering services available.

Open every day except Christmas Day.

Palace House and Gardens; Beaulieu Abbey and Exhibition of Monastic Life; The National Motor Museum featuring more than 250 exhibits including motor cars, commercial vehicles and motorcycles; 'Wheels' – a fantastic ride on 'space age' pods through 100 years of motoring from 1895 to the present day. Monorail, veteran bus and miniature veteran car rides, 'Driving Experience' simulator and display, model railway, radio-controlled cars, mini racing car and motorcycle rides. Daily cavalcades of historic vehicles during peak summer season and many other events throughout the year.

Location: In Beaulieu 7 m SE of Lyndhurst; 14 m S of Southampton; 6 m NE of Lymington.
Opening Times: All facilities open throughout the year. Easter to Sept—Daily 10–6; Oct to Easter—Daily 10–5. *Closed Christmas Day.* Inclusive adm charge. Reduced rates for Children & OAPs.
Parties at special rates.
Refreshments: Lunches and teas at licensed Brabazon Restaurant.

BRAMDEAN HOUSE

Bramdean, nr Alresford   map J3
Telephone: 0962 771214
(Mrs H. Wakefield)

Carpets of Spring bulbs. Walled garden with famous herbaceous borders, working kitchen garden and large collection of unusual plants.

Location: Bramdean. On A272 midway between Winchester & Petersfield.
Opening Times: Suns Mar 15, Apr 19, May 17, June 21, July 19, Aug 16, Mon Apr 20, 2–5. Also by appointment. Adm £1, Chd free. *In aid of the National Gardens Scheme.* Car park. Not suitable for disabled.
Refreshments: Teas.

BREAMORE HOUSE

nr Fordingbridge   map H3   △
Telephone: Downton (0725) 22468
(Sir Westrow Hulse, Bt)

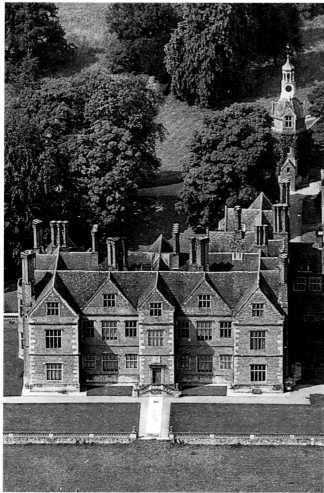

Elizabethan Manor House (1583) with fine collection of paintings, tapestries, furniture. Countryside Museum. Exhibition of Rural Arts and Agricultural machinery. Carriage Museum. 'The Red Rover', and other coaches.

Location: 3 m N of Fordingbridge off the main Bournemouth Road (A338) 8 m S of Salisbury.
Opening Times: Easter Hol, Apr, Tues, Weds, Suns; May, June, July & Sept—Tues, Weds, Thurs, Sats, Suns and all Bank Hols; Aug—Daily, 2–5.30. Adm: Combined ticket £3.50, Chd £2. Reduced rates for parties & OAPs. *Other times by appointment.*
Refreshments: Home-made Teas. Food available. Bat and Ball, Breamore.

BROADLANDS – *See page 83*

CALSHOT CASTLE

map H3
Telephone: (0703) 892023
(English Heritage)

Part of the chain of Henry VIII's coastal defences against the Catholic powers of Europe. Completed in 1540 and still virtually intact, the Castle has played an important role in England's defence from the 16th Century until World War II. From 1912 to the mid 1950's it formed part of a flying boat base, initially a Royal Naval Air station, then RAF Calshot. Site exhibition and restored WWI barrack room.

Location: On Spit 2 m (3.2 km) south-east of Fawley off B3053, 15 m (24 km) south east of Southampton. OS map 196, ref SU488025.
Opening Times: Good Friday or Apr 1 (whichever is earlier) to Sept 30: Open daily 10–6. Adm 95p, Concessions 75p, Chd 45p.

EXBURY GARDENS

nr Southampton   map H3
(E L de Rothschild, Esq)

Unique 200 acre woodland garden created by Lionel de Rothschild, with a superb display of rhododendrons, azaleas, camellias, magnolias, other fascinating flora and new plantings. Well stocked Plant Centre and Gift Shop, artist's studio, licensed tea rooms. Dogs welcome on leads.

Location: Exbury village, 15 m SW of Southampton close to New Forest. Turn W off A326 at Dibden Purlieu towards Beaulieu.
Opening Times: GARDEN: Feb 29 to July 5; Summer July 6 to Sept 4 (53 acre summer garden); Autumn: Sept 5 to Oct 25. **Plant Centre and Gift Shop** open all year except Christmas and Boxing Day. 10–5.30 (or dusk if earlier). Adm charges £3.50, OAPs and parties £3, Chd (10–16) £2.50. Early and late season discounts.
Refreshments: Licensed refreshments. **Also** ample parking and toilet facilities. Dogs on short leads.

FORT BROCKHURST

map J3
Telephone: (0705) 581059
(English Heritage)

One of five forts known as the Gosport Advanced Line, Brockhurst was built in the mid-19th century to protect Portsmouth Dockyard. The traditional star shape was abandoned for a polygonal plan. Norman castles had become obsolete with the use of gunpowder, but some features were retained. Brockhurst has a moat and a draw-bridge. It also has a keep, traditionally the point of last defence. There is an exhibition on the history of Portsmouth's defences.

Location: Off the A32 in Elson on the north side of Gosport. OS map ref SU596020.
Opening Times: Good Friday or Apr 1 (whichever is earlier) to Sept 30: Open Daily 10–6. Oct 1 to Maundy Thursday or Mar 31 (whichever is earlier): Open Tues to Sun 10–4. *Closed* Dec 24–26, Jan 1. Adm £1.50, Concessions £1.10, Chd 75p.

BROADLANDS

Romsey   map H3
Telephone: Romsey (0794) 516878
(Lord and Lady Romsey)

BROADLANDS

Famous for royal honeymoons and as the home of Lord Mountbatten, Broadlands has countless mementoes of the Mountbatten and Palmerston eras and of its many royal visitors.

One of the finest Palladian houses in England, Broadlands is also home to a magnificent collection of paintings and furniture.

Enjoying an idyllic setting on the banks of the Test with superb views from the riverside lawns.

The Mountbatten Exhibition traces the eventful lives of Lord and Lady Mountbatten, while history is brought vividly to life in 'The Life and Times of Lord Mountbatten' multi-screen audio-visual presentation.

SPECTACULAR MOUNTBATTEN AUDIO-VISUAL

Facilities include self-service restaurant, picnic area and two gift shops.

1992 opening 16th April-27th September. Admission 10am - 4pm. Closed Fridays, except Good Friday and in August. All-inclusive admission charge. Children under 12 free when accompanied by parent. Free parking.

For further information, call Romsey (0794) 516878.

OFF A31, ROMSEY. SIGNPOSTED FROM JUNCTIONS 2 AND 3, M27

Famous in recent times as the home of Lord Mountbatten, Broadlands was also the country residence of Lord Palmerston, the great Victorian Prime Minister. Fine example of Palladian architecture set in Capability Brown parkland on the banks of the River Test. Visitors may view interior of house containing many fine works of art including "The Iron Forge" by Joseph Wright of Derby, several Van Dycks and furniture by Ince and Mayhew. Visitors may also relive Lord Mountbatten's life and times in the Mountbatten Exhibition and spectacular Mountbatten Audio-Visual Presentation housed in William and Mary stable block.

Location: 8 m N of Southampton (A3057); entrance from by-pass immediately S of Romsey (A31).
Station: Romsey (1 m).
Opening Times: Apr 16 to Sept 27. Daily 10–5.30 (last adm 4). *Closed* Fri except Good Friday and in Aug. Adm £4.75, Chd 12–16 £3.15, Chd under 12 accompanied by parent/guardian free, OAPs £3.80. Disabled £3.80, Students £3.80. Reduced rates for parties of 15 or more. Free coach and car park.
Refreshments: Self-service restaurant. Kiosk in picnic area.

HIGHCLERE CASTLE

nr Newbury RG15 9RN   map H4
Telephone: (0635) 253210
(The Earl of Carnarvon KCVO, KBE)

Highclere Castle is the ultimate in high Victorian exuberance. Designed by Charles Barry in the 1830s at the same time as he was building the Houses of Parliament, this soaring pinnacled mansion provided the perfect social setting for the 3rd Earl of Carnarvon, one of the great hosts of Queen Victoria's reign. Several prominent Victorian architects, including Barry, George Gilbert Scott and Thomas Allom, are responsible for the extravagant interiors in styles which range from church Gothic through Moorish flamboyance and rococo revival to the solid masculinity in the long library. Old master paintings mix with portraits by Van Dyck and 18th Century painters. Napoleon's desk and chair rescued from St. Helena sits with other 18th and 19th Century furniture.

The 5th Earl of Carnarvon, passionate archaeologist and Egyptologist, was the discoverer of the tomb of Tutankhamun and a special display shows some of his early finds in Egypt which had laid hidden for over 60 years.

GARDENS – The parkland with its massive cedars was designed by Capability Brown. The walled gardens also date from the earlier house at Highclere but the dark yew walks are entirely Victorian in character. The glass Orangery and Fernery add an exotic flavour and an impression of the complexity of the gardens at their peak. Walking through to the Secret Garden, the walled walks unexpectedly open up into a curving, densely planted herbaceous garden laid out in this Century with ornamental trees and flowering plants and shrubs.

Location: 4½ m S of Newbury on A34, junction 13 of M4 about 2 m from Newbury. M3. Basingstoke junction about 15 m. Heathrow via M4 1 hour. Rail from London (Paddington station) 1 hour.

Opening Times: July, Aug, Sept, Wed, Thurs, Sat and Sun 2–6 (last entry 5). Easter, May and Aug Bank Holidays, Sun and Mon. Adm rates not available at time of going to press. Special reductions for parties of 30 or more by application. Car park and picnic area adjacent to Castle. Suitable for disabled persons on ground floor only. One wheelchair available. Visitors can buy original items in Castle Gift Shop and visit the Plant Centre only a short distance away in the Park.

Refreshments: Traditional country cream teas, ices, soft drinks, etc.

THE SIR HAROLD HILLIER GARDENS AND ARBORETUM

Ampfield, nr Romsey   map H3
(Hampshire County Council)

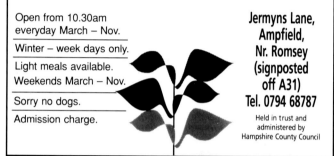
Begun by the famous nurseryman Sir Harold Hillier in 1953, and gifted to Hampshire County Council in 1977, the Gardens and Arboretum now extend to some 160 acres and contain the largest collection of different hardy plants in the British Isles. With this diversity in plants, the Gardens provide something of interest throughout the seasons, from the magnificent floral displays in the spring, followed by the pastel shades of summer which become overwhelmed by the riot of autumnal hues in October to the highly scented winter flowering Witch Hazels.

Location: 3 m north east of Romsey, off A31.

Opening Times: Mon to Fri 10.30–5 (all year round). Weekends and Bank Hols 10.30–6 (Mar to end Nov). Adm £2, OAPs £1.50, Chd (under 16 years) 75p. Groups over 30 £1.50 each. Regret NO DOGS.

Refreshments: Light refreshments at weekends and Bank Hols.

HINTON AMPNER, The National Trust

nr Alresford   map J3
Telephone: Winchester (0962) 771305 or 771023

The house was remodelled in the Georgian style in 1934 by Ralph Dutton but decimated by fire in 1960. Rebuilt and re-furnished with fine regency furniture, pictures and porcelain. The gardens juxtapose formality of design and informality of planting, producing delightful walks and unexpected vistas.

Location: 1 m W of Bramdean Village on A272; 8 m E of Winchester.

Opening Times: Apr 1 to end Sept. GARDEN: Sat, Sun, Tues and Wed (inc. Good Friday and Bank Holiday Mon) 1.30–5.30. HOUSE: Tues & Wed only and Sat & Sun in Aug 1.30–5.30 (last adm 5). Admission: Garden £2, House £1.30 extra. Children half-price. No dogs. Most of garden accessible by wheelchair. Party reductions (£2.80 House & Garden) by prior booking.

Refreshments: Teas.

HOUGHTON LODGE

Stockbridge map H3 &
Telephone: 0264 810 177 or 0264 810 502
(Captain & Mrs M W Busk)

Unique 18th century gothic 'Cottage Orne' set in listed landscaped gardens leading down to River Test with lovely views over the tranquil valley. Within the traditional kitchen garden surrounded by rare chalk cob walls is the HAMPSHIRE HYDRO-PONICUM where flowers, delicious fruits, herbs and vegetables grow WITHOUT SOIL. Believed to be the first Hydroponicum in England primarily intended to delight and inform the visitor. The ease of Hydroponic Gardening (no weeding, or digging, no soil borne pests) makes it an ideal method for the handicapped.

Location: 1½ m S of A30 at Stockbridge on minor road to Houghton village.
Opening Times: Mar to Sept incl, 10–5 on Sat and Sun, 2–5 on Mon, Tues and Fri. Coach tours and parties welcome by prior appointment. Tel. for details. Plants and produce for sale. Free parking.

HURST CASTLE

map H2
Telephone: (0590) 642344

Built by Henry VIII to defend the Solent, Hurst Castle was completed in 1544, and had a garrison of 23 men. During the Civil War it was occupied by Parliamentary forces and Charles I was imprisoned here for a short time. A longer incarceration was that of an unfortunate priest called Atkinson, who was a prisoner here for 29 years in the 18th century. The castle was considerably modernised in the mid-19th century, under the fear of a French invasion, and was still useful in the Second World War.

Location: Approach by ferry from Keyhaven. OS map ref SZ319898.
Opening Times: Good Friday or Apr 1 (whichever is earlier) to Sept 30: Open Daily 10–6. Oct 1 to Maundy Thursday or Mar 31 (whichever is earlier): Open weekends 10–4. *Closed* Dec 24–26, Jan 1. Adm £1.50, Concessions £1.10, Chd 75p.

JENKYN PLACE

Bentley map J3
(Mrs G E Coke)

Beautifully designed garden with large collection of rare plants, roses, double herbaceous borders.

Location: In Bentley 400 yds N of cross roads Heritage signs on A31. *Station: Bentley (1 m).*
Opening Times: GARDEN ONLY. Apr 9 to Sept 6—Thurs, Fris, Sats, Suns & Bank Hol Mons 2–6. Coaches only by prior arrangement. Adm £2, Chd (5–15) 75p. *Open on certain Suns in aid of the National Gardens Scheme.* No dogs. Car park free.

JANE AUSTEN'S HOUSE

Chawton map J3
Telephone: Alton (0420) 83262
(Jane Austen Memorial Trust)

Jane Austen's home with many interesting personal relics of herself and her family.

Location: 1 m SW of Alton off A31 and B3006, sign post Chawton.
Station: Alton (1¾ m).
Opening Times: Daily Apr–Oct; Nov, Dec & Mar: Weds to Suns. Jan & Feb: Sats & Suns only, 11–4.30. *Closed Christmas Day & Boxing Day.* Adm £1.50, Chd (8–18) 50p; Groups (15+) £1.

MEDIEVAL MERCHANTS HOUSE

map H3
Telephone: (0703) 221503

A medieval merchant's house, built in the 1290s is now fully restored to its 14th century appearance. On the ground floor is the restored medieval shop stocked with traditional wines and other produce. The house is furnished with medieval reproductions based on contemporary illustrations.

Location: 58 French St between Castle Way and Town Quay. OS map ref 504 19 112.
Opening Times: Good Friday or Apr 1 (whichever is earlier) to Sept 30: Open Daily 10–6. Oct 1 to Maundy Thursday or Mar 31 (whichever is earlier): Open Tues to Sun 10–4. *Closed* Dec 24–26, Jan 1. Adm £1.80, Concessions £1.40, Chd 90p. Admission price includes a Personal Stereo Guided Tour.

MOTTISFONT ABBEY GARDEN, The National Trust

Mottisfont map H3 △ ♿
Telephone: Lockerley 41220

With a tributary of the River Test flowing through, the garden forms a superb setting for a 12th century Augustinian priory, which, after the Dissolution became a house (tenanted). It contains the spring or 'font' from which the place name is derived, a magnificent collection of trees, and the Trust's unique collection of old roses within walled gardens.

Location: 4½ m NW Romsey ¾ m W of A3057.
Station: Dunbridge (¾ m).
Opening Times: Apr to end Sept: Garden: daily (except Fri & Sat) 2–6, last adm 5. HOUSE: (Whistler Room and Cellarium only): special openings Wed only 2–5. Evening opening of the Rose Garden 7–9pm (last adm 8.30). Tues, Wed, Thurs and Sun during rose season, usually June but check with property first. Adm £2.30, Chd half-price. Shop. Dogs in car park only. Wheelchairs – grounds and cellarium only. Special parking area for disabled people, please ask at kiosk on arrival.

NETLEY ABBEY

map H3
Telephone: (0703) 453076

Extensive picturesque remains of a Cistercian abbey on the east bank of the Southampton Water. Netley Abbey was founded in 1239 by monks from Beaulieu. Remains include the church and cloister buildings.

Location: In Netley, 7 m SE of Southampton, facing Southampton Water. OS map ref 504 53 089.
Opening Times: Good Friday or Apr 1 (whichever is earlier) to Sept 30: Open Daily 10–6. Oct 1 to Maundy Thursday or Mar 31 (whichever is earlier): Open Weekends only 10–4. *Closed* Dec 24–26, Jan 1. Adm £1.10, Concessions 85p, Chd 55p.

OATES MUSEUM AND THE GILBERT WHITE MUSEUM

Selborne map J3
Telephone: Selborne (042 050) 275
(Rev. Gilbert White, 1720–93)

'The Wakes', home of the Rev. Gilbert White, pioneer English naturalist and author of *The Natural History and Antiquities of Selborne*, a classic published 200 years ago and still in print. Historic house, furnished rooms, and museum displays on Gilbert White and Selborne. 5 acre garden. Also includes The Oates Memorial Museum with exhibitions on Frank Oates, 19th century explorer and naturalist, in South America and Africa, and Captain Lawrence Oates who went with Scott to the South Pole.

Location: In Selborne
Opening Times: Mar 21 to Nov 1, Wed to Sun 11–5.30 (last adm 5). Tues to Sun during July, Aug and Sept; open Bank Hols. Parties by arrangement. Adm £1.60, Chd (under 16) 80p. OAPs and students £1.

THE PILGRIMS' HALL

Winchester map H3
(The Dean & Chapter, Winchester Cathedral)

Late 13th century hall with fine hammer-beam roof.

Location: In the Cathedral Close.
Station: Winchester (5 mins walk).
Opening Times: All the year—Daily (except when booked for private meetings, functions, etc). *Parties must give notice in advance.* Adm free.

PORTCHESTER CASTLE

map J3
Telephone: (0705) 378291

A Roman fortress, a Norman castle and a Romanesque church share this same site on the north shore of Portsmouth harbour. The outer walls were built in the 3rd century when Britain was the vulnerable north-west frontier of a declining Roman Empire. Today they are among the finest Roman remains in northern Europe. Eight centuries —and very little repair work—later, the walls were sound enough to encompass a royal castle. Portchester was popular with the medieval monarchs but by the 15th century royal money was being spent on Portsmouth instead. The last official use of the castle was as a prison for French seamen during the Napoleonic wars. An exhibition tells the story of Porchester.

Location: South side of Portchester. OS map ref SU625046.
Opening Times: Good Friday or Apr 1 (whichever is earlier) to Sept 30: Open Daily 10–6. Oct 1 to Maundy Thursday or Mar 31 (whichever is earlier): Open Tues to Sun 10–4. *Closed* Dec 24–26, Jan 1. Adm £1.50, Concessions £1.10, Chd 75p.

STRATFIELD SAYE HOUSE

Reading   map J4   ♿
Telephone: Basingstoke (0256) 882882
(The Duke of Wellington)

This Stuart house is filled with the Great Duke's possessions and personality. THE HOUSE: Rebuilt in the reign of Charles I replacing an older residence, the house has been home of the Dukes of Wellington since it was presented to the Great Duke in 1817. It contains a unique collection of paintings, prints, furniture, effects and personal belongings of this most famous soldier and statesman. THE EXHIBITION: The Wellington Exhibition re-creates many scenes from the life of the Great Duke and the Battle of Waterloo. 'The Last Journey', a special display, features the Duke's magnificent Funeral Carriage. THE GROUNDS: Include a wildfowl sanctuary, gardens, and Copenhagen's grave. Stratfield Saye is situated on the Hampshire/Berkshire borders.

Location: 1 m W of A33 between Reading & Basingstoke (turn off at Wellington Arms Hotel); signposted. Close to M3 & M4.
Opening Times: HOUSE AND GARDENS; open daily (except Fris) from May 1 to last Sun in Sept 11.30–4 (last adm 3.30). Wellington Country Park (3 m from House) — Nature trails, adventure playgrounds, animals, boating, windsurfing, fishing, deer park miniature steam railway. National Dairy Museum, Thames Valley Time Trail—Mar to Oct daily 10–5. Nov–Feb Sats & Suns only. Please telephone for admission charges to House and Park.
Refreshments: Tea and snacks, licensed restaurant.

ROTHERFIELD PARK   🏛

Alton   map J3
Telephone: Tisted (042 058) 204
(Lt Col Sir James and Lady Scott)

Victorian Gothic House, built 1820. Romanticised 1880s. Fine position, many original contents. Large garden. Plants for sale.

Location: On A32, East Tisted. 4½ m S of Alton.
Opening Times: Suns, Mons of Bank Hol Weekends and June 1 to June 7, July 1 to July 7, Aug 1 to Aug 7 2–5. Also Garden open Easter to end Sept, Thurs and Sun 2–5. Adm House/Garden £2.50, Chd 50p. Garden only £1, Chd free. Other times for groups by appointment with Lady Scott (042 058) 204, or preferably in writing. Also available for wedding receptions, still photography and filming. Plants for sale.
Refreshments: Teas (often for charity). Picnic area.

SANDHAM MEMORIAL CHAPEL, The National Trust 🌺

Burghclere, nr Newbury   map H4   ♿
Telephone: Burghclere 394 or 292

Walls covered with paintings by Stanley Spencer depicting war scenes in Salonica.

Location: In village of Burghclere 4 m S of Newbury ½ m E of A34.
Opening Times: Apr 1 to end Oct: Wed–Sun 11.30–6. Open Good Friday and Bank Holiday Mon. Nov to end Mar: Sat & Sun only 11.30–4. Adm £1.20. No cameras allowed in Chapel. Parties must book. No reduction for parties. No dogs. Wheelchair access.

STRATFIELD SAYE HOUSE – *See above*

THE VYNE, The National Trust 🌺

Basingstoke   map J4   ♿
Telephone: Basingstoke 881337

THE VYNE, The National Trust − *continued*

An important early 16th century house with classic portico added 1654. Tudor panelling, 18th century ornamented staircase. Extensive lawns, lake, trees, herbaceous border.

Location: 4 m N of Basingstoke between Bramley & Sherborne St John (1½ m from each). *Station: Bramley (2½ m).*
Opening Times: Apr 1 to end Oct daily except Mon and Fri (open Good Friday and Bank Hol Mons). HOUSE: 1.30−5.30; GARDEN: 12.30−5.30. Bank Hol Mon 11−5.30. Last adm 5. *Closed Tues, following Bank Hol Mons.* Adm House and Garden: £3.80. Garden only: £1.90, *Chd half price. Reduced rates for pre-booked parties Tues, Weds & Thurs only* £2.50. Shop. Dogs in car park only. Wheelchair provided.
Refreshments: Light lunches and teas in the Old Brewhouse (12.30−5.30). *Closed 2−2.30* (last orders 5).

WOLVESEY: OLD BISHOP'S PALACE ⌗

map H3
Telephone: (0962) 54766

Ruins of an extensive palace of the Bishops of Winchester, built round a quadrangular courtyard.

Location: ¼ m (0.5 km) south east of Winchester Cathedral, next to the Bishop's Palace. OS map ref SU484291.
Opening Times: Good Friday or Apr 1 (whichever is earlier) to Sept 30: Open Daily 10−6. Adm £1.10, Concessions 85p, Chd 55p.

HEREFORD & WORCESTER

ABBERLEY HALL

nr Worcester   map G6
Telephone: (0299) 896634 (office hours only)
(Mrs Atkinson)

Five principal rooms show ornate decoration of mid-Victorian period.

Location: 12 m NW of Worcester on A443.
Opening Times: HOUSE ONLY. May 25; July 22−24 and 27−31; Aug 3−7, 10−14, 17−21, 24−28 and 31, 1.30−4.30. Adm £1. Unsuitable for wheelchairs. No dogs.

AVONCROFT MUSEUM OF BUILDINGS

Stoke Heath, Bromsgrove   map G6   Ⓢ
Telephone: Bromsgrove 31886 or 31363
(Council of Management)

An open-air Museum containing buildings of great interest and variety. Exhibits include a working windmill, a 15th century timber-framed house, a cockpit theatre, a 1946 prefab, from the 18th century, an ice house, an earth closet and a cider mill, and also a 19th century toll house. New exhibit: the magnificent 14th century Guesten Hall roof from Worcester.

Location: At Stoke Heath 2 m S of Bromsgrove off A38 between junctions 4 & 5 of M5 and 3½ m S of M42 junction 1.
Opening Times: Mar & Nov 11−4.30, closed Mons & Fris; Apr, May, Sept & Oct 11−5.30, *closed Mons;* June, July & Aug daily 11−5.30. Open Bank Holidays. *Closed Dec to Feb.* Adm £2.80, Chd £1.40, OAPs £1.95. Family ticket (2 adults and 2 Chd) £7.40. Parties at reduced rates by arrangement. Free car park & picnic site.
Refreshments: Available at Museum tea room. Souvenir and Bookshop.

BERNITHAN COURT

Llangarron   map G5
Telephone: Llangarron (098984) 477
(M.J. Richardson Esq.)

William & Mary house built for Hoskyns family in 1692: some surviving panelling, fine staircase, walled gardens.

Location: 4 m Ross on Wye, 1½ m from A40 Ross−Monmouth road.
Opening Times: By prior appointment, contact Mrs James, 1 Bernithan Farm Cottage, Llangarron, Ross on Wye HR9 6NG. Adm £2.

BERRINGTON HALL, The National Trust 🦋

Leominster   map F6   △   &
Telephone: Leominster (0568) 615721

Built 1778−1781 by Henry Holland, the architect of Carlton House. Painted and plaster ceilings. "Capability" Brown laid out the park.

Location: 3 m N Leominster, 7 m S of Ludlow, W of A49.
Opening Times: Apr, Sat & Sun, Easter Sat−Mon, 1.30−5.30; May to end of Sept− Weds to Suns & Bank Hol Mons 1.30−5.30; Oct: Sat & Sun 1.30−4.30. Grounds & restaurant open from 12.30. Adm £3, Chd £1.50, grounds only £1.20. Family ticket £8.25. Parties by prior written arrangement only. No dogs. Wheelchair available. Wheelchair access grounds only. No photography. Last admission ½hr before closing.
Refreshments: Light luncheons and afternoon teas in restaurant.

BREDON SPRINGS

Ashton-under-Hill, nr Evesham   map G5
(Ronald Sidwell, Esq)

1¾ acre garden. Large plant collection in natural setting.

Location: 6 m SW of Evesham, turn off A435; in Ashton turn right then 1st left.
Opening Times: GARDEN ONLY. Mar 31 to Oct 27−Sats, Suns, Weds, Thurs, Bank Hol Mon & Tues, 10−dusk. Adm 75p (Chd free). *In aid of National Gardens Scheme.* Coach parties alight at church−6 mins walk through churchyard and over 2 fields. Limited parking at house. Plants for sale. Dogs welcome.

BROBURY GARDEN & GALLERY

Brobury, nr Hereford   map F6
Telephone: Moccas (09817) 229
(Eugene Okarma, Esq)

8 acres of garden around a 100 years' old house on the banks of the River Wye. Spacious lawns, rock gardens, terraces, herbaceous borders; mature conifers. The Gallery specialises in old prints and 19th and 20th century watercolours.

Location: 11 m W of Hereford, off A438; signposted Brobury Bredwardine.
Opening Times: GARDEN. May 1 to Sept 30 — Mons to Sats 9–4.30. Adm £1.50, OAPs £1, Chd 50p. GALLERY: Open all the year — Mons to Sats 9–4.30 (closes at 4 in winter). Adm free.

BURFORD HOUSE GARDENS

Tenbury Wells   map G6
Telephone: (0584) 810777
(Treasures of Tenbury Ltd.)

The gardens at Burford were created by John Treasure over a period of 35 years and are filled with a wealth of rare and interesting plants many of which are grown by the adjoining world famous nursery which bears his name.

Location: 1 m W of Tenbury Wells on the A456.
Opening Times: Mar 16 to Oct 20, Mon to Sat 10–5, Sun 1–5. At other times by prior arrangement. Adm £1.95, Chd 80p. Parties of 25 or more by prior arrangement – Adm £1.60 each. No wheelchairs available.
Refreshments: Tea Rooms situated near entrance, serving morning coffee, light lunches and teas with locally baked cakes and scones.

BURTON COURT 🏛

Eardisland   map F6   ♿
Telephone: Pembridge 231
(Lt-Cmdr & Mrs R. M. Simpson)

A typical squire's house, built around the surprising survival of a 14th century hall. The East Front re-designed by Sir Clough Williams-Ellis in 1912. An extensive display of European and Oriental costume, natural history specimens, and models including a working model fairground. Pick your own soft fruit in season.

Location: 5 m W of Leominster between A44 & A4112.
Opening Times: Spring Bank Hol to end Sep — Weds, Thurs, Sats, Suns & Bank Hol Mons 2.30–6. Adm £2, Chd £1.50. Coach parties £1.50.
Refreshments: Coach parties catered for. Teas.

CROFT CASTLE, The National Trust 🌱

nr Leominster   map F6   ♿
Telephone: Yarpole 246

Welsh Border castle mentioned in Domesday. Inhabited by the Croft family for 900 years. Fine 18th century Gothic interior. Extensive wooded parkland.

Location: 5 m NW of Leominster just N of B4362 signposted from Ludlow/Leominster road (A49), and from A4110 at Mortimers Cross.
Opening Times: Apr & Oct Sat & Sun 2–5; Easter Sat, Sun & Mon 2–6; May to end Sept — Weds to Suns & Bank Hol Mons 2–6. Adm £2.70, Chd £1.35. Family ticket £7.40. Parties by prior written arrangement. Access for disabled to ground floor and part of grounds. Wheelchair available. Last admission 30 mins before closing.
Refreshments: Lunches and teas available in restaurant at Berrington Hall (5½m).

CWMMAU FARMHOUSE, BRILLEY, The National Trust

Whitney-on-Wye   map F5   🌱

Early 17th century timber-framed and stone tiled farmhouse.

Location: 4 m SW of Kington between A4111 and A438. Approached by a long narrow lane.
Opening Times: Easter, May, Spring & Summer Bank Hol weekends only — Sats, Suns & Mons 2–6. *At other times by prior written appointment with the tenant Mr S M Joyce.* Adm £2, Chd £1. *No reduction for parties.* No dogs. Unsuitable for wheelchairs & coaches.

EASTNOR CASTLE

nr Ledbury   map G5
Telephone: Ledbury (0531) 2302, 2849 or (0648) 567103 (*Administrator*)
Fax: (0531) 631030.
(*James Hervey-Bathurst, Esq*)

Splendid Norman Revival Castle built in 1812 in a dramatic setting within the Malvern Hills, Eastnor Castle captures the spirit of medieval chivalry and romance. The lavish interiors, in Italianate, Norman and Gothic style, display a unique collection of armour, tapestries, fine furniture and pictures by Van Dyck, Kneller, Romney, Watts and others. Castellated terraces descend to a lake. There is a renowned arboretum in the pleasure grounds, and a 500 acre park with red deer.

Location: 5 m from M50 (exit 2) 2 m E of Ledbury on Hereford/Tewkesbury Road A438.
Station: Ledbury (2 m).
Opening Times: Bank Hol Sun & Mons. Easter to Sept. Suns May to mid-Oct: Tues, Wed, Thurs July and Aug, 2–5 last admissions. Parties by appointment on any day, Easter to Oct. Adm £3, Chd £1.50. Reduced rates for parties of 20 or more. Dogs on leads allowed.
Refreshments: Home-made teas.

DINMORE MANOR

nr Hereford   map F5   &
(*R.G. Murray*)

Spectacular hillside location. A range of impressive architecture dating from 14th to 20th century. Chapel, Cloisters, Great Hall (Music Room) and extensive roof walk giving panoramic views of the countryside and beautiful gardens below. Large collection of stained glass. Interesting and unusual plants for sale in plant centre.

Location: 6 m N of Hereford on (A49).
Opening Times: All the year – Daily 9.30–5.30. Adm £2, OAPs £1, children under 14 admitted free when accompanied.
Refreshments: Available in the Plant Centre most afternoons.

EASTGROVE COTTAGE GARDEN NURSERY

Sankyns Green, nr Shrawley, Little Witley   map G6
Telephone: (0299) 896389
(*Mr & Mrs J. Malcolm Skinner*)

A peaceful old world country flower garden displaying a specialist collection of hardy plants maintained by the owners since 1970. This cottage garden is sensitively arranged with great emphasis laid on colour and form, and with the 17th century cottage and timber framed barn, it blends into the unspoiled country of meadow and woodland. The owners are on hand to offer advice and a wide range of good quality and unusual plants are grown at the nursery.

Location: Near Shrawley – 4 m SW of Stourport; 8 m NW of Worcester on road between Shrawley (on B4196) and Great Witley (on A443).
Opening Times: Open afternoons – Apr 2 to Nov 1, 2–5; (except Tues & Weds); *closed throughout Aug.* Adm £1, Chd 20p *in aid of National Gardens Scheme.*

EASTNOR CASTLE – *See above*

GOODRICH CASTLE

map G5
Telephone: (0600) 890538

The castle was built to command the ancient crossing of the Wye by the Gloucester/Caerleon road. Among the extensive remains of the original castle the keep survives, which largely dates from the late 13th century. For almost 300 years from the mid-14th century it was held by the Earls of Shrewsbury.

Location: 3 m (4.8 km) south west of Ross-on-Wye. OS map ref SO579199.
Opening Times: Good Friday or Apr 1 (whichever is earlier) to Sept 30: Open Daily 10–6. Oct 1 to Maundy Thursday or Mar 31 (whichever is earlier): Open Tues to Sun 10–4. *Closed* Dec 24–26, Jan 1. Adm £1.50, Concessions £1.10, Chd 75p.

THE GREYFRIARS, The National Trust

Worcester   map G6   △
Telephone: Worcester 23571

A richly timber-framed house built c. 1480, was rescued from demolition at the time of World War II. Carefully restored and refurbished; interesting textiles and furnishings add character to panelled rooms; an archway leads through a delightful garden.

Location: In Friar Street, Worcester.
Station: Worcester, Foregate Street (1/2 m).
Opening Times: Apr to end Oct – Weds & Thurs and Bank Holiday Mons 2–5.30. Other times adult parties by written application only. Adm £1.40, Chd 70p. Family ticket £3.80. Parties of children (inc schools) not admitted. No dogs. Unsuitable for wheelchairs.

HANBURY HALL, The National Trust

nr Droitwich   map G6   &
Telephone: (0527) 821214

William and Mary red brick house c. 1700 built for a wealthy lawyer. Outstanding painted ceilings and staircase by Sir James Thornhill. The Watney Collection of porcelain; Orangery c. 1730.

Location: 4½ m E of Droitwich, 1 m N of B4090.
Opening Times: Apr to end Oct, Sats, Suns and Mons 2–6. Adm £2.80, Chd £1.40. Family ticket £7.70. *Parties by prior written arrangement only.* Shop. No dogs. Wheelchair available. Braille guidebook available. Last admission 30 mins before closing.
Refreshments: Teas in the house.

HARTLEBURY CASTLE

nr Kidderminster   map G6
Telephone: Hartlebury (0299) 250410
(The Church Commissioners)

Historic home of the Bishops of Worcester for over 1,000 years. Fortified in 13th century, rebuilt after sacking in the Civil War and Gothicised in 18th century. State Rooms include medieval Great Hall, Hurd Library and Saloon. Fine plaster-work and remarkable collection of episcopal portraits. Also County Museum in North Wing.

Location: In village of Hartlebury, 5 m S of Kidderminster, 10 m N of Worcester off A449.
Opening Times: State Rooms Easter Mon to Sept 4 — First Sun in every month but please telephone to check. Every Wed Easter to end of August Bank Hol Sun & Mon 2 – 4. Adm 75p, Chd 25p, OAPs 50p. Guided tours for parties of 30 or more on weekdays by arrangement.
County Museum Mar to Nov — Mons to Thurs 10 – 1; Fris and Sun 2 – 5. *Closed* Sats and Good Friday. Open Bank Holidays 10 – 5. Adm 80p, OAPS, Students & Chd 40p. Family tickets (2 adults and up to 3 children) £2. School parties please telephone for information. Picnic area.
Refreshments: Available.

HARVINGTON HALL

nr Kidderminster DY10 4LR   map G6
Telephone: Chaddesley Corbett (0562 777) 267
(The Roman Catholic Archdiocese of Birmingham)

Moated medieval and Elizabethan manor-house containing secret hiding-places and rare wall-paintings. Georgian Chapel in garden with 18th century altar, rails and organ. Harvington Festival July 17, 18 and 19 1992. Other events throughout the summer.

Location: 3 m SE of Kidderminster, ½ m from the junction of A448 and A450 at Mustow Green.
Opening Times: Mar 1 to Oct 31 daily except Good Friday, 11.30 – 5.30. *Closed Nov to Feb except by appointment.* Adm £2.50, Chd £2, OAPs £1.50. Parties by arrangement with the custodian. Free car parking.
Refreshments: Licensed restaurant in the medieval wing overlooking the moat, open Apr 4 to Sept 30 daily (except Mons and Fris) and on Suns in Oct. Light refreshments on other afternoons. Bookings taken for Sunday lunch and evening functions.

HELLEN'S

Much Marcle   map G6   △
('The Pennington-Mellor-Munthe Trust)

Built as a stone fortress in 1292 by Mortimer, Earl of March, this manorial house has been lived in since then by descendants of original builder. Visited by Black Prince and Bloody Mary.

Location: In village of Much Marcle on Ledbury/Ross Road. Entrance opp church.
Opening Times: Good Fri to Oct 2 — Weds, Sats, Suns and Bank Hol Mons 2 – 6 (guided tours each hour). *Other times by written appointment with the Custodian).* Adm £2.50, Chd (must be accompanied by adult) £1.

HERGEST CROFT GARDENS

Kington   map F5
Telephone: Kington (0544) 230160
(W L & R A Banks, Esq)

Photograph Andrew Morris.

The gardens of fifty acres contains 'one of the finest and most thriving collections of exotic trees in the British Isles'. Many of the trees and shrubs brought back from China in the early 1900's have grown to great size and the scope of the collection continues to expand with many recently introduced species. The wide range of maples

HERGEST CROFT GARDENS – *continued*

and birches have been named as National Collections of these two genera. The trees are under-planted with rhododendrons and azaleas which include many rare species, some now more than thirty feet tall. The gardens are a rare survival of the school of William Robinson, in addition to the woodland garden there is a traditional kitchen garden, conservatory and herbaceous borders which are at their best in the summer months. From spring bulbs to autumn colour in October the gardens have much to interest the visitor at any season.

Location: On outskirts W of Kington off Rhayader Road (A44) *(signposted to Hergest Croft at W end of bypass).*

Opening Times: Daily – Apr 17 to Oct 25, 1.30 – 6.30. Adm £2, Chd under 15 free. Reduced rates for pre-booked parties of over 20 by appointment at any time.

Refreshments: Home-made teas daily and for parties of over 20 by arrangement.

HILL COURT GARDENS & GARDEN CENTRE

Hom Green, Ross on Wye   map G5   ♿
Telephone: Ross 763123
(Mr J C Rowley)

Set in the beautiful grounds of a William and Mary Mansion. An avenue of white limes line the drive up to the house, gardens, and garden centre. The two and a half acres of ornamental gardens include an 18th century Yew Walk, colourful herbaceous borders, water garden with gazebo, rose gardens and monthly shrub borders. Set in one of the walled gardens these borders are designed to assist the visitors in their choice of shrubs for their own gardens throughout the year. The garden centre offers the gardener excellent choice in plants and products, professional advice from horticulturally trained staff, a relaxing environment and the pleasure of strolling through the gardens too. There is a tea garden serving light lunches and afternoon teas within another of the lovely walled gardens.

Location: B4228 from Ross on Wye, fork right at the Prince of Wales public house, drive for 2½ miles.

Opening Times: Open daily 9.30 – 5.30, open all Bank Holidays. Adm free. All parties by appointment only, particularly coach parties. Ample car parking. Suitable for disabled, although shingled ground does sometimes cause problems.

Refreshments: A delightful tea garden set in one of the walled gardens with indoor and patio seating. Open Spring & Summer season, weekends only during early Spring season. Light lunches and afternoon teas available, all cakes homemade. Special group bookings possible. The house is not open to the public.

HOW CAPLE COURT GARDENS 🏛

How Caple   map G5
Telephone: How Caple 626
(Mr & Mrs P L Lee)

11 acres overlooking the river Wye. Formal terraced Edwardian gardens, extensive plantings of mature trees and shrubs, water features and a sunken Florentine garden undergoing restoration. Norman church with 16th century Diptych. Specialist nursery plants for sale. Fabrics shop.

Location: B4224, Ross on Wye (4½ m) to Hereford (9 m).

Opening Times: Apr 1 to Oct 31 Mons to Sats 9.30 – 5. May to Sept 30 also Suns 10 – 5. Adm £2, Chd £1. Parties by appointment. Car parking. Toilets.

KENTCHURCH COURT

Hereford   map F5
Telephone: Golden Valley 240228
(J E S Lucas-Scudamore, Esq)

Fortified border manor house altered by Nash. Gateway and part of the original 14th century house still survives. Pictures and Grinling Gibbons carving. Owen Glendower's tower.

Location: Off B4347, 3 m SE of Pontrilas; 12 m Monmouth; 14 m Hereford; 14 m Abergavenny, on left bank River Monnow.

Opening Times: May to Sept. *Parties only by appointment.* Adm £3, Chd £1.50.

Refreshments: At Kentchurch Court by appointment.

KINNERSLEY CASTLE

Kinnersley   map F5
Telephone: (05446) 407
(H Garratt-Adams)

Medieval Welsh border Castle, reconstructed about 1588. Little changed since then, retaining fine plasterwork and panelling, leaded glass and stone tiled roof. Yew hedges, walled garden and fine trees including probably the largest example of a Ginkgo tree in the United Kingdom. Art and other exhibitions. Still a family home, used out of season for courses and conferences. Early home of the De Kinnardsley and De le Bere families, remodelled by Roger Vaughan and later home of parliamentary General Sir Thomas Morgan.

Location: 4 m W of Weobley on A4112 (Black and White Village Trail).

Opening Times: Bank Holiday Sat, Sun, Mons – May to Aug. Selected weekends in June, and daily from Aug 1 to Sept 13 *except Tues* 2 – 4. Adm: £2, Chd £1, OAPs £1.50, Groups £1.50 (by arrangement throughout the year). Gardens only £1.

Refreshments: Tea room.

LANGSTONE COURT

Llangarron HR9 6NR   map G5
(R.M.C. Jones Esq.)

Mostly late 17th century house with older parts. Interesting staircases, panelling and ceilings.

Location: Ross on Wye 5m, Llangarron 1m.

Opening Times: By prior appointment, write to R.M.C. Jones at the above address. Adm free.

LITTLE MALVERN COURT AND GARDENS 🏛

nr Great Malvern   map G5
Telephone: Malvern (0684) 892988
(Mr and Mrs T M Berington)

14th century Prior's Hall once attached to 12th-century Benedictine Priory, and principal rooms in Victorian addition by Hansom. Family and European paintings and furniture. Collection of 18th and 19th century needlework. Home of the Berington family by descent since the Dissolution. 10 acres of former monastic grounds. Magnificent views, lake, garden rooms, terrace. Wide variety of spring bulbs, old fashioned roses, shrubs and trees.

Location: 3 m S of Great Malvern on Upton-on-Severn Road (A4104).

Opening Times: Apr 22 to July 23 – Weds and Thurs 2 – 5. Parties by prior arrangement. Adm £3 for house and garden, GARDEN ONLY £2. Chd aged 5 – 14 £2 house and garden, £1 garden only. No concession for OAPs. Unsuitable for wheelchairs. Guided Tours last adm 4.30.

Refreshments: Home made teas only available for parties by arrangement.

LOWER BROCKHAMPTON, The National Trust 🌿

Bromyard   map G6   ♿

Small half-timbered manor house c. 1400 with unusual detached 15th century gate house and ruins of 12th century chapel.

Location: 2 m E of Bromyard N of A44 Bromyard/Worcester Road.

Opening Times: Medieval Hall and Parlour only: Apr to end of Sept – Weds, Thurs, Fris, Sats, Suns & Bank Hol Mons 10 – 1, 2 – 6. *Closed* Good Friday. Oct – Wed to Sun 10 – 1, 2 – 4. Adm £1.30, Chd 65p. Family ticket £3.50. Parties by prior written arrangement only. N.B. Hall reached by narrow road through 1½ m woods & farmland. No dogs in Hall. Wheelchair access.

MOCCAS COURT

Moccas   map F5
Telephone: Moccas (098 17) 381
(R T G Chester-Master, Esq)

Designed by Adam, built by Keck in 1775 and has been in the ownership of the Cornewalls, and the present owner, for three centuries. The House stands in 'Capability' Brown parkland on the south bank of the River Wye.

Location: 13 m W of Hereford by River Wye. 1 m off B4352.
Opening Times: HOUSE & GARDENS. Apr to Sept—Thurs 2−6. Adm £1.50. Picnics in garden allowed.
Refreshments: Food and drink available at the Red Lion Hotel, Bredwardine, by prebooking only.

MORTIMER'S CROSS WATER MILL, LUCTON ✳

map F6
Telephone: (056881) 8820

Erected in the 18th century, this watermill was still in use in the 1940s. The outer housing is of sandstone rubble and the mechanism, which could be worked by one man, is located on three floors.

Location: 4½ m (7.2 km) north west of Leominster. OS map ref SO426637.
Opening Times: Apr 1 to Sept 30: Open Thurs, Suns and Bank Hols only 2−6 Adm 60p, Concessions 45p, Chd 30p.

THE PRIORY

Kemerton   map G5
(The Hon Mrs Peter Healing)

4 acre garden; main features are long herbaceous borders planned in colour groups; stream and sunken garden; many interesting and unusual plants and shrubs.

Location: NE of Tewkesbury, turn off A435 (Evesham/Cheltenham) at Beckford.
Opening Times: GARDEN ONLY. Every Thurs May 28 to end Sept; also Suns Aug 9, 30; Sept 13: 2−7. Adm £1. Accompanied chd free. *In aid of National Gardens Scheme & other charities.* Plants for sale.

SPETCHLEY PARK

Worcester   map G5
(Mr & Mrs R J Berkeley)

This lovely 30 acre garden is a plantsman's delight, with a large collection of trees, shrubs and plants, many of which are rare or unusual. There is colour and interest throughout the months that the garden is open to visitors. The park contains red and fallow deer.

Location: 3 m E of Worcester on Stratford-upon-Avon Road (A422).
Opening Times: Gardens & Garden Centre: Apr 1 to Sept 30 — Tues, Wed, Thurs, Fri 11−5; Suns 2−5; Bank Hol Mons 11−5. *Closed* other Mons and all Sats. Adm £1.80, Chd 90p. Reduced rates for pre-booked parties of 25 or more. Regret no dogs. Plants and shrubs for sale. House not open.
Refreshments: Tea in the garden.

STONE HOUSE COTTAGE GARDENS

Kidderminster   map G6   ♿
Telephone: Kidderminster 69902
(Major & The Hon Mrs Arbuthnott)

Sheltered wall garden with towers. Rare wall shrubs and climbers also interesting herbaceous plants, all labelled. Adjacent Nursery.

Location: 2 m SE of Kidderminster on A448 to Bromsgrove; next to Stone Church.
Station: Kidderminster (2 m).
Opening Times: GARDEN & NURSERY ONLY. Mar to Oct: Weds, Thurs, Fris, Sats. Also open Sun Aug 30 and Bank Holiday Mons Apr 20, May 4, 25, Aug 31 (10−6); Suns, May and June. Adm £1.50, accompanied Chd free. Coaches by appointment only. *In aid of National Gardens Scheme and Mother Teresa.*
Refreshments: Food & drink available at Harvington Hall.

THE WEIR, The National Trust 🌿

Swainshill, nr Hereford   map F5

Delightful riverside garden, particularly spectacular in early spring. Fine views of the river Wye and Black Mountains.

Location: 5 m W of Hereford on A438.
Opening Times: Feb 14 to end Oct — Wed to Sun & Bank Hol Mon 11−6. (incl Good Friday). Adm £1.50. No reduction for parties. Unsuitable for coach parties. No dogs. Unsuitable for wheelchairs or visually handicapped.

WHITE COTTAGE

Earls Common Road, Stock Green   map G6   ♿
Telephone: 0386 792414
(Mr and Mrs S. M. Bates)

Two acre garden developed since 1981. Large herbaceous and shrub borders, many unusual varieties. Specialist collection of hardy geraniums. Stream and natural garden carpeted with primroses, cowslips and other wild flowers. Nursery featuring plants propagated from the garden.

Location: Droitwich 5 m, Worcester 10 m. A422 Worcester/Alcester, turn left at Red Hart pub (Dormston), 1½ m to T junction. Turn left for 75 yards. Or Droitwich/ Feckenham B4030, turn right through Bradley Green, right at first T junction, right at second T junction, continue ¼ m.
Opening Times: GARDEN ONLY: Apr 17 to Oct 4 — Daily 10−5. (August by prior appointment only). *Closed* Thurs. Sun openings are Apr 19, May 3, 17, 24, 31; June 14, 28, July 12, 26, Sept 6, 20, Oct 4. Nursery open daily Mar 15 to Oct 4. *Closed* Thurs. Adm 75p, Chd free. Parties by arrangement only. *In aid of National Gardens Scheme.* Car parking. Suitable for disabled persons. No dogs please.
Refreshments: Teas at Jinney Ring Craft Centre, Hanbury.

WITLEY COURT ⚜

Map G6
Telephone: (0299) 896636
(English Heritage)

This is one of the most spectacular country house ruins. Cast in the Victorian Italian style of the 1860s, it is on a huge scale, with a glorious facade. Looking from the house to the gardens, a view enjoyed by Edward VII, who as Prince of Wales often stayed at the house, the scene is dominated by the immense Perseus Fountain.

Location: 10 m NW of Worcester on the A443.
Opening Times: Good Fri or Apr 1 (whichever is earlier) to Sept 30, open daily 10–6. Oct 1 to Maundy Thurs or Mar 31 (whichever is earlier), open Tues to Sun 10–4. *Closed* Dec 24 to 26 and Jan 1. Adm 95p, Concessions 75p, Chd 45p.

WORCESTER CATHEDRAL

Worcester map G6 △ ♿
Telephone: Worcester (0905) 28854
(The Dean and Chapter of Worcester)

Beside the River Severn opposite the Malvern Hills. Built between 1084 and 1375. Norman Crypt and Chapter House. Early English Quire, Perpendicular Tower. Monastic buildings include refectory (now College Hall and open on request during August), cloisters, remains of guesten hall and dormitories. Tombs of King John and Prince Arthur. Cloister herb garden, Elgar memorial window, misericords. Edgar Tower gatehouse.

Location: Centre of Worcester. Main roads Oxford and Stratford to Wales. 3 m junction 7 (M5).
Opening Times: Every day 7.30–6. Choral Evensong daily (except Thurs and school hols). No admission charge but donations of £1.50 accepted. Parties: suggested minimum donation of £2 (Chd 50p) per head for guided tours. No cathedral car parking—City centre parking. Disabled visitors most welcome—some steps, but help and wheelchair available. Information Desk, shop and toilets. **Refreshments:** Light refreshment in Cloister Tea Room. Special arrangements made for parties.

HERTFORDSHIRE

ASHRIDGE

Berkhamsted map J5
Telephone: Little Gaddesden (044 284) 3491
(Governors of Ashridge Management College)

150 acres of both Parkland and intimate smaller gardens. The landscape influenced by Humphrey Repton. Mature trees combined with unique features e.g. Beech Houses with Windows and doors, in a Pink and Grey Garden, Grotto – Ferns planted between Herts Pudding Stone.

Location: 3½ m N of Berkhamsted (A41), 1 m S of Little Gaddesden.
Opening Times: Gardens open Apr to Oct—Sats & Suns 2–6. Adm: Gardens: £2, Chd/OAP £1.

BENINGTON LORDSHIP GARDENS 🏛

nr Stevenage map K5
Telephone: Benington (043 885) 668
(Mr & Mrs C. H. A. Bott)

Photograph A. F. Kersting.

Laid out in 1906 around a Norman castle this hilltop garden has changed little and is very 'English'. Full of atmosphere the entrance is through a magnificent neo-Norman gate house. Sweeping lawns stretch downhill towards lakes and parkland. A broad terrace cuts across the lawn and leads to a Spring rock/water garden, double herbaceous borders outstanding in mid-Summer, kitchen garden and nursery. There are also masses of old and modern roses and many unusual plants with interest all the year.

Location: 4 m E of Stevenage in village of Benington between Walkern (B1037) & Watton-at-Stone (A602).
Opening Times: GARDENS ONLY: Snowdrops, Weds & Suns in Feb, 12–5 (weather permitting). Rest of the year. Easter, Spring and Summer Bank Hol Mons 12–5. Every Wed beginning of Apr to end Sept, 12–5. Every Sun beginning of Apr to end of Aug 2–5. Floral Festival with adjoining church June 27 & 28, 12–6. Nursery and garden open by appointment on weekdays Apr to Sept. Free parking (coaches please book). Regret unsuitable for wheel chairs and disabled. No dogs. Adults £2, Chd free.
Refreshments: Teas every Sun and Wed, June to Aug.

HATFIELD HOUSE

Hatfield   map K5   △
Telephone: (0707) 262823
(The Marquess of Salisbury)

This celebrated Jacobean house, which stands in its own great park, was built between 1607 and 1611 by Robert Cecil, 1st Earl of Salisbury and Prime Minister to King James I. It has been the family home of the Cecils ever since. The Staterooms are rich in world-famous paintings, fine furniture, rare tapestries and historic armour. The beautiful stained glass in the chapel is original. Within the delightful gardens stands the surviving wing of the Royal Palace of Hatfield (1497) where Elizabeth I spent much of her girlhood and held her first Council of State in November 1558. She appointed William Cecil, Lord Burghley as her Chief Minister. Some of her relics can be seen in the house. 25 minutes by regular fast train service from Kings Cross to Hatfield (station faces Park gates). The Moorgate to Hatfield electric train service has direct Underground links; Victoria Line at Highbury, Circle Line at Moorgate, Piccadilly Line at Finsbury Park. Hatfield House Lodge is opposite the station. Further particulars from The Curator, Hatfield House.

Location: In Hatfield, close to A1(M), 7 m M25.
Station: Hatfield (opposite house).
Opening Times: Mar 25–Oct 11, 1992. Hatfield House: Daily except Mon and Good Friday. Weekdays from 12. Guided tours only, last tour 4.15. Sun 1.30–5–no guided tours, guides in each room. Also open on Easter, May Day, Spring and Aug Bank Hol Mon, 11–5, no guided tours–guides in each room. Park: 10.30–8, daily except Good Friday. West Gardens: 11–6, daily except Good Friday. East Gardens: 2–5, Mon only (except Bank Hol Mons). Adm £4.30, OAP £3.50, Chd £2.90. Reductions for pre-booked parties, 20 or more. Coach and car park free. Guided Tour (Tues–Sat) takes about 1 hour. LIVING CRAFTS EXHIBITION: May 7–10, 10–6; A FESTIVAL OF GARDENING: June 20–21, 10–6; NATIONAL PATCHWORK CHAMPIONSHIPS: June 4–7, 10–6.
Refreshments: Available in adjacent restaurant–coffee shop. ELIZABETHAN BANQUETING IN THE OLD PALACE THROUGHOUT THE YEAR. Dogs not admitted to House or garden.
Telephone: (0707) 262823 (Curator); Banqueting and Restaurant (0707) 262055/262030. Telex: 26527 OLD PAL G.

CAPEL MANOR

nr Enfield   map K5
Telephone: Lea Valley (0992) 763849
(London Borough of Enfield)

A 100 acre estate used extensively by one of the country's leading Horticultural and Environmental Colleges. The 30 acres of historical and modern theme gardens are all richly planted and include the 17th Century garden, large Italian style maze, Rock and Water features, a 5 acre Trials and Demonstration garden run by the Consumers' Association. Walled garden with rose collection and display glasshouses, tree collection and woodland walks. The National Gardening Centre features more theme gardens including the 'Sunday Times' Chelsea '90 winner, a 'Garden for Beginners'. The Gardens offer seasonal interest to all keen gardeners looking for inspiration or just a relaxing day out. Mostly level surface, disabled persons – 2 wheelchairs available. Unfortunately the House is not open to viewing. The educational farm is on a neighbouring site 1 mile from the gardens and shows a small range of livestock. Usually baby animals and milking demonstrations to see (cow permitting!)

Location: 3 min from M25 junction M25/A10 S and turn right at traffic lights. Nearest station Turkey Street/Liverpool Street line.
Opening Times: GARDENS: Weekdays (except Christmas Day, Boxing Day and New Year's Day) 10–4.30. Weekends: Apr to Oct 10–5.30. FARM: Weekdays during school holidays only and weekends Apr to Oct 1–5. Adm: £1.50, concessions 75p. SPECIAL SHOWS: May, June, July, Sept (please check for dates). Adm: usually £2.50, concessions £1.25 (this price includes a visit to the Farm). Special rates for coaches, garden tours. Show this entry and receive a free garden's guide leaflet. Further details from the Resources Officer, Capel Manor College, Bullsmoor Lane, Enfield, Middx EN1 4RQ, tel (0992) 763849.

CROMER WINDMILL

Ardeley, Stevenage, Hertfordshire SG2 7QA   map K5
Telephone: (0438) 861293
(Hertfordshire Building Preservation Trust)

Hertfordshire's unique 17th century Post Windmill, under restoration to working order. Static display, guided visits.

Location: Adjoins the B1037 between Walkern and Cottered, 4 m NE of Stevenage.
Opening Times: Sun May 10 'National Mill Day', and Suns to Sept 13, Bank Holiday Mons, second and fourth Weds May 13 to Sept 9, 2.30–5. Adm 75p, Chd 25p. Individual appointments possible with prior arrangement. Groups by prior appointment with Mr and Mrs Hughes, 0438 886 1293. Parking limited. Not suitable for disabled visitors.
Refreshments: None, public houses with catering in Walkern (2m) and Cottered (2m).

THE GARDENS OF THE ROSE

Chiswell Green, St Albans   map K5   &
Telephone: St Albans (0727) 50461
(Royal National Rose Society)

The Showgrounds of the R.N.R.S. containing some 30,000 roses of over 1,650 different varieties.

Location: Off B4630 (formerly A412) St Albans/Watford Road.
Stations: St Alban's City (2 m).
Opening Times: June 13 to Oct 18—Mons to Sats 9–5; Suns & Bank Holidays 10–6. Facilities for the disabled.
Refreshments: Licensed cafeteria.

GORHAMBURY

St Albans   map K5   △
Telephone: St Albans (0727) 54051
(The Earl of Verulam)

Mansion built 1777-84 in modified classical style by Sir Robert Taylor. 16th century enamelled glass and historic portraits.

Location: 2 m W of St Albans. Entrance off A4147 at St. Michael's, near Roman Theatre.
Opening Times: May to Sept—Thurs 2–5. Adm £2.50, Chd & OAPs £1.50. Guided tours only. Parties by prior arrangement Thurs £2, other days £3.

HATFIELD HOUSE – *See page 95*

KNEBWORTH HOUSE

Knebworth   map K5
Telephone: Stevenage 812661   Fax: Stevenage 811908
(The Lord Cobbold)

Home of the Lytton family for over 500 years. The original Tudor Manor House was transformed 150 years ago by the spectacular high gothic decoration of Victorian novelist and statesman, Sir Edward Bulwer-Lytton. There are many beautiful rooms, important portraits and furniture, and a fine collection of manuscripts and letters asso iated with many famous visitors to the House. Charles Dickens acted here in private theatricals and Winston Churchill painted at his easel in the superb Jacobean Banqueting Hall. It was the home of Constance Lytton, the suffragette, and Robert Lytton, Viceroy of India. Lord Lytton's Viceroyalty and the great Delhi Durbar of 1877 are commemorated in a fascinating exhibition and audio-visual display. The Lutyens

gardens include a Jekyll herb garden. The house is situated in a 250 acre country park with deer herds. Large Adventure Playground with Fort Knebworth and Miniature Railway.

Location: 28 m N of Central London. Own direct access off A1(M) Junction 7 (Stevenage South A602). 12 miles north of M25.
Stations: Stevenage (2 m).
Opening Times: HOUSE, GARDENS AND PARK, Weekends, Bank Hols and School Hols from Apr 4 to May 17; then daily (except Mons) May 23 to Sept 6, plus weekends only to Oct 4. *(Closed June 27 and July 31 to Aug 3 incl.)* Open Park: 11–5.30. House & Gardens: 12–5. House, Gardens & Park: £4, Chd/OAPs £3.50. Park only: £2.50 (no reductions for Chd/OAPs). Reductions for pre-booked parties of 20 or more (Apr 4 to Oct 4). Opening times & prices subject to special events. Coach and Car park free. Dogs admitted to Park only on leads. Telephone above number for further details.
Refreshments: Licensed Cafeteria in 16th Century Tithe Barns close to House & Gardens (Tel: Stevenage 813825). Oakwood Restaurant in hotel at Park entrance (Tel: Stevenage 742299).

LEVERSTOCK GREEN VILLAGE GARDENS AND HILL END FARM

map K5

A village opening of an interesting variety of four village gardens.

Hill End Farm
Beech Tree Lane, Gorhambury   &
(Mr and Mrs Alban Warwick)

Part dates back to 1275. Mature garden; herbaceous borders; duck pond; grass walk flanked by coniferous and deciduous specimen trees; new sunken area with C16 plants. Lunches and picnic facilities. Plant stall.

King Charles II Cottage
Westwick Row   &
(Mr and Mrs F. S. Cadman)

A one acre garden; roses a special feature; small well stocked ornamental pond; part of the house is also open (weather permitting), with flower arrangements by Mrs Sheila Macqueen (no extra charge). Mrs Macqueen is an internationally known flower decorator.

Swedish Cottage
Westwick Row
(Doug and Barbara Wiles)

Young half acre garden specialising in scented and wild flowers, plants to attract bees, butterflies, birds etc. Aviaries with parakeets, owls and wild fowl.

Westwick Cottage
Westwick Row   &
(Mrs Sheila Macqueen)

Medium-sized garden specialising in plants for flower arranging; many unusual specimens. Flower arrangements in the house (weather permitting) by Mrs Sheila Macqueen (no extra charge). Plant stall.

Location: Via A4147 mid-way between Hemel Hempstead and St Albans.
Opening Times: All the above village gardens open June 28 (11–5). Car parking free. Combined admission charge for all gardens £2, Chd free. *In aid of National Gardens Scheme.*
Refreshments: Lunches and picnic facilities at Hill End Farm, Gorhambury. Light refreshments, teas and coffee at Westwick Cottage.

MOOR PARK MANSION

nr Rickmansworth   map J4
Telephone: Rickmansworth (0923) 776611
(Three Rivers District Council)

Palladian house reconstructed in 1720 by Sir James Thornhill and Giacomo Leoni incorporating house built in 1678/79 for James, Duke of Monmouth. Magnificent interior decorations by Verrio, Sleker and others. Club House of Moor Park Golf Club. Being restored by the District Council.

Location: 1 m SE of Rickmansworth.
Stations: Rickmansworth or Moor Park.
Opening Times: All the year except Bank Holidays—Mons to Fris 10–12, 2–4; Sats 10–12 noon. *Restricted viewing may be necessary on occasions.* Visitors are requested to report to reception. Adm free. Descriptive leaflet available. Guided tours during summer months. Telephone Council's Information Centre for more details.

SCOTT'S GROTTO

Ware   map K5
Telephone: Ware (0920) 464131/Hertford (0992) 584322
(East Hertfordshire District Council)

Grotto, summerhouse and garden built 1760-73 by Quaker poet, John Scott. Described by English Heritage as "one of the finest grottos in England". Now extensively restored by The Ware Society.

Location: Scott's Road, Ware (off A119 Hertford Road). Nearest station Ware/ Liverpool Street line.
Opening Times: New extended opening times. Every Sat beginning of Apr to end of Sept and Easter, Spring and Summer Bank Hol Mons 2–4.30. Adm free but donation of £1 requested. Please park in Amwell End car park by level crossing (300 yards away) and walk up Scott's Road. Advisable to wear flat shoes and bring a torch. Parties by prior arrangement.

SHAW'S CORNER, The National Trust ✂

Ayot St Lawrence, Nr Welwyn map K5
Telephone: Stevenage (0438) 820307

Home of George Bernard Shaw from 1906–1950. The rooms downstairs remain as in his lifetime; Shaw's bedroom, bathroom and display room upstairs.

Location: SW end of village of Ayot St Lawrence. 3 m NW Welwyn; 2 m NE of Wheathampstead.

Opening Times: Apr to end Oct—Wed to Sat 2–6; Suns & Bank Hol Mons 12–6. *Closed Good Friday & Mons & Tues.* Last adm 5.30. Adm £2.50, Chd £1.25. Parties must book. *On busy days adm may be by timed ticket.* Dogs in car park only. Unsuitable for wheelchairs.

HUMBERSIDE

BEVERLEY GUILDHALL

Beverley map J9
Telephone: 0482 867430
(East Yorkshire Borough of Beverley Borough Council)

Beverley's **heritage** spans a period of 1300 years which is reflected in its fine old buildings and outstanding Market Square, in particular, in Register Square, is the Guildhall. Bought by the Council for use as a Town Hall in 1500 and extended in 1762, containing the Mayor's Parlour and the Tourist Information Centre. Doric portico leads to 18th century Courtroom and Magistrates' Room. Fine collection of civic regalia, charters, period furniture and other exhibits. Notable features – medieval wall and outstanding work of Italian stuccoist Cortese in beautiful ceiling depicting all-seeing figure of Justice.

Location: In Town Centre, off pedestrianised zone, Register Square.
Opening Times: Easter to Oct and Oct to Easter. Various sections open/closed according to time of year. Adm free most dates but for full details enquire The Tourist Information Office, The Guildhall, Register Square, Beverley HU17 9AU. Car parking very limited. Free car parks in near vicinity. Ground floor only suitable for disabled.
Refreshments: Facilities in near proximity.

BLAYDES HOUSE

Hull map J9
Telephone: Hull (0482) 26406
(The Georgian Society for East Yorkshire)

Mid-Georgian merchants house, fine staircase and panelled rooms. Restored by the Society in 1974-5.

Location: 6 High Street, Hull.
Station: Hull.
Opening Times: Staircase, Blaydes and Partners' Rooms—all the year Mons to Fris (except Bank Hols) 10.30–1, 2–4. By appointment only with Blackmore Son & Co, Chartered Architects at Blaydes House. Adm 50p.

BURNBY HALL GARDENS

Pocklington map J9 &
Telephone: Pocklington (0759 30) 2068
(Stewart's Burnby Hall Gardens & Museum Trust)

Large gardens with 2 lakes. Finest display of hardy water lilies in Europe – 65 varieties, **designated National Collection.** Museum housing Stewart Collection—sporting trophies, ethnic material. Picnic area, rose garden. Sales kiosk.

Location: 13 m E of York on A1079.
Opening Times: Sat Apr 4 to mid Oct—daily 10–6. Adm £1.50, Chd (under 5) free, (5–16) 50p, OAPs & Parties £1 (1992 rates). Free coach and car park. Disabled facilities.
Refreshments: Teas in the garden.

BURTON AGNES HALL – *See page 98*

BURTON CONSTABLE 🏛

nr Hull map K9
Telephone: (0964) 562400
(J Chichester Constable, Esq)

Magnificent Elizabethan House, built c1570. Outstanding collection of furniture, pictures, works of art. and eighteenth century scientific instruments. Eighteenth century decoration by Robert Adam and Thomas Lightoler. Unusual chapel converted from billiard room, and an outstanding eighteenth century Chinese room. Parkland by 'Capability' Brown.

Location: At Burton Constable; 1½ m N of Sproatley; 7½ m NE of Hull (A165); 10 m SE of Beverley (A1035).
Opening Times: Easter, May Day and Spring Bank Holiday Suns and Mons. Suns in June and July; July 19 to Sept 6: Sun to Thurs incl. Parties anytime by arrangement. For further details write to: The Administrator, Burton Constable Hall, Hull, HU11 4LN, or Tel: (0964) 562400.
Refreshments: Coffee shop. Gift shop.

BURTON AGNES HALL

nr Bridlington map J10
Telephone: Burton Agnes (0262 89) 324
(Preservation Trust Ltd)

BURTON AGNES HALL
near BRIDLINGTON, Humberside
Described by 'Everybody's' as a Yorkshire Treasure House

Burton Agnes Hall, built AD 1598-1610, is filled with treasures collected during four centuries. Antique furniture, Elizabethan carved ceilings, oriental china and the largest private collection in the North of French Impressionist and Modern paintings—Renoir, Pissaro, Corot, Utrillo, Gauguin, Augustus John, etc.

Open to the public daily from 1st April – 31st October 1992. Admittance to Hall and Gardens £2.50. Children & OAP's £2. Group rates on application. Gardens only–£1.00 Hours of opening 11am to 5pm. Licensed Cafeteria, Teas, light lunches and refreshments served. Guides and guide books are available and there is a free car park within a few yards of the Hall. Bus service 200 yards from Hall. Bridlington 6 miles, Scarborough 18 miles, York 34 miles. Toilets for the Disabled.

For further particulars apply: Estate Office, Burton Agnes, Driffield, East Yorkshire. Tel: Burton Agnes (0262 89) 324.

The Hall is a magnificent example of late Elizabethan architecture – still lived in by descendants of the family who built it in 1598. There are wonderful carvings, lovely furniture and fine collection of modern French and English paintings of the Impressionist Schools – Renoir, Pissaro, Corot, Utrillo, Gauguin, Augustus John, etc. The recently redeveloped walled garden contains a potager, maze, herbaceous borders, campanula collection, jungle garden and giant games set in coloured gardens. Also woodland gardens and walk, children's corner, Norman manor house, donkey wheel and gift shop.

Location: In village of Burton Agnes, 6 m SW of Bridlington on Driffield/Bridlington Road (A166).
Opening Times: Apr 1 to Oct 31 – Daily 11–5. Hall and Gardens: Adm £2.50, OAPs £2. Group rates on application. GARDEN ONLY £1. *The management reserves the right to close the house or part thereof without prior notice; adm charges will be adjusted on such days.*
Refreshments: Licensed cafeteria. Teas, light lunches & refreshments. Toilet for the disabled.

CARLTON TOWERS – *See page 99*

THE CHARTERHOUSE

Hull map J9
Telephone: (0482) 20026
(Charterhouse Trustees)

Charterhouse, was founded in 1384 by Michael de la Pole, Earl of Suffolk. The Charterhouse is an almshouse which provides accommodation for the elderly, and visitors are requested not to enter areas other than the Chapel and Gardens.

Location: Charterhouse Lane, Hull.
Opening Times: CHAPEL & GARDENS open daily during July and on Good Friday, Easter Day, Easter Monday, Spring and Summer Bank Holidays 10–8. No adm charge but prior notice should be given for parties of 10 or more. Children should be accompanied by an adult. Dogs not permitted. Limited car parking available.
Refreshments: Facilities in nearby City centre.

CARLTON TOWERS

Goole map J9 △
Telephone: (0482) 20026
(Duke of Norfolk)

The most complete Victorian Gothic House, still a family home and includes beautiful china, silver, carved woodwork, etc and a Priest's Hiding Hole.

Location: 20 m S of York; 6 m S of Selby and 1 m N of Snaith (A1041) and 6 m from M62 exits 34 & 36.
Station: Snaith (1m).
Opening Times: All Suns from the beginning of May to the end of Sept plus usual Bank Holidays, 1–5 (last adm 4.30); Parkland/Rose Garden 12.15–6. Adm £2.50, OAPs £1.50, Chd £1. PARTY BOOKINGS ON OTHER DAYS & EVENINGS, by appointment, (min of 20 visitors); guided tour (1½ hours) at £2.50 per person.

THE CHARTERHOUSE – *See page 98*

ELSHAM HALL COUNTRY PARK 🏛

Brigg map J8 △ ♿
Telephone: (0652) 688698
(Capt J Elwes, DL)

Beautiful English park with lakes and wild gardens. Giant Carp. Domestic animals, Wild Butterfly walkway. Adventure playground, Arts and Craft Centre, Granary Tearooms, Animal farm, Wrawby Moor Art Gallery, Falconry Centre. Caravan site. Eight National Awards for Catering and Conservation. An excellent unspoilt venue for a good day out.

Location: Near Brigg on Barton-on-Humber Road A15. 8 m S of the Humber Bridge.
Stations: Elsham (1½ m); Barnetby (2½ m); Humberside Airport Airport 3½ m.
Opening Times: PARK. Easter to mid-Sept—Mons to Sats 11–5; Suns & Bank Hols 11–5.30. *Park closes 6 pm or dusk.* Mid-Sept to Easter—Suns & Bank Hols only 11–4 or dusk. Park closes early in bad weather. Closed Good Friday & Christmas Day. Admission: Price subject to review. Please telephone for Party bookings.
Refreshments: The Granary Tea Room—lunches & fresh teas daily in summer. The special restaurant caters for Sunday lunches. Parties by arrangement. Specialist conference and wedding facilities. Coach parties welcome by arrangement with Administrator.

EPWORTH

The Old Rectory map J8 △
Telephone: Epworth (0427) 872268
(Trustees of the World Methodist Council)

Built 1709. Restored 1957. Childhood home of John & Charles Wesley, oldest Methodist shrine.

Location: In Epworth, 3 m N of Haxey on A161, 18 m E of Doncaster M180 exit 2.
Opening Times: Mar to Oct—Weekdays 10–12, 2–4; Suns 2–4. Adm £1.50, Chd 75p. A/V presentation. Coaches by arrangement only. Accommodation by arrangement.
Refreshments: At the House *by arrangement only.*

MAISTER HOUSE, The National Trust 🌿

Hull map J9
Telephone: Hull (0482) 24114

Rebuilt 1744 with a superb staircase-hall designed in the Palladian manner.

Location: 160 High Street, Hull.
Station: Hull (¾ m).
Opening Times: Staircase and entrance hall only. All the year—Mons to Fris 10–4. *Closed Bank Hols.* Adm by guide book 80p. No dogs. Unsuitable for wheelchairs & parties.

NORMANBY HALL COUNTRY PARK

Scunthorpe map J9
Telephone: Scunthorpe (0724) 720588
(Scunthorpe Borough Council)

A Regency mansion set in 350 acres of beautiful parkland and gardens. Normanby Hall was designed by Sir Robert Smirke (architect of the British Museum) and completed in 1830. It is now leased from the Sheffield family, formerly Dukes of Buckingham and owners of Buckingham Palace, and has been decorated and furnished in period by Scunthorpe Museums and Art Gallery. The spacious Country Park surrounding the Hall provides interest for all the family, with herds of red and fallow deer, wild and exotic birds, lakeside and woodland nature trails, a gift shop, picnic areas, farming museum, and special events.

Location: 4 m N of Scunthorpe on B1430, turn right at Normanby village. Car Park off Thealby Lane.
Opening Times: HALL: Easter to Oct—Mons to Fris 11–5, Sat & Sun 1–5, Nov to Mar—by appointment only. *Closed Sats all year.* Adm FREE. Wheelchairs—ground floor only. Guided tours and parties by appointment. PARK: Open during daylight hours, daily throughout the year.
Refreshments: Café in grounds, summer only. Lunches and cream teas by arrangement for Groups.

SEWERBY HALL

Bridlington map K10
(Borough of East Yorkshire)

Built 1714–20 by John Greame with additions 1803. Sewerby Hall occupies a dramatic setting overlooking Bridlington Bay. The 50 acres of gardens of great beauty and botanical interest include fine old English walled garden and small zoo and aviary. There is also an art gallery and a museum which includes the Amy Johnson Trophy Room dedicated to the pioneer woman aviator.

Location: In Bridlington on the cliffs, 2 m NE from centre of town.
Stations: Bridlington (2½ m); Bempton (2 m).
Opening Times: Park open all year—Daily 9–dusk. Art Gallery open Easter to Sept—Suns to Fris 10–12.30, 1.30–6; Sats 1.30–6. Provisional adm £1.20, Chd 60p (including zoo and art gallery). (Concessions granted to organised parties.)
Refreshments: Self-service snack bar in the Hall (summer season only).

SLEDMERE HOUSE 🏛

Driffield   map J10
Telephone: (0377) 86028
(Sir Tatton Sykes, Bart)

A Georgian house begun in 1751 with important additions attributed to Samuel Wyatt in conjunction with Sir Christopher Sykes, containing superb library 100ft long. The entire building was burnt to the ground in 1911 and splendidly restored with an Edwardian feeling for space by York architect Walter Brierley during the first world war. The latter copied Joseph Rose's fine ceilings and inserted a magnificent Turkish room. The House contains much of its original furniture and paintings. An unusual feature is the great organ, which is played daily 2–4. Capability Brown Park. 18th century walled rose garden. Main garden under reconstruction.

Location: 24 m E of York on main York/Bridlington Road; 8 m NW of Driffield at junction of B1251 & B1253.
Opening Times: Easter weekend, Apr 17 to Sept 27 – Daily (except Mons and Fris); open all Bank Hols; 1.30–5.30 (last adm 5). Adm £2.75, Chd £1.50, OAPs £2.30. Special rates for booked parties; grounds only £1, Chd 60p. Private parties arranged by appointment on Weds evenings. Free Car Park and Coach Parks. Illustrated brochure from The House Secretary, Sledmere House, Driffield, East Yorkshire.
Refreshments: Self service licensed restaurant, Driffield (0377) 86208.

THORNTON ABBEY ⊞

map J9
Telephone: (0469) 40357

The great crenellated gatehouse demonstrates that Thornton was one of the richer monasteries of the Augustinian Order. It was founded about 1139 by William le Gros, Earl of Albemarle, who is buried here. The dissolution of the monastery in the 16th century gave rise to a macabre legend – that the remains of a monk had been found walled up in a room, seated at a table with a book, pen and ink.

Location: 2 m (3.2 km) north east of Thornton Curtis. OS map ref TA115190.
Opening Times: Good Friday or Apr 1 (whichever is earlier) to Sept 30: Open Daily 10–6. Oct 1 to Maundy Thursday or Mar 31 (whichever is earlier): Open Weekends only 10–4. *Closed* Dec 24–26, Jan 1. Adm £1.10, Concessions 85p, Chd 55p.

WILBERFORCE HOUSE

Hull   map J9   ⓢ
Telephone: Hull (0482) 593902
(Hull City Council)

17th century Merchant's house, now a local history museum with period furniture. Hull silver, costume, dolls, toys and adjoining chemists' shop. New displays were opened in 1983 to commemorate the 150th Anniversary of the Death of William Wilberforce, the slave emancipator, born in the house in 1759. Secluded gardens.

Location: 25 High Street, Hull.
Station: Hull.
Opening Times: All the year – Weekdays 10–5; Suns 1.30–4.30. *Closed Good Friday, Christmas Day, Boxing Day & New Year's Day.* Adm free.

ISLE OF WIGHT

APPULDURCOMBE HOUSE ⊞

map J2
Telephone: (0983) 852484

The only house in the 'grand manner' on the Island, Appuldurcombe (pronounced 'Applercombe') was a status symbol and not a home. Sir Robert Worsley started the house in 1701 but ran out of money. The east façade, a beautiful example of English baroque, dates from this year. The house was not completed until the end of the century. The house is now an empty shell but still stands in its fine park, moulded by 'Capability' Brown.

Location: ½ m (0.8 km) west of Wroxall. OS map ref SZ543800.
Opening Times: Good Friday or Apr 1 (whichever is earlier) to Sept 30: Open Daily 10–6. Oct 1 to Maundy Thursday or Mar 31 (whichever is earlier): Open Tues to Sun 10–4. *Closed* Dec 24–26, Jan 1. Adm £1.10, Concessions 85p, Chd 55p.

CARISBROOKE CASTLE ⊞

map H2
Telephone: (0983) 522107

Here are seven acres of castle and earthworks to explore. The oldest parts of the castle are 12th century, but the great mound – 71 steps high – bore a wooden castle before that, and there are fragments of Roman wall at its base. Fortified against the French, then the Spaniards, the castle is best known as the prison of Charles I in 1647/8. A bold escape plan failed when the King became wedged between the bars of the great chamber window. The castle contains the island's museum. A personal stereo guided tour is available.

Location: 1¼ m (2 km) south west of Newport. OS map ref SZ486877.
Opening Times: Good Friday or Apr 1 (whichever is earlier) to Sept 30: Open Daily 10–6. Oct 1 to Maundy Thursday or Mar 31 (whichever is earlier): Open Daily 10–4. *Closed* Dec 24 –26, Jan 1. Adm £3, Concessions £2.30, Chd £1.50.

THE NEEDLES OLD BATTERY, The National Trust

West Highdown, Totland Bay   map H2
Telephone: Isle of Wight 754772

A former Palmerstonian fort built in 1862, 77m above sea level; 60m tunnel to spectacular view of the Needles. Exhibition on history of the Needles Headland.

Location: West Highdown, Totland Bay.
Opening Times: Mar 29 to Nov 1 – Daily, except Fris & Sats but open Good Friday, Apr 17 to Apr 30, Easter Sat, and daily from May 24 to Oct 1 10.30–5. (Last admission 4.30). Adm £2, Chd half price. No reduction for parties.
Refreshments: Tearoom open same days as Battery.

NEWTOWN OLD TOWN HALL, The National Trust

Newtown   map H2

18th century building of brick and stone. One of the buildings surviving from the island's former ancient borough.

Location: In Newtown, midway between Newport and Yarmouth.
Opening Times: Apr 1 to end Sept: Mons, Weds & Suns 2–5; (also open Good Friday, Easter Sat and Sun, and Tues and Thurs in July and Aug), (last adm 4.45). *Closed Oct to end March.* Adm £1, Chd half price. No reduction for parties. No dogs. Unsuitable for wheelchairs.

NUNWELL HOUSE AND GARDENS

Brading   map J2
Telephone: Isle of Wight (0983) 407240
(Colonel & Mrs J A Aylmer)

Nunwell with its historic connections with King Charles I is set in beautiful gardens and parkland with channel views. A finely furnished home with Jacobean and Georgian wings. Home Guard museum and family military collection.

Location: 1 m from Brading, turning off A3055; 3 m S of Ryde.
Station: Brading.
Opening Times: HOUSE AND GARDENS: July 5 to Sept 24, Sun–Thurs 10–5. Adm £2.30, OAP £1.80, accompanied Chd 60p, school parties £1.15. *Closed* Fri and Sat. Coach and School parties welcome at all times by appointment. No dogs.
Refreshments: Large parties may book catering in advance. Picnic areas.

OSBORNE HOUSE

East Cowes   map H3
Telephone: (0983) 200022
(English Heritage)

This was Queen Victoria's seaside residence built at her own expense, in 1845. The Prince Consort played a prominent part in the design of the house, it was his version of an Italian villa, and the work was carried out by Thomas Cubitt, the famous London builder. The Queen died here in 1901 and her private apartments have been preserved more or less unaltered. Crowded with furniture and bric-a-brac they epitomise the style we call 'Victorian'. Also see the Queen's bathing machine. There is a carriage drawn by horse running from House to the Swiss Cottage Gardens and Museum. This is included in the adm price, see below for details.

Location: 1 m SE of East Cowes. OS map ref SZ 516948.
Station: Ferry terminal East Cowes (1 m).
Opening Times: Good Friday or Apr 1 (whichever is earlier) to Sept 30: daily 10–6, Oct 1 to 31 daily 10–5. House: *closed*, but Swiss Cottage, Grounds and carriage run open. Adm: £2, Concessions £1.50, Chd £1. June 9 to Oct 31: open daily. House 10–5, grounds 10–6. Adm £5, Concessions £4, Chd £3.

YARMOUTH CASTLE

map H2
Telephone: (0983) 760678

Part of the coastal defences of Henry VIII, Yarmouth embodied the very latest fashion in military engineering. Completed in 1547, it is square in plan, and washed on two sides by the sea. During the Civil War the island was strongly royalist and throughout the Commonwealth Cromwell kept a large garrison here. When Sir Robert Holmes was appointed Captain of the Island in 1667, the castle was already outmoded and ineffective. He reduced it in size, filled in the moat and built himself a house – now the hotel – on the site. There is a site display and an exhibition of paintings.

Location: Yarmouth. OS map ref SZ354898.
Opening Times: Good Friday or Apr 1 (whichever is earlier) to Sept 30: Open Daily 10–6. Adm £1.50, Concessions £1.10, Chd 75p.

KENT

BEDGEBURY NATIONAL PINETUM

nr Goudhurst   map L3
Telephone: (0580) 211044
(Forestry Commission Research Station)

Has the most comprehensive collection of conifers in Europe. Conifers from all continents are planted in generic groups within 160 acres. Landscaped with grass avenues, paths, stream valleys, ridges and a lake. Rhododendrons, azaleas, maples and uncommon oak species add colour in spring and autumn.

Location: On B2079, 1 m from A21 London to Hastings travelling towards Goudhurst.
Opening Times: Daily 10 till dusk. Adm £1.50, OAP £1, Chd 75p. Visitor centre: open daily Easter to 11–5, and daily during Oct 12–4. Car parking. Difficult for wheelchairs.
Refreshments: In nearby villages, ice cream vendor in car park and light refreshments available in visitor centre.

BELMONT 🏛

nr Faversham   map L4   &dh;   △
Telephone: (0795) 890202
(Harris (Belmont) Charity)

Belmont was built in the late 18th century to the design of Samuel Wyatt, in a splendid elevated position with commanding views over the attractive and unspoilt countryside. It has been the seat of the Harris family since it was acquired in 1801 by General George Harris, the victor of Seringapatam. The Mansion remains in its original state and contains interesting mementos of the family's connections with India and the finest collection of clocks in any English country house open to the public.

Location: 4 m SSW of Faversham. W of A251 follow signs from Badlesmere.
Opening Times: Easter Sun to end Sept — Sat, Sun and Bank Hol Mons. Guided tours 2–5. Last adm 4.30. Telephone 079 589 202 to confirm availability. Groups (minimum 10) by prior arrangement only, Tues and Thurs. Adm to Mansion, Grounds and Clock Museum £3.50, Chd £2. Car parking. Shop.
Refreshments: Teas in the Stables Tearoom Sat, Sun and Bank Hol Mons June 1 to end Sept. Pre-booked parties by arrangement.

BLACK CHARLES

nr Sevenoaks   map K4
Telephone: Hildenborough (0732) 833036
(Mr & Mrs Hugh Gamon)

Charming 14th century home of John de Blakecherl and his family. A hall house with beautiful panelling, fireplaces and many other interesting features.

Location: 3 m S of Sevenoaks off A21; 1 m E in the village of Underriver.
Opening Times: Open to groups by appointment (minimum of 10).

BOUGHTON MONCHELSEA PLACE – *See page 103*

CHARTWELL, The National Trust 🦋

Westerham   map K4   &dh;
Telephone: Edenbridge 866368

The home for many years of Sir Winston Churchill.

Location: 2 m S of Westerham off B2026.
Opening Times: House. Mar to end Nov: Mar & Nov — Sats, Suns & Weds only 11–4.30 except Mar 21 when house will be closed; Apr to end Oct — Tues, Weds, Thurs 12–5.30; Sats, Suns & Bank Hol Mons 11–5.30 (last adm 30 minutes before closing). Closed Good Fri and Tues following Bank Hol. All Tues mornings (except after Bank Hols) reserved for prebooked parties and guided tours.
Garden & Studio: Apr to end Oct — Same times as house. Adm House & Garden £3.80, Chd £1.90. Garden only £1.60, Chd 80p. Studio 50p extra (Chd no reduction). Pre-booked parties, Tues mornings only, £3.10, Chd £1.60. Parties welcome on other days; no need to book, no reduction. Write to the Administrator, Chartwell, Westerham, Kent. Car Park. Lavatory for disabled.
Refreshments: Restaurant open from Apr to end Oct — 10.30–5 (Mar & Nov: 10.30–4) on days when house is open. Self-service, licensed (no spirits).

CHIDDINGSTONE CASTLE – *See page 104*

CHILHAM CASTLE GARDENS 🏛

nr Canterbury   map L4
Telephone: Canterbury 730319
(Viscount Massereene & Ferrard DL)

25 acre garden with formal terraces first made by Tradescant when the Jacobean house was built by the side of the old Norman Castle Keep. Informal lake garden. Magnificent views and many fine trees. Birds of Prey on display and flying free, afternoons daily except Mon and Fri. Gift shop. Medieval banquets, dinners, wedding receptions in Gothic Hall. Special events as advertised. House open by appointment only.

Location: In Chilham village, 6 m W of Canterbury (A252); 8 m NE of Ashford (A28); 22 m NW of Dover, Faversham turn off M2.
Station: Chilham (1 m).
Opening Times: Apr to mid-Oct—Daily (inc Bank Hols). Open from 11 am. Adm weekdays £2,80. Chd half-price. Free parking. Coaches welcome. Special rates for parties on application.
Refreshments: Jacobean tea room.

COBHAM HALL — *See below*

BOUGHTON MONCHELSEA PLACE

nr Maidstone   map L4   △
Telephone: Maidstone (0622) 743120
(Charles W. Gooch)

Battlemented Elizabethan Manor of Kentish ragstone built in 1567, with interesting Regency alterations. Dramatically situated with breathtaking view over its own landscaped park, in which fallow deer have roamed for at least 300 years, and beyond, to the whole Weald of Kent. The beautiful interior is still that of an intimate and inhabited home to which successive generations have added new treasures. Dress display and early farm implements. Manor records. Walled flower gardens with interesting plants. Tudor kitchen and Garden tearooms. The House and Grounds are available for private hire, wedding receptions, lunches, suppers and dinners. Also clay shoots, ballooning, archery. Further land is available for other activities. Contact (0622) 743120,

Location: On B2163. In village of Boughton Monchelsea 5 m S of Maidstone. Turn off Maidstone/Hastings Road (A229) at Linton.
Opening Times: Good Fri to early Oct—Suns & Bank Hols (also Weds during July & Aug) 2.15–6. House & Grounds Adm £3, Chd (under 14) £1.75. Grounds only Adm £2, Chd (under 14) £1.50. *Parties welcome any day, at special rates, but only by previous engagement.*
Refreshments: Tea rooms at the House. For parties lunch or supper can be ordered in advance.

COBHAM HALL

nr Rochester   map L4
Telephone: Shorne 3371
(Westwood Educational Trust Ltd)

Charming mixture of Gothic and Renaissance architecture. The 150 acres of grounds with giant cedars, other specimen trees and 100 year old lawns provide a good example of Repton's landscape gardening. Fine example of work of James Wyatt. Family gilded State Coach built in 1715, and gilt Banqueting Hall. Now an independent girls' school.

Location: 4 m W of Rochester on Watling Street & Rochester Way (B2009 off A2). 27 m from London.
Station: Sole Street (1¹/₂ m).
Opening Times: Apr 5, 8, 9, 12, 17, 19, 20, 22, 23; July 26, 29, 30; Aug 5, 6, 9, 12, 13, 16, 19, 20, 23, 26, 27, 31, 2–5 (last tour 5). Adm £2, Chd & OAPs £1. No reduction for parties.
Refreshments: Teas and light refreshments, enquiries (0474 82) 3371.

CRITTENDEN HOUSE

Matfield   map L3
(B P Tompsett, Esq)

Garden completely planned and planted since 1956 on labour-saving lines. Spring shrubs, roses, lilies, foliage, waterside planting of ponds in old iron workings. Of interest from the early Spring bulbs to Autumn colour. Garden featured in RHS Journal Apr 1990.

Location: 5 m SE of Tonbridge off B2160.
Opening Times: GARDENS ONLY. Suns Mar 29, Apr 5, 19, June 21, Mons Apr 20, May 4, 25 in aid of *National Gardens Scheme.* Sun, May 17; RSPCA; Sun June 7; *Save the Children Fund* 2–6. Adm £1.25, Chd under 12 yrs 25p. Cars free. **No dogs.**

CHIDDINGSTONE CASTLE

nr Edenbridge   map K4   ♿
Telephone: Penshurst (0892) 870347
(Trustees of the Denys Eyre Bower Bequest)

Chiddingstone Castle: the dream-child of two romantics. Squire Henry Streatfeild, who c.1805 had his family seat transformed into a fantasy castle, and whose money ran out; and Denys Eyre Bower, inspired and eccentric art collector, who never had any money at all. Entranced with the (by then) semi-ruinous Castle, he made it his home in 1955. When he died in 1977 he left it and its fascinating contents to the Nation. It is still a home, lovingly restored and cared for, untouched by commercialism. An afternoon is all too short to enjoy fully the fine furniture and pictures, Egyptian antiquities, Stuart and Jacobite memorabilia, and the Japanese swords and armour and incomparable lacquer. The landscaped park and grotto are still in course of restoration. Souvenir Shop. The grounds and Goodhugh Wing available (with catering) for functions and small conferences. For information, apply to Administrator. Good coarse fishing in lake in season £8 per day. One onlooker allowed per fisherman, £3. Picnics allowed adjacent car park, but not in grounds. Dogs on lead in grounds.

Location: in Chiddingstone village, off the Edenbridge–Tonbridge road B2027 at Bough Beech. Approximately ten miles Sevenoaks, Tonbridge and Tunbridge Wells.
Stations: Penshurst 2½ miles, Edenbridge 4 miles.
Opening Times: Apr 4 to Oct 31. Apr, May and Oct: public holidays, Weds, Sats and Suns only. June to Sept: Tues to Suns and public holidays. Weekdays (inc. Sats) 2–5.30, Suns and public holidays 11.30–5.30. Last adm 5. Open all year round for booked parties of 20 or more, by special arrangement. Adm for House, Grounds and Car Park: £3, Chd (between 5–15) £1.50 – under 5 free. All children to be in charge of adult. Booked parties of 20 or more £2.75 at times when Castle open to public. Special fee at other times.
Refreshments: Tea, coffee and cookies in tearoom (seats 25). Special teas, lunches and light refreshments for parties of 20 or more in private room must be booked.

DEAL CASTLE ▓

map M4
Telephone: Deal Castle (0304) 372762
(English Heritage)

When Henry VIII divorced Catherine of Aragon he defied the Pope and broke with Catholic Europe. Deal and Walmer were built under the threat of a 'crusade' against Henry—an invasion which never came. Deal contains an exhibition on the coastal defences of Henry VIII. At Walmer the atmosphere is country house rather than martial, for this has long been the official residence of the Lords Warden of the Cinque Ports. One of the best remembered is the Duke of Wellington (the original 'Wellington boot' may be seen here), and one of the best loved, Queen Elizabeth the Queen Mother.

Location: Deal Castle is near the town centre. OS map ref TR378521.
Opening Times: Deal: Good Friday or Apr 1 (whichever is earlier) to Sept 30: Open Daily 10–6. Oct 1 to Maundy Thursday or Mar 31 (whichever is earlier): Open Tues to Sun 10–4. *Closed* Dec 24–26, Jan 1. Adm £1.60, Concessions £1.20, Chd 80p. Admission price includes a Personal Stereo Guided Tour.

DODDINGTON PLACE GARDENS

nr Sittingbourne ME9 0BB   map L4
Telephone: Doddington (079586) 385
(Mr Richard and The Hon. Mrs Oldfield)

Large landscaped gardens in the grounds of a Victorian country house with good views over surrounding countryside. Edwardian rock garden and formal garden, rhododendrons and azaleas in a woodland setting, fine trees and yew hedges.

Location: 4 m from A2 and A20. 5 m from Faversham. 6 m from Sittingbourne. 12 m from Canterbury.
Opening Times: 11–6 every Wed and Bank Holiday Mon from Easter to end Sept. Also Suns in May only 11–6. Adm £1.50, Chd 25p. Groups of 25 or more and coaches by prior arrangement only. Present shop.
Refreshments: Restaurant serving morning coffee, lunches, afternoon teas.

DOVER CASTLE

map M4
Telephone: (0304) 201628
(English Heritage)

Castle Hill dominates the shortest passage between Britain and the Continent, and has been the scene of military activity from the Iron Age to the present day. Here is extensive proof from every age of man's ingenuity in devising ways to repel invaders. Dover Castle had its narrowest escape in 1216 when in an heroic siege it just managed to hold out against the French. There is much to see, including the Roman lighthouse (now the bell tower of a fine Saxon church) and the great keep itself and a spectacular exhibition 'All the Queen's Men'. The secret war tunnels of the castle are now open to the public. The evacuation of the troops from Dunkirk was planned by Vice-Admiral Ramsay from this once secret base. Entry is by guided tours only; for full details of Hellfire Corner see below.

Location: East side of Dover. OS map ref TR326416.
Opening Times: Good Friday or Apr 1 (whichever is earlier) to Sept 30 daily 10–6. Oct 1 to Maundy Thursday or Mar 31 (whichever is earlier) daily 10–6. *Closed* Dec 24–26, Jan 1. Adm £4.50, Concessions £3.40, Chd £2.30.
Refreshments: in the Keep Yard.

EMMETTS GARDEN, The National Trust

nr Brasted   map K4
Telephone: Ide Hill 429

Hillside shrub garden of 5 acres. Lovely spring and autumn colours, rock garden, formal garden and roses. Further areas of garden being restored and re-planted.

Location: 1½ m S of A25 on Sundridge/Ide Hill Road.
Opening Times: GARDEN ONLY. Apr to end Oct – Wed to Sun, Good Fri, Bank Hol Mon 2–6. Last adm 5. Adm £2.20, Chd £1.10. Pre-booked parties: £1.70, Chd 90p (15 or more). Dogs admitted on lead. Wheelchair access to level parts of garden only. Tearoom.

FINCHCOCKS

Goudhurst   map L3
Telephone: Goudhurst (0580) 211702
(Mr & Mrs Richard Burnett)

Finchcocks, dated 1725, is a fine example of Georgian baroque architecture, noted for its fine brickwork, with a front elevation attributed to Thomas Archer. It is set in beautiful gardens and parkland near the village of Goudhurst. The house contains a magnificent collection of historic keyboard instruments which are restored to full playing condition, and provides a unique setting where visitors can hear music performed on the instruments for which it was written. Demonstration tours and music whenever the house is open.

Location: 1½ m W of Goudhurst, 10 m E of Tunbridge Wells off A262.
Opening Times: Easter to Sept 27 – Suns; also Bank Hol Mons & Weds to Suns in Aug: 2–6. Demonstrations & Music on instruments of the collection on Open Days. Adm £4.20, Chd £2.80. Family ticket £10. Free parking.
Refreshments: Teas available.

GAD'S HILL PLACE

Rochester map L4
(Gads Hill School Ltd)

Grade 1 listed building, built in 1780. Home of Charles Dickens from 1857 to 1870. Adm £1.50, Chd/OAPs £1, parties by arrangement. Proceeds to restoration fund.

Location: On A226; 3 m from Rochester, 4 m from Gravesend.
Station: Higham (1 m).
Opening Times: By prior appointment only. Apply to the Headmistress, Gad's Hill School, Higham, Rochester. Tel. 047482 2366.
Refreshments: Food & Drink available at Sir John Falstaff Inn opposite House.

GODINTON PARK – *See below*

GOODNESTONE PARK 🏛

nr Canterbury map M4
(The Lord & Lady FitzWalter)

The garden is approximately 14 acres, with many fine trees, a woodland garden and the walled garden with a large collection of old roses and herbaceous plants. The house has a fine collection of family portraits and furniture. Jane Austen was a frequent visitor, her brother Edward having married a daughter of the house.

Location: 8 m SE of Canterbury; 4 m E of A2; ¼ m SE of B2046; S of A257.
Station: Adisham (2 m).
Opening Times: GARDEN ONLY. **Weekdays:** Mar 30 to Oct 30 (incl. Bank Holidays), Mon to Fri 11–5. Apr 5 to Sept 27: Suns 2–6. July and Aug: Sats 2–6. Adm £1.50, Chd (under 12) 20p, OAP £1.30. Disabled in wheelchairs £1. Parties over 25 £1.30, if guided £1.50. House: Parties only £1. **No dogs.**
Refreshments: Teas. Enquiries: Tel: (0304) 840/218.

GREAT COMP – *See page 107*

GREAT MAYTHAM HALL

Rolvenden map L3
(Country Houses Association Ltd)

Built in 1910 by Sir Edwin Lutyens.

Location: ½ m E of Rolvenden village, on road to Rolvenden Layne.
Opening Times: May to Sept – Weds & Thurs 2–5. Last entry 4.30. Adm £1.50, Chd 50p. Free car park. No dogs admitted.

HAXTED MILL & MUSEUM 🏛

Haxted, nr. Edenbridge map K4
Telephone: Curator, Summer months Edenbridge (0732) 865720. Mr. D.G. Neville. Dorking (0306) 887979 during winter months.

An ancient working watermill and dynamic museum of functioning mill machinery combining to provide a unique illustration of the history, development and uses of water power throughout the centuries. The galleries contains artefacts and working models relating to all aspects of milling. There are special attractions for children – including a den of lions and tigers with their cubs.

Location: 1½ m W of Edenbridge beside road joining B2029 at Lingfield Common with B2026 at Edenbridge.
Opening Times: April to Sept: Weds, Sat, Sun & Bank Hols, 1–5. Guided parties at any time by prior appointment. Adm £2, Chd 75p, OAPs £1. Reductions for parties booked in advance.
Refreshments: Licensed restaurant adjacent, open daily *except Mon.*

GODINTON PARK 🏛

Ashford map L4 △
(Alan Wyndham Green, Esq)

The existing house belongs mostly to Jacobean times though there are records of another house being here in the 15th century. The interior of Godinton contains a wealth of very fine panelling and carving, particularly in the Hall and on the Staircase. The house contains interesting portraits and much fine furniture and china. The gardens were originally laid out in the 18th century and were further extended by Sir Reginald Blomfield with topiary work and formal gardens giving a spacious setting to the house.

Location: 1½ m W of Ashford off Maidstone Road at Potter's Corner (A20).
Station: Ashford (2 m).
Opening Times: Easter Sat, Sun & Mon; then June to Sept – Suns & Bank Hols only 2–5. Adm House & Gardens £1.50, Chd (under 16) 70p. Weekdays by appointment only. Parties of 20 or more £1.20 per person.

GREAT COMP

nr Borough Green   map L4
Telephone: Borough Green 882669
(The Great Comp Charitable Trust)

This outstanding garden of seven acres has been expertly developed by Mr and Mrs Cameron since 1957 to provide interest throughout the year. In a setting of well maintained lawns the carefully designed layout and good use of plants allows the visitor to wander through areas of different character. Around the 17th century house are formal areas of paving, terraces, old brick walls and hedges. These are surrounded by less formal planting providing winding paths, vistas and woodland glades with occasional ornaments and constructed "ruins" for additional interest. A wide variety of trees, shrubs, herbaceous plants and heathers offer inspiration and pleasure and include many which are rarely seen. Good Autumn colour. Nursery open daily with wide range of plants from garden for sale. Music festival and other events in July & September. S.A.E. to R. Cameron, Great Comp, Borough Green, Sevenoaks, Kent TN15 8QS.

Location: 2 m E of Borough Green B2016 off A20. First right at Comp crossroads ½ m on left.
Station: Borough Green & Wrotham (1½ m).
Opening Times: GARDEN AND NURSERY ONLY. Apr 1 to Oct 31 – Daily 11 – 6. Free parking. *Parties by prior arrangement (coaches welcome)*. Adm £2, Chd £1. Guide book £1. Annual tickets £7.50. Annual ticket holders may visit any day Apr to Oct, and out of season on any Sun in Nov, Feb and Mar. *No dogs.* Guided tours and lectures by arrangement.
Refreshments: Teas on Sun and for parties by arrangement.

HEVER CASTLE & GARDENS 🏛

nr Edenbridge map K4
Telephone: Edenbridge (0732) 865224; Fax (0732) 866796
(Broadland Properties Limited)

Enchanting 13th century double-moated castle, childhood home of Queen Anne Boleyn, set in magnificent gardens of 40 acres. The gardens feature fine topiary including a maze, the magnificent Italian garden with statuary and sculpture dating back 2000 years, and the 35 acre lake alongside which visitors can walk and picnic. The Castle was restored and filled with treasures by William Waldorf Astor in 1903. Exhibitions on the Astors of Hever and the life and times of Anne Boleyn. Regimental Museum. Open-air theatre season.

Location: Mid-way between London and S coast, between Sevenoaks and East Grinstead, 3 m SE Edenbridge off B2026. M25 — junction 5/6, 20 mins. M23 — junction 10, 20 mins. *Station: Hever (1 m walk, no taxis available), Edenbridge Town (3 m, taxis available).*
Opening Times: CASTLE & GARDENS open daily — Mar 17 — Nov 8. GARDENS: 11 – 6 (last entry 5pm). CASTLE: opens 12 noon. Dogs on leads gardens only. Adventure playground. Facilities for disabled visitors. Special pre-booked private tours available all year. Special rate for groups. Residential Conferences, private dining, day meetings and receptions available in the Tudor Village linked to the Moated Castle.
Refreshments: Large self-service licensed restaurant. Picnics welcome.

IGHTHAM MOTE, The National Trust

Ivy Hatch map K4
Telephone: Plaxtol 810378

One of the most complete remaining examples of a medieval moated manor house. Major exhibition of building conservation in action.

Location: 3 m S of Ightham, off A227, 4½ m E of Sevenoaks off A25.
Opening Times: Apr to end Oct—Mons, Weds, Thurs, Fris 12–5.30; Suns and Bank Hol Mons 11–5.30 (last adm 5); pre-booked guided tours 11–12 weekdays, no reduction, open Good Friday. Adm weekdays £3.20, Chd £1.60. Sun and Bank Hols £3.70, Chd £1.90. Pre-booked parties (20 or more) weekdays £2.70, Chd £1.40. Pre-booked guided tours, 11–12 weekdays only, no reductions.
Refreshments: Tea pavilion in car park.

KNOLE, The National Trust

Sevenoaks map K4   △
Telephone: Sevenoaks 450608

One of the largest private houses in England, dating mainly from 15th century, with splendid Jacobean interior and fine collection of 17th century furniture.

Location: At the Tonbridge end of Sevenoaks, just E of A225; 25 m from London.
Station: Sevenoaks (1½ m)
Opening Times: Apr to end of Oct—Weds to Sats (inc Good Fri) & Bank Hol Mons 11–5; Suns 2–5. Last Adm 4. Guided tours Tues only, for pre-booked parties of 25 or more, no reduction. GARDEN: May to Sept, first Wed in every month. Adm: £3.50, Chd £1.80 (£4, Chd £2 Fri – extra rooms shown). GARDEN ONLY: 50p. Pre-booked parties of 25 or more £2.30, Chd £1.20. Wheelchairs: park and gardens only. Parking £6 (£6.50 Fri) includes one admission.

LADHAM HOUSE

Goudhurst map L3
(Betty, Lady Jessel)

10 acres of rolling lawns, fine specimen trees, rhododendrons, azaleas, camellias, shrubs and magnolias. Newly planted arboretum. Spectacular twin mixed borders. Fountain garden and bog garden. Fine view.

Location: 11 m E of Tunbridge Wells off A262 on NE of village.
Opening Times: Garden only. Suns May 3, 10, July 19: (11–6). *Open other times by appointment and for coaches:* Adm £2, Chd (under 12) 50p. *In aid of National Gardens Scheme.* Free parking.
Refreshments: Teas served on the 3 open days, but not on days arranged by appointment.

LEEDS CASTLE

nr Maidstone map L4
Telephone: Maidstone (0622) 765400. Telex: 965737. Fax: (0622) 735616
(Leeds Castle Foundation)

Leeds Castle stands as one of the most beautiful and ancient Castles in the Kingdom, rising from its two small islands in the middle of a lake and surrounded by 500 acres of magnificent parkland and gardens. Dating back to the 9th century and rebuilt by the Normans in 1119, Leeds Castle was then a Royal Palace for over three centuries. It now contains a superb collection of mediaeval furnishings, French and English furniture, tapestries and paintings. You can wander down through the Duckery into the woodland and water gardens, where peacocks and swans roam free. Visit the aviaries with rare tropical birds and the Culpeper Garden full of old fashioned flowers and fragrance. See a fascinating underground grotto at the centre of the maze and visit the greenhouses and vineyard. There's also a museum of Medieval Dog Collars in the 13th century Gate Tower. Or, come and play our 9-hole golf course. Beautiful gifts available from the Castle Shop and Plant Shops. Now owned by the Leeds Castle Foundation, a private Charitable Trust, the Castle is also used as a high level residential conference centre.

Special Events: New Year's Day Treasure Trail: Wed, Jan 1; **Easter Egg Hunt:** Sat Apr 18 to Mon Apr 20; **Wine Festival:** Sat May 16 to Sun May 17; **Balloon and Bentley Fiesta:** Sat June 6 to June 7; **Open Air Concerts:** (Advance ticket sales only) Sat June 27 and Sat July 4; **Flower Festival:** Fri Sept 18 to Mon Sept 21; **Grand Firework Display:** Sat Nov 7; **Kentish Evening Dinners:** Sats all year except Aug (by reservation); **Special Christmas Shop:** daily from Nov 1 to Dec 23.

Location: 4 m E of Maidstone; access on B2163 at junction 8 of the M20.
Station: Bearsted or Hollingbourne (2 m). Inclusive rail/admission tickets from British Rail, Victoria Station to Bearsted.
Opening Times: Mar 16 to Oct 31—Daily 11–5*. Nov to Mar—Sats & Suns only 11–4* (*last admission to grounds). Also daily in Christmas week (Dec 26 to Jan 1). Special events programme. Kentish Evening Dinners Sats throughout year except Aug. Reduced prices for Chd (under 16) Students & OAPs, Family tickets, also for Groups and School Parties who are welcomed at any time all year round, by appointment. Picnic area. Car park. Passenger trailer takes elderly visitors from car park to Castle. Facilities for the disabled. Regret no dogs.
NB The Trustees reserve the right to close all or parts of the Castle for Government seminars. Closed June 27, July 4 & Nov 7 for Open Air Concerts & Fireworks Display.
Refreshments: Lunch and refreshments available in licensed restaurants and the Fast Food outlets in the Stable Courtyard.

LULLINGSTONE CASTLE

Eynsford   map L4
Telephone: Farningham (0322) 862114
(Guy Hart Dyke, Esq)

Family portraits, armour, Henry VII gateway. Church.

Location: In the Darenth valley via Eynsford on A225.
Station: Eynsford (1/2 m).
Opening Times: CASTLE & GROUNDS. Apr to Oct, Sats, Suns, Bank Hols 2–6. Adm £3, Chd £1, OAPs
£2.50, Weds, Thurs & Fris 2–6 by arrangement. No dogs. Free car parking. Telephone for
enquiries or bookings.
Refreshments: In the gatehouse tea rooms.

LULLINGSTONE ROMAN VILLA ⛩

map K4
Telephone: (0322) 863467
(Closed for refurbishment in 1990.)

The ancient Romans understood the art of gracious living. In this country villa they
walked on mosaic floors, dined off fine tableware and commissioned elaborate wall
paintings to decorate one of the earliest churches in Britain.

Location: 1/2 m (0.8 km) south west of Eynsford. OS map ref TQ529651.
Opening Times: Good Friday or Apr 1 (whichever is earlier) to Sept 30: Open Daily 10–6.
Oct 1 to Maundy Thursday or Mar 31 (whichever is earlier): Open Tues to Sun 10–4. *Closed*
Dec 24–26, Jan 1. Adm £1.50, Concessions £1.10, Chd 75p. Admission prices include a
Personal Stereo Guided Tour.

LYMPNE CASTLE

nr Hythe   map M3
Telephone: Hythe (0303) 267571
(Harry Margary, Esq)

This romantic medieval castle with an earlier Roman, Saxon and Norman history was
once owned by the Archdeacons of Canterbury. It was rebuilt about 1360, and
restored in 1905, 300 feet above the well known Roman Shore Fort – Stutfall Castle.
Four miles from the ancient Cinque Port of Hythe, it commands a tremendous view
across Romney Marshes to Fairlight over the great sweep of the coast from Dover to
Dungeness and across the sea to France. Terraced gardens with magnificent views out
to sea.

Location: 3 m NW of Hythe off B2067, 8m W of Folkestone.
Station: Sandling (2 1/2 m).
Opening Times: Easter to Sept 30 – Daily 10.30–6. *Parties by appointment.* Adm £1.50, Chd
50p. *Closed, occasionally on Sats.*

MOUNT EPHRAIM 🏛

Hernhill, nr Faversham   map L4
Telephone: Canterbury (0227) 751310 or 751496.
(Mrs M N Dawes & Mr & Mrs E S Dawes)

Mount Ephraim has been the Dawes home for 300 years but the present gardens were
laid out around 1912. By the end of the Second World War they were badly overgrown
and it has taken many years to reclaim them. With some simplifications their old
beauty and serenity have been restored. The site is magnificent, with views over the
Thames estuary and rose terraces sloping down to a small lake and woodland area.
There are many fine trees, a topiary garden, a herbaceous border and an extensive
Japanese rock garden with a series of pools and a diversity of plants and shrubs. A
new vineyard and water garden are added attractions.

Location: 6 m W of Canterbury, 3 m E of Faversham; 1/2 m N of A2 at Boughton.
Opening Times: GARDENS ONLY. Apr 19 to end Sept 2–6. Adm £1.50, Chd 25p. Parties by
prior arrangement.
Refreshments: Teas available. Suns only.

NEW COLLEGE OF COBHAM

Cobham   map L4   ♿
Telephone: Meopham (0474) 814280
(Presidents of the New College of Cobham)

Almshouses based on medieval chantry built 1362, part rebuilt 1598. Originally
endowed by Sir John de Cobham and descendants.

Location: 4 m W of Rochester; 4 m SE of Gravesend; 1 1/2 m from junction Shorne/ Cobham
(A2). In Cobham rear of Church of Mary Magdalene.
Station: Sole St (1 m).
Opening Times: Apr to Sept – Daily (except Thurs) 10–7. Oct to Mar – Mons, Tues, Weds,
Sats & Suns 10–4.
Refreshments: Afternoon teas by prior arrangement

NORTHBOURNE COURT GARDENS

Deal   map M4
Telephone: (0304) 611281
(The Lord Northbourne)

Northbourne Court is on the site of a palace which belonged to Eadbald, son of
Ethelbert Saxon King of Kent. In 618 he gave it to the monks of St Augustines Abbey
who used the produce from the farms and fish ponds for the support of the poor. After
the dissolution it reverted to the crown and finally King James I gave it to Sir Edwyn
Sandys. Sir Edwyn built a large house facing three tiers of terraces, which were
probably built by Edwin Saunders. These terraces and their high flanking walls are
still standing and provide the principal architectural feature of the gardens. The
terrace forms a mount which is a rarely surviving characteristic of Tudor Gardens.
These gardens are planted with a wide range of old fashioned and grey foliage plants
on chalk soil to provide interest and colour all year round.

Location: A256 (Dover to Sandwich). Turn right towards Deal/Mongeham and continue for
approximately 2 m.
Opening Times: Suns May 3, 24, June 7, 21, July 5, 19, Aug 2, 16, 30, Sept 13: 2–6. Adm
£2.50, Chd/OAP £1.50 in aid of *National Gardens Scheme.* Plenty of car/coach parking
nearby. Limited access for disabled persons (no wheelchairs available).
Refreshments: Pub in village serves good food.

OWL HOUSE GARDENS

Lamberhurst map L3
(Maureen, Marchioness of Dufferin & Ava)

PENSHURST PLACE – *See page 112*

PORT LYMPNE
ZOO PARK, MANSION & GARDENS

Lympne, Hythe map M3
Telephone: Hythe (0303) 264646/264647
(John Aspinall, Esq)

Built for Sir Philip Sassoon between 1911 and 1915, and described as the 'last historic house built this century', Port Lympne encompasses the essence of Roman villas and the English country house. Overlooking the Romney Marsh and Channel and set in 15 acres of terraced gardens around the Trojan Stairway of 125 steps, the interior of the Mansion features a Moorish Patio, marble columns, an intriguing mosaic hall floor, plus the rare Rex Whistler Tent Room, and the new Spencer Roberts Mural Room and other wildlife Exhibitions. The principal architect was Sir Herbert Baker who designed New Delhi. Bought and restored by Mr John Aspinall in 1973, it is now open to the public together with its 300 acre rare wildlife park. Gorillas, lions, tigers, rhinos and many more rare animals. Gift shop. Picnic areas. Safari trailer, check for service times.

Location: 3 m W of Hythe; 6 m W of Folkestone; 7 m SE of Ashford off A20.
Opening Times: All the year – Daily. Summer 10–5*; Winter 10–one hour before dusk* (*last admissions). *Closed Christmas Day.* Reduced prices for OAPs and Chld 4–14 (3 and under free). Special party rates. Free car park. (Some areas not suitable for disabled.)
Refreshments: Licensed restaurant and kiosks in summer.

13 acres of romantic gardens surround this 16th century timber framed wool smuggler's cottage. Spring flowers, roses, rare flowering shrubs and ornamental fruit trees. Expansive lawns lead to leafy woodland walks graced by English and Turkish oaks, elm, birch and beech trees. Rhododendrons, azaleas, camellias encircle peaceful informal sunken water gardens.

Location: 8 m SE of Tunbridge Wells; 1 m from Lamberhurst off A21.
Opening Times: GARDENS ONLY. All the year – daily and weekends including all Bank Hol weekends 11–6. Adm £2, Chd £1. (Proceeds towards Lady Dufferin's charity, Maureen's Oast House for Arthritics.) Dogs on lead. Free parking. Coach parties welcome.

PENSHURST PLACE

Tunbridge Wells   map K4   △
Telephone: Penshurst (0892) 870307
(The Rt Hon Viscount De L'Isle, MBE)

The early house, including the Great Hall, dates from 1340. There were later additions but the whole house conforms to the English Gothic style in which it was begun. Regarded as one of Britain's outstanding Stately Homes, with fine State Rooms and famous medieval Great Hall. Ten acre walled garden with hedged enclosures. Farm museum. Park, Venture Playground with Tuckshop and Nature Trail.

Location: In Penshurst village on B2176, W of Tonbridge & Tunbridge Wells.
Station: Penshurst (2 m).
Opening Times: Penshurst Place is open every day from Apr 1 to Oct 4. Grounds only open weekends in Mar and Oct, 11 to dusk. Grounds 11–6. House 1–5.30 (last entry to House is 5). Reduced adm rates for groups, OAPs and Chd. Free car park for visitors. No dogs admitted. For all enquiries and party bookings please contact Penshurst Place, Penshurst, Tonbridge, Kent TN11 8DG. Tel: (0892) 870307.
Refreshments: Light luncheons and teas available.

QUEBEC HOUSE, The National Trust 🦌

Westerham   map K4
Telephone: Westerham 62206

Probably early 16th century in origin, now mainly 17th century. Mementos of General Wolfe, and colourful exhibition about the Battle of Quebec.

Location: At junction of Edenbridge & Sevenoaks Roads (A25 & B2026).
Opening Times: Apr to end Oct – Daily (except Thurs & Sats), inc Good Fri and Bank Hol Mon 2–6. Last adm 5.30. Adm £2, Chd £1. *Pre-booked parties £1.40, Chd 70p.* No dogs. Unsuitable for wheelchairs.

QUEX HOUSE, QUEX PARK 🏛

Birchington   map M4
Telephone: Thanet (0843) 42168
(Trustees of the Powell-Cotton Museum)

Wander through the period rooms of P.H.G. Powell-Cotton's mansion, Quex House, the only stately home in Thanet, with its superb woodcarving and panelling, beautiful plasterwork and an air of mellow maturity. The rooms are arranged much as they were in his lifetime and contain fine 17th and 18th century English furniture and many family treasures. The unique Chinese Imperial porcelain collection, however, has been moved into its own gallery in the Powell-Cotton Museum as have the English and Continental porcelain collections. This purpose-built museum, adjoining the Mansion, now extends to nine large galleries; here Powell-Cotton created huge dioramas showing 500 African and Asian animals, all mounted by Rowland Ward, in scenes re-creating their natural habitats. He assembled the world's finest collection of African ethnography gathered on his 28 expeditions, and displayed it at Quex, together with superb weapons collections, cannon, local archaeological material and outstanding fine arts from many countries of the Orient.

Location: In Birchington, ½ m S of Birchington Square (signposted). SW of Margate; 13 m E of Canterbury.
Station: Birchington (1 m).
Opening Times: Easter to Sept 30 – Weds, Thurs & Suns (also Fris in Aug): 2.15–6. Open Bank Hols in summer. Adm £1.50, OAPs £1, Chd £1 (last entry 5). Museum only open in winter Sun afternoons, reduced rates. Parties on other days by arrangement. Ground floor rooms & museum only, suitable for disabled. Free car and coach parking.
Refreshments: Tea-room, light refreshments, summer only.

RICHBOROUGH CASTLE ⬚

map M4
Telephone: (0304) 612013

The sea has deserted Richborough, but as Rutupiae it was well-known in Roman times as a seaport. It was here that the conquering Roman army landed in AD 43. The massive stone walls were built in the 3rd century to combat the ferocious attacks of Saxon sea-raiders. A personal stereo guided tour is available.

Location: 1½ m (2.4 km) north of Sandwich. OS map ref TR324602.
Opening Times: Good Friday or Apr 1 (whichever is earlier) to Sept 30: Open Daily 10–6. Oct 1 to Maundy Thursday or Mar 31 (whichever is earlier): Open Tues to Sun 10–4. *Closed* Dec 24–26, Jan 1. Adm £1.40, Concessions £1.10, Chd 75p.

RIVERHILL HOUSE 🏛

Sevenoaks   map K4   △
Telephone: Sevenoaks (0732) 452557/458802
(John Rogers Esq)

Small Ragstone house built in 1714 and home of the Rogers family since 1840. Panelled rooms, portraits and interesting memorabilia. An historic garden with rare trees and shrubs. Sheltered terraces and rhododendrons and azaleas in woodland setting. Bluebells. Ancient trackway known as "Harold's Road".

Location: 2 m S of Sevenoaks on road to Tonbridge (A225).
Station: Sevenoaks (2 m).
Opening Times: Garden: Apr 1 to June 30: every Sun and the Sat and Mon of all Bank Holiday weekends during this period, 12–6. Picnics allowed. No dogs. Unsuitable for the disabled. Adm £1.50, Chd 50p. **The HOUSE is now only open to party bookings** and for a limited period when the gardens are at their best. Any day in April, May or June except Sun and Bank Holidays. Adults only. Entrance £2. Minimum number 20.
Refreshments: Home made teas in the old stable from 2.30 on Suns. Special Catering for booked parties – Ploughman's Lunches, teas etc – by arrangement. All enquiries to Mrs Rogers (0732) 452557/458802.

ROCHESTER CASTLE ⬚

Rochester   map L4
Telephone: (0634) 402276
(English Heritage)

Large 11th century castle partly founded on the Roman city wall, with a splendid keep of c. 1130, the tallest in England. A Personal, Stereo Guided Tour is available.

Location: By Rochester Bridge (A2).
Opening Times: Good Friday or Apr 1 (whichever is earlier) to Sept 30 daily 10–6. Oct 1 to Maundy Thursday or Mar 31 (whichever is earlier) Tues to Sun 10–4. *Closed* Dec 24–26, Jan 1. Adm £1.50, Concessions £1.10, Chd 75p.

ST AUGUSTINE'S ABBEY ⬚

map M4
Telephone: (0227) 767345

This was founded in 598 by St Augustine, the first Archibishop of Canterbury. The excavated finds from this early building are rare memorials of the Anglo-Saxon church. The remains we see today are from the later Norman church, its well-preserved crypt, and the medieval monastery.

Location: Canterbury, near the Cathedral. OS map ref TR154578.
Opening Times: Good Friday or Apr 1 (whichever is earlier) to Sept 30: Open Daily 10–6. Oct 1 to Maundy Thursday or Mar 31 (whichever is earlier): Open Tues to Sun 10–4. *Closed* Dec 24–26, Jan 1. Adm £1.10, Concessions 85p, Chd 55p.

ST JOHN'S JERUSALEM GARDEN, The National Trust

Sutton-at-Hone, Dartford   map K4
Telephone: Lamberhurst (0892) 890651

Garden and the former chapel of a Commandery of the Knights Hospitallers.

Location: 3 m S of Dartford on E side of A225.
Opening Times: Apr to end Oct. Weds only 2–6 (last adm 5.30). Adm £1 – no reductions. Parties by prior arrangement.

SCOTNEY CASTLE GARDEN, The National Trust

Lamberhurst   map L3   &
Telephone: Lamberhurst (0892) 890651

Romantic landscape garden framing moated castle.

Location: 1½ m SE of Lamberhurst (A21).
Opening Times: Garden: Apr to Nov 8 – Weds to Fris 11 – 6 or sunset if earlier *(closed Good Fri)*; Sats, Suns & Bank Hol Mons 2 – 6 or sunset if earlier. Last adm one hour before closing. Old Castle: May to Aug 23 – days & times as for Garden. Adm Sun & Bank Hol Mon: £3, Chd £1.50; Wed to Sat: £2.40, Chd £1.20. Parties by prior appointment £1.80, Chd £1. *No reduction on Sats, Suns or Bank Hol Mons. No dogs.* Picnic area next to car park. Shop. Wheelchairs available. (Steep entrance to garden.)

SISSINGHURST CASTLE GARDEN, The National Trust

Sissinghurst   map L3
Telephone: Cranbrook 712850

The famous garden created by the late Vita Sackville-West and Sir Harold Nicolson between the surviving parts of an Elizabethan mansion.

Location: 2 m NE of Cranbrook; 1 m E of Sissinghurst village (A262).
Opening Times: Apr to Oct 15 – Tues to Fris 1 – 6.30; Sats, Suns & Good Fri 10 – 6.30. (Last adm 6.) *Closed Mons, incl Bank Hol Mons.* Because of the limited capacity of the garden, visitors will often have to wait before admission. The property is liable to be closed at short notice once it has reached its visitor capacity for the day. Adm Tues to Sats £4.50, Chd £2.30; Suns £5; Chd £2.50. Parties by appointment only; reductions on weekdays only. No dogs. No picnics in garden. Adm to wheelchair visitors is restricted to 2 at any one time. Shop.
Refreshments: In the Granary Restaurant. Apr to Oct 15 – Tues to Fri 12 – 6, Sat & Sun 10 – 6, also Oct 28 to Dec 21 – Wed to Sat 11 – 4. Closed Mons.

SMALLHYTHE PLACE, The National Trust

Tenterden   map L3
Telephone: Tenterden 2334

The Ellen Terry Memorial Museum. Half-timbered 16th century yeoman's home. Mementoes of Dame Ellen Terry, Mrs Siddons, etc.

Location: 2½ m S of Tenterden on E side of Rye Road (B2082).
Opening Times: Apr to end of Oct – Daily (except Thurs & Fris) 2 – 6 or dusk if earlier. Open Good Fri. Last adm half-hour before closing. Adm £2, Chd £1. *Parties should give advance notice – no reduction. No parties in August.* No indoor photography. No dogs. Unsuitable for wheelchairs. Can only take 25 at a time in house.
Refreshments: Tea available at The Spinning Wheel & the Tudor Rose, Tenterden.

SOUTH FORELAND LIGHTHOUSE

On the cliff top between Dover and St. Margaret's Bay.

Location: 1.5 m SW of St. Margaret's at Cliffe village. Visitors are advised to park in village car park (2 miles).
Opening Times: Apr to end Oct. Sat, Sun & Bank Hol Mon, 2 – 5.30. Last adm 5. Adm £1.20, Chd 60p.

SQUERRYES COURT

Westerham   map K4
Telephone: Westerham (0959) 562345 or 563118
(J St A Warde, Esq)

William and Mary manor house built in 1681. Home of the Warde family who have lived there since 1735. Period furniture, paintings, tapestries and china. Objects of interest connected with General Wolfe. Landscape grounds in a parkland setting include lake, formal garden, rhododendrons and azaleas.

Location: Western outskirts of Westerham on A25.
Opening Times: Mar: Suns only 2 – 6. Apr 1 to Sept 30: Weds, Sats, Suns and Bank Hol Mons 2 – 6 pm (last adm 5.30). Adm House & Grounds £2.80, Chd (under 14) £1.40; Grounds only £1.60, Chd (under 14) 80p. Parties over 20 (any day except Suns) by arrangement at reduced rates. Dogs on leads in grounds only. Free parking at house.
Refreshments: Homemade teas at weekends & for booked parties.

STONEACRE, The National Trust

Otham   map L4

A half-timbered small manor house, c. 1480. Small garden.

Location: In Otham, 3 m SE of Maidstone; 1 m S of A20.
Station: Bearsted (2 m).
Opening Times: Apr to end Oct – Weds & Sats 2 – 6 (last adm 5). Adm £1.50, Chd 80p. No reduction
for parties. No dogs. Unsuitable for wheelchairs. Narrow access road.

WALMER CASTLE ⬚

Walmer   map M4
Telephone: (0304) 364288
(English Heritage)

One of the coastal castles built by Henry VIII and the official residence of The Lords Warden of The Cinque Ports, including Queen Elizabeth, the Queen Mother and the Duke of Wellington who died at Walmer and whose furnished rooms have been preserved unaltered. (The original 'Wellington Boot' may be seen here).

Location: On coast at Walmer 2 m S of Deal off the Dover/Deal Road.
Station: Walmer (1½ m).
Opening Times: Good Friday or Apr 1 (whichever is earlier) to Sept 30 daily 10−6. Oct 1 to Maundy Thursday or Mar 31 (whichever is earlier). Tues−Sun 10−4. *Closed* Dec 24−26, Jan 1 to Feb 29. Adm £2.50, Concessions £1.90, Chd £1.30. Admission price includes a Personal Stereo Guided Tour.

TONBRIDGE CASTLE

Tonbridge   map K4
Telephone: Tonbridge (0732) 770929
(Tonbridge & Malling Borough Council)

Built by Richard de Fitzgilbert, remains of Norman Motte and Bailey Castle with 13th century Gatehouse overlooking River Medway. Reputedly England's finest example of the layout of a Norman Motte and Bailey Castle with 13th century Gatehouse set in landscaped gardens overlooking the River Medway. The site is clearly interpreted for your enjoyment. Audio tours are available from the Tourist Information Centre. New exhibition opening Easter 1992 (Prov.) A Re-creation of Medieval Life in the 13th Century Castle Gatehouse as it was over 700 years ago.

Location: In town centre off High Street.
Opening Times: Apr to Sept: Mon to Sat 9−5, Sun & Bank Hol 10.30−5. Oct to Mar: Mon to Fri 9−5, Sat 9−4. Sun 10.30−4. *Closed* Christmas Day and New Year's Day (last tours leave 1 hr before closing time).

UPNOR CASTLE ⬚

map L4
Telephone: (0634) 718742

The Castle was built in 1559 on the orders of Elizabeth I, to protect her warships moored in the Medway alongside the new dockyards at Chatham. Within a century the castle was out of date, and was used as a magazine for gunpowder and munitions.

Location: At Upnor, on unclassified road off A228. OS map ref TQ758706.
Opening Times: Good Friday or Apr 1 (whichever is earlier) to Sept 30: Open Daily 10−6. Adm £1.50, Concessions £1.10, Chd 75p.

WALMER CASTLE − *See above*

WAYSTRODE MANOR GARDEN

Cowden, nr Edenbridge   map K4
Telephone: (0342) 850 695
(Mr & Mrs Peter Wright)

8 acre garden, large range of herbaceous plants, trees and shrubs. Featured in many magazines and journals.

Location: ½ m N of Cowden village. 4½ m S of Edenbridge, off B2026.
Opening Times: Wed May 27, 1.30−5,30. June 10, 1.30−5.30. Adm £1.50, Chd 50p. Suns May 31 and June 28 2−6. *In aid of National Gardens Scheme.* Last adm 30 mins before closing time. Groups by appointment, minimum 20.
Refreshments: Home made teas. Plant stall. **No dogs.**

WILLESBOROUGH WINDMILL

Ashford   map L4
(Ashford Borough Council)

Willesborough Windmill, built in 1869, has now been restored as a working smock mill. Visitors can view the turn-of-the-century miller's cottage, enjoy guided tours of the mill and visit the mill's own tea room and shop.

Location: 2 m E of Ashford town centre, just off A292 and approx ¼ m from Junction 10 of the M20.
Opening Times: All year, Sun 2−5. Adm £1, Chd/OAP 50p. Group rates available on application. Limited parking. Not suitable for disabled.
Refreshments: Tea shop in restored barn adjacent to the mill. Light refreshments available − suitable for disabled.

LANCASHIRE

ASTLEY HALL

Chorley   map G9
(Chorley Borough Council (1922))

Elizabethan house c. 1666. Furniture, pottery, tapestries, pictures.

Location: 2 m NW town centre on A6 (footpath access only to Hall ¾ m) or A581 (car access, turn right after 1½ m—signposted).
Opening Times: All the year Apr to Sept—Daily 12–5.30; Oct to Mar—Mons to Fris 12–3.30; Sats 10–3.30; Suns 11–3.30. Adm £1.55, Chd, OAPs & registered unemployed 75p, Family ticket £3.55. Reduced rates for parties. Large free car park.
Refreshments: At the Hall (summer months).

BROWSHOLME HALL

nr Clitheroe   map G9   △
Telephone: Stonyhurst (0254) 826719

Home of the Parker family, Bowbearers of the Forest of Bowland. Tudor with Elizabethan front, Queen Anne Wing and Regency additions. Portraits furniture and antiquities. Guided tours by members of the family.

Location: 5 m NW of Clitheroe; off B6243; Bashall Eaves—Whitewell signposted.
Opening Times: Easter: Good Friday to Mon. Late May Bank Hol weekend. July: Every Sat; Aug: every Sat & Sun, and Aug Bank Hol weekend 2–5. Reductions for booked parties at other times by appointment with A. Parker, Tel. as above.

GAWTHORPE HALL, The National Trust

Padiham   map G9
Telephone: Padiham (0282) 78511

House built in 1600-1605, restored by Barry in 1850; Barry's designs newly re-created in principal rooms. Display of Rachel Kay-Shuttleworth textile collections; private study by arrangement. Major display of late 17th century portraits on loan from the National Portrait Gallery. Estate building, recently restored, houses a broad programme of craft and management courses.

Location: On E outskirts of Padiham (¾ m drive to house is on N of A671).
Station: Rose Grove (2 m).
Opening Times: Apr 1 to Nov 1. HALL: Tues, Weds, Thurs, Sats & Suns, 1–5, last adm 4.15. Open Good Fri & Bank Holiday Mons. GARDEN: Open daily all year 10–6. SHOP: Daily *(except Mons & Fris)* Apr 1 to Dec 22, 11–5. Adm House: £2.30, Chd £1. Reductions for pre-booked parties of 15 or more (except Bank Holidays). No dogs. Access for disabled: Ground floor of Hall, Shop & Gallery. W.C.
Refreshments: Refectory in Estate Building open as shop.

HOGHTON TOWER

nr Preston   map F9
Telephone: Hoghton (025 485) 2986
(Sir Bernard de Hoghton, Bt)

Dramatic 16th century fortified hilltop mansion with the magnificent Banqueting Hall where James I knighted the 'Sirloin' of Beef in 1617. The seat of Sir Bernard de Hoghton, Bt. Spend a few hours in this delightful historic mansion where there are permanent exhibitions, Chinese teapots, Dolls Houses and historic Hoghton documents. Underground passages, dungeons and Lancashire witches' kitchen. Gift shop. Walled gardens and Old English Rose Garden.

Location: 5 m E of Preston on A675.
Station: Preston (5 m).
Opening Times: Easter Sat, Sun & Mon, then Suns to end of Oct, also Sats in July & Aug. Wed, 11–4.30 June, July, Aug. All Bank Hols: 2–5. Adm £2.50, Chd £1. School parties—Chd £1. Private visits welcome (minimum 25 persons) throughout week. Apply Administrator, Hoghton Tower, Preston PR5 0SH. Souvenir & Craft Shop.
Refreshments: Tea rooms.

LEIGHTON HALL

Carnforth   map F10   △
Telephone: 0524 734474
(Mr & Mrs R. G. Reynolds)

Mid 12th century House rebuilt in the late 18th century with a neo Gothic façade added in 1800. Extensive grounds, garden and labyrinth. **Displays with trained eagles and falcons at 3.30 pm unless raining.**

Location: 2 m W of A6 through Yealand Conyers; signposted from M6, exit 35 junction with A6.
Stations: Silverdale (1½ m, bridlepath only); Carnforth (2½ m).
Opening Times: May to Sept—Suns, Bank Hol Mons & Tues to Fris 2–5 (last tour of House 4.30). Other times by appointment for parties of 25 or more. Special Educational Programme for Schools—mornings from 10 am. Adm House & Grounds £2.50 (OAPs and parties £2), Chd £1.50, Chd parties £1.20. Teachers with schools free. Inquiries: Mrs Reynolds at the Hall. Schools Programme—Mr A Oswald Tel: 0524 701353. Disabled visitors welcome.
Refreshments: Teas at the Hall. Salad lunches/high teas for booked parties.

MARTHOLME

Great Harwood, Blackburn   map G9

Screens passage and service wing of medieval manor house altered 1577 with 17th century additions. Gatehouse built 1561, restored 1969.

Opening Times: Exterior: Fri & Sat. Interior: by appointment only.

MEOLS HALL

Southport   map F9
(R. F. Hesketh, Esq.)

A 17th century house, with subsequent additions, containing an interesting collection of pictures, furniture, china etc.

Location: 1 m N of Southport; 16 m SW of Preston; 20 m N of Liverpool; near A565 & A570.
Opening Times: Mid July to mid Aug 2–5. Adm £2, Chd 75p. Chd under 10 accompanied by adult free.

RUFFORD OLD HALL, The National Trust

Rufford, nr Ormskirk   map F9
Telephone: Rufford (0704) 821254

One of the finest 15th century buildings in Lancashire. The Great Hall is remarkable for its ornate hammer-beam roof and unique screen. There are fine collections of 17th century oak furniture, 16th century arms, armour and tapestries.

Location: 7 m N of Ormskirk at N end of Rufford village on E side of A59.
Stations: Rufford (1/2 m) (not Suns); Burscough Bridge (2 1/2 m).
Opening Times: Apr 1 to Nov 1 – Daily (except Fris) 1 – 5. Last adm 4.30. Garden and shop: open 12 – 5.30 on same days, Suns 1 – 5. Refreshments same days 12 – 5, Sun 2 – 5. Adm Hall & Garden £2.60, Chd £1.30. Reduced rate for parties of 15 or more by arrangement. Access for disabled garden only. Guide dogs.
Refreshments: At the Hall (parties should book).

SAMLESBURY HALL

nr Preston   map G9
(Samlesbury Hall Trust)

14th century Manor House owned and administered by private trust.

Location: On A677; 6 m E of Preston; 5 m W of Blackburn.
Opening Times: All the year – Tues to Suns 11.30 – 5 (summer), 11.30 – 4 (winter). *Closed Mons.* Adm £2, Chd (under 16) 80p. Coach & organised parties by appointment Tues to Fris only. Ongoing sales of antiques and collectors' items. Also various craft, at work and other exhibitions.
Refreshments: Restaurant open 12 – 4.

SELLET HALL GARDENS

Kirkby Lonsdale   map G10
Telephone: (05242) 71865

Herbs, shrubs, herbaceous, trees including the National Collection of Japanese maples and associated plants. Also wide variety of primulas. Garden open. Mail order catalogue.

Location: 1 m SW of Kirkby Lonsdale off A65.
Opening Times: 10 – 5 daily except Christmas, Boxing and New Year's Day. Adm Nursery free, Garden 50p. Parties by appointment. Car parking. Suitable for disabled.

STONYHURST COLLEGE

Hurst Green   map G9
Telephone: Stonyhurst (0254) 826345

TOWNELEY HALL ART GALLERY & MUSEUM and MUSEUM OF LOCAL CRAFTS & INDUSTRIES

Burnley   map G9
Telephone: Burnley 24213
(Burnley Borough Council)

The House dates from the 14th century, with 17th and 19th century modifications. The furnished rooms include an Elizabethan Long Gallery, and a fine entrance hall with plasterwork by Vassali completed in 1729. Collections include oak furniture, 18th and 19th century paintings and Zoffany's painting of Charles Towneley. Loan exhibitions are held throughout the summer. There is a Museum of Local Crafts and Industries in the old Bew House, and the Natural History Centre, with an aquarium in the grounds.

Location: 1/2 m SE of Burnley on the Burnley/Todmorden Road (A671).
Station: Burnley Central (1 3/4 m).
Opening Times: All the year – Mons to Fris 10 – 5, Suns 12 – 5. *Closed Sats throughout year.* Adm free. *Closed Christmas – New Year.*
Refreshments: At café in grounds during the summer.

TURTON TOWER

Chapeltown Road, Turton, Bolton   map G9
Telephone: Bolton (0204) 852203
(Lancashire County Council)

Medieval Pele Tower with Elizabethan extensions. Stuart and Victorian revisions. Permanent collections of 17th century furniture, Some arms and armour, period rooms, wood collections. Temporary exhibtions and events.

Location: Chapeltown Road, Turton. 5 m N of Bolton on B6391.
Station: Bromley Cross.
Opening Times: May to Sept: Mon to Fri 10 – 12, 1 – 5; Sat and Sun 1 – 5; Mar, Apr, Oct: Sat to Wed 2 – 5; Nov and Feb: Sun 2 – 5; Open Bank Holidays. *Closed* Dec, Jan. Adm charges. Parties, guided tours by appointment. Car parking. Nine acres of woodland gardens. Shop.
Refreshments: Tearoom.

The original house, (situated close to the picturesque village of Hurst Green in the beautiful Ribble Valley) dates from the late 16th century. Set in extensive grounds which include ornamental gardens. The College has an impressive approach down a long avenue flanked by man made rectangular ponds constructed in the 17th century. The Parish Church of St. Peters built in 1832, is linked to the main building which is a boys' Catholic boarding school, founded by the Society of Jesus in 1593.

Location: Just off the B6243 (Longridge – Clitheroe) on the outskirts of Hurst Green. 10 m from junction 31 on M6.
Opening Times: House: weekly from Aug 4 to Sept 5, Tues to Sun only (plus Aug Bank Hol Mon) 1 – 5. Grounds & Gardens: weekly from July 11 to Sept 5, Tues to Sun only (plus Aug Bank Hol Mon) 1 – 5. Adm: House and Grounds £3, Chd (4 – 14) £2 (under 4 free), OAPs £2; Grounds only £1. No dogs permitted.
Refreshments/Gift Shop. Limited facilities for disabled. Coach parties by prior arrangement.

LEICESTERSHIRE

ASHBY DE LA ZOUCH CASTLE

map H7
Telephone: (0530) 413343

In 1464 Edward IV granted the Norman manor house of Ashby to his Lord Chamberlain, Lord Hastings, who built the impressive four-storey tower. His enjoyment of it was short-lived, alas, for in 1483 he was beheaded by Richard III. His successors fared better and among royal visitors were Henry VII, Mary Queen of Scots, James I and Charles I. In 1649 the tower was partially destroyed by Parliamentary forces.

Location: In Ashby de la Zouch. OS map ref SK363167.
Opening Times: Good Friday or Apr 1 (whichever is earlier) to Sept 30: Open Daily 10–6. Oct 1 to Maundy Thursday or Mar 31 (whichever is earlier): Open Tues to Sun 10–4. *Closed* Dec 24–26, Jan 1. Adm £1.10, Concessions 85p, Chd 55p.

BELGRAVE HALL

Belgrave   map J7

Small Queen Anne house of 1709–13, with period room settings from late 17th to mid 19th century. Coaches in stable block. Outstanding period and botanic gardens with over 6,500 species of plants.

Location: Church Road, Belgrave, off Thurcaston Road in Leicester.
Opening Times: Open weekdays 10–5.30, Sun 2–5.30. *Closed Good Friday, Christmas Day and Boxing Day.* Access for disabled to all gardens, but ground floor only of 3-storey house. Unrestricted street parking outside.

BELVOIR CASTLE – *See below*

BOSWORTH BATTLEFIELD VISITOR CENTRE & COUNTRY PARK

Market Bosworth   map H6   &
Telephone: Market Bosworth (0455) 290429
(Leicestershire County Council)

Site of the famous Battle of Bosworth Field (1485) with extensive Visitor Centre including exhibitions, models, film theatre, book and gift shops and cafeteria; and outdoor interpretation of the Battle. Series of special mediaeval attractions during summer months.

Location: 15 m W of Leicester; 2 m S of Market Bosworth (sign posted off M42, A5, A447, A444 and B585).
Opening Times: BATTLEFIELD VISITOR CENTRE. Apr 1 to Oct 31 – Mons to Sats 1–5.30; Suns and Bank Hols 1–6. July 1 to Aug 31: open from 11 a.m. Admission £1.50, Chd (under 16 years) and OAPs £1. (Special charges apply on main Special Event days.) Parties at any time by appointment at reduced rates. COUNTRY PARK & BATTLE TRAILS: Open all year during daylight hours.
Refreshments: Bosworth Buttery Cafeteria.

THE GUILDHALL

Leicester   map H7   &
Telephone: (0533) 532569

14th to 16th century Hall of Corpus Christi Gild, used as Town Hall from late 15th century to 1876. 19th century Police Station with cells.

Location: In Leicester
Opening Times: Open weekdays 10–5.30, Sun 2–5.30. *Closed* Good Friday, Christmas Day and Boxing Day. Access for disabled throughout except for Old Town Library. Public car park in St. Nicholas Circle, 30 yards.

KIRBY MUXLOE CASTLE

map H7
Telephone: (0533) 386886

William, Lord Hastings, was a very wealthy man, so he was able to indulge his passion for building. He developed his moated brick mansion from a fortified manor house, but it was never completed. A striking feature is the patterned brickwork, clearly visible on the gatehouse walls.

Location: 4 m (6.4 km) west of Leicester. OS map ref SK524046.
Opening Times: Good Friday or Apr 1 (whichever is earlier) to Sept 30: Open Daily 10–6. Oct 1 to Maundy Thursday or Mar 31 (whichever is earlier): Open Tues to Sun 10–4. *Closed* Dec 24–26, Jan 1. Adm £1.10, Concessions 85p, Chd 55p.

LYDDINGTON BEDE HOUSE

map J6
Telephone: (057 282) 2438
(English Heritage)

The building is the only surviving part of the medieval palace of the Bishops of Lincoln. After the Reformation it passed to Thomas, Lord Burghley, who turned it into an almshouse. It was used as such until the present century.

Location: In Lyddington 6m (9.6 km) north of Corby. OS map ref SP875970.
Opening Times: Good Friday or Apr 1 (whichever is earlier) to Sept 30 – daily 10–6. Adm £1.10, Concessions 85p, Chd 55p.

THE MANOR HOUSE

Donington-le-Heath   map H7

Fine medieval manor house circa 1280 with 16th to 17th century alterations. Now restored as period house.

Location: In Donington-le-Heath, Hugglescote nr Coalville.
Opening Times: Wed before Easter to Sept 30 inc: Wed to Sun 2–6, and all Bank Holidays. Access for disabled to ground floor only. Visitors' car park.
Refreshments: Cream teas in adjoining stone barn.

BELVOIR CASTLE

nr Grantham   map J7
Telephone: Grantham (0476) 870262
(His Grace the Duke of Rutland)

Seat of the Dukes of Rutland since Henry VIII's time, and rebuilt by Wyatt in 1816. A castle in the grand style, commanding magnificent views over the Vale of Belvoir. The name dates back to the famous Norman Castle that stood on this site. Many notable art treasures, and interesting military relics. The Statue gardens contain many beautiful 17th century sculptures. Flowers in bloom throughout most of the season. Medieval Jousting Tournaments. Conference and filming facilities. Banquets, school visits, private parties.

Location: 7 m WSW of Grantham, between A607 (to Melton Mowbray) and A52 (to Nottingham).
Opening Times: Apr 1 (Good Friday) to Oct 1 1992, Tues Wed, Thurs, Sat–11–5 (all days). Sun and Bank Holiday Mons. Last adm 4.30. Oct Sun only. Other times for groups by appointment. Adm £3.20, Chd/OAP £2.20. All coach tours and excursions £2.50 (coach driver free). Parties of 30 or more adults £2.50 (organiser free). School parties £1.80 (teacher free). On Jousting Tournament days an extra charge of 50p per person will apply. Ticket office and catering facilities in the Castle close approximately 30 mins before the Castle. Guide books are on sale at the ticket office or inside the Castle, or by post (£2.50) including postage and packing. We regret that dogs are not permitted (except Guide Dogs).

We've Travelled Back In Time

Travel back in time with a visit to one of Leicestershire's 15 museums.

You'll find plenty to amaze and amuse you — from the Rutland Dinosaur at New Walk to the Rutland rural life exhibition at Oakham, and from the Roman remains at Jewry Wall to the Regency elegance of Belgrave Hall.

There's so much to enjoy that we think you'll keep coming back time after time.

LEICESTERSHIRE MUSEUM AND ART GALLERY, New Walk, Leicester.

JEWRY WALL MUSEUM AND SITE, St. Nicholas Circle, Leicester.

NEWARKE HOUSES MUSEUM, The Newarke, Leicester.

HARBOROUGH MUSEUM, Council Offices, Adam and Eve Street, Market Harborough.

WYGSTON'S HOUSE MUSEUM OF COSTUME, Applegate, St. Nicholas Circle, Leicester.

MELTON CARNEGIE MUSEUM, Thorpe End, Melton Mowbray.

THE GUILDHALL, Guildhall Lane, Leicester.

LEICESTERSHIRE MUSEUM OF TECHNOLOGY, Corporation Road, Abbey Lane, Leicester.

LEICESTERSHIRE RECORD OFFICE, 57 New Walk, Leicester.

RUTLAND COUNTY MUSEUM, Catmos Street, Oakham.

OAKHAM CASTLE, Market Place, Oakham.

MUSEUM OF THE ROYAL LEICESTERSHIRE REGIMENT, The Magazine, Oxford Street, Leicester.

BELGRAVE HALL, Church Road, Belgrave, Leicester.

THE MANOR HOUSE, Donington-le-Heath, Coalville.

SNIBSTON – THE INDUSTRIAL ADVENTURE, Ashby Road, Coalville (opening July 1992).

You'll keep coming back to...

LEICESTERSHIRE MUSEUMS, ARTS & RECORDS SERVICE

STANFORD HALL

Lutterworth map J6 △
Telephone: Rugby (0788) 860250
(The Lady Braye)

A William and Mary House built in the 1690's containing a fine collection of pictures (including the Stuart Collection), antique furniture and family costumes dating from Queen Elizabeth I's time. There is a full-size replica of the 1898 Flying Machine of Percy Pilcher who is officially recognised as England's Pioneer Aviator. He experimented at Stanford where he was killed whilst flying in 1899. The Motorcycle Museum contains an outstanding collection of Vintage and historic motorcycles. Walled Rose Garden leading to Old Forge. Nature Trail. Craft Centre most Sundays.

Location: 7½ m NE of Rugby; 3½ m from A5; 6 m from M1 at exit 18; 5 m from M1 at exit 20; 6 m from M6 at exit 1; 1¼ m from Swinford.
Opening Times: Easter Sat to end of Sept — Sats & Suns also Bank Hol Mons & Tues following 2.30–6. Adm House & Grounds, etc, £2.80, Chd £1.30; Grounds, Rose Garden, Flying Machine, Old Forge, Craft Centre (most Suns) £1.50, Chd 70p. Parties of 20 or more (min £50) £2.50, Chd £1.15. OAPs with a party of 20 or more £2.20. School parties of 20 or more (one teacher adm free) £2.50, Chd £1.15. Adm prices subject to increase on occasional Event Days. Motorcycle Museum 90p, Chd 20p.
NB On Bank Hols and Event Days open 12–6 (House 2.30).
Refreshments: Home-made teas. Light lunches most Suns. Lunches, Teas, High Teas or Suppers for pre-booked parties any day during season.

OAKHAM CASTLE

Market Place, Leicester map J7
Telephone: (0572) 723654

12th century Great Hall of Norman castle in castle grounds with earlier motte. Unique collection of horseshoes presented by visiting Peers of the Realm.

Location: In Leicester
Opening Times: Castle Grounds: Apr to Oct — daily 10–5.30. Nov to Mar — daily 10–4. Sun 2–4. Great Hall: Apr to Oct — Tues to Sat and Bank Holiday Mon 10–1, 2–5.30. Sun 2–5.30. Nov to Mar — Tues to Sat 10–1, 2–4. *Closed* Good Friday, Christmas Day and Boxing Day. Access for disabled to Great Hall. Parking for disabled visitors **only** on request.

ROCKINGHAM CASTLE — SEE UNDER NORTHANTS.

STANFORD HALL — *See above*

WYGSTON'S HOUSE, MUSEUM OF COSTUME

Applegate, St Nicholas Circle, Leicester map J7 &
Telephone: (0533) 554100

Important late medieval building, with later additions to house. Costume from 1750 to present day. Reconstruction of drapers, dress and shoe shops of 1920s.

Location: St Nicholas Circle, in Leicester
Opening Times: Weekdays 10–5.30, Sun 2–5.30. Closed Good Friday, Christmas Day and Boxing Day. Access for disabled on ground floor only. Public car park adjacent.

LINCOLNSHIRE

AUBOURN HALL

nr Lincoln map J8
(H. N. Nevile, Esq.)

Late 16th century house attributed to J. Smythson (Jnr). Important carved staircase and panelled rooms. New rose garden.

Location: In Aubourn village 7 m S of Lincoln
Opening Times: July and Aug: Wed, 2–6. Also Sun June 7 and June 21, or by appointment. Adm £2, Chd/OAF £1.50.

BELTON HOUSE, The National Trust

nr Grantham map J7 ⓢ
Telephone: Grantham (0476) 66116

The crowning achievement of Restoration country house architecture, built 1685–88 for Sir John Brownlow, heir to the fortunes of a successful Elizabethan lawyer; alterations by James Wyatt 1777, plasterwork ceilings by Edward Goudge, fine wood carvings of the Grinling Gibbons school. Family portraits, furniture, tapestries, Speaker Cust's silver and silver-gilt, Duke of Windsor memorabilia. Formal gardens, orangery by Jeffrey Wyattville, 17th century stables, magnificent landscape park. Extensive Adventure Playground for children.

Location: 3 m NE of Grantham on A607 Grantham/Lincoln Road; easily accessible from A1.
Opening Times: Apr 1 to end of Oct — Weds to Suns & Bank Hol Mons 1–5.30. *Closed* Good Friday. Gardens open 11. Parkland opens daily with free access on foot (may be closed for special events). Last adm 5. Adm House £3.80. School parties contact the Administrator for details. 1992 Events — details from the Administrator.
Refreshments: Counter service licensed restaurant open 12–5.30 for lunches and teas.

BISHOP'S PALACE

map J8
Telephone: (0522) 27468

When James I visited Lincoln in 1617 the palace was a ruin. It was not until the 1880s that it was partially restored by Bishop King. Excavations have revealed most of the medieval layout which largely dates from the 12th, 13th and 15th centuries.

Location: South side of Lincoln cathedral. OS map ref SK981717.
Opening Times: Good Friday or Apr 1 (whichever is earlier) to Sept 30: Open Daily 10–6. Adm 75p, Concessions 55p, Chd 40p.

BELVOIR CASTLE — SEE UNDER LEICESTERSHIRE

BURGHLEY HOUSE

Stamford map J7 △
Telephone: Stamford (0780) 52451
(Burghley House Trustees)

The finest example of later Elizabethan architecture in England. Eighteen State rooms open containing fine furniture, porcelain, silver and the largest private collection of Italian art. Also magnificent painted ceilings by Verrio and Laguerre. Much of the renowned Burghley collection of Oriental porcelain is on display within the State Rooms. There is also a Special Exhibition which changes annually. During 1992 this will feature a selection of the many items that have been discovered during the restoration and conservation programme that has taken place at Burghley over the last decade. These exciting discoveries include rare ceramics, miniatures, furniture, textiles and jewellery and, as with all of the annual exhibitions, will include many

Burghley House Stamford

THE LARGEST AND GRANDEST HOUSE OF THE ELIZABETHAN AGE

Home of the Cecils for over 400 years.

Built in 1587 by William Cecil, first Lord Burghley and Lord High Treasurer to Queen Elizabeth I and occupied by his descendants ever since. Eighteen treasure filled State Rooms are on view including the Heaven Room – the finest painted room in England. Of special interest are the silver fireplaces, needlework, painted ceilings, medieval kitchen with over 260 copper utensils, and one of the largest private art collections in Britain. The house is set in a Deer Park landscaped by 'Capability' Brown. Home of the famous Burghley Horse Trials.

Easily reached – just 1 mile from the Great North Road (A1) at Stamford.

Refreshments available in the Orangery.

Open daily from Good Friday to October 4 (not September 12) 11 am to 5 pm.

For further information and details of special party rates and menus contact: The Manager, telephone Stamford (0780) 52451.

BURGHLEY HOUSE − *Continued from page 120*

items not normally displayed. The 'Capability' Brown Deer Park is open to visitors at no extra charge nor is there a charge for car parking.

Location: 1 m SE of Stamford clearly signposted from the A1.
Station: Stamford (1m).
Opening Times: Good Friday to Oct 4 − Daily 11−5. *Closed Sept 12.* Adm £4.10, Chd £2.50, OAP £3.80. Family ticket £11. Party rates available.
Refreshments: Snacks, lunches and teas in the Orangery. Enquiries for bookings, party rates & menus tel: (0780) 52451.

DODDINGTON HALL

Doddington   map J8   △   Ⓢ
Telephone: Lincoln (0522) 694308
(Mr & Mrs A. G. Jarvis)

One of the Elizabethan gems of England. A romantic house set in 5 acres of superb gardens, with beautiful contents which reflect 400 years of unbroken family occupation. Fine furniture, porcelain, tapestries and pictures, and still very much a family home.

Location: 5 m W of Lincoln on the B1190 & signposted off the A46 Lincoln by-pass.
Opening Times: Easter Mon then May to Sept − Weds, Suns & Bank Hol Mons 2−6. Adm £3.30, Chd £1.65. Gardens only: £1.65, Chd 80p. Minimum charge per booked party, 20 people, £66.
Refreshments: The Littlehouse Restaurant opens from noon on open days, 'phone (0522) 510333 for bookings.

FULBECK HALL

Grantham   map J7   ♿
Telephone: Loveden (0400) 72205
(Mrs M. Fry)

Home of the Fane family since 1632, with alterations and additions by nearly every generation. This is a friendly, lived-in house where visitors receive a personal welcome from the owners. It is mainly 18th century with an older service wing and later additions to the main block. Links with Wellington, the Raj and Arnhem. In the eleven acre garden there has been much recent planting of unusual subjects within the Edwardian design. Planting plans may be borrowed. Plants for sale, nature trail with free leaflet, peacocks, Hebridean sheep, picnic area. Fulbeck Hall and Fulbeck Manor (see list at back) will open together for groups of more than 20 at any time by prior arrangement.

Location: On A607. Lincoln 14 m, Grantham 11 m. 1 m S of A17.
Opening Times: House and Garden: Easter, May and Aug Bank Holiday Mons. Daily from July 1 to 26 incl, 2−5. Adm £2.50, OAPs £2, Chd £1. Parties of more than 20 by agreement. Garden only: Every weekday from May 5 to June 30. Adm £1.50, Chd £1. Car parking free. Suitable for disabled persons (no wheelchairs available).
Refreshments: Teas in house during July opening. At other times at local craft workshops (*closed* Mons) less than 300 yards from House. Special catering of any kind available for groups − lunch, tea or dinner.

GRANTHAM HOUSE, The National Trust ❧

Grantham   map J7

Dating from 1380 but extensively altered and added to throughout the centuries. Ground floor only open to the public. The grounds run down to the river.

Location: In Castlegate, immediately E of Grantham Church.
Station: Grantham (1 m).
Opening Times: Apr to end of Sept, Weds only − 2−5 by written appointment only with Maj-Gen Sir Brian Wyldbore-Smith, Grantham House, Castlegate, Grantham NG1 6SS. Adm £1, Chd 50p. No reduction for parties. No dogs. Unsuitable for wheelchairs. No lavatories.

GRIMSTHORPE CASTLE AND GARDENS

Bourne   map J7
(Grimsthorpe & Drummond Castle Trust)

The home of the Willoughby de Eresby family since 1516. Examples of early 13th century architecture, the Tudor period of the reign of Henry VIII and work by Sir John Vanbrugh. State Rooms and Picture Galleries open to the Public.

Location: 4 m NW of Bourne on A151 Colsterworth/Bourne Road, SE of Grantham.
Opening Times: Park and Gardens: Easter Sun, and Mon Apr 19, 20, 12−6. Last entry 5. May 2 to Sept 13: every Sat, Sun, Bank Hol 12−6, last entry 5. Adm £1, Chd (under 16) 50p. (Those visiting the Castle will be refunded these charges). Castle − Suns and Bank Hols May 31 to Sept 13: 2−6. Adm £3, under 16 yrs £1.50, Chd under 5 free. Conference Room available.
Refreshments: The Coach House cafeteria serves home made teas.

GUNBY HALL, The National Trust ❧

Burgh-le-Marsh   map K8

Built by Sir William Massingberd in 1700. Reynolds' portraits, contemporary wainscoting. Ground floor only open to the public. Walled gardens full of flowers and roses.

Location: 2½ m NW of Burgh-le-Marsh; 7 m W of Skegness on S side of A158.
Opening Times: House & Garden. Apr 1 to end of Sept − Weds 2−6; Tues, Thurs & Fris by prior written appointment only to J. D. Wrisdale, Esq., Gunby Hall, nr Spilsby, Lincs. Gardens only also on Thurs 2−6. Adm House & Gardens £2.30, Chd £1.10. Garden only: £1.50, Chd 70p. No reduction for parties. Dogs in garden only, on leads. Wheelchairs in garden only.

LINCOLN CASTLE − *See page 124*

MARSTON HALL − *See page 124*

THE OLD HALL

Gainsborough   map J8   ∧   Ⓔ   Ⓢ
Telephone: 0427 612669.
(Lincolnshire County Council and English Heritage)

An unspoilt 15th century timber framed manor house, built between 1460 and 1480 by Thomas Burgh. Superb medieval kitchen and great hall. Kitchen displayed to portray its use in 1483, on the eve of Richard III's visit. Henry VIII held court here in 1541. Manor house sold to William Hickman in 1597 who allowed the early Separatists to worship here. They were later the core of the Mayflower Pilgrims. John Wesley preached at the Hall several times. 17th and 18th century Hickman portraits and furniture. Medieval, Tudor, and Stuart room settings. Displays on Richard III, Henry VIII's Lincolnshire, history of the building and the Mayflower Pilgrims. Soundalive sound tour. Regular living history events, and school re-enactments.

Location: In centre of Gainsborough.
Stations: Gainsborough Lea Road and Gainsborough Central.
Opening Times: All the year—Mons to Sats 10–5; Suns (Easter to Oct) 2–5.30. *Closed Christmas Day, Boxing Day, New Year's Day & Good Friday.* Adm charge. Organised parties welcome outside normal opening hours.
Refreshments: Tea shop open daily. Meals by arrangement. We look forward to seeing you!

LINCOLN CASTLE

Castle Hill map J8
Telephone: Lincoln (0522) 511068
(Recreational Services Dept, Lincolnshire County Council)

Visitors can enjoy the impressive walls, towers and gatehouses that enclose beautiful and peaceful lawns and gardens. There are fine views of Lincoln and the surrounding countryside from the walls, and particularly from the Observatory Tower. The Castle, built in 1068, also houses a unique Victorian Prison Chapel which is open to visitors. During the summer the Castle is the ideal setting for a wide range of special events, including historical reconstructions, jousting tournaments, rallies and concerts. Further details regarding this year's special events can be obtained from the Manager, Lincoln Castle, or Recreational Services Department, Lincolnshire County Council, Telephone Lincoln (0522) 511068. The Castle has a well stocked gift shop and is close to Lincoln Cathedral and other museums run by the Recreational Services Department.

Location: Above Hill, Lincoln.
Opening Times: Open Bank Hols, except Christmas, British Summer Time: Mons to Sats 9.30–5.30, Suns 11–5.30. Winter Time: Mons to Sats 9.30–4, Sun 11–4. Adm 80p concessionary 50p (until Apr 1992). Reduced rates for parties of 20 or more. No public car parking inside Castle, adequate parking in car parks close to walls. Suitable for disabled persons but not on walls and towers.
Refreshments: Available at Castle. The Castle Tea Room has a selection of homemade organic cakes, in addition to the usual snacks. Picknicking is encouraged within the grounds.

MARSTON HALL

Grantham map J7
Telephone: Loveden (0400) 50225
(The Rev Henry Thorold, FSA)

Tudor Manor house with Georgian interiors, held by Thorolds since 14th century; interesting pictures and furniture. Romantic garden with long walks and avenues, high hedges enclosing herbaceous borders and vegetables, Gothick gazebo and ancient trees.

Location: 6 m NW of Grantham; 1½ m off A1.
Opening Times: Suns May 19, June 16, 23, July 21 2–6, in aid of local charities, and at other times by appointment. Adm House and Garden £1.50.
Refreshments: Cream teas and other local fare on opening days.

THE OLD HALL – *See page 123*

TATTERSHALL CASTLE, The National Trust ❧

Lincoln map K8
Telephone: Coningsby (0526) 42543

The Keep is one of the finest examples of a fortified brick dwelling, although built more for show than defence, c. 1440, for Ralph Cromwell. Museum and shop in Guardhouse.

Location: 12 m NE of Sleaford on Louth Road (A153); 3½ m SE of Woodhall Spa.
Opening Times: Daily–Apr 1 to end of Oct, 10.30–6. Nov to end Mar 1993 12–4.30 *Closed Christmas Day & Boxing Day.* Adm £1.90, Chd 90p. Parties of 15 or more – details from Custodian. Dogs in grounds only, on leads. Wheelchair access.
Refreshments: Fortescue Arms Hotel, Tattershall.

WOOLSTHORPE MANOR, The National Trust ❧

nr Grantham map J7
Telephone: Grantham (0476) 860338

17th century farm house, birthplace of Sir Isaac Newton. Traditionally it was under an apple tree in this garden that Newton was struck with the theory of gravity.

Location: 7 m S of Grantham, ½ m NW of Colsterworth; 1 m W of A1 (not to be confused with Woolsthorpe, nr Belvoir).
Opening Times: Apr 1 to end of Oct–Sat–Wed 1–5.30, last adm 5. *Closed Thur & Fri.* Adm £2.30, Chd £1.10. No reduction for parties. *Closed Good Friday.* No dogs. Wheelchair access to garden & ground floor only. Parking for coaches limited to one at a time – must book. *NB In the interests of preservation numbers admitted to rooms at any one time must be limited; liable to affect peak weekends & Bank Hols.*

LONDON

APSLEY HOUSE

Wellington Museum map K4 ♿
Telephone: 071-499 5676
(Trustees of the Victoria & Albert Museum)

Built 1771–8, the Iron Duke's London Palace housing his famous collection of paintings, porcelain, silver and personal relics.

Opening Times: *Closed from 1/1/92 for refurbishment. Due to re-open mid 1993 during Waterloo week.*

ASHBURNHAM HOUSE

Westminster map K4
Telephone: 071-222 3116
(Westminster School)

Closed for major renovation work during 1991, re-opens 1992.

THE BLEWCOAT SCHOOL, The National Trust ❧

Westminster map K4
Telephone: 071-222 2877

Built in 1709 at the expense of William Green, a local brewer, to provide an education for poor children; in use as a school until 1926, the building was bought by the Trust in 1954; it was restored in 1975 and now houses a National Trust shop and information centre.

Location: No 23 Caxton Street, Westminster, SW1.
Stations: Victoria ¼ m; Underground St James's Park (Circle and District Lines) less than 100 yards.
Opening Times: All year, Mon to Fri 10–5.30, (Dec 24, closes 4.30). Late night shopping Thurs until 7. Also Sats Dec 5, 12, 19, 11–4.30. *Closed Bank Holiday Mondays, Dec 25–31, Jan 1 and Good Friday.* Adm free.

BOSTON MANOR – *See page 125*

BURGH HOUSE

Hampstead map K4
Telephone: 071-431 0144
(Burgh House Trust)

Built 1703. Used for art exhibitions, concerts. Hampstead Museum. Terrace Garden.

Location: New End Sq E of Hampstead Underground Station.
Station: Hampstead (Underground). Hampstead Heath (BR North London Link).
Opening Times: Weds to Suns 12–5; Bank Hol Mons 2–5. Adm free.
Refreshments: Coffee, lunches and Teas. Licensed Buttery (for reservations and enquiries about catering for functions at the House Tel: 071-431 2516).

BOSTON MANOR

Brentford map K4
Telephone: 081-862 5805
(London Borough of Hounslow)

Jacobean house (1622) with elaborate plaster ceiling in the State Room which also contains a fireplace and mantelpiece dating from 1623. Original oak staircase. The house is set in a small park.

Location: In Boston Manor Road.
Opening Times: May 24 to Sept 20 — Sun afternoons only 2–4.30. Adm free.

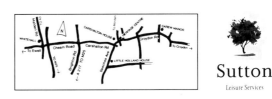

CAREW MANOR AND DOVECOTE

Beddington map K4
(London Borough of Sutton)

This building, formerly known as Beddington Park or Beddington Place, contains a late-medieval Great Hall, with an arch-braced hammer-beam roof, which is listed Grade I. The house is used as a school, but the Hall is now accessible (details below), together with the restored early 18th century Dovecote, with its 1,288 nesting boxes and potence, which is a scheduled ancient monument. Guided tours are given of the Dovecote, the Great Hall and the cellars of the house which contain medieval, Tudor, and later features (cellars accessible on guided tours only). Some tours take in the late 14th century Church of St Mary, Beddington, with its Norman font and its 15th century Carew Chapel containing important Carew memorials (the Carews of Beddington were lords of the manor for over four hundred years). Carew Manor and Beddington Church stand on the edge of Beddington Park, the landscaped home park of the Carews, through which a Heritage Trail has been established giving details of the history, historic buildings, garden features, and wildlife of this important conservation area. Guide book, trail leaflet and other publications and souvenirs available.

Location: Church Road, Beddington. Off A232 ¾ m E of junction with A237.
Opening Times: Suns & Bank Hol Mons. Guided tours from Easter to Nov 1 (phone Sutton Heritage Service 081-773 4555). Adm charge.

CARLYLE'S HOUSE, The National Trust 🌿

Chelsea map K4
Telephone: 071-352 7087

Home of Thomas and Jane Carlyle 1834-1881. *Note: Certain rooms have no electric light, visitors wishing to make a close study of the interior should avoid dull days.*

Location: At 24 Cheyne Row, Chelsea SW3 (off Cheyne Walk on Chelsea Embankment).
Stations: Sloane Sq (Underground 1 m); Victoria (BR 1½ m).
Opening Times: Apr to end of Oct—Weds to Suns & Bank Hol Mons 11–5. Last adm 4.30. *Closed Good Friday.* Adm £2.50, Chd £1.25. No reduction for parties, which should not exceed 20 and must book. No dogs. Unsuitable for wheelchairs.

CARSHALTON HOUSE (Daughters of the Cross) St Philomena's School, Pound Street

Carshalton map K4

An important listed building, built by about 1707 around the core of an older house and with grounds laid out originally by Charles Bridgeman, Carshalton House is open on a limited number of occasions each year. Its garden buildings include the unique Water Tower, now in the care of the Carshalton Water Tower Trust. The former lake is leased to the London Wildlife Trust. The house contains principal rooms with 18th century decoration, including the important Blue Room and the Painted Parlour (attributed to Robert Robinson). Openings are organised by Sutton Heritage Service in conjunction with the Water Tower Trust, the London Wildlife Trust, and the Daughters of the Cross. Tours of the house and grounds and a programme of short talks on the house and its people, and the lake project are given during the open days (included in entrance fee). Refreshments and publications are available. Carshalton House is close to Sutton's Heritage Centre at Honeywood, in the Carshalton conservation area.

Location: Pound Street, Carshalton, at junction with Carshalton Road, on A232.
Station: Carshalton (¼ m).
Opening Times: 1992: Mon Apr 20 (Easter Monday), Mon May 25 (Spring Bank Hol), Mon Aug 31 (Aug Bank Hol) 10–5 (last admission 4.30). Adm charge. For further details telephone Sutton Heritage Service on 081-773 4555.
Refreshments: Available.

CHAPTER HOUSE AND PYX CHAMBER ⬛ WESTMINSTER ABBEY

map K4
Telephone: 071-222 5897

Described as 'incomparable' when it was finished in 1253, with some of the finest of English medieval sculpture, the chapter house was one of the largest in England and could seat 80 monks around its walls. It was converted to a record office in the 16th century, but by 1740 the roof had decayed and been removed. Restoration of the whole building took place in 1865 and again after it was bombed in 1941. The 11th century Pyx Chamber now houses the Abbey Treasures. A joint ticket admits to the Abbey Museum.

Location: East side of the abbey cloister.
Opening Times: Good Friday or Apr 1 (whichever is earlier) to Sept 30: Open Daily 10–6. Oct 1 to Maundy Thursday or Mar 31 (whichever is earlier): Open Daily 10–4. *Closed* Dec 24 –26, Jan 1. Adm £1.80, Concessions £1.40, Chd 90p. Liable to be closed at short notice on state occasions.

CHELSEA PHYSIC GARDEN

Chelsea map K4

The second oldest Botanic garden in the country, founded 1673 including notable collection of medicinal plants, comprises 4 acres densely packed with c. 5,000 plants, many rare and unusual.

Location: 66 Royal Hospital Road, Chelsea; nr junction of Royal Hospital Road & Chelsea Embankment.
Station: Sloane Square (Underground).
Opening Times: Mar 22 to Oct 18—Suns and Weds, 2–5. Also Tues 19 to Fri May 22 (Chelsea Flower Show Week) 12–5. Adm (1992 prices) £2.50, Chd, unemployed & students (with cards) £1.30. Open at other times for subscribing Friends and groups by appointment. No dogs. Garden accessible for disabled & wheelchairs via 66, Royal Hospital Road. Parking in street Suns, other days across Albert Bridge in Battersea Park, free.

CHISWICK HOUSE ⬛

Chiswick map K4
Telephone: 081-995 0508
(English Heritage)

Architect and patron of the arts, the third Earl of Burlington set a fashion with this Italian-style villa, built to house his library and art collections. The gardens were landscaped by William Kent.

Location: Burlington Lane (½ m) NE of Chiswick Station.
Opening Times: Good Friday or Apr 1 (whichever is earlier) to Sept 30 daily 10–6. Oct 1 to Maundy Thursday or Mar 31 (whichever is earlier) daily 10–4. *Closed* Dec 24, 25. Adm £2, Concessions £1.50, Chd £1.

COLLEGE OF ARMS

City of London EC4V 4BT map K4 △
Telephone: 071-248 2762
(The Corporation of Kings, Heralds & Pursuivants of Arms)

Mansion built in 1670s to house the English Officers of Arms and their records, and the panelled Earl Marshal's Court.

Location: On N side of Queen Victoria Street; S of St Paul's Cathedral.
Opening Times: EARL MARSHAL'S COURT ONLY. Open all the year (except Public holidays & on State & special occasions) Mons to Fris 10–4. Group visits (up to 10) by arrangement only. RECORD ROOM open for tours (groups of up to 20) by special arrangement in advance with the Officer in Waiting. Adm free (parties by negotiation). *No coaches, parking, indoor photography or dogs.* Shop—books, souvenirs.

DE MORGAN FOUNDATION

Old Battersea House map K4 △
Telephone: 081-788 1341
(De Morgan Foundation)

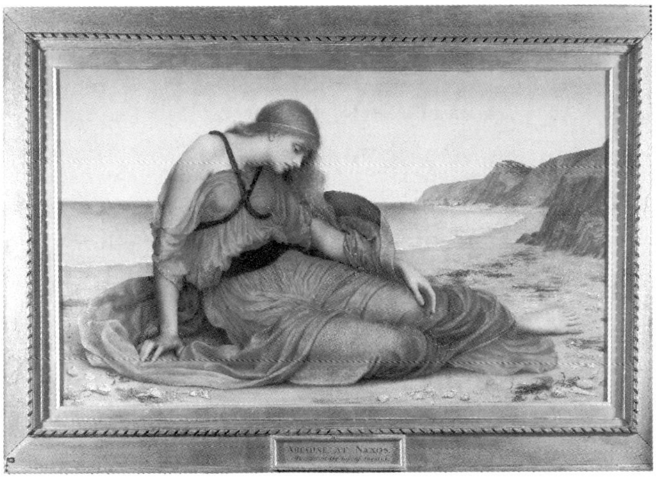

A substantial part of the De Morgan Foundation collection of ceramics by William De Morgan and paintings and drawings by Evelyn De Morgan (nee Pickering), her uncle Roddam Spencer Stanhope, J. M. Strudwick and Cadogan Cowper are displayed in the ground floor rooms of elegantly restored Old Battersea House – a Wren building. The setting is that of a privately occupied house.

Location: Vicarage Crescent, Battersea.
Opening Times: Admission by appointment only – usually Weds afternoons. All visits are guided. Adm £1, optional catalogue £1.50. No special reductions. Parties – maximum 30 (split into two groups of 15). Car parking in Vicarage Crescent. Suitable for disabled, (no special facilities for wheelchairs) front steps are the only obstacle. Adm by writing in advance to De Morgan Foundation, 21 St Margaret's Crescent, London SW1 6HL.
Refreshments: No catering at house. Many facilities in Battersea/Wandsworth.

THE DICKENS HOUSE MUSEUM, WC1N 2LF

map K4
Telephone: 071-405 2127
(The Trustees of the Dickens House)

House occupied by Dickens and his family 1837-39. Relics displayed include manuscripts, furniture, autographs, portraits, letters and first editions.

Location: 48 Doughty Street, near Grays Inn Road/Guilford Street.
Opening Times: All the year—Mons to Sats 10–5. *Closed Suns, Bank and Christmas week Holidays.* Adm £2, Students £1.50, Chd £1; Families £4 (subject to alteration). Parties by appointment. Ground floor only (2 rooms) suitable for disabled—reduced adm charge.

FENTON HOUSE, The National Trust

Hampstead map K4
Telephone: 071-435 3471

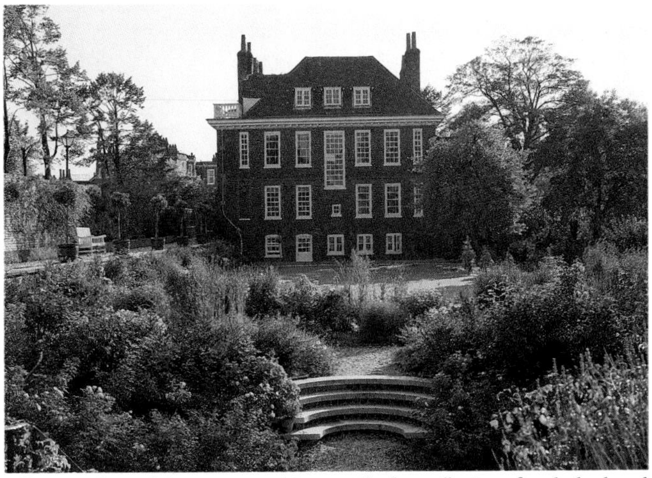

Collection of porcelain, pottery and Benton Fletcher collection of early keyboard musical instruments. Late 17th century house, walled garden.

Location: On W side of Hampstead Grove.
Stations: Hampstead (Underground 300 yards); Hampstead Heath (BR 1 m).
Opening Times: Mar—Sat & Sun only 2–6; Apr to end Oct—Sats, Suns and Hol Mons 11–6; Mon, Tues, and Wed 1–7. Last adm ½ hour before closing time. *Closed Good Friday.* Adm £3, Chd half-price. No reductions for parties, which must book. No dogs. Suitable for wheelchairs on ground floor only.

FULHAM PALACE

Fulham map K4
Telephone: 071-736 5821; 071-736 3233 (Museum and tours only).
(London Borough of Hammersmith and Fulham)

Former residence of the Bishops of London since the 8th century. Buildings now date from 15th century and stand on the site of a Roman Settlement. The gardens gained major importance during the 17th century, when many American species of trees and shrubs were first introduced to Europe through Fulham Palace. Museum of the history of the Palace open in 1992.

Location: In Bishop's Ave, ½ m N of Putney Bridge underground station (District Line).
Opening Times: Grounds, Botanic Garden and herb collection open daily, daylight hours. Adm free. Free tours of principal rooms and gardens are conducted by the Museum Curator on every second Sunday throughout the year at 2. Private tours at other times by arrangement (£2.50 per head, incl tea). Function rooms available for private hire, incl receptions and filming (071-736 7181).

GUNNERSBURY PARK MUSEUM

Gunnersbury Park W3 map K4 ♿
Telephone: 081-992 1612
(London Boroughs of Ealing & Hounslow)

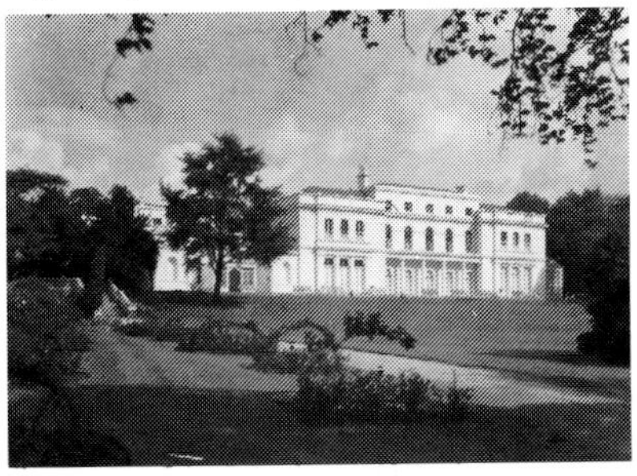

Large mansion built c.1802 by architect owner Alexander Copland. Fine rooms by Sydney Smirke and painted ceilings by E. T. Parris for N. M. Rothschild c.1836. Now a local history museum which includes Rothschild carriages. Original Victorian kitchens open summer by arrangement and on selected weekends. Large park with other buildings of interest, and sporting facilities.

Location: Mansion at NE corner of Park; alongside North Circular (A406); N of Great West Road & M4; Kew Bridge 1¼ m; Chiswick Roundabout ½ m. Bus: E3 (daily), 7 (Suns only).
Station: Acton Town (Underground ¼ m).
Opening Times: House & Museum. Mar to Nov—Mons to Fris 1–5; Sats, Suns & Bank Hols 1–6. Nov 1 to Feb—Mons to Fris 1–4; Sats, Suns & Bank Hols 1–4. *Closed Christmas Eve (variable), Christmas Day, Boxing Day & Good Friday.* Gardens. Daily dawn till dusk. Adm free. Special facilities for school parties by arrangement with Interpretative Officer. Vehicle access Popes Lane. Pedestrians – many entries to Park.
Refreshments: Cafeteria in Park (daily, winter weekends according to weather).

HALL PLACE

Bexley map K4
(Bexley London Borough Council)

Historic mansion (1540). Outstanding Rose, Rock, Water, Herb, Peat gardens and Floral bedding displays, Conservatories, Parkland, Topiary designed in the form of the Queen's Beasts.

Location: Near the junction of A2 and A223.
Station: Bexley (1/2 m).
Opening Times: MANSION. Weekdays 10–5; Suns 2–6 (except from Nov to Mar). Museum & other exhibitions. PARK & GROUNDS. Daily during daylight throughout the year. Adm free.
Refreshments: At café.

HAM HOUSE, The National Trust

Ham, Richmond TW10 7RS map K4
Telephone: 081-940 1950

Outstanding Stuart house, built about 1610, redecorated and furnished in 1670s in the most up to date style of the time by the Duke and Duchess of Lauderdale; restored 17th century garden.

Location: On South bank of the river Thames, W of A307 at Petersham.
Stations: Richmond 2 m by road. Kingston 2 m.
Bus: LT 65 Ealing Broadway-Kingston. 371 Richmond-Chessington Zoo (both passing BR Richmond and Kingston), 71 also passing BR Surbiton.
Opening Times: House: Closed throughout 1992 for major restoration. Garden: all year: daily except Mon 10.30–6 (or dusk if earlier), garden free. Disabled visitors may park near entrance. Lavatory for disabled in garden.
Refreshments: Teas – limited facilities only serving tea, coffee daily except Mon, Apr to end Oct 11.30–5.30. Please check in advance (tel: 081-940 1950).

HERITAGE CENTRE

Honeywood, Carshalton map K4
(London Borough of Sutton)

Honeywood is a late 18th century listed building, containing the core of an earlier house, with later additions. (The London Borough of Sutton includes Beddington, Carshalton, Cheam, Sutton and Wallington.) A permanent exhibition and a/v, plus a changing programme of exhibitions, cover many aspects of local life – social and domestic history, architecture, sport, famous people, transport, local industries, including lavender and herbs. Honeywood stands at the head of Carshalton's picturesque town ponds, one of the sources of the Wandle, and at the heart of a conservation area. Gift shop and tea room available.

Location: Honeywood Walk, Carshalton. By Carshalton Ponds, opp. the Greyhound Inn.
Station: Carshalton (1/4 m).
Opening Times: Tues to Sun and Bank Hol Mon 10–5.30. *Closed* Mons. Adm charge.
Further details: Phone Sutton Heritage Services 081-773 4555.
Refreshments: Access to Tea Room free.

HOGARTH'S HOUSE

Chiswick map K4 △
Telephone: 081-994 6757
(London Borough of Hounslow)

The artist's country house for 15 years containing many prints and some relics associated with the artist.

Location: In Hogarth Lane, Great West Road, Chiswick W4 2QN (200 yards Chiswick House).
Stations: Chiswick (1/2 m) (Southern Region); Turnham Green (1 m) (District Line).
Opening Times: Apr to Sept–Mons to Sats 11–6; Suns 2–6. Oct to Mar–Mons to Sats 11–4; Suns 2–4. *Closed* Tues, Good Friday, Aug 31 to Sept 13, last 3 weeks in Dec & New Year's Day.

KEATS HOUSE

Wentworth Place, Keats Grove, Hampstead NW3 2RR map K4
Telephone: 071-435 2062
(London Borough of Camden)

Keats House was built in 1815–1816 as Wentworth Place, a pair of semi-detached houses. John Keats, the poet, lived here from 1818 to 1820; here he wrote 'Ode to a Nightingale', and met Fanny Brawne, to whom he became engaged. Keats' death early in Italy prevented the marriage. Keats House was completely restored in 1974–1975. It houses letters, books and other personal relics of the poet and his fiancee.

Location: S end of Hampstead Heath nr South End Green.
Station: (BR Hampstead Heath). Underground: Belsize Park or Hampstead. Bus: 24, 46, 168, C11 (alight South End Green). 268 (alight Downshire Hill).
Opening Times: All the year—Apr 1 to Oct: Mon–Fri 10–1, 2–6, Sat 10–1, 2–5; Sun and Bank Holiday 2–5. Nov to Mar: Mon–Fri 1–5, Sat 10–1, 2–5; Sun 2–5. Adm free. *Closed Christmas Eve, Christmas Day, Boxing Day, New Year's Day, Good Friday, Easter Eve & May 4.*

KENWOOD, THE IVEAGH BEQUEST ⊞

Hampstead   map K4
Telephone: 081-348 1286
(English Heritage)

Adam mansion, once the seat of Lord Mansfield. The Iveagh Bequest of Old Master and British paintings, including works by Rembrandt, Vermeer, Hals, Gainsborough, Turner and Reynolds. Fine collection of neo-classical furniture.

Location: Hampstead Lane, NW3.
Station: Archway or Golders Green Underground (Northern Line), then Bus 210.
Opening Times: Good Friday or Apr 1 (whichever is earlier) to Sept 30 daily 10–6. Oct 1 to Maundy Thursday or Mar 31 (whichever is earlier) daily 10–4. *Closed* Dec 24, 25. Adm free.
Refreshments: At the Coach House.

KEW GARDENS

Kew   map K4   ♿
Telephone: 071-940 1171
(Royal Botanic Gardens)

300 acres in extent containing living collection of over 50,000 different plant species. Greenhouses. Museums.

Location: On south bank of Thames at Kew 1 m from Richmond.
Station: Kew Gardens (¹/₂ m).
Opening Times: All the year—Daily, open at 9.30. *Closed Christmas Day & New Year's Day.* Museums open from 9.30. Closing times vary according to season but not later than 6.30 Mons to Sats & 8.30 Suns.
Refreshments: At Pavilion (Mar–Nov); at Tea Bar (all year). Orangery Restaurant.

LEIGHTON HOUSE MUSEUM – *See page 130*

LINLEY SAMBOURNE HOUSE, W8

map K4
Telephone: 081-994 1019
(The Victorian Society)

The home of Linley Sambourne (1844–1910), chief political cartoonist at 'Punch'. A unique survival of a late Victorian town house. The original decorations and furnishings have been preserved together with many of Sambourne's own cartoons and photographs, as well as works by other artists of the period.

Location: 18 Stafford Terrace, W8 7BH.
Station: (Underground) Kensington High Street.
Opening Times: 1 Mar to 31 Oct—Weds 10–4, Suns 2–5. Parties at other times by prior arrangement. Apply to The Victorian Society, 1 Priory Gardens, London W4. Telephone: 081-994 1019. Adm £2.

LITTLE HOLLAND HOUSE

Carshalton   map K4
(London Borough of Sutton)

The home of Frank Dickinson (1874–1961), follower of the Arts and Crafts movement: artist, designer and craftsman in wood and metal who built the house himself to his own design and in pursuance of his philosophy and theories. Features his interior design, paintings, hand-made furniture and other craft objects.

Location: 40 Beeches Avenue, Carshalton. On B278 (off A232).
Station: Few minutes from Carshalton Beeches BR.
Opening Times: Mar to Oct—first Sun in the month plus Bank Hol Suns & Mons 1–6. Further information from Sutton Heritage Service on 081-773 4555. **Admission free.**

MARBLE HILL HOUSE ⊞

Twickenham   map K4
Telephone: 081-892 5115
(English Heritage)

A complete example of an English Palladian villa. Early Georgian paintings and furniture.

Location: Richmond Road.
Stations: St Margaret's (¹/₂ m); Twickenham (1 m); Richmond (2 m).
Opening Times: Good Friday or Apr 1 (whichever is earlier) to Sept 30 daily 10–6. Oct 1 to Maundy Thursday or Mar 31 (whichever is earlier) daily 10–4. *Closed* Dec 24, 25. Adm free.
Refreshments: In Stable Block.

MARLBOROUGH HOUSE

Pall Mall

Will be closed indefinitely for repairs.

LEIGHTON HOUSE MUSEUM

12 Holland Park Road   map K4
Telephone: 071-602 3316
(Royal Borough of Kensington and Chelsea)

Leighton House Museum from the Garden

LEIGHTON HOUSE MUSEUM

The Arab Hall

Royal Borough of Kensington Libraries and Arts Service

Adjacent to Holland Park in Kensington lies the Artists' Colony, a group of remarkable Studio Houses, built by some of the leading figures of the Victorian art world. Leighton House Museum was the first of these to be built, and is today a museum of high Victorian art. The opulent fantasy of Frederic Lord Leighton, President of the Royal Academy, the house was designed by George Aitchison. Leighton lived here from 1866 until his death in 1896. His unique collection of Islamic tiles is displayed in the walls of the Arab Hall, and the Victorian interiors, restored to their original splendour, are hung with paintings by Leighton, Millais, Watts, Burne-Jones and others. Fine 'New Sculpture' by Leighton, Brock and Thornycroft is displayed in the house and garden. The study collection of Leighton drawings may be seen by appointment. Temporary exhibitions of modern and historic art throughout the year.

Location: Kensington.
Opening Times: All year. Mon–Sat 11–5.30. **Garden:** Apr–Sept *(Closed Bank Holidays)*. Parties by arrangement with the Curator. Chd under 16 must be accompanied by an adult.

MUSEUM OF GARDEN HISTORY

Lambeth   map K4
Telephone: 071-373 4030 (between 7 and 9 am)
and 071-261 1891 (between 11 and 3)
(The Tradescant Trust)

The former church of St Mary-at-Lambeth has been converted into the first museum of Garden History in the world. The tomb of John Tradescant, gardener to Charles I, lies in the former churchyard where a 17th century Garden has been created, planted with species shrubs and flowers of the period. Lectures, concerts, exhibitions, shop. Permanent exhibition of aspects of garden history, including a fine collection of antique tools.

Location: Lambeth Palace Road.
Station: Waterloo or Victoria, then 507 Red Arrow bus, alight Lambeth Palace.
Opening Times: Mons to Fris 11–3; Suns 10.30–5. *Closed Sat. Closed from second Sun in Dec to first Sun in Mar.* Adm free. Donation requested. Literature is sent on request.
Refreshments: Tea, coffee, light lunches; parties catered for but prior booking essential.

THE OCTAGON, ORLEANS HOUSE GALLERY

Riverside Twickenham   map K4   &
Telephone: 081-892 0221
(London Borough of Richmond upon Thames)

The magnificent Octagon built by James Gibbs in c.1720 for James Johnston, Joint Secretary of State for Scotland under William III. An outstanding example of baroque architecture. The adjacent wing has been converted into an art gallery which shows temporary exhibitions and the whole is situated in an attractive woodland garden.

Location: Access from Richmond Road (A305).
Stations: St Margaret's (¹/₂ m); Twickenham (¹/₂ m); Richmond (underground 2 m)
Opening Times: Tues to Sats 1–5.30 (Oct to Mar, 1–4.30); Suns 2–5.30 (Oct to Mar, 2–4.30). Easter, Spring, Summer Bank Hols 2–5.30. *Closed Christmas.* Adm and parking free. Disabled access. W,S.

THE OLD PALACE

Old Palace Road, Croydon   map K4   △
Telephone: 081-680 5877
(Old Palace School (Croydon) Ltd)

Seat of Archbishops of Canterbury since 871. 15th century Banqueting Hall and Guardroom, Tudor Chapel, Norman undercroft.

Location: In central Croydon. Adjacent to Parish Church.
Stations: East Croydon or West Croydon (few mins walk).
Opening Times: Conducted Tours only. Doors open 2 pm. Last tour commences 2.30. Tues Apr 21 to Sat Apr 25, Mon May 25 to Fri May 29. Mon July 13 to Sat July 18, Mon July 20 to Sat July 25. Adm £3.50, Chd & OAPs £2.50, this includes home made tea served in the undercroft. Car park. Souvenir shop. Parties catered for, apply Bursar. Unsuitable for wheelchairs.

OLD ROYAL OBSERVATORY

Greenwich SE10   map K4
Telephone: 081-858 4422
(National Maritime Museum)

Part of the National Maritime Museum it includes Flamsteed House, designed by Sir Christopher Wren, the Meridian Building and the Greenwich Planetarium.

Location: In Greenwich Park, N side of Blackheath.
Station: Maze Hill (short walk).
Opening Times: Mon to Sat 10–6 (10–5 in winter); Sun 12–6 (2–5 in winter). *Closed* Christmas Eve, Christmas Day, Boxing Day. Adm (1991): Each site £3.25, Chd/OAP/Student £2.25. Passports to four attractions including Cutty Sark £5.95, Chd/OAP/Student £3.95, Family £11.95.
Refreshments: In Park cafeteria and museum main buildings.

OSTERLEY PARK The National Trust ✹

Isleworth, Middlesex TW7 4RB   map K4   △   &
Telephone: 081-560 3918

Elizabethan mansion transformed by Robert Adam 1760-80; with Adam decorations and furniture; 140 acres of parkland.

Location: ¹/₄ m E of Osterley Underground station (Piccadilly Line) and ¹/₂ m W of Gillette Corner, access from Thornbury Road, N side of Great West Road (A4)
Station: Syon Lane (1³/₄ m); Underground: Osterley (³/₄ m).
Bus: LT 91 Hounslow-Wandsworth (¹/₂ m.)
Opening Times: House: Mar: Sat and Sun 1–5; Apr to end Oct: Wed to Sat 1–5; Sun and Bank Holiday Mon 11–5. House closed Good Friday. Last admission 4.30. Park: all year 9–7.30 or sunset if earlier. Car park closed Dec 25, 26. Adm £3. Parties must book, rates on application to Administrator. Park free. Car park 250 yards £1. Guided tours may be arranged in advance with the Administrator. Park suitable for disabled. Lavatory for disabled. Dogs in park only.
Refreshments: Teas and light lunches in stables, Tues to Sun and Bank Holiday Mon, Mar to end Oct 12–5. Also open Good Friday.

PITSHANGER MANOR MUSEUM

Mattock Lane, Ealing W5   map K4
Telephone: 081-567 1227 or 081-579 2424 ext 42683
(London Borough of Ealing)

Set in an attractive park, Pitshanger Manor was built 1800-04 by the architect Sir John Soane (1753-1837) as his family home. The house incorporates a wing of the late 1760s by George Dance. The interiors are being restored. All rooms are open to the public after 1pm. *Please enquire in advance as to which rooms are open in the mornings.* A Victorian room holds a changing and extensive display of Martinware

PITSHANGER MANOR MUSEUM – *Continued from page 131*

pottery including a unique chimney-piece of 1891. Exhibitions and cultural events are held regularly. Adm free. Parties by arrangement in advance. Limited disabled access – further details available on request.

Location: ⅓ m from Ealing Broadway Tube Station (Central and District Lines). On the A3001 (Ealing Green). No parking.
Opening Times: Tues to Sat 10–5. *Closed Sun & Mon.* (but open Sun afternoons in July and Aug). *Also closed Christmas, Easter and New Year.*
Refreshments: Tea and coffee vending machine.

THE QUEEN'S HOUSE

Greenwich SE10 map K4
Telephone: 081-858 4422
(National Maritime Museum)

THE QUEENS HOUSE
GREENWICH
A Royal Palace by the Thames

Visit the House of Delights designed by Inigo Jones for the wife of Charles I. Admire the sumptuous Royal Apartments that recreate the original seventeenth century splendour, and learn the fascinating history of the House in the special display in the vaulted brick basement.

A combined ticket allows you to visit the Old Royal Observatory, National Maritime Museum and *Cutty Sark* which are nearby

ADMISSION – SEE EDITORIAL REFERENCE

Royal Palace designed by Inigo Jones for Anne of Denmark, wife of James I, and Henrietta Maria, wife of Charles I. Now restored to its former 17th century glory, after a £5M refurbishment. Highlights include the sumptuous Royal Apartments and the Great Hall, a perfect 40ft cube. The vaulted brick basement houses a display on the history of the house, and the treasury, showing the NMM's richest trophies, swords and ornamental silver.

Location: Greenwich, London.
Station: Maze Hill (BR); Island Gardens (Docklands Light Railway); River Buses.
Opening Times: Mon to Sats 10–6 (10–5 in winter), Suns 12–6 (2–5 in winter). *Closed* Christmas Eve, Christmas Day, Boxing Day. Adm (1991): Each site £3.25, Chd/OAP/Student £2.25. Passport to all sites including Cutty Sark £5.95, Chd/OAP/Student £3.95; Family £11.95. Wheelchair access to ground floor and basement. Wheelchairs available.
Refreshments: Licensed restaurant.

RANGER'S HOUSE ⌗

Blackheath map K4 Ⓢ
Telephone: 081-853 0035
(English Heritage)

A Gallery of English Portraits in the 4th Earl of Chesterfield's house, from the Elizabethan to the Georgian period. Dolmetsch Collection of musical instruments in period rooms on restored first floor.

Location: Chesterfield Walk, SE10.
Stations: Greenwich or Blackheath (15 mins walk).
Opening Times: Good Friday or Apr 1 (whichever is earlier) to Sept 30 daily 10–6. Oct 1 to Maundy Thursday or Mar 31 (whichever is earlier) daily 10–4. *Closed* Dec 24, 25. Adm free.

ROYAL INSTITUTE OF BRITISH ARCHITECTS: Drawings Collection and Heinz Gallery

W1 map K4
Telephone: 071-580 5533
(Royal Institute of British Architects)

Study room open 10–1 weekdays, by appointment only for serious enquiries. Changing architectural exhibitions throughout most of the year freely open to the public, 11–5 weekdays, 10–1 Sats.

Location: 21 Portman Square W1H 9HF.
Opening Times: Weekdays 11–5, Sats 10–1. Adm free. Unsuitable for disabled persons. No car parking.

RSA (The Royal Society for the encouragement of Arts, Manufacturers and Commerce)

8 John Adam Street WC2N 6EZ
Telephone: 071-930 5115

Founded in 1754, the RSA moved to its bespoke house, designed and built by Robert Adam, in 1774. The most interesting features of the Society's premises are its Great Room, a lecture hall, capacity 200, with murals by James Barry and the recently restored vaults.

Location: 8 John Adam Street, London WC2N 6EZ.
Opening Times: Mon to Fri 10–1, adm free. Visitors who wish to see any of the Society's rooms are requested to telephone in advance in order to avoid disappointment if the rooms are in use and therefore inaccessible.

ST JOHN'S GATE

Clerkenwell map K4 △
Telephone: 071-253 6644, Ext 35
(The Order of St John)

Headquarters of the Order in England, the 16th century gatehouse contains the most comprehensive collection of items relating to the Order of St John outside Malta. Together with the nearby Priory Church and 12th century Crypt it now forms the headquarters of the modern Order of St. John, whose charitable foundations include St. John Ambulance and the Ophthalmic Hospital in Jerusalem. The collection includes Maltese silver, Italian furniture, paintings, coins and pharmacy jars.

Location: In St John's Lane, EC1M 4DA.
Stations: (Underground) Farringdon, Barbican.
Opening Times: Mon to Fr 10–5, Sats 10–4. Tours of the building, including the Grand Priory Church and Norman crypt on Tues, Fri and Sat 11 & 2.30.

SIR JOHN SOANE'S MUSEUM

13 Lincoln's Inn Fields, WC2A 3BP map K4
Telephone: 071-405 2107; Information line 071-430 0175

Built by Sir John Soane, RA, in 1812–13 as his private residence. Contains his collection of antiquities and works of art. Tues to Sat 10–5 (lecture tours Sat 2.30, maximum 22 people, no groups): Groups welcome at other times, but must book in advance. Late evening opening on the first Tues of each month, 6–9pm. Also library and architectural drawings collection: access by appointment. *Closed* Bank Holidays.

SOUTHSIDE HOUSE – *See page 134*

SYON HOUSE

Brentford map K4 △
Telephone: 081-560 0881/3
(His Grace the Duke of Northumberland)

Noted for its magnificent Adam interior and furnishings, famous picture collection, and historical associations dating back to 1415, 'Capability' Brown landscape.

Location: On N bank of Thames between Brentford & Isleworth.
Stations: Brentford (BR 1 m); Syon Lane (BR 1 m).
Opening Times: Apr 1 to Sept 29—Daily (except Fris) 12–5. Last adm 4.15. Also Suns in Oct, 12–5. Adm charges not available at time of going to press.

SOUTHSIDE HOUSE

Wimbledon Common SW19 4RJ   map K4   △
Telephone: 081-947 2491 or 081-946 7643
(The Pennington–Mellor–Munthe Charity Trust, established 1947 – reg no 283266)

SOUTHSIDE HOUSE

(the Kemeys-Pennington-Mellor-Munthe family)

Wimbledon Common, London SW19 4RJ
Telephone: 081-947 2491 & 081-946 7643

OPEN THROUGHOUT THE WINTER
FROM OCTOBER 1st UNTIL MAY 31st

See: Queen Anne Boleyn's Dressing Case collected from the Tower of London after her execution; the sword that killed the King's favourite nephew; the pearl necklace which fell from its hiding place when Queen Marie Antoinette was executed; the room specially created for the stay of Frederick, Prince of Wales, in 1750; pictures dating from 1580 by more than fifty major artists; and much more.....

Hear: how Robert Pennington returned from exile with the Prince of Wales at the end of the Civil War to build Southside House after losing his only son to The Great Plague of London; how Philip, Duke of Wharton, "our dear infamous relative", was kicked out of the Hell Fire Club; how John Pennington became a real-life "Scarlet Pimpernel" during the French Revolution; how Emma Hamilton entertained her hosts and fellow guests, including Admiral Lord Nelson, after dinner, with her famous classical "Attitudes"; and much more.....

hourly guided tours on Tuesdays, Thursdays & Saturdays &
Bank Holiday Mondays (closed Christmas)
special Connoisseur's, School and Group Tours bookable

Historic home built by Robert Pennington after his little son had perished in the great plague of London, 1665. Still lived in by his descendants today. Much original furniture, pictures, works of art and personal belongings of ancestors remain here – including Anne Boleyn's vanity box with comb used on her last day in the Tower of London – Philip, Duke of Wharton's portrait wearing Hell Fire Club uniform, also his Order of the Garter suit and snuff box – Frederick, Prince of Wales's bedroom as prepared for his visit, 1750 – Queen Marie Antoinette's last pearl necklace which fell from its hiding place when her head was cut off – and other gifts to John Pennington (the family "Scarlet Pimpernel") by grateful Frenchmen whom he helped escape. In 1802 and 1803 Sir William Hamilton used to dine here with his Emma and Lord Nelson. In 1907, the heiress of this house, Hilda Pennington Mellor, married Axel Munthe, the Swedish Doctor and philanthropist who later wrote part of his "Story of San Michele" here.

Location: On S side of Wimbledon Common (B281), opposite The Crooked Billet Inn – off Wimbledon High Street (A219).
Stations: Wimbledon (British Rail & Underground) 1 m.
Buses: No 93, alight Rose & Crown Inn, Wimbledon High Street – six minutes walk along Southside of Common to Crooked Billet Inn and Southside House.
Opening Times: From Oct 1 until May 31. Guided tours only on Tues, Thurs, Sat & Bank Holiday Mons *(Closed Christmas)* on the hour from 2–5 (last admission), lasting approximately 1¼ hours. Connoisseur's Private Tours can be arranged at other times (Charity Trust engagements permitting) by applying to the Administrator in writing. Adm £5, Chd (over 10 and under 18 accompanied by responsible adult) £3. Organised school groups accompanied by responsible teachers free by appointment in writing.

SYON HOUSE – *See page 133*

SYON PARK GARDENS

Brentford   map K4
Telephone: 081-560 0881/3
(His Grace the Duke of Northumberland)

Includes the Great Conservatory by Dr Fowler. Within the Estate is the London Butterfly House and the British Heritage Motor Museum (telephone details below); also the Syon Art Centre.

Location: On N bank of Thames between Brentford & Isleworth.
Stations: Waterloo to Kew Bridge, nearest tube Gunnersbury.
Buses: 267 or 237 to Brentlea.
Opening Times: All the year – Mar to Oct – Daily 10–6. Oct to Feb – Daily 10–dusk; Last adm 1 hour before closing. *Closed Christmas Day & Boxing Day.* Adm charges not available at time of going to press. Free car park. Telephone 081-560 0881/3.
London Butterfly House – opening times & adm charges: Telephone 081-560 7272.
British Heritage Motor Museum – opening times & adm charges: Telephone 081-560 1378.
Syon Art Centre – free admission: Telephone 081-568 6021. (Gift shop – National Trust.)
Refreshments: Cafeteria and Restaurant. Telephone 081-568 0778/9. Enquiries to Administrator, Syon Park.

THE TRAVELLERS' CLUB

Pall Mall   map K4
Telephone: 071-930 8688 *(by prior appointment)*

Built in 1829-33 by Sir Charles Barry. (Roof restored in 1986).
Location: 106 Pall Mall.
Station: Piccadilly Circus Underground.
Opening Times: By prior appointment Mon to Fri only from 10–12 and 3–5.30. Weekends by negotiation. *Closed Bank Hols, Aug and Christmas.* Adm £5.50.

VALE MASCAL BATH HOUSE

Bexley   map K4
Telephone: (0322) 554894

Gothic style Bath House built circa 1766. Grade II. Situated on an island beside the River Cray and reached by crossing a small wooden bridge from the garden.
Location: About 16 miles from central London, A2 & A20 off M25.
Opening Times: First sun in month. Small amount of car parking. Not suitable for wheelchairs. Teas supplied if requested.

WHITEHALL

1 Malden Road, Cheam   map K4
Telephone: 081-643 1236
(London Borough of Sutton)

A unique timber-framed house built c 1500. A feature is the revealed sections of original fabric. Displays include medieval Cheam pottery; Nonsuch Palace; timber-framed buildings and Cheam School. Changing exhibitions throughout the year.

Location: On A2043 just N of junction with A232.
Station: Cheam (¼ m).
Opening Times: Apr to Sept – Tues to Fris, Sun 2–5.30. Sat 10–5.30. Oct to Mar – Wed, Thurs, Sun 2–5.30. Sat 10–5.30. Also open Bank Holiday Mons 2–5.30. *Closed Dec 24 to Jan 2 incl.* Further information from Sutton Heritage Service on 081-773 4555. Adm charge. Party bookings, guided tour facilities, tea room and gift shop available.

MERSEYSIDE

BLUECOAT CHAMBERS

Liverpool   map F8
Telephone: 051-709 5297
(Bluecoat Arts Centre)

Fine Queen Anne building, cobbled quadrangle, garden courtyard, gallery, concert hall, artists studios.

Location: School Lane, in the City centre.
Station: Liverpool Lime Street (½ m).
Opening Times: Mons to Sats 10–5. *(Gallery closed Mon).* Adm free.
Refreshments: Cafe bar.

CROXTETH HALL & COUNTRY PARK

Liverpool   map F8   ⑤
Telephone: 051-228 5311

500 acre Country Park centred on the ancestral home of the Molyneux family, Earls of Sefton. Hall rooms with character figures on the theme of an Edwardian houseparty. Victorian Home Farm and Walled Garden both with quality interpretive displays; superb collection of farm animals (Approved Rare Breeds Centre). Miniature Railway. Special events and attractions most weekends. Picnic areas and play areas.

Location: 5 m NE of Liverpool City Centre; Signposted from A580 & A5088 (ring road).
Opening Times: Parkland open daily throughout the year, adm free. Hall, Farm & Garden open 11–5 daily in main season, please telephone to check exact dates. Inclusive admission to Hall, Farm & Gardens; £2, Chd/OAPs £1 (provisional prices). Reduced rates for parties. Wheelchair access to Farm, Garden and Café but to ground floor only in Hall.
Refreshments: 'The Old Riding School' cafe during season.

SPEKE HALL, The National Trust 🌿

Liverpool   map F8   △   &
Telephone: 051-427 7231

Richly half-timbered Elizabethan house around a courtyard; features include Great Hall, Priest holes; Jacobean plasterwork and Victorian restoration and decoration. Attractive gardens and extensive woodlands.

Location: On N bank of Mersey 8 m from City centre. 1 m off A561 on W side of Liverpool Airport. Follow airport signs from M62; M56 junction 12.
Station: Garston (2 m); Hunts Cross (2 m).
Opening Times: Apr 1 to Oct 30—daily except Mons, but open Bank Holiday Mons, 1–5.30. *Closed Good Fri.* Oct 31 to Dec 13—Sats & Suns 1–4.30. Garden Apr 1 to Oct 31: as house 12 –5.30. Nov to Mar 1993: daily except Mon 12–4. *(Closed 24–26 Dec and Jan 1).* Adm £3, Family ticket £7.50. Garden only 60p. Discount for parties. Guided tours and school visits by prior arrangement with Administrator.
Refreshments: Tea room and shop.

NORFOLK

BEESTON HALL 🏛

Beeston St Lawrence   map M7
Telephone: (0692) 630771
(Sir Ronald & Lady Preston)

18th century 'Gothick' country house with Georgian interiors in picturesque setting.

Location: 2½ m NE of Wroxham on S side of A1151; 11 m NE of Norwich.
Station: Wroxham (2¾ m). Also accessible from Broads at Neatishead.
Opening Times: Principal Rooms, Gardens, Wine Cellars and Woodland Walks. Apr 19 to Sept 13—Fris & Suns, also Bank Hols 2–5.30, Aug also Weds. Adm £2, Chd (accompanied by adult) £1. Parties by arrangement.
Refreshments: Teas and light refreshments in the Orangery.

BERNEY ARMS WINDMILL ✪

map M7
Telephone: (0493) 700605

At one time the Norfolk and Suffolk marshes were drained entirely by wind-power, a function carried out by this 'tower' mill after it was no longer used for its original purpose of grinding cement clinker. The mill has seven floors, making it the highest marsh-mill in the area and a landmark for miles around.

Location: North bank of River Yare, 3½ m (5.6 km) north east of Reedham. OS map ref TG465051. Accessible only by boat, or ½ m walk.
Opening Times: Good Friday or Apr 1 (whichever is earlier) to Sept 30: Open Daily 10–6. Adm 75p, Concessions 55p, Chd 40p.

BLICKLING HALL, The National Trust 🌿

Aylsham   map M7   &
Telephone: Aylsham 733084

Great Jacobean house, altered 1765-70. State rooms include Peter the Great Room with fine Russian tapestry, Long Gallery with exceptional ceiling and State bedroom. The Formal Garden design dates from 1729. Temple and Orangery, park and lake.

Location: 1½ m NW of Aylsham on N side of B1354 (which is 15 m N of Norwich on A140).
Opening Times: Hall: Mar 28 to Nov 1 *(Closed* Good Friday): Tues, Wed, Fri, Sat, Sun, 1–5. Bank Holiday Sun & Mon 12–5. Garden: as Hall but open 12 noon. Adm House and Garden: £4.90, Chd (with adult) £2.40. Pre-booked parties £3.75. Garden only £2.30, Chd £1.10. Free car park. Shop. Dogs in Park & Picnic area only, on leads. Wheelchair access—2 provided. Lift to first floor.
Refreshments: Teas, coffee and lunches 11–5. *(Parties by arrangement;* table licence). Picnic area in walled orchard. Restaurant, shop and garden open daily in July & Aug. Plant centre in orchard open all year. Buckinghamshire Arms Inn open all year.
NB Free access to the South Front, shop and restaurant when Hall is open.

BRESSINGHAM GARDENS

Bressingham, Diss IP22 2AB   map L6
Telephone: (037988) 464/8133

Five acres of display gardens open seasonally. Leading Plant Centre stocking over 4,000 varieties of hardy plants including perennials, shrubs, conifers and alpines.

Location: A1066 3 m from Diss on Thetford Road.
Opening Times: All year, seven days a week 10–5.30.

CASTLE ACRE PRIORY

map L7
Telephone: (07605) 394

William de Warenne and his wife were so impressed with the great Abbey of Cluny in Burgundy that they determined to found the Order in England. This they did—at Lewes. The priory at Castle Acre was probably established by their son and it survived, not without friction, until 1537 when it was surrendered to Henry VIII. The gaunt ruins span seven centuries and include a 16th century gatehouse, a church of mixed origins and a prior's lodging almost fit to be lived in. The castle, at the other end of the village started as an undefended Norman manor house but later evolved into a conventional keep. Ruins of this keep and outer earthworks can be seen.

Location: 3½ m (5.6 km) north of Swaffham. OS map ref TF814148.
Opening Times: Good Friday or Apr 1 (whichever is earlier) to Sept 30: Open Daily 10–6. Oct 1 to Maundy Thursday or Mar 31 (whichever is earlier): Open Tues to Sun 10–4. *Closed* Dec 24–26, Jan 1. Adm £1.80, Concessions £1.40, Chd 90p.

CASTLE RISING CASTLE

map K7
Telephone: (055387) 330

The long and distinguished history of Castle Rising began in 1138. It was then that William de Albini started to build a grand castle to mark the upturn in his fortunes which followed his marriage to Henry I's widow. Later owners were no less notable and included Isabella 'the She-Wolf of France', wife of Edward II, the Black Prince, Prince Hal and the Howard Dukes of Norfolk. The 12th century keep, reached through a handsome decorated doorway is the finest part of the castle. Outside, there is a gatehouse of the same date and the remains of a church.

Location: 4 m (6.4 km) north of King's Lynn. OS map ref TF666246.
Opening Times: Good Friday or Apr 1 (whichever is earlier) to Sept 30: Open Daily 10–6. Oct 1 to Maundy Thursday or Mar 31 (whichever is earlier): Open Tues to Sun 10–4. *Closed* Dec 24–26, Jan 1. Adm £1.10, Concessions 85p, Chd 55p.

THE FAIRHAVEN GARDEN TRUST

Nr Norwich   map M7   &
Telephone: 060549 449
(G. E. Debbage)

Unique woodland and water gardens with private broad. Primroses and bluebells in profusion. Many rare and unusual plants. Wild flowers and cultivated varieties grow happily together. Spectacular display of candelabra primulas in May and June and azaleas and rhododendrons. Giganteum lilies end of June, early July. 900 year old oak. Lots to interest naturalists and horticulturists in a lovely peaceful part of the Norfolk Broads.

Location: 9 m NE of Norwich on the B1140.
Opening Times: Apr 12 to May 3: Sun and Bank Holidays 11–6; May 6 to Sept 13: Wed to Sun and Bank Holidays 11–6, Sat 2–6; Sept 20 and 27, Sun only 11–6. Special openings 1992: Primrose weekend: Apr 17, 18, 19, 20: Frid and Sat 2–6; Sun and Mon 11–6; Candelabra Primula weekend: May 23, 24, Sat 2–6, Sun, Mon 11–6; Walks with the Warden each Sun in July at 2.30 (up to 50 people). Adm £3, OAPs £2.50 – price includes gardens, bird sanctuary, tea and cream scone. To book, telephone 060549 449. Autumn Colours: Nov 1 10 to dusk. Adm £1.80, OAPs £1.30, Chd 80p. Season ticket £6. Parties by arrangement, telephone 060549 449. Car parking for 450 on grass. Mainly suitable for disabled persons. Plants for sale grown in the gardens.
Refreshments: South Walsham Hall Hotel and Country Club. Small tea room on car park. Cream teas, all cakes home-made.

FELBRIGG HALL, The National Trust ❧

nr Cromer   map M7   &
Telephone: West Runton 444   (Restaurant: West Runton 8237)

17th century country house with Georgian interiors set in a fine wooded park. Important 18th century Library and Orangery. Traditional walled garden. Woodland and Lakeside walks.

Location: 2 m SW of Cromer on S side of A148.
Station: Cromer (2¼ m).
Opening Times: Hall & Gardens—Mar 28 to Nov 1: Mons, Weds, Thurs, Sats and Suns, 1.30 –5.30. Bank Hol Suns and Mons 11–5.30. Gardens 11–5.30. Adm £4.30, Chd (with adult) £2.15. Gardens only £1.60. Pre-booked parties of 15 or more £3.10. Shop. No dogs. Wheelchair access, 2 provided. Picnic area.
Refreshments: 11–5.15, coffee, lunches, teas in the Park restaurant, open daily Mar 28 to Nov 1. Note: Free access to restaurant, shop, park and picnic area.

GRIME'S GRAVES

map L6
Telephone: (0842) 810656

This is an intricate network of pits and shafts sunk by our neolithic ancestors some 4000 years ago. The purpose of all this industriousness was to find flints for the world's first farmers—flints to make axes to fell trees so that the cleared ground could be sown with seed. Between 700 and 800 pits were dug, some of them to a depth of 30 or 40ft (9–12m). Two of the 16 excavated shafts have been left open; they give an idea of those early miners' working conditions.

Location: 2¾ m (4.4 km) north east of Brandon. OS map ref TL818898.
Opening Times: Good Friday or Apr 1 (whichever is earlier) to Sept 30: Open Daily 10–6. Oct 1 to Maundy Thursday or Mar 31 (whichever is earlier): Open Tues to Sun 10–4. *Closed* Dec 24–26, Jan 1. Adm £1.10, Concessions 85p, Chd 55p.

HOLKHAM HALL – *See page 137*

HOUGHTON HALL – *See page 137*

MANNINGTON GARDENS AND COUNTRYSIDE 🏛

Saxthorpe, Norfolk   map L7
Telephone: Saxthorpe (026 387) 4175
(Lord and Lady Walpole)

15th century moated house and Saxon church ruin set in attractive gardens. Outstanding rose gardens. Extensive walks and trails around the estate.

Location: 2 m N of Saxthorpe, nr B1149; 18 m NW of Norwich. 9 m from coast.
Opening Times: GARDEN. Apr to Oct: Suns 12–5. Also June to Aug: Weds, Thurs and Fris 11–5. Adm £2, Chd (accompanied children under 16) free, Senior Citizens/Students £1.50. House open by prior appointment only.
Refreshments: Coffee, salad lunches and home-made teas.

NORWICH CASTLE

Norwich   map M7   &
Telephone: (0603) 222222
(Norwich City Council/Norfolk Museums Service)

Norwich Castle houses one of the finest regional museums in Britain. The castle keep built by the Normans between 1100 and 1130 contains displays of medieval objects and an exhibition illustrating Norfolk's links with Europe. Galleries displaying art (the Norwich School) natural history, archaeology and ceramics.

Location: In the centre of Norwich.

HOLKHAM HALL 🏛

Wells map L7
Telephone: Fakenham (0328) 710227

HOLKHAM HALL – *Continued*

Fine Palladian mansion. Pictures, Tapestries, Statuary, Furnishings. Bygones Museum.

Location: 2m W of Wells; S of the Wells/Hunstanton Road (A149).
Opening Times: Daily (except Fris/Sats) from May 24 to Sept 30: 1.30–5, also Easter, May, Spring and Summer Bank Holiday: Suns and Mons 11.30–5 (last adm 4.40). Adm £2.70, Chd (5–15) £1.20. Bygones and Park: £2.70, Chd £1.20. All inclusive: £4.70, Chd £2. 10% reduction on pre-paid parties of 20 or more.
Refreshments: Served in tea rooms.

OXBURGH HALL, The National Trust 🦋

Swaffham map L7   ♿
Telephone: Gooderstone 258

Late 15th century moated house. Outstanding gatehouse tower. Needlework by Mary Queen of Scots. Unique French parterre laid out circa 1845. Woodland walk and traditional herbaceous garden. Chapel with fine altar piece.

Location: 7 m SW of Swaffham on S side of Stoke Ferry Road.
Opening Times: House: Mar 28 to Nov 1 – Sat to Wed, 1.30–5.30. Garden: 12–5.30. Bank Hol Mons 11–5.30. Adm £3.50, Chd (with adult) £1.75. Pre-booked parties of 15 or more £2.60. Shop. No dogs. Wheelchair access, 2 provided.
Refreshments: In Old Kitchen. Light lunches and teas 12–5.

HOUGHTON HALL 🏛

Kings Lynn map L7   ♿
Telephone: East Rudham 528569
(The Marquess of Cholmondeley)

The Home of the Marquess and Marchioness of Cholmondeley, Houghton Hall was built in the 18th century for Sir Robert Walpole by Colen Campbell and Thomas Ripley, with interior decoration by William Kent, and is regarded as one of the finest examples of Palladian architecture in England. Houghton was later inherited by the 1st Marquess of Cholmondeley through his grandmother, Sir Robert's daughter. Situated in beautiful parkland, the house contains magnificent furniture, pictures and china. Pleasure grounds. Shetland ponies, heavy horses on show in the stables. A private collection of 20,000 model soldiers and militaria.

Location: 13 m E of King's Lynn; 10 m W of Fakenham off A148.
Opening Times: Easter Sun (Apr 19) to Sept 27 – Suns, Thurs & Bank Hols. HOUSE opens 1–2 5.30. Last adm 5. Gates, Picnic Area. Children's Playground, stables and Model Soldier & Militaria Collection opens Suns, Thurs & Bank Hols 12.30–5. Adm charges £4, OAPs £3.50, Chd £2 (under 5 free). No additional charges except for special events which will be advertised. Reduction of 10% for pre-booked parties of 20 or more. Car park near House, toilets & lift to State floor for the disabled. Free parking for coaches & cars.
Refreshments: Tea room.

SANDRINGHAM HOUSE & GROUNDS 🏛

Sandringham   map L7
Telephone: King's Lynn (0553) 772675
(Her Majesty The Queen)

A fine country residence, the private home of four generations of monarchs. All the principal rooms normally occupied by the Royal Family when in residence are open to the public during the times shown below. These include the Saloon, the Small Drawing Room (used by the Lady-in-Waiting in attendance), the Main Drawing Room, the Dining Room, the Lobby, the Ballroom Corridor and the Ballroom. Superb grounds laid out by W.B. Thomas in 1862, with two lakes and extensive woodland walks. The Grounds are particularly colourful during the rhododendron season (mid-May – end-June). The Museum contains exhibits of gifts presented to the Royal Family, part of the Royal Doll Collection, Big Game trophies, commemorative china and glass relating to royal events, local archaeological finds and vehicles used by members of the Royal Family. Outside the House and Grounds is Sandringham Country Park, a free attraction open all year round.

Location: 8 m NE of King's Lynn (off A149).
Opening Times: House, Grounds and Museum open Good Fri, then daily except Fri and Sat from Apr 19 to Oct 1 inclusive (except the period stated below and when H.M. The Queen or any member of the Royal Family is in residence). House *closed* from July 20 to Aug 8 inclusive. Grounds *closed* from July 24 to Aug 5 inclusive. Adm: House, Grounds and Museum £2.50, OAPs £2, Chd £1.50. Grounds and Museum: £2, OAPs £1.50, Chd £1. Free coach and car parks.
Refreshments: Available in Country Park in restaurant (capacity 60 people) serving teas and lunches. Self-service cafeteria also available.

RAINTHORPE HALL & GARDENS 🏛

Flordon, nr Norwich   map M6   △   ♿
(George Hastings, Esq.)

Rebuilt in 1503 after a fire, and modernised during the reign of Elizabeth, Rainthorpe Hall is one of the very few half-timbered houses of its period in East Anglia. Its chimney breasts are placed in the French manner, at either end of the Great Hall – a pattern rare in this country. It is set in large gardens, with a conservation lake. Rainthorpe Hall has appeared in several Television productions. In both 1982 and 1987 it was used for 'Tales of the Unexpected'. It served as the principal location for the six hour murder mystery 'Cover Her Face', which was shown in England in 1985 and in the United States in 1987. Its drive and gates were used in 'The Black Tower' in 1986, and it was the scene of the Hunt Ball in 'Menace Unseen', a three-hour drama shown in 1988. In 1989, ITV used it for the live show 'Ghost Train', and the BBC for Omnibus.

Location: 1 m SSW of Newton Flotman (A140) on Flordon Road, 8 m S of Norwich.
Opening Times: GARDENS. Easter to Oct: Weds, Sats, Suns & Bank Hol Mons 10–5. Adm £1.50, Chd 75p, OAPs 75p. Car park free. Plants on sale. House open by appointment. Gardens only suitable for disabled.
Refreshments: Home-made teas.

RAVENINGHAM HALL GARDENS

Norwich NR14 6NS   map M6
Telephone: (050846) 206
(Sir Nicholas Bacon Bt.)

An extensive garden laid out at the turn of the century surrounding original Georgian house. In the last thirty years a large number of new areas have been designed and brought into cultivation, many in the traditional style, with plantings of unusual shrubs, herbaceous plants and roses. An Arboretum planted in March 1990 contains many unusual trees. In recent years an important and extensive Nursery and Plant Centre has grown, to include many rare and exotic plants that can be seen in the garden. (Catalogue 3 x first class stamps, refundable on orders over £10). Also Victorian Conservatory and walled vegetable garden. The house is not open to the public.

Location: 4 m from Beccles off the B1136 between Beccles and Loddon.
Opening Times: Plant Centre: Mon to Fri 9–4 all year; Sats 9–4 and Suns 2–5.30 mid-Mar to mid-Sept. Garden: Every Sun and Bank Hol Mon from Mar 24 to Sept 15, 2–5.30. Adm £1.70, Chd free, in aid of local charities. Free car park.
Refreshments: Home-made teas served on Garden Open Days only.

SANDRINGHAM HOUSE & GROUNDS – *See above*

TRINITY HOSPITAL

Castle Rising   map L7
(Trustees)

Nine 17th century brick and tile Almhouses with court, chapel and treasury.

Location: 4 m NE of King's Lynn on A149.
Opening Times: All the year—Tues, Thurs & Sats. Summer: 10–12, 2–6. Winter: 10–12, 2 –4. Adm free.

WOLTERTON PARK

Erpingham   map M7
Telephone: Saxthorpe 4175
(Lord and Lady Walpole)

Extensive historic park with lake, Hawk and Owl Trust display.

Location: Nr Erpingham, signposted from A140 Norwich to Cromer road.
Opening Times: Park open all year, daily 9–5 or dusk if earlier. Adm £2 per car. See local press for details of special events, and garden and Hall tours.
Refreshments: Saracens Head (near drive gates).

NORTHAMPTONSHIRE

ALTHORP

Northampton　map J6　△
(The Earl Spencer)

Home of the Spencer family since 1508, Althorp was built by Sir John Spencer in that year, altered by Henry Holland in 1790, and entirely redecorated in 1982. Rooms in rotation. Maintained as a private home where visitors are welcome. Magnificent picture collection of English and European Masters – Reynolds, Gainsborough, Rubens, Van Dyck, Lely, Lotto, Lucidel, Maratti. French furniture by Weisweiler, Saunier Boulle. Rare porcelain from the Bow, Chelsea, Sevres and Meissen factories. Presents shop for fashion jewellery. Antique china and glass. Victorian, Edwardian and Art Deco in the historic Georgian stables. Wine shop with French, German and English wines. Tearoom with home made iced cakes and scones. Group luncheons by arrangement. Functions in main house, weddings, luncheons, dinners and seminars. Heating in house and stables all winter. Please respect times when house and grounds are closed. No early arrival except by appointment.

Location: 6 m NW of Northampton on Northampton/Rugby Road (A428); 6 m from M1 exit 16.
Opening Times: Sept to June: HOUSE 1–5; July to Aug: HOUSE 11–6, Bank Holidays 11–6. Open all year daily except Christmas Day. Weds – Connoisseurs day throughout the year (extra rooms, longer tour). Adm House and Grounds: £2.95; pre-booked groups of 8 or more £2.75, Chd £1.75. Connoisseurs day £3.95, Chd £2. Jan, Feb, Mar £2.70. Grounds and Lake only: Adm 50p, Chd 25p. Coach parking fees £10 in advance please, booking essential. Groups of more than 8 people during Jan and Feb £1.50. Mon only Mar to Dec: £2.20, Chd £1. Cars free. Wine shop & Gift shop. Private morning visits by arrangement at extra cost. Weddings, 21st Birthdays, business or private lunches and dinners our speciality. Light lunches in Stables Restaurant for groups. For booking (enclosing sae) write to: The Countess Spencer, Althorp, Northampton NN7 4HG. *Information & prices are subject to alteration without notice as details submitted well in advance of printing.*
Refreshments: Tea room; home-made cakes & scones available at counter.
NB – *For security reasons House & Grounds may be closed without notice; Coach parties will be informed.* House unsuitable for small children and frail & disabled people.

AYNHOE PARK

Aynho　map H5
(Country Houses Association Ltd)

17th century mansion. Alteration by Soane.

Location: 6 m SE of Banbury on A41.
Opening Times: May to Sept – Weds & Thurs 2–5. Last entry 4.30. Adm £1.50, Chd 50p. Free car park. No dogs admitted.

BOUGHTON HOUSE – *See page 140*

CANONS ASHBY HOUSE, The National Trust 🌿

Canons Ashby　map H5
Telephone: Blakesley (0327) 860044

The home of the Dryden family since the 16th century; a manor house c. 1580 and altered for the last time in 1710; Elizabethan wall paintings and outstanding Jacobean plasterwork; formal garden with terraces, walls and gatepiers of 1710: medieval Priory Church, privately owned since the Reformation. 70 acre park.

Location: Easy access from either M40 junction 11 or M1 junction 16. From M1 signposted from A5 2 m S of Weedon crossroads, along unclassified road (13 m) to Banbury. From M40 at Banbury take A422 exit, then left along unclassified road.
Opening Times: Apr 1 to end of Oct – Weds to Suns & Bank Hol Mons 1–5.30. *Closed Good Friday.* Adm £2.80, Chd £1.40. Parking for cars & coaches which must pre-book (discount for parties). Dogs on leads, in Home Paddock only. 1992 events – details from the Administrator.
Refreshments: Party bookings afternoon tea 2.30–5 in Brewhouse.

BOUGHTON HOUSE

Kettering   map J6   △   &   ⑤
Telephone: Kettering (0536) 515731
(His Grace the Duke of Buccleuch & Queensberry KT and the Living Landscape Trust)

A 500 year old Tudor monastic building gradually enlarged around 7 courtyards until the French style addition of 1695. Outstanding collection of 17/18th century French and English furniture, tapestries, 16th century carpets, porcelain, painted ceilings – notable works by El Greco, Murillo, Caracci and 40 Van Dyck sketches – celebrated Armoury and Ceremonial Coach. Exhibition and lecture rooms in Stable block with audio/visual facilities. Beautiful parkland with avenues and lakes – picnic area – gift shop – exciting adventure woodland play area – garden centre. For details of our specialist one, three and five day Fine Art Courses run in conjunction with Sotheby's and our Schools Education Facilities (Sandford Award Winner), please telephone the Living Landscape Trust at Kettering (0536) 515731.

Location: 3 m N of Kettering on A43 at Geddington; 75 m N of London by A1 or M1.
Opening Times: House and grounds: Aug 1 to Sept 1. Daily, grounds 1–5; House 2–5. Staterooms strictly by prior booking. Grounds: Apr 25 to Sept 27 – Daily except Fris, 1–5.
Facilities: Garden Centre open daily throughout year. Adventure play area and tearooms open 1–5 at weekends and public holidays from May to Sept and daily throughout Aug, at other times by appointment. Museum and educational groups welcome by appointment at other times.

COTON MANOR GARDENS

map J6　&

Telephone: Northampton (0604) 740219

(Ian Pasley-Tyler Esq)

An outstanding old English Garden exquisitely laid out on different levels. Old hedges, herbaceous borders, lawns and water gardens lend it a special charm and character enhanced by flamingoes, cranes and waterfowl roaming at large.

Location: 10 m N of Northampton & 11 m SE of Rugby. Follow tourist signs on A428 and A50.

Opening Times: Easter to end of Sept: Weds, Suns and Bank Hol Mons (and Tues following), also Thurs in July & Aug, 2–6. Adm £2.50, OAP £2, Chd 50p. Unusual plants for sale.

Refreshments: Home-made teas.

COTTESBROOKE HALL AND GARDENS

nr Northampton　map J6

Telephone: 060 124 808/515

(Captain & Mrs John Macdonald-Buchanan)

Architecturally magnificent Queen Anne house commenced in 1702. Renowned picture collection, particularly of sporting and equestrian subjects. Fine English and Continental furniture and porcelain. Main vista aligned on celebrated 7th century Saxon church at Brixworth. House reputed to be the pattern for Jane Austen's 'Mansfield Park'. Notable gardens of great variety including fine old cedars and specimen trees, herbaceous borders, water and wild gardens.

Location: 10 m N of Northampton nr Creaton on A50, nr Brixworth on A508.

Opening Times: Thurs from Apr 23 to Sept 24, Easter Mon, May day, Spring Bank Holiday, Aug Bank Holiday 2–5.30. Last adm 5. Adm £3.50. Gardens only £1.50. Chd half price. Parties accommodated by appointment, when possible. Car parking. Gardens but not house suitable for disabled. No dogs.

Refreshments: In the Old Laundry 2.30–5.

DEENE PARK – *See page 142*

DELAPRE ABBEY

nr Northampton　map J6

(Northamptonshire Borough Council)

House rebuilt or added to 16th to 19th centuries. Converted for use as The County Record Office.

Location: On London Road (A508) 1 m due S of centre of Northampton.

Station: Northampton (1 m).

Opening Times: All the year–Thurs 2.30–5 (closes 4.30 Oct to Apr). Adm free 'public rooms and passages only'.

HOLDENBY HOUSE GARDENS

Northampton　map J6　Ⓢ

Telephone: Northampton (0604) 770074

(James Lowther, Esq.)

Once the largest house in Elizabethan England, Holdenby secured its place in history when it became the prison of Charles I during the Civil War. Today Holdenby's Falconry Centre and collection of rare farm animals complement the beauty and history of the grounds with their Elizabethan and fragrant borders. As buzzards and other birds of prey capture the attention in the sky above, train rides and a 'cuddle farm' ensure an enjoyable day for the children on the ground. This year, there will be a special series of events and activities to commemorate the 350th anniversary of the Civil War. Craft shop.

Location: 7 m NW of Northampton, off A428 & A50; 7 m from M1 exit 18.

Opening Times: GARDENS. Apr to end Sept–Suns & Bank Hol Mons 2–6; also Thurs July & Aug, 2–6. Adm Gardens: £2.40, Chd £1.20, OAP £1.80. House and Gardens: £3.50, Chd £1.50. HOUSE. Open by arrangement to pre-booked parties Mons to Fris Adm £3, Chd £1. Enquire for special rates for school parties. Plant & Souvenir shop.

Refreshments: Home-made teas in Victorian Kitchen.

DEENE PARK

nr Corby map J6 △ &
Telephone: Bulwick 278 or 361 (office hours)
(Edmund Brudenell, Esq.)

Deene is a 16th and 17th century transformation of a mediaeval manor house with extensive 19th century additions and has belonged to the Brudenell family since 1514. It is still the 'elegant habitation of the Brudenells' as William Camden described it in the 16th century, and was the home of the Earl of Cardigan who led the Charge of the Light Brigade. Its special appeal lies in its indefinable atmosphere of a home cherished by the same family for over four centuries. The house which is of considerable architectural importance and historical interest, overlooks a large park and lake and has extensive gardens with old fashioned roses, rare trees and shrubs.

Location: 8 m NW of Oundle; 6 m NE of Corby on Kettering/Stamford Road (A43).
Opening Times: Easter, May, Spring & Summer Bank Hol Suns & Mons, also every Sun in June, July & Aug 2–5. Adm charges not available at time of going to press. Upstairs rooms now on view. *Special guided tours to parties of 20 or more may be arranged throughout the year on application to the House Keeper.*

KIRBY HALL

map J6
Telephone: (0536) 203230
(English Heritage)

Richness and variety of architectural detail distinguish this Elizabethan country house from others. Begun by Sir Humphrey Stafford in 1570, it was completed by Sir Christopher Hatton, a talented courtier to Queen Elizabeth. The fourth Sir Christopher Hatton devoted his energies to the garden in the late 17th century. The gardens are currently undergoing a complete restoration.

Location: 2 m (3.2 km) north of Corby. OS map ref SP926927.
Opening Times: Good Friday or Apr 1 (whichever is earlier) to Sept 30 daily 10–6. Oct 1 to Maundy Thursday or Mar 31 (whichever is earlier) Tues to Sun 10–4. *Closed* Dec 24–26, Jan 1. Adm £1.10, Concessions 85p, Chd 55p.

LAMPORT HALL – *See page 143*

LYVEDEN NEW BIELD, The National Trust

Oundle map J6
Telephone: Benefield (083 25) 358

The shell of an unusual Renaissance building erected about 1600 by Sir Thomas Tresham to symbolize the Passion. He died before the building could be completed and his son was then imprisoned in connection with the Gunpowder Plot. A viewing platform allows visitors to look from the East Window.

Location: 4 m SW of Oundle via A427. 3 m E of Brigstock (A6116) (½ m walk from roadside parking).
Opening Times: All the year – Daily. *Property approached via two fields. Parties by arrangement with Custodian, Lyveden New Bield Cottage, nr Oundle, Northants.* Adm £1, Chd 50p. *No parking for coaches but which may drop & return to pick up passengers.* Dogs admitted on leads. Unsuitable for disabled or visually handicapped.

THE PREBENDAL MANOR HOUSE

Nassington map J6
Telephone: (0780) 782575

Probably the earliest surviving Manor in Northamptonshire, dating from the early 13th century. The present Manor overlays one of King Canute's Royal Manors and the site is of significant archaeological interest. The Manor forms the focus of a group of stone buildings which include a fine 16th century Dovecote, and an archaeological exhibition.

Location: 6 m N of Oundle. A605-614, 7 m S of Stamford. A1 to Wansford 614. 9 m E of Peterborough. A47-614.
Opening Times: Tues and Wed 2–6 from June 1 to Aug 31. Bank Hol Mons 2–6 and last Sun of each month from June to end of Aug. Adm £2.50, Chd/OAP £1.25. Parties by arrangement. Free car parking. Not suitable for disabled.
Refreshments: Teas by arrangement.

PRIEST'S HOUSE – *See page 144*

LAMPORT HALL

Northampton   map J6   ⑤
Telephone: (060128) 272
(Lamport Hall Trust)

Lamport Hall was the home of the Isham family from 1560 to 1976. The South West front is a rare example of the work of John Webb, pupil and son-in-law of Inigo Jones and was built in 1655 (during the Commonwealth) with wings added in 1732 and 1740. High Room with plaster ceiling by John Woolston, an outstanding library, and thirteen other fine rooms containing the Ishams' collections of superb paintings, furniture and china. The Hall is set in spacious wooded parkland with tranquil gardens including a remarkable rock garden. Teas in Victorian dining room. Now run by the Lamport Hall Trust, school visits, group and private bookings are especially encouraged and a programme of fairs, music, art and craft events is put on throughout the season – details from the Director.

Location: 8 m N of Northampton on A508 to Market Harborough. M1 J15/16/18/20.
Opening Times: House & Gardens. Easter to end of Sept – Suns & Bank Hol Mons 2.15–5.15. Also Thurs in July & Aug, 2.15–5.15. School & private parties any time by appointment. Adm £2.50, OAPs £2, Chd £1. Group rates on application. Coach parties welcome. Free car park and coach parking. Dogs on leads in picnic area only.
Refreshments: Home-made teas at the house.

ROCKINGHAM CASTLE

nr Corby   map J6   △   ⑤
Telephone: Corby (0536) 770240
(Commander Michael Saunders Watson)

A Royal Castle till 1530, since then the home of the Watson family. Rockingham Castle was built by William the Conqueror on the site of an earlier fortification and was used by the early Kings of England until the 16th century when it was granted by Henry VIII to Edward Watson whose family still live there today. The house itself is memorable not so much as representing any particular period, but rather a procession of periods. The dominant influence in the building is Tudor within the Norman walls, but practically every century since the 11th has left its mark in the form of architecture, furniture or works of art. There is a particularly fine collection of English 18th, 19th and 20th century paintings, and Charles Dickens, a frequent visitor, was so captivated by Rockingham that he used it as a model for Chesney Wold in Bleak House. The Castle stands in 12 acres of formal and wild garden and commands a splendid view of five counties. Particular features are the 400 year old elephant hedge and the rose garden marking the foundations of the old keep. See also the Special Exhibition: Castles in Northamptonshire.

Location: 2 m N of Corby; 9 m from Market Harborough; 14 m from Stamford on A427; 8 m from Kettering on A6003.
Opening Times: Easter Sun to Sept 30 – Suns & Thurs also Bank Hol Mons & Tues following and Tues during Aug: 1.30–5.30. Adm £3.30, Chd £2. Gardens only £2. OAPs £2.70. *Any other day by previous appointment for parties.*
Refreshments: Teas – home-made at Castle.

PRIEST'S HOUSE, The National Trust

Easton-on-the-Hill   map J7
Telephone: Stamford (0780) 62506

Pre-Reformation priest's house given to the National Trust by The Peterborough Society. Contains a small museum of village bygones.

Location: 2 m SW of Stamford off A43.
Station: Stamford (2 m).
Opening Times: Access only by prior appointment with Mr. R. Chapman, Glebe Cottage, 45 West St., Easton-on-the-Hill, nr Stamford. Adm free. No dogs. Unsuitable for disabled or visually handicapped & Coaches.

ROCKINGHAM CASTLE – *See page 143*

RUSHTON HALL

Rushton, nr Kettering   map J6
(Royal National Institute for the Blind)

Dates from c. 1500, with earlier wing and later additions.

Location: 4 m NW of Kettering, off A6003.
Opening Times: Grounds & exterior of premises only (with a limited inspection of the interior) by prior appointment with the Head Teacher.

RUSHTON TRIANGULAR LODGE

map J6
Telephone: (0536) 710761

Three walls with three windows and three gables to each . . . three storeys topped by a three-sided chimney. What is the reason for this triangular theme? The building is the brainchild of Sir Thomas Tresham and every detail is symbolical of the Holy Trinity and the Mass. Tresham's religious beliefs, unpopular in Elizabethan England, earned him many years' imprisonment. The lodge, begun on his return home in 1593, was finished four years later.

Location: ¾ m (1 km) west of Rushton; 4 m (6.4 km) north west of Kettering. OS map ref SP830831.
Opening Times: Good Friday or Apr 1 (whichever is earlier) to Sept 30: Open Daily 10–6. Adm £1.10, Concessions 85p, Chd 55p.

SOUTHWICK HALL

nr Oundle   map J6
Telephone: Oundle (0832) 274064
(Christopher Capron, Esq.)

A family home since 1300, retaining medieval building dating from 1300, with Tudor re-building and 18th century additions. Exhibitions:– Victorian and Edwardian life; collections of agricultural and carpentry tools, named bricks and local archaeological finds and fossils.

Location: 3 m N of Oundle 4 m E of Bulwick.
Opening Times: Bank Holidays, Sun & Mon (Apr 19, 20; May 3, 4, 24, 25; Aug 30, 31). Weds from May 6 to Aug 26: 2–5. Adm £2, Chd £1, OAPs £1.30. Parties at other times by arrangement with Secretary at Southwick Hall, Peterborough PE8 5BL.
Refreshments: Teas available.

STOKE PARK PAVILIONS

Towcester   map J5
(A. S. Chancellor, Esq)

Two pavilions and colonnade. Built in 1630 by Inigo Jones.

Location: Stoke Bruerne village; 7 m S of Northampton just W of Stony/Northampton Road A508.
Opening Times: June, July & Aug—Sats, Suns & Bank Hols 2–6. *Exterior only on view.* Adm £1. Car park free.

SULGRAVE MANOR

Banbury   map H5   △
Telephone: Sulgrave (0295) 760205
(The Sulgrave Manor Board)

The Washington ownership dates from 1539 when Lawrence Washington purchased the land upon the Dissolution by Henry VIII, of St. Andrew's Priory, Northampton. The House was completed in 1558 (the year Elizabeth I came to the throne of England) and was lived in by descendants of the Washington family for 120 years. Today it is an excellent example of a small Manor House, typical of a wealthy man's home and gardens in Elizabethan times, restored and refurbished with scholarly care and attention to detail which makes a visit both a delight and an education. Sulgrave Manor has been open to the public since 1921 when it was established as a 'Token of Friendship' between the people of Britain and the United States. It is now held in trust for the peoples of both nations, the trustees being the American Ambassador in London, the British Ambassador in Washington, and the Regent of Mount Vernon, Virginia. Endowed by the National Society of Colonial Dames of America.

Location: Sulgrave Village is off Banbury/Northampton Road (B4525); 5 m from Banbury junction of M40, 12 m from Northampton junction of M1. 7 m NE of Banbury; 28 m SE of Stratford-upon-Avon; 30 m N of Oxford; 70 m NW of London.
Opening Times: Mar to Dec 31—Daily (except Weds); Apr to Sept (inc) 10.30–1, 2–5.30. Other months 10.30–1, 2–4. *Closed Sun June 21 for private function. Closed Christmas Day, Boxing Day, and all January.* February: Groups only by appointment. Adm £2.50, Chd £1.25. Free car & coach parking.
Refreshments: At Thatched House Hotel opposite, Tel Sulgrave (029 576) 232. Light refreshments in Brewhouse.

NORTHUMBERLAND

ALNWICK CASTLE

Alnwick   map H12
Telephone: Alnwick (0665) 510777
(His Grace the Duke of Northumberland)

ALNWICK CASTLE

Ancient Fortress Home of
the Duke of Northumberland

Home of the Percy family since 1300.

In spite of its rugged medieval appearance, it has a rich interior, housing the most exquisite art treasures.

For opening times
please contact
The Supervisor, Estates Office,
Alnwick Castle,
Alnwick, NE66 1NQ

Telephone: (0665) 510777

Important example of medieval fortification restored by Salvin, dating to 12th century. Including the Keep, Armoury, Guard Chamber, Library and other principal apartments, Dungeon, State Coach and Museum of British and Roman antiquities. Pictures by Titian, Canaletto, Van Dyck, and other famous artists. Fine furniture, Meissen china and various historical heirlooms.

Location: In the town of Alnwick, 30 m N of Newcastle off the A1.
Opening Times: For 1992 opening times contact: The Supervisor, Estates Office, Alnwick Castle. Tel: Alnwick 510777.

AYDON CASTLE

map G11
Telephone: (043 471) 2450

Built as a manor house at the end of the 13th century, Aydon Castle fortified almost immediately afterwards as a result of the insecurity of the borders with Scotland. Captured by the Scots in 1315, it was pillaged and burned, and seized again by English rebels two years later. It has survived as a result of its conversion to a farmhouse in the 17th century.

Location: 1 m (1.6 km) north east of Corbridge, on minor road off B6321 or A68. OS map 87, ref NZ002663.
Opening Times: Good Friday or Apr 1 (whichever is earlier) to Sept 30: Open Daily 10–6. Adm £1.50, Concessions £1.10, Chd 75p.

BAMBURGH CASTLE

Bamburgh   map H13   △
Telephone: Bamburgh 208

BAMBURGH CASTLE

AND ARMSTRONG MUSEUM
The home of Lady Armstrong

The Norman Keep has stood for eight centuries and its setting upon The Crag, which is referred to as a Royal Centre by A.D. 547, is certainly one of the most dramatic of all Castles in Britain.

Featuring:
● **Magnificent Seascapes including Holy Island and the Farne Islands, and Landscapes extending to the Cheviot Hills.**
● **Public Rooms with exhibition of porcelain, china, paintings, furniture and items of interest.**
● **The Armoury, including loan collections from H.M. Tower of London, The John George Joicey Museum, Newcastle-upon-Tyne, and others.**
● **Fine Paintings including some from the Duke of Cambridge's collection.**

Open to the Public from Maundy Thursday to the last Sunday in October.
— Concessionary Rates for Parties in or out of Season —
Restaurant – Tea Room in the Castle Clock Tower
Operators – All at one stop. Tour. Food. Cloakrooms. Free Coach Parking at Entrance to Walled Castle.
CUSTODIAN – TEL: BAMBURGH (066 84) 208

Fine 12th century Norman Keep with its setting upon The Crag, and referred to as a Royal Centre by AD 547, is certainly one of the most dramatic of all Castles in Britain. Remainder of the Castle considerably restored. Magnificent seascapes including Holy Island and the Farne Islands, the landscapes extending to the Cheviot Hills. Public rooms with exhibition of porcelain, china, paintings, furniture and items of interest. The Armoury includes loan collections from HM Tower of London, The John George Joicey Museum, Newcastle upon Tyne and others. Fine paintings, including some from the Duke of Cambridge's collection.

Location: Coastal – 16 m N of Alnwick 6 m from Belford; 3 m from Seahouses.
Opening Times: Easter to last Sun of Oct – Daily (incl Suns) open at 1; Adm £2.20, Chd £1 (1991 prices). *Parties may be booked out of normal hours.* For closing times enquire The Custodian.
Refreshments: Clock Tower tea rooms.

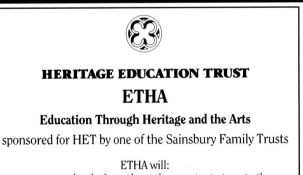

BELSAY HALL CASTLE AND GARDENS ⬚

map G12
Telephone: (066 181) 636
(English Heritage)

19th-century Neo-Classical mansion lies at the entrance to 30 acres of exciting gardens, which in turn lead on to the 14th-century castle and ruined manor. Important collections of rare and exotic flowering trees grow in the meandering, deep ravines of the "picturesque" Quarry Gardens. Massed plantings of rhododendrons. Large heather garden. Spring bulbs. Exhibition of Belsay's architectural and landscape history in stable block.

Location: 14 m (22.4 km) north west of Newcastle upon Tyne. OS map ref NZ088785.
Opening Times: Good Friday or Apr 1 (whichever is earlier) to Sept 30 daily 10–6. Oct 1 to Maundy Thursday or Mar 31 (whichever is earlier) Tues to Sun 10–4. *Closed* Dec 24–26, Jan 1. Adm £2.10, Concessions £1.60, Chd £1.10.

BERWICK BARRACKS ⬚

map G13
Telephone: (0289) 304493

The barracks were designed in 1717 to accommodate 36 officers and 600 men, first being occupied in 1721. The buildings consist of three blocks of accommodation around a square, the fourth side having a splendidly decorated gatehouse. The barracks' new exhibition, the award winning 'Beat of Drum' traces the history of the British infantryman from 1660 to the end of the 19th century. The regimental museum of the King's Own Scottish Borderers and Borough Museum of Berwick on Tweed are also housed here.

Location: On the Parade, off Church St, Berwick town centre.
Opening Times: Good Friday or Apr 1 (whichever is earlier) to Sept 30: Open Daily 10–6. Oct 1 to Maundy Thursday or Mar 31 (whichever is earlier): Open Tues to Sun 10–4. *Closed* Dec 24–26, Jan 1. Adm £1.80, Concessions £1.40, Chd 90p.

BRINKBURN PRIORY ⬚

map G12
Telephone: (066 570) 628

The priory church stands within a loop of the River Coquet, in beautiful surroundings. Founded about 1130, the priory suffered badly from Scottish raids. In the last century the church was carefully restored by the Newcastle architect, Thomas Austin, and is still in occasional use. It is a fine example of early Gothic architecture.

Location: 5 m (8 km) east of Rothbury. OS map ref NZ116984.
Opening Times: Good Friday or Apr 1 (whichever is earlier) to Sept 30: Open Daily 10–6. Adm £1.10, Concessions 85p, Chd 55p.

CHERRYBURN, The National Trust 🌿

Mickley map G11 ♿
Telephone: Stocksfield (0661) 843276

Birthplace of Northumbria's greatest artist, wood engraver and naturalist, Thomas Bewick, in 1753. His family cottage is restored and the adjacent farmyard has a display of animals. The museum explores his famous works and life and in the Printing House demonstrations of hand printing from wood blocks can be seen.

Location: 11 m W of Newcastle on A695 (200 yards signed from Mickley Square).
Opening Times: Apr 1 to Oct 31 – daily except Tues 1–5.30. Last adm 5. Adm £2.40. No party rate. Wheelchair access and WC.

CHESTERS FORT

map G12
Telephone: (043481) 379

An impressive bath-house, buildings of great interest inside the fort, the remains of the bridge carrying Hadrian's Wall across the Tyne, a museum full of Roman inscriptions and sculptures, all set in one of the most beautiful valleys in Northumberland—these are among the attractions of Chesters, once garrisoned by a regiment of Roman cavalry.

Location: ½ m (0.8 km) south west of Chollerford. OS map NY913702.
Opening Times: Good Friday or Apr 1 (whichever is earlier) to Sept 30: Open Daily 10–6. Oct 1 to Maundy Thursday or Mar 31 (whichever is earlier): Open Daily 10–4. *Closed* Dec 24 –26, Jan 1. Adm £1.80, Concessions £1.40, Chd 90p.

CHILLINGHAM CASTLE AND GARDENS

Alnwick NE66 5NJ   map G13
Telephone: (06685) 359
(Sir Humphry Wakefield Bt)

This medieval family fortress has been home since the 1200's to the Earls Grey and their relations. Complete with jousting course, alarming dungeon and even a torture chamber, the Castle displays many remarkable restoration techniques in action, alongside antique furnishings, paintings, tapestries, arms and armour. The Italian ornamental garden, landscaped avenues and gate lodges were created by Sir Jeffrey Wyatville, fresh from his triumphs at Windsor Castle. There are attractive woodland walks and a lake, tea room, gift shop and antique shop.

Location: 12 m N of Alnwick, signposted from the A1 and A697.
Opening Times: Good Friday to Easter Mon; May 1 to Sept 30: 1.30–5 (*closed* Tues). Adm £2.50, OAPs £2, Chd over 5 £1.80. Parties (over 20) £1.80 per head. Unlimited free car parking. Access for disabled difficult due to number of stairs. Wheelchairs available only by arrangement.
Refreshments: Tea room serving light refreshments available within the Castle during opening hours. Nearest restaurant – Percy Arms, Chatton (2 m). Restaurant facilities available by arrangement. Fishing and clay pigeon shooting by arrangement. Musical and theatrical events regularly planned.

CORBRIDGE ROMAN SITE

map G11
Telephone: (043471) 2349

For nearly a century this was the site of a sequence of Roman forts, since Corbridge was an important junction of roads to Scotland, York and Carlisle. It developed into a prosperous town and supply base for Hadrian's Wall, with shops, temples, houses, granaries and an elaborate fountain. Among the rich collection of finds in the museum is a remarkable fountainhead—the Corbridge Lion.

Location: ½ m (0.8 km) north west of Corbridge. OS map ref NY983649.
Opening Times: Good Friday or Apr 1 (whichever is earlier) to Sept 30: Open Daily 10–6. Oct 1 to Maundy Thursday or Mar 31 (whichever is earlier): Open Tues to Sun 10–4. *Closed* Dec 24–26, Jan 1. Adm £1.80, Concessions £1.40, Chd 90p.

CRAGSIDE HOUSE, COUNTRY PARK AND GARDEN, The National Trust

Rothbury   map G12
Telephone: Rothbury (0669) 20333

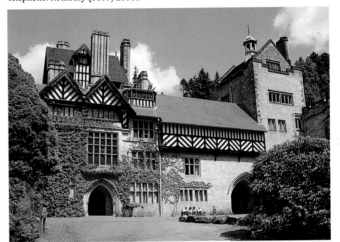

The House was designed by Richard Norman Shaw for the first Lord Armstrong and built between 1864–95. It contains much of its original furniture and Pre-Raphaelite paintings. It was the first house in the world to be lit by electricity generated by water power. The Country Park is famous for its rhododendrons, magnificent trees and the beauty of the lakes. The Armstrong Energy Centre displays the past and future stories of 'energy' and the 'Power Circuit Walk' includes restored hydraulic and hydroelectric machinery. Formal garden with Orchard House, Rose loggia, Ferneries open in 1992.

Location: ½ m E of Rothbury; 30 m N of Newcastle-upon-Tyne. Entrance off Rothbury/ Alnwick Road B6341; 1 m N of Rothbury at Debdon Burn Gate.
Opening Times: HOUSE: Apr 1 to Oct 31—daily except Mon (open Bank Holiday Mons), 1– 5.30. Last adm 5. COUNTRY PARK AND GARDEN: Apr 1 to Oct 31—daily except Mon (open Bank Holiday Mon) 10.30–7. Nov and Dec: Tues, Sat & Sun 10.30–4. Adm House & Country Park and Garden, Museum & Power Circuit £5.20; Country Park £3.20. Parties £4.80; Country Park £2.80. Parties by prior arrangement only with the Administrator. Armstrong Energy Centre & shop in Visitor centre. Dogs in Country Park only. Wheelchair access to House—lift available (wheelchairs provided). Toilets for disabled. Fishing.
Refreshments: Restaurant in Visitor Centre. Telephone Rothbury (0669) 20134.

DUNSTANBURGH CASTLE

map H13
Telephone: (066576) 231

Isolated and unspoilt, the ruins stand on a large, rocky cliff top rising steeply from the sea. Begun by Thomas, Earl of Lancaster, in 1313, the castle was attacked by the Scots and besieged during the Wars of the Roses. The keep gatehouse is still impressive and the south wall an enduring memorial to the workmanship of Earl Thomas's masons.

Location: 8 m (13 km) north east of Alnwick. OS map ref NU258220.
Opening Times: Good Friday or Apr 1 (whichever is earlier) to Sept 30: Open Daily 10–6. Oct 1 to Maundy Thursday or Mar 31 (whichever is earlier): Open Tues to Sun 10–4. *Closed* Dec 24–26, Jan 1. Adm 95p, Concessions 75p, Chd 45p.

HADRIAN'S ROMAN WALL IN NORTHUMBERLAND AND TYNE AND WEAR

map G12

The wall runs from Bowness to Wallsend-on-Tyne, a distance of 73 miles (117 km). Although parts of the wall have been lost over the centuries, fine sections remain at Walltown Crags, Cawfields, Sewingshields and Heddon-on-the-Wall. At Denton, near Newcastle, there is a well-preserved turret, and there are others at Brunton, where the wall is still 7ft (2m) high, at Sewingshields and Black Carts. These turrets, or observation towers, punctuated the wall at every third of a Roman mile between

HADRIAN'S ROMAN WALL IN NORTHUMBERLAND AND TYNE AND WEAR – *Continued from page 147*

milecastles, good examples of which may be seen at Cawfields and Sewingshields. At Benwell and Carrawburgh there are Roman temples; at Chesterholm a milestone and the great fort Vindolanda, for which there is an admission fee. Other sites may be visited free of charge.

Locations: OS map references. Heddon-on-the-Wall NZ136669; Planetrees Farm, Chollerford NY928696; Brunton Turret, Chollerford NY921698; Chesters Bridge Abutment, Chollerford NY913701; Black Carts NY884713; Carrawburgh, Temple of Mithras NY869713; Sewingshields, Haydon Bridge NY813702; Chesterholm, Vindolanda Roman Fort and Milestone NY771664; Winshields Milecastle, Bardon Mill NY745676; Cawfields Milecastle NY726669; Walltown Crags, Greenhead NY674664; Benwell Condercum NZ215646; Benwell Roman Temple NZ217646; Denton Hall Turret NZ198655 and West Denton NZ195656.

HOUSESTEADS ROMAN FORT

map G12
Telephone: (04984) 363

This is the best-preserved Roman troop-base on Hadrian's Wall. In the museum, a model shows the layout of barracks, headquarters buildings, commandant's house and granaries. Also displayed are relics from the fort and the settlement that grew up outside the walls in the 3rd and 4th centuries.

Location: 2¾ m (4.4 km) north east of Bardon Mill. OS map ref NY790687.
Opening Times: Good Friday or Apr 1 (whichever is earlier) to Sept 30: Open Daily 10–6. Oct 1 to Maundy Thursday or Mar 31 (whichever is earlier): Open Daily 10–4. *Closed* Dec 24 –26, Jan 1. Adm £1.80, Concessions £1.40, Chd 90p.

HOWICK HALL GARDENS

Alnwick   map H12
(Howick Trustees Ltd)

Extensive grounds including a natural woodland garden in addition to the formal gardens surrounding the Hall.

Location: 6 m NE of Alnwick, nr Howick village.
Opening Times: Mar to Oct – Daily 1–6. Adm charge.

KIRKLEY HALL COLLEGE

Ponteland   map H12
Telephone: (0661) 860808
(Dr R. McParlin)

Prestigious gardens, greenhouses, plantsman's paradise, wide selection of plants – all labelled, high standards of maintenance. Trees, shrubs, ornamental borders, herbaceous perennials, sunken garden, wide range dwarf conifers, alpines. Wall trained fruit trees. National collections – fagus, hedera, dwarf salix. Propagation, biological pest control. Practical demonstrations (prior notice). Conducted tours (prior arrangement). Guided walks 2 pm second Sun every month.

Location: 3 m N of Ponteland off A696, 4 m S of B6524 Morpeth (A192/197) Belsay road, RAC signposted.
Opening Times: Daily 10 till dusk. Adm £1.20, Chd/OAPs 60p, Family £3. Reduced rates for parties, prior notice only. Free car and coach parking. Disabled welcome. Toilet facilities. No dogs.
Refreshments: Refreshments available.

LINDISFARNE CASTLE, The National Trust

Holy Island   map G13
Telephone: Berwick (0289) 89244

Built about 1550. Sympathetically restored as a comfortable house by Lutyens in 1903.

Location: 5 m E of Beal across causeway.
Opening Times: Apr 1 to Sept 30 – Daily (closed Fris, open Good Fri) 1–5.30; Oct – Weds, Sats & Suns 1–5.30. Last adm 5. Adm £3. No party rate. No dogs in Castle. Unsuitable for wheelchairs.

LINDISFARNE PRIORY – *See page 149*

NORHAM CASTLE

map G13
Telephone: (028982) 329

Built in the 12th century by the Bishop of Durham, this massive castle stands on a site of great natural strength. It withstood repeated attacks in the 13th and 14th centuries and was thought to be impregnable. But in 1513 it was stormed by the forces of James IV and partially destroyed. Although later rebuilt, the castle lost its importance as a defensive stronghold by the end of the 16th century.

Location: 8 m (13 km) south west of Berwick. OS map ref NT907476.
Opening Times: Good Friday or Apr 1 (whichever is earlier) to Sept 30: Open Daily 10–6. Oct 1 to Maundy Thursday or Mar 31 (whichever is earlier): Open Tues to Sun 10–4. *Closed* Dec 24–26, Jan 1. Adm £1.10, Concessions 85p, Chd 55p.

PRESTON TOWER

Chathill   map H13
(Major T. H. Baker-Cresswell)

One of the few survivors of 78 Pele Towers listed in 1415. The tunnel vaulted rooms remain unaltered and provide a realistic picture of the grim way of life under the constant threat of 'Border Reivers'. Two rooms are furnished in contemporary style and there are displays of historic and local information.

Location: 7 m N of Alnwick; 1 m E from A1. Follow Historic Property signs.
Station: Chathill (1 m).
Opening Times: All year – Daily during daylight hours. Adm £1, Chd and OAPs 50p. Free car park.
No dogs (except those left in car).

PRUDHOE CASTLE

map G11
Telephone: (0661) 33459

Extensive remains of 12th century castle with gatehouse, curtain wall and keep enclosed within surrounding earthworks. In the 19th century a gothick house was built within the ruins, now containing an exhibition on the history of the castle and video about Northumberland Castles.

Location: In Prudhoe, on minor road off A695. OS map ref NZ092634.
Opening Times: Good Friday or Apr 1 (whichever is earlier) to Sept 30: Open Daily 10–6. Oct 1 to Maundy Thursday or Mar 31 (whichever is earlier): Open Tues to Sun 10–4. *Closed* Dec 24–26, Jan 1. Adm £1.50, Concessions £1.10, Chd 75p.

SEATON DELAVAL HALL

Whitley Bay   map H12
Telephone: Tyneside (091) 2373040/2371493
(The Lord Hastings)

The house was designed by Sir John Vanbrugh in his most theatrical manner for Admiral George Delaval and built between 1718–1728. Regarded by many as Sir John Vanbrugh's masterpiece. Built on a small budget it is ducal magnificence in miniature. Relatively small, the house gives the impression of being vast, which is of course what was intended. It is the theatre again – Vanbrugh the playwright using stones, columns and pediments instead of words. It comprises a centre block between two arcaded and pedimented wings, the centre block being gutted by fire in 1822 and for

LINDISFARNE PRIORY

map G13
Telephone: (028989) 200

Roofless and ruined, the priory is still supremely beautiful, its graceful arches and decorated doorways commemorating the craftsmanship of their Norman builders. This has been sacred soil since 634 when the missionary Bishop Aidan was sent from Iona, to spread Christianity through northern England. New visitor centre with atmospheric exhibition and shop.

Location: On Holy Island, which can be reached at low tide across a causeway. Tide tables are posted at each end of the causeway. OS map ref NU126418.
Opening Times: Good Friday or Apr 1 (whichever is earlier) to Sept 30: Open Daily 10–6 subject to tides. Oct 1 to Maundy Thursday or Mar 31 (whichever is earlier): Open Tues to Sun 10–4 subject to tides. *Closed* Dec 24–26, Jan 1. Adm £1.80, Concessions £1.40, Chd 90p.

---

many years stood a gaunt ruin, but it was partially restored in 1862–63 and again in 1959–62. The East Wing contains very fine stables and in the grounds are extensive gardens and statues.

Location: ½ m from coast at Seaton Sluice, and between Blyth and Whitley Bay (A190). (Northumbria Bus from Newcastle 363, 364.)
Opening Times: May 1–Sept 30: Wed, Sun, and Bank Holidays 2–6. Adm £1.50, Chd (accompanied by adult).

WALLINGTON HOUSE, WALLED GARDEN and GROUNDS, The National Trust

Cambo   map G12
Telephone: Scots Gap (067 074) 283 (House)

Built 1688, altered 18th century. Central Hall added in 19th century, decorated by William Bell Scott, Ruskin and others. Fine porcelain, furniture and pictures in series of rooms including a late Victorian nursery and dolls' houses. Museum. Coach display in West Coach House. Woodlands, lakes, walled terraced garden and conservatory with magnificent fuchsias.

Location: Access from N, 12 m W of Morpeth on B6343. Access from S, A696 from Newcastle; 6 m NW of Belsay B6342 to Cambo.
Opening Times: HOUSE: Apr 1 to Oct 31, daily 1–5.30. Last adm 5. *Closed* Tues. WALLED GARDEN: Open all year daily. Apr 1 to Sept 10.30–7 (or dusk if earlier). Oct to Mar 10.30–4. GROUNDS: Open all year during daylight hours. Adm House and Grounds £3.80, Grounds only £1.80. Party rate House & Grounds £3.30. Grounds £1.30. No dogs in house; on leads in walled garden. Shop & Information Centre. Wheelchairs provided. *Parties by prior arrangement with the administrators.*
Refreshments: Available at Clock Tower Restaurant. Telephone Scots Gap (067 074) 274.

WARKWORTH CASTLE

map H12
Telephone: (0665) 711423

From 1332 the history of Warkworth was the history of the Percy family. In 1399 this became the history of England, when the third Percy lord of Warkworth and his son Harry Hotspur put Henry IV on the throne. Three scenes from Shakespeare's Henry IV Part 1 are set at Warkworth. Norman in origin, the castle has some very fine medieval masonry. Part of the keep was restored and made habitable in the 19th century.

Location: 7½ m (12 km) south of Alnwick. OS map ref NU247057.
Opening Times: Good Friday or Apr 1 (whichever is earlier) to Sept 30: Open Daily 10–6. Oct 1 to Maundy Thursday or Mar 31 (whichever is earlier): Open Tues to Sun 10–4. *Closed* Dec 24–26, Jan 1. Adm £1.10, Concessions 85p, Chd 55p.

WARKWORTH HERMITAGE

map H12
Telephone: (0665) 711423

The hermitage and chapel of Holy Trinity is situated in a peaceful, retired place, overshadowed and surrounded by trees upon the left bank of the River Coquet half a mile above the castle, in that part of the manor of Warkworth anciently called Sunderland Park. It can be approached by boat up the river from the landing place below the castle or by a pleasant footpath through woods and meadows up the right bank and across by ferry from the upper boat landing.

Location: 7½ m (12 km) south of Alnwick.
Opening Times: Summer weekends only 10–6. Adm 75p, concessions 55p, Chd 40p.

NOTTINGHAMSHIRE

CARLTON HALL

Carlton-on-Trent map J8 △
(Trustees of G H Vere-Laurie dec'd)

George III house built c.1765 by Joseph Pocklington of Newark, banker, 1736–1817. Beautiful drawing room. Magnificent ancient cedar in grounds. Stables attributed to Carr of York.

Location: 7 m N of Newark just off A1.
Opening Times: Any day, telephone (0636) 821421 to be certain of being shown round. Adm House and Garden £1.50.

CLUMBER PARK, The National Trust

nr Worksop map J8 &
Telephone: Worksop (0909) 476592

4,000 acre landscaped park with lake and woods. Classical bridge, temples, lawned Lincoln Terrace and pleasure grounds. Walled kitchen garden and tools exhibition.

Location: Clumber Park 4½ m SE of Worksop; 6½ m SW of East Retford.
Opening Times: Open daily all year. The Estate Office, Gardens Cottage, Clumber Park, Worksop,
Notts S80 3AZ. Vehicle parking charges. Dogs admitted. Shop. Cycle hire. Fishing bank. Wheelchairs
& special fishing platform for disabled. **1992 Events:** July 18, 'Jazz in the Park'.
Refreshments: Cafeteria open all year daily. Licensed restaurant for lunches daily, evening meals
available for pre-booked parties. Telephone: Worksop 484122.

HODSOCK PRIORY GARDENS

Blyth, nr Worksop map J8
Telephone: Worksop (0909) 591204
(Sir Andrew and Lady Buchanan)

Enjoy a very special afternoon out in these romantic gardens on the historic site mentioned in the Domesday Book. Five acres of beauty and peace bounded by dry moat. Grade I listed gatehouse c.1500. Mature trees include huge cornus, catalpas, tulip tree, swamp cypress. Small lake, bog garden, spring bulbs, mixed borders, roses old and new, established holly hedges. Featured in 'The Rose Gardens of England', 'The Shell Guide to the Gardens of England and Wales', 'Country Life' (Nov 1990), and the 'Good Gardens Guide' (1 star).

Location: 1 m from A1 at Blyth. Off B6045 Blyth to Worksop road.
Opening Times: Easter Sun, then May Day, Spring and Aug Bank Holiday (Sun and Mon); also Weds & Thurs from mid-June to mid-July. 'Special Spectaculars' – for Snowdrops Feb/Mar; Daffodils Apr. Blossom and Bluebells May; Autumn Colour Oct/Nov, with reduced price sale of plants. All 10–5. Adm £1.50, Chd 25p. Visitors in wheelchairs free. For dates, details and group bookings please telephone.
Refreshments: Home-made teas.

HOLME PIERREPONT HALL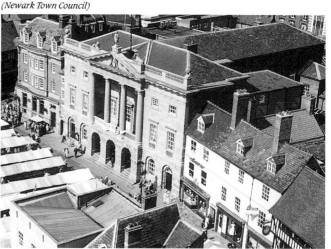

Radcliffe-on-Trent, nr Nottingham map J7 △
Telephone: (0602) 332371
(Mr & Mrs Robin Brackenbury)

Medieval brick manor house. Historic Courtyard garden with box parterre, 1875. Regional 17th, 18th, 19th and 20th century furniture, china and pictures. Quiet and free from crowds. Jacob sheep. Shop with Jacob wool products.

Location: 5 m SE from centre of Nottingham by following all signs to the National Water Sports Centre and continue for 1½ m.
Opening Times: June, July & Aug – Tues, Thurs, Fri, Sun 2–6. Easter, Spring & Summer Bank Hol Sun, Mons & Tues 2–6. Groups by appointment throughout the year, including evenings. Adm £2.50, Chd £1, subject to alteration.
Refreshments: Home-made teas. Other refreshments by arrangement.

NEWARK TOWN HALL

Newark map J7
Telephone: (0636) 640100
(Newark Town Council)

One of the finest Georgian Town Halls in the country, the building has recently been refurbished in sympathy with John Carr's original concept. On display is the Town's collection of Civic Plate, silver dating generally from the 17th and 18th century, including the 'Newark Monteith' and the Newark Siege Pieces. Other items of interest are some early historical records and various paintings including a collection by the artist Joseph Paul.

NEWSTEAD ABBEY

Linby map H7
Telephone: Mansfield (0623) 793557
(Nottingham City Council)

Newstead Abbey is best known as the home of the poet Lord Byron who made the house and its ghostly legends famous. Visitors can see Byrons apartments and mementos of the poet including letters, manuscripts and first editions. Splendid 19th century rooms bring the lives of later Victorian residents of the house to life. The early history of Newstead as a religious building can be seen in the remains of the medieval priory. The cloisters of the priory surround a secret garden, in the centre is an ancient stone foundation carved with fantastic beasts. Newstead Abbey stands amongst 300 acres of parkland, magnificent in all seasons, that includes lakes, waterfalls, rock and rose gardens.

Location: 12 m N of Nottingham on A60 (Mansfield Rd). Close to junction 27 of the M1.
By Bus: (Trent no's 63 and X2) from Nottingham Victoria Coach Station, drops off at Abbey gates (1 m from house).
Opening Times: HOUSE: Easter to Oct, daily 12–6. GARDENS: all year daily 10–dusk (except last Fri in Nov). Adm: House and gardens £3.50, £1.90 reductions. Gardens only £1.50, 90p reductions.
Refreshments: Tea room and licensed restaurant in grounds, tel (0623) 797392.

NEWARK TOWN HALL – *Continued*

Location: Market Place, Newark; located on A1 and A46.
Station: Newark Castle; Northgate (¹/₂ m).
Opening Times: All the year–Mons to Fris 10–12, 2–4. Open at other times for groups by appointment. *Closed* Sats, Suns, Bank Holiday Mons and Tues following and Christmas week. Adm free.

NEWSTEAD ABBEY – *See page 150*

PAPPLEWICK HALL

Near Nottingham   map H7
Telephone: (0602) 633491
(Dr R. B. Godwin-Austen)

Fine Adam house built 1784 with park and woodland garden.

Location: 6 m N of Nottingham, 2 m from exit 27 M1.
Opening Times: By appointment only, all year.

THRUMPTON HALL

Nottingham   map H7   △
Telephone: Nottingham 830333
(George FitzRoy Seymour, Esq)

Fine Jacobean house, built 1607, incorporating earlier manor house. Priest's hiding hole, magnificent Charles II carved staircase carved and panelled saloon and other fine rooms containing beautiful 17th and 18th century furniture and many fine portraits. Large lawns separated from landscaped park by ha-ha and by lake. This house retains the atmosphere of a home, being lived in by owners who will show parties around.

Location: 7 m S of Nottingham; 3 m E of M1 at junction 24; 1 m from A453.
Opening Times: By appointment for parties of 20 or more persons. Adm House & Gardens £3, Chd £1.50. Minimum charge of £60. Open all year including evenings.
Refreshments: By prior arrangement.

WOLLATON HALL

Nottingham   map H7
Telephone: Nottingham 281333 or 281130
(City of Nottingham)

Fine example of late Elizabethan Renaissance architecture. Natural History Museum – one of the finest in the country.

Location: 2¹/₂ m W of City centre.
Station: Nottingham (2³/₄ m).
Opening Times: All the year. Apr to Sept: weekdays 10–7, Suns 2–5; Oct to Mar: weekdays 10–dusk, Suns 1.30–4.30. Adm free (small charge Suns & Bank Hols). Conducted tours by arrangement £1, Chd 50p (subject to alteration). *Closed Christmas Day.*
Refreshments: Tea at refreshment pavilion all year.

OXFORDSHIRE

ARDINGTON HOUSE   🏛

nr Wantage   map H4
Telephone: (0235) 833244
(Mrs Desmond Baring)

Early 18th century of grey brick with red brick facings. Hall with Imperial staircase, panelled dining room with painted ceiling.

Location: 12 m S of Oxford; 12 m N of Newbury; 2¹/₂ m E of Wantage.
Station: Didcot (8 m).
Opening Times: May to Sept–Mons & all Bank Hols 2.30–4.30. Parties of 10 or more welcomed any day by appointment. Adm House & Grounds £2.
Refreshments: Coffee & Teas by arrangement.

ASHDOWN HOUSE, The National Trust   🦋

nr Lambourn   map H4   △

17th century house built by 1st Lord Craven and by him 'consecrated' to Elizabeth, Queen of Bohemia; great staircase rising from hall to attic; portraits of the Winter Queen's family; access to roof, fine views; box parterre and lawns. Avenues and woodland walks.

Location: 2¹/₄ m S of Ashbury; 3¹/₂ m N of Lambourn on W side of B4000.
Opening Times: Hall, stairway & roof only (fine views). Apr to end Oct–Weds & Sats 2–6. Guided tours only: at 2.15, 3.15, 4.15 and 5.15, from front door. *Closed* Easter and Bank Holiday Mon. Adm Grounds, hall, stairway & roof £2, Chd half-price. **Woodlands** open all year–Sats to Thurs, dawn to dusk, adm free. No reduction for parties (which should pre-book in writing). No dogs allowed in house or grounds. Wheelchair access to garden only. No WCs or refreshments available.

BLENHEIM PALACE   🏛

Woodstock   map H5   △   Ⓢ
Telephone: Woodstock (0993) 811325 (24 hr information)
(His Grace the Duke of Marlborough)

The Long Library

Masterpiece of Sir John Vanbrugh in the classical style. Fine collection of pictures and tapestries. Gardens and park designed by Vanbrugh and Queen Anne's gardener, Henry Wise. Later construction was carried out by 'Capability' Brown, who also created the famous Blenheim lake. Exhibition of Churchilliana and Sir Winston Churchill's birth room. Churchill paintings on exhibition.

A visit to Blenheim Palace is a wonderful way to spend a day. An inclusive ticket covers the Palace Tour, Park and Gardens, Butterfly House, Motor Launch, Train, Adventure Play Area and Nature Trail. Optional are the new Marlborough Maze and Boat Hire on Queen Pool. Events planned for 1992 include the Annual Grand Charity Cricket Match, in aid of the Oxfordshire Association of Boys' Clubs, between a Lords Taverners XI and Oxford University XI on 24th May. The Blenheim Audi International Horse Trials take place on 3rd, 4th, 5th and 6th September. Further details from The Administrator, Blenheim Palace, Woodstock, Oxon OX20 1PX. Telephone: (0993) 811091.

Location: SW end of Woodstock which lies 8 m N of Oxford (A44).
Opening Times: mid-Mar to Oct 31–Daily 10.30–5.30 (last adm 4.45). Special prices apply on Spring Bank Holiday Sunday when the Lord Taverners Charity Cricket Match takes place. *Reduced rates for parties.* Educational service for school parties–Palace, Farm, Forestry, Horticulture & Nature Trail. Blenheim Audi International Horse Trials Sept 3, 4, 5 & 6. Adm charges not available at time of going to press. The right to close the Palace or Park without notice is reserved.
Refreshments: Licensed Restaurant & self service cafeteria at the Palace. Self Service Cafeteria at the Garden Centre.

BOTANIC GARDENS

Oxford   map H5
(University of Oxford)

Oldest botanic garden in Britain, founded 1621.

Location: High Street.
Station: Oxford (1 m).
Opening Times: All the year—9–5, (closes 4.30 winter). Adm £1 during July and Aug.
Closed Good Fri and Christmas day.

BROOK COTTAGE

Well Lane, Alkerton   map H5
Telephone: Edge Hill (029 587) 303 or 590
(Mr & Mrs David Hodges)

4-acre hillside garden, formed since 1964, surrounding 17th century house. Wide variety of trees, shrubs and plants of all kinds in areas of differing character; water garden; alpine scree; one-colour borders; over 200 shrub and climbing roses; many clematis. Interesting throughout season.

Location: 6 m NW of Banbury; ½ m A422 (Banbury/Stratford-upon-Avon). In Alkerton take Well Lane (opposite war memorial) then right fork.
Opening Times: GARDEN ONLY. Apr 1–Oct 31, Mon–Fri 9–6. Adm £1.50, OAPs £1, Chd free. Evenings, weekends and all group visits by appointment. *In aid of National Gardens Scheme.*
Refreshments: For parties by prior arrangement; otherwise DIY coffee/tea. Unusual plants for sale.

BROUGHTON CASTLE 🏠

Banbury   map H5
Telephone: Banbury (0295) 262624
(The Lord Saye & Sele)

The home of Lord and Lady Saye and Sele and owned by the family for 600 years. A moated medieval Castle greatly enlarged in 1550. Fine panelling and fireplaces, splendid plaster ceilings and good period furniture. Interesting Civil War connections including the secret meeting room of the parliamentary leaders.

Location: 2 m SW of Banbury on the Shipston-on-Stour Road (B4035).
Opening Times: May 20 to Sept 13—Weds & Suns 2–5; also Thurs in July & Aug 2–5; Bank Hol Suns & Bank Hol Mons including Easter 2–5. Adm £2.80, Chd £1.40, OAPs/ Students £2.10. Groups on other days throughout the year by appointment (reduced rates).
Refreshments: Buffet teas on open days; by arrangement for groups.

BUSCOT OLD PARSONAGE, The National Trust 🌿

nr Lechlade   map H4

Built in 1703 of Cotswold stone and stone tiles. On the banks of the Thames. Small garden.

Location: 2 m SE of Lechlade; 4 m NW of Faringdon on A417.
Opening Times: Apr to end Oct—Weds 2–6, by appointment in writing with the tenant. Adm £1. *No parties.* No dogs. No WCs. Unsuitable for wheelchairs.

BUSCOT PARK, The National Trust 🌿

nr Faringdon   map H4   △
Telephone: Faringdon (0367) 240786 (not weekends)

Built 1780. Fine paintings and furniture. Burne-Jones room. Attractive garden walks, lake. Administered for the National Trust by Lord Faringdon.

Location: 3 m NW between on Lechlade/Faringdon road (A417).
Opening Times: Apr to end Sept (incl Good Friday, Easter Sat & Sun)—Weds, Thurs, Fris and every 2nd and 4th Sat, and immediately following Sun, 2–6, i.e. Apr 11, 12, 18, 19, 25, 26; May 9, 10, 23 & 24; June 13, 14, 27, 28; July 11, 12, 25, 26; Aug 8, 9, 22, 23; Sept 12, 13, 26, 27. Adm House & Grounds £3.50, Chd £1.75. Grounds only £2.50, Chd £1.25. *No dogs. No indoor photography.* Unsuitable for wheelchairs.
Refreshments: Tea room.

THE CHANTRY HOUSE

Henley-on-Thames   map J4
Telephone: Henley (0491) 577340
(St Mary's Church PCC)

Church Hall, formerly school, dating back to 1400.

Location: Next to church, by bridge over the river Thames (A423).
Station: Henley-on-Thames.
Opening Times: All the year – by appointment.

DITCHLEY PARK

Enstone   map H5
Telephone: Enstone (0608) 677346
(Ditchley Foundation)

Third in size and date of the great 18th century houses of Oxfordshire, Ditchley is famous for its splendid interior decorations (William Kent and Henry Flitcroft). For three and half centuries the home of the Lee family and their descendants – with whom Robert E. Lee was directly connected – Ditchley was frequently visited at weekends by Sir Winston Churchill during World War II. It has now been restored, furnished and equipped as a conference centre devoted to the study of issues of concern to the people on both sides of the Atlantic.

Location: 1½ m W of A44 at Kiddington; 2 m from Charlbury (B4437).
Station: Charlbury (2 m).
Opening Times: Visits by arrangement with The Bursar, afternoons only. *Closed* mid-July to mid-Sept.

FAWLEY COURT – MARIAN FATHERS HISTORIC HOUSE & MUSEUM – *See page 153*

THE GREAT BARN, The National Trust 🌿

Great Coxwell   map H4

13th century, stone built, stone tiled roof, exceptionally interesting timber roof construction. Magnificent proportions.

Location: 2 m SW of Faringdon between A420 & B4019.
Opening Times: All year daily at reasonable hours. Adm 50p. Dogs on leads admitted. Wheelchair access.

GREYS COURT – *See page 154*

FAWLEY COURT – MARIAN FATHERS HISTORIC HOUSE & MUSEUM 🏛

Henley-on-Thames RG9 3AE   map J4
(Marian Fathers)

Designed by Sir Christopher Wren, Fawley Court was built in 1684 for Colonel William Freeman as a family residence. The Mansion House, decorated by Grinling Gibbons and later by James Wyatt, is situated in a beautiful park designed by Lancelot 'Capability' Brown. The Museum consists of a library, various documents of the Polish kings, a very rare and well preserved collection of historical sabres and many memorable military objects of the Polish Army. There are classical sculptures, and paintings from Renaissance and later times. Fawley Court also serves nowadays as a seat of religious community, and from 1953 has been cared for, maintained and restored by the Congregation of Marian Fathers.

Location: 1 m N of Henley-on-Thames via A4155 to Marlow.
Station: Henley-on-Thames (1½ m).
Opening Times: Mar to Oct: Weds, Thurs, Suns 2–5. *Closed Easter and Whitsuntide weeks.* Adm £2, Chd £1, OAPs £1.50. Car park. No dogs. Nov, Feb: open to groups by pre-booked appointment.
Refreshments: Tea, coffee & home-made cakes available July & Aug.

KINGSTON BAGPUIZE HOUSE – *See page 155*

MAPLEDURHAM HOUSE AND WATERMILL

nr Reading RG4 7TR   map J4
Telephone: Reading (0734) 723350
(J J Eyston and Lady Anne Eyston)

MAPLEDURHAM HOUSE   MAPLEDURHAM WATERMILL

Late 16th century Elizabethan home of the Blount family. Original moulded ceilings, great oak staircase, fine collection of paintings and private chapel in Strawberry Hill Gothic added in 1797. Interesting literary connections with Alexander Pope, John Galsworthy's Forsyte Saga and Kenneth Graham's Wind in the Willows. Unique setting in grounds running down to the Thames. The 15th century Watermill is fully restored and producing flour and bran which are sold in the gift shop. Walkman audio tours included in the entry to Mill.

Location: 4 m NW of Reading on North Bank of Thames. Signposted off Caversham/Woodcote Road on A4074. Boats from Caversham Bridge 2pm on open days. (Caversham Bridge is ½ m from Reading Station).
Opening Times: House. Easter to end of Sept – Sats, Suns & Bank Hols. Country Park/Picnic Area: 12.30–7. Watermill: 1–5. House: 2.30–5, (last adm 5). Winter Suns: Watermill only open 2–4. Midweek party visits by prior arrangement include guided tours.
Refreshments: Tea room serving home made cream teas, cakes, and ice cream in original old manor built in 1390.

MILTON MANOR HOUSE 🏛

nr Abingdon map H4 △ ㋡
Telephone: Abingdon (0235) 831287 or 831871
(Anthony Mockler-Barrett Esq)

Photograph Jeremy Grayson.

Mellow restoration house, with Georgian wings, traditionally designed by Inigo Jones and much admired by Tsar Peter the Great of All the Russias, a frequent visitor. Seat of the Barrett family for six generations. Exquisite Roman Catholic Chapel where mass is still celebrated. "Like all the best things in England" wrote the late Poet Laureate Sir John Betjeman, "this is hidden. Milton village street is true Berkshire. The Manor House is splendid. Inside are handsome rooms and an exciting contrast – a Chapel and Library in Strawberry Hill Gothick. Do go and see it".

Walled garden. Stables. Dovecote. Dusty cellars full of attractions for children. Outdoor chess, croquet, ping-pong and swings usually available, at no extra charge. Pygmy goats, peacocks, rare breed pigs and other animals to see. Headquarters of the 'Back to Berkshire' campaign. "A perfect gem of an historic house – the interior is a delight" says Elizabeth de Stroumillo, writing in the Daily Telegraph. "Milton Manor is not to be missed".

Location: 9 m S of Oxford. A34 leading S towards Newbury and the M4. Turning off signposted Milton. Village ½ m. Entrance gates by church. 3 m S of Abingdon. 1 m from Sutton Courtney on B4016. 1½ hrs from London via M4 or M40.
Station: Didcot (2 m).
Opening Times: Easter Sat to end Sept – Sats & Suns only plus Bank Holidays: 2–5.30, last adm 5. Guided tours. (Guided evening tours and coach tours outside these times may be booked). All parking free (except for special events). Adm House and Gardens: £2.50; Gardens only £1.20, Chd under 14 half price. Shop with walled garden, organic fruit and vegetables also for sale in season.
Refreshments: Home made teas in the old kitchens, where the famous teapot collection of Mrs Marjorie Mockler, the present owner's late mother, may be seen. Lunches, buffets and receptions (including wedding parties) by special arrangement.

GREYS COURT, The National Trust 🍃

Henley-on-Thames map J4
Telephone: Rotherfield Greys (04917) 529

Jacobean house with Georgian additions set amid the remains of the courtyard walls and towers of a 14th century fortified house; beautiful gardens; Tudor donkey wheel well-house; Archbishop's Maze.

Location: At Rotherfield Greys 3 m W of Henley-on-Thames E of B481.
Opening Times: House: Apr to end Sept – Mons, Weds, Fris 2–6. Garden: Apr to end of Sept – Mon to Wed, Fri and Sat 2–6. *Closed* Good Friday. Last admissions half-hour before closing. Adm House & Garden £3.50. Garden only £2.50, Chd half-price. Parties must book in advance. No reduction for parties. *Closed Good Friday*. Dogs in car park only.
Refreshments: Teas, Apr and May – Weds & Sats; June to end Sept – Mons, Weds, Fris & Sats 2.30–5.15, also for booked parties at other times by arrangement.

KINGSTON BAGPUIZE HOUSE 🏛

Kingston Bagpuize   map H4
Telephone: (0865) 820259
(Lady Tweedsmuir)

A superb Charles II manor house surrounded by parkland, a large garden and attractive 17th century stable buildings. The house has a magnificent cantilevered staircase and well-proportioned panelled rooms with fine furniture and pictures. The large and interesting garden contains beautiful trees, lawns, a woodland garden, herbaceous and shrub borders and many lovely bulbs.

Location: 5½ m W of Abingdon at junction of A415 & A420.
Opening Times: Apr 1 to Sept 30, Suns and Bank Holiday Mons 2.30–5.30 (last adm 5). Adm House and Gardens: £2.50, OAPs, £2, Chd £1. Garden only: 50p. (Chd under 5 free adm to Gardens, not admitted to House). Groups welcome by appointment. Group rates on request. Wheelchairs garden only. No dogs. Gifts, books, plants for sale. Car parking.
Refreshments: Teas.

MAPLEDURHAM HOUSE AND WATERMILL – *See page 153*

MILTON MANOR HOUSE – *See page 154*

MINSTER LOVELL HALL AND DOVECOTE ✿

map H5
Telephone: (0993) 75315
(English Heritage)

Originally a 15th century manor house, the Hall was built around a courtyard. The medieval dovecote, complete with nesting boxes, has recently been restored. When the hall was dismantled in the 18th century, a skeleton was found in the cellars. This is thought to have been the Yorkist Lord Lovell who disappeared after the Battle of Bosworth 1485, where he fought on the losing side.

Location: 2½ m (4 km) north west of Witney. OS map ref SP324114.
Opening Times: Good Friday or Apr 1 (whichever is earlier) to Sept 30 daily 10–6. Adm 95p, Concessions 70p, Chd 50p.

NUFFIELD PLACE

Nettlebed   map J4
Telephone: (0491) 641224
(Nuffield College, Friends of Nuffield Place)

The home from 1933–1963 of Lord Nuffield, founder of Morris Motors, Nuffield Place is a rare survival of a complete upper-middle class home of the 1930s. Built in 1914, the house was enlarged in 1933 for Lord Nuffield. Several rooms are still decorated in the '30s style, and all rooms contain furnishings acquired by Lord and Lady Nuffield when they took up residence. Clocks, rugs and some tapestries are of fine quality. Some of the furniture is antique but much was custom made by Cecil A. Halliday of Oxford, and is of skilled craftsmanship. The gardens, with mature trees, stone walls and rockery, were laid out during and just after the First World War. Lady Nuffield's Wolseley car is also on display.

Location: Approximately 7 m from Henley-on-Thames, just off A423 to Oxford.
Opening Times: May to Sept, every 2nd and 4th Sun 2–5. Adm £2, concessions £1.50, Chd 50p. Parties by arrangement. Tel: (0491) 39422. Ground floor and garden suitable for the disabled.
Refreshments: Teas.

ROUSHAM HOUSE – *See page 156*

STANTON HARCOURT MANOR 🏛

Stanton Harcourt   map H5
(Mr Crispin & The Hon Mrs Gascoigne)

Unique medieval buildings in tranquil surroundings—Old Kitchen, Pope's Tower and Domestic Chapel. House maintained as family home, contains fine collection of pictures, furniture, silver and porcelain. 12 acres of Garden with Great Fish Pond and Stew Ponds.

Location: 9 m W of Oxford; 5 m SE of Witney; on B4449, between Eynsham & Standlake.
Opening Times: House & Gardens. Apr 5, 16, 19, 20, 30; May 3, 4, 14, 17, 21, 24, 25; June 4, 7, 18, 21; July 2, 5, 16, 19, 30; Aug 2, 13, 16, 27, 30, 31; Sept 10, 13, 24, 27; 2–6. HOUSE & GARDEN £3, Chd (12 and under) and OAPs £2. GARDEN ONLY £1.50, Chd (12 and under) and OAPs £1. Large parties and coaches by prior arrangement. Disabled visitors welcome. Home container-grown shrubs & pot plants for sale.
Refreshments: Teas on Suns and Bank Hols in aid of Parish Church.

STONOR PARK – *See page 156*

ROUSHAM HOUSE

Steeple Aston map H5 △
Telephone: Steeple Aston (0869) 47110 or (0860) 360407
(C Cottrell-Dormer, Esq)

Rousham House was built by Sir Robert Dormer in 1635 and the shooting holes were put in the doors while it was a Royalist garrison in the Civil War. Sir Robert's successors were Masters of Ceremonies at Court during eight reigns and employed Court artists and architects to embellish Rousham. The house stands above the River Cherwell one mile from Hopcrofts Holt, near the road from Chipping Norton to Bicester. It contains 150 portraits and other pictures and much fine contemporary furniture. Rooms were decorated by William Kent (1738) and Roberts of Oxford (1765). The garden is Kent's only surviving landscape design with classic buildings, cascades, statues and vistas in thirty acres of hanging woods above the Cherwell. Wonderful herbaceous borders, pigeon house and small parterre. Fine herd of rare Long-Horn cattle in the park. Wear sensible shoes and bring a picnic, and Rousham is yours for the day.

Location: 12 m N of Oxford off Banbury Road (A423) at Hopcrofts Holt Hotel (1 m).
Station: Heyford (1 m).
Opening Times: Apr to Sept inclusive: Weds, Suns & Bank Hols 2–4.30. Gardens only, every day all year, 10–4.30. No children under 15. No dogs. *Parties by arrangement on other days.*

STONOR PARK 🏛

nr Henley-on-Thames map J4
Telephone: Turville Heath (049 163) 587
(Lord & Lady Camoys)

Ancient home of Lord and Lady Camoys and the Stonor family for over eight hundred years, and centre of Catholicism throughout the Recusancy Period, with its own medieval Chapel where mass is still celebrated today. Sanctuary for St. Edmund Campion in 1581. An exibition features his life and work. The house is of considerable architectural interest, built over many centuries from c.1190, and the site of prehistoric stone circle, now recreated within the grounds. A family home containing fine family portraits and rare items of furniture, paintings, drawings, tapestries, sculptures and bronzes from Britain, Europe and America. Peaceful hillside gardens with magnificent roses and ornamental ponds. Souvenir gift shop and afternoon tearoom serving home-made cakes. Parties welcome, lunches available by prior arrangement.

Location: On B480; 5 m N of Henley-on-Thames, 5 m S of Watlington.
Opening Times: Apr: Suns and Bank Hol Mons only; May, June and Sept: Weds, Suns and Bank Hol Mons; Jul: Weds, Thurs, Suns; Aug: Weds, Thurs, Sats, Suns and Bank Hol Mons 2–5.30 (Bank Hol Mons 12.30–5.30). Last adm 5. Parties by prior arrangement any Tues, Wed or Thur (morning, afternoon or evening with supper) and Sun (afternoon only). Adm (1992) £3.25, OAPs £2.65, Chd (under 14 with adult) free. Party rates on application. Discount for NT and English Heritage members, HHA members free on production of card.

WATERPERRY GARDENS

nr Wheatley map J5
Telephone: (0844) 339226 and 339254

WATERPERRY GARDENS
Nr. WHEATLEY, OXFORDSHIRE

The peaceful gardens at Waterperry feature a magnificent herbaceous border, shrub and heather borders, alpine and rock gardens, and a new formal garden. Together with stately trees, a river to walk by and a quite Saxon Church to visit – all set in 83 acres of unspoilt Oxfordshire – the long established herbaceous and alpine nurseries provide year round interest. For the experienced gardener, the novice, or those who have no garden of their own, here is a chance to share, enjoy and admire the order and beauty of careful cultivation.

Garden Shop and Plant Centre with exceptionally wide range of plants, shrubs and fruit produced in the nurseries for sale. Expert care and training is shown in all stages of development. Pots, tubs and sundries also available.

The Teashop provides a delicious selection of home-made food, tea, coffee, fruit juices, etc. Light lunches, morning coffee, teas with scones and cream, cakes, etc. Wine licence.

Open all year from 10 am. Closed for Christmas and New Year Holidays. Open only to visitors to ART IN ACTION between 16th and 19th July.

Enquiries Telephone: (0844) 339226/339254

ADMISSION SEE EDITORIAL REFERENCE

Spacious and peaceful ornamental gardens of 6 acres. Church of Saxon origin and historical interest in grounds with famous old glass, brasses and woodwork. Many interesting plants. Shrub, Herbaceous and Alpine Nurseries.

Location: 2½ m from A40, turn off at Wheatley. 50 m from London, 9 m from Oxford. 62 m Birmingham M40, junction 8. Well signposted locally with Tourist Board 'Rose' symbol.
Opening Times: All the year. Daily—Mar to Oct 10–5.30 (weekdays); 10–6 (weekends); Nov to Feb 10–4.30 *(Teashop closes 30 mins earlier)*. *Closed* for Christmas and New Year Hols. Open only to visitors to ART IN ACTION (enquiries 071-381 3192) July 16–19. Adm to Ornamental Gardens & Nurseries Mar to Oct £1.85, Nov to Feb 60p. Parties and coaches at all times by appointment only. High quality Plant Centre and Garden Shop, telephone: (0844) 339226. *In aid of National Gardens' Scheme & Gardeners' Sun, June 7 & Aug 9.*
Refreshments: Teashop for morning coffee, light lunches and teas. Wine licence.

SHROPSHIRE

ACTON ROUND HALL

Bridgnorth map G6
(H L Kennedy, Esq)

Built in 1714 for Sir Whitmore Acton by the Smith Brothers of Warwick and abandoned from 1717–1918, the house remains little altered from its original state.

Location: 6 m W of Bridgnorth; 15 m SE of Shrewsbury.
Opening Times: May, June, July Aug—Thurs 2.30–5.30. Adm £2. Opening hours and catering for organised parties by arrangement.

ADCOTE

Little Ness, nr Shrewsbury map F7
Telephone: (0939) 260202
(Adcote School Educational Trust Ltd)

"Adcote is the most controlled, coherent and masterly of the big country houses designed by Norman Shaw" (Mark Girouard, 'Country Life' Oct 1970).

Location: 7 m NW of Shrewsbury off A5.
Opening Times: Apr 22 to July 10 (except May 23–26 inclusive); 2–5. Re-open Sept 7–30. All other times by appointment. Adm free but the Governors reserve the right to make a charge.

ATTINGHAM PARK, The National Trust ❧

nr Shrewsbury SY4 4TP map G7   ♿
Telephone: Upton Magna (0743 77) 203

Designed in 1785 by George Steuart for the 1st Lord Berwick. Elegant classical interior decoration. Famous painted boudoir. Nash Picture Gallery. Fine collection of Regency Silver. Park landscape designed by Humphry Repton, 1797. Extensive deer park. House closing early in the season due to major internal work.

Location: At Atcham; 4 m SE of Shrewsbury, on N side of Telford Road (A5, re-numbered B4380 from summer 1992).
Opening Times: Apr 18 to Sept 6: Sats to Weds 1.30–5, (Bank Hol Mons 11–5). Last adm 4.30. Adm House & Grounds £3, Chd £1.50. Family ticket £7.50. Deer Park & Grounds only £1. Pre-booked parties, including evening opening, by arrangement. Dogs in grounds only (not in deer park). Wheelchairs available. Shop. Mother and Baby room.
Refreshments: Home-made lunches and refreshments in tearoom 12.30–5, Bank Holiday Mon 11–5. Licensed. Lunches and suppers at other times for pre-booked parties.

BENTHALL HALL, The National Trust ❧

Broseley TF12 5RX map G6
Telephone: Telford (0952) 882159

16th century stone house with mullioned windows. Interior improved in 17th century. Fine oak staircase and plaster ceilings. Interesting small garden.

Location: 1 m NW of Broseley; 4 m NE of Much Wenlock; 6 m S of Wellington, (B4375).
Opening Times: Apr 1 to end Sept —Weds, Suns and Bank Hol Mons 1.30–5.30 (last adm 5). House visits and garden visits at other times for groups by appointment. Adm £2.20, Chd £1.10. Garden only £1. *No reduction for parties.* No dogs. Wheelchair access.

BOSCOBEL HOUSE ⚑

Shifnal map G6
Telephone: (0902) 850244
(English Heritage)

When John Giffard built his hunting lodge in the 17th century, he little knew that it would become a refuge for the future King Charles II after his defeat at the battle of Worcester in 1651. It is now fully re-furnished with historic tapestries, paintings and antique furniture as the Victorians thought it would have appeared when Charles II hid in the priest's hole and took refuge in the oak tree in the grounds. Exhibition, shop and tea room.

Location: 8 m NW of Wolverhampton; 3¾ m N of Albrighton. O.S. map ref SJ 837083.
Opening Times: Good Friday or Apr 1 (whichever is earlier) to Sept 30, daily 10–6. Oct 1 to Maundy Thursday or Mar 31 (whichever is earlier), Tues to Sun 10–4. *Closed* Dec 24–26, Jan 1 to 31. Adm £2.80, Concessions £2.10, Chd £1.40.

BUILDWAS ABBEY ⚑

map G7
Telephone: (095 245) 3274

Founded in 1135 as an offshoot of Furness Abbey in Cumbria, the abbey belonged briefly to the Savignac Order, then to the Cistercians. Building continued throughout the 12th century and, once completed, the abbey changed little until the Dissolution. The almost complete church typifies the austere style favoured by the Cistercians.

Location: 3¼ m (5.2 km) north east of Much Wenlock. OS map ref SJ642044.
Opening Times: Good Friday or Apr 1 (whichever is earlier) to Sept 30: Open Daily 10–6. Oct 1 to Maundy Thursday or Mar 31 (whichever is earlier): Open Tues to Sun 10–4. *Closed* Dec 24–26, Jan 1. Adm £1.10, Concessions 85p, Chd 55p.

CARDING MILL VALLEY & LONG MYND, The National Trust ✿

Church Stretton map F6
Telephone: Church Stretton 722631

Chalet Pavilion in the magnificent scenery of Carding Mill Valley.

Location: 15 m S of Shrewsbury; W of Church Stretton Valley & A49.
Station: Church Stretton (1 m).
Opening Times: Moorland open all year. Chalet Pavilion Information Centre, Shop & Café. Mar 31 to end June and Sept: Tues to Sat 12–5, Suns and Bank Hol Mons 10.30–5.30. July to end Aug: Mon to Sat 12–5.30, Suns and Bank Hol Mons 10.30–5.30. Oct: Sat and Sun 2–5. Booked parties at other times by arrangement. Entrance charge per car £1.20. Coaches free. Dogs allowed if kept under control.
Refreshments: Snacks, light lunches, teas, etc at Chalet Pavilion (Dogs not allowed in Pavilion).

CASTLE GATES LIBRARY

Shrewsbury map F7
Telephone: Shrewsbury 241487

Former premises of Shrewsbury Grammar School, from 16th and 17th centuries. Now used as a public library. Also houses Shropshire's Local Studies Library. Granted a Civic Trust award for a recent restoration scheme.

Opening Times: Public part of the building Mon–Sat 9–5. Private areas by prior appointment only.

CONDOVER HALL

nr Shrewsbury map F6
(Royal National Institute for the Blind)

'E' shaped building, an excellent example of masons' craft of the late 16th century.

Location: 5 m S of Shrewsbury; 1½ m from A49.
Opening Times: Grounds & exterior of premises (with a limited inspection of the interior) Aug only, by prior appointment.

DUDMASTON, The National Trust ✿

Quatt, Bridgnorth map G6 &
Telephone: Quatt 780866

Late 17th century house; collections of Dutch flower paintings, modern art, botanical paintings and family history. Extensive grounds, woodlands and lakeside garden.

Location: 4 m SE of Bridgnorth on A442.
Opening Times: Apr 1 to end of Sept–Weds & Suns 2.30–6 (last adm 5.30). Special opening for pre-booked parties Thur 2.30–6. Adm House & Garden £2.80, Family £7. Garden only £1.80. Parties must book in advance. Dogs in garden only, on leads. Shop.
Refreshments: Home-made teas 2.30–5.30.

HAUGHMOND ABBEY ⚑

map F7
Telephone: (074 377) 661

William FitzAlan re-established this house for Augustinian canons in 1135. It was rebuilt when FitzAlan became abbot, and further changes and additions were made over the centuries. In 1539 the church was demolished and the abbot's lodging, great hall and kitchens were converted into a private house. Some fine Norman doorways and 14th century statues repay a visit.

Location: 3½ m (5.6 km) north east of Shrewsbury. OS map ref SJ542152.
Opening Times: Good Friday or Apr 1 (whichever is earlier) to Sept 30: Open Daily 10–6. Oct 1 to Maundy Thursday or Mar 31 (whichever is earlier): Open Tues to Sun 10–4. *Closed* Dec 24–26, Jan 1. Adm £1.10., Concessions 85p, Chd 55p.

BOSCOBEL HOUSE

HODNET HALL GARDENS

nr Market Drayton   map G7   &
Telephone: (063 084) 202
(Mr & the Hon Mrs Heber Percy)

HODNET HALL GARDENS

HODNET, MARKET DRAYTON, SHROPSHIRE
Home of Mr and the Hon Mrs A. Heber Percy

These beautiful landscape gardens with their series of lakes and pools occupy some 60 acres and rank among the finest in the country. Magnificent forest trees, flowers and shrubs in endless variety provide an exciting show of colour throughout the seasons. Featured on television and radio. Picturesque 17th Century tea rooms contains a unique collection of Big Game Trophies. Gift shop. Plants, flowers and vegetables are on sale at the garden centre.

From the glorious daffodils of Spring to the magnificent roses of Summer, each season brings fresh delights to these award winning gardens. Over 60 acres of magnificent forest trees, sweeping lawns and tranquil pools ensure plentiful wildlife and brilliant natural colour within this beautiful setting.

Location: 12 m NE of Shrewsbury; 5½ m SW of Market Drayton, at junction of A53 to A442; M6 18½ m (junction 15) leading to A53 or M54 (junction 3).
Opening Times: Apr 1 to Sept 30, Mon to Sat 2–5; Suns & Bank Hols 12–5.30. Adm £2.25, OAPs £2, Chd £1. *Reduced rates for organised parties of 25 or over.* Season tickets on application. Free car & coach park. Dogs allowed, but must be kept on leads.
Refreshments: Tearooms open daily 2–5. Suns and Bank Holidays 12–5.30. *Parties to pre-book (menu on request). Gift shop, kitchen garden sales.*

LUDFORD HOUSE

Ludlow SY8 1PJ   map F6
(Mr D. F. A. Nicholson)

House dating back to 12th century.

Location: ½ m S of Ludlow, B4361 road.
Opening Times: Grounds and exterior by written permission, with limited inspection of interior. Adm £2. Unsuitable for disabled.
Refreshments: Hotels and Restaurants in Ludlow available.

LUDLOW CASTLE – *See page 161*

MAWLEY HALL

Cleobury Mortimer   map G6

18th century house.

Location: 1 m S of Cleobury Mortimer (A4117); 7 m W of Bewdley.
Opening Times: By written appointment to Mrs R. Sharp, 43 Dover Street, London W1X 3RE. Adm £3.

MOAT HOUSE

Longnor, Nr Shrewsbury SY5 7PP   map F6
Telephone: Dorrington (074 373) 434
(Mr & Mrs C. P. Richards)

Small timber framed manor house c1390 with unique timber work and wooden masks. Surrounded by a water filled moat of c1250 and also a fish pool.

Location: 8 m S of Shrewsbury 1 m East of A49 on edge of village.
Opening Times: Apr to Sept. Thurs & Spring & Summer Bank Hols 2.30–5, other times by arrangement for parties of 20 plus. Adm £1.50. Not suitable for the disabled. No dogs. Accommodation for six, dinner if pre-booked, licensed, brochure available.

PITCHFORD HALL – *See page 162*

SHIPTON HALL

Much Wenlock   map G6
Telephone: Brockton (074 636) 225
(J N R N Bishop, Esq)

Delightful Elizabethan stone manor c. 1587 with Georgian additions. Interesting Roccoco and Gothic plasterwork by T. F. Pritchard. Georgian stable block containing working pottery. Stone walled garden, medieval dovecote and Parish Church, dating from late Saxon period.

Location: In Shipton; 6 m SW of Much Wenlock junction B4376 & B4368.
Opening Times: Easter to end Sept: Thurs, Bank Holiday Suns and Mons (except Christmas and New Year) 2.30–5.30. Also by appointment for parties of 20 or more any time of year. Adm: House & Garden £2, Chd £1. Special rate for parties.
Refreshments: Teas/buffets by prior arrangement.

STOKESAY CASTLE

Craven Arms   map F6
Telephone: Craven Arms (0588) 672544
(Lady Magnus-Allcroft)

Finest example of a moated and fortified manor house, dating from the 13th century.

Location: 8 m from Ludlow; ¾ m S of Craven Arms on 3rd class Road off A49.
Station: Craven Arms (1 m).
Opening Times: First Wed in Mar to Oct 31 – Daily (except Tues) 10–5.30 (10–4.30 in Mar and Oct); Nov 1 to Nov 30 – weekends only 10–2.30. Last adm half an hour before closing. *Closed Dec, Jan & Feb.* Adm £2, Chd (under 15) £1. Party bookings in advance. Toilets. Car park. Enquiries to The Custodian, Stokesay Castle, Craven Arms, Shropshire SY7 9AH.

UPTON CRESSETT HALL

Bridgnorth   map G6
Telephone: Morville 307
(William Cash, Esq)

Elizabethan Manor House and magnificent Gatehouse in beautiful countryside by Norman church. Unusually fine medieval timber work and interesting brick and plaster work; 14th century Great Hall.

Location: 4 m W of Bridgnorth; 18 m SE of Shrewsbury off A458.
Opening Times: May to Sept – Thurs 2.30–5. Adm £2, Chd £1. *Parties at other times throughout the year by appointment.*

WALCOT HALL

Lydbury North   map F6
Telephone: 071-581 2782
(C.R.W. Parish)

Built by Sir William Chambers for Lord Clive of India. This Georgian House possesses a free-standing and recently restored ballroom, stable yard with matching clock towers, extensive walled garden, in addition to its icehouse, meat safe and dovecote. There is a fine arboretum, noted for its rhododendrons and azaleas and specimen trees.

Location: 3 m E of Bishop's Castle, on B4385, ½ m outside Lydbury North.
Opening Times: May to Sept: Thurs, also Suns in July and Aug, Bank Hols Sun & Mon 2.30–5.30 (except Christmas & New Year). Adm £2.50, Chd under 15 free; groups of 10 or more by appointment. Suitable for disabled.
Refreshments: Powis Arms; teas when available.

WENLOCK PRIORY

Much Wenlock   map G6
Telephone: (0952) 727466
(English Heritage)

The long history of Wenlock stretches back to the 7th century, although nothing visible remains of the religious house founded by St Milburge. After the Norman Conquest, a Cluniac priory was established, which came to be regarded as alien during the Hundred Years' War with France. Decorative arcading from the 12th century chapter house survives and some unusual features in the later, rebuilt church.

Location: In Much Wenlock.
Opening Times: Good Friday or Apr 1 (whichever is earlier) to Sept 30 daily 10–6. Oct 1 to Maundy Thursday or Mar 31 (whichever is earlier) Tues to Sun 10–4. *Closed Dec 24–26, Jan 1.* Adm £1.50, Concessions £1.10, Chd 75p. Admission price includes a Personal Stereo Guided Tour.

LUDLOW CASTLE

Castle Square, Ludlow   map F6
Telephone: (0584) 873947
(The Trustees of the Powis Castle Estate)

Originally a Norman Castle of which the remains include the round nave of a Chapel with fine Norman doorways. Then a fortified Royal Palace and headquarters of the Council of the Marches. An unusually complete range of medieval buildings still stands. Visitors can enjoy the large open space of the outer bailey.

Location: Castle Square, Ludlow.
Opening Times: Daily Feb 1 to Apr 30, 10.30–4. May 1 to Sept 30, 10.30–5. Oct 1 to Nov 30, 10.30–4. *Closed* Dec and Jan. Adm £2, Chd £1, OAP's £1.50. Family ticket £6. Discounts for school parties by arrangement with Custodian. Public car park off Castle Square. Suitable for disabled.
Refreshments: In Castle Square.

PITCHFORD HALL

nr Condover map F6
Telephone: (06944) 205
(Mr & Mrs Colthurst)

A Grade I Listed half timber framed House of Historic and National importance, dating from 1473. 4 acre garden with tree house dating from 1692 in 500 year old Lime tree. Queen Victoria stayed here as a child of thirteen.

Location: 6½ m S of Shrewsbury off A5/A458 signposted to Pitchford and Acton Burnell.
Opening Times: Aug 1–31, daily 2–5. Adm House and Gardens £3. Gardens only £1.50. Chd (under 12) half price. No dogs except guide dogs for the blind. Groups by appointment only, all months except Aug. Apply Mrs O. Colthurst.
Refreshments: Home made teas.

WESTON PARK

nr Shifnal map G7
Telephone: Weston-under-Lizard 207
(Weston Park Foundation)

WESTON PARK

17th Century House family seat of the Earls of Bradford in "Capability" Brown landscape.

Museum of Country Bygones, Woodland Adventure Playground, Pets Corner, Miniature Railway and Tropical House.

Enquiries to
Miss Helen Howat, Administrator,
Weston Park, Weston-under-Lizard,
Nr. Shifnal, Shropshire. TF11 8LE
Tel: Weston-under-Lizard (095 276) 207

Built 1671 by Lady Wilbraham and contains a superb art collection. Miniature Railway, Adventure Playground, Museum, Woodland Walks and Pets Corner.

Location: Entrance from A5 at Weston-under-Lizard, 6 m W of Junction 12, M6 (Gailey); 3 m N of Junction 3, M54 (Tong).
Opening Times: House & Park. Apr 17 to June 14—weekends; Bank Hols, June 22 to July 31 Daily (except Mon & Fri). Aug 1 to Aug 31: daily; Sept 1 to Sept 20: weekends only. Park 11–7. Last admission 5. Adm Grounds, Museum, Adventure Playground, Pets Corner, Tropical House, £3, Chd & OAPs £2. House extra. Special rates for pre-booked parties and school visits. Entry charges may be adjusted on certain days for special events. Free coach and car park. Dogs (on leads) admitted to Park.
Refreshments: In the Old Stables licensed bar and cafeteria. Restaurant service for pre-booked parties.

WILDERHOPE MANOR, The National Trust

Wenlock Edge map G6 &
Telephone: Longville 363

Elizabethan manor house with 17th century plaster ceilings. House now run as a Youth Hostel.

Location: 7 m SW of Much Wenlock; ½ m S of B4371.
Opening Times: Apr 1 to end of Sept—Weds & Sats 2–4.30; Oct to Mar—Sats only 2–4.30. Adm £1, Chd 50p. *No reduction for parties.* Dogs around Manor on leads.

WROXETER (VIROCONIUM) ROMAN CITY

map G6
Telephone: (074375) 330

Viroconium was the fourth largest city in Roman Britain and the largest to escape modern development. Deep beneath the exposed walls of the market-hall excavations are revealing a legionary fortress of the first century; while nearby the timber buildings of later settlers are being examined. The most impressive feature is the huge wall dividing the exercise yard from the baths.

Location: 5½ m (8.8 km) south east of Shrewsbury. OS map ref SJ568088.
Opening Times: Good Friday or Apr 1 (whichever is earlier) to Sept 30: Open Daily 10–6. Oct 1 to Maundy Thursday or Mar 31 (whichever is earlier): Open Tues to Sun 10–4. *Closed* Dec 24–26, Jan 1. Adm £1.50, Concessions £1.10, Chd 75p.

SOMERSET

BARFORD PARK

Enmore map F3
Telephone: Spaxton (0278) 671269
(Mr & Mrs Michael Stancomb)

Set in a large garden and looking out across a ha-ha to a park dotted with fine trees, it presents a scene of peaceful domesticity, a miniature country seat on a scale appropriate today. The well proportioned rooms, with contemporary furniture, are all in daily family use. The walled flower garden is in full view from the house, and the woodland and water gardens and archery glade with their handsome trees form a perfect setting for the stone and red-brick Queen Anne building.

Location: 5 m W of Bridgwater.
Opening Times: May 1 to Sept 19—Weds, Thurs and Bank Hol weekends 2–6, or other times by appointment. Please telephone above number. Adm charges not available at the time of going to press.

BARRINGTON COURT

Nr Ilminster, TA19 0NQ map F3
(National Trust)

Beautiful garden influenced by Gertrude Jekyll and laid out in a series of 3 rooms. Tudor manor house restored in 1920s by the Lyle family. Now sub-let to Stuart Interiors, the furniture reproducers.

Location: In Barrington village, 5 m NE of Ilminster off A303, 6 m S of Curry Rivel on A378 between Taunton and Langport (193: ST397182).
Opening Times: Barrington Court Garden, Apr 1 to Nov 1, Sun to Thurs inclusive, 12–5.30; Court House, Apr 1 to Nov 1, Weds only, 1.30–5. Adm Garden £3, Chd £1.50; parties £2.50, Chd party £1.20. Court House 50p (guided tours only).
Refreshments: Licensed restaurant open same days as Garden.

THE BISHOP'S PALACE

Wells map G3
Telephone: Wells (0749) 78691
(The Church Commissioners)

The fortified and moated Palace comprises Jocelin's Hall (early 13th century), the Bishop's Chapel and the ruins of the Banqueting Hall (both late 13th century) and the Bishop's Residence (15th century). The grounds which include the wells from which Wells derives its name, provide a beautiful setting for gardens of herbaceous plants, roses, shrubs, mature trees and the Jubilee Arboretum. On the Moat are waterfowl and swans.

Location: City of Wells, at end of Market Place (enter through Bishop's Eye).
Opening Times: Palace, Chapel and Grounds and Wells. Easter to end of Oct—Bank Holiday Mons, Thurs & Suns; Aug—Daily: 2–6. Special exhibitions are announced from time to time in the press, when different admission charges may apply. Last admission 5.30. Adm £1, Chd 50p. Party rates by appointment.
Refreshments: Available in Undercroft.

BRYMPTON d'EVERCY 🏛

nr Yeovil map G3
Telephone: Yeovil (0935) 862528
(Charles E B Clive-Ponsonby-Fane, JP)

Mansion house with 17th century South front and Tudor West front. State Rooms, prize-winning gardens and Vineyard, Priest House, Britain's smallest legal distillery, painting and photographic exhibitions. Estate produce, wine, cider and Brympton Apple Brandy. 14th century Parish Church alongside. **Winner HHA/Christie's Garden of The Year Award.**

Location: Just W of Yeovil. Follow signs off A30 or A3088.
Opening Times: Easter weekend (Fri to Mon incl) then May 2 to Sept 30 – Daily (except Thurs & Fris) 2 – 6. *Further details from Brympton Estate Office, Yeovil.* DISCOUNT RATES FOR OAPs, NATIONAL TRUST MEMBERS.
Refreshments: Freshly made cream teas in Old Stables.

THE CHURCH HOUSE

Crowcombe map F3
(The Charity Commissioners)

Historic 15th century stone building with graceful open timber roof.

Location: Opposite Crowcombe Church; off A358 Taunton/Minehead Road.
Opening Times: End of May to end of Aug – Mons to Fris 2.30 – 4.30. Adm free.

CLAPTON COURT GARDENS AND PLANT CENTRE 🏛

Crewkerne map F3 &
Telephone: Crewkerne (0460) 73220/72200
(Capt S J Loder)

One of the West Country's most beautiful and interesting 10 acre gardens in lovely park-like setting. Immaculate formal gardens with terraces, rockery, rose and water gardens. Fascinating woodland garden with natural streams and glades. Fine collection of rare and unusual plants, shrubs and trees of botanical interest. Largest and oldest Ash in Great Britain, an original Metasequoia now over 80 feet. Dazzling display of spring bulbs, glorious autumn colours, worth visiting at all seasons. Recently featured in BBC Gardeners World, Country Life and House and Garden. PLANT CENTRE selling high quality, rare and choice plants, shrubs and trees.

Location: 3 m S of Crewkerne on B3165 to Lyme Regis.
Opening Times: GARDENS AND PLANT CENTRE ONLY. Mar to Oct inclusive– Mons to Fris 10.30 – 5; Suns 2 – 5. *Closed* Sats (except Easter Sat 2 – 5). Parties must be pre-booked. No dogs. Free car parking.
Refreshments: Home-made lunches and teas, licensed Apr to Sept, times as garden. Meals by arrangement for parties.

CLEEVE ABBEY ▣

map F3
Telephone: (0984) 40377

Although little remains of the church, most of the buildings surrounding the cloister of this Cistercian abbey are remarkably complete. A timber roof of outstanding workmanship survives in the 15th century dining hall; also preserved are fragments of pavements, tiles and wall paintings of earlier date.

Location: Washford. OS map ref ST047407.
Opening Times: Good Friday or Apr 1 (whichever is earlier) to Sept 30: Open Daily 10 – 6. Oct 1 to Maundy Thursday or Mar 31 (whichever is earlier): Open Tues to Sun 10 – 4. *Closed* Dec 24 – 26, Jan 1. Adm £1.50, Concessions £1.10, Chd 75p.

COLERIDGE COTTAGE, The National Trust 🌿

Nether Stowey, nr. Bridgwater map F3
Telephone: Nether Stowey 732662

Home of S T Coleridge from 1797 – 1800, where he wrote 'The Ancient Mariner'.

Location: At W end of village on S side of A39; 8 m W of Bridgwater.
Opening Times: PARLOUR AND READING ROOM ONLY. Apr 1 to Oct 4: Tues to Thurs and Suns 2 – 5. Adm £1.40, Chd 70p. No reduction for parties. Parties must book beforehand. *Adm in winter by written application to the tenant.* No dogs. Unsuitable for wheelchairs & coaches.
Refreshments: In village.

COMBE SYDENHAM COUNTRY PARK 🏛

Monksilver map F3 Ⓢ
Telephone: Stogumber (0984) 56284
(Mr and Mrs W. Theed)

Built in 1580 on the site of a monastic settlement and home of Elizabeth Sydenham, wife of Sir Francis Drake. The Cannon Ball associated with their wedding can be seen in the Court Room which has now been beautifully restored, and onsite work is continuing including the old Corn Mill. Elizabethan-style gardens, Country Park walks and Deer Park. Fly fishing available on valley ponds. Children's play area. Speciality smoked trout/pate. Gift Shop, tea room, free car/coach park.

Location: 5 m N of Wiveliscombe; 3 m S of Watchet on B3188.
Station: Stogumber (2½ m) (West Somerset Railway).
Opening Times: Easter to Oct, 10 – 5 Sun to Fri. (Court Room and gardens closed each weekend.) Sun Special admission ticket. Sat morning Gift Shop and Fish sales only. Court Room: Last entry to Court Room two hours before closing time. School parties welcomed by arrangement throughout the year for activity days. (Winner 1984 and 1990 Sandford Award for Heritage Education.)

CRICKET ST. THOMAS

Chard map F3
Telephone: (0460) 30755

Estate of Cricket St. Thomas recorded in Domesday Book of 1087. Today it is a wildlife and leisure park of outstanding natural beauty, with animals and birds from all over the world, many leading a free natural life. Visitors can also enjoy the Tropical Aviary, the Heavy Horse Centre, the Victorian Shopping Arcade, Craft Workshops, lakeside walks, woodland railway and children's Adventure Playground. Film location for BBC TV series 'To The Manor Born'.

Location: 4 m E of Chard on A30. Nearest M5 junction No. 25.
Opening Times: All year round. Daily from 10 am.
Refreshments: Waitress service in the Tythe Barn. Self service in the licensed Pavilion Restaurant. Bar meals in the Black Swan Inn. Outdoor meals at the Heavy Horse Centre.

DODINGTON HALL

nr. Nether Stowey, Bridgwater map F3
Telephone: Holford (0278 74) 422
(Lady Gass, occupier Mrs Webber)

Small Tudor Manor House on the lower slopes of the Quantock Hills. Great hall with oak roof. Carved stone fireplace.

Location: ½ m from A39. 11 m from Bridgwater; 7 m from Williton.
Opening Times: Suns July 5 to Sept 6 (inclusive) 2 – 4. Donations for Dodington Church. Parking for 15 cars. Regret unsuitable for disabled.

DUNSTER CASTLE, The National Trust 🌿

nr. Minehead map F3 &
Telephone: Dunster (0643) 821314

Castle dating from 13th century, remodelled by Anthony Salvin in 19th century. Fine 17th century staircase and plaster ceilings. Terraced Gardens.

Location: In Dunster, 3 m SE of Minehead on A396.
Station: Dunster (West Somerset Railway) (1½ m).
Opening Times: Castle: Apr 1 to Oct 4 – Sat to Wed 11 – 5. Oct 5 to Nov 1: Sat to Wed 11 4.
Garden and Park: Feb 1 to Dec 13: daily. Feb, Mar, Oct, Nov, Dec 11 – 4; Apr to Sept 11 – 5.
Adm castle, garden and park £4.30. Chd under 16 £2.10. Parties £3.80 by prior arrangement.
Garden and park only £2.20, Chd (under 16) £1.10. Shop. Ten minute steep climb from NT
car park. No dogs in garden, in park area on leads. Battri Car available from car park. Areas of
the house can be visited by wheelchair, and assistance given if needed.
Refreshments: In village (not N.T.). National Trust Shop.

FARLEIGH HUNGERFORD CASTLE

map G4
Telephone: (0225) 754026

Sir Thomas de Hungerford, Speaker of the House of Commons, fortified the original
manor house without permission; he was later pardoned. His mailed effigy, sur-
rounded by the tombs of other Hungerfords, lies in the chapel, a place to stir the
imagination.
Location: Farleigh Hungerford 3½ m (5.6 km) west of Trowbridge. OS map ref ST801577.
Opening Times: Good Friday or Apr 1 (whichever is earlier) to Sept 30: Open Daily 10 – 6.
Oct 1 to Maundy Thursday or Mar 31 (whichever is earlier): Open Tues to Sun 10 – 4. *Closed*
Dec 24 – 26, Jan 1. Adm 95p, Concessions 75p, Chd 45p.

GAULDEN MANOR

Tolland, nr Taunton   map F3   △
Telephone: Lydeard St Lawrence (09847) 213
(Mr & Mrs James LeGendre Starkie)

Small historic red sandstone Manor House of great charm. A real lived-in home. Past
Somerset seat of the Turberville family, immortalised by Thomas Hardy. Great Hall
has magnificent plaster ceiling and oak screen to room known as the Chapel. Fine
antique furniture. Interesting grounds include bog garden with primulas and other
moisture loving plants. Herb garden.
Location: 9 m NW of Taunton; 1 m E of Tolland Church. Gaulden Manor signposted from
A358 Taunton/Williton Rd just N of Bishops Lydeard and from B3188 Wivelscombe/Watchet
Rd (cars only). Nearest village Lydeard St Lawrence (1½ m).
Opening Times: May 3 to Sept 6 – Suns & Thurs; also Easter Sun and Mon and all Bank
Hols: 2 – 5.30 (last adm 5). House & Garden Adm £2.50, Chd (under 14) £1. Garden only £1
(1991 rates). *Parties on other days by prior arrangement. Mornings, afternoons or evenings
& out of season.* Shop – books, rare and unusual plants.
Refreshments: Teas in Garden Tearoom.

GLASTONBURY TRIBUNAL

map G3
Telephone: (0458) 32949

Justice was administered here by the Abbot of Glastonbury until the Dissolution. Later
a kitchen was added and the building converted to a private house. It is well
preserved, with decorative details from three centuries.
Location: High Street. OS map ref ST499390.
Opening Times: Good Friday or Apr 1 (whichever is earlier) to Sept 30: Open Daily 10 – 6.
Oct 1 to Maundy Thursday or Mar 31 (whichever is earlier): Open Tues to Sun 10 – 4. *Closed*
Dec 24 – 26, Jan 1. Adm £1.10, Concessions 85p, Chd 55p.

HADSPEN GARDEN & NURSERY

Castle Cary   map G3
Telephone: (0963) 50939

Specialising in choice garden plants – herbaceous, old fashioned and modern shrub
roses, clematis, damp land plants. Very old hosta collection and National Collection of
Rodgersias. All to be viewed in the 8 acre adjoining garden..
Location: 2 m E of Castle Cary on the A371.
Opening Times: Mar 1 to Oct 1: Thurs, Fri, Sat, Sun and Bank Holiday Mon. Adm £2, Chd
50p. Wheelchairs free. Car parking.
Refreshments: Sunday afternoons.

HATCH COURT – *See page 166*

KELWAYS NURSERIES LTD

Langport
Telephone: (0458) 250521

The Royal Nurseries of Langport – special open fields in May and June During the
Paeony Festival.
Location: On Somerton Road from Langport (B31530 just 200 yards from A372.
Opening Times: Nursery all year; please telephone for dates of Paeony Festival.

KENTSFORD HOUSE

Watchet   map F3
(Mrs Wyndham. Occupier: Mr H Dibble)

House open **only** by written appointment with Mr H. Dibble.
Opening Times: Gardens: Tues and Bank Hols Apr 14 – Sept 29. Donations towards
renovation of fabric.

LYTES CARY MANOR, The National Trust

nr Ilchester   map G3

Mediaeval manor house with chapel; fine furnishings; formal garden.
Location: On W side of Fosse Way (A37); 2½ m NE of Ilchester signposted on bypass
(A303).
Opening Times: Apr 1 to Oct 31 – Mons, Weds & Sats 2 – 6 or dusk if earlier (last adm 5.30).
Adm £3, Chd £1.50. No dogs. No lavatories. NB. Large coaches cannot pass gate piers, so
must stop in road. ¼ m walk.
Refreshments: Refreshments and National Trust Shop at Montacute.

MAUNSEL HOUSE – *See page 166*

MIDELNEY MANOR

Drayton, nr Langport   map F3   △
(Mr John Cely Trevilian)

16th to 18th century Manor House. Originally island manor of Abbots of Muchelney
and property of Trevilian family since 1500. 17th century Falcons Mews. Gardens;
Woodland walks; Heronry.
Location: Signposted from A378 at Bell Hotel; Curry Rivel & from B3168 Hambridge/ Curry
Rivel Road & in Drayton.
Opening Times: Every Thurs, Apr 30 to Sept 24 and all Bank Holiday Mons 2.30 – 5.30 (last
tour 4.30). Adm £2, Chd £1. Coach parties and teas by appointment.

MILTON LODGE GARDENS

Wells   map G4
Telephone: (0749) 72168
(Mr & Mrs David Tudway Quilter)

"The great glory of the gardens of Milton Lodge is their position high up on the slopes
of the Mendip Hills to the north of Wells . . . with broad panoramas of Wells Cathedral
and the Vale of Avalon." *Lanning Roper.* Mature alkaline terraced garden of great
charm dating from 1909. Replanned 1962 with mixed shrubs and herbaceous plants,
old fashioned ,roses and ground cover; numerous climbers; old established yew
hedges. Fine trees in garden and in separate 7 acre arboretum on opposite side of Old
Bristol Road.
Location: ½ m N of Wells. From A39 Bristol–Wells turn N up Old Bristol Road; free car park
first gate on left.
Opening Times: GARDEN AND ARBORETUM ONLY: Easter to end Oct: daily (except Sat) 2 – 6.
Parties and coaches by prior arrangement. Adm £2, Chd under 14 free. Open on certain Suns
in aid of National Gardens scheme. No dogs.
Refreshments: Teas available Suns only in May, June and July.

HATCH COURT

Hatch Beauchamp   map F3
Telephone: Hatch Beauchamp (0823) 480120
(Dr and Mrs Robin Odgers)

A fine Bath stone mansion in the Palladian style, designed in 1755 by Thomas Prowse of Axbridge. Curved wings, magnificent stone staircase and much of the internal decoration carried out around 1800. The house has a good collection of pictures, 17th and 18th century furniture and unusual semicircular china room. Small Canadian Military Museum. Gardens with fine walled kitchen garden. The medieval parish church of St. John the Baptist is situated nearby.

Location: 6 m SE of Taunton midway between Taunton & Ilminster off A358.
Opening Times: July 2 to Sept 10 – Thurs and Aug Bank Holiday Mon 2.30–5.30. *(No coaches)*. Adm £2.50. Organised parties by prior appointment – at all times *(unless open as above)*.
Refreshments: Full catering by arrangement. Teas available Thurs.

MAUNSEL HOUSE

North Newton, nr Bridgwater   map F3
Telephone: (0278) 663398
(Maggie Lennie)

MAUNSEL HOUSE

Nr BRIDGWATER, SOMERSET

*ADMISSION
SEE EDITORIAL REFERENCE*

Imposing 13th century Manor House, partly built before the Norman Conquest but mostly built around a great Hall erected in 1420. Two further wings were added by Slade family between 1772 and 1868. St Michaels Church, the family church, was purchased by John Slade in 1772 for use by the employees to the estate, and is still used by the Parish for regular Sunday Services. Extensive restoration has taken place since 1986 to return the house to its original excellence and Maunsel now has a fascinating collection of antique beds and unusual baths. The mediaeval kitchen, Tudor bedrooms and original Victorian wallpaper are still on show. Geoffrey Chaucer was a frequent visitor and guest. He wrote part of the Canterbury Tales whilst staying at the house. Also the ancestral house of Madeline Slade (Mira Behn), devotee to the great Indian leader Mahatma Gandhi. Maunsel House is the ancestral seat of the Slade family and is now the home of 7th Baronet, Sir Benjamin Slade.

Location: Bridgwater 4 m, Bristol 20 m, Taunton 7 m, junction 24 M5, turn left North Petherton 1½ m North Newton, ½ m S St. Michael Church.
Opening Times: Mar to Sept – Sun & Mon 2–5.30. Adm £2, Chd £1. Other days by appointment only. Coach and group parties welcome by arrangement. Reception, private parties and banqueting rooms available. Free car parking. Picnic and Barbecue area. Dogs on leads in grounds only. Fishing £1 – bring own tackle. Boating £1 – bring own boat.

MONTACUTE HOUSE, The National Trust

Yeovil   map G3
Telephone: Martock (0935) 823289

Magnificent Elizabethan house of Ham Hill stone begun in the 1590s by Sir Edward Phelips. Fine heraldic glass, tapestries, panelling and furniture. National Portrait Gallery Exhibitions of Elizabethan and Jacobean portraits. Fine formal garden and park.

Location: In Montacute village 4 m W of Yeovil on E side of A3088; 3 m E of A303 nr Ilchester.
Opening Times: House: Apr 1 to Nov 1: Daily (except Tues) 12–5.30. *Closed* Good Friday. Last adm 5 (or sunset if earlier). *Parties by written appointment with the Administrator.* Garden & Park: Apr 1 to Apr 1993 – Daily (except Tues) 11.30–5.30 or dusk if earlier. Adm House, Garden & Park £4.30, Chd £2.20; Parties £4, Chd £2. Garden & Park only: Apr 1 to Nov 1 £2.20, Chd £1.10 Nov 2 to Apr 1993 £1, Chd 50p. Dogs in park only. Wheelchairs in garden only.
Refreshments: Light lunches & teas. *Parties catered for by arrangement with the Administrator. National Trust Shop.*

ORCHARD WYNDHAM

Williton, nr Taunton   map F3
(Mrs Wyndham)

Modest English Manor House. Family home for 700 years encapsulating continuous building and alteration between 14th and 20th centuries.

Location: 1 m from A39 at Williton.
Opening Times: House and Gardens: Guided tours only – Aug 1992 – Thur & Fri 2–4.30. Last tour begins at 4. *(Property undergoing restoration, please telephone 0984 32309 before planning a visit.)* Adm £2.50, Chd under 12 £1. Limited parking. No coaches – narrow access road. Maximum of 15 people in house at any one time. No dogs. Not suitable for the disabled.
Refreshments: Available in Williton.

STOKE-SUB-HAMDON PRIORY, The National Trust

nr Montacute   map G3   ⚹

Complex of buildings begun in 14th century for the priests of the chantry chapel of St Nicholas (destroyed).

Location: Between A303 & A3088; 2 m W of Montacute between Yeovil & Ilminster.
Opening Times: All the year – Daily 10–6 (or sunset if earlier). Adm free. *Great Hall only open to the public.* No dogs.

TINTINHULL HOUSE GARDEN, The National Trust

nr. Yeovil   map G3   △   ⚹

20th century formal garden surrounding 17th century house (house not open).

Location: 5 m NW of Yeovil; ½ m S of A303 on outskirts Tintinhull village.
Opening Times: Apr 1 to Sept 30 – Weds, Thurs & Sats, also Bank Hol Mons 2–6 (last adm 5.30). Adm £2.80. *No reductions for parties or children.* Coach parties by written arrangement with the tenant. No dogs. Wheelchairs provided.
Refreshments: In courtyard (not NT).

STAFFORDSHIRE

ANCIENT HIGH HOUSE

Stafford   map G7

The Ancient High House is the largest timber-framed town house in England, and was built in 1595 by John Dorrington from local oak. It has been in the hands of several famous Staffordshire families, inlcuding the Sneyds and Dyotts, and has enjoyed a long and varied history. It has recently been restored to its Elizabethan splendour and houses a permanent collection of furniture, costume, paintings and ceramics, all in period room settings. A special feature of interest is the collection of rare 18th and 19th century wallpapers, found during the restoration. The house also has an exhibition area, along with a video theatre, heritage shop selling traditional gifts made by local craftsmen, and a children's costume wardrobe. Heritage Exhibition and Tourist Information Centre.

Location: M6 Off junction 13 – A449 to Stafford and junction 14 – A5013 to Stafford off M6.
Opening Times: House and Exhibition Centre: Mon to Fri 9–5; Sat Apr to Oct: 10–4. Nov to Mar: 10–3. Adm £1.20, Chd/OAPs 60p, reduced rate for parties. Tourist Information Centre: Mon to Fri 9–5; Sat Oct to Mar: 10–3. Apr to Sept: 10–4. No car park. Contact: The Heritage Manager (0785) 223181 ext 352, or (0785) 40204.

BIDDULPH GRANGE GARDEN, The National Trust ⚹

Biddulph, Stoke-on-Trent   map G7
Telephone: (0782) 517999

An exciting and rare survival of a high Victorian garden, acquired by the National Trust in 1988. The garden has undergone an extensive restoration project, which will continue for a number of years. Conceived by James Bateman, the 15 acres are divided into a number of smaller gardens which were designed to house specimens from his extensive and wide-ranging plant collection. An Egyptian Court, Chinese Pagoda, Bridge, Joss House and Pinetum, together with many other settings, all combine to make the garden a miniature tour of the world.

Location: ½ m N of Biddulph, 5 m SE of Congleton, 7 m N of Stoke-on-Trent. Access from A527 (Tunstall Road). Entrance on Grange Road.
Station: Kidsgrove or Congleton, both 4 m. Stoke-on-Trent 7m.
Opening Times: Apr 1 to end Oct – Wed to Fri 12–6 (last adm 5.30 or dusk if earlier). *Closed* Good Friday. Sat, Sun and Bank Holiday Mon 11–6. Pre-booked guided tours at 10 Wed, Thurs, Fri £5 (inc NT members); Nov 1 to Dec 20 – Sat and Sun 12–4. £3.50, Chd half price. Family ticket £8.75. Parking free, car park 50 yards. Access for disabled visitors is extremely difficult, unsuitable for wheelchairs, please contact Head Gardener for details.
Refreshments: Coffee, light refreshments including teas. Tea room and shop open same time as garden.

CHILLINGTON HALL 🏛

nr Wolverhampton   map G7   △
Telephone: Brewood 850236
(Mr & Mrs Peter Giffard)

Georgian house. Part 1724 (Francis Smith); part 1785 (Sir John Soane). Fine saloon. The lake in the Park is believed to be the largest ever created by 'Capability' Brown. The bridges by Brown and Paine, and the Grecian and Roman Temples, together with the eyecatching Sham House, as well as many fine trees and plantations add great interest to the four mile walk around the lake. Dogs welcome in grounds if kept on lead.

Location: 4 m SW of A5 at Gailey; 2 m Brewood; 8 m NW of Wolverhampton; 14 m S of Stafford. Best approach is from A449 (Junction 12, M6, Junction 2, M54) through Coven and follow signposts towards Codsall (no entry at Codsall Wood).
Opening Times: May to Sept 14 — Thurs (also Suns in Aug) 2.30 – 5.30. Open Easter Sun & Suns preceding May and late Spring Bank Holidays 2.30 – 5.30. Adm £1.80; Grounds only 90p. Chd half price. *Parties of at least 15 other days by arrangement.*

DOROTHY CLIVE GARDEN

Willoughbridge   map G7
(Willoughbridge Garden Trust)

7 acre woodland and rhododendron garden; shrub roses, water garden and a large scree in a fine landscape setting.

Location: 9 m SW Newcastle-under-Lyme. On A51 between junctions with A525 & A53, 1 m E of Woore.
Opening Times: Garden only. Apr to Oct: daily 10 – 5.30. Adm £2, Chd 50p. Large car park.

MOSELEY OLD HALL, The National Trust 🌿

Wolverhampton   map G6   △   Ⓢ   ♿
Telephone: Wolverhampton (0902) 782808

A 17th century formal garden surrounds this mainly Elizabethan house where Charles II hid after the battle of Worcester.

Location: 4 m N of Wolverhampton mid-way between A449 & A460 Roads. Off M6 at Shareshill then via A460. Traffic from S via. M6 and M54 take junction 1 to Wolverhampton and Moseley is signposted after ½ m. Coaches via. A460 to avoid low bridge.
Opening Times: Apr 1 to Oct 31, Wed, Sat, Sun & Bank Hol Mons (and Tues in July & Aug) 2 – 5.30. Bank Hol Mon 11 – 5. Pre-booked parties at other times including evening tours. Adm £2.80, Chd half price. Family ticket £7. Educational facilities. Wheelchair access ground floor only. Shop as Hall; also open Nov 8 to Dec 20 Sun only 2 – 4.30.
Refreshments: Tearoom in 18th century barn. Teas as house 2 – 5.30, and Nov 8 to Dec 20: Sun only 2 – 4.30; other times for parties by prior arrangement. Licensed. Light lunches Bank Hol Mons.

PILLATON OLD HALL

Penkridge   map G7   ♿
Telephone: Penkridge (0785) 712200
(Mr R. W. & The Hon Mrs Perceval)

15th century gatehouse wing and chapel.

Location: 1 m E of Penkridge on Cannock Road (B5012); turn right at Pillaton Hall Farm.
Opening Times: Open by appointment. Adm 50p.

SHUGBOROUGH, The National Trust – *See page 169*

TAMWORTH CASTLE

Tamworth   map H7
Telephone: Tamworth 63563
(Tamworth Borough Council)

One of the few remaining shell-keeps in the country, Tamworth's sandstone castle was occupied almost continually for 800 years. Period room settings depicting scenes from the life and times of its former occupants include a tudor timber framed Great Hall, Chapel, Jacobean and Victorian period apartments. Audio-visual presentation and museum collections. Haunted room, Dungeon and Norman exhibition.

Location: In Tamworth; 15 m NE of Birmingham.
Station: Tamworth (¾ m).
Opening Times: All the year — Weekdays 10 – 5.30, Suns 2 – 5.30. Last adm 4.30. Open Bank Hols. *Closed Christmas Day & Boxing Day.* Adm £2.15, Senior Citizens £1.15, Chd (up to 16 years) 70p; family ticket £5 (1992 prices).

WALL (LETOCETUM) ROMAN SITE ✜

map H7
Telephone: (0543) 480768

Much of the business of Imperial Rome depended on official couriers who travelled the comprehensive road network. Posting stations were built for them at regular intervals. At Wall, on Watling Street, traces of the hostel and a large part of the bath-house survive.

Location: 2 m (3.2 km) south west of Lichfield. OS map ref SK099067.
Opening Times: Good Friday or Apr 1 (whichever is earlier) to Sept 30: Open Daily 10 – 6. Oct 1 to Maundy Thursday or Mar 31 (whichever is earlier): Open Tues to Sun 10 – 4. *Closed* Dec 24 – 26, Jan 1. Adm £1.10, Concessions 85p, Chd 55p.

WESTON PARK — SEE UNDER SHROPSHIRE

WHITMORE HALL 🏛

Whitmore, nr Newcastle-under-Lyme   map G7
Telephone: (0782) 680478
(Mr G. Cavenagh-Mainwaring)

Carolinian Manor House, owner's family home for over 800 years. Family portraits dating back to 1624. Outstanding Tudor Stable Block.

Location: Four miles from Newcastle-under-Lyme on the A53 Road to Market Drayton.
Opening Times: Open 2 – 5.30 every Tues & Weds, May to Aug inclusive (last tour 5). Adm £2. *No reduction for parties. Free car parking. Not suitable for disabled. No wheelchairs available.*
Refreshments: Mainwaring Arms Inn, Whitmore & also at Whitmore Art Gallery & Tea rooms, Whitmore.

SHUGBOROUGH, The National Trust

Stafford   map G7   Ⓢ   ♿
Telephone: Little Haywood (0889) 881388
(Administered by Staffordshire County Council)

Seat of the Earls of Lichfield. Architecture by James Stuart and Samuel Wyatt. Rococo plasterwork by Vassalli. Extensive parkland with neo-classical monuments. Beautiful formal gardens. Victorian terraces and rose-garden. Guided garden and woodland walks. Working rare breeds farm. Restored Mill. Working Brewhouse.

Location: 6 m E of Stafford on A513, entrance at Milford common 10 mins drive from M6, junction 13.

Opening Times: House, Museum, Farm, Working Brewhouse and Mill. Grade I Historic Garden: Mar 27 to Oct 30 — daily inc. Bank Holiday Mons 11 – 5. Site open all year round to pre-booked parties only from 10.30. (Mansion House open for 'Good Housekeeping Tours' from Jan to Mar. Booked parties only). Adm: House £3 (reduced rate £2). Museum £3 (reduced rate £2). Farm £3 (reduced rate £2). All-in ticket (House, Museum and Farm) £7.50 (reduced rate £5). Family All-in ticket (2 adults and 2 Chd) £15. Coach parties All-in ticket £5 or £2 per site. (Adm prices subject to change). Reduced rates available for Chd, OAPs and registered unemployed. Chd under 5 free. NT members free entry to the House. Party bookings for guided tours. Specialist tour (A Servant's Place). School parties guided tour £1.30 per head, per site (all 3 sites for £3.50 inc. of guide). Working School demonstrations Oct to Easter £2.30 per head, per demo. When Special Events are held charges may vary. Guide Dogs admitted to House and Museum. Site access for parking, picnic area, gardens, monuments and woodland trails £1 per vehicle. Coaches free. National Trust Shop and toilets.

Refreshments: Tea-rooms restaurant.

SUFFOLK

AKENFIELD

Charsfield Woodbridge   map M6
Telephone: (047337) 402

A quarter acre garden, originally council house garden comprising vegetable plot, two greenhouses, flower garden of separate 'rooms' and pond (new).

Location: 3 m W of Wickham Market on B1078 – turn N to Charsfield.
Opening Times: May to Sept: 10–dusk, daily. Adm £1, OAP 75p, Chd free. Coach loads 75p each. Parties by arrangement. Car parking on field opposite house. Not suitable for disabled.
Refreshments: By arrangement. Cream teas at Village Hall/Ploughmans suppers by WI members.

BELCHAMP HALL – SEE UNDER ESSEX

BLAKENHAM WOODLAND GARDEN

Little Blakenham, nr Ipswich   map L6
(Lord Blakenham)

5 acre wood with many rare trees and shrubs. Lovely throughout the year, with bluebells, camellias and magnolias followed by azaleas, rhododendrons, roses, hydrangeas and fine autumn colouring.

Location: 4 m NW of Ipswich. The garden is signposted from Little Blakenham which is 1 m off the old A1100 now called B1113.
Opening Times: Apr to Sept – Weds, Thurs, Suns and Bank Hols 1–5. Adm £1. Free car-park. No dogs.

CHRISTCHURCH MANSION – *See page 171*

EUSTON HALL   🏛

Thetford   map L6
Telephone: (0842) 766366
(The Duke and Duchess of Grafton)

Euston Hall – Home of the Duke and Duchess of Grafton. The 18th century house contains a famous collection of paintings including works by Stubbs, Van Dyck, Lely and Kneller. The pleasure grounds were laid out by John Evelyn and William Kent. The garden and nearby 17th century parish church in Wren style. Teas and Craft Shop in Old Kitchen. Picnic area.

Location: A1088; 3 m S Thetford.
Opening Times: June 4 to Sept 24 – Thurs only 2.30–5. Also Sun June 28 & Sept 6, 2.30–5. Adm £2.25, Chd 50p, OAPs £1.50. Parties of 12 or more £1.50 per head.
Refreshments: Teas in Old Kitchen. Craft shop. Picnic area.

FRAMLINGHAM CASTLE – *See page 171*

GAINSBOROUGH'S HOUSE

Sudbury   map L5
Telephone: Sudbury (0787) 72958
(Gainsborough's House Society)

Thomas Gainsborough's birthplace. Large collection of his work in 18th century setting. Temporary exhibitions of historic and contemporary art and craft throughout the year. Print workshop, charming town garden containing Mulberry tree planted in 1600s.

Location: 46 Gainsborough Street, Sudbury.
Station: Sudbury (¼ m).
Opening Times: Open all the year. Easter to Oct – Tues to Sats 10–5; Sun & Bank Hol Mons 2–5; Nov to Maundy Thursday – Tues to Sats 10–4; Sun and Bank Hol Mons 2–4. *Closed Mons, Good Fri & between Christmas & New Year.* Adm £2, OAP £1.50, Students/Chd £1.

CHRISTCHURCH MANSION

Christchurch Park, Ipswich map M5
Telephone: Ipswich (0473) 253246
(The Borough of Ipswich)

A fine Tudor house set in beautiful parkland. Period rooms furnished in styles from 16th to 19th century; outstanding collections of china, clocks and glass. Paintings by Gainsborough, Constable and other Suffolk artists. Attached Wolsey Art Gallery showing contemporary works.

Location: In Christchurch Park, near centre of Ipswich.
Station: Ipswich (1¹/₄ m).
Opening Times: All the year—Tues to Sats 10–5 *(dusk in winter)*; Suns 2.30–4.30 *(dusk in winter)*. Open Bank Hol Mons. *Closed Dec 24, 25 & 26 and Good Fri.* Adm free.

GUILDHALL OF CORPUS CHRISTI, The National Trust 🌿

Lavenham map L6

Early 16th century timber-framed Tudor building; originally hall of Guild of Corpus Christi. Display of local history, industry and farming including a unique exhibition of 700 years of the woollen cloth trade. Delightful walled garden.

Location: Market Place Lavenham, Sudbury.
Opening Times: Mar 28 to Nov 1—Daily 11–5. Adm £2, Chd 60p. Parties £1.60, please book with sae to Administrator. *Closed* Good Friday. School parties 50p by prior arrangement. Shop.
Refreshments: Coffee, light lunches and teas.

HAUGHLEY PARK

nr Stowmarket map L6
(Mr & Mrs A J Williams)

Jacobean manor house. Gardens and woods, fine trees and shrubs.

Location: 4 m W of Stowmarket signed on A45 nr Wetherden (not Haughley).
Opening Times: May to Sept—Tues 3–6. Adm £2, Chd £1.

FRAMLINGHAM CASTLE ⊞

map M6
Telephone: (0728) 723330
(English Heritage)

The present massive walls and their 13 towers were built by Roger Bigod, second Earl of Norfolk, on a site given to his father by Henry I. The ornamental brick chimneys were added in Tudor times when the arch of the entrance gateway was rebuilt. In 1636 the castle passed to Pembroke College, Cambridge, and in later years the great hall was converted to a poor-house and many of the buildings inside the walls were demolished. It was here, in 1553, that Mary Tudor learned she had become Queen of England.

Location: North side of Framlingham. OS map ref TM287637.
Opening Times: Good Friday or Apr 1 (whichever is earlier) to Sept 30 daily 10–6. Oct 1 to Maundy Thursday or Mar 31 (whichever is earlier) Tues to Sun 10–4. *Closed* Dec 24–26, Jan 1. Adm £1.50, Concessions £1.10, Chd 75p.

HELMINGHAM HALL GARDENS

Ipswich   map M6
Telephone: Helmingham (0473) 890363
(The Lord & Lady Tollemache)

The Hall, which was completed in 1510, has been the home of the Tollemache family from that date to the present day. It is one of the finest houses of the Tudor period, surrounded by a wide moat with drawbridges raised every night. There are two superb gardens which extend to several acres all set in 400 acres of ancient park containing herds of Red and Fallow deer and Highland Cattle. The main garden is surrounded by its own moat and 1740 wall, with wide herbaceous borders and planted tunnels intersecting an immaculate kitchen garden; the second is a very special rose garden enclosed within high yew hedges with a herb and Knot garden containing plants grown in England before 1750. English Heritage Grade I Garden.

Location: 9 m N of Ipswich on B1077.
Opening Times: GARDENS ONLY. May 3 to Sept 15 – Suns only 2–6. Adm £2, Chd (15 and under) £1.10, OAPs £1.80. Safari rides. Gift shop. *House not open to the public.*
Refreshments: In the Coach House Tea Rooms. Cream teas. Home-grown plants and produce for sale.

ICKWORTH, The National Trust

nr Bury St Edmunds   map L6   &
Telephone: Bury St Edmunds 735270

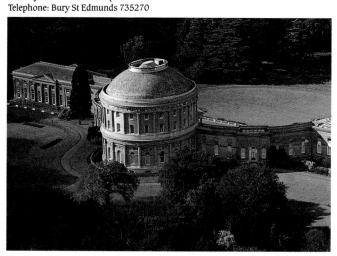

The house, begun c. 1794, was not completed until 1830. Contents of this architectural curiosity include late Regency and 18th century French furniture, magnificent silver, pictures. Formal gardens, herbaceous borders, orangery. Extensive waymarked park walks.

Location: 3 m SW of Bury St Edmunds on W side of A143.
Opening Times: House & Garden. Mar 28 to Apr 30: Sats and Suns. May 1 to Sept 30: Tues, Weds, Fris, Sats and Suns 1.30–5.30. Oct to Nov 1: Sats and Suns 1.30–5.30. Open Bank Hol Mons: 1.30–5.30. Adm £4.10, Chd £2. Access to Park, Garden, Restaurant and Shop £1.50, Chd 50p. Parties £3.50. Park open daily 7–7. Dogs in park only, on leads. Wheelchair access, one provided. Shop.
Refreshments: Lunch & tea in old Servants' Hall. Table licence, restaurant opens 12 noon on House open days.

KENTWELL HALL

Long Melford   map L6
(J. Patrick Phillips, QC)

KENTWELL
Spend an hour or a day & share the magic of its spell

THE HALL *Magnificent mellow redbrick moated Tudor manor still a family home*
MOAT HOUSE *Surviving part of 15th C. house, furnished & equipped as then*
GARDENS *Ancient Walled Garden & large Herb Garden*
MAZE *Unique brick-paved mosaic Tudor Rose*
TUDOR FARM *Working Farm - traditional buildings, rare breeds, early tools & equipment*

FOR ADMISSION AND STANDARD OPENING TIMES SEE EDITORIAL ENTRY

DIARY OF MAIN SPECIAL EVENTS FOR 1992

Easter: Fri 17-Mon 20 Apr	**Great Easter Egg Quiz; Tudor Bakery & Dairy**
May Day: Sat 2-Mon 4 May	**Tudor May Day Celebrations**
Whitsun: Sat 23-Mon 25 May	**Re-Creation of Tudor Life** in Moat House & Barns
Sun 31 May	**Wool Day -** *Sheep Shearing etc*
June 14-July12 (Sats, Suns & Fri 10 Jul only)	**Re-Creation of 1578 -** *200 'Tudors' take the whole Manor back to how it was in the year 1578*
Aug BH: Fri 29-Mon 31 Aug	**Re-Creation of Tudor Life** in Moat House & Barns
September 19-20	**Michaelmas Craft Market -** *Quality craft stalls*

KENTWELL HALL, LONG MELFORD, SUFFOLK. TEL 0787 310207

Romantic mellow red brick moated Tudor manor, in lovely setting. Still a family home. Moat House: unaltered 15th c house, furnished and equipped as then. Walled garden and large Herb garden. Mosaic brick maze and separate "Tudor" farm.

Location: Entrance on W of A134, N of Green in Long Melford; 3 m N of Sudbury.
Opening Times: HOUSE, MOAT HOUSE AND GARDENS: Mar 22 to June 7 Suns only 12–5; plus Apr 21 to 24 daily 12–5; plus May 26 to 31 daily 12–5; plus Bank Hol weekends Sat to Mon 11–6. Main Historical Re-Creation of Everyday Tudor Life – June 14 to July 12, Sats, Suns and Fri July 10: 11–5. Special adm prices. HOUSE, MOAT HOUSE AND GARDENS open daily July 15 to Sept 20 12–5; Sept 21 to Oct 31: Suns only 12–5. WORKING "TUDOR" FARM: open daily Easter to Oct 31. Adm (except for special events): House and Garden £3.25, Chd £1.90, OAP £2.70. "Tudor" Farm: £1.75, Chd £1, OAP £1.50. Reduction of 20% for pre-booked parties over 20 on open days. Guided tours available for parties of 30 or more by arrangement. No dogs.
Refreshments: Light lunches and afternoon teas available.

IPSWICH MUSEUM

Ipswich map M6
Telephone: Ipswich (0473) 213761/2
(Ipswich Borough Council)

Geology and natural history of Suffolk; Mankind galleries covering Africa, Asia, America and the Pacific. 'Romans in Suffolk' gallery showing local archaeology. Temporary exhibitions in attached gallery.

Location: High Street, in town centre.
Station: Ipswich.
Opening Times: Tues to Sats 10–5. Temporary exhibition programme. Adm free.

IXWORTH ABBEY

nr Bury St Edmunds map L6 △
(John Rowe, Esq)

House contains 12th century monastic buildings with 15th to 19th century additions. 13th century Undercroft and 15th century Priors Lodging recently restored.

Location: 6 m NE of Bury St Edmunds; 8 m SE of Thetford; at junction of A143 & A1088.
Opening Times: May 1 to June 8: weekdays only 2–4. Also Spring and Summer Bank Holidays 2–4. Adm £4.25, Chd over 5 £1. Guided visits only.
Refreshments: Meals by prior arrangement only.

KENTWELL HALL – *See page 172*

LITTLE HALL 🏠

Lavenham map L6
(Suffolk Preservation Society)

15th century "hall" house, rooms furnished with Gayer Anderson collection of furniture, pictures, china, books, etc.

Location: E side Lavenham Market Place.
Opening Times: Good Friday to mid-Oct—Weds, Thurs, Sats, Suns & Bank Hols 2.30–6. *Groups by appointment tel: (0787) 247179.* Adm £1, Chd 50p.

MELFORD HALL, The National Trust 🌿

nr Sudbury map L5 ♿

Built between 1554 and 1578 by Sir William Cordell, contains fine pictures, furniture and Chinese porcelain. Interesting garden and gazebo. Beatrix Potter display.

Location: In Long Melford on E side of A134; 3 m N of Sudbury.
Opening Times: Principal Rooms & Gardens. Mar 28 to Apr 30: Sats and Suns. May 1 to Sept 30: Weds, Thurs, Sats, Suns and all Bank Holiday Mons 2–5.30. Oct to Nov 1: Sats and Suns 2–5.30. Adm £2.50, Chd (with adult) £1.25. Pre-booked parties of 15 or more £2.40, Weds & Thurs only. No dogs. Wheelchair access, one provided.
Refreshments: In Long Melford.

NETHER HALL

Cavendish, nr Sudbury map L5
(B. T. Ambrose, Esq)

15th century Manor House with gallery museum and vineyard. Prize-winning Estate white wines.

Location: 12 m S of Bury St Edmunds; beside A1092. N of church.
Opening Times: Daily 11–4. Adm £2. Parties by appointment.

ORFORD CASTLE ▣

map M6
Telephone: (039 44) 50472

No sooner had Henry II built this castle on the Suffolk coast than rebellion broke out (in 1173). The castle's powerful presence helped to uphold the King's authority and it continued to be an important royal residence for more than 100 years. In 1280 it was granted to the Earl of Norfolk for his lifetime, and from then on it remained in private hands. The design was very advanced for its time, and the keep, much of which remains, is unique in England. The outer wall of the castle, the last section of which collapsed in 1841, was punctuated by rectangular towers, an innovation that provided excellent cover for the defenders.

Location: In Orford. OS map ref TM419499.
Opening Times: Good Friday or Apr 1 (whichever is earlier) to Sept 30: Open Daily 10–6. Oct 1 to Maundy Thursday or Mar 31 (whichever is earlier): Open Tues to Sun 10–4. *Closed Dec 24–26, Jan 1.* Adm £1.50, Concessions £1.10, Chd 75p.

OTLEY HALL

Otley, nr Ipswich, IP6 9PA map M6 △
Telephone: (0473) 890264; Fax: (0473) 890803
(Mr J G Mosesson)

Stunning 15th century moated Hall (Grade I) and gardens. Fine timbers, herringbone brick, pargetting, linenfold, fresco-work. Built by, and home for 250 years, of Gosnold family. Much historical association: Royal households of Elizabeth I, James I, Charles I. Civil War (Captain Robert Gosnold – Siege of Carlisle). Bartholomew Gosnold settled and named Cape Cod and Martha's (Gosnold) Vineyard, and later a founder of Jamestown.

Location: 10 m N of Ipswich, via B1077/B1078; ¼ m NE of Otley village.
Opening Times: Easter Fri to Mon, (Apr 17, 18, 19, 20); Spring Bank Hol Sun & Mon (May 24 and 25); Summer Bank Hol Sun & Mon (Aug 30 and 31): 2–6. Adm £3.50, Chd (with adult) £2.50. Also open by appointment to parties, special interest groups, etc. Guided tours. Lectures available on associated history, architectural background, etc.
Refreshments: Tea & light refreshments and meals available by arrangement.

THE PRIORY – *See page 174*

SAXTEAD GREEN POST MILL ▣

map M6
Telephone: (0728) 82789

In the 13th century Framlingham was a thriving farming community, whose wealth derived from cereals, particularly wheat. This corn-mill, one of the finest in the world, probably dates from 1287 and produced flour until the First World War. The upper part of the mill, containing the machinery, was rotated by a track-mounted fantail. This ensured that the sails always faced square into the wind.

Location: 2 m (3.2 km) west of Framlingham. OS map ref TM253645.
Opening Times: Good Friday or Apr 1 (whichever is earlier) to Sept 30: Mon–Sat 10–6. Adm £1.10, Concessions 85p, Chd 55p.

THE PRIORY

Lavenham map L6
Telephone: Lavenham (0787) 247417
(Mr & Mrs A Casey)

Through the ages the home of Benedictine monks, medieval clothiers, an Elizabethan rector, and now of the Casey family, who rescued the house from a derelict ruin. Beautiful timber-framed building (Grade 1) with stimulating interior design blending old and new, enhanced by paintings, drawings and stained glass by Ervin Bossanyi (1891–1975). Lovely herb garden of unique design. Work still continues on parts of the building. On display is an exhibition of photographs illustrating the restoration.

Location: In Water Street, Lavenham; 10 m S of Bury St Edmunds.
Opening Times: Apr to end Oct – Daily 10.30–5.30. Adm £2, Chd £1. Open by appointment for groups, morning, afternoon or evening, please telephone above number. Guided tours can emphasise timber framed buildings and their restoration, history of the house and the area, the Bossanyi collection, interior decor – according to your interests.
Refreshments: Coffee, lunches and teas served in the Refectory. Gift shop. Selection of unusual gifts and woven tapestries.

SOMERLEYTON HALL

nr Lowestoft map M6
(The Lord & Lady Somerleyton)

Somerleyton Hall is an extravagantly splendid early Victorian mansion built around a Tudor and Jacobean shell, epitomising an era of self confident expansion. No expense was spared in the building or the fittings. Stone was brought from Caen and Aubigny and the magnificent carved stonework created by John Thomas (who worked on the Houses of Parliament) has been recently fully restored. In the State rooms there are paintings by Landseer, Wright of Derby and Stanfield, together with fine wood carving by Willcox of Warwick and from the earlier house, Grinling Gibbons. Twelve acres of gardens surround the Hall with magnificent specimen trees, azaleas, rhododendrons and splendid statuary. There are handsome glass houses designed by Paxton. The most notable feature is the MAZE, planted in 1846, which ranks amongst the finest in the country. The stable tower clock by Vulliamy made in 1847 is the original model for a great clock to serve as the Tower Clock in the new Houses of Parliament, now world famous as Big Ben. A quarter mile long MINIATURE RAILWAY carries passengers at the edge of the park on most days. Free car parking. No dogs allowed.

Location: 5 m NW Lowestoft off B1074; 7 m Yarmouth (A143).
Station: Somerleyton (1½ m).
Opening Times: House, Maze and Gardens open – Easter Sun to end of Sept, Thurs, Suns and Bank Holidays. Also Tues & Wed in July & Aug 2–5.30. Adm £3.40, Chd £1.65, OAPs £2.70.
Refreshments: Tea in the loggia.

WINGFIELD COLLEGE

Nr Eye map M6 △
Telephone: Stradbroke (037 984) 505
(Ian Chance, Esq)

Founded in 1362 on the 13th century site of the Manor House by Sir John de Wingfield, a close friend of the Black Prince. Magnificent Medieval Great Hall. Surrendered to Henry VIII in 1542 and seized by Cromwell's Parliament in 1549. Mixed period interiors with 18th century neo-classical façade. Walled gardens (and Topiary). Teas. Celebrated Arts and Music Season. Adjacent church with tombs of College founder and Benefactors, The Dukes of Suffolk.

Location: Signposted off B1118; 7 m SE of Diss.
Opening Times: Easter Sat to Sept 30 – Sats, Suns & Bank Hols 2–6.
Refreshments: Home-made teas.

SURREY

ALBURY PARK

Albury, Guildford map J4
(Country Houses Association Ltd)

Country mansion by Pugin.

Location: 1½ m E of Albury off A25 Guildford to Dorking road.
Stations: Chilworth (2 m); Gomshall (2 m); Clandon (2 m)
Bus Route: Tillingbourne No 25 Guildford–Cranleigh
Opening Times: May to Sept – Weds & Thurs 2–5. Last entry 4.30. Adm £1.50, Chd 50p.
Free car park. No dogs admitted.

ASGILL HOUSE

Richmond map K4
(Asgill House Trust Ltd)

Palladian villa designed by Sir Robert Taylor.

Location: Richmond, Surrey
Opening Times: By written application. Unsuitable for disabled. Car parking on street only.

BROOKLANDS MUSEUM

Brooklands Road, Weybridge KT13 0QN
Telephone: (0932) 857381

THE BIRTHPLACE OF BRITISH MOTORSPORT AND AVIATION

THE *Spirit* OF
BROOKLANDS

BROOKLANDS MUSEUM
WEYBRIDGE, SURREY

Brooklands is the site of the world's first purpose built motor circuit. The museum features the famous banked racetrack, Motoring Village, Edwardian Clubhouse and a unique collection of historic Brooklands cars, aircraft, motorcycles, cycles and the Wellington bomber recovered from Loch Ness.
Brooklands is celebrating its 85th Birthday this year with an exciting programme of motoring and aviation events.
For further details telephone (0932) 857381.

OPENING HOURS: October to March, Saturday and Sunday, 10am–4pm. From April, Saturday and Sunday, 10am–5pm. Pre-arranged tours Tuesday to Friday.

ADMISSION: Adults £3.50, Students and Senior Citizens £2.50. Children under 16 £1.50, Children under 5 free. The Brooklands Museum Shop is located in the Visitors Reception area. Light refreshments are also available.

CHILWORTH MANOR

nr Guildford map J4
(Lady Heald)

Garden laid out in 17th century on site of 11th century monastery, 18th century walled garden, spring flowers, flowering shrubs, herbaceous border, 11th century stewponds.

Location: 3¾ m SE of Guildford off A248 in Chilworth Village turn at Blacksmith Lane.
Station: Chilworth (¾ m).
Opening Times: GARDEN ONLY: Sat to Wed Apr 4–8; May 9–13; June 13–17; July 18–22; Aug 15–19. Other times by appointment. Car park open 12.30 for picnics. Adm Garden £1, House with floral arrangements (on the above Sats & Suns only) £1, accompanied Chd free. Cars free. *In aid of National Gardens Scheme.*
Refreshments: Tea at the house, Sats & Suns only.

CLANDON PARK, The National Trust

nr Guildford map J4 &
Telephone: Guildford 222482

A Palladian house built 1731–35 by Giacomo Leoni. Fine plasterwork. Collection of furniture, pictures and porcelain. Museum of the Queen's Royal Surrey Regiment. Garden with parterre, grotto and Maori house.

Location: At West Clandon 3 m E Guildford on A247; S of A3 & N of A246.
Station: Clandon (1 m).
Opening Times: Apr 1 to end Oct: daily (except Thurs and Fris) 1.30–5.30 (last adm 5). Open Bank Hol Mons and preceding Suns 11–5.30; open Good Friday. Parties & guided tours by arrangement with the Administrator *(no reduced rate at weekends and Bank Hols)*. Adm House and Museum £3.30, Chd half price. Parties (Mons, Tues, Weds only) £2.70. Shop. Picnic area. Dogs in car park and picnic area only, on leads. Wheelchairs provided.
Refreshments: Restaurant in house 12.30–2 & 3.15–5.30. Prior booking advisable for luncheon,
Tel Guildford 222502.

CLAREMONT

Esher map K4
Telephone: Esher (0372) 467841
(The Claremont Fan Court Foundation Ltd)

Excellent example of Palladian style; built 1772 by "Capability" Brown for Clive of India; Henry Holland and John Soane responsible for the interior decoration. It is now a co-educational school run by Christian Scientists.

Location: ½ m SW from Esher on Esher/Cobham Road A307.
Opening Times: Feb to Nov: first complete weekend (Sats and Suns) in each month 2–5. Adm £2, Chd/OAPs £1. Reduced rates for parties. Souvenirs.
Refreshments: Not available.

CLAREMONT LANDSCAPE GARDEN, The National Trust

Esher map K4 &

The earliest surviving English landscape garden, recently restored. Begun by Vanbrugh and Bridgemen before 1720, extended and naturalized by Kent. Lake, island with pavilion, grotto and turf amphitheatre, viewpoints and avenues. House not National Trust property.

Location: ½ m SE of Esher on E side of A307. NB: no access from A3 by-pass.
Stations: Esher (2 m) (not Suns); Hersham (2 m); Hinchley Wood (2½ m).
Opening Times: All the year daily: Apr to end of Oct 9–7 *(July 15 to July 19 closes 4 pm).* Nov to end of Mar: daily 9–5 (or sunset if earlier). *Closed Christmas Day and New Year's Day.* Adm Sun and Bank Hols £2.50; Mons to Sats £1.50 (Chd half price). Guided tours (minimum 15 persons) £1.10 plus admission price by prior booking, telephone (0372) 469421. Wheelchairs provided. No reduction for parties. No dogs. Shop.
Refreshments: Tea room open Jan 11 to end Mar: Sats and Suns 11–4.30; Apr to end Oct: daily (except Mons) 11–5.30 (open Bank Hol Mon); Nov to Dec 15: daily (except Mons) 11–4.

COVERWOOD LAKES

Peaslake Road, Ewhurst map K4
Telephone: (0306) 731103
(Mr & Mrs C G Metson)

Landscaped water and cottage gardens in lovely setting between Holmbury Hill to the north and Pitch Hill to the south. Rhododendrons, azaleas, primulas, fine mature trees. New 3½ acre arboretum, planted 1990. Four small lakes and bog garden. Herd of pedigree Poll Hereford cattle and flock of mule sheep in the adjoining farm (Mr and Mrs Nigel Metson).

Location: ½ m from Peaslake village. 8 m from Guildford. 8 m from Dorking (A25). 3 m from A25.
Opening Times: GARDEN ONLY: For *National Gardens Scheme* Suns May 10, 17, 2–6.30. Adm £1.50, Chd (5 to 16) 75p. GARDEN AND FARM: Wed May 27, Sun May 24, 31, June 7, 14, 2–6.30. Oct 25, 11–4.30. Adm £2 Chd (5 to 16) 75p. Chd under 5 free. Special reductions for large parties if arrangements made prior to visit. Plenty of free parking space. No dogs please. Suitable for disabled persons (no wheelchairs available). Plant stall.
Refreshments: Teas and home-made cakes available, plus hot soup and sandwiches on Oct 25. Nearest hotel is the Hurtwood, (THF) at Peaslake village (½ m away from garden).

CROSSWATER FARM

Churt, Farnham   map J4
Telephone: Frensham (025 125) 2698
(Mr & Mrs E. G. Millais)

6-acre woodland garden surrounded by acres of National Trust property. Plantsman's collection of Rhododendrons and Azaleas including many rare species collected in the Himalayas, and hybrids raised by the owners. Pond, stream and companion plantings. Plants for sale from adjoining Rhododendron nursery. (See Millais Nurseries entry in Garden Specialists section).

Location: Farnham/Haslemere 6 miles. From A287 turn East into Jumps Road ½ m north of Churt village centre. After ¼ m, turn left into Crosswater Lane, and follow Nursery signs.
Opening Times: May 16 to June 14 daily 10–5. Adm £1, Chd free. No dogs. In aid of the *National Gardens Scheme* on May 23, 24, 25, 30, 31, June 6, 7.
Refreshments: Teas available on NGS days.

FARNHAM CASTLE

Farnham   map J4   △
(The Church Commissioners)

Bishop's Palace built in Norman times by Henry of Blois, with Tudor and Jacobean additions. Formerly the seat of the Bishops of Winchester. Fine Great Hall re-modelled at the Restoration. Features include the Renaissance brickwork of Wayne-fleter's tower, and the 17th century chapel.

Location: ½ m N of Town Centre on A287.
Station: Farnham.
Opening Times: Castle—All year Weds 2–4. Parties at other times by arrangement. Adm £1, OAP, Chd and Students 50p. Reductions for parties. All visitors are given guided tours. Centrally heated in winter.

FARNHAM CASTLE KEEP ⊞

map J4
Telephone: (0252) 713393

Farnham formed part of the estate of the Bishops of Winchester long before the Norman Conquest. And there was still a bishop in residence until 1955—an impressive tenancy. But why should the massive keep be built *around* the mound of earth, and not on top of it? Your guess is as good as the archaeologists'!

Location: ½ m N of Farnham town centre on A287. OS map ref SU839474.
Opening Times: Good Friday or Apr 1 (whichever is earlier) to Sept 30: Open Daily 10–6. Adm £1.40. Concessions £1, Chd 70p. Adm price includes a Personal Stereo Guided Tour.

GODDARDS

Abinger Common, Dorking   map K4
Telephone: Dorking (0306) 730487
(The Lutyens Trust)

Edwardian country house by Sir Edwin Lutyens, with Gertrude Jekyll garden, in beautiful setting on slopes of Leith Hill. Recently given to The Lutyens Trust by the family whose home it has been since 1953.

Location: 4½ m SW of Dorking in Abinger Common. Open: Newly open to visitors from Apr – please telephone for details.

GREATHED MANOR

Lingfield   map K4
(Country Houses Association Ltd)

Victorian Manor house.

Location: 2½ m SE of Lingfield on B2028 Edenbridge road, take Ford Manor road beside Plough Inn, Dormansland for final 1 m.
Stations: Dormans (1½ m); Lingfield (1½ m).
Bus Route: No. 429 to Plough Inn, Dormansland.
Opening Times: May to Sept—Weds & Thurs 2–5. Last entry 4.30. Adm £1.50, Chd 50p. Free car park. No dogs admitted.

HATCHLANDS PARK, The National Trust 🌿

East Clandon   map K4   ♿
Telephone: Guildford 222787

Built by Admiral Boscawen in 18th century, interior by Robert Adam, with later modifications. Contains Cobbe collection of keyboard instruments, paintings and furniture. Garden.

Location: E of East Clandon on N side of Leatherhead/Guildford Road (A246).
Station: Clandon (2 m).
Opening Times: Apr 1 to Oct 18: Tues, Weds, Thurs, Suns and Bank Hol Mons, but also open Sats in Aug, 2–5.30 (no admission after 5). Adm £3.20, Chd half price. Pre-booked parties £2.40 (Tues, Weds and Thurs only). No dogs. Wheelchair access to ground floor and part of the garden. Shop.
Refreshments: Teas, and light lunches.

LITTLE HOLLAND HOUSE, CHEAM—SEE UNDER LONDON

LOSELEY HOUSE – *See page 177*

PAINSHILL PARK

Portsmouth Road, Cobham   map K4
Telephone: (0932) 868113
(Painshill Park Trust)

Painshill, contemporary with Stourhead & Stowe, is one of Europe's finest eighteenth century landscape gardens. It was created by The Hon Charles Hamilton, plantsman, painter and brilliantly gifted designer, between 1738 and 1773. He transformed barren heathland into ornamental pleasure grounds and parkland of dramatic beauty and contrasting scenery, dominated by a 14 acre meandering lake fed from the river by an immense waterwheel. Garden buildings and features adorned the Park, including a magnificent Grotto, Temple, ruined Abbey, Chinese Bridge, castellated Tower, and a Mausoleum. Well maintained for 200 years in private ownership, the Park was neglected after 1948 and sank into dereliction. In 1981 the Painshill Park Trust, a registered charity, was formed to restore the gardens to their original splendour, raising the extensive funds needed for such an ambitious project. Already, after nearly 10 years, the Trust has made enormous progress, and this masterpiece is re-emerging from the wilderness.

Location: W of Cobham on A245. 200 yards E of A3/A245. Roundabout.
Opening Times: Apr 12 to Oct 18: Suns (only) 11–6 (last ticket 5). Adm £3, OAP's, Students and UB40s £2, Chd under 16 free. Season tickets available. Pre-booked parties (min. 10) on any day except Suns. Please ring (0932) 864674 for more information. School parties particularly welcome by arrangement with Painshill Park Education Trust, (0932) 866743. Much of Park accessible for disabled (wheelchairs available). Limited facilities and parking. No dogs please.
Refreshments: Light refreshments available.

POLESDEN LACEY, The National Trust 🌿

nr Dorking   map K4   ♿
Telephone: Bookham 58203 or 52048

Originally a Regency villa altered in Edwardian period. Greville collection of pictures, tapestries, furniture. 18th century garden extended 1906, with herbaceous borders, rose garden, clipped hedges, lawns, beeches. Views.

Location: 3 m NW of Dorking, reached via Great Bookham (A246) & then road leading S (1½ m).
Stations: Boxhill or Bookham (both 2½ m).
Opening Times: Mar and Nov: Sats and Suns 1.30–4.30; Apr 1 to end of Oct: Weds to Suns 1.30–5.30. Last adm half hour before closing. Open Good Friday. Open Bank Hol Mons and preceding Suns 11–5.30. Garden open daily all year, 11–6. No dogs in formal gardens. Adm Garden only Apr 1 to end Oct £2, Nov to end Mar £1.50. House: Sun and Bank Holiday Mons £3.20 extra. Other open days £2.50 extra. Chd half-price. *Party reductions on Weds, Thurs & Fris only by prior arrangement with the Administrator £4.* Wheelchairs admitted & provided. Shop open same days as house, from 11.
Refreshments: Licensed Restaurant in the grounds; Jan 18 to end Mar: Sats and Suns only 11–4 *(Closed 2–2.30)*. Apr 1 to end Oct: Weds to Suns and Bank Hol Mons 11–5.30. Nov to Dec. Special times before Christmas. Tel Bookham 456190.

LOSELEY HOUSE 🏛

Guildford   map J4   ♿   △
Telephone: Guildford (0483) 304440
(Mr and Mrs James More-Molyneux)

The Elizabethan country house with the friendly atmosphere. Built of stone from Waverley Abbey in a glorious parkland setting by an ancestor of the present owner and occupier. Queen Elizabeth I stayed here three times, James I twice. Queen Mary visited in 1932. Panelling from Henry VIII's Nonsuch Palace. Fine ceilings, unique carved chalk chimney piece, inlaid cabinets, tapestries, needlework, but Loseley is a home, not a museum. Moat walk. Farm tours. Restaurant and farm shop housed in the 17th century Tithe Barn. Wholefood lunches, teas and organic wine. Farm Shop selling Loseley ice cream, yoghurt and cream as well as Loseley organic bakery products and organic vegetables.

Location: 2½ m SW of Guildford (take B3000 off A3 through Compton); 1½ m N of Godalming (off A3100).
Station: Farncombe (2 m).
Opening Times: May 25 to Oct 3: Weds, Thurs, Fris and Sats 2–5; also Summer Bank Hol Mon Aug 31 2–5. Adm £3.50, Chd £2. Parties of 20 and over £2.75 per person. School parties £2 per person. Gardens and grounds £1.50, Chd 50p. Parties of 20 or more £1.20 per person. Farm shop. Farm Tours when house is open; at other times, booked parties only. Tithe Barn Restaurant and Farm Shop open same days as House, 11–5.
Refreshments: Home produce, morning coffee, home made lunches and teas in Tithe Barn. Open May 25 to Oct 3: Wed, Thurs, Fri & Sat; also Bank Hol Mon (Aug 31).

PYRFORD COURT

nr Woking   map J4
Telephone: Woking (0483) 765880
(Mr C Laikin)

Twenty acres of wild and formal gardens, azaleas, wisteria, rhododendrons, pink marble fountain, venetian bridge.

Location: 2 m E of Woking, B367 junction with Upshott Lane, M25 (exit 10) on to A3 towards Guildford, off to Ripley signposted Pyrford.
Opening Times: Suns, May 24, 31 2–6.30. Sun, Oct 18 12–4. Adults £1.50, Chd 50p. Open in aid of *National Gardens Scheme and Cancer Research Campaign.* For details of operas/concerts and other events in the house please phone above number.
Refreshments: Tea and cakes.

RAMSTER

Chiddingfold   map J3
Telephone: (0428) 644422
(Mr & Mrs Paul Gunn)

Mature 20 acre woodland garden of exceptional interest. Laid out by Gauntlett Nurseries of Chiddingfold in early 1900's. Fine rhododendrons, azaleas, camellias, magnolias, trees and shrubs in lovely setting.

Location: On A283 1½ m S of Chiddingfold.
Opening Times: GARDEN ONLY. Apr 25 to June 7 – Daily 2–6. Adm £1.50, Chd under 16 free. Parties by arrangement. *Share to National Gardens Scheme.*
Refreshments: Teas Sats, Suns & Bank Hol Mons in May only.

VANN

Hambledon   map J3
Telephone: Wormley (0428) 683413
(Mr & Mrs M. B. Caroe)

16th to 20th century house surrounded by 5 acre 'paradise' garden. Water garden by Gertrude Jekyll 1911.

Location: 6 m S of Godalming; A283 to Wormley, turn left at Hambledon cross roads and follow signs along Vann Lane for 2 m.
Station: Witley (2 m).
Opening Times: GARDENS ONLY: Easter Mon Apr 20, Bank Holiday Mon May 4, Sun June 7 2 –7. Tues to Sun, Apr 21–26, Tues to Sun May 5–10, Mon to Sat June 8–13, 10–6. Easter to Sept: by prior appointment. Plant and vegetable stall. Party bookings and guided tours with morning coffee, lunches or home made teas in house or garden by arrangement. Adm £1.30, Chd 30p. *In aid of National Gardens Scheme and Hambledon Village Hall.*
Refreshments: Home made teas in house, Apr 20, May 4, June 7 only.

WHITEHALL, CHEAM – SEE UNDER LONDON

WINKWORTH ARBORETUM, The National Trust 🌿

nr Godalming   map J3   ♿

99 acres of trees and shrubs planted mainly for Spring and Autumn colour. Two lakes, fine views.

Location: 2 m SE of Godalming on E side of B2130.
Station: Godalming (2 m).
Opening Times: Open all the year during daylight hours. Adm £2, Chd half price. No reduction for parties. *Coach parties by prior appointment* Tel: (048632) 477. Bookings Tearoom Concessionaire, Winkworth Arboretum, nr Godalming, Surrey. Dogs must be kept under control. Wheelchair access.
Refreshments: Apr 1 to Nov 15: daily (except Mons) 2–6 or dusk if earlier, Sats and Suns only 11–6. *Open Bank Hol Mons and closed Tues following Bank Hols.* Also open weekends in Nov to Dec 22, plus weekends in Mar, and open daily in May and Oct 11–6 for light lunches and teas.

WISLEY GARDEN

Wisley   map K4   ♿
(The Royal Horticultural Society)

British gardening at its best in all aspects. 250 acres of glorious garden. The wooded slopes with massed rhododendrons and azaleas, the wild daffodils of the alpine meadow, the calm of the pinetum, the gaiety of the herbaceous border, the banked mounds of heathers, the new alpine house, the panorama of the rock garden, the model fruit and vegetable gardens and the range of greenhouse displays are there waiting for you to enjoy them and to learn from them.

Location: In Wisley just off M25 Junction 10, on A3. London 22 m, Guildford 7 m.
Opening Times: The garden is open to the public Mon to Sat throughout the year (except Christmas Day) from 10–sunset (or 10–7 during the summer). ON SUNDAYS THE GARDEN IS OPEN ONLY TO MEMBERS of RHS. Adm £3.95, Chd 6–14 yrs £1.75 (under 6 free). Groups of more than 20, Mon to Fri £2.95, Sat £3.25. Tickets for parties must be obtained 14 days in advance of visit. Dogs not admitted other than guide dogs. Information centre, Shop & Plant sales centre.
Refreshments: Licensed restaurant in garden (Jan 6 to mid Dec) & licensed cafeteria.

EAST SUSSEX

ALFRISTON CLERGY HOUSE, The National Trust

Alfriston, nr Seaford   map K3
Telephone: Alfriston (0323) 870001

Bought in 1896, the first building acquired by the Trust. Wealden hall-house, possibly a parish priest's house, c. 1350.

Location: 4 m NE of Seaford just E of B2108; adjoining The Tye & St Andrew's Church. *Station: Berwick (2¹/₂ m).*
Opening Times: Exhibition Room, Medieval Hall, two other rooms & Garden. Apr to end Oct—Daily 11–6 (or sunset if earlier). Last adm half-hour before closing. Adm Mar, Apr, May, Sept, Oct: £1.20, Chd 60p; June, July, Aug: £1.70, Chd 90p. Pre-booked parties low season 90p, Chd 50p. High season £1.30, Chd 70p. Shop (open until Christmas). No dogs. Unsuitable for wheelchairs.

BATEMAN'S, The National Trust

Burwash   map L3   △
Telephone: Burwash 882302

Built 1634. Rudyard Kipling lived here. Water-mill restored by the National Trust. Attractive garden, yew hedges, lawns, daffodils and wild garden.

Location: ¹/₂ m S of Burwash on the Lewes/Etchingham Road (A265).
Opening Times: Apr to end of Oct—Daily (except Thurs & Fris but open Good Fri) 11–5.30. Last adm 4.30. Adm House, Mill & Garden £3.20, Chd £1.60, weekends & Bank Hols £3.70, Chd £1.90. Pre-booked parties £2.60, Chd £1.30, weekends and Bank Holidays £3, Chd £1.50. No dogs.
Refreshments: Tea room: coffees, light lunches and teas, open as House. Shop.

BATTLE ABBEY

map L3
Telephone: (04246) 3792
(English Heritage)

The Battle of Hastings, 1066—the best-known date in English history. Battle Abbey was built by William the Conqueror as a thanksgiving for his victory, with the high altar on the spot where King Harold died. The church has yet to be fully excavated, but visitors may walk over the battlefield, and see the remains of many of the domestic buildings of the monastery and see an audio-visual show. A new exhibition is open in the newly restored 14th century gatehouse. A Personal Stereo Guided Tour is available.

Location: Battle. OS map ref TQ749157.
Opening Times: Good Friday or Apr 1 (whichever is earlier) to Sept 30, daily 10–6. Oct 1 to Maundy Thursday or Mar 31 (whichever is earlier), daily 10–4. *Closed* Dec 24–26, Jan 1. Adm £2.50, Concessions £1.90, Chd £1.30.

BAYHAM ABBEY

map L3
Telephone: (0892) 890381

Built by monks in the 13th century, the abbey owes its survival not to historical or archaeological interest, but to its being a picturesque ruin. By the 18th century the building was in a desperate condition, but then came the Gothic revival and the structure was repaired and landscaped to provide a romantic vista for the nearby Dower House.

Location: 1³/₄ m (2.8 km) west of Lamberhurst. OS map ref TQ651366.
Opening Times: Good Friday or Apr 1 (whichever is earlier) to Sept 30: Open Daily 10–6. Adm £1.50, Concessions £1.10, Chd 75p.

BENTLEY HOUSE & GARDENS

Halland   map K3

Bentley House dates back to Tudor times and was built on land granted to James Gage by the Archbishop of Canterbury with the permission of Henry VIII. The family of Lord Gage was linked with Bentley from that time until 1904. The estate was purchased by Gerald Askew in 1937, and during the 1960's he and his wife, Mary, added two large double height Palladian rooms to the original farmhouse. The architect who advised them was Raymond Erith, who had previously worked on 10 Downing Street. The drawing room in the East wing contains 18th century Chinese wallpaper and gilt furniture, and the Bird room in the West wing contains a collection of wildfowl paintings by Philip Rickman. The Gardens at Bentley have been created as a series of 'rooms' divided by Yew hedges, one room leading into the next, specialising in many old fashioned roses including the Bourbons, the Gallicas and the Damask. Nearby six stone sphinxes stand along a broad grass walk where daffodils bloom in spring.

Location: 7 m NE of Lewes signposted on A22, A26 & B2192.
Opening Times: Apr 1 to Oct 31 daily. HOUSE: 12–5. ESTATE: 10.30–5. Adm: £3.10, OAPs £2.40, Chd 4–15 £1.50. Family ticket (2 adults, 4 Chd) £8. Special rates for disabled (wheelchairs available). Parties of 11 + 10% discount. Admission price allows entry to the House, Garden and Grounds, Wildfowl reserve, Motor Museum, Woodland Walk, Animal section, Children's adventure play area, Picnic area, Tea Room, Gift Shop and Education Centre. Ample free parking – dogs allowed in this area only. Special arrangements can be made for parties outside normal hours. Please contact the Manager for details. Tel: Halland (0825) 840573.
Refreshments: Tea Rooms on site (licensed).

BODIAM CASTLE, The National Trust ✲

nr Robertsbridge   map L3   ♿
Telephone: Staplecross (058 083) 436

Built 1385–9, one of the best preserved examples of medieval moated military architecture.

Location: 3 m S of Hawkhurst; 1 m E of A229.
Opening Times: Apr to Oct 31 incl. Good Fri. Daily 10–6 (or sunset if earlier). Nov to end Mar – Mons to Sats only. 10–sunset. Last adm half-hour before closing. *Closed Dec 25 to 29.* Adm £2, Chd £1. *Parties of 15 or more by prior arrangement £1.50, Chd 80p.* Car park free to members. Museum. Audio visual. Shop. Dogs admitted except in shop & museum. Wheelchair access.
Refreshments: Restaurant, Apr to Dec 24.

BORDE HILL GARDEN

Haywards Heath   map K3
Telephone: Haywards Heath (0444) 450326

Large garden with woods and parkland of exceptional beauty. Rare trees and shrubs, herbaceous borders and fine views. Woodland Walk, water feature, picnic area by lake..

Location: 1½ m N of Haywards Heath on Balcombe Road. Brighton 17 m; Gatwick 10 m.
Opening Times: Open daily from Mar 28 to Oct 25 10–6. Adm £2, Chd 75, Senior Citizen £1.25; parties of 20 or more £1.25. Parking free. Interesting plants for sale. Entry to lake, children's playground, picnic area only (incl restaurant and plant sales): £1 per car (does not apply to special events). Dogs allowed on lead.
Refreshments: Licensed – morning coffee, light lunches, cream teas; parties by arrangement.

BRICKWALL HOUSE

Northiam, Rye   map L3
Telephone: Northiam (0797) 252494 or Curator (0797) 223329
(Frewen Educational Trust)

Home of the Frewen family since 1666. 17th century drawing room with superb 17th century plaster ceilings, and family portraits spanning 400 years of history. Grand staircase. Chess garden and arboretum.

Location: 7 m NW of Rye on B2088.
Opening Times: Apr to end Sept – Sats and Bank Holiday Mons 2–5; Adm £1.50. Open at other times by prior arrangement with the curator.

CHARLESTON FARMHOUSE

Firle, nr Lewes map K3
Telephone: Ripe (0323) 811265 (Visitor information),
(0323) 811626 (Administration)
(The Charleston Trust)

17/18th century farmhouse, the home of Vanessa and Clive Bell and Duncan Grant from 1916 until Grant's death in 1978. Virginia and Leonard Woolf 'discovered' Charleston in 1916, when her sister Vanessa was looking for a house in the country, 'If you lived there, you could make it absolutely divine' Virginia wrote prophetically. Here over the decades Maynard and Lydia Keynes, David Garnett, Roger Fry, Lytton Strachey, Raymond Mortimer, Desmond MacCarthy, T.S. Eliot and E.M. Forster were residents or constant visitors. Others included G.E. Moore, Bertrand Russell, Georges Duthuit, Charles Mauron, Andre Dunoyer de Segonzac, Matthew Smith, Ernest Ansermet, Kenneth Clark, Benjamin Britten, Peter Pears and Frederick Ashton. As a habitation of genius and talent, a theatre of intellectual activity for over half a century, it would be remarkable. But Charleston is far more: from the start Vanessa Bell and Duncan Grant, her children, and other artists, adorned the house and garden. The place was enriched by an accumulation of decorative achievements; a particular style, now a part of art history, is found here, in its finest and most characteristic form.

Location: 6 m E of Lewes, on A27, between Firle and Selmeston.
Station: Lewes 6 m; Berwick 3 m.
Opening Times: Apr 1 to Oct 31 — Weds, Thurs, Sats (Guided Tours) and Suns and Bank Hol Mons (unguided), 2–6 (last adm 5). Kitchen open Thurs only. Adm £3.50; car park 50p (no parking charge midweek Apr, May, Oct). Numbers in the House will be limited; no dogs. Student/OAP/UB40 concessions midweek throughout the season, also weekends Apr, May, Oct. Coaches by prior appointment only. Contact Charleston Office at Farmhouse.

COBBLERS GARDEN

Crowborough map K3
Telephone: (0892) 655969
(Mr & Mrs Martin Furniss)

Designed by architect Martin Furniss and described as a 'work of art' by Anita Periére, this superb 2 acre garden on a sloping site was created for all season interest, and has all the intimacy and character of an English cottage garden. Large range of herbaceous and shrub species; natural pool with waterside plants chosen to give a long season of colour and variety. Featured in RHS Journal 1978 and two BBC television programmes, August 1978 'Country Life' and 'Homes and Gardens' 1981 and TVS 'That's Gardening' 1991.

Location: At Crowborough Cross (A26) turn on to B2100 (signposted Crowborough station & Rotherfield); at 2nd crossroads turn right into Tollwood Road.
Station: Crowborough (1 m).
Opening Times: GARDEN ONLY — Mon May 25, Suns May 31; June 14, 28; July 12, 26; Aug 9. Coaches by appointment. Open 2.30–5.30. Adm £2.50, Chd £1 (including home made tea). *In aid of National Gardens Scheme and The National Trust.* No dogs please. Excellent range of plants for sale. Car park.
Refreshments: Home-made teas.

FIRLE PLACE — *See page 181*

GLYNDE PLACE — *See page 181*

FIRLE PLACE

nr Lewes   map K3   △
Telephone: Glynde (0273) 858335
(Viscount Gage)

Home of the Gage family since the 15th century, the original Tudor house was largely altered about 1730. The House contains an important collection of European and British Old Masters. The pictures are further enhanced with French and English furniture by famous craftsmen. There is also a quantity of Sèvres porcelain of the finest quality. These are largely derived from the Cowper collection, and can be seen in a spacious family setting. Items of particular interest to visitors from the USA through General Gage, Commander-in-Chief of the British Forces at the beginning of the War of Independence, and his wife Margaret Kemble of New Jersey. The House is set in parkland under the South Downs, 55 miles from London by road. Hourly rail service Victoria to Lewes, takes 64 minutes, thence by taxi (5 miles).

Location: 5 m SE of Lewes on the Lewes/Eastbourne Road (A27).
Station: Glynde (1¹/₂ m) or Lewes (5 m, taxis available).
Opening Times: May 3, June, July, Aug & Sept—Weds, Thurs & Suns. Also Easter, May, Spring & Summer Bank Hol Suns & Mons: 2 last tickets 5. First Wed in month longer, unguided Connoisseurs' tour of House. Pre-booked group parties of 25 on Open Days (except first Wed in month) at reduced rate. Special exclusive viewings at other times of year for parties over 25 by arrangement. *Party bookings in writing to Showing Secretary, Firle Place, Nr Lewes, East Sussex BN8 6LP (0273) 858335.*
Refreshments: Cold buffet luncheon 12.30–2 daily *except Sat.* Sussex cream teas from 3, only on house open days. Shop and contemporary pictures exhibition. Car park adjacent to house.

GLYNDE PLACE

nr Lewes   map K3   △
Telephone: Glynde (0273) 858337
(Viscount Hampden)

Beautiful example of 16th century architecture. The house, which is built around a Courtyard, is of flint and brick and stands in the picturesque village of Glynde. Interesting collection of pictures by Kneller, Lely, Snyders, Weenix and Zoffany. Bronzes by Francesco Bertos. Historical documents.

Location: 4 m SE of Lewes on Eastbourne/Lewes Road (A27) or A265.
Station: Glynde (¹/₂ m).
Opening Times: June to Sept—Weds & Thurs and first and last Sun of each month 2.15–5.30 (last adm 5). Open Easter Sun & Mon and Bank Hols. House open for guided tours by prior arrangement (25 or more £2.50 per person). Adm £3, Chd £1.50. Garden only 75p (rebate on entry into house). Free parking.
Refreshments: Home-baked teas in Coach House (parties to book in advance).

GREAT DIXTER 🏠

Northiam   map L3   △
Telephone: (0797) 253160
(Quentin Lloyd, Esq)

A beautiful example of a 15th century half-timbered manor house with a Great Hall of unique construction in a truly 'English' garden setting. Restorations and the addition of a smaller 16th century hall house were carried out by Sir Edwin Lutyens who also designed the gardens. Yew hedges, topiary and garden buildings create a delightful setting for flower borders. These contain a rich diversity of plants of horticultural interest. Naturalised daffodils and fritillaries; paeonies; primulas, fuchsias, rose garden, clematis, herbaceous and bedding plants informally arranged.

Location: ½ m N of Northiam; 8 m NW of Rye; 12 m N of Hastings. Just off A28.
Opening Times: Apr 1 to Oct 11 – Daily except Mons (but open all Bank Hol Mons) also weekends Oct 17, 18, 24, 25; open 2 until last adm at 5. Gardens open at 11 on May 23, 24, 25. Suns in July & Aug, also Aug 31. Adm House & Gardens £3.20, Chd 50p. Gardens only £2, Chd 25p. Concessions to OAPs and NT members on Fris – House and Gardens ask for details. No dogs.
Refreshments: At Garden Cottage, next to nurseries.

HASTINGS CASTLE AND 1066 STORY

Hastings   map L3
Telephone: (0424) 717963
(Hastings Heritage Ltd)

Majestic ruins of England's first Norman castle, with panoramic views of the coastline. William of Normandy's original mound – or motte – of earth and sand, with a deep ditch to the east side, was the site of the pre-fabricated wooden fort originally erected here, and can still be seen today. Also remaining are the walls of the collegiate Church of St. Mary, within the grounds, and the north and east curtain walls incorporating the magnificent eastern gateway. The famous 'whispering' dungeons beneath the mound also open for viewing. Within the grounds is an 11th Century siege tent, home of the '1066 Story' – a hi-tec audio/visual experience, incorporating surround sound and scenic effects, and depicting the story of the Battle of Hastings, and the 900 year dramatic history of the castle.

Location: On West Hill Cliff, adjacent Hastings Town Centre ½m from A259 and A21.
Opening Times: Apr 11 to Sept 27 1992 – Daily 10 – last adm 5. Open during winter by arrangement – tel. (0424) 422964. Adm £2, Students/OAPs £1.75, Chd £1.50. Parties £1.25, Chd etc £1 (min party size 10). Seafront car park, access via cliff railway (West Hill). Unsuitable for disabled persons.
Refreshments: Numerous seafront and town centre restaurants nearby. West Hill Cafe 200m from entrance, on cliff top.

KIDBROOKE PARK WITH REPTON GROUNDS

Forest Row   map K3
(The Council of Michael Hall School)

Sandstone house and stables built in 1730s with later alterations.

Location: 1 m SW of Forest Row, off A22, 4 m S of East Grinstead.
Opening Times: Spring Bank Hol Mon (May 30) then Aug – Daily (inc Bank Hol Mon), 11 – 6. Application for admission to the Bursar.

LAMB HOUSE, The National Trust 🌿

Rye   map L3

Georgian house with garden. Home of Henry James from 1898 to 1916.

Location: In West Street facing W end of church.
Station: Rye (¹/₂ m).
Opening Times: House (Hall & 3 rooms only) & Garden. Apr to end of Oct – Weds & Sats 2 – 6 (last admission 5.30). Adm £1.50. No reduction for children or parties. No dogs. Unsuitable for wheelchairs. No lavatories.

MICHELHAM PRIORY 🏠

nr Hailsham   map L3   △   ♿
(Sussex Archaeological Society)

Founded in 1229 this Augustinian Priory is surrounded by one of the largest moats in England. Elizabethan wing and 14th century gatehouse. Special exhibitions and events. Tudor barn. Working Watermill restored, grinding wholemeal flour.

Location: ½ m E of Upper Dicker just off London/Eastbourne Road (A22); 10 m N of Eastbourne.
Opening Times: Mar 25 to Oct 31 – Daily 11 – 5.30; Nov, Feb and Mar Sun only, 11 – 4. Adm (inc Watermill) £3, OAPs £2.70, Chd (5 – 16) £1.70, Family ticket (2 adults & 2 Chd) £8. Booked parties of 20+ £2.50. *No dogs.* Sussex Crafts & Small Industries Aug 5 – 9 inclusive. Activities week in Aug & many other events including 5 art exhibitions.
Refreshments: Morning coffees, farmhouse lunches and Sussex teas at licensed restaurants in Grounds.

MONKS HOUSE, The National Trust

Rodmell   map K3

A small village house and garden. The home of Virginia and Leonard Woolf from 1919 until his death in 1969. House administered and largely maintained by tenants.

Location: 3 m SE of Lewes, off C7 in Rodmell village.
Station: Southease (1 m).
Opening Times: Apr to end Oct—Weds & Sats 2–5.30 (last adm ½ hour before closing time). Adm £2. No reduction for children or parties. No dogs. Unsuitable for wheelchairs. Maximum of 15 people in house at any one time. Narrow access road. Car park 50 yards.

MOORLANDS

Crowborough   map K3
Telephone: (0892) 652474
(Dr and Mrs Steven Smith)

Three acres set in lush valley adjoining Ashdown Forest; water garden with ponds and streams; herbaceous border, primulas, rhododendrons, azaleas and many unusual trees and shrubs; good autumn colour.

Location: Friar's Gate. 2m N of Crowborough. Approach via B2188 at Friar's Gate – take L fork signposted 'Crowborough Narrow Road', entrance 100 yards on left. From Crowborough crossroads take St Johns Road to Friar's Gate.
Opening Times: Suns May 24 and June 7. 2–6. Also by appointment only; Apr 1 to Oct 31. *In aid of National Gardens Scheme.* Sun July 19 2–6 *in aid of Ashdown Forest;* Sun July 12 2–6 *in aid of East Sussex Home Physiotherapy Service.* Adm £1.50, Chd 30p. Limited free car parking. Unsuitable for disabled persons.
Refreshments: Teas in garden on open days; and for parties by prior arrangement.

PEVENSEY CASTLE

map L3
Telephone: (0323) 762604

The walls that enclose this 10-acre site are from the 4th century Roman fort, Anderida. The inner castle, with its great keep, is medieval. With the fall of France in 1940, Pevensey was put into service again, after centuries of neglect. A Personal Stereo Guided Tour is available.

Location: Pevensey. OS map ref TQ645048.
Opening Times: Good Friday or Apr 1 (whichever is earlier) to Sept 30: Open Daily 10–6. Oct 1 to Maundy Thursday or Mar 31 (whichever is earlier): Open Tues to Sun 10–4. *Closed* Dec 24–26, Jan 1. Adm £1.50, Concessions £1.10, Chd 75p.

PRESTON MANOR

Brighton   map K3
Telephone: (0273) 603005
(Borough of Brighton)

A Georgian house built in 1738 and added to in 1905; the house of the Stanford family for nearly 150 years. The house is fully furnished and illustrates the way of life of a rich gentry family and their servants. Delightful grounds with walled garden and pets' cemetery.

Location: On main Brighton to London Road at Preston Park.
Station: Preston Park.
Opening Times: All the year—Tues–Sat 10–5. Sun 2–5. Closed Mons (except Bank Hols) Good Fri, Christmas & Boxing Day. Admission charge. *Reduced rates for parties, families, Chd and OAPs.* Garden free. Parties by arrangement.

ROYAL PAVILION

Brighton   map K3   &

Telephone: (0273) 603005

Spectacular seaside palace of the Prince Regent, transformed by John Nash (1815–1822) into one of the most dazzlingly exotic buildings in the British Isles. Interiors furnished in the Chinese style. The ten years structural restoration programme is now complete. NEW – Queen Victoria's apartments. Pavilion shop.

Location: In centre of Brighton (Old Steine).

Station: Brighton (³/₄ m).

Opening Times: All the year – Daily 10–5 (June to Sept 10–6). *Closed Christmas Day & Boxing Day.* Admission charge. *Reduced rates for parties, families, children and OAPs.* Ground floor accessible for the disabled.

Refreshments: Tearoom with balcony overlooking the gardens.

SHEFFIELD PARK GARDEN, The National Trust 🌿

nr Uckfield   map K3   &

Telephone: Danehill 790655

Large garden with series of lakes linked by cascades; great variety of unusual shrubs.

Location: Midway between East Grinstead & Lewes on E side of A275; 5 m NW of Uckfield.

Opening Times: Apr to Nov 8 – Tues to Sats (closed Good Fri) 11–6 or sunset if earlier; Suns and Bank Hol Mons 2–6 or sunset if earlier. Suns during Oct & Nov: 1 – sunset. Last adm one hour before closing. *Closed Tues following Bank Hol Mons.* Adm May, Oct & Nov £3.70, Chd £1.90; Mar, Apr & June to Sept £3.20, Chd £1.60. Pre-booked parties £2.60 & £2.10 according to season. *No reduction for parties on Sats, Suns & Bank Hols.* No dogs. Shop. Wheelchairs available.

WEST SUSSEX

ARUNDEL CASTLE

Arundel   map J3   &

Telephone: Arundel 883136

(Arundel Castle Trustees Ltd.)

Tʜɪs ɢʀᴇᴀᴛ ᴄᴀsᴛʟᴇ, ʜᴏᴍᴇ ᴏғ ᴛʜᴇ Dᴜᴋᴇs ᴏғ Nᴏʀғᴏʟᴋ, ᴅᴀᴛᴇs ғʀᴏᴍ ᴛʜᴇ Nᴏʀᴍᴀɴ Cᴏɴǫᴜᴇsᴛ. Cᴏɴᴛᴀɪɴɪɴɢ ᴀ ᴠᴇʀʏ ғɪɴᴇ ᴄᴏʟʟᴇᴄᴛɪᴏɴ ᴏғ ғᴜʀɴɪᴛᴜʀᴇ ᴀɴᴅ ᴘᴀɪɴᴛɪɴɢs Aʀᴜɴᴅᴇʟ Cᴀsᴛʟᴇ ɪs sᴛɪʟʟ ᴀ ғᴀᴍɪʟʏ ʜᴏᴍᴇ, ʀᴇғʟᴇᴄᴛɪɴɢ ᴛʜᴇ ᴄʜᴀɴɢᴇs ᴏғ ɴᴇᴀʀʟʏ 1000 ʏᴇᴀʀs.

Iᴛ ɪs ᴏᴘᴇɴ ғʀᴏᴍ 1sᴛ Aᴘʀɪʟ ᴜɴᴛɪʟ 30ᴛʜ Oᴄᴛᴏʙᴇʀ Sᴜɴᴅᴀʏs ᴛᴏ Fʀɪᴅᴀʏs ғʀᴏᴍ 12.00 ᴛᴏ 5.00ᴘᴍ. Lᴀsᴛ ᴀᴅᴍɪssɪᴏɴ ᴏɴ ᴀɴʏ ᴅᴀʏ ɪs 4.00ᴘᴍ. Tʜᴇ Cᴀsᴛʟᴇ ɪs ɴᴏᴛ ᴏᴘᴇɴ ᴏɴ Sᴀᴛᴜʀᴅᴀʏs.

Tʜᴇ ʀᴇsᴛᴀᴜʀᴀɴᴛ sᴇʀᴠᴇs ʜᴏᴍᴇ ᴍᴀᴅᴇ ғᴏᴏᴅ ғᴏʀ ʟᴜɴᴄʜ ᴀɴᴅ ᴀғᴛᴇʀɴᴏᴏɴ ᴛᴇᴀ. Pʀᴇ-ʙᴏᴏᴋᴇᴅ ᴘᴀʀᴛɪᴇs ᴀʀᴇ ᴡᴇʟᴄᴏᴍᴇ. Mᴇɴᴜs ᴀʀᴇ ᴀᴠᴀɪʟᴀʙʟᴇ ᴏɴ ʀᴇǫᴜᴇsᴛ.

Tʜᴇ Sʜᴏᴘ sᴇʟʟs ᴍᴀɴʏ ɪᴛᴇᴍs ᴄʜᴏsᴇɴ ʙʏ ᴛʜᴇ Cᴏᴜɴᴛᴇss ᴏғ Aʀᴜɴᴅᴇʟ ᴀɴᴅ ɪs ᴀʟᴡᴀʏs ᴏᴘᴇɴ ᴀᴛ ᴛʜᴇ sᴀᴍᴇ ᴛɪᴍᴇ ᴀs ᴛʜᴇ Cᴀsᴛʟᴇ.

Arundel Castle

Fᴏʀ ғᴜʀᴛʜᴇʀ ɪɴғᴏʀᴍᴀᴛɪᴏɴ ᴀᴘᴘʟʏ ᴛᴏ: Tʜᴇ Cᴏᴍᴘᴛʀᴏʟʟᴇʀ, Aʀᴜɴᴅᴇʟ Cᴀsᴛʟᴇ, Sᴜssᴇx, BN18 9AB. Tᴇʟᴇᴘʜᴏɴᴇ (0903) 883136/882173.

This great castle, situated in magnificent grounds overlooking the River Arun, was built at the end of the 11th century by Roger de Montgomery, Earl of Arundel. It has been the seat of the Dukes of Norfolk and their ancestors for over seven hundred years. Badly damaged in 1643, the castle was restored by the 8th, 11th and 15th Dukes in the 18th and 19th centuries. Fine furniture, tapestries, clocks and portraits by Van Dyck, Gainsborough, Reynolds, Mytens, Lawrence etc. Fitzalan Chapel. Host to Arundel Festival at the end of August each year, which attracts international artists.

Location: In Arundel 9 m W of Worthing: 10 m E of Chichester. Entrance for cars and pedestrians: Lower Lodge Mill Road.

Station: Arundel (³/₄ m).

Opening Times: Mar 29 to last Fri in Oct – Suns to Fris 1–5 (during June, July & Aug and all Bank Hols 12–5). Last adm any day 4 pm. *The Castle is NOT open on Sats.* Adm charges not available at time of going to press. No dogs. *Special rates for organised parties.*

BERRI COURT

Yapton   map J3

Telephone: (0243) 551 663

(Mr & Mrs J. C. Turner)

3-acre garden of wide interest, trees, flowering shrubs, heathers, eucalyptus, daffodils, shrub roses, hydrangeas and lily ponds.

Location: Centre of Yapton village.

Station: Barnham (1³/₄ m).

Opening Times: Suns, Mons, Apr 7 & 8, May 12 & 13, June 30 & July 1, 2–5; Oct 20 & 21, 12–4. Adm 80p, Chd 30p. *In aid of National Gardens Scheme.* Dogs on leads.

CHAMPS HILL

Coldwaltham, Nr Pulborough   map J3

(Mr & Mrs David Bowerman)

27 acres of formal garden and woodland walks around old sandpits. Conifers and acid-loving plants. Many species labelled. Superb views across Arun Valley. Special

CHAMPS HILL – *Continued from page 185*

Continued from page 185

features:– March – Winter heathers and Spring flowers. May/June – Rhododendrons, Azaleas, Wild Flowers etc. August – Heaths and other specialities.

Location: S of Pulborough on A29 in Coldwaltham turn right to Fittleworth; garden 300 yds on right.
Opening Times: 11–5 (Suns 1–5). March 29, May 3, 15, 16, 17, 24, June 7, Aug 16, 21, 22, 23. Adm £1, Chd free. *In aid of National Gardens Scheme.* No dogs.
Refreshments: Coffees, Teas (Not March).

CHICHESTER CATHEDRAL

West Street map J3
Telephone: Chichester 782595
(The Dean & Chapter of Chichester)

In the heart of the city, this fine Cathedral has been a centre of Christian worship and community life for 900 years. Site of Shrine of St Richard of Chichester; Romanesque stone carvings; works by Sutherland, Feibusch, Procktor, Chagall, Skelton, Piper, and Anglo/German tapestry. Treasury. Cloister. Refectory. Shops in Bell Tower and South Street. Schools should contact the Education Adviser. Vicars' Close and hall.

Location: Centre of city; British Rail; A27, A286.
Opening Times: All year 7.40–7 (5 in winter except for those attending Evensong). Choral Evensong daily (except Weds) during term time; occasionally visiting choirs at other times. Ministry of welcome operates. Guided tours must be booked. No dogs except guide dogs. Wheelchair access (one wheelchair available on application to Vergers). Loop system for the hard of hearing. Touch and hearing Centre for the blind. Adm free: suggested donations Adults £1, Chd 20p. Parking in city car parks.
Refreshments: Refectory off Cathedral Cloisters with lavatory facilities (including those for the disabled).

COATES MANOR

nr Fittleworth map J3
(Mrs G. H. Thorp)

One acre garden, mainly shrubs and foliage of special interest.

Location: ½ m S of Fittleworth; SE of Petworth; turn off B2138 signposted 'Coates'.
Opening Times: GARDEN ONLY. Sun, Mon & Tues June 14, 15 & 16, 11–6. Adm £1, Chd 20p. Also by appointment. *In aid of National Gardens Scheme.*
Refreshments: Tea & cakes.

COKE'S BARN

West Burton, Nr Pulborough map J3
(Mr & Mrs Nigel Azis)

Major part of existing garden redesigned surrounding converted stone barn. S facing conservatory with gravelled courtyard garden; old roses, herbaceous, shrubs and water area.

Location: West Burton 5 m SW of Pulborough/Petworth. At foot of Bury Hill turn W off A29 to W. Burton for 1 m then follow signs.
Opening Times: Suns, Mons, Tues May 10, 11, 12, 24, 25, 26, June 28, 29, 30, Aug 16, 17, 18. Adm 75p, Chd 20p. *In aid of the National Gardens Scheme.* Suitable for wheelchairs, No dogs. Plants for sale.
Refreshments: Tea.

DANNY

Hurstpierpoint map K3
(Country Houses Association Ltd)

Elizabethan E-shaped house, dating from 1593.

Location: Between Hassocks and Hurstpierpoint (B2116) – off New Way Lane.
Station: Hassocks (1 m).
Opening Times: May to Sept—Weds & Thurs 2–5. Last entry 4.30. Adm £1.50, Chd 50p. Free car park. No dogs admitted.

DENMANS

Fontwell map J3 &
Telephone: Eastergate (0243) 542808
(Mrs J. H. Robinson)

Unique 20th century walled garden extravagantly planted for overall, all-year interest in form, colour and texture; areas of glass for tender species. John Brookes School of Garden Design at Clock House, short courses throughout the season.

Location: Between Arundel and Chichester; turn off A27 into Denmans Lane (W of Fontwell racecourse).
Station: Barnham (2 m).
Opening Times: Open daily throughout the year including all Bank Holidays except Christmas Day and Boxing Day 9–5. Coaches by appointment. Adm £1.95, Chd £1, OAPs £1.70. Groups of 15 or more £1.55. Plant centre. The Country Shop. No dogs. National Gardens Scheme.
Refreshments: Tea & shop open 10–5.

GOODWOOD HOUSE 🏛

Chichester map J3
Telephone: Chichester (0243) 774107
(Duke of Richmond)

Bought by the first Duke of Richmond (son of King Charles II and a French female spy!) and home of the Dukes of Richmond ever since, Goodwood House is filled with the treasures collected by all ten Dukes. They include Canaletto's first London paintings, snuff boxes, tapestries, family portraits by Van Dyck, Kneller, Lely, Reynolds, etc; French commodes (!) and a collection of Sèvres porcelain bought by the Third Duke when (a very bad) British Ambassador at Versailles. There are royal relics, Napoleonic booty and the bits and pieces inevitable after a family has stayed put for 300 years. Chambers, then Wyatt, enlarged the House to hold these Collections. Country Park near the Racecourse on crest of South Downs. Pleasure flights available from the Goodwood Aerodrome together with flying instruction to top standards. Dressage Championships (National & International) and other events in Goodwood Park. Glorious Goodwood Racecourse.

Location: 3½ m NE of Chichester, approach roads A283 & A286, A27. Aerodrome 1 m from House.
Opening Times: Easter Sun & Mon then May 4 to Sept 28—Suns & Mons (except June 14, and event days, prospective visitors should check these dates before setting out); also Tues, Weds & Thurs in Aug, 2–5. Large free car park for visitors to House during open hours; House suitable for wheelchairs (no steps); a wheelchair available; Goodwood souvenirs and prints for sale. For all information & group rates contact the House Secretary. Goodwood House, Chichester, West Sussex, PO18 0PX.
Refreshments: Teas in one of the State Rooms for pre-booked parties (min 20); unbooked teas for individuals and families on days when no evening function, or tea and biscuits at The Goodwood Park Hotel Golf and Country Club at the Park Gate (east).

HAMMERWOOD PARK 🏛

nr East Grinstead map K3
Telephone: East Grinstead (0342) 850594, Facsimile: 850864
(David Pinnegar, Esq)

HAMMERWOOD PARK CELEBRATES ITS BI-CENTENARY THIS YEAR with the completion of one of the most ambitious trompe-l'oeil decoration schemes of this century in the staircase hall. Built in 1792, the house was the first work of Latrobe, the architect of The White House and The Capitol, Washington D.C., U.S.A Set in Reptonesque parkland on the edge of Ashdown Forest, the house is an early example of Greek Revival. In 1982 David Pinnegar purchased the house as a near ruin from the pop-group Led Zeppelin. A decade of award winning restoration works has been completed. Just one room remains spectacularly derelict. Various collections include photographica, musical instruments, nurseries, and a copy of the Elgin Marbles. Guided tours by the family, luscious cream teas and musical evenings bring the house to life.

Location: 3½ m E of East Grinstead on A264 Tunbridge Wells; 1 m W of Holtye.
Opening Times: Easter Mon to end Sept—Weds, Sats & Bank Holiday Mons 2–5.30. Guided tour starts just after 2. Coaches (21 seats or more) by appointment. School groups welcome. Adm House and Park – excluding July & Aug: Adults £3, Chd £1.50. July & Aug £3.50, Chd £1.50, OAP £3.
Refreshments: Luscious cream teas in the Elgin Room.

HEASELANDS

Haywards Heath   map K3
(R. D. Kleinwort, Esq)

Over 30 acres of garden with flowering shrubs and trees; water gardens; woodland; small collection of waterfowl.

Location: 1 m SW of Haywards Heath Hospital on A273 to Burgess Hill.
Station: Haywards Heath (1 m).
Opening Times: GARDEN ONLY: Parties of 15 or more by appointment from May 1 to June 12 and Oct for Autumn colour except at weekends and Bank Hols. Telephone: (0444) 458084. Adm £2, Chd 50p. In aid of *National Gardens Scheme*. No dogs.
Refreshments: Available.

HIGH BEECHES GARDENS 🏛

Handcross   map K3
Telephone: Handcross (0444) 400589
(High Beeches Gardens Conservation Trust)

Twenty acres of enchanting woodland valley gardens, planted with Magnolias, Camellias, Rhododendrons, and Azaleas, for Spring. In Autumn, this is one of the most brilliant gardens for leaf colour, superbly landscaped with Maples, Liquidambers, Amelanchiers and Nyssas. Gentians, Primulas, and Iris are naturalised, with Royal Fern and Gunnera in the Water Gardens. There are four acres of Wildflower Meadows, with cowslips and many Orchids.

Location: 1 m E of A23 at Handcross, on B2110.
Opening Times: GARDENS ONLY. Easter Mon to June 27, and Sept 5 to Oct 31, daily 1–5 except Weds & Suns. EVENTS. Mon Apr 20, Daffodil day, 10–5. Mon May 4, Wine Tasting 10–5. Mon May 25, Plant Sale, 10–5. Traditional Haymaking, Aug 16, 11–6. Autumn Event for Marie Curie Cancer Care, Sun Oct 18. Adm £2, accompanied Chd free. £3 for guided groups, by appointment, at any time.
Refreshments: Homemade lunches and teas on Event Days only, or by appointment for Groups.

LEONARDSLEE GARDENS

Horsham   map K3
(The Loder Family)

One of the most beautiful gardens in the country. Fantastic setting of natural valley with 6 lakes. Famous for camellias & magnolias in April, glorious rhododendrons and azaleas in May, tranquil Summer foliage; brilliant Autumn tints. Rock garden, Bonsai exhibition, Alpine house. Wallabies, Deer parks. Souvenirs & plants for sale.

Location: In Lower Beeding at junction of A279 & A281: 5 m SE of Horsham or 3 m SW of Handcross at bottom of M23.
Opening Times: Apr 17 to June 30; every day 10–6. July to Oct; Mon to Fri 2–6, Sat, Sun 10–6. Adm: May £3.50 (May Suns & Hol Mons £4). Chd £2. Apr, June & Oct £3. July to Sept £2.50, Chd £1. No dogs please.
Refreshments: Licensed Restaurant and Tea Room.

MALT HOUSE

Chithurst, nr Midhurst   map J3
Telephone: Rogate (0730) 821433
(Mr & Mrs Graham Ferguson)

Approximately 4 acres; flowering shrubs including exceptional rhododendrons and azaleas, leading to 60 acres of lovely woodland walks.

Location: 3½ m W of Midhurst via A272, turn N to Chithurst cont 1½ m; or via A3, 2 m S of Liphook turn SE to Milland and Chithurst.
Opening Times: GARDEN ONLY. Suns—Apr 26 to May 31; Bank Hol Mons; May 4 & 25, 2–6. Adm £1, Chd 50p. *In aid of National Gardens Scheme.* Also open by appointment for parties. Plants for sale.
Refreshments: Tea and biscuits.

NEWTIMBER PLACE

Newtimber   map K3
Telephone: Hurstpierpoint (0273) 833104
(His Honour & Mrs John Clay)

Moated house—Etruscan style wall paintings.

Location: Off A281 between Poynings and Pyecombe.
Opening Times: May to Aug—Thurs 2–5. Adm £1.50.

NYMANS GARDEN, The National Trust 🌼

Handcross   map K3   ♿
Telephone: Handcross 400321 or 400002

Extensive garden, partly enclosed by walls, with exceptional collection of rare trees, shrubs and plants, herbaceous borders, bulbs. Exhibition on the history of the garden.

Location: At Handcross just off London/Brighton M23/A23.
Opening Times: Apr 1 to end Oct—Daily (except Mons & Fris) and open B.H. Mon and Good Friday 11–7 or sunset if earlier. Last adm 1 hour before closing. Adm £3. Chd half price. Parties of 15 or more by prior arrangement with Head Gardener. No dogs. Wheelchair provided. Shop and exhibition, same days as garden 12–6.
Refreshments: Teas.

PARHAM HOUSE AND GARDENS 🏠

Pulborough map J3
Telephone: Storrington (0903) 742021

Beautiful Elizabethan House with important collection of Elizabethan and Stuart portraits, fine furniture, carpets, tapestries and a profusion of rare needlework. Fresh flowers in each room. Eleven acres of gardens including a 4 acre walled garden with lake, fine statuary, brick and turf maze. New for 1992 – a vegetable garden or pôtager. Also new plant sales shop.

Location: A283 Storrington/Pulborough road.
Opening Times: Weds, Thurs, Sun and Bank Hol Mon afternoons from Easter Sun to first Sun in Oct. Gardens 1–6, House 2–6 (last adm 5.30). Adm (1991 rates, 1992 not yet available) House & Gardens £3.20, OAP £2.50, Chd £1.50. Group rates for both guided (Weds & Thurs mornings by arrangement) and unguided visits available on application. Gardens only £1.50, Chd 75p. Church. Shop. Picnic area close to house. Large car park. Access for disabled, garden only, 1 wheelchair available.
Refreshments: Self service teas in Big Kitchen. Some outside seating. Bookings and all enquiries to Administrator.

PETWORTH HOUSE, The National Trust 🦋

Petworth map J3 ♿
Telephone: Petworth 42207

Rebuilt 1688-96 by the 6th Duke of Somerset. Later reconstruction by Salvin, in large and beautiful deer park, landscaped by 'Capability' Brown and painted by Turner. 14th century chapel. Important collection of paintings, sculpture and furniture.

Location: In centre of Petworth 5½ m E of Midhurst.
Opening Times: Apr 1 to end Oct daily (except Mon and Fri) (open Good Friday and Bank Hol Mon, *closed* Tues following) 1–5.30 (last adm 5). Adm £3.80, Chd half price. Pre-booked parties of 15 or more welcome on Weds, Thurs & Sats only, £3. No dogs in House or Pleasure Grounds. Car park for visitors to House during open hours, 800 yds. Shop. Wheelchairs provided. No prams or pushchairs in showrooms. Deer Park open daily all year–8–sunset, adm free (*closed* June 26, 27, 28). Car park for Park only on A283, 1½ m N of Petworth. Dogs must be kept under control.
Refreshments: Light lunches 12.30–2.30, and teas 3–5 (last orders 4.30) in House on open days. Shop 1–5.

ST MARY'S HOUSE AND GARDENS – *See page 189*

SACKVILLE COLLEGE

East Grinstead map K4
Telephone: East Grinstead (0342) 323279/326561
(Patron Earl De La Warr)

Jacobean Almshouses founded in 1609. Common Room, Dining Hall, Chapel and Study. Original furniture.

Location: High Street, East Grinstead off A22.
Opening Times: June 1 to Aug 31 daily 2–5. Adm £1.25, Chd 65p. Parties by arrangement Apr to Oct with teas available to order at time of booking.

STANDEN, The National Trust 🦋

East Grinstead map K3
Telephone: East Grinstead (0342) 23029

Built 1894 by Philip Webb. William Morris wallpapers and textiles. Period furniture, paintings. Hillside garden with fine views across Medway Valley.

Location: 1½ m S of East Grinstead signposted from the Turners Hill road (B2110).
Station: East Grinstead (2 m).
Opening Times: Apr 1 to end Oct, Wed to Sun (incl Good Friday) 1.30–5.30 (last adm 5). Open Bank Holiday Mon (*closed* Tues following). Access may be restricted at busy times. Adm House and Garden £4. Garden only £2. Chd half-price. Pre-booked parties £2.50 Weds, Thurs & Fris only; telephone Administrator. *Dogs admitted to car park & woodland walks only.* Wheelchairs provided; disabled drivers may park near house with prior permission from administrator. Shop.
Refreshments: Light lunches and teas served from 12–5.30, last admission 5.

STANSTED PARK – *See page 189*

TELEGRAPH HOUSE

North Marden, Nr Chichester map J3
Telephone: (0730) 825 206
(Mr & Mrs David Gault)

1 acre enclosed chalk garden 700 asl; chalk-tolerant shrubs, shrub roses, herbaceous plants; 1 m avenue of copper beeches; walks through 150-acre yew wood; lovely views. House (not shown) in small park, built on site of semaphore keeper's cottage.

Location: North Marden, 9 m NW of Chichester. Entrance on B2141. From Petersfield to South Harting for 2 m from Chichester via A286 for 4 m N of Lavant turn W on to B2141.
Opening Times: Sats, Suns June 20, 21; July 18, 19 (2–6); also by appointment May to Aug (2–5). Adm £1.50 Chd 75p. Wheelchairs. *In aid of the National Gardens Scheme.*
Refreshments: Teas.

WAKEHURST PLACE GARDEN, The National Trust 🦋

nr Ardingly map K3 ♿
Telephone: Ardingly (0444) 892701
(Administered by Royal Botanic Gardens, Kew)

A wealth of exotic plant species including many fine specimens of trees and shrubs. Picturesque watercourse linking several ponds and lakes. Heath garden and rock walk.

Location: 1½ m NW of Ardingly on B2028.
Opening Times: All the year–Daily Nov to end Jan, 10–4; Feb & Oct, 10–5; Mar, 10–6; Apr to end of Sept, 10–7. Last adm ½ hour before closing. *Closed Christmas Day & New Year's Day.* Adm £3, Chd 16 and under £1. Reduced rates for students, OAPs and pre-booked parties but prices and opening times may be subject to alteration. Visitors should check with Wakehurst Place for 1992 prices. No dogs. Wheelchairs provided. Exhibition in Mansion. Book shop open, not NT.
Refreshments: Light refreshments.

THE WEALD AND DOWNLAND OPEN AIR MUSEUM

Singleton, nr Chichester map J3
Telephone: Singleton (024 363) 348

Continued on page 190

ST MARY'S HOUSE AND GARDENS

Bramber   map K3
Telephone: Steyning 816205
(Peter Thorogood Esq)

ST. MARY'S HOUSE
Bramber
c. 1470

Magnificent Grade I medieval house, classified as "the best late 15th century timber-framing in Sussex". Rare 16th century painted wall-leather. Fine panelled rooms, including the unique trompe l'oeil 'Painted Room', decorated for the visit of Queen Elizabeth I. Furniture, marquetry, books manuscripts. Charming gardens with Topiary. Teas.

Tourist Board "Warmest Welcome" commendation.

ADMISSION–SEE EDITORIAL REFERENCE

The foundations of St Mary's go back to the 12 century when land at Bramber was granted to the Knights Templar. The present house (c 1470) was re-fashioned by William Waynflete, Bishop of Winchester, founder of Magdalen College, Oxford, and is classified as "the best late 15th century timber-framing in Sussex". Fine panelled rooms, including unique 'Painted Room' decorated for Elizabeth I's visit. The 'King's Room' has connections with Charles II's escape to France in 1651. Also other Royal and historic associations. Rare 16th century painted wall-leather, splendid carved oak fireplaces, massive 'dragon-beam' in the 'Warden's Room', superb marquetry decoration and strapwork doors. Furniture, pictures, manuscripts. Library contains largest private collection of first editions and illustrated books by celebrated 19th century comic poet and artist, Thomas Hood. Victorian Music room, with elaborate medieval Gothic stone fireplaces, added in 1896 by Hon. Algernon Bourke, son of the Earl of Mayo. Sherlock Holmes connection during ownership (1903–13) of Alfred Musgrave. Ring for details of concerts and other events, May to December.

Location: 10 m NW of Brighton in village of Bramber off A283.
Station: Shoreham-by-Sea (4 m). Trains from London (Victoria).
Opening Times: Easter Sun to last Sun in Sept—Suns & Thurs 2–6. Bank Hol Mons 2–6. Also Mons in July, Aug & Sept 2–6. Adm £3.30, OAP £3, Chd £2, **Coach party bookings** daily by prior arrangement from Apr 1 to Oct. Reduced rates for parties £3 (25 or over). Free coach and car parking in grounds.
Refreshments: Morning coffee, homemade afternoon tea in the Music Room. Catering for parties including "Palm Court" teas by arrangement. Seating for 60.

STANSTED PARK

Rowlands Castle   map J3
Telephone: 0705 412265
(Stansted Park Foundation)

This Neo-Wren house with its ancient chapel and walled gardens and arboretum is surrounded by an enchanting forest through which runs the longest beech avenue in the South of England. John Keats describes the interior of the chapel in his Eve of St. Mark. Cricket matches are played in front of the house on most Sundays throughout the season.

Location: Rowlands Castle, 4 m by road; 2 m walking through forest; Westbourne 3 m; Havant 5 m and Chichester 8 m.
Station: Rowlands Castle (2 m).
Opening Times: Easter Sun and Mon then from May to Sept —Suns, Mons & Tues only 2–5. Bus parties by arrangement only. Ample free car parking. Grounds, Chapel, Shop and Tearoom only suitable for disabled at present. Adm £3.50, Chd, OAPs £1.50. Party rate (by prior arrangement). Grounds, Chapel and tearoom and shop only £2, Chd £1, OAPs £2.
Refreshments: Home made cakes and cream teas.

THE WEALD AND DOWNLAND OPEN AIR MUSEUM –

Continued from page 188

The Museum is rescuing and re-erecting historic Buildings from South-East England. The Collection illustrates the history of vernacular architecture in the Weald and Downland area. Exhibits include a Medieval Farmstead, Garden and History of Farming Exhibition centred on Bayleaf Farmhouse (above), a Tudor Market Hall, a 16th century Treadwheel. Farm Buildings include two 18th century Barns and a Granary, a Blacksmith's Forge, Plumber's and Carpenter's Workshops, a Charcoal Burner's Camp and a Village School.

Location: 6 m N of Chichester on A286 just S of Singleton.
Opening Times: Mar 1 to Oct 31 – Daily 11 – 5. Nov 1 to Feb 28 – Weds, Suns and Bank Hols only 11 – 4. Adm charge. Parties by arrangement. (Group rates available.)
Refreshments: Light refreshments during main season.

WEST DEAN GARDENS

nr Chichester   map J3
Telephone: Singleton (0243 63) 301
(The Edward James Foundation)

Extensive garden in a downland setting with specimen trees, 300ft pergola, summer-houses, herbaceous borders, wild garden, extensive walled garden under restoration and Mower museum. Circuit walk (2¼ miles) through parkland and the 45 acre St. Roches Arboretum. House not open to visitors.

Location: 6 m N of Chichester on A286, nr Weald & Downland Open Air Museum.
Opening Times: Mar to Oct incl. – Daily 11 – 6 (last adm 5). Parties by arrangement. Coach & car parking. Sorry no dogs. Adm £2.25, OAPs £2, Chd £1, Parties £1.70 per person.

TYNE & WEAR

GIBSIDE CHAPEL & GROUNDS, The National Trust

Gibside   map H11
Telephone: Consett (0207) 542255

Built to James Paine's design soon after 1760. Outstanding example of Georgian architecture approached along a terrace with an oak avenue.

Location: 6 m SW of Gateshead; 20 m NW of Durham between Rowlands Gill and Burnopfield.
Opening Times: Apr 1 to Oct 31 daily except Mons (open Bank Hol Mons) 11 – 5. Adm to Chapel & Grounds £2, Chd half price. Shop, tea room, picnic area, circular walk.

HYLTON CASTLE

map H11

Heraldic shields and carved figures adorn this splendid castle, shaped like an enormous gatehouse and designed more for comfort than defence. Sir William Hylton built it about 1400 but it was much altered in the 1860s and transformed into a suburban villa. These later additions have since been removed and the castle is a ruin in a parkland setting.

Location: 3¾ m (6 km) west of Sunderland. OS map ref NZ358588.
Opening Times: Good Friday or Apr 1 (whichever is earlier) to Sept 30: Open Daily 10 – 6. Oct 1 to Maundy Thursday or Mar 31 (whichever is earlier): Open Tues to Sun 10 – 4. *Closed* Dec 24 – 26, Jan 1. Adm 75p, Concessions 55p, Chd 40p.

KIRKLEY HALL COLLEGE – SEE NORTHUMBERLAND

SOUTER LIGHTHOUSE, The National Trust

Whitburn   map H11
Telephone: (091) 529 3161

Shore based lighthouse and associated buildings, built in 1871 – the first to be powered by an alternative electric current.

Location: 2½m S of South Shields on A183, 5m N of Sunderland.
Opening Times: Apr 1 to Oct 31 – Daily except Mon (open Bank Holiday Monday) 11 – 5. Last adm 4.30. Adm £2, Chd half price. Pre-booked parties £1.50. Shop, picnic area.
Refreshments: Tea room.

TYNEMOUTH CASTLE AND PRIORY

map H12
Telephone: 091-257 1090

Two saints were buried within the walls of this Benedictine priory, established in the 11th century on the site of an earlier abandoned monastery. Two walls of the presbytery still tower to their full height and the 15th century chantry chapel has a splendid collection of roof bosses. A fortified gatehouse was added during the Border wars, which persuaded Henry VIII to retain the priory as a royal castle after the Dissolution. The headland remained in use for coastal defence until 1956, one restored battery is open to the public.

Location: Tynemouth. OS map ref NZ374695.
Opening Times: Good Friday or Apr 1 (whichever is earlier) to Sept 30: Open Daily 10 – 6. Oct 1 to Maundy Thursday or Mar 31 (whichever is earlier): Open Tues to Sun 10 – 4. *Closed* Dec 24 – 26, Jan 1. Adm £1.10, Concessions 85p, Chd 55p.

WASHINGTON OLD HALL, The National Trust

Washington   map H11
Telephone: Washington (091) 4166879

Jacobean manor house incorporating portions of 12th century house of the Washington family.

Location: In Washington on E side of Ave; 5 m W of Sunderland (2 m from A1); S of Tyne Tunnel, follow signs for Washington New Town District 4 & then village.
Opening Times: Apr 1 to Oct 31 – Daily (except Fri, but open Good Friday) 11 – 5; (last adm 4.30). Adm £1.80; Chd half price. *Parties of 15 or more £1.40 each, by prior arrangement only with the Custodian.* Shop. Dogs in garden only, on leads. Wheelchair access.

WARWICKSHIRE

ARBURY HALL

Nuneaton   map H6   △
Telephone: Nuneaton (0203) 382804
(The Rt Hon the Viscount Daventry)

Photograph English Life Publications

16th century Elizabethan House, gothicized late 18th century, pictures, period furniture etc. Park and landscape gardens. Arbury has been the home of the Newdegate family since the 16th century. For a country house the Gothic architecture is unique, the original Elizabethan house being Gothicised by Sir Roger Newdigate between 1750 and 1800, under the direction of Sanderson Miller, Henry Keene, and Couchman of Warwick. Beautiful plaster ceilings, pictures and fine specimens of period furniture, china and glass. Fine stable block with central doorway by Wren. Arbury Hall is situated in very large grounds and is about 1½ miles from any main road. Excellent carriage drives lined with trees. George Eliot's "Cheveral Manor".

Location: 2 m SW of Nuneaton off B4102.
Opening Times: Suns from Easter Sun to end of Sept. Bank Hol Mons. Gardens 2–6, Hall 2–5.30 (last adm 5). Adm Hall and Gardens £3, Chd £1.60, Gardens & Park £1.60, Chd 80p. The Arbury dining room can also be available for exclusive luncheons and dinner functions. Organised parties most days (25 or over) special terms by prior arrangement with Administrator. School parties also welcome. Free car park.
Refreshments: Available on all open days. Set meals arranged for parties.

BADDESLEY CLINTON, The National Trust

Solihull   map H6   &
Telephone: Lapworth (0564) 783294

A romantically sited medieval moated manor house, with 120 acres, dating back to the 14th century and little changed since 1634.

Location: ¾ m W of A41 Warwick to Birmingham Road, nr Chadwick End; 7½ m NW of Warwick; 15 m SE of Birmingham.
Station: Lapworth (2 m) (not Suns).
Opening Times: Mar 4 to end of Sept–Weds to Suns & Bank Hol Mons 2–6. Grounds, shop and restaurant open from 12.30. *Closed Good Fri;* Oct–Weds to Suns 12.30–4.30. Last admissions 30 mins before closing. Adm £3.50, Chd £1.75, grounds only £2. Family tickets £9.60. Coach parties (weekdays only) by prior arrangement only. No prams or pushchairs in the house. No dogs. Wheelchair available. Shop.
NB: Timed tickets are issued for entry into the house.
Refreshments: Lunches from 12.30 and teas.

CHARLECOTE PARK, The National Trust

Warwick   map H6   △   &
Telephone: Stratford-upon-Avon (0789) 470277

Originally built by the Lucy family, 1550s. Refurbished 1830s in Elizabethan Revival style. Deer park.

Location: 5 m E of Stratford-upon-Avon on the N side of B4086.
Opening Times: Apr to end Oct–Daily (except Mon & Thurs) House: 11–1 & 2–5.30, Park 11–6 (*Closed* Good Friday, open Bank Hol Mons 11–6). Last adm to house 5 (*closed* 1–2). Parties (including schools) by prior arrangement only. Evening guided tours for pre-booked parties Tues, May to Sept 7.30–9.30. Full price for evening visits (including NT members). Adm £3.40, Chd £1.70. Family tickets £9.40. No dogs. Wheelchairs provided. Shop.
Refreshments: Refreshments in Orangery.

COUGHTON COURT, The National Trust

Alcester map H6
Telephone: Alcester (0789) 762435

Impressive central gatehouse dating from 1530. Two mid-Elizabethan half-timbered wings. Jacobite relics. The home of the Throckmorton family since 1409. Tranquil lake and riverside walk.

Location: 2 m N of Alcester just E of A435.
Opening Times: Apr—Sats, Suns 1.30–5.30, Easter Sat to Thurs 1.30–5. May to end Sept—Daily except Mon & Fri, 1.30–5.30, but open Bank Hol Mons 12.30–5.30. Oct—Sats & Suns 1.30–5. Also open Oct 27–29 (half-term) also Nov 5. Adm £3, Chd £1.50. Family ticket £8. Parties by prior arrangement. Shop. Limited access for wheelchairs. Dogs on leads in grounds.

FARNBOROUGH HALL, The National Trust

nr Banbury map H5
(The National Trust)

Mid 18th century house incorporates fine plasterworks and ancient sculpture. ¾ mile terrace walk feature temples and obelisk.

Location: 6 m N of Banbury; ½ m W of A423.
Opening Times: April to end of Sept—Weds and Sats & May 3 & 4, 2–6. Adm House, Grounds & Terrace Walk £2.50, Garden and Terrace Walk £1.50, 2–6. Terrace Walk only 90p (Thurs & Fris). Chd half-price. (Last adm ½ hr before closing). *No reduction for parties.* Parties by prior written arrangement only. Dogs in grounds only, on leads. No indoor photography. NB: The tenants are responsible for the showing arrangements.

HONINGTON HALL

Shipston-on-Stour map M5
Telephone: Shipston-on-Stour (0608) 61434
(Sir John Wiggin, Bart.)

Originally built by the Parker family in 1680. Contains fine 18th century plasterwork.

Location: 10 m S of Stratford-on-Avon; ½ m E of A3400.
Opening Times: June, July, Aug—Weds & Bank Hol Mons 2.30–5. Parties at other times by appointment. Adm £2, Chd 50p.

KENILWORTH CASTLE

map H6
Telephone: (0926) 52078
(English Heritage)

One of the grandest ruins in England, this castle was made famous by Sir Walter Scott. Gone now is the great lake that once surrounded it, but still standing is the huge Norman keep with walls nearly 20ft (6m) thick in places. Inside the encircling walls built by King John are the remains of John of Gaunt's chapel and great hall, the Earl of Leicester's stables and gatehouse. The most splendid royal occasion took place in 1575 when Queen Elizabeth I was entertained lavishly by the Earl with music and dancing, fireworks and hunting, for 19 days.

Location: West side of Kenilworth. OS map ref SP278723.
Opening Times: Good Friday or Apr 1 (whichever is earlier) to Sept 30 daily 10–6. Oct 1 to Maundy Thursday or Mar 31 (whichever is earlier) Tues—Sun 10–4. *Closed* Dec 24–26, Jan 1. Adm £1.50, Concessions £1.10, Chd 75p.

THE GRAMMAR SCHOOL

Church Street, Stratford-upon-Avon map H6

Present-day schoolboys assist your visit to this picturesque half-timbered Guildhall (1417) which includes Shakespeare's schoolroom.

Location: Church Street, Stratford-upon-Avon between the Guild Chapel and almshouses.
Opening Times: Occasionally at weekends and during school holidays or by appointment – details from the Guild School Association. Adm charge.

LORD LEYCESTER HOSPITAL

Warwick map H6 △
Telephone: Warwick (0926) 492797
(The Governors of Lord Leycester Hospital)

In 1100 the chapel of St. James was built over the West Gate of Warwick and became the centre for the Guilds established by Royal Charter in 1383. In 1571 Robert Dudley, Earl of Leycester, founded his Hospital for twelve 'poor' persons in the buildings of the Guilds, which had been dispersed in 1546. The Hospital has been run ever since for retired or disabled ex-Servicemen and their wives. The buildings have been recently restored to their original condition including the Great Hall of King James the Guildhall (museum), the Chaplain's Hall (Queen's Own Hussars Regimental Museum) and the Brethren's Kitchen.

Location: W gate of Warwick (A46).
Station: Warwick (³/₄ m).
Opening Times: All the year—Mons to Sats 10–5.30 (summer) 10–4 (winter). Last admission 15 mins earlier. *Closed Suns, Good Fri & Christmas Day.* Adm £2, Chd (under 14) 50p, OAPs and students £1. Free car park.
Refreshments: (Easter to Oct) morning coffee, light lunches, afternoon teas.

PACKWOOD HOUSE – *See page 194*

RAGLEY HALL

Alcester map H6
Telephone: Alcester (0789) 762090 or 762455
(The Earl and Countess of Yarmouth)

Built in 1680. Superb baroque plasterwork, fine paintings, china, furniture and works of art including the mural 'The Temptation'. Gardens, park and lake. Farm and woodland trails, lakeside picnic areas. Superb Adventure Wood playground and maze for children.

Location: 2 m SW of Alcester on Birmingham/Alcester/Evesham Road (A435); 8 m from Stratford-upon-Avon; 20 m from Birmingham.
Opening Times: Apr 18 to Sept 27. PARK & GARDENS: Open daily 10–6 (except Mon & Fri, but open Bank Holiday Mons). HOUSE: Open daily except Mon and Fri 12–5 (open Bank Holiday Monday). ADMISSION: (1991 prices) HOUSE, GARDENS & PARK (includes Adventure Wood and Woodland Trails) £4, Chd, OAPs £3 and Group Rate adults £3. GARDEN & PARK ONLY: £3, Chd/OAPs £2. Free car park. Dogs welcome on leads in Park and on Woodland Trails, not in House, Gardens or Adventure Wood.
Refreshments: Licensed Cafeteria open daily except Mon and Fri. Please telephone for group reservation of Restaurant. Refreshments available in park.
Advance Bookings: (at any time of the year). Coach parties welcome by arrangement. Lunches and teas – parties please write for menus. Private dinner parties for any number up to 150 can be arranged. For further information please contact: The Business Manager, Ragley Hall, Alcester, Warwickshire B49 5NJ. Telephone: Alcester (0789) 762090.

PACKWOOD HOUSE, The National Trust

Hockley Heath　map H6
Telephone: Lapworth (0564) 782024

Elizabethan house with mid-17th century additions. Tapestry, needlework, Carolean formal garden, and yew garden of c. 1650 representing the Sermon on the Mount.

Location: 2 m E of Hockley Heath (which is on A3400) 11 m SE of Birmingham. *Stations: Lapworth (1½ m); Dorridge (2 m).*
Opening Times: Apr to end of Sept—Weds to Suns & Bank Hol Mons 2–6. *Closed* Good Friday. Oct—Wed to Suns 12.30–4.30. Last adm ½ hr before closing. Adm £2.80, Chd £1.90. Family tickets £7.70. Garden only £1.90. Parties by prior written arrangement only. No dogs. No prams in House. Wheelchair access to part of garden & ground floor (difficult).

RAGLEY HALL – *See page 193*

SHAKESPEARE'S BIRTHPLACE

Stratford-upon-Avon　map H6　　△　&

The half-timbered house where Shakespeare was born, containing many rare Shakespearian exhibits, also BBC Television Shakespeare Costume Exhibition.

Location: Henley Street.
Opening Times: Jan 1 to Feb 28, 29 & Nov 1 to Dec 31: weekdays 9.30–4.30, Suns 10.30–4.30. Mar 1 to Oct 31: weekdays 9–6, Suns 10–6. Last admission 30 mins before closing time. Adm incl Exhibition £2.40, Chd £1.

ANNE HATHAWAY'S COTTAGE

Stratford-upon-Avon　map H6　　△

The picturesque thatched home of Anne Hathaway before her marriage to Shakespeare. Attractive garden and Shakespeare Tree Garden. Refreshments all year.

Location: Shottery (1¼ m).
Opening Times: Jan 1 to Feb 28, 29 & Nov 1 to Dec 31: weekdays 9.30–4.30, Suns 10.30–4.30. Mar 1 to Oct 31: weekdays 9–6, Suns 10–6. Last adm 30 mins before closing time. Adm £2, Chd 90p.

HALL'S CROFT

Stratford-upon-Avon　map H6　　△　&

A fine Tudor house complete with period furniture and walled garden where Shakespeare's daughter Susanna and Dr John Hall lived.

Location: Old Town.
Opening Times: Jan 1 to Feb 28, 29 & Nov 1 to Dec 31: weekdays 10–4.30, Suns 1.30–4.30. Mar 1 to Oct 31: weekdays 9.30–5.30, Suns 10.30–5.30. Last admission 30 mins before closing time. Adm £1.60, Chd 70p.

THE SHAKESPEARE BIRTHPLACE TRUST PROPERTIES

All the properties are open daily except on Good Friday morning, Christmas Eve, Christmas Day, Boxing Day and the morning of Jan 1st. For those needing transport there is a regular guided bus tour service all the year round connecting the town properties with Anne Hathaway's Cottage and Mary Arden's House.

THE SHAKESPEARIAN PROPERTIES

STRATFORD-UPON-AVON

5 historic houses associated with **William Shakespeare** and his family **open all year round.**

Besides the world famous attractions of **Shakespeare's Birthplace** and **Anne Hathaway's Cottage** there are also **The Shakespeare Countryside Museum at Mary Arden's House,** Wilmcote. Tudor farmstead home of Shakespeare's mother plus turn-of-the-century Glebe Farmhouse. Exhibits illustrating country life over 400 years. Gipsy caravans, dovecote, duck pond, field walk, and daily displays of falconry. Refreshments and picnic area. Ideally allow 2 hours.

Hall's Croft. A delightful Elizabethan town house, once the home of Dr. Hall, Shakespeare's physician son-in-law. Exceptional furniture and paintings. 17th century-style doctor's consulting room and exhibition about medical life in Shakespeare's time. Lovely secluded garden. Refreshments.

Shakespeare's Birthplace

New Place. Site and grounds of Shakespeare's last home, with colourful Elizabethan-style knott garden, provides quiet oasis in the heart of Stratford.
Nash's House adjoining contains fine Tudor furniture.

Single admission fees available but particularly good value offered by **3 Property Town Heritage Trail** or **5 Property Inclusive Tickets**

Anne Hathaway's Cottage

See editorial for opening times and admission fees

NEW PLACE/NASH'S HOUSE

Stratford-upon-Avon   map H6   △   &

Foundations of Shakespeare's last home, preserved in an Elizabethan garden setting with Nash's House adjoining which is furnished in period style.

Location: Chapel Street.
Opening Times: Jan 1 to Feb 28, 29 & Nov 1 to Dec 31: weekdays 10–4.30, Suns 1.30–4.30. Mar 1 to Oct 31: weekdays 9.30–5.30, Suns 10.30–5.30. Last admission 30 mins before closing time. Adm £1.60, Chd 70p.

THE SHAKESPEARE COUNTRYSIDE MUSEUM at MARY ARDEN'S HOUSE

Stratford-upon-Avon   map H6   △   &

The Tudor farmhouse where Shakespeare's mother lived, with a farming and Shakespeare countryside museum now extended to include the adjoining Glebe Farm. Interesting dovecote. Rural Crafts. Daily falconry displays. Light refreshments all year.

Location: Wilmcote (3½ m).
Opening Times: Jan 1 to Feb 28, 29 & Nov 1 to Dec 31: weekdays 10–4.30, Suns 1.30–4.30. Mar 1 to Oct 31: weekdays 9.30–5.30, Suns 10.30–5.30. Last admission 30 mins before closing time. Adm £2.75, Chd £1.10. Also, at this property only: Family ticket £6.50, admitting 2 adults and 2/3 children. Inclusive ticket admitting to all five properties: £6.50, Chd £3. Shakespeare's Town Heritage Trail. Ticket includes combined admission to the three town Properties (Birthplace, New Place and Hall's Croft) and a self-guiding Town Heritage Trail leaflet £4.50, Chd £2.
Educational Groups: For admission to single properties all organised school (primary and secondary) parties will be admitted at the normal children's rates and all student groups will be admitted at the normal adult rates. The Trust also offers special inclusive visit permits as follows: Inclusive admission permit for accompanied school parties £2.75 per pupil. Inclusive admission permit for organised college and university student parties £4 per student. One member of staff to each 10 pupils/students is admitted free. Large groups may wish to divide into parties of 10 or more but all groups must be accompanied by staff throughout.

UPTON HOUSE, The National Trust

Edge Hill   map H5   &
Telephone: Edge Hill (0295 87) 266

17th century house containing one of the National Trust's finest collections of paintings and porcelain. Tapestries and 18th century furniture. Beautiful terraced garden descending to lakes and bog garden in deep valley.

Location: 1 m S of Edge Hill; 7 m NW of Banbury on the Stratford Road (A422).
Opening Times: Apr, and Oct: Sat, Sun & Bank Hol Mon 2–6. May to end Sept: Sat to Wed 2–6. Last adm to House 5.30. Adm House & Garden £3.50, Chd £1.00. Family ticket £9.60. Garden only £2. Parties by prior arrangement with the Administrator. Motorized buggy with driver available for access to/from lower garden, manned by volunteers of the Banbury Association. No indoor photography. Wheelchair available. Wheelchair access ground floor only.
Refreshments: Tearoom in House.

WARWICK CASTLE   🏛

Warwick   map H6   △
Telephone: Warwick (0926) 495421

WARWICK CASTLE
The finest mediaeval castle in England

R ising majestically from the banks of the River Avon, Warwick Castle spans one thousand years of history. The site was selected and fortified by William the Conqueror in 1068 and to this day Warwick Castle remains the finest mediaeval castle in England with commanding Battlements and Towers, Dungeon and Torture Chamber.

The magnificently appointed State Rooms contain a wealth of historic treasures and in the former Private Apartments there is a unique award-winning exhibition by Madame Tussaud's entitled 'A Royal Weekend Party 1898'.

The castle is set in 100 acres of parkland landscaped by 'Capability' Brown, and is a delight in all seasons. The magnificently restored Conservatory with views across the Pageant Field and River Avon, plus the faithfully recreated Victorian Rose Garden – one of many evocative attractions.

Warwick Castle offers an unforgettable day out for all the family.

Open every day
except Christmas Day

Tel: (0926) 495421

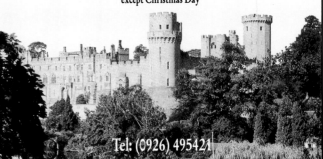

One of the finest medieval castles, standing on a steep rock cliff beside the River Avon, 8 miles from Stratford. The present castle is a fine example of 14th century fortification with towers and dungeons open to visitors all the year round. The State Rooms contain a magnificent collection of pictures by Rubens, Van Dyck and other Masters. Surrounded by acres of parkland landscaped by 'Capability' Brown, gardens where peacocks roam freely and a river island.

Location: In the centre of Warwick.
Stations: Warwick (½ m); Leamington Spa (2 m).
Opening Times: Open daily (except Christmas Day) all year. Mar 1 to Oct 31–Daily 10–5.30. Nov 1 to Feb 29–Daily 10–4.30. Adm charges not available at time of going to press. Car park.
Refreshments: Licensed restaurant & cafeteria in the Castle. Medieval Banquets.

WEST MIDLANDS

ASTON HALL

Birmingham   map H6   △
Telephone: 021-327 0062
(Birmingham City Council)

A fine Jacobean house built 1615-35, with many rooms furnished as period settings. Home of the Holte family for 200 years, with outstanding Jacobean plasterwork, panelling and great staircase. Long Gallery, paintings, tapestry and furniture of 17-19th centuries. James Watt the Younger lived here. Summer events, bi-ennial Candlelight evenings. Pre-booked parties by arrangement. Admission is free. A branch of Birmingham Museums and Art Galleries.

Location: 2½ m from centre of city. Entrance for coaches at Frederick Road; entrance for cars at Witton Lane.
Station: Aston (³/4 m).
Opening Times: Mar 28 to Nov 3 1992 – Daily 2–5. Adm free. School parties can arrange to visit throughout the year.

BADDESLEY CLINTON – SEE UNDER WARWICKSHIRE

BLAKESLEY HALL

Birmingham   map M6
Telephone: 021-783 2193
(Birmingham City Council)

A timber-framed yeoman's farmhouse c.1590 carefully furnished to an inventory of the period. Built for Richard Smallbroke, a leading merchant in late 16th century Birmingham, with original wall paintings and diminutive Long Gallery. Also contains displays of building methods and 17th century pottery from a single excavation. In walking distance of Yardley Village (medieval church, trust school, Georgian cottages). Pre-booked parties by arrangement. Summer events. Admission is free. A branch of Birmingham Museums and Art Gallery.

Location: 3 m from city centre; entrance in Blakesley Road.
Stations: Stechford (³/4 m); Birmingham New Street. Buses: 16 & 17, 11 on Outer Circle.
Opening Times: Mar 28 to Nov 3 1992 – Daily 2–5. Adm free. School parties can arrange to visit throughout the year.

CASTLE BROMWICH HALL GARDENS

Birmingham   map H6   &
Telephone: 021-749 4100

A vision of England more than 250 years ago. The ongoing restoration, started six years ago, now provides visitors, academics and horticulturists the opportunity of seeing a unique collection of historic plants, shrubs, medicinal and culinary herbs and a fascinating plant collection. The Gardens are a cultural gem and an example of the Formal English Garden of the 18th century.

Location: 4 m E of Birmingham, 1 m from exit 5 of the M6 (exit Northbound only).
Opening Times: Mainly Apr to Sept (others by arrangement), Mon to Thur 1.30–4.30 *(closed* Friday). Sat, Sun, Public Holidays 2–6. Adm £2, concessions for seniors and Chd. Guided tours Wed, Sat, Sun. Gift shop.
Refreshments: Coffee shop, but also light meals by arrangement.

HAGLEY HALL – *See page 197*

PERROTT'S FOLLY

Edgbaston   map G6
(The Perrott's Folly Company – a registered charity)

Perrott's Folly, 'Birmingham's most eccentric building' is a striking 96ft high Tudor style tower with seven floors, built 1758.

Location: Waterworks Road, Edgbaston. Situated 2m W of Birmingham city centre at the junction of Waterworks Road and Monument Road (which leads off the A456).
Opening Times: Easter to Sept: Suns, Bank Hol Mons 2–5. Adm £1.50, Chd free.

RYTON GARDENS

Ryton-on-Dunsmore   map H6
(Henry Doubleday Research Association)

10 acres organic demonstration gardens open to the public every day for small admission charge. Displays include herb garden, wildlife garden, composting displays, bee garden, rose garden, special needs garden.

Location: Coventry 5 m B4129, off A45.
Opening Times: £3 adults with concessions. Parties £2 (by previous arrangement). Car parking. Suitable for disabled (1 wheelchair available). Shop on site. Picnic area. Guided tours for pre-arranged parties.
Refreshments: Organic wholefood cafe listed in Good Food Guide.

HAGLEY HALL

nr Stourbridge   map G6
Telephone: Hagley (0562) 882408
(The Viscount & Viscountess Cobham)

The last of the great Palladian Houses, designed by Sanderson Miller and completed in 1760. The House contains the finest example of Rococo plasterwork by Francesco Vassali, and a unique collection of 18th century furniture and family portraits including works by Van Dyck, Reynolds and Lely. Teas in the House. Receptions and private dinner parties by arrangement throughout the year.

Location: Just off A456 Birmingham to Kidderminster; 12 m from Birmingham within easy reach M5 (exit 3 or 4), M6 or M42.
Stations: Hagley (1 m) (not Suns); Stourbridge Junction (2 m).
Opening Times: From Jan 2 to Mar 1 daily except Sats. Thereafter only Apr 19, 20, 21, May 24, 25, 26, Aug 30, 31, Sept 1, 2–5. Open for pre-booked parties by arrangement. For further details, please telephone Hagley (0562) 882408.
Refreshments: Tea available in the House.

WIGHTWICK MANOR, The National Trust

Wolverhampton   map G6   △   ⑤
Telephone: (0902) 761108

Strongly influenced by William Morris the interiors of this late 19th century house include Morris wallpapers and fabrics, Kempe glass, de Morgan ware and a connoisseurs' collection of pre-Raphaelite paintings. Victorian/Edwardian gardens, terraces & pools.

Location: 3 m W of Wolverhampton, up Wightwick Bank (A454).
Opening Times: House: Mar to Dec 31: Thur and Sat 2.30–5. Also open Bank Holiday Sun and Mon 2.30–5.30 (Ground floor only, no guided tours). Also open for pre-booked parties Weds & Thurs, also special evening tours. *Closed* Dec 25, 26. School visits on Wed & Thurs, contact Administrator for details. Adm £3.50. Chd half price. Students £1.75. Gardens only £1.50. *Parties must book in advance (no reductions).* Owing to the fragile nature of their contents and the requirements of conservation, some rooms cannot always be shown. Tours of the house will vary, therefore, during the year. Dogs in garden only, on leads.

WILTSHIRE

AVEBURY MANOR & GARDEN

Nr Marlborough   map H4

Opening Times: The Manor is open subject to restoration work, please telephone 06723 388 (answer phone from March) to check opening times. Garden: Apr 1 to Nov 1 daily except Mon & Thurs 11–5.30. Last adm 5. Adm Garden £2, Chd £1.30. Parties £1.80, Chd £1.10. House and garden: £3, Chd £2.30. Parties £2.80, Chd £2.

AVEBURY MUSEUM

map H4
Telephone: (06723) 250

No one knows quite why our ancient ancestors built Silbury Hill or the Sanctuary. But fortunately some of their tools, pottery and weapons have survived and are housed in the museum, which lies at the heart of Britain's earliest beginnings.

Location: In Avebury, 7 m (11.2 km) west of Marlborough. OS map ref SU100700.
Opening Times: Good Friday or Apr 1 (whichever is earlier) to Sept 30: Open Daily 10–6. Oct 1 to Maundy Thursday or Mar 31 (whichever is earlier): Open Daily 10–4. *Closed* Dec 24 –26, Jan 1. Adm £1.20, Concessions 90p, Chd 60p.

BOWOOD HOUSE & GARDENS

Calne   map G4
Telephone: Calne (0249) 812102
(The Earl and Countess of Shelburne)

Outstanding example of 18th century architecture, set in one of the most beautiful parks in the country, landscaped by 'Capability' Brown and not altered since his time. On display in the House is a remarkable collection of family heirlooms built up over 250 years, including Victoriana, Indiana, silver, porcelain, fine paintings and water-colours. Interesting rooms include Robert Adam's famous Library, Dr. Joseph Priestley's Laboratory where he discovered oxygen gas, and the Chapel. The 100 acre park contains many exotic trees, a 40 acre lake, Cascade, Grotto, caves and a Doric Temple, arboretum, pinetum, rose garden and Italian garden. For children, a massive Adventure Playground. From mid-May to mid-June a separate garden of 50 acres features spectacular rhododendron walks.

Location: 2½ m W of Calne; 5 m SE of Chippenham. Immediately off A4 at Derry Hill village between Calne and Chippenham.
Opening Times: House, Gardens & Grounds. Apr 1 to Nov 1 – Daily incl Bank Hols 11–6. Rhododendron Walks (entrance off A342 at Kennels Lodge) mid-May to mid-June (depending on season) 11–6. Adm to House, Garden and Grounds: £4.30, OAPs £3.50, Chd £2.10.
Refreshments: Licensed restaurant & Garden Tearoom.
Advance Bookings: Coach parties welcome by arrangement. Lunches and Teas – please write for party menus and further information: The Estate Office, Bowood Estate, Calne, Wiltshire SN11 0LZ. Free car park. No dogs.

BROADLEAS GARDENS (Charitable Trust)

Devizes   map G4
Telephone: Devizes 722035
(Lady Anne Cowdray)

A delightful garden with rare and unusual plants and trees, many Rhododendrons, Azaleas and Magnolias with interesting perennials and ground cover.

Location: 1½ m SW of Devizes on A360
Opening Times: Apr 1 to Oct 31 – Suns, Weds & Thurs 2–6. Adm £1.50, Chd (under 12) 50p. Discount for parties. Plants propagated for sale.
Refreshments: Home-made teas on Sundays – also by prior arrangement.

CHARLTON PARK HOUSE

Malmesbury   map G4
(The Earl of Suffolk and Berkshire)

Jacobean/Georgian mansion, built for the Earls of Suffolk, 1607, altered by Matthew Brettingham the Younger, c. 1770.

Location: 1½ m NE Malmesbury. Entry only by signed entrance on A429, Malmesbury/Cirencester Road. No access from Charlton village.
Opening Times: May to Oct, Mon & Thurs 2–4. Viewing of Great Hall, Staircase and saloon. Adm £1, Chd/OAPs 50p. Car parking limited. Unsuitable for wheelchairs. No dogs. No picnicking.

CORSHAM COURT

Chippenham   map G4
Telephone: Corsham (0249) 712214
(The Lord Methuen)

Elizabethan (1582) and Georgian (1760–70) house, fine 18th century furniture. British, Spanish, Italian and Flemish Old Masters. Park and gardens laid out by "Capability" Brown and Humphrey Repton. Contains one of the oldest and most distinguished collections of Old Masters and furniture.

Location: In Corsham 4 m W of Chippenham off the Bath Road (A4).
Opening Times: Staterooms. Jan 1 to Nov 30 – Daily except Mons and Fris 2–4. (From Good Friday to Sept 30, 2–6 (including Fri and Bank Hols); *Closed* Dec. Last adm 30 minutes before closing time. Other times by appointment. Parties welcome. Adm (incl gardens) £3, Chd £1.50; Parties of 20 or more by arrangement. Gardens only £1.50, Chd £1.
Refreshments: Methuen Arms, Corsham *(parties by prior arrangement)*.

THE COURTS GARDEN, The National Trust

Holt   map G4
Telephone: North Trowbridge (0225) 782340

7 acre garden of mystery – of interest to amateur and botanist. Borders, lily pond and arboretum carpeted with wild flowers.

Location: 2½ m E of Bradford-on-Avon on S side of B3107; 3 m N of Trowbridge. *Station: Bradford-on-Avon (2½ m).*
Opening Times: GARDEN ONLY. Apr 1 to Nov 1 – Daily (except Sat), 2–5. Adm £2, Chd £1. Other times by appointment; please telephone the Head Gardener. House not open. No dogs. Wheelchair access. No lavatory.

FITZ HOUSE GARDEN

Teffont Magna, nr Salisbury   map H3
Telephone: (0722) 716257
(Major & Mrs Mordaunt-Hare)

Lovely hillside terraced gardens frame a listed group of beautiful ancient stone buildings in one of Wiltshire's prettiest villages. 16th/17th century House (not shown) admired by Nikolaus Pevsner in his Wiltshire Guide. One time home of Edith Olivier the authoress, and of Siegfried Sassoon, the author. The gardens, bordered by yew and beech hedges and a stream, are a haven of tranquillity, planted with spring bulbs and blossom, azaleas, roses and clematis of all types, honeysuckles, vines and mixed borders. Something of interest throughout the season including much new planting during the last three years. Many scented plants. Featured in *English Private Gardens* by Judy Johnson and Susan Berry published May 1991, and *Country Life* July 1990.

Location: On B3089 Barford St Martin (A30) to Mere Road (A303) in the village; 10 m W of Salisbury on direct route Wilton House-Stourhead.
Opening Times: GARDEN ONLY: May 2 to Sept 27: Sats and Suns 2–5.30. No dogs. No coaches.

GREAT CHALFIELD MANOR, The National Trust 🌾

nr. Melksham   map G4

15th century moated manor house restored in the 20th century. Set across a moat between Parish Church and stables.

Location: 2½ m NE Bradford-on-Avon via B3109, signposted in Holt village.
Opening Times: Apr 1 to Oct 29 — Tues to Thurs. Guided tours only starting at 12.15, 2.15, 3, 3.45 & 4.30. Adm £3.10. *Closed* Public Holidays. *Historical & other Societies by written arrangement. No reductions for parties or children.* No dogs. Unsuitable for wheelchairs. No lavatory.
Refreshments: Bradford-on-Avon; Melksham.

HAMPTWORTH LODGE 🏛

Landford, Salisbury SP5 2EA   map H3
Telephone: Romsey (0794) 390215
(Mr N. Anderson)

Reproduction Jacobean Manor.

Location: 10 m SE of Salisbury on the C44 road between Redlynch and Landford, which is a link road joining the A36 Salisbury–Southampton and the A338 Salisbury– Bournemouth.
Opening Times: House and garden open daily, except Suns, Mar 30 to Apr 30, 2.15–5. Conducted parties only 2.30 and 3.45. Adm £3, under 11 free. No special arrangements for parties, but about 15 is the maximum. Car parking. Suitable for disabled ground floor only. Coaches only by arrangement.
Refreshments: Nearest Hotel is in Salisbury. No refreshments at house.

HEALE GARDENS AND PLANT CENTRE 🏛

Woodford, Salisbury   map H3   ♿
Telephone: Middle Woodford (072 273) 504
(Mr. Guy & Lady Anne Rasch)

Winner of Christie's/HHA Garden of the Year award 1984. Early Carolean manor house where King Charles II hid during his escape. The garden provides a wonderfully varied collection of plants, shrub, musk and other roses, growing in the formal setting of clipped hedges and mellow stonework, at their best in June and July. Particularly lovely in Spring and Autumn is the water garden, planted with magnificent Magnolia and Acers, surrounding an authentic Japanese Tea House and Nikko Bridge which create an exciting focus in this part of the garden. Many of these plants are for sale in the plant centre.

Location: 4 m N of Salisbury on the Woodford Valley road between A345 and A360. Midway between Salisbury, Wilton and Stonehenge.
Opening Times Garden Plant Centre and Shop open throughout the year, 10–5. Tours of the house, lunches and teas for parties of over 20 by arrangement.
Refreshments: Lunches & Teas in the House for parties over 20 by arrangement.

IFORD MANOR GARDENS 🏛

Bradford-on-Avon   map G4
Telephone: Bradford-on-Avon (02216) 3146 or 2840
(Mrs Cartwright-Hignett)

Iford Manor, a Tudor house with an 18th century façade, stands beside a medieval bridge over the River Frome. Once a busy centre of the woollen trade, it is now surrounded by a peaceful terraced garden of unique character. Designed in the Italian style, it was the creation of Harold Peto, the Edwardian landscape architect who lived at Iford from 1899–1933. There are pools, statues, a colonnade, antique carvings, cloisters and many plants of botanical interest.

Location: 7 m SE of Bath on A36, signpost Iford 1 m; or from Bradford-on-Avon and Trowbridge via Westwood.
Opening Times: GARDENS ONLY: 2–5 Tues, Weds, Thurs, Sats and Suns in May, June, July, Aug and Sept and Summer Bank Holidays. Also Apr and Oct Suns and Easter Mon. Adm £2, Chd/OAPs £1. Coaches and groups by arrangement. Dogs on leads. Free car parking.
Refreshments: On the premises. Sun and Bank Holiday Mons May–Sept.

THE KING'S HOUSE

65, The Close, Salisbury   map H3   ♿
Telephone: Salisbury (0722) 332151
(Salisbury & South Wiltshire Museum)

The King's House is a Grade 1 listed building dating from the 13th century and is one of the finest houses in the Cathedral Close. It is also the home of the award-winning Salisbury Museum with highly-praised galleries on Stonehenge, Early Man, Old Sarum and Salisbury (with its famous Giant and Hob Nob), the Pitt Rivers collection, pictures (five Turners), ceramics, a pre-N.H.S. surgery and Wedgwood room. **Costume, lace and embroidery gallery now open.**

Location: In Salisbury Cathedral Close opposite the west front.
Station: Salisbury.
Opening Times: House & Museum. All year. Mon to Sat 10–5; Suns in July, Aug and during Salisbury Festival 2–5. *Closed* Christmas. Adm £2.25, Chd 50p, Concessions £1.50 (Tickets give unlimited visits throughout calendar year). Gift shop. Coffee Shop Apr to Oct.
Refreshments: Apr to Oct. Party bookings all year.

LACOCK ABBEY, The National Trust

nr Chippenham   map G4   △
Telephone: Lacock (0249) 730227

13th century abbey converted into a house in 1540, with 18th century "Gothick" alterations for the Talbot family whose home it still is. The medieval cloisters, the brewery and the house are also open to the public. Fine trees.

Location: In the village of Lacock; 3 m N of Melksham; 3 m S of Chippenham just E of A350.
Opening Times: House: Apr 1 to Nov 1 daily (except Tues) 1–5.30. Daily 12–5.30 (last adm 5). *Closed* Good Friday. Adm House, Grounds & Cloisters £3.80, Chd £1.90. Parties (15 or more) £3.20, Chd party £1.60 per person. Cloisters & Grounds only £1.60, Chd 80p.

LONGLEAT HOUSE

Warminster   map G3   △
Telephone:
Longleat House: Warminster (0985) 844551
Safari Park: Warminster (0985) 844328
Caravan Club site: Warminster (0985) 844663
(The Marquess of Bath)

Longleat House, built by Sir John Thynne in 1580, and still owned and lived in by the same family, was the first truly magnificent Elizabethan House to be built in the Italian Renaissance style. Longleat was also the first Stately Home to be opened to the public in 1949, it is still actively run by the 6th Marquess of Bath and other members of the Thynne family, thus keeping Longleat alive with their presence. Throughout its existence, ancestors have commissioned alterations within the House; ceilings by Italian craftsmen, rooms and corridors by Wyatville, additional libraries to house the vast collection of rare books and of course, the beautiful parkland landscaped by Lancelot 'Capability' Brown. In 1966, Lord Bath, in conjunction with Jimmy Chipperfield established the first drive through wild animals reserve outside Africa and it remains the model for Safari Parks throughout the world. Many other attractions have since been opened, making Longleat a full day's entertainment for all the family. Attractions include, Victorian Kitchens, Lord Bath's Bygones, Dolls Houses, Dr. Who Exhibition, Butterfly Garden, Railway, World's Largest Maze, Pets Corner, Safari Boat Ride, Lord Bath's V.I.P. Vehicle Exhibition. 'Adventure Castle' for children. 1:25 scale model of Longleat House.

Opening Times: Longleat House open all year – Daily (Except Christmas Day) incl. Suns Easter to September 10–6, remainder of year 10–4. Safari Park every day from mid Mar to end Oct, 10–6. (Last cars admitted 5.30 or sunset if earlier.) All other attractions every day from Easter–Oct 30, 11–6 – for Maze, Railway & Adventure Castle last entry 5.30. School Parties welcome at all times of the year – reduced rates for Parties booking in advance. Helicopter landing facilities provided advance notice given.
Refreshments: At the Old Cellar Restaurant at the House and in the Restaurant Complex.

LUCKINGTON COURT

Luckington   map G4
Telephone: Malmesbury 840 205
(The Hon Mrs Trevor Horn)

Mainly Queen Anne with magnificent group of ancient buildings. Beautiful mainly formal garden with fine collection of ornamental trees and shrubs.

Location: 6 m W of Malmesbury on B4040 Bristol Road.
Opening Times: All the Year–Weds 2–6. Outside only, 50p. Inside view by appointment 3 weeks in advance, £1. Open Sun, May 17, 2.30–6. *Collection box for National Gardens' Scheme.*
Refreshments: Teas in garden or house (in aid of Luckington Parish Church). May 12 only.

LYDIARD HOUSE

Lydiard Park, Lydiard Tregoze, Swindon   map H4   △   ♿
(Borough of Thamesdown)

Ancestral home of St John family, remodelled in 1743, set in country parkland. Fine period furniture, family portraits (16th to 19th century), exceptional plasterwork, original wallpaper and fascinating painted glass window.

Location: 5 m W of Swindon just N of Junction 16 M4; signpost Lydiard Park.
Opening Times: Weekdays 10–1, 2–5.30; Suns 2–5.30. (Early closing 4 pm, Oct 27 to Feb 9). Children under 14 must be accompanied by an adult.

MOMPESSON HOUSE, The National Trust

Salisbury   map H3
Telephone': (0722) 335659

Fine Queen Anne town house, furnished as the home of a Georgian gentleman; walled garden.

Location: In Cathedral Close on N side of Choristers' Green.
Station: Salisbury (1/2 m).
Opening Times: Apr 1 to Nov 1 daily except Thurs & Fri 12–5.30. Last adm 5. Adm £2.60, Chd £1.30, parties £2.30. No dogs. Visitors sitting room.
Refreshments: Garden tea room.

NEWHOUSE

Redlynch   map H3
Telephone: Downton 20055
(Mr & Mrs George Jeffreys)

Brick Jacobean "Trinity" house, c. 1619, with two Georgian wings. Contents include costume collection, and "Hare" picture.

Location: 9 m S of Salisbury; 3 m from Downton, off B3080.
Opening Times: Aug 1 to Aug 31, excluding Sun, 2–5.30. Open by arrangement at other times between May and Sept for groups of 25+. Telephone (0725) 20055. Adm £2, Chd (under 15) £1.

OLD SARUM

map H3
Telephone: (0722) 335398

On the summit of a hill north of Salisbury, huge ramparts and earth mounds are silhouetted against the skyline. Ancient Britons fortified the hill-top which was later inhabited by Romans, Saxons and Normans. Parts of an 11th century castle remain and the foundations of two successive cathedrals are marked on the grass.

Location: 2 m (3.2 km) north of Salisbury. OS map ref SU138327.
Opening Times: Good Friday or Apr 1 (whichever is earlier) to Sept 30: Open Daily 10–6. Oct 1 to Maundy Thursday or Mar 31 (whichever is earlier): Open Tues to Sun 10–4. *Closed* Dec 24–26, Jan 1. Adm £1.20, Concessions 90p, Chd 60p.

OLD WARDOUR CASTLE

map G3
Telephone: (0747) 870487

The ruins stand in a romantic lakeside setting as a result of landscaping and planting in the 18th century. French in style and designed more for living than defence, the castle was built in 1393 by the fifth Lord Lovel, a campaigner in France. It was badly damaged in the Civil War and never repaired. The 18th century Banqueting House contains a small display about the 'Capability' Brown landscape.

Location: 2 m (3.2 km) south of Tisbury. OS map ref ST939263.
Opening Times: Good Friday or Apr 1 (whichever is earlier) to Sept 30: Open Daily 10–6. Oct 1 to Maundy Thursday or Mar 31 (whichever is earlier): Open Weekends only 10–4. *Closed* Dec 24–26, Jan 1. Adm £1.20, Concessions 90p, Chd 60p.

PHILIPPS HOUSE, The National Trust

Dinton   map G3   ఉ
Telephone: Teffont 208

Classical house completed in 1816 by Sir Jeffry Wyattville for the Wyndham family.

Location: 9 m W of Salisbury; on N side of B3089.
Opening Times: By prior written appointment only with the Warden. Adm £1.40. *No reduction for parties or children.* House leased to YWCA for residential conferences. No dogs.

PYTHOUSE

Tisbury   map G3
(Country Houses Association Ltd)

Palladian style Georgian mansion.

Location: 2½ m W of Tisbury; 4½ m N of Shaftesbury.
Station: Tisbury (2½ m).
Opening Times: May to Sept—Weds & Thurs 2–5. Last entry 4.30. Adm £1.50, Chd 50p. Free car park. No dogs admitted.

SHELDON MANOR – *See below*

STONEHENGE

map H3
(English Heritage)

Built between 3100 and 1100 BC, this is Britain's most famous ancient monument and one of the world's most astonishing engineering feats. Many of the stones, some weighing 4 tons each, were brought from the Preseli Mountains in Wales to Salisbury Plain, there to be erected by human muscle power. Refreshments are available.

Location: 2 m (3.2 km) west of Amesbury. OS map ref SU123422.
Opening Times: Good Friday or Apr 1 (whichever is earlier) to Sept 30 daily 10–6. Oct 1 to Maundy Thursday or Mar 31 (whichever is earlier) Daily 10–4. *Closed* Dec 24–26, Jan 1. £2.50, Concessions £1.90, Chd £1.30.

SHELDON MANOR

Chippenham   map G4   ⑤   ఉ
Telephone: Chippenham (0249) 653120
(Major Martin Gibbs, DL, JP)

Plantagenet Manor House, lived in as a family home for 700 years. There has been a house here since early Plantagenet times. The present Great Porch and Parvise above, dating from 1282, were built by Sir Geoffrey Gascelyn, Lord of the Manor and Hundred of Chippenham and were 700 years old in 1982. Sheldon is the sole survivor of a vanished medieval village. Succeeding generations and other families, notably the Hungerfords, have added to the beautiful house, its forecourt and surrounding buildings. All the house is lived in and it is shown by the family. There are good collections of early oak furniture, Mailsea glass, porcelain and Persian saddlebags. There are beautiful informal terraced gardens with ancient yew trees, water, interesting trees and shrubs and connoisseur collection of old fashioned roses. Home-made lunches and cream teas served in the Barn or on the lawn. Visitors to Sheldon will find the food "a major consideration". "In nominating an eating place with an intimate atmosphere, I could do no better than to recommend Sheldon". Hugh Montgomery-Massingberd, Weekend Telegraph, July 11th, 1987.

Location: 1½ m W of Chippenham, signposted from A420; eastbound traffic also signposted from A4, E of Corsham (2½ m). M4 exit 17 4 m.
Station: Chippenham (2½ m).
Opening Times: Open Easter Sun and Easter Mon then every Sun, Thurs and Bank Hol to Oct 4 12.30–6. House opens 2. Most of property suitable for wheelchairs.
Refreshments: Home-made lunches & cream teas. Coaches welcome by appointment.

STOURHEAD, The National Trust 🌿

Stourton, nr Mere   map G3   △   ♿
Telephone: Bourton (0747) 840348

The world famous garden was laid out 1741–80; its lakes, temples and rare trees forming a landscape of breath-taking beauty throughout the year. Palladian House designed in 1722 by Colen Campbell. Furniture by Thomas Chippendale the Younger.

Location: 3 m NW of Mere (A303) in the village of Stourton off the Frome/Mere Road (B3092).
Opening Times: Garden all year daily 8–7 or sunset if earlier (except July 22–25, when garden closes at 5). House Apr 1 to Nov 1 daily except Thur & Fri, 12–5.30 or dusk if earlier. Last adm 5. Other times by written arrangement with the Administrator. Adm House £4, Chd £2. Parties by prior written appointment only. Garden Mar to Oct 30 £3.60, Chd £1.70, Parties £3.20. Nov to end Feb £2.60, Chd £1.30. Wheelchairs provided – access to gardens only. No dogs in garden except on leads from Nov to end Feb only. In woods throughout the year.
Refreshments: Accommodation, Spread Eagle Inn at Garden entrance, (0747) 840587. National Trust Shop.

TOTTENHAM HOUSE

Savernake Forest, Marlborough   map H4
Telephone: Marlborough 870331
(The Trustees of the Savernake Estate)

Tottenham House, built by the Marquess of Ailesbury, was originally designed by Burlington and built in the early 18th century. About one hundred years later the house was completely rebuilt by Thomas Cundy although some evidence of Burlington's work still remains. The house is let to Hawtreys Preparatory School.

Location: 3 m A4; 6 m Marlborough.
Opening Times: HOUSE ONLY. Open in School holidays—Jan 8–12 10.30–1.30; Mar 21–25; Apr 16–20; July 5–9; Aug 31; Sept 1–4; Dec 15–19: 10.30–1.30. Adm £1, Chd (under 14) 50p. No reductions. There are steps to the front door (although there is assistance permanently available), thereafter every room open to the public is on one floor, and the property could not strictly be described as unsuitable for the disabled. Car park.
Refreshments: Savernake Forest Hotel ½ m.

WESTWOOD MANOR, The National Trust 🌿

nr. Bradford-on-Avon   map G4   △

15th century stone manor house altered in the late 16th century. Fine furnishings. Gardens of clipped yew. Administered for the National Trust by a tenant.

Location: Beside Westwood Church 1½ m SW of Bradford-on-Avon off Frome Road (B3109).
Stations: Avoncliff (1 m); Bradford-on-Avon (1½ m).
Opening Times: Apr 1 to end Sept: Suns, Tues, Wed 2–5. Adm £2.80. *Other times parties of up to 20 by written application to the tenant. No reduction for parties or children. No photography.* No dogs. Unsuitable for wheelchairs. No lavatory.

WILTON HOUSE 🏛

Salisbury   map H3   △
Telephone: (0722) 743115
(The Earl of Pembroke)

Superb 17th Century State Rooms including magnificent Double and Single Cube Rooms. World famous collection of paintings and other treasures. The New Earls Time theatre incoporating the latest technology to present an exciting and entertaining documentary drama film on The Lives & Times of the Earls of Pembroke. Superb exhibition of toy soldiers and other fascinating displays. A true-to-life reconstruction of a Tudor Kitchen with all the utensils and equipment. Superb gardens and grounds with notable cedar trees and the Palladian Bridge. Adventure playground.

Location: In town of Wilton – 2½ m W of Salisbury on A30. Trains from Waterloo and many other southern and western region stations to Salisbury. Buses from Salisbury Centre. Station: Salisbury 2 miles.
Opening Times: HOUSE, GROUNDS, EXHIBITIONS AND ADVENTURE PLAYGROUND: Seven days a week, Mon to Sat 11–6. Sun 12–6. Last entrance 4.45. Ticket options: £5, Pensioners and Students (with student card) £4.50, Chd over 5 and under 16 years £3.50. Parties (min 15 persons) £4.50, Pensioners and Students £4.20, Chd £3.50. Family ticket – two adults and two children £15. Grounds only: £2, Chd £1.50. Special parties – guided tours by appointment only. Over 15 people £8, fewer than 15 people £10, fewer than 10 people £15.
Refreshments: Licensed self-service restaurant and Gift Shop. Garden Centre and nearby Pembroke Arms Hotel.

NORTH YORKSHIRE

ALDBOROUGH ROMAN TOWN

map H10
Telephone: (0423) 322768

The little village of Aldborough lies within the bounds of what was once the rich Roman city Isurium Brigantum, Aldborough has even retained part of the Roman street plan—a regular grid with a central open space, once the forum. Part of the Roman town walls survive, and two mosaic pavements may be seen in their original positions. A remarkable collection of Roman objects is on display in the Museum.

Location: ¾ m (1 km) east of Boroughbridge. OS map ref SE405667.
Opening Times: Good Friday or Apr 1 (whichever is earlier) to Sept 30: Open Daily 10–6. Oct 1 to Maundy Thursday or Mar 31 (whichever is earlier): Grounds only free. *Closed* Dec 24 –26, Jan 1. Site only. Adm £1.10, Concessions 85p, Chd 55p.

ALLERTON PARK

nr. Knaresborough   map H9   △
Telephone: (0423) 330927
(The Gerald Arthur Rolph Foundation for Historic Preservation and Education)

The grandest of the surviving Gothic revival stately homes. Its Great Hall and Dining Room are considered amongst the finest carved wood rooms in England. Allerton Park is the ancestral home of Lord Mowbray (c. 1283), Segrave (c. 1283) and Stourton (c. 1448), the premier Baron in England. House designed by George Martin, some interior rooms by Benjamin Baud. Temple of Victory built by Frederick, Duke of York (brother to King George IV) in 18c. The setting for Sherlock Holmes film 'The Sign of Four'. Private collection of mechanical music machines and luxury antique motor cars. World War II museum dedicated to Number 6 Group (RCAF).

Location: 14½ m W of York; ¼ m E of A1 on York Road (A59); 4½ m W of Knaresborough, 6 m N of Wetherby; 7 m S of Boroughbridge; 14 m N of Leeds.
Opening Times: Easter Sun to end Sept – Suns and Bank Holiday Mons 1–6: last house tour 5. Adm House, Grounds and Car Museum: £3. Students, OAPs and accompanied Chd under 16 £2. Parties (25 and over) £2.50. School groups £2. Free car parking. No dogs, except guide dogs for the blind. Other days by appointment for parties of 25 or more and events. Enquiries to: Mr. Farr, Administrator, Allerton Park, nr. Knaresborough, N. Yorkshire HG5 0SE. Tel: (0423) 330927.
Refreshments: Lunch and refreshments available in licensed tearoom.

THE BAR CONVENT

York   map H9
Telephone: (0904) 643238
(The Bar Convent Museum Trust)

Impressive Georgian town house (1787) enclosing neo-classical Chapel (1769), both by Thomas Atkinson. 19th century covered courtyard with Coalbrookdale floor tiles and cast iron furniture. Museum tells story of the Convent. Exhibition programme.

Location: At Micklegate Bar on the A1036 from A64 which links to A1.
Opening Times: Feb 1 to Dec 23, Tues to Sat 10–5 and Bank Hol Mons. *Closed* Good Friday. Adm £1.75, Concessions £1.50, Chd £1, Family Ticket £3.50. Disabled access. Nearby public parking. Shop.
Refreshments: Cafe; home made fare.

BENINGBROUGH HALL The National Trust

nr York   map H9   △   &
Telephone: York (0904) 470666

This handsome Georgian house has been completely restored and in the principal rooms are 100 famous portraits on loan from the National Portrait Gallery. Victorian laundry, potting shed and exhibitions. Garden and wilderness play area.

Location: 8 m NW of York; 3 m W of Shipton (A19); 2 m SE Linton-on-Ouse; follow signposted route.
Opening Times: Apr 4 to Nov 1: Apr, May, June, Sept and Oct. Tues, Weds, Thurs, Sats, Suns amd Bank Hol Mons July and Aug: daily except Mon. House 11–5 (last adm 4.30); grounds, shop and restaurant 11–5.30. Shop and restaurant also open Nov 28 to Dec 13, 11–4 weekends. Adm House, Garden and Exhibitions £4, Chd (accompanied) £2. Family ticket (2 adults, 2 Chd) £10, Parties £3.20, Chd £1.60. Garden and Exhibitions £2.50, Chd (accompanied) £1.20. Family ticket £6.20. No dogs. Wheelchairs provided. Baby changing facilities.
Refreshments: The Restaurant serves homemade hot & cold lunches, teas, special suppers. Wheelchair access. Picnic area. Kiosk. Special functions catered for, details from the Administrator.

BOLTON CASTLE

nr Leyburn   map G10
Telephone: (0969) 23981/23674
(The Hon. Harry Orde-Powlett)

One of Britain's best preserved medieval castles now in the first stages of restoration. Recently redecorated and refurbished with period tapestries, arms and armour, and tableaux depicting everyday life in the fifteenth and sixteenth centuries.

Location: Situated within the Yorkshire Dales National Park, 5 m W of Leyburn, 10 m E of Hawes, road signs from the A684.
Opening Times: Daily, Mar to end Oct: 10–5; Nov to Mar, weekends and holiday periods open, otherwise by special arrangement. Party visits welcomed, discount for groups of 25 and over (10 per cent) plus one person free. Car park. Modern toilet facilities. Gift shop.
Refreshments: Tea room with homemade light refreshments. (Under cover.)

BYLAND ABBEY

map H10
Telephone: (03476) 614

Built in the shadow of the Hambleton Hills, this 12th century Cistercian monastery is still magnificent, both in size and workmanship. The area of the cloister, for example, is larger than either Fountains or Rievaulx Abbeys. Some of the carved stone details are particularly fine, and sections of medieval green and yellow glazed tile floor may be seen.

Location: 1 m (1.6 km) north east of Coxwold. OS map ref SE549789.
Opening Times: Good Friday or Apr 1 (whichever is earlier) to Sept 30: Open Daily 10–6. Oct 1 to Maundy Thursday or Mar 31 (whichever is earlier): Open Tues to Sun 10–4. *Closed* Dec 24–26, Jan 1. Adm £1.10, Concessions 85p, Chd 55p.

CASTLE HOWARD – *See page 204*

CLIFFORD'S TOWER, YORK

map H9
Telephone: (0904) 646940
(English Heritage)

York Castle, like the city itself, has had a long and turbulent history. Clifford's Tower was built on an earlier motte (or mound) in the 13th century. The tower is named after a Lancastrian leader from the Wars of the Roses, Sir Robert Clifford, who was defeated in 1322, and his body hung in chains from the tower.

Location: Near Castle Museum. OS map ref SE605515.
Opening Times: Good Friday or Apr 1 (whichever is earlier) to Sept 30 daily 10–6. Oct 1 to Maundy Thursday or Mar 31 (whichever is earlier) daily 10–4. *Closed* Dec 24–26, Jan 1. Adm £1.10, Concessions 85p, Chd 55p.

CASTLE HOWARD

York map J10
Telephone: Coneysthorpe (065 384) 333
(The Hon. Simon Howard)

Designed by Vanbrugh 1699–1726 for the 3rd Earl of Carlisle, assisted by Hawksmoor, who designed the Mausoleum. Has been open to the public since the day it was built. Impressive Great Hall and many other magnificent rooms filled with fine collections of pictures, statuary and furniture. Interesting rooms include The Castle Howard Bedroom, Lady Georgiana's Bedroom and Dressing Room, The Antique Passage, The Music Room, The Tapestry Room, The Museum Room, The Long Gallery, and the Chapel. Costume Gallery features tableaux of authentic historical costumes which are changed annually. Beautiful park and grounds with nature walks, rose gardens in season, superb Atlas fountain, Temple of The Four Winds. Lakeside Adventure Playground for children. Plant Centre. Boat trips on the lake in Victorian style launch in season.

Location: 15 m NE of York; 3 m off A64; 6 m W of Malton; 38 m Leeds; 36 m Harrogate; 22 m Scarborough; 50 m Hull.
Opening Times: Daily Mar 25 to Nov 1. House and Costume Galleries open from 11. Plant centre, rose gardens, grounds and cafeteria open from 10. Last admissions: 4.30. Adm £5.50, Chd £2.50, OAPs £4.50. Special terms for adult booked parties.
Refreshments: Cafeteria. Licensed restaurant available for families and booked parties.

Sir Edwin Landseer Lutyens
Architect

His work can be seen at the following properties included in Historic Houses Castles and Gardens:

> *Castle Drogo*
> *Goddards*
> *Great Dixter*
> *Great Maytham Hall*
> *Hestercombe House and Gardens*
> *Knebworth*

Gertrude Jekyll
writer and gardener
(1843–1932)

Her designs were used at the following properties included in Historic Houses Castles and Gardens:

> *Hestercombe House and Gardens*
> *Knebworth*
> *Vann*

CONSTABLE BURTON HALL

Leyburn   map H10
Telephone: Bedale 50428
(M. C. A. Wyvill, Esq.)

Extensive borders, interesting alpines, large informal garden. John Carr house completed in 1768.

Location: On A684, between Leyburn (3 m) & Bedale; A1 (7 m).
Opening Times: Gardens. May 1 to Sept 1 — Daily 9—6. Adm £1 (1992 charge), collecting box. House: opening dates & adm charges not available at time of going to press. Party rates by arrangement.

DUNCOMBE PARK

Helmsley   map H10
(The Rt Hon Lord Feversham)

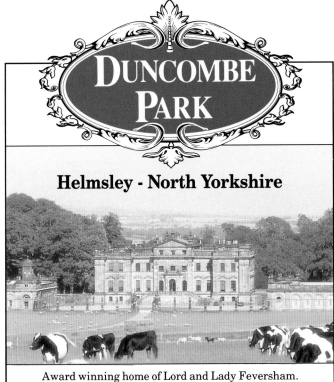

DUNCOMBE PARK

Helmsley - North Yorkshire

Award winning home of Lord and Lady Feversham.
Originally built in 1713, recently restored to a family home.
Unique 18th century landscape gardens. Visitor Centre.
Country Walks. Adventure Playground. Licensed Tea Room.

Further information: Tel: 0439 70213.

**Country Fair - 27 May; Craft Festivals - June-September;
Flower Festival 19-21 June; Steam Fair 4-5 July.**

Admission: see editorial

Home of the Duncombes for 300 years; 60 years a school, now restored to family home and open to public for first time. Fine 19th century interiors, family pictures, English and Continental furniture. Unique 18th century landscape garden with lawns, temples, tree-lined terraces, woodland and riverside walks. Visitor Centre, gift shop, children's playground, car park.

Location: 3 mins from Helmsley market square.
Opening Times: Apr: Suns 11—6, Easter weekend (Apr 17—21) 11—6; May 3 to Oct 25: Sun to Thurs 11—6; Bank Hol Sats and all events Sats.
Refreshments: Tea room.

EBBERSTON HALL

Scarborough   map J10
(W. de Wend Fenton, Esq.)

Palladian Villa of 1718 designed by the architect Colin Campbell. Water gardens attributed to William Benson and Switzer. Elaborate woodwork and cornices comparable to Castle Howard and Beningbrough.

Location: 11 m W of Scarborough on A170 Scarborough/Pickering Road.
Opening Times: Easter to Oct 1 — Daily 10—6. Adm £2.50.

FAIRFAX HOUSE

Castlegate, York   map H9
Telephone: (0904) 655543
(York Civic Trust)

An 18th century house designed by John Carr of York and described as a classic architectural masterpiece of its age. Certainly one of the finest townhouses in England and saved from near collapse by the York Civic Trust who restored it to its former glory during 1982/84. In addition to the superbly decorated plasterwork, wood and

FAIRFAX HOUSE – *Continued from page 205*

wrought iron, the house is now home for an outstanding collection of 18th century Furniture, and Clocks, formed by the late Noel Terry. Described by Christie's as one of the finest private collections of this century, it enhances and complements the house and helps to create a very special 'lived in' feeling. The gift of the entire collection by Noel Terry's Trustees to the Civic Trust has enabled it to fill the house with appropriate pieces of the period and has provided the basis for what can now be considered a fully furnished Georgian Townhouse.

Location: Centre of York, follow signs for Castle Area and Jorvik Centre.
Opening Times: Mar 1 to Dec 31: Mon to Thurs and Sat 11–5; Sun 1.30–5 (last admission 4.30). *Closed* on Fridays except during August. Adm £2.50, Chd and Student £1, OAP £2.25. Parties, Adult (pre-booked 15 or more) £2, Chd 75p. Special evening tours, connoisseur visits and receptions welcomed by arrangement with the Director. Public car park within 50 yards. Suitable for disabled persons only with assistance (by telephoning beforehand staff can be available to help). A small gift shop offers selected antiques, publications and gifts. Opening times are the same as the house.

FOUNTAINS ABBEY & STUDLEY ROYAL, The National Trust ❧

Ripon   map H10   &
Telephone: Ripon (0765) 86333/620333

Extensive ruins of Cistercian monastery. Ornamental gardens laid out by John Aislabie, 1720. 400 acre deer park with fine Burges church. Awarded World Heritage status.

Location: 2 m W of Ripon; 9 m W of Harrogate; NW of A61.
Opening Times: Open all year during daylight hours, adm free. ABBEY AND GARDENS: Jan, Feb, Mar, Nov & Dec – daily except Christmas Eve, Christmas Day and Fris in Jan, Nov and Dev, 10–5 or dusk if earlier; Apr, May, June & Sept: 10–7; July & Aug: 10–8; Oct: 10–6 or dusk if earlier. FOUNTAINS HALL: Apr to Oct: 11–6; Nov to Mar: 11–4. Adm free. ABBEY AND GARDEN ONLY: Jan 1 to Mar 31 1992: £2.70, Chd £1.30, Family £6.70; group over 15 £2.30, Chd £1. Apr 1 to Oct 31: £3.50, Chd £1.60, Family £8.60, group over 15 £3.10, Chd £1.50; Nov 1 to Mar 31 1993: £3, Chd £1.50, Family £7.50; group over 15 £2.50, Chd £1.30. PARKING (all day) from Apr 1 1992: Studley Park £1.50 (refundable if adm ticket purchased), other parking free. Powered runaround bookable in advance, and adapted lavatories at each entrance.
Refreshments: Light lunches, sandwiches, cakes, soup, tea, coffee, cold drinks available Studley tea room Jan to Mar 10–5 daily (or dusk if earlier); Apr 1 to Nov 10–6 daily (or dusk if earlier); Nov 7 to Dec 31 10–5 weekends. Abbey Cafe: daily Apr 4 to Nov 1, 10–6 or dusk if earlier. Visitor Centre: Restaurant: open daily 9.30–6, June, Sept and Oct; July & Aug: 9.30–8. Nov & Dec 10–5. Wheelchair access. Picnics can be taken anywhere on Estate. Dogs on leashes only. Visitor Centre shop: open daily June to Oct 10–6, Nov & Dec 10–5. Note: It is expected that the new Visitor Centre will operate from May 1992 – look out for new direction signs.

GEORGIAN THEATRE ROYAL

Richmond   map H10
Telephone: (0748) 823710
(The Georgian Theatre (Richmond) Trust Ltd.)

Built in 1788. Historically very important being country's oldest theatre in original form. Beautiful intimate interior; also Theatre Museum.

Location: 4 m from Scotch Corner (A1) on the A6108.
Opening Times: Theatre & Museum – Easter weekend to Oct, daily Mon to Sat 11–4.45; Sun 2.30–4.45. Adm charge. Party rates on application. Seasons of Plays, Recitals, etc. *Theatre may be viewed during winter months; apply in writing to the Manager.*

HARLOW CARR BOTANICAL GARDENS

Harrogate   map H9
(The Northern Horticultural Society)

68 acres of ornamental gardens and woodlands.

Location: 1½ m from centre of Harrogate, Otley Road B6162.
Station: Harrogate (1½ m).
Opening Times: All the year – Daily 9–7.30 (or dusk if earlier). Adm charge. Free car park. Restaurant. Shop and plant sales. Museum of Gardening.

HELMSLEY CASTLE ⌗

map H10
Telephone: (0439) 70442

Even in its ruined state, Helmsley Castle is spectacular. Begun by Walter Espec shortly after the Norman Conquest, the huge earthworks – now softened to green valleys – are all that remain of this early castle. The oldest stonework is 12th century. Like many English castles, Helmsley rendered indefensible during the Civil War, when it belonged to the notorious George Villiers, Duke of Buckingham. It was abandoned as a great house when its owners built nearby Duncombe Park. The 17th century domestic buildings contains an exhibition about the castle.

Location: Helmsley. OS map ref SE611836.
Opening Times: Good Friday or Apr 1 (whichever is earlier) to Sept 30: Open Daily 10–6. Oct 1 to Maundy Thursday or Mar 31 (whichever is earlier): Open Tues to Sun 10–4. *Closed* Dec 24–26, Jan 1. Adm £1.50, Concessions £1.10, Chd 75p.

HOVINGHAM HALL

York   map J10
(Sir Marcus & Lady Worsley)

Palladian house designed c. 1760 by Thomas Worsley. Unique Riding School, magnificent yew hedges, dovecot, private cricket ground. Family portraits.

Location: 20 m N of York on Malton/Helmsley Road (B1257).
Opening Times: Open for parties of 15 or more **by written appointment only** – Apr 21 to Sept 24, 1992, Tues, Weds & Thurs 11–7. Adm £2.50, Chd £1.25.
Refreshments: At the Hall by arrangement. Meals at The Worsley Arms, Hovingham.

KIRKHAM PRIORY ⌗

map J10
Telephone: (065381) 768

The patrons of this monastery, the Lords of Helmsley, are still much in evidence. Their coats of arms adorn the gatehouse, and four family graves have survived amid the ruins of the Church. Built for the monks the Augustinian Order, or Black Canons, Kirkham was founded early in the 12th century by Walter Espec, who also founded Rievaulx Abbey.

Location: 5 m (8 km) south west of Malton. OS map ref SE735657.
Opening Times: Good Friday or Apr 1 (whichever is earlier) to Sept 30: Open Daily 10–6. Oct 1 to Maundy Thursday or Mar 31 (whichever is earlier): Open Tues to Sun 10–4. *Closed* Dec 24–26, Jan 1. Adm £1.10, Concessions 85p, Chd 55p.

MARKENFIELD HALL

Ripon   map H10
(The Lord Grantley, MC)

Fine example of English manor house 14th, 15th & 16th century buildings surrounded by moat.

Location: 3 m S of Ripon off the Ripon/Harrogate Road (A61). Access is up a road marked 'Public Bridleway Hell Wath Lane'.
Opening Times: Apr to Oct – Mons 10–12.30, 2.15–5. Adm 50p, Chd (accompanied by adult) free. Exterior only outside courtyard and moat all other days in May – times as above. Adm free.

MIDDLEHAM CASTLE ⌗

map H10
Telephone: (0969) 23899

The great days of Middleham were in the 14th and 15th centuries, when it was the stronghold of the mighty Neville family. After the death of Richard Neville – 'Warwick the Kingmaker' – in 1471, the castle was forfeited to the Crown and was the childhood home of Richard III. The dominant feature of the castle is the great keep, one of the largest in England. A replica of the famous Middleham jewel is on display.

Location: 2 m (3.2 km) south of Leyburn. OS map ref SE128875.
Opening Times: Good Friday or Apr 1 (whichever is earlier) to Sept 30: Open Daily 10–6. Oct 1 to Maundy Thursday or Mar 31 (whichever is earlier): Open Tues to Sun 10–4. *Closed* Dec 24–26, Jan 1. Adm £1.10, Concessions 85p, Chd 55p.

MOUNT GRACE PRIORY ✿

map H10
Telephone: (0609) 83249

These 14th century ruins provide a rare opportunity to study the plan of a Carthusian monastery, or 'charterhouse'. The Carthusian monks lived like hermits—in seclusion not only from the world, but from each other. They met together only in chapel, and for religious feasts. Every monk had his own cell—21 in all—a tiny two-storey house with its own garden and workshop. And each cell had running water—a remarkable luxury in the Middle Ages. A fully restored cell with hand-carved furniture and exhibition gives a fascinating insight into the lives of the monks.

Location: 7 miles (11.3 km) north east of Northallerton. OS map ref SE453982.
Opening Times: Good Friday or Apr 1 (whichever is earlier) to Sept 30: Open Daily 10–6. Oct 1 to Maundy Thursday or Mar 31 (whichever is earlier): Open Tues to Sun 10–4. *Closed* Dec 24–26, Jan 1. Adm £1.80, Concessions £1.40, Chd 90p.

NEWBURGH PRIORY

Coxwold   map H10
Telephone: Coxwold (034 76) 435
(Sir George Wombwell Bt)

One of the North's most interesting Historic Houses. Originally built in 1145 with alterations in 1568 and 1720-1760, the Priory has been the home of one family and its descendants since 1538. The house contains the tomb of Oliver Cromwell (his third daughter, Mary, was married to Viscount Fauconberg – owner 1647-1700). In the grounds there is a really beautiful Water Garden full of rare alpines, plants and rhododendrons. Afternoon tea is served in the original kitchen.

Location: 5 m from Easingwold off A19, 9 m from Thirsk.
Opening Times: May 17 to Aug 30—Weds and Suns, Easter Mon and Aug Bank Hol Mon. House open 2.30–4.45. Grounds 2–6. Adm House & Grounds £2.50, Chd £1.10. Grounds only £1, Chd 50p. *Other days for parties of 25 or more by appointment with the Administrator.*
Refreshments: In the Old Priory Kitchens.

NEWBY HALL & GARDENS 🏛

Ripon   map H10   &
Telephone: (0423) 322583
(R. E. J. Compton, Esq.)

The family home of Mr and Mrs Robin Compton is one of Yorkshire's renowned Adam houses. It is set amidst 25 acres of award-winning gardens full of rare and beautiful plants. The contents of the house are superb and include an unique Gobelins Tapestry Room, a gallery of classical statuary and some of Chippendale's finest furniture. Other attractions are railway rides beside the river, adventure gardens for children, a woodland discovery walk, Newby shop and plants stall, and picnic area. Coach and car park free.

Location: 4m SE of Ripon on Boroughbridge Road (B6265). 3m W of A1; 14m Harrogate; 20m York; 35m Leeds; 32m Skipton.
Opening Times: Apr 1 to Sept 30—Daily except Mons (but open Bank Holidays) from 11am. Full visitor information from the Administrator, The Estate Office, Newby Hall, Ripon HG4 5AE. See colour photograph in preliminary section.
Refreshments: Lunches & teas in the licensed Garden Restaurant.

NORTON CONYERS 🏛

Ripon HG4 5EH   map H10   △   ♿
Telephone: Melmerby (0765) 640333
(Sir James Graham, Bt)

Late medieval house with Stuart and Georgian additions. Family pictures, furniture and wedding dresses. Friendly atmosphere, remarked on by many visitors, resulting from over 360 years of occupation by the same family. Visited by James I, Charles I and James II. Charlotte Brontë stayed in 1839; the house is one of the originals of Thornfield Hall in 'Jane Eyre', and a family legend was reputedly the inspiration for the mad Mrs Rochester. 18th century walled garden in full cultivation, with Orangery and herbaceous borders. Small Garden Centre specialising in unusual hardy plants. Pick Your Own Fruit in July and August.

Location: 3½ m NW of Ripon nr Wath. 1½ m from A1; turn off at the Baldersby Flyover, take A61 to Ripon, turn right to Melmerby.
Opening Times: Suns from May 17 to Sept 13, also all Bank Holiday Suns & Mons, and daily from July 27 to Aug 1, 2 – 5.30. Any time for booked parties; inquiries to Beatrice, Lady Graham at above address. Adm £2, Chd (4 – 14) £1, OAPs £1.50, parties of 20 or more £1.50. Parking is free. Small gift shop in house. Guided tours by previous arrangement only. Dogs (excluding guide dogs) in grounds and garden only and must be on a lead. Visitors are requested not to wear high-heeled shoes. Disabled visitors welcome.
The garden is open all year Mon – Fri 9 – 5, Sat & Sun Mar 28 to Oct 3 2 – 5.30. Admission free.
Refreshments: Teas served Bank Holidays and Charity openings. Teas, light refreshments and buffet lunches for booked parties by request.

NUNNINGTON HALL The National Trust 🌸

nr Helmsley   map J10
Telephone: Nunnington (043 95) 283

Sixteenth century manor house with fine panelled hall and staircase. Carlisle Collection of Miniature Rooms on display.

Location: In Ryedale; 4½ m SE of Helmsley; 1½ m N of B1257.
Opening Times: Apr 4 to Nov 1. Apr: weekends and 18 to 23 incl, 2 – 6. May, June, Sept & Oct – Tues, Weds, Thurs, Sats & Suns 2 – 6; July & Aug – Tues, Weds, Thurs 2 – 6; Sats & Suns 12 – 6. Bank Hol Mons 12 – 6. Last admission 5. Shop and tearoom open as house. School Parties on weekdays by arrangement with administrator. Adm House and Gardens £3, Chd £1.50. Adult party £2.50, Chd party £1.10. Gardens only: £1.50, Chd 70p. Access to Ground Floor and tearoom only for Wheelchairs. Lavatory for disabled at rear of house. Access to main gardens via ramp. Guide dogs permitted. Dogs in car park only. Baby changing facilities.
Refreshments: Afternoon teas available at all times when house is open 2 – 5.30 in indoor tearooms or tea garden. Lunches July & Aug. Shop.

PICKERING CASTLE ⛉

map J10
Telephone: (0751) 74989

Most of the medieval kings visited Pickering Castle. They came to hunt deer and wild boar in the neighbouring forest. It was a sport of which they were inordinately fond, and the royal forests were zealously guarded. Romantics may like to speculate as to why Rosamund's Tower has been linked with 'Fair Rosamund', mistress of Henry II. They should, however, be aware that the tower was built in 1323, a century after the lady died.

Location: Pickering. OS map ref SE800845.
Opening Times: Good Friday or Apr 1 (whichever is earlier) to Sept 30: Open Daily 10 – 6. Oct 1 to Maundy Thursday or Mar 31 (whichever is earlier): Open Tues to Sun 10 – 4. *Closed* Dec 24 – 26, Jan 1. Adm £1.50, Concessions £1.10, Chd 75p.

RICHMOND CASTLE ⛉

map H10
Telephone: (0748) 822493

Surrounded on three sides by high moorland, Richmond Castle is in a strongly defensible position. However, the castle has seen little active service, which accounts for the remarkable amount of early Norman stonework that has survived. Built by Alan the Red, shortly after 1066, the castle went with the title 'Duke of Richmond' and has had many royal and powerful owners. The 100 foot high keep provides fine views over the ruins and surrounding countryside.

Location: Richmond. OS map ref NZ174006.
Opening Times: Good Friday or Apr 1 (whichever is earlier) to Sept 30: Open Daily 10 – 6. Oct 1 to Maundy Thursday or Mar 31 (whichever is earlier): Open Tues to Sun 10 – 4. *Closed* Dec 24 – 26, Jan 1. Adm £1.50, Concessions £1.10, Chd 75p.

RIEVAULX ABBEY ⛉

map H10
Telephone: (043 96) 228

The fluctuating fortunes of the abbey may be read from the ruins. Within two decades of its foundation in 1131, Rievaulx—the first Cistercian monastery in the north—was vast, with 140 monks and 500 lay brothers. A costly building programme followed, and it is little wonder that by the 13th century the monastery was heavily in debt, and buildings were being reduced in size. By the Dissolution in the 16th century, there were only 22 monks. The church is a beautiful example of early English Gothic. New visitor centre with exhibition and shop.

Location: 3 miles (4.8 km) north west of Helmsley. OS map ref SE577849.
Opening Times: Good Friday or Apr 1 (whichever is earlier) to Sept 30: Open Daily 10–6. Oct 1 to Maundy Thursday or Mar 31 (whichever is earlier): Open Tues to Sun 10–4. *Closed* Dec 24–26, Jan 1. Adm £1.80, Concessions £1.40, Chd 90p.

RIEVAULX TERRACE, The National Trust

Helmsley   map H10
Telephone: Bilsdale (04396) 340

Beautiful half mile long grass terrace with views of Rievaulx Abbey. Two 18th century Temples and permanent exhibition.

Location: 2½ m NW of Helmsley on Stokesley Road (B1257).
Opening Times: Apr 1 to Nov 1 – Daily 10.30–6 or dusk if earlier. Last adm 5.30. Ionic Temple closed 1–2. Adm £1.80, Chd 90p, Adult party £1.60. Chd party 80p. All dogs on leash. Battery operated 'Runabout' available.
Refreshments: Teas available at Nunnington Hall, 7 m E.

RIPLEY CASTLE

Ripley   map H9
Telephone: Harrogate (0423) 770152
(Sir Thomas Ingilby Bt)

Ripley Castle and Gardens

Home of the Ingilby Family for over 650 years, the castle is situated ten minutes north of Harrogate, in the centre of one of England's most beautiful and historic estate villages. The castle itself overlooks a seventeen acre lake and deer park, and the setting is wonderful. The rooms are packed with anecdote, humour and items of fascination, and the knight's chamber in the 1555 tower remains one of the most startlingly complete medieval rooms in the country, complete with waggon roof ceiling, ancient panelling, Royal Greenwich armour and secret priest's hiding hole.

The famous gardens contain the national hyacinth collection and a magnificent assortment of tropical and semi tropical plants in the greenhouse.

The village is quite unique and well worth a visit, and the four star **Boar's Head Hotel** with its first class restaurant and bar would make an excellent base for touring Yorkshire's stately homes, almost all of which are within one hour's drive.

Has been the home of the Ingilby family since early 14th century. Priests secret hiding place and Civil War armour. Main gateway dates from reign of Edward IV. Extensive gardens. National Hyacinth and tropical plant collections.

Location: In Ripley 3½ m N Harrogate; 7½ m from Ripon.
Opening Times: Castle: Apr, May and Oct – Sats & Suns, 11.30–4.30; June to Sept (incl) – Daily except Mons and Fri 11.30–4.30. Good Friday and all Bank Holidays in season 11–4.30. Booked parties: Groups can visit the castle on any day during the year, by prior appointment. Gardens: Daily Apr 1 to Oct.
Refreshments: Licensed restaurant and public bar (The Boar's Head Hotel) in village: Tearoom in castle courtyard, serving teas and refreshments.

SCARBOROUGH CASTLE

map J10
Telephone: (0723) 372451

Standing on the massive headland between the North and South Bays, the castle commands magnificent views. There was a prehistoric settlement here, and a Roman signal station, but the first mention of the castle is in the 12th century, when it was seized by Henry II. During the Civil War the castle was besieged and changed hands several times. A hundred years later it was still in use to detain political prisoners – notably George Fox, founder of the Society of Friends (Quakers).

Location: East of town centre. OS map ref TA050893.
Opening Times: Good Friday or Apr 1 (whichever is earlier) to Sept 30: Open Daily 10–6. Oct 1 to Maundy Thursday or Mar 31 (whichever is earlier): Open Tues to Sun 10–4. *Closed* Dec 24–26, Jan 1. Adm £1.50, Concessions £1.10, Chd 75p.

SHANDY HALL

Coxwold   map H10
Telephone: Coxwold 465
(The Laurence Sterne Trust)

Here in 1760-67 the witty and eccentric parson laurence Sterne wrote *Tristram Shandy* and *A Sentimental Journey*, 'novels that jump clean out of the 18th century into the 20th', influencing Dickens, Goethe, Tolstoy, Balzac, Proust, Melville, Joyce, Virginia Woolf, and other great writers. Shandy Hall was built as a timber-framed open-hall in the mid-15th century, modernised in the 17th, curiously added to by Sterne in the 18th. It survives much as he knew it, almost as full of surprises and odd digressions as his novels, most of which he wrote in his little book-lined study. Not a museum but a lived-in house where you are sure of a personal welcome. Surrounded by a walled garden full of old-fashioned roses and cottage-garden plants.

Location: 20 m from York via A19; 6 m from A19 at Easingwold; 8 m from Thirsk; 13 m from A1 at Dishforth.
Opening Times: June to Sept – Weds 2–4.30. Suns 2.30–4.30. *Any other day or time all year by appointment with Hon Curators.* Adm £2, Chd (accompanied) half-price. Book & handicrafts shop. Plants for sale.
Refreshments: Close by in village.

SKIPTON CASTLE

Skipton map G9 △
Telephone: Skipton (0756) 792442

At the gateway to the Yorkshire Dales
stands one of England's best-preserved castles,
nine hundred years old and fully roofed:
in its beautiful Conduit Court flourishes
the Yew planted by Lady Anne Clifford in 1659.

Come & explore

Skipton Castle

Free Castle Explorer's badge
for everyone under 18!

Open all year

Open **10am** (Sun. **2pm**) *tel* 0756-792442

Nine-hundred-year-old Skipton Castle is still fully roofed! It is one of the most complete and best-preserved medieval castles in England. Explore the massive round towers and beautiful Conduit Court with its famous yew.

Location: Head of High Street.
Railway Station: (¹/₂ m).
Bus Station: (town centre).
Opening Times: Every day from 10 (Sunday 2). Last admission 6 (Oct–Feb 4). *Closed* Christmas Day. Adm with illustrated Tour Sheet £2.40; under-18's with Tour Sheet and new Castle Explorer's badge, half price; under-5's with badge, free! Party visits welcomed: school parties, including accompanying adults, £1.20 per head; other parties of 15 or more, less 10%. Guides available for pre-booked parties, otherwise illustrated Tour Sheets are provided in a choice of **seven languages:** English, Dutch, French, German, Italian, Japanese or Spanish. Large coach and car park off nearby High Street.

Robert Adam – architect

His work can be seen at the following properties included in Historic Houses Castles and Gardens:

Bowood
Culzean Castle
Hatchlands
Kedleston Hall
Kenwood
Kimbolton Castle
Luton Hoo
Mellerstain

Moccas Court
Newby Hall
Nostell Priory
Osterley Park House
Papplewick Hall
Saltram House
Syon House

SION HILL HALL

Kirby Wiske, nr Thirsk   map H10
Telephone: Thirsk (0845) 587206
(The H W Mawer Trust)

Charming neo-Georgian country house designed by the York Architect Walter H. Brierley in the Lutyens style, one of the last country mansions. Now houses the beautiful Mawer bequest of fine furniture, paintings, porcelain, clocks etc. The house also contains collections of specialised interest more recently acquired. R.I.B.A. Award Winner for outstanding architectural merit.

Location: 6 m S of Northallerton, 4 m W of Thirsk, ½ m off A167 signpost Kirby Wiske.
Opening Times: First Sun in each month, May to Oct 2–5 (last adm 4.30). Adm £3, Concessions £2.50, Chd free if accompanied. Organised groups by arrangement with the Curator at any reasonable time. Tel: Thirsk (0845) 587206.
Refreshments: Teas served in our Granary Tearoom.

SKIPTON CASTLE – *See page 210*

STOCKELD PARK 🏛

Wetherby   map H9
Telephone: Wetherby (0937) 586101
(Mr and Mrs P. G. F. Grant)

This small country mansion is set amidst an extensive rural estate of farms, wood and parklands on the edge of the Vale of York and is one of the finest examples of the work of the celebrated architect James Paine and a splendid example of the Palladian style. Stockeld Park was built for the Middleton family during the period 1758–63 and purchased in 1885 by Robert John Foster. Mr Foster was the great grandson of John Foster who founded John Foster & Son based at the Black Dyke Mills. Visitors have an opportunity to see the house as it is lived in at present, together with furniture and pictures collected by the Foster family over many years.

Location: 2 m N of Wetherby; 7 m SE of Harrogate on A661.
Opening Times: July 1 to 31 1992 (*except Mons*) 2.30–5.30 (other times by appointment in writing to the Estate Office or tel: (0937) 586101. Adm £2.20, Chd £1.20, OAPs £1.50. Gardens only £1.20.
Refreshments: Home-made teas available every day.

SUTTON PARK 🏛

Sutton-on-the-Forest   map H10
Telephone: 0347 810249
(Mrs Sheffield)

Most welcoming early Georgian house, the home of Mrs Nancie Sheffield, built in 1730. Historical contents include Chippendale, Sheraton and French furniture, decorative plasterwork by Cortese, fine paintings and porcelain, with fresh flower arrangements in every room. Very beautiful landscaped gardens and parkland created by Capability Brown. Georgian Ice House, Woodland/Daffodil Walks, Nature Trail and Gift Shop.

Location: 8 m N of York; on the B1363 York/Helmsley road. Also signposted from the A19 York/Thirsk road in the Easingwold area.
Opening Times: GARDENS: open daily from Easter to Oct 1 from 11–5.30. HOUSE AND GARDENS: open all Easter weekend, May 6 to Sept 9: Weds and Bank Holiday Sun and Mons from 1.30. Adm charges not available at time of going to press. Booked parties of 20 or more welcome every day (*except Sat*). Contact: The Secretary, Sutton Park, Sutton-on-the-Forest, York, YO6 1DP. Tel: (0347) 810249.
Refreshments: Tea room/restaurant.

THORP PERROW ARBORETUM

nr Snape   map H10
(Sir John Ropner)

Thorp Perrow, the country home of Sir John Ropner, contains a magnificent arboretum – a collection of over 1,000 varieties of trees and shrubs, including some of the largest and rarest in England. It has rapidly become a popular attraction in the area and can be enjoyed by all members of the family, who may wander amidst these 85 acres of landscaped grounds. Lake, grassy glades, tree trails and woodland walks. Milbank Pinetum, within the arboretum, is now open to the public.

Location: N of Ripon on the Well/Bedale Road. O.S. map ref. SE258851.
Opening Times: All year, dawn to dusk. Adm £2, Chd under 16 & OAPs £1. Free car park. Picnic area. Toilets. Dogs permitted on leads.

TREASURER'S HOUSE, The National Trust

York   map H9
Telephone: York (0904) 624247

Large 17th century house of great interest. Fine furniture and paintings. Exhibition.
Location: Behind York Minster.
Station: York (½ m).
Opening Times: Apr 1 to Nov 1 – Daily 10.30–5. Last adm 4.30. Guided tours by arrangement. Adm £2.60, Chd £1.30. Adult party £2.20, Chd party £1.10. Wheelchair access – part of ground floor only. No car parking facilities. Dogs not allowed, except for guide dogs. Baby changing facilities. Shop and tearoom open as house.
Refreshments: Available in licensed tea rooms serving morning coffee, light lunches, teas. Open for pre-booked parties during and outside normal opening hours and for private functions. Tel: York 646757.

WHITBY ABBEY

map J10
Telephone: (0947) 603568

Founded in 657 and presided over by the Abbess Hilda, Whitby was a double monastery for both men and women – a feature of the Anglo-Saxon church. This early history has been chronicled by the Venerable Bede, who tells us that here the poet Caedmon lived and worked. Destroyed by invading Danes in 867, the monastery was refounded after the Norman Conquest, but its exposed cliff-top site continued to invite attack by sea pirates. The building remains are from the later Benedictine monastery.

Location: Whitby. OS map ref NZ904115.
Opening Times: Good Friday or Apr 1 (whichever is earlier) to Sept 30: Open Daily 10–6. Oct 1 to Maundy Thursday or Mar 31 (whichever is earlier): Open Tues to Sun 10–4. *Closed* Dec 24–26, Jan 1. Adm £1.10, Concessions 85p, Chd 55p.

SOUTH YORKSHIRE

CANNON HALL

Cawthorne   map H8
Telephone: Barnsley 790270
(Barnsley Metropolitan Borough Council)

18th century house by Carr of York. Collections of fine furniture, paintings, glassware, pewter and pottery. Also the Regimental Museum of the 13th/18th Royal Hussars. 70 acres of parkland.

Location: 5 m W of Barnsley on A635; 1 m NW of Cawthorne.
Opening Times: All the year – Tues to Sat 10.30–5; *Closed Mon.* Suns 2.30–5. Adm free. *Closed from Dec 23 re-opening Jan 2. Also closed Good Friday.*

CONISBROUGH CASTLE

map H8
Telephone: (0709) 863329

Sir Walter Scott's novel 'Ivanhoe' made Conisbrough Castle famous. The magnificent keep – still largely intact – is one of the finest examples of 12th century building in England. Sited by the River Don, the castle we see today was probably the work of Hamelin Plantagenet, illegitimate half-brother of Henry II.

Location: 4½ m (7.2 km) south west of Doncaster. OS map ref SK515989.
Opening Times: Good Friday or Apr 1 (whichever is earlier) to Sept 30: Open Daily 10–6. Oct 1 to Maundy Thursday or Mar 31 (whichever is earlier): Open Tues to Sun 10–4. *Closed* Dec 24–26, Jan 1. Adm £1.50, Concessions £1.10, Chd 75p.

MONK BRETTON PRIORY

map H9
Telephone: (0226) 204089

The monastery was founded about 1153, initially for monks of the Cluniac Order. The priory was involved in violent arguments with another Cluniac monastery at Pontefract, and more than once an armed force was sent to occupy Monk Bretton. Their differences were only resolved by Monk Bretton leaving the Order to become a Benedictine house. The remains show the layout of the monastery. One of the bestpreserved buildings is the 14th century prior's lodging, which stands three storeys high.

Location: 2 m (3.2 km) north east of Barnsley. OS map ref SE373065.
Opening Times: Good Friday or Apr 1 (whichever is earlier) to Sept 30: Open Daily 10–6. Oct 1 to Maundy Thursday or Mar 31 (whichever is earlier): Open Tues to Sun 10–4. *Closed* Dec 24–26, Jan 1. Adm 75p, Concessions 55p, Chd 40p.

ROCHE ABBEY

map H8
Telephone: (0709) 812739

Most medieval monasteries are near running water, since the monks were more fastidious about sanitation than their contemporaries. The two founders of Roche gave land on either side of a stream, and parts of the building bridge the water. Founded in 1147 for monks of the Cistercian Order, the name 'Roche' derives from its rocky site. Sadly, the only part of the abbey's history of which we know any detail, is the Dissolution. When the monks left, the monastery was plundered and the carved wood from the church burnt in order to melt the lead taken from the roof.

Location: 1½ m (2.4 km) south of Maltby. OS map ref SK544898.
Opening Times: Good Friday or Apr 1 (whichever is earlier) to Sept 30: Open Daily 10–6. Oct 1 to Maundy Thursday or Mar 31 (whichever is earlier): Open Weekends only 10–4. *Closed* Dec 24–26, Jan 1. Adm £1.10, Concessions 85p, Chd 55p.

SHEFFIELD BOTANIC GARDENS

Clarkehouse Rd, Sheffield   map H8
(Sheffield City Council)

Begun as a private venture in 1833, transferred to the Town Trust in 1898, and to Sheffield Corporation 1951. Demonstration gardens, conservation area and garden, and garden and chalet for the disabled, together with the Paxton Pavilion complex, which includes aviary, aquarium and half hardy house.

Location: 1 m from centre of Sheffield.
Opening Times: Daily all year. Admission free.

THE SUE RYDER HOME, HICKLETON HALL

nr Doncaster map H8
(The Sue Ryder Foundation)

This Home cares for 50 physically handicapped and others who are homeless and unable to cope on their own.

Location: 6 m NW of Doncaster; on A635 Doncaster/Barnsley Road (behind Hickleton Church).
Opening Times: Individuals wishing to visit the Home may do so, Mons to Fris 2–4 without prior appointment. Please report your arrival to the Office in the main entrance.
Refreshments: Hotels & Restaurants in Doncaster.

WEST YORKSHIRE

BAGSHAW MUSEUM

Wilton Park, Batley map H9
Telephone: (0924) 472514
(Kirklees Metro Council)

The museum is housed in 'The Woodlands' a High Victorian mansion built for a local mill-owning family in 1875. The architect, Walter Hamstock, and his patron, George Sheard, were responsible for the interior decoration. Fine pitch pine and oak panelling, marble fireplaces, tiles, plasterwork and painted friezes have survived and have been or are being restored. The museum houses displays of local and natural history, Oriental ceramics, and objects from around the world. New galleries explore Ancient Egypt and animals in myth, art and religion.

Location: Batley.
Opening Times: Open daily, please phone for details. Gift Shop.

BRAMHAM PARK

Wetherby map H9
Telephone: Boston Spa (0937) 844265
(Mr & Mrs George Lane Fox)

The house was created during the first half of the 18th century and affords a rare opportunity to enjoy a beautiful Queen Anne mansion containing fine furniture, pictures and porcelain—set in magnificent grounds with ornamental ponds, cascades, tall beech hedges and loggias of various shapes—unique in the British Isles for its grand vistas design stretching out into woodlands of cedar, copper beech, lime and Spanish chestnut interspersed with wild rhododendron thickets.

Location: 5 m S of Wetherby on the Great North Road (A1).
Opening Times: GROUNDS ONLY. Easter weekend, May Day, Spring Bank Hol weekend. HOUSE & GROUNDS. June 14 to Aug 31 (Bank Holiday Mon)—Suns, Tues, Weds & Thurs also Bank Hol Mon 1.15–5.30. Last adm 5 pm. For adm charges concessionary rates contact The Estate Office, Bramham Park, Wetherby, W. Yorks LS23 6ND.
BRAMHAM HORSE TRIALS—June 4–7, 1992.

BRONTË PARSONAGE AND MUSEUM

Haworth map G9
Telephone: Haworth 642323
(The Brontë Society)

BRONTË PARSONAGE AND MUSEUM – *Continued from page 213*

Once the home of the Brontë family, this Georgian parsonage has rooms furnished as in the Brontës' day, with many relics of the family, including furniture, clothes, manuscripts and drawings. Small formal garden.

Location: 4 m SW of Keighley on A6033 at Haworth.
Opening Times: All the year – Daily Apr to Sept, 10–5; Oct to Mar, 11–4.30. Adm £2.50, OAP/Student/UB40 £1, Chd 50p. *Closed Dec 24, 25, 26, 27 and Jan 13 to Feb 7 inclusive.*

EAST RIDDLESDEN HALL, The National Trust 🌿

Keighley   map H9   ♿
Telephone: Keighley (0535) 607075

17th century manor house. Magnificent tithe barn. Small formal garden.

Location: 1 m NE of Keighley on S side of A650, on N bank of Aire.
Station: Keighley (1½ m).
Opening Times: Apr 4 to Nov 1. Apr: weekends and 17 to 22 incl., 12–5.30. May to Nov 1, Sat to Wed, 12–5.30, last adm 5 (School groups and parties on weekdays by prior arrangement.) Shop and tearoom open as house and Nov to Dec 13 weekends, 12–4. Adm £2.50, Chd £1.30, Adult Parties £2, Chd Parties £1. Dogs, with the exception of guide dogs, allowed in grounds only and must be on leash. Only ground floor and garden accessible for disabled visitors. Braille guide. Baby changing facilities. Shop. Large camera bags are not allowed in house – photography by permission only.
Refreshments: Afternoon teas and refreshments in Bothy Tearoom adjacent to house (on first floor), special arrangements for disabled visitors contact Administrator.

HAREWOOD HOUSE AND BIRD GARDEN – *See page 215*

LEDSTON HALL

nr Castleford   map H9
(G. H. H. Wheler, Esq.)

17th century mansion with some earlier work.

Location: 2 m N of Castleford off A656.
Station: Castleford (2¾ m).
Opening Times: Exterior only. May, June, July and Aug – Mon to Fri 9–4. Other days by appointment.
Refreshments: Chequers Inn, Ledsham (1 m).

LOTHERTON HALL

Aberford   map H9
(Leeds Metro District Council)

Lotherton Hall was built round an earlier house dating from the mid-eighteenth century. The extensions to the east were completed in 1896 and those to the west in 1903. The Hall, with its art collection, park and gardens, was given to the City of Leeds by Sir Alvary and Lady Gascoigne in 1968 and opened as a country house museum in 1969. The Gascoigne collection, which contains pictures, furniture, silver and porcelain of the 17th and 18th centuries, as well as works of a later period, includes a magnificent portrait of Sir Thomas Gascoigne by Pompeo Batoni and an impressive group of silver race cups ranging in date from 1776 to 1842. The first floor and costume galleries were opened in 1970 and the oriental gallery in 1975. There is also a Museum shop and audio visual room.

Location: 1 m E of A1 at Aberford on the Towton Road (B1217).
Opening Times: All the year – Tues to Sun 10.30–6.15 (or dusk if earlier); Thurs from May to September 10.30–8.30. *Closed Mons except Bank Hol Mons.* Adm £1, Chd & OAPs 45p. Students 45p. Season ticket £4.35 (includes Temple Newsam, see below).

NOSTELL PRIORY, The National Trust 🌿

Wakefield   map H9   ♿
Telephone: Wakefield 863892

Built for Sir Rowland Winn by Paine; a wing added in 1766 by Robert Adam. State rooms contain pictures and famous Chippendale furniture made especially for the house.

Location: 6 m SE of Wakefield, on N side of A638.
Station: Fitzwilliam (1½ m).
Opening Times: Apr 4 to Nov 1: Apr, May, June, Sept, Oct – Sats 12–5, Suns 11–5; July & Aug – Daily (except Fris) 12–5, Sun 11–5. Bank Hol Openings (*closed* Good Friday): Easter – Mon & Tues; May Day – Mon; Spring Bank Hol – Mon & Tues; Aug Bank Hol – Mon: Mons 11–5, Tues 12–5. Adm House & Grounds £3.30, Chd £1.70; Adult party £2.80, Chd party £1.40. Grounds only £2, Chd £1. Guided tours on weekdays only (last tour 4). Parking free. Pre-booked parties welcome outside normal published opening times. However, on these occasions, a charge will be made to National Trust members. *Dogs in grounds on leashes, not in house (except guide dogs). Lift available for disabled.*
Refreshments: Lunches and afternoon teas available in stable tea rooms (not NT).

HAREWOOD HOUSE AND BIRD GARDEN

Leeds   map H9   ⓢ
Telephone: (0532) 886225
(The Earl of Harewood)

18th century house designed by John Carr and Robert Adam and still the home of the Lascelles family. As well as superb ceilings, plasterwork and Chippendale furniture it contains fine English and Italian paintings and Sevres and Chinese porcelain. In the grounds, landscaped by 'Capability' Brown, are lakeside and woodland walks, displays of roses and rhododendrons and a herbaceous border running the length of the Terrace.

Location: 7 m S of Harrogate; 8 m N of Leeds on Leeds/Harrogate road; Junction A61/659 at Harewood village; 5 m from A1 at Wetherby 22m from York.
Opening Times: HOUSE, GROUNDS, BIRD GARDEN AND ALL FACILITIES — Apr 5 to Oct 31 daily. Gates open 10 House open 11. Concession rates for Coach parties, school parties welcome at all times. Adm charges and details of Summer and Weekend Events — including Car Rallies and Leeds Championship Dog Show available from Gerald Long, Visitors Information, Estate Office, Harewood, Leeds LS17 9LQ. State Dining Room (max 48) available.
Refreshments: Cafeteria; Restaurant; also Courtyard Functions Suite for Conference/Product launches throughout the year.

Sir Peter Lely – portrait painter

His paintings can be seen at the following properties included in Historic Houses Castles and Gardens:

Althorp
Aynhoe Park
Belton House
Browsholme Hall
Dalmeny House
Euston Hall
Goodwood House
Gorhambury

Hinwick House
Kedleston Hall
Ragley Hall
St Osyth Priory
Stoneleigh Abbey
Stanford Hall
Weston Park

OAKWELL HALL

Birstall   map H9

Sixteenth century manor house (built 1583) now displayed as the home of the Batt family in the 1690s. Period gardens. Civil War and Brontë connections. Set in 87 acres of country park featuring an adventure playground, equestrian arena, Visitor Centre and Shop, Countryside Information Centre, picnic areas, wildlife garden and aboretum, Events programme. Telephone for details or see Events Leaflet.

Location: Birstall, Batley.
Opening Times: Open daily. Please phone for details. Adm charge (seasonal).
Refreshments: Oaktree Cafe.

SHIBDEN HALL

Halifax   map G9
Telephone: Halifax (0422) 352246 or (0422) 321455
(Calderdale Metropolitan Borough Council)

An early 15th century half-timbered house with later additions, furnished with 17th and 18th century material. The 17th century barn and outbuildings are equipped with early agricultural implements and craft workshop. The museum is set in a large park and surrounded by terrace gardens. Café facilities.

Location: ¼ m SE of Halifax on the Halifax/Hipperholme Road (A58).
Opening Times: Mar to Nov—Mons to Sats 10–5, Suns 12–5. Feb—Suns only 2–5. *Closed December to January.* Adm £1.50, Chd, OAPs 75p. *Conducted tours after normal hours* (Fee payable).
Refreshments: At the Hall.

TEMPLE NEWSAM

Leeds   map H9
(Leeds Metro District Council)

RED HOUSE

Gomersal, Nr Cleckheaton   map H9
Telephone: (0274) 872165
(Kirklees Metropolitan Council)

Period house with Brontë connections. Built in 1660, Red House was completely restored in 1990. It is now displayed as the 1830s home of Yorkshire wool clothier and merchant Joshua Taylor and his family. Home of Mary Taylor, 19th century writer and feminist. Charlotte Brontë, Mary's lifelong friend, often stayed at Red House in the 1830s, later featuring it as 'Briarmains' and the Taylors as the 'Yorkes' in her novel 'Shirley'. Attractive museum shop. Re-created early 19th century gardens. Lively events and activities programme.

Location: Gomersal, Nr Cleckheaton.
Opening Times: Open daily. Please ring for details.

The Temple Newsam estate belonged to the Knights Templar and later passed to the D'Arcy family who retained it until 1537. The house was the birthplace of Lord Darnley and a centre of English and Scottish intrigue during the reign of Elizabeth I. It was later acquired by Sir Arthur Ingram, whose descendants became Viscounts Irwin. It was eventually inherited by the late Lord Halifax who sold it to Leeds Corporation in 1922. The house has many fine features of 16th and 17th century date, as well as a magnificent suite of Georgian rooms, and contains some superb furniture, silver, ceramics and a fine collection of pictures. There is also a Museum shop in the house.

Location: 5 m E of Leeds; 1 m S of A63 (nr junction with A642).
Station: Cross Gates (1³/₄ m).
Opening Times: All the year—Tues to Sun 10.30–6.15 (or dusk if earlier); Weds from May to Sept 10.30–8.30. *Closed Mons except Bank Hol Mons.* Adm £1, Chd & OAPs 45p. Students 45p. Season tickets £4.35 (includes Lotherton Hall, see above).

TOLSON MEMORIAL MUSEUM

Ravensknowle Park, Huddersfield, HD5 8DJ   map H9
Telephone: (0484) 530591

Fine Italianate mansion built as Ravensknowle Hall in 1859-62, by a local textile manufacturer, and set in a public park. It now houses attractive modern displays on the natural history, archaeology and local history of the Huddersfield district. Special attractions include the Farming, Transport and Woollen Industry galleries. A full range of special exhibitions is offered, with many workshops, events and children's activities. Access and toilets for disabled people. Shop.

Location: Huddersfield.
Opening Times: Open daily please phone for details. Adm free.

WALES

CLWYD

BODELWYDDAN CASTLE

Bodelwyddan LL18 5YA   map E8
Telephone: (0745) 583539
(Clwyd County Council)

Bodelwyddan Castle has been authentically restored as a Victorian Country House and contains a major collection of portraits and photography on permanent loan from the National Portrait Gallery. The collection includes works by many eminent Victorian Portraitists such as G. F. Watts, William Holman Hunt, John Singer Sargeant, Sir Edwin Landseer and Sir Thomas Lawrence. The portraits are complemented by furniture from the Victoria & Albert Museum and sculptures from the Royal Academy. The extensive formal gardens have been restored to their former glory and provide a magnificent display of flowering plants, water features, maze, aviary and woodland walks. For children there is an adventure woodland and play area.

Location: Just off the A55 near St. Asaph (opposite the Marble Church).
Opening Times: Easter to June 30 and Sept 1 to Nov 1. Open daily except Fri July 1 to Aug 31, open daily 10–5. Williams Hall opens 10.30. Last admission one hour before closing. For details of winter openings please ring. Discount rates available for groups of 20 or more. Ample car parking. Suitable for disabled persons (wheelchairs available). Gift shop. Picnic Area. Woodland Walk. Maze and Aviary. Adm £3.50, concessions £2, Family £9. Discount rates available for groups of 20 or more. Ample car parking. Suitable for disabled persons (wheelchairs available). Gift shop, Picnic area, Woodland walk.
Refreshments: Victorian Tea Room, Pavilion Restaurant, Cafeteria.

CHIRK CASTLE, The National Trust ❧

nr Wrexham   map F7
Telephone: Chirk (0691) 777701

Built 1310; a unique example of a border castle of Edward I's time, inhabited continuously for 660 years. Interesting portraits, tapestries etc. Gardens.

Location: ½ m from Chirk (on A5 trunk road) then 1½ m private driveway; 20 m NW of Shrewsbury 7 m SE of Llangollen.
Station: Chirk (2 m).

CHIRK CASTLE, The National Trust – *Continued from page 217*

Opening Times: Apr 1 to Sept 27 – Daily except Mons & Sats but open Bank Holiday Mon. Oct 3 to Nov 1, Sat & Sun only, 12–5, Gardens open 12–6. (Open Bank Holiday Mons 12–5). Castle 12–5, Grounds open 12–6. (Last adm to Castle 4.30.) Adm £3.40, Chd £1.70, Group £2.70, Family £8.50. No dogs. Very limited access for wheelchairs.
Refreshments: Tea rooms (light lunches & teas).

ERDDIG, The National Trust

nr Wrexham map F7
Telephone: Wrexham (0978) 355314

Late 17th century house with 18th century additions and containing much of the original furniture, set in a garden restored to 18th century formal design and containing varieties of fruit known to have been grown there during that period. Range of domestic outbuildings include laundry, bakehouse, sawmill and smithy, all in working order; the extensive restoration work on house and garden is now complete. Visitor Centre containing early farm implements.

Location: 2 m S of Wrexham off A525.
Stations: Wrexham Central (1³/4 m); Wrexham General (2¹/2 m), includes 1 m driveway to House.
Opening Times: Apr 1 to Sept 30 daily except Thurs and Fris (open Good Friday), 11–6, (house 12–5). Last adm 4. Oct 3 to Nov 1: Belowstairs, servants' quarters only daily except Thurs & Fri 11–6, last adm 4.
NB: Certain rooms have no electric light; visitors wishing to make a close study of pictures & textiles should avoid dull days early & late in season. Due to extreme fragility the Tapestry & Chinese Rooms will be open only on Weds & Sats.
Refreshments: Light lunches & teas.

EWLOE CASTLE

nr Hawarden map F8
(Cadw: Welsh Historic Monuments)

Native Welsh castle with typical round and aspidal towers.

Location: 1 m NW of Ewloe.

GYRN CASTLE

Llanasa, Holywell map F8
Telephone: (0745) 853500
(Sir Geoffrey Bates, BT, MC)

Dating, in part, from 1700; castellated 1820. Large picture gallery, panelled entrance hall. Pleasant woodland walks.

Location: 26 m W of Chester (off A55); 4 m SE of Prestatyn.
Opening Times: All the year – by appointment. Adm £3, parties welcome.
Refreshments: By arrangement.

VALLE CRUCIS ABBEY

Llangollen map F7
(Cadw: Welsh Historic Monuments)

The lovely ruins of this 13th century Abbey are set beside the Eglwyseg stream in a narrow valley.

Location: B5103 from the A5, west of Llangollen, or A542 from Ruthin.
Opening Times: Mar 29 to Oct 25, daily 9.30–6.30. Oct 26 to Mar 28, weekdays 9.30– 4; Sun 2–4.

DYFED

CARREG CENNEN CASTLE

Trapp map E5
(Cadw: Welsh Historic Monuments)

A 13th century castle dramatically perched on a limestone precipice.

Location: Minor roads from A483 (T) to Trapp Village, near Llandeilo.
Opening Times: Mar 29 to Oct 25 daily 9.30–6.30; Oct 26 to Mar 28 weekdays 9.30–4, Sun 2–4.

CILGERRAN CASTLE

Cilgerran map E5
(Cadw: Welsh Historic Monuments)

Picturesque remains that date essentially from the time of William Marshall the Younger, chiefly early 13th century.

Location: 3 m S of Cilgerran off A478.
Opening Times: Mar 29 to Oct 25 daily 9.30–6.30; Oct 26 to Mar 28 weekdays 9.30–4, Sun 2–4.

COLBY WOODLAND GARDEN, The National Trust

Amroth map D5
Telephone: Llandeilo 822800, Saundersfoot (0834) 811885

Formal and woodland gardens; walks through a secluded valley along open and wooded pathways with rhododendrons and azaleas. Mr and Mrs A. Scourfield Lewis kindly allow access to the Walled Garden during normal visiting hours.

Location: NE of Tenby off A477; E of junction A477/A478.
Station: Kilgetty (2¹/2 m).
Opening Times: Mar 30 to Oct 31 daily 10–5. Adm £2, Chd 70p.

KIDWELLY CASTLE

Kidwelly map D5
(Cadw: Welsh Historic Monuments)

One of the finest castles in west Wales, an outstanding example of late 13th century castle design.

Location: Kidwelly via A484 (between Carmarthen & Burry Port).
Opening Times: Mar 29 to Oct 25, daily 9.30–6.30. Oct 26 to Mar 28, weekdays 9.30– 4; Sun 2–4.

LAMPHEY BISHOP'S PALACE

Lamphey map D4
(Cadw: Welsh Historic Monuments)

Substantial remains of the medieval Bishops of St David's country residence.

Location: 2¹/2 m E of Pembroke on A4139.
Opening Times: Mar 29 to Oct 25, 9.30–6.30 daily; Oct 26 to Mar 28 weekdays 9.30–4, Sun 2–4.

LLAWHADEN CASTLE

Llawhaden map D5
(Cadw: Welsh Historic Monuments)

A fortified palace at the centre of a manorial estate belonging to the Bishops of St Davids.

Location: Llawhaden, off A40(T) 3m NW of Narberth.
Opening Times: Mar 29 to Oct 25, 9.30–6.30 daily; Oct 26 to Mar 28 weekdays 9.30–4, Sun 2–4.

PICTON CASTLE

Haverfordwest map D5
(The Picton Castle Trust)

A scheduled ancient monument, but also a beautiful home, occupied continuously since the 15th century by the Philipps family who are still in residence.

Location: 4 m SE of Haverfordwest S of A40 via the Rhos.
Opening Times: CASTLE: Easter Sun & Mon, and following Bank Hols. Also every Sun & Thurs from
mid-July to mid-Sept: 2–5. GROUNDS: Easter Sat to Sept 30 – Daily 10.30–5, except Mon.
GRAHAM
SUTHERLAND GALLERY (tel: (0437) 751296): Easter Sat to Sept 30 daily 10.30–12.30, 1.30–5
except Mon, but open Bank Hol Mons. Dates and times of opening under review. Craft Shop. Free car
park. Adm: Grounds £1, Castle & Grounds £2, Chd half price. (Subject to review.)
Refreshments: Tea room. *Closed* Mon.

ST DAVIDS BISHOP'S PALACE

St Davids   map C5
(Cadw: Welsh Historic Monuments)

A most impressive medieval Bishop's Palace within the Cathedral Close.

Location: Near the centre of St Davids.
Opening Times: Mar 29 to Oct 25 daily 9.30–6.30; Oct 26 to Mar 28, weekdays 9.30–4, Sun 2–4.

STRATA FLORIDA ABBEY

Strata Florida   map E6
(Cadw: Welsh Historic Monuments)

Founded in 1164, the ruins of this Cistercian abbey stand in a lovely valley.

Location: 1¼ m SE of Pontrhydfendigaid.
Opening Times: Mar 29 to Oct 25 daily 9.30–6.30; Oct 26 to Mar 28, weekdays 9.30–4, Sun 2–4.

TALLEY ABBEY

Talley   map E5
(Cadw: Welsh Historic Monuments)

A small early 13th century monastic site founded for the Premonstratensian Order.

Location: Talley on B4302 6m N of Llandeilo.
Opening Times: Mar 29 to Oct 25 daily 9.30–6.30; Oct 26 to Mar 28, weekdays 9.30–4, Sun 2–4.

TUDOR MERCHANT'S HOUSE, The National Trust

Tenby   map D4
Telephone: (0834) 2279

An example of a merchant's house of the 15th century.

Location: Quay Hill, Tenby.
Station: Tenby (8 mins walk) (not Suns, except June–Aug).
Opening Times: Mar 30 to Oct 30 Mon–Fri 11–6. Sun 2–6. *Closed Sat.* Adm £1.50, Chd 70p. Group discount 20%.

MID GLAMORGAN

CAERPHILLY CASTLE

Caerphilly   map F4
(Cadw: Welsh Historic Monuments)

Caerphilly Castle is one of the largest surviving castles of the medieval western world, with extensive water defences covering over 30 acres.

Location: A468 (from Newport), A470/A469 (from Cardiff).
Opening Times: Mar 29 to Oct 25, daily 9.30–6.30. Oct 26 to Mar 28, weekdays 9.30–4; Suns 2–4.

COITY CASTLE

Coity   map E4
(Cadw: Welsh Historic Monuments)

Although originally established soon after 1100, much of the castle dates from 14th century and later.

Location: Coity 2 m NE of Bridgend.
Opening Times: Mar 29 to Oct 25, daily 9.30–6.30. Oct 26 to Mar 28, weekdays 9.30–4; Suns 2–4.

LLANCAIACH FAWR

Treharris   map F4
Telephone: (0443) 412248
(Rhymney Valley District Council)

Llancaiach Fawr is a fine example of a Tudor period semi-fortified manor house which was built by the Prichard family in the 1530's. It has been lived in continuously to the present day and is unique in South Wales for having survived virtually unaltered from its original form. The house and gardens have been carefully restored to how they would have appeared in the mid-seventeenth century. Llancaiach Fawr is now a superb living history museum of the Civil War period. Visitors step back in time to the gentry household of Colonel Edward Prichard, master of Llancaiach Fawr during the Civil War. Costumed stewards each taking on the character of one of Prichard's servants show guests around their master's house. Visitors to Llancaiach Fawr can try out the reproduction furniture, try on period clothes or even try a turn in the stocks! Excellent visitor centre facilities include exhibition, audio visual display, gift shop, restaurant, toilets, baby changing room and teaching rooms. There is disabled access to the Visitor Centre, gardens and ground floor of the house. Ample car and coach parking.

Location: Thirty minutes north of Cardiff (M4 Jtn 32) just off the A470 at Nelson on the B4254.
Opening Times: All year except Dec 25, 26, Jan 1. Mon to Fri 10–5, Sat 10–6, Sun 2–6 *(last adm 1 hr before closing).* Adm charge.
Refreshments: Conservatory Cafe in the Visitor Centre which serves seventeenth century recipes as well as more contemporary cuisine. Available for hire. Period banquets in the manor house.

SOUTH GLAMORGAN

CARDIFF CASTLE

Cardiff   map F4   △
(Cardiff City Council)

Begun 1090 on remains of Roman Fort. Rich interior decorations. Location for Cardiff Searchlight Tattoo.

Location: In centre of Cardiff city.
Station: Cardiff Centre (¹/₂ m).

CASTELL COCH

Tongwynlais, nr Cardiff   map F4
(Cadw: Welsh Historic Monuments)

This late 19th century castle – a combination of Victorian Gothic fantasy and timeless fairytale – peeps unexpectedly through the trees on the north hills of Cardiff.

Location: M4 (Junction 32), A470 and signposted.
Opening Times: Mar 29 to Oct 25, daily 9.30–6.30. Oct 26 to Mar 28, weekdays 9.30–4; Suns 2–4.

WELSH FOLK MUSEUM

St. Fagans, Cardiff   map F4

One of Europe's foremost open-air museums, in 100 acres of parkland, featuring dwellings from an elegant mansion house to humble quarrymen's cottages. This unique collection of re-erected buildings includes farmhouses, cottages, a Victorian shop, a chapel and a toll house, with craftsmen demonstrating their traditional skills within. Festivals include Old May Day Fair, Mid Summer Festival, Harvest Festival and Christmas.

Location: M4, junction 33, signposted.
Opening Times: Apr to Oct daily 10–5; Nov to Mar Mon to Sat 10–5. Telephone (0222) 569441 for information and admission prices.

WEST GLAMORGAN

MARGAM PARK

nr Port Talbot   map E4   Ⓢ
Telephone: (0639) 881635; Fax: (0639) 895897
(West Glamorgan County Council)

This 850 acre country park has historic buildings including the famous Orangery, a deer herd, one of Europe's largest hedge mazes, and outdoor sculpture park, audio visual theatre, putting, gift shop, and cafeteria plus Fairy Tale Land – a nursery rhyme village for the under 8s. Large coach and car park.

Location: Easy access on A48 ¼ m from Exit 38 off M4 near Port Talbot.
Opening Times: Apr to Sept: daily 10–6 (last adm 4); Oct to Mar: Wed to Sun 10–6 (last adm 3). Adm charge: Apr to Sept – entry and use of certain facilities – all classes £2.50 under 3s free. Special rates for families and pre-booked parties. Adm charge: Oct to Mar £1, Chd and OAPs 50p.
Refreshments: Charlotte's Pantry. The magnificent Orangery can be hired. Please telephone for details.

NEATH ABBEY

Neath   map E4
(Cadw: Welsh Historic Monuments)

Originally founded as a daughter house of Savigny by Richard de Granville in 1130, the abbey was absorbed into the Cistercian order in 1147.

Location: 1 m W of Neath off A465. M4 (Jn 44), A48(T), A483, A4109, A474 all leading to A465.
Opening Times: Mar 29 to Oct 25 daily 9.30–6.30. Oct 26 to Mar 28 weekdays 9.30–4; Sun 2–4.

WEOBLEY CASTLE

Weobley   map E4
(Cadw: Welsh Historic Monuments)

Picturesque fortified medieval manor house.

Location: 2 m W of Llanrhidian.
Opening Times: Mar 29 to Oct 25 daily 9.30–6.30. Oct 26 to Mar 28 weekdays 9.30–4; Sun 2–4.

GWENT

CAERLEON ROMAN FORTRESS

Caerleon   map F4
(Cadw: Welsh Historic Monuments)

Impressive remains of the fortress baths, amphitheatre, barracks and fortress wall.

Location: B4236 to Caerleon, from M4 (junction 25).
Opening Times: Mar 29 to Oct 25 daily 9.30–6.30. Oct 26 to Mar 28 weekdays 9.30–4; Sun 2–4.

CHEPSTOW CASTLE

Chepstow   map G4
(Cadw: Welsh Historic Monuments)

This strategic fortress – one of the earliest stone built castles in Britain – guards one of the main crossings from England to Wales.

Location: Chepstow via A466, B4235, A48 or M4 (Junction 22).
Opening Times: Mar 29 to Oct 25, daily 9.30–6.30. Oct 26 to Mar 28, weekdays 9.30–4; Suns 2–4.

PENHOW CASTLE – *See page 221*

RAGLAN CASTLE – *See page 221*

TINTERN CASTLE – *See page 221*

TREDEGAR HOUSE

Newport   map F4
Telephone: Newport (0633) 815880
(Newport Borough Council)

One wing of the 16th century house survives, but Tredegar House owes its character to lavish 17th century rebuilding in brick. Ancestral home of the Morgan family, Lords of Tredegar. The Country Park includes gardens, lake adventure play farm, carriage rides and craft workshops.

Location: SW of Newport; signposted from M4 junction 28, A48.
Station: Newport (2¾ m).
Opening Times: PARK. Daily 6.15–Sunset. HOUSE AND ATTRACTIONS. Good Fri to last Sun in Sept. Weds to Suns and Public Hols and Tues, school hols and weekends in Oct. House Tours every ½ hour from 11.30–4. House open at other times by appointment. Adm to house and walled gardens (1992 rates) £3.20, Chd/OAPs £2.20, Family £7.20. Coach and school parties welcome if booked in advance.
Refreshments: Lunch and teas at the Old Brewhouse Bar and Tea Room.

PENHOW CASTLE

Nr Newport map F4
Telephone: Penhow (0633) 400800 and
Recorded Information: (0633) 400469
(Stephen Weeks Esq.)

Penhow Castle

WALES' OLDEST LIVED-IN CASTLE: The Most Stimulating Castle Tour in Britain

Penhow Castle is Wales' oldest lived-in Castle, and was the first home in Britain of the famous Seymour family. The buildings date from the early 12th century (the Norman Keep) and building continued around its courtyard until the late 17th century (the Charles II panelled rooms). The restoration of the Castle since 1973 has been substantial and includes the Great Hall with its minstrels' gallery, the kitchens, the excavation of the moat, and many period rooms. Visitors are guided by the award-winning "Time Machine" Walkman Tours, included in the admission price.

Location: On A48, midway between Chepstow and Newport. M4 junctions 22 or 24.
Opening Times: Good Fri to end of Sept – Weds to Suns inclusive and Bank Holidays; Aug: open 7 days 10–6 (last adm 5). Winter opening: Wed only, 10–5. Adm £2.75, Chd £1.50. Family tickets (2 + 2): £7. *Price includes TIME MACHINE Walkman Tour.* 'Candlelit Tours' by appointment; open all year round for educational visits. Gift shop.
Refreshments: At tour point.

RAGLAN CASTLE

Raglan map F5
(Cadw: Welsh Historic Monuments)

This 15th century castle with its Great Tower or 'Yellow Tower of Gwent', was as much a product of social grandeur as it was military necessity.

Location: Via the A40 (between Monmouth and Abergavenny).
Opening Times: Mar 29 to Oct 25, daily 9.30–6.30. Oct 26 to Mar 28, weekdays 9.30–4; Suns 2–4.

TINTERN ABBEY

Tintern map G4
(Cadw: Welsh Historic Monuments)

Impressive ruins of Cistercian abbey, founded in 1131, set in the picturesque Wye valley.

Location: Tintern via A466 (between Chepstow and Monmouth), from the M4 (Junction 22).
Opening Times: Mar 29 to Oct 25, daily 9.30–6.30. Oct 26 to Mar 28, weekdays 9.30–4; Suns 2–4.

TREDEGAR HOUSE – *See page 220*

WHITE CASTLE

Llantilio Crosseny map F5
(Cadw: Welsh Historic Monuments)

Imposing moated remains of 12th century castle, probably the work of Henry II.

Location: 6 m E of Abergavenny, off B4233.
Opening Times: Mar 29 to Oct 25 daily 9.30–6.30. Oct 26 to Mar 28 weekdays 9.30–4; Sun 2–4.

GWYNEDD

ABERCONWY HOUSE, The National Trust

Conwy map E8
Telephone: Conwy (0492) 592246

Town house that dates from 14th century. Furnished rooms and an audio-visual presentation show daily life from different periods in its history.

Location: In the town at junction of Castle Street & High Street.
Station: Conwy 300 yds.
Opening Times: Apr 1 to Nov 1 – Daily (except Tues) 11–5.30 (last admission 5); Adm £1.40, Chd 70p, Family £3.50. Pre-booked parties £1. Shop.

BEAUMARIS CASTLE (World Heritage Listed Site)

Beaumaris, Anglesey map E8
(Cadw: Welsh Historic Monuments)

The last and largest of the castles built by King Edward I, Beaumaris is the most perfect example of a concentrically planned castle in Britain.

Location: A545 (Menai Bridge), A5 (Bangor).
Opening Times: Mar 29 to Oct 25, daily 9.30–6.30. Oct 26 to Mar 28, weekdays 9.30– 4; Suns 2–4.

BODNANT GARDEN, The National Trust

Tal-y-Cafn map E8
Telephone: Tyn-y-Groes (0492) 650460

Begun in 1875 by Henry Pochin. Amongst the finest gardens in the country. Magnificent collections of rhododendrons, camellias, magnolias and conifers.

Location: 8 m S of Llandudno & Colwyn Bay on A470; Entrance along Eglwysbach Road.
Station: Tal-y-Cafn (1½ m).
Opening Times: Mar 14 to Oct 31 – Daily 10–5 (last adm 4.30). Adm £3, Chd £1.50, Group £2.60 (for groups over 20 adults). Free car park. *No dogs (except guide dogs for the blind).* Wheelchairs provided but garden is steep & difficult. Braille guide.
Refreshments: Pavilion in car park.

BRYN BRAS CASTLE

Llanrug map E8
Telephone: Llanberis (0286) 870210
(Mr & Mrs N E Gray-Parry)

The Castle, Grade II* listed, was built in c.1830 in the Romanesque style on an earlier structure built before 1750. There are fine examples of stained glass, panelling, interesting ceilings and richly carved furniture in this romantic castle, which was built by a Welshman, and is still a Welsh family home. The extensive and tranquil landscaped gardens of natural beauty, with much wild life, gradually merge into the

BRYN BRAS CASTLE – *Continued from page 221*

foothills of Snowdon. They include peaceful lawns, herbaceous borders, roses, walled Knot Garden, stream and pools, woodland walks and a ¼ mile mountain walk with magnificent panoramic views of Snowdon, Anglesey and the sea.

Location: 4½ m E of Caernarfon; 3½ m NW of Llanberis; ½ m off A4086.
Opening Times: Spring Bank Hol to mid-July & Sept — Daily (except Sats) 1 – 5. Mid- July to end Aug — Daily (except Sats) 10.30 – 5. Adm £2.50, Chd £1.25 (1991 rates). *10% reduction for parties.* Free car park. No dogs.
Refreshments: Home made Welsh teas (including Bara Brith) in charming tea room & the tea garden. Picnic area.
Castle Apartments for holidays available all year.

CAERNARFON CASTLE (World Heritage Listed Site)

Caernarfon   map D2
(Cadw: Welsh Historic Monuments)

This mighty medieval fortress, built by King Edward I was planned as both a royal residence and seat of government for north Wales. The castle earned itself a place in modern history on July 1, 1969 as the setting for the Investiture of HRH Prince Charles as Prince of Wales.

Location: A4085, A487(T), A4086 and B4366.
Opening Times: Mar 29 to Oct 25, daily 9.30 – 6.30. Oct 26 to Mar 28, weekdays 9.30 – 4; Suns 2 – 4.

COCHWILLAN OLD HALL

Talybont, Bangor   map E8
Telephone: Bangor 364608
(R. C. H. Douglas Pennant, Esq)

Fine example of medieval architecture (restored 1971).

Location: 3½ m Bangor; 1 m Talybont village off A55.
Opening Times: Open by appointment.

CONWY CASTLE (World Heritage Listed Site)

Conwy   map E8
(Cadw: Welsh Historic Monuments)

Imposing fortress built between 1283 and 1287. Conwy castle remains a masterpiece of medieval architecture.

Location: Conwy via A55 or B5106.
Opening Times: Mar 29 to Oct 25, daily 9.30 – 6.30. Oct 26 to Mar 28, weekdays 9.30 – 4; Suns 2 – 4.

CRICCIETH CASTLE

Criccieth   map D7
(Cadw: Welsh Historic Monuments)

Perched in a commanding position above Tremadog Bay, the castle was established in around 1230 by the Welsh prince Lleywelyn the Great.

Location: A497 to Criccieth from Porthmadog or from Pwllheli.
Opening Times: Mar 29 to Oct 25, daily 9.30 – 6.30. Oct 26 to Mar 28, weekdays 9.30 – 4; Suns 2 – 4.

CYMER ABBEY

Cymer   map E7
(Cadw: Welsh Historic Monuments)

Substantial remains of Cistercian abbey founded in 1199.

Location: 2 m N of Dolgellau off A494.
Opening Times: Mar 29 to Oct 25 daily 9.30 – 6.30. Oct 25 to Mar 28 weekdays 9.30 – 4; Sun 2 – 4.

GWYDIR UCHAF CHAPEL

Llanrwst   map E7
(Cadw: Welsh Historic Monuments)

A 17th century chapel with elaborately painted ceilings and walls.

Location: On Forestry Commission land ½ m SW of Llanrwst.
Opening Times: Mar 29 to Oct 25 daily 9.30 – 6.30. Oct 26 to Mar 28 weekdays 9.30 – 4; Sun 2 – 4.

HARLECH CASTLE (World Heritage Listed Site)

Harlech   map D7
(Cadw: Welsh Historic Monuments)

The powerful walls and towers of this magnificent castle were built by King Edward I, during his conquest of Wales in 1283 and were mainly complete by 1289.

Location: A496 from Blaenau Ffestiniog or from Barmouth.
Opening Times: Mar 29 to Oct 25, daily 9.30 – 6.30. Oct 26 to Mar 28, weekdays 9.30 – 4; Suns 2 – 4.

PENRHYN CASTLE, The National Trust

Bangor   map E8
Telephone: (0248) 353084

The 19th century Castle is a unique and outstanding example of neo-Norman architecture. The garden and grounds have exotic and rare trees and shrubs. There is an Industrial Railway Museum and exhibition of dolls. Victorian formal garden. Superb views of mountains and Menai Strait.

Location: 1 m E of Bangor, on A5122.
Station: Bangor (3 m).
Opening Times: Apr 1 to Nov 1 — Daily except Tues Castle 12 – 5, July & Aug 11 – 5 (last adm 4.30). Grounds: 11 – 6, (last audio tour 4). Adm £3.80, Chd £1.90, Family £9.50, Groups £3. Garden only: £2, Chd £1.
Refreshments: Light lunches & teas at Castle.

PLAS BRONDANW GARDENS

Nr Penrhyndeudraeth   map E7
Telephone: (0766) 771136

Created by Sir Clough Williams-Ellis, architect of Portmeirion, below his ancestral home. Italian inspired gardens with spectacular mountain views, topiary and folly tower.

Location: 2 m N of Penrhyndeudraeth. ¼ m off the A4085 on Croesor Road.
Opening Times: Open all year, daily 9 – 5. Adm £1, Chd 25p.

PLAS MAWR

Conwy   map E8
(Royal Cambrian Academy of Art)

Built by Robert Wynne 1577 – 80.

Location: High Street Conwy.
Station: Conwy (200 yards).
Opening Times: Nov, Feb & Mar — Weds to Suns 10 – 4; Apr to Sept — All week 10 – 6; Oct — All week 10 – 4. *Closed Dec & Jan.* Adm £1, Chd 25p, OAPs/Students 50p.

PLAS NEWYDD, The National Trust

Isle of Anglesey   map D2
Telephone: Llanfairpwll (0248) 714795

18th century house by James Wyatt in unspoilt position adjacent to Menai Strait. Magnificent views to Snowdonia. Fine spring garden. Rex Whistler exhibition and mural painting. Military museum.

Location: 1 m SW of Llanfairpwll on A4080 to Brynsiencyn; turn off A5 to Llanfairpwll at W end of Britannia Bridge.
Station: Llanfairpwll (1¾ m).
Opening Times: Apr 1 to Sept 27 — Daily except Sats 12 – 5 (garden 11 – 5 in July and Aug), last adm 4.30. Oct 2 to Nov 1 Fri and Sun Sun only 12 – 5. Adm £3.30, Chd £1.65, Family £8.25, Group £2.65.
Refreshments: Tea rooms (light lunches & teas).

TŶ MAWR WYBRNANT, The National Trust

nr. Penmachno   map E7
Telephone: Penmachno (069 03) 213

The birthplace of Bishop William Morgan. (c. 1545 – 1604), the first translator of the Bible into Welsh.

Location: At the head of the little valley of Wybrnant, 3½ m SW of Betws-y-Coed; 2 m W of Penmachno.
Opening Times: Apr 1 to Sept 27 — Weds, Thurs, Fris, Suns 12 – 5. Oct to Nov 1: Fri and Sun 12 – 4. Last adm 30 mins before closing. Oct 4 to Nov 3: Fris and Suns only 12 – 4. Last adm 30 mins before closing. May to Aug 31, Fri evenings by arrangement only. Adm £1.20, Chd 60p, Family £3, Group £1.

POWYS

GREGYNOG
Newtown map F6
Telephone: (0686) 650224
(The University of Wales)

A Victorian mansion, in 750 acres of wooded parkland with extensive gardens, including one of the most striking displays of rhododendrons in Wales; the Western red cedar 'Zebrina' is probably the biggest tree of this variety in the U.K. Many walks in the grounds. The Hall has an exceptionally fine carved parlour of 1636, retained when the old hall was rebuilt in the 1840s. The works of art still remaining from the collections of the Davies sisters include two Rodin bronzes. On show also are books by the Gregynog Press, one of the best-known private presses of the 1920s and 30s, and by the present Gwasg Gregynog, where fine printing is still carried on. This is a working Press and visitors can only be accepted occasionally by prior appointment. Accommodation is sometimes available in the Hall, depending on the nature and size of the resident conference. Since 1963, The Hall has operated as an intercollegiate course and conference centre for the various colleges and institutions of the University of Wales. During the last week in June, an important annual Music Festival is held here.

Location: Near the village of Tregynon, 5 m N of Newtown, off B4389.
Opening Times: Gardens always open. Hall: Jun 5 – Sept 30, Mon to Sat. *Guided tours only at 11 and 3,* adm £1.50, including morning coffee or afternoon tea. Chd under 15 half price. Parties by arrangement. Free car parking. Suitable for disabled persons (no wheelchairs provided). Hall and Gardens may very exceptionally have to be closed for a day.

TREBINSHWN HOUSE
nr Brecon map F5
(Robin Watson, Esq)

A medium sized 16th century manor house which underwent extensive restoration in 1800. Fine courtyard and walled garden.

Location: 7 m SE of Brecon; 1½ m from Bwlch & A40; 4 m from Llangorse (B4560).
Opening Times: May 1 to Aug 31 – Mons & Tues 10 – 5. Adm charge not available at time of going to press.
Refreshments: Red Lion Hotel, Llangorse (4 m).

POWIS CASTLE, The National Trust 🦋
Welshpool map F6 &
Telephone: Welshpool (0938) 554336

The medieval stronghold of the Welsh princes of Upper Powys, the home of the Herbert family since 1587. Clive of India Museum. Fine plaster work, murals, furniture, paintings and tapestry. Historic terraced garden; herbaceous borders, rare trees and shrubs.

Location: 1 m S of Welshpool on A483; Pedestrian access from High Street (A490); Cars enter road to Newtown (A483); 1 m.
Stations: Welshpool (1¼ m); Welshpool Raven Square (1¼ m); BR service Aug only.
Opening Times: Apr 1 to June 30 and Sept 1 to Nov 1: daily except Mons and Tues. July 1 to Aug 31: daily except Mons 12 – 5, last adm 30 mins prior to closing. Museum and Garden: 11 – 6. Adm All-inclusive ticket £5.40, Chd £2.70, Group £5. Museum/Garden: £3.20, Chd £1.60, Family £8, Group £2.60.
Refreshments: Tea rooms (light lunches & teas).

TRETOWER COURT & CASTLE ⚙️
Crickhowell map F5
(Cadw: Welsh Historic Monuments)

One of the finest medieval houses in Wales. The castle is located across an open meadow to the rear.

Location: 3 m NW Crickhowell off A479, and A470.
Opening Times: Mar 29 to Oct 25 daily 9.30 – 6.30. Oct 26 to Mar 28 weekdays 9.30 – 4; Sun 2 – 4.

IRELAND (REPUBLIC OF)

ANNES GROVE GARDENS 🏛️
Castletownroche map (i)V
Telephone: 022-26145
(Mr & Mrs Patrick Grove Annesley)

Extensive Robinsonian woodland and riverside gardens with notable collection of rhododendrons and other exotica. Edwardian flower garden.

Location: 1 m N of Castletownroche, signposted from N72 Fermoy/Killarney road.
Opening Times: Apr 1 to Sept 30 – Mons to Fris 10 – 5; Sats and Suns 1 – 6. Guided tours for pre-booked groups. Adm £2, OAPs/Students £1.50, Chd £1, disabled free. Free car park, adjacent picnic site.
Refreshments: Lunches and teas for pre-booked groups by arrangement.

AYESHA CASTLE 🏛️
Killiney, Co. Dublin map (iii)Z
(Mr & Mrs Aylmer)

A romantic 19th century Victorian Castle of ashlar with a round tower and various turrets affording the finest views of Killiney Bay and Sugar Loaf. Built in 1840 by Robert Warren who named it Victoria Castle, commemorating Queen Victoria's accession to the throne. The Castle was damaged by fire in 1924, purchased in 1928 by Sir Thomas Power who restored and renamed it "Ayesha" after the goddess in Ryder Haggard's Book "She" – purchased by Colonel Aylmer in 1947 and has remained in that family to present day. Notable features include the fine oak panelling in the entrance hall and dining room coupled with the magnificent oak spiral staircase. Ayesha is situated in 4½ acres of garden and woodland containing most unusual and exotic plants, flowers and shrubs. Exhibitions include family lace (English and Irish), Military Exhibition and Historical/Pictorial Record of Killiney/Dalkey and its environs.

Location: 7 m from Dublin on Victoria Road, Killiney (just below Killiney Village through Gothic Archway).
Opening Times: House/Gardens and Craftshop/Exhibitions: Mar 1 – 31 10 – 2; Apr and May 2 – 5 (Tues, Wed & Thur); June and July 11 – 3 (weekends only). All other times by special arrangement. Adm IR£2, Group rate £1.50.
Refreshments: Afternoon teas/lunches/dinner/Victorian Evenings by pre-booking. For full details Tel: Mrs Aylmer 01-2852323.

BANTRY HOUSE – *See page 226*

BIRR CASTLE DEMESNE 🏛️
Co Offaly map (iii)Y
Telephone: + 353 509 20056

Over 100 acres of gardens, rivers with waterfalls, lake and lake walks, terraces and parkland, scenically laid out and planted with most important collection of plants, many introduced directly from the wild. The Park contains the nineteenth century's largest telescope. Facilities include exhibition gallery, educationally explained tree trail, picnic and play area, coffee shop and tourist office.

Opening Times: Jan to Apr and Oct to Dec: Adm £2, Chd £1. Exhibition season (May 1 to Sept 30): daily 10.5 to 5.30. Adm £3, Chd £1.50. Group rates £2, Chd £1. Expo '90 – Irish Tri-Colour: the discovery of colour photography by Offaly, born John Joly. Open daily throughout the year: 9 – 1 and 2 – 6 (or dusk in winter). Note: Bureau de change can be found in the tourist office at the gates of the Castle.
Refreshments: Morning coffee, lunch, afternoon teas from Apr to Sept.

BLARNEY CASTLE AND BLARNEY HOUSE

Blarney, Co. Cork map (i) X   ♿
(Sir Richard Colthurst, Bart)

Blarney Castle and Rock Close. Situated 5 miles from Cork City, the Castle is famous for its Stone which has the traditional power of conferring eloquence on all who kiss it. The word "Blarney" has found its way into the English language and has been described as conferring upon anyone who kisses it "a cajoling tongue and the art of flattery, or of telling lies with unblushing effrontery". The battlements crowning the fine intact keep are typically Irish in form and set in the walls below the battlements is the Stone. To kiss it one has to lean backwards out from the parapet walk. Adjacent to the Castle is the Rock Close, said to have Druidic connections and containing the gardens laid out by the Jefferies family in 1759 and now containing many old specimens and much new planting of shrubs, trees and beds, amongst the fine old limestone rocks scattered in 25 acres. **Blarney House & Gardens:** 200 yards from the Castle is Blarney House and Gardens, a fine Scottish Baronial type house, with distinguished corner turrets and bartizans with conical roofs and now restored inside with fine rooms and stairwell. Outside, the formal gardens and fine view of Blarney Lake together with the walk down to it and between the House and the Castle a large area of new planting, with shrubs, trees, beds and walks.

Location: 7 m from Cork City. 9 m from Cork Airport; 9 m from Ringaskiddy Port.
Opening Times: Blarney Castle & Rock Close: Mon to Sat, May, 9–6. June, July, Aug 9–7; Sept 9–6; Oct to Apr 9–5 (or sunset). Sun, Summer 9.30–5.30. Winter 9.30–5.30 (or sunset). **Blarney House & Gardens:** June–mid Sept Mons to Sat only 12–6. (Last adm 30 mins before stated closing times.) Adm **Blarney Castle and Rock:** IR £3, Chd IR £1, OAPs and Students IR £2. **Blarney House & Gardens:** IR £2.50, Chd IR £1, OAPs and Students IR £2. Car and Coach Parking.
Refreshments: Sweet and soft drink kiosk; three hotels, three public houses; tea houses.

BUNRATTY CASTLE & FOLK PARK

Bunratty, Co. Clare map (ii) X
(Shannon Free Airport Development Company)

Bunratty Castle, built in 1469, is the most complete and authentic example of a Medieval Castle in Ireland. Its furniture, tapestries and works of art are displayed to give the visitor an idea of the furnishings and arrangement of a Castle of the late 16th or early 17th century. The Folk Park, in the grounds of the Castle, contains typical rural dwellings recreated and furnished to reflect life in Ireland at the turn of the century. The Park also features the complete reconstruction of a 19th century Irish village street, including craft shops, post office and general stores. **Bunratty House** (1805) has also been restored and furnished.

Location: 7 m from Shannon International Airport – N18 on Map.

BIRR CASTLE

CASTLETOWN HOUSE

CRATLOE

DUNKATHEL

DUNLOE CASTLE

Irish Heritage Properties

Historic Irish Tourist Houses & Gardens Association Ltd. (H.I.T.H.A.)
Under the auspices of Bord Failte (Irish Tourist Board) to promote
Houses, Castles and Gardens open to the public
3a Castle Street, Dalkey, Co. Dublin.   Tel: 2859323
More than 50 properties in Ireland including those listed on these pages.

 JAPANESE GARDENS

 MOUNT USHER GARDENS

KYLEMORE

NEWBRIDGE HOUSE

LISMORE

POWERSCOURT TOWNHOUSE

 MALAHIDE

POWERSCOURT GARDENS

BANTRY HOUSE

Bantry Co. Cork   map (i) X
Telephone: (027) 50047
(Mr & Mrs Egerton Shelswell-White)

Partly-Georgian mansion standing at edge of Bantry Bay, with beautiful views. Seat of family of White, formerly Earls of Bantry. Unique collection of tapestries, furniture etc. Terraces and Statuary in the Italian style in grounds.

Location: In outskirts of Bantry (½ m); 56 m SW of Cork.
Opening Times: Open all year – Daily 9–6 *(open until 8 on most summer evenings)*. Adm House & Grounds £2.50, Chd (up to 14) accompanied by parents, free, OAPs/ Students £1.50. Parties of 20 or more £2. Craft shop.
Refreshments: Tea room. Bed and Breakfast.

CARRIGGLAS MANOR 

Longford   map (iv) Y
Telephone: Ireland (043) 45165   Fax: (043) 45875
(Mr & Mrs Lefroy)

Tudor Gothic Revival House with beautifully furnished interiors. Fine Georgian stableyard by James Gandon with costume museum. Tea room & shop. Woodland Garden.

Location: 3 m from Longford on T15/R194 Ballinalee/Granard Road. 2 m N of main N4 Route on signed turn-off avoiding Longford Town congestion.
Opening Times: House, Stableyard, Costume Museum, Tea Room & Shop. June 15 to Sept 9, daily except Tues & Weds 12.30–4.30 (Aug 5.30). Pre-booked parties at other times by arrangement. Hourly House Tours – Last Tour 3.30 (Aug 4.30). Adm IR £3, Chd IR £2, Adult Group rate IR £2, Chd Group rate IR £1.
Refreshments: Tea room, light lunches & afternoon teas. Hotels, pubs etc. in Longford (3m). Dinner, Bed & Breakfast available. Pre-booking absolutely essential. Self catering apartments in Gandon Stableyard. For all details contact Mrs Lefroy: Tel. Longford (043) 45165. International code (010 353 43) 45165. Fax: 043 45875.

CASTLE MATRIX

Rathkeale, Co. Limerick   map (ii) X
Telephone: (069) 64284

This Norman tower was built upon a Celtic Santuary from which the original name *Matres* was derived: later Anglicized to *Matrix*. Constructed in 1440 by the 7th Earl of Desmond who along with his father are the earliest recorded Norman poets in the Irish language. Here in 1580, Raleigh and Spenser first met and began their lifelong friendship.

Location: 18 m SW of Limerick City on the main Killarney road; the castle is at the SW edge of Rathkeale village.
Opening Times: May 15 to Sept 15, Sats to Tues 1–5. Open at other times by prior arrangement. Adm £2, Chd £1. Spit-roasted mediaeval banquets available to groups by arrangement.
Refreshments: Teas and luncheons available to groups by arrangement.

CASTLETOWN HOUSE

Celbridge, Co. Kildare   map (iii) Z
(Castletown Foundation)

Built in 1722, the finest Georgian country house in Ireland.

Location: 12 m W of Dublin. 27 'bus to gates.
Opening Times: Open daily all year. Mon to Fri 10–5; Suns and Bank Hols 2–5.
Refreshments: Coffee shop and West Wing restaurant.

CLONALIS HOUSE 

Castlerea, Co. Roscommon   map (iv) X
Telephone: (0907) 20014

Clonalis is the ancestral home of the O'Conor's of Connaught, descendants of the last High Kings of Ireland and traditional kings of Connaught. The Gaelic history of the family is recorded through the collection of archives, documentation and portraits in the house.

Location: Situated to the W of Castlerea town.
Opening Times: June 1 to Sept 10 – Daily 11–5.30. Suns 12–5. Other times by arrangement. Craft shop.
Refreshments: Tea room.

THE CRAGGAUNOWEN PROJECT 

Craggaunowen, Quin, Co. Clare   map (ii) X
(Shannon Free Airport Development Company)

The Craggaunowen project is pleasantly situated in the wooded farmland of County Clare. The site consists of a mediaeval Tower House containing a display of furniture and art objects, including some rare Irish pieces. There are two iron-age dwellings – a lake dwelling and a ring fort – and the leather boat 'Brendan' sailed by Tim Severin from Ireland to Newfoundland. In the summer months experiments and displays are conducted on the techniques associated with milling, pottery making and weaving in the iron age.

Location: 6 km E of Quin, 4 km N of Sixmilebridge. 24 km NW of Limerick.

CRATLOE WOODS HOUSE 

Cratloe, Co. Clare   map (ii) X
Telephone: Ireland (061) 327028. Fax: (061) 327031
(Mr & Mrs J.G. Brickenden)

One of the few roofed examples of an Irish Longhouse, this is a home of special architectural and historical interest. Displays of antiquities, decorative arts, memorabilia and period farm machinery. Guided tours, farm animals and rare breeds, craft shop.

Location: 5 m from Limerick and 10 m from Shannon Airport on the Limerick-Shannon and Ennis dual carriageway.
Opening Times: June 1 – Mid Sept – daily 2–6 except Suns. Group rates available. Car park. Suitable for disabled persons.
Refreshments: Afternoon Teas.

DUNGUAIRE CASTLE

Kinvara, Co. Galway　map (iii) X

Dunguaire was the stronghold of Guaire, King of Connaught in the 7th century. The 15th century Dunguaire Castle, now beautifully restored overlooks Galway Bay and gives an insight into the lifestyles of those that lived there. Dunguaire features mediaeval banquets nightly, May to September.

Location: The Castle is on the Ennis/Galway road.

DUNLOE CASTLE HOTEL GARDENS

Beaufort, Killarney, Co. Kerry　map (i) W
Telephone: (064) 44111　Telex: 73833　Fax: (064) 44583

The gardens at Dunloe Castle contain an extensive and interesting collection of plants, several of which are rarely, if at all, found elsewhere in Ireland. Each season brings its own specialities, camelias and rhododendron in spring, magnolias and sun roses in summer, Irish heaths and richly tinted leaves in autumn, are just a few of the many attractions. This combination of wild grandeur and garden exotica is situated in a setting of incomparable views of mountains and lakes.

Location: Situated adjacent to the Deluxe 140 bedroomed Hotel Dunloe Castle, off the main Killarney/Killorglin road, on the route to the Gap of Dunloe, approximately 8 km from Killarney.
Opening Times: May 1 to end Sept. Adm free. Catalogue of plants and trees available at hotel reception for £1.
Refreshments: Available at Hotel Dunloe Castle.

EMO COURT

Portlaoise, Co. Leix　map (iii) Y
Telephone: Ireland (0502) 26110
(C.D. Cholmeley-Harrison)

Outstanding neo-classical house by James Gandon completed in 1792. Extensive gardens containing a wealth of specimen trees & flowering shrubs, spectacular in spring and autumn.

Location: Portlaoise 6 m on N7.
Opening Times: GARDENS— daily 10.30–5.30 (last entry), Adm £2, Students & OAPs £1. HOUSE—Mon 2–6, Adm £2.50 *(no reductions and no children)*. Free car park. Suitable for disabled persons.
Refreshments: Suns or by arrangement.

FERNHILL GARDEN

Sandyford　map (iii) Z
Telephone: Ireland (01) 956000
(Mrs Sally Walker)

A Garden for all seasons, 200 years old in Robinsonian style with over 4,000 species and varieties of trees, shrubs and plants. Dogs not allowed.

Location: 7 m S centre Dublin on the Enniskerry Rd, or 4 m inland from Dun Laoghaire. T43.
Opening Times: Mar 1 to Nov 30, Tues–Sat 11–5, Suns 2–6, Bank Holidays 11–5. Adm £2.50, OAP/Students £1.50, Chd (under 5) £1, Groups (20+) £2.
Refreshments: Stepeside & Dundrum.

FOTA

Fota Island, Carrigtwohill, Co. Cork　map (i) Y
(Richard Wood)

Regency mansion with fine neo-classical and French Revival rooms, contains an important collection of Irish period landscapes. Furnished with Irish 18th and 19th century pieces. Also world famous arboretum and 70 acre wildlife park. **European Museum of the Year Award Winner.**

Location: 10 m E of Cork City, on Cobh Road, off main Waterford Road.
Station: Fota.

GLIN CASTLE

Glin　map (ii) X
Telephone: Ireland (068) 34173/34112　Fax: (068) 34364
(The Knight of Glin and Madam Fitz-Gerald)

A Georgian Gothic castle with a series of battlemented folly lodges on lands held by the Knights of Glin for over 700 years. The interiors possess elaborate neo-classical plaster ceilings, a flying grand staircase and a notable collection of 18th century Irish mahogany furniture, family portraits and Irish landscapes. Formal gardens.

Location: On N69 32 m W of Limerick and 3 m E of Tarbert.
Opening Times: May 1 to May 31, 10–12, 2–4, and at other times. Groups by arrangement. Adm IR £2, Chd IR £1, groups IR £1.50. Car Parking. Suitable for disabled persons. Luncheon, dinner and overnight stays can be arranged in the Castle. Contact Mrs O'Sullivan (068) 36230 or Nancy Ellis (068) 34112.

GPA-BOLTON LIBRARY

John St, Cashel, Co. Tipperary　map (ii) Y
Telephone: 062-61944
(The Very Revd the Dean of Cashel, Custodian)

Founded by Archbishop Theophilus Bolton in 1744, his Library of 12,000 titles is today housed in an early 19th century building, situated beside the small Georgian Cathedral. This was recently extensively renovated due to the generosity of the Irish aircraft leasing firm, Guinness Peat Aviation. The collection covers printed books from 1473, and includes examples from the houses of Caxton and Pynson (London); and from the great continental houses of Koberger, Froschover, Estienne (Stephanus), Aldus, Plantin, Elzevir and others. There are many very rare books, some 800 not recorded elsewhere in Ireland and about 50 believed to be unique to Cashel. A selection from these can be seen daily, in two displays. One is representative of the whole collection, the other covers a special topic. These are announced in the press, and include Mathematics, Eastern Europe, Medicine, Rare Books, Conservation, and Bindings. Authors include Berkeley, Swift, Euclid, Archimedes, the writers of Greek and Latin antiquity, Drayton, Trussel, Sidney, Burton, More, Raleigh, Donne, Milton, Dante, Cervantes, and Macchiavelli. There is also a small but fine collection of Silver on display, dating from 16th century to 19th century. A genealogical service is available on request.

Location: The Library is 300 yards up John Street, immediately opposite the Cashel Palace Hotel.
Opening Times: Sat 9.30–5.30, Sun 2.30–5.30 throughout the year. Adm £1, OAP/Students 70p, Chd 50p. Ample parking. Group rates on application. Groups and students welcome.

THE JAMES JOYCE TOWER

Sandycove　map (iii) Z
Telephone: Ireland (01) 2809265/2808571
(Dublin Tourism)

Martello Tower built in 1804 as part of defence system against threatened Napoleonic invasion. Lived in briefly by James Joyce in 1904, and made the setting for the opening of his famous novel *Ulysses*. Opened as the James Joyce Museum in 1962. First and rare editions, personal possessions and other Joyce memorabilia, various military fittings preserved. Commanding view of Dublin Bay. Books of Joycean and Irish interest, posters, cards etc. on sale. Occasional evening lectures, slide shows etc.

Location: 1¼ m SE of Dun Laoghaire, Turn L from Sandycove Road along Sandycove Avenue west to Sandycove Harbour and footpath to the Tower.
Opening Times: Apr 1 to Oct 31 (including Bank Holidays), Mon–Sat 10–1, 2–5, Suns 2.30–6. Rest of the year by appointment. Tel. Ireland (01) 2808571. Adm £1.70, Students and OAPs £1.40, Chd 90p. Parties (20+) £1.20. School parties negotiable. Guided tours for parties by arrangement in advance. Suitable for disabled persons on ground floor only.
Refreshments: Fitzgerald's Pub, Sandycove: Wishbone Restaurant, Glasthule: Carney Arms Hotel, Dun Laoghaire: Royal Marine Hotel, Dun Laoghaire.

JAPANESE GARDENS

Tully　map (iii) Y
Telephone: (045) 21617
(Irish National Stud)

Created between 1906–1910, the Japanese Gardens symbolise the Life of Man from the Cave of Birth to the Gateway to Eternity. Special features include the Tea House, Bridge of Life and some very old bonsai trees.

Location: Co. Kildare 1 m from Kildare Town and 5 m from Newbridge.
Opening Times: Easter to Oct 31 – Mon to Fri 10–5, Suns 2–5.30, Sat and Bank Holidays 10–5.30. Adm Adults £2, Students and OAPs £1.50, Chd £1. Family (2 adults and 2 children under 12) £5. Unsuitable for the disabled. Entrance to The Irish National Stud is at the same gate. (Suitable for disabled.)
Refreshments: Tea, coffee, soup, salads, sandwiches etc. Groups can be catered for with some notice.

THE JOHN F. KENNEDY ARBORETUM

New Ross　map (ii) Z
Telephone: (051) 88171
(Coillte Teoranta, The Irish Forestry Board)

A comprehensive, scientifically laid-out arboretum with plant collections arranged in botanical circuits. Incorporated are forest plots and areas devoted to plant research. Reception building with display panel, Lecture Hall with A/V. Special collections of conifers, rhododendrons etc. A road gives access to a view point (890 ft) from which six counties may be seen.

Location: 12 km (7½ m) S of New Ross on R733.
Opening Times: Daily all year, except Christmas Day and Good Friday. May to Aug 10–8; Apr & Sept 10–6.30; Oct to Mar 10–5. Adm 90p (IR £1). Family £2.70 (IR £3). Car, Season ticket £13.50 (IR £15). Coach £10.80 (IR £12). Minibus £5.40 (IR£6). Suitable for the disabled.
Refreshments: Cafe/Shop (May to Sept and weekends Apr). Tea, coffee, soup, sandwiches, salads etc. Five counties Hotel, New Ross 11km (7 m), Horse & Hound, lounge bar, Ballynabola 10km (6 m).

JOHNSTOWN CASTLE DEMESNE

Wexford　map (ii) Z　&
Teagasc (Soils and Environment Centre)

Grounds and gardens only. 50 acres of well laid out grounds, with artificial lakes and fine collection of ornamental trees and shrubs. Agricultural museum.

Location: 5 m SW of Wexford.
Opening Times: All the year—Daily 9–5. Guidebook available at Castle. Although the grounds will continue to be open throughout the year, an adm charge will apply only from May 1 to Oct 4 1992. Adm: Car (and passengers) £2.30; coach (large) £16 coach (small) £8. Adults (pedestrian/cyclists) £1.20, Chd/Students 60p. Wedding parties for photography £16.
Refreshments: Coffee shop during July & Aug at museum.

KNAPPOGUE CASTLE

Quin, Co. Clare　map (ii) X
Telephone: (061) 71103
(Mr and Mrs M E Andrews)

Knappogue Castle is one of the forty-two Castles built by the great McNamara Tribe which ruled over the territory of Clancullen from the 5th to the mid-15th centuries. The Castle has undergone extensive restoration work with its furnishings giving an authentic 15th century atmosphere. Craftshop.

Location: Quin—R469 on Map.

KYLEMORE ABBEY

Kylemore, Connemara　map (iii) W
Telephone: (095) 41146, or shops (095) 41113. Fax: (095) 41123.

The only home of the Benedictine Nuns in Ireland. The Castle was acquired by the Nuns in 1920, and a precious heirloom was preserved, both for and on behalf of the people of Ireland, and visitors from all over the world. Built by Mr Mitchell Henry, MP for County Galway, and a native of Manchester. The Abbey is set amidst the lakes and mountains of Connemara in an area of outstanding beauty.

Location: 50 m from Galway city, between Galway and Clifden, near Letterfrack.
Opening Times: The grounds and part of the Abbey are open daily, Mar to Nov 10–6. Adm free. Pottery, Gift and Craft shop.
Refreshments: Restaurant.

LISMORE CASTLE

Lismore, Co. Waterford　map (ii) Y
Telephone: Dungarvan (058) 54424
(Trustees of the Lismore Estates)

Beautifully situated walled and woodland gardens, containing a fine collection of camellias, magnolias and other shrubs. There is a remarkable yew walk.

Location: In town of Lismore; 45 m W of Waterford; 35 m NE of Cork.
Opening Times: GARDENS ONLY. May 11 to Sept 11—Daily (except Sats) 1.45–4.45. Adm £1.80, Chd (under 16) 90p. Reduced rates for parties.

LISSADELL

Sligo　map (iv) X
(Josslyn Gore-Booth, Esq)

The finest Greek-revival country house in Ireland. Splendid views of the surrounding countryside. The home of Countess Markiewicz.

Location: 8 m NW of Sligo overlooking Sligo Bay.
Opening Times: June 1 mid-Sept—Weekdays 10.30–12.15, 2–4.15. *Closed Suns.* Adm £2, Chd 50p.

LOUGH GUR VISITOR CENTRE

Lough Gur　map (ii) X

Lough Gur Visitor Centre is modelled on Neolithic circular and rectangular houses and illustrates the story of man and his landscape through audio-visuals, artifacts and replicas of materials found in this historic place.

Location: Lough Gur – 16 m SE of Limerick City on the road to Kilmallock.

LOUGH RYNN ESTATE & GARDENS

Mohill, Co. Leitrim　map (iv) Y

Formerly the home of the Earls of Leitrim, Lough Rynn makes for a wonderful stopping off point when travelling to or from the North West. Terraced 19th century gardens, extensive walks and nature trails, interesting Victorian rock garden and fernery, many 19th century buildings, castle ruins from 17th century, dolmen and crannog site. Full restaurant facilities, fast food, craft shop, picnic area, plant sales, guided tours.

Opening Times: May 1 to Sept 1, 10–7. Adm £1.25, Chd 75p, Group rates on request.

MALAHIDE CASTLE

Malahide　map (iii) Z
Telephone: 452655/452371
(Ann Chambers, Administrator)

One of Ireland's oldest and most historic castles containing a unique collection of Irish period furniture and Irish historical portraits, most of which are on permanent loan from the National Gallery of Ireland. In the adjacent gardens there are in excess of 5000 species and varieties of shrubs.

Location: 8 m from centre of Dublin.
Opening Times: Jan to Dec: Mon to Fri 10–5; Nov to Mar: Sat, Sun and Public Holidays 2–5; Apr to Oct: Sat 11–6, Sun and Public Holidays 2–6. Closed for tours 12.45–2 weekdays. Adm £2.45, OAPs/Students (12–17 yrs) £1.85, Chd (3–11 yrs) £1.25. Family ticket (2 adults, 3/4 Chd) £7. Group rates: £2.10, OAPs/Students (12–17 yrs) £1.60, Chd £1.15.
Refreshments: Restaurant.

MOUNT USHER GARDENS

Ashford　map (iii) Z
Telephone: (0404) 40205/40116
(Mrs Madelaine Jay)

The Gardens (20 acres) extend along the Vartry river in beautiful County Wicklow. They are laid out in the informal 'Robinsonian' style comprising rare plants, shrubs and trees, collected from many parts of the world.

Location: Ashford, 1 m from Wicklow on Dublin-Bray-Wexford Road.
Opening Times: Mar 17 to Oct 31, open daily including Suns and Bank Holidays 10.30–6. Adm IR £2.20, OAPs, Chd, Students IR £1.50. Groups (20) IR £1.70, OAPs, Chd, Students IR £1.20. Car parking. Suitable for the disabled. No wheelchairs provided. Shopping courtyard.
Refreshments: Tea room at entrance, snacks, light lunches.

MUCKROSS HOUSE AND GARDENS

Killarney, Co. Kerry　map (i) X
Telephone: (064) 31440　Fax: (064) 33926

Muckross House is a 19th century manor house, beautifully situated close to Muckross Lake, second largest of Killarney's three lakes. The house has many items of historic interest including locally carved period furniture, prints, maps and items which illustrate a traditional way of life of the people of Kerry. Skilled craftworkers at Muckross House carry on some of the traditional crafts of Kerry as their predecessors did in bygone days. The gardens, informal in design, are noted for their fine collection of rhododendrons and azaleas, extensive water gardens and an outstanding rock garden on natural limestone.

Location: 6 km (3.5 m) from Killarney on the Kenmare road.
Opening Times: Open all year. Mar 17 to June 30 daily 9–6. July 1 to Aug 31 daily 9– 7. Sept 1 to Oct 31 daily 9–6; Rest of year daily, 9–5.30. Free car park, suitable for buses. Adm IR £2.50, Chd IR £1, group rates for 20+ IR £1.75. Family ticket £6. Free adm to the gardens.
Refreshments: Restaurant located in the old coach-house, serving teas, coffees, soup, sandwiches, pastries, hot and cold lunches.

NATIONAL BOTANIC GARDENS

Glasnevin, Dublin 9　map (iii) Z
(Department of Agriculture)

Founded 1795. 47 acres in extent containing 25,000 different living plant species and varieties. Flowering shrubs. Dwarf conifers. Orchids. Herbarium, 500,000 specimens.

Location: 2 m from city centre.
Opening Times: All the year—Daily (except Christmas Day); Weekdays 9–6 (summer); 10–4.30 (winter). Sundays 11–6 (summer); 11–4.30 (winter). Conservatories. Mons to Fris 9–12.45, 2.15–5 (summer); 10–12.45, 2.15–4.15 (winter). Sats 9–12.15, 2.15–5.45 (summer); 10–12.15, 2.15–4.15 (winter). Suns 2–5.45 (summer); 2–4.15 (winter). Adm free.

NEWBRIDGE HOUSE

Donabate   map (iii)Z
Telephone: Dublin 436534/5
(Ann Chambers, Administrator)

Newbridge House is an 18th century mansion in its own magnificent parkland of 300 acres. The Great Drawing room, in its original state, is one of the finest Georgian interiors in Ireland. Kitchen and laundry capture the 'below stairs' atmosphere of the big house, and the courtyard, with its coach house and various workshops, connect the past with the present.

Location: 12 m from the centre of Dublin.
Opening Times: Apr to Oct – Tues–Fri 10–5. Sats 11–6. Suns & Bank Holidays 2–6. *Closed* for lunch weekdays 1–2, restaurant remains open. Nov to Mar – Sat, Suns & Bank Holidays 2–5. Open on request outside these hours for groups of 20 or more. Traditional farm open during above hours. Adm £2.20, OAPS & Students £1.80, Chd £1.20, Family ticket £6.50 (2 adults & 3/4 Chd); Parties £2, OAPs & Students £1.60, Chd £1.10. Bus & public car parks. Unsuitable for the disabled.
Refreshments: Coffee Shop serving teas, coffees, cakes, sandwiches.

POWERSCOURT GARDENS & WATERFALL

Enniskerry, Co. Wicklow   map (iii)Z   &
Telephone: Dublin 867676/7/8   Fax: 863561

Powerscourt is owned by the Slazenger family and has been welcoming visitors for more than fifty years. Powerscourt is a magnificent example of an aristocratic garden laid out with taste and imagination. The breathtaking location nestling under the Great Sugar Loaf, the beauty of its Italian and Japanese Gardens, the splendid statuary and the incomparable iron work make it a fairytale demesne. The Waterfall is 398 feet high, which makes it one of the most spectacular in Ireland. Restaurant, souvenir gift and craft shop and children's play areas, garden centre and house-plant shop.

Location: ¼ mile Enniskerry, 12 miles S of Dublin.
Opening Times: Gardens: Mar 1 to Oct 31 – Daily 9–5.30. Garden Centre open all year. Waterfall open all year 10.30–7. Closes dusk wintertime. Guided tours for specialist groups on request. Adm charges Gardens: £2.50, Student/OAP £2, Chd £1; Waterfall: £1, Student/OAP 80p, Chd 50p. Group reductions, season tickets. Wheelchair available.
Refreshments: Gardens: small restaurant (50 people) serving lunches, teas etc. Waterfall: Teas, light lunches available in high season.

POWERSCOURT TOWNHOUSE CENTRE.

59 South William Street, Dublin 2
Telephone: Dublin 687477

Built in 1771 for Richard Wingfield – Third Viscount Lord Powerscourt. Designed by Robert Mack and contains fine plasterwork by James McCullagh and Michael Stapleton.

Location: 59 South William Street, Dublin 2.
Opening Times: Open daily 9.30–5.30. *Closed* Bank Holidays. Adm free. Wheelchair access to three floors.

RIVERSTOWN HOUSE

Glanmire, Co. Cork   map (i)X

The House was originally built in 1602. It became the seat of Doctor Jemmett Brown, Bishop of Cork, who rebuilt it in 1745 with fine plasterwork by the Francini brothers.

Location: 6 km from Cork City on the Cork/Dublin road.
Opening Times: May to Aug, Thurs to Sat 2–6. At other times by appointment. Adm £1.50.

THE ROYAL HOSPITAL KILMAINHAM/THE IRISH MUSEUM OF MODERN ART

Kilmainham   map (iii)Z
Telephone: (01) 718666, Fax: (01) 7186 95

Founded in 1680 by the Duke of Ormond as a hospice for pensioner soldiers, the Royal Hospital Kilmainham is the earliest surviving public building in the country. Now the new Irish Museum of Modern Art, it comprises an important collection of Irish and international art.

Location: Situated 2 m W of Dublin city; 300 metres from Heuston Station.
Opening Times: Tues to Sun 10–5.30. Entrance to museum free, except when there is a special exhibition. Guided tours of North Range Sun 12–5, £1 per person.
Refreshments: Coffee shop open 7 days a week 10–5.

RUSSBOROUGH

Blessington, Co. Wicklow   map (iii)Z
Telephone: (045) 65239
(Alfred Beit Foundation)

Palladian house in romantic setting in the Wicklow mountains, built 1740–50 and housing the Beit Art Collection.

Location: 20 m SW of Dublin; 2 m S of Blessington on N81.
Opening Times: Easter to Oct 31: Easter to May 31, and Sept to Oct 31: Suns and Bank Holidays only 10.30–5.30. June 1 to Aug 31: daily 10.30–5.30. Adm £2.50, Chd (accompanied) 50p. Chd (over 12 accompanied) £1, Student/OAP £1.50. Upstairs – £1, Chd (accompanied) free. Shop. Children's playground. Extensive wooded parkland. Adjacent lakeside amenity and picnic area.
Refreshments: Restaurant.

SLANE CASTLE

Slane   map (iv)Z
Telephone: Drogheda (041) 24207   Fax: (041) 24401
(The Earl of Mount Charles)

Dramatic 18th century Castle on river Boyne, featuring work of James Wyatt, Francis Johnston, James Gandon and Capability Brown, with fine pictures and furniture.

Location: 29 m from Dublin. 8 m from Navan. 9 m from Drogheda. Slane village on N2. Castle entrance on N51 (to Navan).
Opening Times: Mar 17 to Oct 30. Suns and Bank Holiday Mons 2–6. Adm IR £2, Family Rate (2 Adults 2 Chd) IR £5, Parties (20+) IR £1.50 (by prior arrangement). Car park for 100. Suitable for the disabled, no wheelchairs available.
Refreshments: Steak bar/restaurant fully licensed. Open Wed–Sun 12–10.30 pm.

STROKESTOWN PARK HOUSE

Strokestown, Co. Roscommon   map (iv)X
Telephone: (078) 33013

Ancestral home of the Pakenham Mahon family from 1660s to 1979. The house, built in the Palladian style, is complete with its original contents and has fine examples of 17th, 18th and 19th century interiors including extensive staff quarters. Incorporated into the tour is a display of documents relating to the Great Famine of the 1840s.

Opening Times: June 1 to mid-Sept, Tues to Sun, 12–5.

THOOR BALLYLEE

Gort   map (iii)X
Telephone: (091) 31436

16th Century Norman Tower with thatched cottage attached. Summer home of W.B. Yeats for 12 years 1917–1929. Location of inspiration of the 'Tower' and 'Winding Stair' poems.

Location: 4 m from Gort Town. 1 m from N18 Galway/Gort road. 1 m from N66 Gort/Loughrea road.
Opening Times: Open daily Apr–Sept 10–6. Large car park suitable for buses. Unsuitable for the disabled. Audio visual presentation on Yeats and the Tower. Bookshop specialising in Anglo-Irish literature. Gift shop.
Refreshments: Tea room in cottages attached to Tower supplying tea, coffee, soup, sandwiches, cakes, pastries, biscuits etc. Ample toilet facilities.

TIMOLEAGUE CASTLE GARDENS

Bandon   map (i)X
Telephone: (023) 46116 or (021) 831512
(Mr N.R.E. Travers)

Seven acres of old fashioned gardens in a beautiful and historic setting. Palm trees and other frost-tender shrubs flourish in the mild climate of this beautiful part of West Cork.

Location: Adjoining Timoleague village, Bandon 8 m.
Opening Times: GARDEN ONLY Easter Weekend, then daily mid May to mid Sept 12–6. Adm IR £1.50, Chd IR 75p. Parties by arrangement. Car park. Suitable for the disabled.
Refreshments: At local hotels.

TULLYNALLY CASTLE

Castlepollard, Co. Westmeath   map (iii)Y
Telephone: 044-61159 or 044-61425

Home of the Pakenhams (later Earls of Longford) since the 17th century; the original house is now incorporated in a huge rambling Gothick castle. Approximately 30 acres of woodland and walled gardens are also open to the public.

Location: 12 m NE Mullingar, 1½ m from Castlepollard on Granard Rd (signposted).
Opening Times: Gardens: May to Sept, 10–6, Adm £1, Chd 50p. Castle rooms: July 15 to Aug 15, 2–6, £2.50 (to include gardens), Chd £1.50. Open to groups at other times by arrangement.

IRELAND (NORTHERN)

ARDRESS HOUSE, The National Trust

Co Armagh　map (v)Z　△　&
Telephone: Annaghmore 851236

17th century country house with fine plasterwork. Small garden, agricultural display in farmyard. Woodland play area.

Location: 7 m W of Portadown on Portadown/Moy Road (B28); 2 m from Loughgall intersection on M1.
Opening Times: Apr: weekends and Good Friday to Easter Tues (Apr 17–21); May, June: weekends and Bank Hols only; July and Aug: daily except Tues Sept: weekends only 2–6. (Picnic area available from 12 noon.) Farmyard open May, June & Sept weekdays 12–4. Adm House Grounds and Farmyard: £1.80, Chd 90p, groups £1.30 (after hours £2.30). Grounds and Farmyard only: £1.30, Chd 65p, groups £1.10 (after hours £2.10). Wheelchairs admitted. Picnic areas.
Refreshments: Picnickers welcome.

THE ARGORY, The National Trust

Co Armagh　map (v)Y　△　&
Telephone: Moy 84753

295 acre estate with neo-classical house, built c. 1820.

Location: 4 m from Moy on Derrycaw Road; 3 m from Coalisland intersection.
Opening Times: Easter (Apr 17–21); Apr, May, June weekends and Bank Hols only; July and Aug: daily exc Thurs 2–6 (open from 1 on Bank Hols). Last adm 5.15. Adm House and grounds £1.80, Chd 90p, groups £1.30 (after hours £2.30). Car park 50p. Dogs in grounds only on leads. Wheelchairs provided – access to ground floor only.
Refreshments: Shop/Tea Room open as house 2–6; Bank Holidays 1–6; weekdays July & Aug 3–5.

CASTLE COOLE, The National Trust

Co Fermanagh　map (iv)Y　△
Telephone: Enniskillen 322690

Magnificent 18th century mansion by James Wyatt with plasterwork by Joseph Rose.

Location: 1½ m SE of Enniskillen on Belfast/Clogher/Enniskillen Road (A4).
Opening Times: The estate is open from dawn to dusk free of charge from Apr 1 to Sept 30. House: Easter (Apr 17–21); Apr, May: weekends and Bank Hols; June, July & Aug: daily exc Thurs Sept: weekends only, 2–6. Adm House and Grounds: £2.20, Chd £1.10, groups £1.70 (after hours £2.70).

CASTLE WARD, The National Trust

Co Down　map (v)Z　△　&　⑤
Telephone: Strangford 204

Built by the first Lord Bangor in 1765 in a beautiful setting. Laundry museum. Wildfowl collection on lake. Strangford Lough Information Centre in converted barn on edge of shore.

Location: 7 m NE of Downpatrick; 1½ m W of Strangford village (A25).
Opening Times: Apr: weekends and Good Friday to Sun after Easter (apr 17–26); May to Aug: daily (including Bank Hols) except Thurs 1–6. Sept, Oct: weekends only. Estate and grounds open all year dawn to dusk daily. Shop and Restaurant: open as house: weekends and Bank Holidays 1–6, weekdays 1–5. Strangford Lough Barn: weekends and Good Friday – Sun after Easter; Apr, May, June, Sept: weekends and Bank Holidays only; July and Aug, daily except Thurs 2–6. Adm: House £2.30, Chd £1.15, groups £1.60 (after hours £2.80). Estate £3 per car (Nov to end Mar £1.50 per car). Coaches: Booked groups to house, no charge; others £10. Horses (using bridlepath) £5 per single horsebox.
Refreshments: Shop & Tearoom open same days as house weekends and Bank Hois 1–6, weekdays 1–5.

DOWNHILL CASTLE, The National Trust

Londonderry　map (v)Y　&

Built by the Earl of Bristol, Bishop of Derry, in 1783 with Mussenden Temple, the Bishop's Gate, the Black Glen and the Bishop's Fish Pond.

Location: 5 m W of Coleraine on Coleraine/Downhill Road (A2).
Station: Castlerock.
Opening Times: Temple: Apr: weekends and Good Friday to Easter Tues (Apr 17–21); May, June: Sats, Suns and Bank Hols only; July, Aug & Sept: weekends only: daily 12–6. Grounds open all year round, free. Glen open free at all times. Dogs admitted. Wheelchair access.

FLORENCE COURT, The National Trust

Co Fermanagh　map (iv)Y　△　&
Telephone: Florence Court 249

Important 18th century house built by John Cole. Excellent rococo plasterwork. Pleasure Gardens.

Location: 8 m SW of Enniskillen via A4 and A32; 1 m W of Florence Court village.
Opening Times: House: Apr: weekends and Good Friday to Easter Tues (Apr 17–21); May: weekends and Bank Hols; June, July and Aug: daily except Tues; Sept: weekends only, 1–6. Shop and tearoom: open as house 1–6, from 12 noon, June to Aug. Grounds open all year round 10 am to one hour before dusk. Adm House: £2.20, Chd £1.10. Groups, £1.70. After hours £2.70. Estate parking £1. Dogs in pleasure gardens only on leads. Wheelchair access-ground floor only.
Refreshments: Tearoom and shop open as house but open from 12 noon June to Aug.

GRAY'S PRINTING PRESS, The National Trust 🌿

Strabane, Co Tyrone　map (v)Y
Telephone: Strabane 884094

The shop was in existence in 18th century. It has close links with Scots-Irish tradition in America.

Location: In Main Street, Strabane.
Opening Times: Apr to Sept daily 2–5.30 except Thurs, Suns and Bank Hols. At other times by prior arrangement. Shop (not N.T.): all year daily except Thurs, Suns and public hols, 9–1 and 2–5.30. Adm £1.20, Chd 60p. Groups 90p.

HEZLETT HOUSE, The National Trust 🌿

Co Londonderry　map (v)Y　　△
Telephone: Castlerock 848567

Thatched cottage of particular importance because of the unusual cruck/truss construction of the roof.

Location: 4 m W of Coleraine on Coleraine/Downhill Coast Road (A2).
Opening Times: Apr: weekends and Good Friday to Easter Tues (Apr 17–21); May, June: weekends and Bank Hols only; July and Aug: daily except Tues. Sept weekends only: 1–5. Adm £1.20, Chd 60p, Groups 90p. After hours £1.70. No dogs. Unsuitable for wheelchairs.

MOUNT STEWART HOUSE, GARDEN AND TEMPLE, The National Trust 🌿

Co Down　map (v)Z　　△　　&
Telephone: Greyabbey 387

Interesting house with important associations with Lord Castlereagh. Gardens designed by Lady Edith, Marchioness of Londonderry. Fine topiary work, flowering shrubs and rhododendrons. Temple of the Winds, modelled on that at Athens, built 1783.

Location: On E shore of Strangford Lough; 5 m SE of Newtownards; 15 m E of Belfast (A20).
Opening Times: Apr: weekends and Good Friday to Sun after Easter (Apr 17–26); May to Aug: daily except Tues 1–6. Sept and Oct: weekends only 1–6. Garden: Apr 1 to end Aug: daily; Sept and Oct: weekends only 12–6. Temple of the Winds: Days open as House, but from 2–5. Shop and Tea Room: Apr: weekends and Apr 17–26; May: weekends and Bank Holidays June, July and Aug: daily except Tues. Sept: weekends only 2–6. Bank Hols 1–6. Adm: House, Garden and Temple: £3.30, Chd £1.65, groups £2.60; after hours £4.30. Garden and Temple: £2.70. Chd £1.35, groups £2; after hours £3.70; Temple only: 90p. Wheelchairs provided. Booked parties by arrangement throughout the season.
Refreshments: Tea room open as house.

ROWALLANE GARDEN, The National Trust 🌿

Saintfield, Co Down　map (v)Z　　&
Telephone: Saintfield 510131

Beautiful gardens containing large collection of plants, chiefly trees and shrubs. Of particular interest in spring and autumn.

Location: 11 m SE of Belfast; 1 m S of Saintfield on the W of the Downpatrick Road (A7).
Opening Times: Apr 1 to end Oct: Mons–Fris, 10.30–6. Sats and Suns 2–6. Nov to end Mar 10.30–5 Mons–Fris. *Closed* Dec 25 and 26, Jan 1. Adm Easter to end Oct: £2.30, Chd £1.15. Parties £1.60. After hours £2.80. Nov to end Mar: £1.20. Groups 60p. Dogs admitted on leads, to indicated areas. Wheelchair access (1 provided).
Refreshments: Shop and Tearoom: Apr: weekends and Good Friday to Easter Tues (Apr 17–21); May to Aug: daily 2–6. Sept: weekends only.

SPRINGHILL, The National Trust 🌿

Moneymore, Co Londonderry　map (v)Z　　△　　&
Telephone: Moneymore 48210

House dating from 17th century. Magnificent oak staircase and interesting furniture & paintings. Costume museum. Cottar's kitchen.

Location: On Moneymore/Coagh Road (1 m from Moneymore).
Opening Times: Apr: weekends and Good Friday to Easter Tues (Apr 17–21); May, June: weekends and Bank Hols only; July and Aug: daily except Thurs. Sept: weekends only 2–6. Adm House £1.80, Chd 90p. Groups £1.30. After hours £2.30. Booked parties to house: no Estate charge.

TEMPLETOWN MAUSOLEUM, The National Trust 🌿

Co Antrim　map (v)Z

Built 1783 by Robert Adam.

Location: Castle Upton Graveyard, Templepatrick (A6).
Opening Times: All year during daylight hours. Adm free. Dogs admitted. Access difficult for wheelchairs.

WELLBROOK BEETLING MILL, The National Trust 🌿

Cookstown, Co Tyrone　map (v)Y
Telephone: Tulnacross 51735

A water-powered mill built in 18th century with 19th century modifications.

Location: 3 m from Cookstown on Cookstown/Omagh Road.
Opening Times: Apr: weekends and Good Friday to Easter Tues (Apr 17–21); May, June: weekends and Bank Holidays. July and Aug: daily except Tues 2–6. Sept: weekends only. Adm £1.20, Chd 60p. Groups 90p. After hours £1.70. Unsuitable for wheelchairs.

SCOTLAND

BORDERS REGION

NATIONAL TRUST FOR SCOTLAND
Last admissions to most NTS properties are 45 minutes before the advertised closing times. Other than guide-dogs for the blind and deaf, dogs are not generally permitted inside Trust buildings, walled and enclosed gardens or in the immediate area beside buildings which are open to the public. At a number of properties special 'dog walks' are signposted.

ABBOTSFORD HOUSE

Melrose map 13F &
Telephone: (0896) 2043
(Mrs P. Maxwell-Scott)

The home of Sir Walter Scott, containing many historical relics collected by him.

Location: 3 m W of Melrose just S of A72; 5 m E of Selkirk.
Opening Times: 3rd Mon of Mar to Oct 31 — Daily 10–5; Suns 2–5. *Cars with wheelchairs or disabled visitors enter by private entrance.* Gift shop.
Refreshments: Teashop.

AYTON CASTLE

Eyemouth map G13
Telephone: (089 07) 81212

Victorian castle in red sandstone.

Location: 7 m N of Berwick-upon-Tweed on A1.
Opening Times: May to Sept — Suns 2–5 or by appointment. Adm £1, Chd (under 15) free.

BOWHILL

nr Selkirk map F13 △ &
Telephone: Selkirk (0750) 20732
(His Grace the Duke of Buccleuch & Queensberry KT)

Border home of the Scotts of Buccleuch. Famous paintings include 8 Guardis, Canaletto's Whitehall, Claudes, Gainsboroughs, Reynolds, Raeburns and the world famous Buccleuch collection of portrait miniatures. Superb French furniture and porcelain. Monmouth, Sir Walter Scott and Queen Victoria relics. For details of our specialist art courses, please tel: Buccleuch Heritage Trust Selkirk (0750) 20732. Restored Victorian kitchen. Audio-Visual programme. Lecture Theatre. Exciting Adventure Woodland Play Area. Walks to historic Newark Castle and by lochs and rivers along nature trails.

Location: 3 m W of Selkirk on A708 Moffat–St. Mary's Loch road. Edinburgh, Carlisle, Newcastle approx 1½ hours by road.
Opening Times: House open July 1 to July 31 — Daily 1–4.30 (Suns 2–6). Country Park (includes Adventure Woodland Play Area, Nature Trails) — Apr 28 to Aug 28 — Daily except Fri 12–5 (Suns 2–6). Last entry 45 mins before closing time. Riding Centre and Pony Trekking (0750) 20192 open all day all year. Mountain bike hire (0721) 20336. Adm House & Grounds £3. Parties over 20 £2.50. Grounds only £1. Wheelchair users and Chd (under 5) free. Free car and coach parking. Open by appointment at additional times for museums and specialist or educational groups.
Refreshments: Gift shop and licensed tea room open daily during 'House open' period. Tea room open weekends during 'Country Park open' period. Mini shop in playground all seasons.

DAWYCK BOTANIC GARDEN

nr Peebles map 13F
(Royal Botanic Garden, Edinburgh)

Impressive woodland garden.

Location: 8 m SW of Peebles; 28 m S of Edinburgh.
Opening Times: Mar 15 to Oct 22 — Daily 10–6. Adm £1, Chd/concessions 50p. No animals (except guide dogs).

DRYBURGH ABBEY

Dryburgh map 13F
(Historic Scotland)

Sir Walter Scott and Field Marshal Earl Haig are buried in this 12th century Abbey.

Location: 5 m SE of Melrose, nr St Boswells.
Opening Times: Apr 1 to Sept 30 — Weekdays 9.30–6.30; Suns 2–6.30. Oct 1 to Mar 31 — Weekdays 9.30–4.30; Suns 2–4.30. *Closed Dec 25, 26 & Jan 1 & 2.* Adm £1.70, Chd & OAPs 90p. Family ticket £4.50. Prices subject to change 1992 season.

FLOORS CASTLE — *See page 234*

HERMITAGE CASTLE

Liddlesdale map F12
(Historic Scotland)

Here in 1566. Queen Mary visited her wounded lover Bothwell.

Location: In Liddlesdale; 5½ m NE of Newcastleton.
Opening Times: Apr 1 to Sept 30 — Mon to Sat 9.30–6.30, Suns 2–6.30; Oct 1 to Mar 31 — Weekends only. Sat 9.30–4.30, Sun 2–4.30. *Closed Dec 25, 26; Jan 1, 2.* Adm £1, Chd and OAPs 50p. Prices subject to change 1993 season.

THE HIRSEL GROUNDS & DUNDOCK WOOD

Coldstream map G13
Telephone: Coldstream (0890) 2834; 2965; 3160

Snowdrops, aconites and daffodils in Spring in grounds. Fantastic rhododendrons and azaleas May/June Dundock wood and grounds. Marvellous Autumn colouring. Picnic areas. Parking. Playground. Homestead museum, Craft Centre and workshops. Emu Park.

Opening Times: All reasonable daylight hours throughout the year. Adult adm charge.
Refreshments: In main season.

JEDBURGH ABBEY

Jedburgh map F13
(Historic Scotland)

Founded by David I this Augustinian Abbey is remarkably complete. Recent excavations are now open to the public. New Visitor Centre.

Location: In Jedburgh.
Opening Times: Apr to Sept — Mon to Sat 9.30–6.30; Suns 2–6.30. Oct to Mar — Mon to Sat 9.30–4; Suns 2–4. Adm £1.70, Chd and OAPs 90p. Family ticket £4.50. Prices subject to change 1993 season.

MANDERSTON — *See page 234*

MELLERSTAIN

Gordon map G13
Telephone: Gordon (057 381) 225
(The Mellerstain Trust)

Scotland's famous Adam mansion. Beautifully decorated and furnished interiors. Terraced gardens and lake. Gift shop.

Location: 9 m NE of Melrose; 7 m NW of Kelso; 37 m SE of Edinburgh.
Opening Times: Easter weekend (Apr 17 to Apr 20) then May 1 to Sept 30 — Daily (except Sats) 12.30–5. Last adm to House 4.30. Adm charges not available at time of going to press. Free parking. *Special terms for organised parties by appointment, apply Curator.*
Refreshments: Tea rooms.

MELROSE ABBEY

Melrose map F13
(Historic Scotland)

Beautiful Cistercian Abbey founded by David I.

Location: In Melrose.
Opening Times: Apr 1 to Sept 30 — Mon to Sat 9.30–6.30, Suns 9.30–6.30. Oct 1 to Mar 31 — Mon to Sat 9.30–4, Suns 2–4. *Closed Dec 25, 26; Jan 1, 2.* Adm £1.70, Chd and OAPs 90p. Family ticket £4.50. Prices subject to change 1993 season.

MERTOUN GARDENS

St Boswells map F13
Telephone: St Boswells 23236
(His Grace the Duke of Sutherland)

20 acres of beautiful grounds with delightful walks and river views. Fine trees, herbaceous plants and flowering shrubs. Walled garden and well-preserved circular dovecot.

Location: 2 m NE of St Boswells on the B6404.
Opening Times: Garden only. Sats and Suns, and Mons on Public Holidays only — Apr to Sept 2–6 (last entry 5.30). Parties by arrangement. Adm £1, Chd 50p, OAPs 50p. No dogs. Car parking.
Refreshments: Dryburgh Abbey Hotel, Buccleuch Arms Hotel, St Boswells.

NEIDPATH CASTLE

Peebles map F13
Telephone: Peebles (0721) 20333

Medieval castle updated in the 17th century, situated on a bluff above the River Tweed. Pit prison, well hewn out of solid rock and fine views.

Location: 1 m W of Peebles on A72.
Opening Times: Thurs before Easter to Sept 30 — Mons to Sats 11–5; Suns 1–5. Adm £1.50, Chd 75p, OAP £1. Parties at reduced rates — enquiries to The Custodian, Neidpath Castle, Peebles (0721) 20333.
Refreshments: Hotels in Peebles.

OPEN HOUSE TO A SPLENDID HERITAGE

ere, in the beautiful Scottish Borders, stand some of the finest homes and gardens you could wish to see. Many still in private, and proud, family hands. And all within no more than a 50-mile radius.

Abbotsford

Bowhill

Floors

The Hirsel

Manderston

Mellerstain

Paxton

Thirlestane

Traquair

Experience the eloquence of *Abbotsford* – where the walls echo with the words of one of Scotland's celebrated authors. Picture yourself at *Bowhill* – taking in the delights of one of the finest private art collections. Feast your eyes on *Floors* – where you'll see furniture that is genuine 17th-18th century French. Walk into a haven at *The Hirsel* – where beautifully stocked and maintained grounds extend to fully 3,000 acres. Marvel at *Manderston* – with the splendid sweep of its celebrated silver staircase. Delight in the magnificence of *Mellerstain* – with its masterly ceilings and decorations by Robert Adam. Soak up the history of *Paxton* – a Palladian mansion built for a daughter of Frederick the Great. Treat yourself to *Thirlestane* – and the glorious sight of its sumptuous state rooms. Take in centuries-old *Traquair* – where you follow in the footsteps of 27 kings and queens.

Step inside the coupon and send for the leaflet that opens all the doors invitingly wider.

PLEASE SEND ME MORE INFORMATION ON
RETURN TO:–
SCOTLAND'S BORDER HERITAGE
c/o SBTB, HIGH STREET, SELKIRK TD7 4JX

SCOTLAND'S BORDER

HERITAGE

NAME _____

ADDRESS _____

_____

_____ POST CODE _____

FLOORS CASTLE

Kelso map G13
Telephone: Kelso (0573) 23333
(The Duke of Roxburghe)

Built in 1721 by William Adam and later added to by Playfair. Magnificent tapestries, fine French and English furniture, paintings, porcelain.

Location: N of Kelso.

Opening Times: Easter weekend to end Oct: Suns to Thurs inclusive, except July and Aug: 7 days 10.30–5.30 (last admission to House 4.45). Oct: Suns and Weds 10.30–4. Coach parties by special arrangement during Apr and Oct. Adm £3, OAPs £2.40, OAPs pre-booked parties £2.20, pre-booked parties £2.40, Chd 8 and over £1.50, Family ticket £8. Grounds: £1.50. Pipe Bands May 3, 24; June 7; July 12. Massed Pipe Bands Aug 30. Garden Centre and Coffee Shop open 7 days.

Refreshments: Licensed restaurant, gift shop and coffee shop.

MANDERSTON

Duns map G12
Telephone: Duns (0361) 83450
(Lord and Lady Palmer)

The swan-song of the great classical house. Georgian in its taste but with all the elaborate domestic arrangements designed for Edwardian convenience and comfort. Superb classical yet luxurious rooms and the only silver staircase in the world, in a house on which the architect was ordered to spare no expense. The extensive 'downstairs' domestic quarters are equally some of the grandest of their type. Outside, the grandeur is continued. See the most splendid stables and picturesque marble dairy. 56 acres of formal woodland garden and lakeside walks.

Location: 2 m E of Duns on A6105; 14 m W of Berwick upon Tweed.

Opening Times: May 14 to Sept 27 — Thurs and Suns, also Bank Hol Mons May 25 and Aug 31 2–5.30. Adm charges not available at time of going to press. Parties at any time. Gift shop.

Refreshments: Cream Teas.

PAXTON HOUSE

Paxton, nr Berwick-upon-Tweed   map G13
Telephone: (0289) 86291
(The Paxton Trust)

Scotland's most perfect Palladian country mansion. Built for a daughter of Frederick The Great. Designed by the Adam family and furnished by Chippendale and Trotter. Restored Regency picture gallery (outstation of National Galleries of Scotland). Gardens. Riverside Walks. Adventure Playground. Tearoom.

Location: 5 m from Berwick-upon-Tweed on B6461.
Opening Times: Daily – Good Fri to Oct 31. House: noon – 5. Grounds: 10 – 5. Adm £3, grounds only £1. Family ticket £8. Parties catered for. Car parking. Suitable for disabled persons. No wheelchairs available.
Refreshments: Morning coffee, light lunches, afternoon teas.

PRIORWOOD GARDEN

Melrose   map F13
Telephone: Melrose (089 682) 2965
(The National Trust for Scotland)

Garden featuring flowers suitable for drying. Shop and Trust visitor centre.

Location: In Melrose.
Opening Times: Apr 1 to Apr 30 – Mons to Sats 10 – 5.30. *Closed* Suns. May 1 to Oct 31: Mons to Sats 10 – 5.30, Suns 2 – 5.30. Nov 1 to Dec 24, Mons to Sats 10 – 5.30.

ROBERT SMAIL'S PRINTING WORKS

Tweeddale   map F13
Telephone: Innerleithen (0896) 830206
(The National Trust for Scotland)

The buildings contain vintage working machinery, including a 100-year-old printing press which was originally driven by water wheels. The Victorian office is on display complete with its acid-etched plate-glass windows and examples of historic items printed in the works.

Location: In Innerleithen High Street, 30 m S of Edinburgh.
Opening Times: Shop and Printworks: Apr 1 to Oct 31: Mons to Sats 10 – 1, 2 – 5, Suns 2 – 5. Last adm 1 hr before closing am & pm. Adm £1.50, Chd 80p, adult parties £1.20, schools 60p.

SMAILHOLM TOWER

nr Smailholm   map F13
(Historic Scotland)

Simple tower house displaying a collection of costume figures and tapestries relating to Sir Walter Scotts' 'Minstrelsy of the Scottish Borders'.

Location: nr Smailholm Village 6 m NW of Kelso.
Opening Times: Apr 1 to Sept 30 – Mon to Sat 9.30 – 6.30, Suns 2 – 6.30. Oct 1 to Mar 31, *closed*. Adm £1, Chd & OAPs 50p. Prices subject to change 1993 season.

THIRLESTANE CASTLE

Lauder, Berwickshire   map F13
Telephone: Lauder (05782) 430

Described as one of the oldest and finest Castles in Scotland, Thirlestane has its roots in an original 13th century fort overlooking the Leader Valley. The main keep was built in 1590 by the Maitland family who have lived in the Castle for over 400 years; it was extended in 1670 and again in 1840. The Restoration Period plasterwork ceilings are considered to be the finest in existence. The family nurseries now house a collection of over 7,000 historic toys and children are encouraged to dress up. Visitors see the old kitchens, pantries and laundries as well as the Country Life Exhibitions portraying day to day life in the Borders through the centuries. Grounds, picnic tables, woodland walk, free car park, gift shop and tea room.

Location: 28 m S of Edinburgh off A68 – follow signs on all main approach roads.
Opening Times: Easter (Apr 17 to 20 inclusive), May, June and Sept: Weds, Thurs and Suns only. July and Aug: daily except Sats. Castle 2 – 5 (last adm 4.30). Grounds 12 – 6. Adm £3, party rate £2.50, family ticket (parents and own children only) £8 (1992). Booked party tours at other times by arrangement.
Refreshments: Tea room.

TRAQUAIR

Innerleithen   map F13
Telephone: Innerleithen (0896) 830323
(C. Maxwell Stuart of Traquair)

A house full of beauty, romance and mystery. Rich in associations with Mary Queen of Scots, the Jacobites and Catholic persecution. Priest's room with secret stairs. The world-famous Traquair House Ale is brewed in the 18th-century brewhouse. Extensive grounds, craft workshops and maze.

Location: 1 m from Innerleithen; 6 m from Peebles; 29 m from Edinburgh at junction of B709 & B7062 (40 minutes by road from Edinburgh Turnhouse Airport, 1½ hours from Glasgow).
Opening Times: Easter week Apr 18 – 26 incl. May: Sun and Mon only, then daily from May 30 to Sept 30, 1.30 – 5.30; (July and Aug only 10.30 – 5.30). Last adm 5. Grounds: May to Sept: 10.30 – 5.30. Gift Shop, Antique Shop.
Refreshments: Home cooking at the 1745 Cottage Tea Room from 12.30.

CENTRAL REGION

CASTLE CAMPBELL

Dollar   map E14
(Historic Scotland)

15th century oblong tower with later additions, set in a steep sided glen. Sometimes known as "Castle Gloom".

Location: 1 m N of Dollar; on N slope of Ochil Hills at head of Dollar Glen.
Opening Times: Apr 1 to Sept 30 – Mon to Sat 9.30 – 6.30, Suns 2 – 6.30. Oct 1 to Mar 31 – Mon to Sat 9.30 – 4.30, Suns 2 – 4.30. *(Closed Thurs pm & Fris in winter, also Dec 25, 26; Jan 1, 2).* Adm £1.50, Chd & OAPs 80p. Prices subject to change 1993 season.

LINLITHGOW PALACE

Linlithgow   map E14
(Historic Scotland)

Birthplace of Mary Queen of Scots.

Location: In Linlithgow.
Station: Linlithgow (½ m).
Opening Times: Apr 1 to Sept 30 – Daily 9.30 – 6.30 (Suns 2 – 6.30). Oct 1 to Mar 31 – Daily 9.30 – 4.30 (Suns 2 – 4.30). *Closed Dec 25, 26, Jan 1 & 2.* Adm £1.50, Chd & OAPs 80p. Family ticket £4. Prices subject to change 1993 season.

STIRLING CASTLE

Stirling   map E14
(Historic Scotland)

Royal Castle on a great basalt rock dominating the surrounding countryside.

Location: In Stirling.
Station: Stirling (¾ m).
Opening Times: Apr 1 to Sept 30 – Mon to Sat 9.30 – 6.00. Suns 10.30 – 5.30. Oct 1 to Mar 31 – Mon to Sat 9.30 – 5.05. Suns 12.30 – 4.20. *Closed Dec 25, 26; Jan 1, 2 and 3.* Adm £2.30, Chd and OAPs £1.20, Family £6. Prices subject to change 1993 season. Last ticket sold 45 mins before closing time.

DUMFRIES & GALLOWAY

ARBIGLAND GARDENS – *See page 237*

BROUGHTON HOUSE

High Street, Kirkcudbright   map E11
Telephone: (0557) 30437
(The Hornel Trust)

Home of the artist E. A. Hornel 1864 – 1933. Mainly 18th century. Fine furniture, Scottish paintings. George III – Victorian samplers. Special exhibitions: The Artist in his Studio: House Laundry 1920's. Superb town garden and Japanese garden.

Location: 12 High Street, Kirkcudbright DG6 4JX.
Opening Times: Apr 15 to Oct 18: weekdays 11 – 1, 2 – 5, Sun 2 – 5. *Closed* Tues. Adm £1.50, OAPs/Chd half price. Conducted tours for parties available. Car parking nearby in town park.
Refreshments: Many in Kirkcudbright.

CAERLAVEROCK CASTLE

nr Dumfries   map E11
(Historic Scotland)

One of the finest examples of early classical Renaissance building in Scotland and chief seat of the Maxwell family.

Location: 8 m SSE of Dumfries on the Glencaple Road (B725).
Opening Times: Apr 1 to Sept 30 – Mon to Sat 9.30 – 6.30, Suns 2 – 6.30. Oct 1 to Mar 31 – Mon to Sat 9.30 – 4.30, Suns 2 – 4.30. Adm £1.20, Chd & OAPs 60p. Prices subject to change 1993 season.

CARLYLE'S BIRTHPLACE

Ecclefechan   map F12
Telephone: Ecclefechan (057 63) 666
(The National Trust for Scotland)

Thomas Carlyle was born here in 1795. Mementoes and MSS.

Location: 5 m SE of Lockerbie on the Lockerbie/Carlisle Road (A74).
Opening Times: Apr 1 to Oct 25: daily 12 – 5. Other times by appointment. Adm £1.20, Chd 60p (under 5 free). OAPs and Students (on production of their cards) adm at half the standard rate. Adult parties £1, school parties 50p.
Refreshments: Ecclefechan Hotel.

CASTLE KENNEDY GARDENS

Stranraer map D11 &
Telephone: Stranraer (0776) 2024
(The Earl and Countess of Stair)

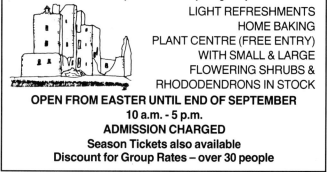

Beautiful gardens laid out on a peninsula between two lochs, Rhododendrons, azaleas, magnolias, embothriums and many other plants from overseas.

Location: 3 m E of Stranraer on A75; Stranraer/Dumfries Road (entrance by Castle Kennedy Lodge only).
Opening Times: Easter to Sept – Daily 10–5. Adm £1.80, Chd (under 16) 50p, OAPs £1. Party rates on application. Free parking. Plant Centre.
Refreshments: Light refreshments only. Hotels Eynhallow, Castle Kennedy & Stranraer.

DRUMLANRIG CASTLE AND COUNTRY PARK

nr Thornhill map E12 △ & ⑤
Telephone: Thornhill (0848) 31682 (24 hr answering service).
Country Park: (0848) 31555.
(Home of the Duke of Buccleuch & Queensberry KT)

Magnificent pink sandstone castle with outstanding art treasures – Leonardo, Rembrandt, Hobein – beautiful silverware, superb furniture and porcelain, Bonnie Prince Charlie's relics. Extensive grounds and woodland includes gardens, exciting adventure woodland play area, nature trails and picnic sites. Tearoom and giftshop. Working craft studios, lecture room and cycle hire. Falconry Centre. Caravan park 1 mile from Castle.

Location: 18 m N of Dumfries; 3 m N of Thornhill off A76; 16 m from A74 at Elvanfoot; approx 1½ hrs by road from Edinburgh, Glasgow & Carlisle.
Opening Times: Castle: Early May to late Aug. Daily (*except Thurs*) 11–5. Suns 1–5. Grounds and Adventure Woodland only – Early May to late Sept. Times subject to change; please telephone to check. Adm charges not available at time of going to press. Discounts for groups of 20 or over, OAPs and students.
Refreshments: Lunches, Afternoon Teas and snacks at above times.

LOGAN BOTANIC GARDEN

Port Logan map D11
(Royal Botanic Garden, Edinburgh)

A unique collection of plants from the warm temperate regions of the world.

Location: 10 m S of Stranraer.
Opening Times: Mar 15 to Oct 31 – Daily 10–6. No animals. Adm £1.50, Concessions £1, Chd 50p.
Refreshments: Salad bar in the garden.

MAXWELTON HOUSE

Thornhill map E12 &
Telephone: (084 82) 385
(M. R. L. Stenhouse)

A stronghold of the Earls of Glencairn in the 13th/14th century, later the birthplace of Annie Laurie of the famous Scottish ballard. House, Chapel, Museum of Agricultural and Early Domestic Life, gardens, tea room and small shop.

Location: 3 m S of Moniaive, 13 m N of Dumfries on B729.
Opening Times: Wed to Sun, Easter to end Sept, 11–5. Car parking free. Suitable for disabled. No wheelchairs available.
Refreshments: Morning coffe, lunch and afternoon tea for 50 people.

RAMMERSCALES

Lockerbie map E12
Telephone: Lochmaben (038 781) 0229
(M. Bell Macdonald, Esq)

Georgian manor house dated 1760 set on high ground with fine views over Annandale. Pleasant policies and a typical walled garden of the period. There are Jacobite relics and links with Flora Macdonald retained in the family. There is also a collection of works by modern artists.

Location: 5 m W of Lockerbie (M6/A74); 2½ m S of Lochmaben on B7020.
Opening Times: 2–5 every day in Aug except Sats.

SWEETHEART ABBEY

New Abbey map E11
(Historic Scotland)

Cistercian monastery famous for the touching and romantic circumstances of its foundation by Lady Dervorgilla.

Location: 7 m S of Dumfries on coast road (A710).
Opening Times: Apr 1 to Sept 30: Mons to Sats 9.30–6.30, Suns 2–6.30. Oct 1 to Mar 31: Mons to Sats 9.30–4.30, Suns 2–4.30 *except* Thurs pm and all day Fris. Adm £1, Chd & OAPs 50p. Prices subject to change 1993 season.

THREAVE GARDEN

nr Castle Douglas map E11 &
Telephone: Castle Douglas (0556) 2575
(The National Trust for Scotland)

The Trust's School of Horticulture. Gardens now among the major tourist attractions of SW Scotland. Visitor centre. Magnificent springtime display of some 200 varieties of daffodil, Trust shop, Restaurant, Exhibition. Ramp into garden for wheelchairs.

Location: 1 m W of Castle Douglas off A75.
Opening Times: GARDENS: All the year, daily 9 – sunset. WALLED GARDEN AND GLASSHOUSES: daily 9–5. Visitor Centre, Exhibition and Shop: Apr 1 to Oct 31 daily 9–5.30. Restaurant: 10–5. Adm £2.80, Chd £1.40. Adult parties £2.20, Schools £1.10, Chd under 5 years free. OAPs & Students (on production of their cards) adm at half the standard adult rate.

ARBIGLAND GARDENS

Kirkbean   map E11
(Captain and Mrs J. B. Blackett)

Built in the 18th century, on land that long ago belonged to the Murrays, the house is set amongst woodland, formal and water gardens arranged round a secluded bay in the Solway Firth. The garden in which John Paul Jones, regarded by history as the father of the United States Navy, worked as a boy. Birthplace of Dr James Craik, Washington's Physician.

Location: 15 m SW of Dumfries on A710.
Opening Times: Gardens: May to Sept incl—Tues, Suns and Bank Hol Mons 2–6. House and Gardens: Fri May 22 to Sun May 31 1992 inclusive 2–6. Adm £2, Chd 50p. Toddlers free. Car park free. Picnic area on sandy beach. Dogs on leads please.
Refreshments: Tea room. Hotels in Dumfries, Southerness (2 m) or New Abbey.

FIFE REGION

ABERDOUR CASTLE

Aberdour   map F14
(Historic Scotland)

A 14th century tower with the remains of a terraced garden and bowling green. There is also a splendid dovecot and panoramic views across the Firth of Forth.

Location: At Aberdour.
Opening Times: Apr 1 to Sept 30—Daily 9.30–6.30 (Suns 2–6.30). Oct 1 to Mar 31—Daily 9.30–4.30 (Suns 2–4.30). *Closed Thurs pm and Fri in winter, also Dec 25, 26; Jan 1, 2.* Adm £1.20, Chd & OAPs 60p. Prices subject to change 1993 season.

BALCARRES

Colinsburgh   map F14
Telephone: 033334 206
(Balcarres Trust)

16th century house with 19th century additions by Burn and Bryce. Woodland and terraced garden.

Location: ½ m N of Colinsburgh.
Opening Times: WOODLANDS AND LOWER GARDEN: Feb 17 to Mar 4; Apr 6 to June 30 (daily except Suns). WEST GARDEN: June 13 to July 1 (Daily except Suns) 2–5. Adm £1.50, OAPs & Chd £1. *House not open except by written appointment* and Apr 27 to May 13 (except Suns). Adm £2. Car park. Suitable for disabled persons, no wheelchairs provided.

FALKLAND PALACE & GARDEN 👑

Fife   map F14   △
Telephone: Falkland (0337) 57397
(Her Majesty the Queen. Hereditary Constable, Capt & Keeper: Ninian Crichton Stuart. Deputy Keeper: The National Trust for Scotland)

Attractive 16th century royal palace, favourite retreat of Stuart kings and queens. Gardens now laid out to the original Royal plans. Town Hall, Visitor Centre, Exhibition and Shop. Original royal tennis court built in 1539. Ramp into garden for wheelchairs.

Location: In Falkland, 11 m N of Kirkcaldy on A912.
Opening Times: Apr 1 to Sept 30: Mons to Sats 10–6, Suns 2–6. Oct: Sats 10–5, Suns 2–5. Adm Palace £3, Chd £1.50. Adult parties £2.50. School parties £1.30. Gardens only £2, Chd £1 (under 5 free). OAPs & Students (on production of their cards) adm at half the standard adult rate. Visitor centre and Trust shop. Display in Town Hall.
Refreshments: Bruce Arms, Falkland.

HILL OF TARVIT 👑

nr Cupar   map F14
Telephone: Cupar (0334) 53127
(The National Trust for Scotland)

Mansion house remodelled 1906. Collection of furniture, tapestries, porcelain and paintings. Gardens.

Location: 2½ m SW of Cupar A916.
Station: Cupar (2½ m).
Opening Times: House: Apr 4 to Apr 30; Sats and Suns 2–6; Apr 17 to 20 and May 1 to Oct 31 daily 2–6. Gardens & grounds: all year 10–sunset. Adm House and Gardens £2.80, Chd £1.40. Adult parties (20 or more) £2.20. School parties £1.10. Gardens only £1, Chd 50p. Chd under 5 free, OAPs & Students (on production of their cards) adm at half the standard adult rate.

KELLIE CASTLE AND GARDEN 👑

Fife   map F14   &
Telephone: Arncroach (033 38) 271
(The National Trust for Scotland)

Fine example of 16th-17th century domestic architecture of Lowland Scotland. Victorian walled garden with wheelchair access. Nursery, video, adventure playground, picnic area, shop, tea room.

Location: 3 m NNW of Pittenweem on B9171.
Opening Times: CASTLE: Apr 4 to Apr 30; Sats and Suns 2–6. Apr 17 to 20 and May 1 to Oct 31 daily 2–6. GARDEN AND GROUNDS open all the year, daily 10–sunset. Adm Castle and Garden £2.80, Chd £1.40. Adult parties (20 or more) £2.20. School parties £1.10. Gardens only £1, Chd (accompanied by adult) 50p (under 5 free). OAPs & Students (on production of their cards) adm at half the standard adult rate. *Gardens only suitable for disabled.* A/V presentation with induction loop for the hard of hearing.

THE TOWN HOUSE & THE STUDY

Culross map E14
Telephone: Newmills (0383) 880359
(The National Trust for Scotland)

Outstanding survival of Scottish 17th century burgh architecture carefully restored to 20th century living standards. Induction loop for the hard of hearing.

Location: 12 m W of Forth Road Bridge, off A985.
Opening Times: Town House (with exhibition and visual presentation) open Apr 17 to 20 and May 1 to Sept 30 daily 11–1, 2–5. Adm 90p, Chd 50p. The Study open Apr 4 to Oct 31, Sats and Suns 2–4. Adm other times by appointment. Adm 60p, Chd 30p. Students (on production of their cards) adm at half the standard adult rate.

GRAMPIAN REGION

BALMORAL CASTLE

nr Ballater map F16
(Her Majesty the Queen)

Grounds and Exhibition open. Country Walks.

Location: 8 m W of Ballater on A93.
Opening Times: Gardens and Exhibitions open during May, June & July—Daily (except Suns) 10–5. Adm (1992 rates) £1.75, OAPs £1.25, Chd free. Donation to charities. Pony trekking. Pony cart rides.
Refreshments: Refreshment room at Balmoral.

BALVENIE CASTLE

Dufftown map F17
(Historic Scotland)

A 13th century castle visited by Mary Queen of Scots in 1562.

Location: At Dufftown.
Opening Times: Apr 1 to Sept 30—Daily 9.30–6.30 (Suns 2–6.30). *Closed Oct to Mar.* Adm £1, Chd & OAPs 50p. Prices subject to change 1993 season.

BRAEMAR CASTLE

Braemar map E16 △
Telephone: Braemar (03397) 41219 – *out of season* 41224
(Captain A A C Farquharson of Invercauld)

BRODIE CASTLE

nr Nairn Moray map E17 &
Telephone: Brodie (030 94) 371
(The National Trust for Scotland)

Built in 1628 by the Earl of Mar. Attacked and burned by the celebrated Black Colonel (John Farquharson of Inverey) in 1689. Repaired by the government and garrisoned with English troops after the rising of 1745. Later transformed by the Farquharsons of Invercauld, who had purchased it in 1732, into a fully furnished private residence of unusual charm. L-plan castle of fairy tale proportions, with round central tower and spiral stair. Barrel-vaulted ceilings, massive iron 'Yett', and underground pit (prison). Remarkable star-shaped defensive curtain wall. Much valuable furniture, paintings and items of Scottish historical interest. Exhibition of International Costumes.

Location: ½ m NE of Braemar on A93.
Opening Times: May to mid Oct—Daily 10–6. Adm £1.45, Chd 75p. Special rates for groups and OAPs. Free car and bus park.

Ancient seat of the Brodies, burned in 1645 and largely rebuilt, with 17th/19th century additions. Fine furniture, porcelain and paintings. Audio-taped guide for the blind.

Location: Off A96 between Nairn & Foress.
Opening Times: Apr 1 to Sept 27: Mons to Sats 11–6; Suns 2–6. Oct 3 to Oct 18: Sats 11–6; Suns 2–6. Grounds open all year 9.30–sunset. Adm £3, Chd £1.50 (under 5 free). Adult parties £2.50, School parties £1.30. OAPs & Students (on production of their cards) adm at half the standard adult rate. Grounds by donation.

CASTLE FRASER

Sauchen map G16
Telephone: Sauchen (033 03) 463
(The National Trust for Scotland)

One of the most spectacular of the Castles of Mar. Z-plan castle begun in 1575 and completed in 1636. Formal garden. Tearoom, picnic area, childrens' adventure playground.

Location: 3 m S of Kemnay off B993; 16 m W of Aberdeen.
Opening Times: May 1 to June 30, and Sept 1 to Sept 30: daily 2–6. July 1 to Aug 31: daily 11–6. Oct 3 to Oct 25, Sats and Suns 2–5. Adm £3, Chd £1.50. Adult parties £2.50, School parties £1.30. Chd under 5 years free. OAPs & Students (on production of their cards) adm at half the standard adult rate. Garden & grounds open all year, 9.30– sunset, adm by donation. Picnic area.

CRATHES CASTLE & GARDEN

Banchory   map G16   △   &
Telephone: Crathes (033 044) 525
(The National Trust for Scotland)

Fine 16th century baronial castle. Remarkable early painted ceilings. Beautiful gardens provide a wonderful display all year. Great yew hedges from 1702. Children's adventure playground.

Location: 3 m E of Banchory on A93; 15 m W of Aberdeen.
Opening Times: CASTLE, VISITOR CENTRE, SHOP, LICENSED RESTAURANT AND PLANT SALES. Apr 17 to Oct 31: daily 11−6, other times by prior appointment only. Adm Grounds only £1.30, Chd 80p. Combined ticket (Castle, Garden & Grounds) £3.50, Chd £1.80, Adult parties £2.80, School parties £1.40. GARDENS AND GROUNDS. All the year−Daily 9.30−sunset. Chd under 5 years free. OAPs & Students (on production of their cards) adm at half the standard adult rate. Visitor Centre.
Refreshments: Shop and licensed Restaurant.

DRUM CASTLE

nr Aberdeen   map G16
Telephone: Drumoak (033 08) 204
(The National Trust for Scotland)

The oldest part of the historic Castle, the great square tower−one of the three oldest tower houses in Scotland−dates from the late 13th century. Charming mansion added in 1619. Historic rose garden.

Location: 10 m W of Aberdeen, off A93.
Opening Times: CASTLE: May 1 to Sept 30: daily 2−6. Oct 3 to Oct 25: Sats and Suns 2−5. WALLED GARDEN OF HISTORIC ROSES: May 1 to Oct 31, daily 10−6. Adm £3, Chd £1.50. Adult parties £2.50, School parties £1.30. Chd under 5 years free. OAPs & Students (on production of their cards) adm at half the standard adult rate. Grounds open all year 9.30−sunset. Adm by donation.

ELGIN CATHEDRAL

Elgin   map F17
(Historic Scotland)

Probably Scotland's most beautiful cathedral with certainly the finest chapter house.

Location: In Elgin.
Opening Times: Apr 1 to Sept 30−Daily 9.30−6.30, Suns 2−6.30. Oct 1 to Mar 31−Daily *(except Thurs pm and Fri)* 9.30−4.30. Suns 2−4.30. *Closed Dec 25, 26; Jan 1, 2.* Adm £1, Chd & OAPs 50p. Prices subject to change 1993 season.

FASQUE

Fettercairn   map G16
Telephone: Fettercairn (05614) 202
(The Gladstone Family)

1809 Home of the Gladstone family with a full complement of furnishings and domestic articles little changed for 160 years.

Location: 1 m N of Fettercairn on the B974 Cairn O Mount pass road; 34 m Aberdeen and Dundee; 17 m Stonehaven; 12 m Montrose; 18 m Banchory.
Opening Times: House open May 1 to end of Sept every day except Fris 1.30−5.30 with last entry at 5 pm. Adults £2, OAP, Chd £1. Parties £1.75 over 25 pre-booked. Evening opening for parties by arrangement.

FYVIE CASTLE

Fyvie   map G17
Telephone: Fyvie (0651) 891266
(The National Trust of Scotland)

The oldest part of the castle dates from the 13th century and its five great towers are the monuments to the five families who owned the castle. The building contains the finest wheel stair in Scotland and a magnificent collection of paintings.

Location: Off A947, 8 m SE of Turriff.
Opening Times: Apr 17 to May 31, Sept 1 to 30: daily 2−6. June 1 to Aug 31: daily 11−6. Oct 3 to Oct 25: Sats and Suns 2−5. Adm £3, Chd £1.50. Adult parties £2.50, School parties £1.30. Parkland free. Chd (under 5) free. OAPs & Students (on production of their cards) adm at half the standard adult rate. Permanent exhibition − Castles of Mar.

HADDO HOUSE

nr Methlick   map G17   △   &
Telephone: Tarves (065 15) 440
(The National Trust for Scotland)

Georgian house designed in 1731 by William Adam. Home of the Gordons of Haddo for over 500 years. Terraced gardens.

Location: 4 m N of Pitmedden; 19 m N of Aberdeen (A981 & B999).
Opening Times: House, permanent exhibition, shop and restaurant open Apr 17 to May 31 and Sept 1 to Oct 31 daily 2−6. June 1 to Aug 31 daily 11−6. Oct 3 to 25 Sats and Suns 2−5. Shop and restaurant Apr 17 to Sept 30 daily 11−6 and weekends in Oct 2−5. Adm £3, Chd £1.50 (under 5 free). Adult parties £2.50, School parties £1.30. OAPs & Students (on production of their cards) adm at half the standard adult rate. Gardens & grounds open all year 9.30−sunset, adm by donation. Wheelchair access.
Refreshments: Restaurant.

HUNTLY CASTLE

Huntly   map F17
(Historic Scotland)

A magnificent ruin of an architectural and heraldic house built in the 16th and 17th centuries.

Location: In Huntly.
Opening Times: Apr 1 to Sept 30: daily 9.30−6.30; Suns 2−6.30. Oct 1 to Mar 31: daily 9.30−4.30, Suns 2−4.30 *except* Thurs pm and all day Fris. *Closed Dec 25, 26; Jan 1, 2.* Adm £1.50, Chd and OAPs 80p. Prices subject to change 1993 season.

KILDRUMMY CASTLE GARDEN

Donside   map F16   &
Telephone: Kildrummy (09755) 71264 or 71277
(Kildrummy Castle Garden Trust)

Approximately 10 acres of garden with shrubs, heaths, gentians, rhododendrons, lilies etc. Alpine and water garden dominated by ruins of 13th century castle. Museum (on request) interesting old stones. Coaches by arrangement.

Location: On A97 off A944 10 m W of Alford; 15 m S of Huntly; 35 m W of Aberdeen.
Opening Times: GARDENS ONLY. Apr to Oct−Daily 10−5. Adm £1.50, Chd (3−8) 20p, (9−16) 50p, (1990 rates). Car park inside hotel main entrance free. Coach park inside hotel trade entrance free. **Plants for sale.** Wheelchairs. **Play area. Video Room.** Walks.
Refreshments: At Kildrummy Castle Hotel in the grounds (please make reservations) Kildrummy (09755) 71288. The Kildrummy Inn, Kildrummy (09755) 71227.

LEITH HALL AND GARDEN

Kennethmont   map F17   &
Telephone: Kennethmont (046 43) 216
(The National Trust for Scotland)

Home of the Leith family from 1650. Jacobite relics, and major exhibition of family's military collection. Charming garden.

Location: 1 m W of Kennethmont on B9002; 34 m NW of Aberdeen.
Opening Times: May 1 to Sept 30: daily 2−6. Oct: Sats and Suns, daily 2−5. Gardens and Grounds: all the year, daily 9.30−sunset. Adm House and garden £3, Chd £1.50 (under 5 free). Adult parties £2.50, School parties £1.30. OAPs & Students (on production of their cards) adm at half the standard adult rate. Admission to gardens & grounds by donation. Picnic area.

PITMEDDEN GARDEN

Udny map G16

Telephone: Udny (065 13) 2352

(The National Trust for Scotland)

Reconstructed 17th century garden with floral designs, fountains and sundials. Display on the evolution of the formal garden. Museum of Farming Life.

Location: 14 m N of Aberdeen on A920.

Opening Times: Grounds open all year—Daily 9.30–sunset. Garden Museum, Visitor Centre & other facilities—May 1 to Sept 30: daily 10–6. Adm Garden & Museum £2.40, Chd £1.20 (under 5 free). Adult parties £1.90, School parties £1. Adm Grounds only £1, Chd 50p. OAPs & Students (on production of their cards) adm at half the standard adult rate. No dogs in garden please. *House not open.*

PROVOST ROSS'S HOUSE

Aberdeen map G16

Telephone: Aberdeen (0224) 572215

(The National Trust for Scotland)

Built in 1593, this is the third oldest house in Aberdeen. It now contains Aberdeen Maritime Museum operated by the City of Aberdeen District Council. Trust Information Centre including a presentation on NTS Grampian properties. Members' Centre shop. Video 'Castle Country'.

Location: City centre.

Opening Times: Open all year Mon to Sat 10–5 (except Christmas and New Year Holidays). Trust Visitor Centre and Shop May 1 to Sept 30, 10–4. Admission free.

HIGHLANDS REGION

ARDTORNISH

Lochaline, Morvern map C15

Telephone: (0967) 421288

(Mrs John Raven)

Garden of interesting mature conifers, rhododendrons and deciduous trees and shrubs set amidst magnificent scenery. ½ m from Kinlochaline Castle 14th century tower house on the river Aline.

Location: Off A82; 41 m SW of Fort William via A82, Corran Ferry & A884.

Opening Times: Apr 1 to Oct 31—Daily 10–6. Adm (by collecting box for garden upkeep) £1, Chd (under 16) free. Also Sun May 24 *in aid of the Scottish Gardens Scheme & Morvern Parish Church* when home made teas are provided in main house.

CAWDOR CASTLE

nr Inverness map E17

Telephone: Cawdor (066 77)615   Fax: 06677 674

(The Earl of Cawdor)

The 14th century Keep, fortified in the 15th century and impressive additions, mainly 17th century, form a massive fortress. Gardens, nature trails and splendid grounds. Shakespearian memories of Macbeth. The most romantic castle in the Highlands.

Location: S of Nairn on B9090 between Inverness and Nairn.

Opening Times: May 1 to Oct 4: daily 10–5.30 (last adm 5). Adm £3.50, Chd (aged 5–15) £1.90, OAPs and disabled £2.80. Parties of 20 or more adults £3.30; 20 or more children (aged 5–15) £1.50. Family ticket (2 adults and up to 5 children) £10. Gardens, grounds and nature trail only £1.80. Blind people, no charge. Free coach and car park. Gift shop. Book shop. Wool shop. Picnic area. 9-hole Pitch and Putt (including hire of clubs and ball) £1.70, Chd 90p. Putting Green (including hire of putter and ball) 80p, Chd 50p. Nature Trails. No dogs allowed in Castle or Grounds.

Refreshments: Licensed restaurant (self-service); Snack bar.

DUNROBIN CASTLE

Golspie map E16

Telephone: (0408) 633177/633268   Fax: (0408) 633800

(The Countess of Sutherland)

One of Scotland's oldest inhabited houses. Historic home of the Sutherland family. Furniture, paintings and china. Exhibits of local and general interest. Victorian Museum in grounds.

Location: ½ m NE of Golspie on A9.

Station: Golspie (2 m).

Opening Times: May: Mons to Thurs 10.30–12.30. June 1 to Oct 15: Mons to Sats 10.30–5.30, Suns 1–5.30. Last admission 5pm (closes 1 hour earlier in Oct). Coaches welcome all year by appointment. Adm £3, Chd £1.50, Parties (10 or more) £2.80, OAPs £2, Family £7.50.

Refreshments: Tearoom.

DUNVEGAN CASTLE

Isle of Skye map B17   △

(John MacLeod of MacLeod)

Dating from the 13th century and continuously inhabited by the Chiefs of MacLeod. Fairy flag. Licensed restaurant; two craft and souvenir shops; castle water garden; audio-visual theatre; clan exhibition; items belonging to Bonnie Prince Charlie; loch boat trips; famous seal colony; pedigree highland cattle fold.

Location: Dunvegan village (1 m); 23 m W of Portree on the Isle of Skye.
Opening Times: Mar 23 to Oct 31: Mon to Sat 10–5.30. Last adm 5. Sun: gardens, craft shop and restaurant open all day 10–5.30. Castle open 1–5.30. Last adm 5. Adm £3.50, Chd £1.90, groups, OAPs, Students £3. Gardens only £2, Chd £1.20.

EILEAN DONAN CASTLE

Wester Ross   map C16   △
Telephone: Dornie (059 985) 202
(Conchra Charitable Trust)

13th century Castle. Jacobite relics—mostly with Clan connections.
Location: In Dornie, Kyle of Lochalsh; 8 m E of Kyle on A87.
Opening Times: Easter to Sept 30: daily (inc Suns) 10–6. Adm £1.50.

FORT GEORGE

Ardersier   map E17
(Historic Scotland)

One of the most outstanding military fortifications virtually unaltered from the 18th century. Re-creations of 18th & 19th century barrack rooms. Seafield collection of arms.

Location: At Ardersier. 11 m NE of Inverness.
Opening Times: Apr 1 to Sept 30—Daily 9.30–6.30, Suns 2–6.30. Oct 1 to Mar 31—Daily 9.30–4.30, Suns 2–4.30. *Closed Dec 25, 26; Jan 1, 2.* Adm £2, Chd & OAPs £1. Family £5. Prices subject to change 1993 season.

HUGH MILLER'S COTTAGE

Cromarty   map E17
Telephone: Cromarty (038 17) 245
(The National Trust for Scotland)

Birthplace (10 Oct 1802) of Hugh Miller, stonemason, eminent geologist, editor and writer. Furnished thatched cottage built c 1711 for his grandfather contains an interesting exhibition on his life and work. Captioned video programme. Cottage garden.

Location: In Cromarty 22m from Inverness A832.
Opening Times: Apr 1 to Sept 27: Mons to Sats 10–12, 1–5; Suns 2–5. Adm £1.20, Chd 60p (under 5 free). Adult parties £1, school parties 50p. OAPs & Students (on production of their cards) adm at half the standard adult rate.

INVEREWE GARDEN

Poolewe, Wester Ross   map C17   &
Telephone: Poolewe (044 586) 229 (Information Centre)
(The National Trust for Scotland)

Remarkable garden created by the late Osgood Mackenzie. Rare and sub-tropical plants.

Location: 7 m from Gairloch; 85 m W of Inverness, A832.
Opening Times: Garden open all the year: daily 9.30–sunset. Visitor Centre: Apr 1 to May 22, Sept 7 to Oct 18: Mons–Sats 10–5, Suns 2–5. May 23 to Sept 6, Mons to Sats 9.30–6, Suns 12–6. Adm £2.80, Chd £1.40, Adult parties £2.20, School parties £1.10. Chd under 5 years free. OAPs & Students (on production of their cards) adm at half the standard adult rate. Ranger Naturalist Service. For disabled: Half garden, greenhouse, toilets, wheelchairs available.
Refreshments: (Licensed) restaurant in garden open during same period, but *closes* 4.30. Guided walks with gardener Apr 1 to Oct 18.

URQUHART CASTLE

Loch Ness   map D16
(Historic Scotland)

Remains of one of the largest Castles in Scotland

Location: On W shore of Loch Ness 1½ m SE of Drumnadrochit.
Opening Times: Apr 1 to Sept 30—Mon to Sat 9.30–6.30, Suns 2–6.30. Oct 1 to Mar 31—Mon to Sat 9.30–4.30, Suns 2–4.30. *Closed Dec 25, 26; Jan 1, 2.* Adm £1.50, Chd & OAPs 80p. Family ticket £4.50. Prices subject to change 1993 season.

LOTHIAN REGION

AMISFIELD MAINS

nr Haddington   map F14
Telephone: Aberlady (08757) 201
(Lord Wemyss' Trust)

Georgian farmhouse with "Gothick" Barn and Cottage.

Location: Between Haddington & East Linton on A1 Edinburgh/Dunbar Road.
Opening Times: Exteriors only. By appointment, Wemyss & March Estates, Estate Office, Longniddry, East Lothian EH32 0PY.

BEANSTON

nr Haddington   map F14
Telephone: Aberlady (08757) 201
(Lord Wemyss' Trust)

Georgian farmhouse with Georgian Orangery.

Location: Between Haddington & East Linton on A1 Edinburgh/Dunbar Road.
Opening Times: Exteriors only. By appointment, Wemyss & March Estates, Estate Office, Longniddry, East Lothian EH32 0PY.

DALMENY HOUSE – *See page 242*

DIRLETON CASTLE & GARDEN

Dirleton   map F14
(Historic Scotland)

Well preserved 13th century castle, attractive gardens.

Location: In the village of Dirleton on Edinburgh/North Berwick Road (A198).
Station: North Berwick (2 m).
Opening Times: Apr 1 to Sept 30—Mon to Sat 9.30–6.30, Suns 2–6.30. Oct 1 to Mar 31—Mon to Sat 9.30–4.30, Suns 2–4.30. *Closed Dec 25 & 26; Jan 1 & 2.* Adm £1.50, Chd & OAPs 80p. Prices subject to change 1993 season.

DALMENY HOUSE

South Queensferry   map F14
Telephone: (031 331) 1888
(The Earl of Rosebery)

Magnificently set in beautiful parkland on the shores of the Firth of Forth, 7 miles from Edinburgh and designed in 1814 by William Wilkins, Dalmeny House was the first Gothic Revival House in Scotland. **Superb Rosebery Collection**: Prime Minister the 5th Earl of Rosebery's important collection of political portraits by Reynolds, Gainsborough, Raeburn and Lawrence. Early Scottish portraits and furniture. Goya tapestries. Exhibition of Adam and other architectural designs. Napoleon Room containing Duke of Wellington's campaign chair together with paintings and furniture associated with the Emperor. **Rothschild Collection** of superb 18th century furniture, fine porcelain and tapestries from Mentmore. Garden Valley Walk with marvellous rhododendrons and azaleas in May and June. Shore Walk with magnificent sea views.

Location: 3 m E of South Queensferry; 7 m W of Edinburgh; on B924 (off A90).
Station: Dalmeny (2 m).
Public Transport: From St. Andrew Sq. Bus Station to Chapel Gate (1 m from house).
Opening Times: May to Sept incl—Suns 1–5.30, Mons to Thurs 2–5.30 (last adm 5). Conducted tours. Adm £3, Chd £1.50, Students £2.50. Party rate £2.50 (minimum 16). Special parties also welcome at other times throughout the year by arrangement with the Administrator.
Refreshments: Tea and Home Baking. Other food and refreshments only by arrangement for special parties.

EDINBURGH CASTLE

Edinburgh   map F14
(Historic Scotland)

Ancient fortress of great importance. St Margaret's Chapel has Norman features.

Location: Castlehill, Edinburgh.
Opening Times: Apr 1 to Sept 30—Mon to Sat 9.30–5.50, Suns 12.30–5.50; Oct 1 to Mar 31—Mon to Sat 9.30–5.05, Suns 12.30–4.20. Last tickets sold 45 mins before closing. *Castle closed Dec 25, 26; Jan 1, 2 & 3.* Adm £3.40, Chd & OAPs £1.70, Family £8.50. Prices subject to change 1993 season.

THE GEORGIAN HOUSE – *See page 244*

GLADSTONE'S LAND – *See page 244*

GOSFORD HOUSE – *See page 244*

HARELAW FARMHOUSE – *See page 244*

HOPETOUN HOUSE

South Queensferry, nr Edinburgh   map E14
Telephone: 031 331 2451
(Hopetoun House Preservation Trust)

Home of the Marquess of Linlithgow. Fine example of 18th century Adam architecture. Magnificent reception rooms, pictures, antiques.

Location: 2 m from Forth Road Bridge nr South Queensferry off A904.
Opening Times: Fri, Apr 17 to Sun, Oct 4: daily 10–5.30 (last adm 4.45). Adm House and Grounds: £3.30. Special concessions for students, children and OAPs, also for groups of 20 or more, and family group. Free parking. Gift shop. Deer park. Picnic areas. Free Ranger service. Roof top viewing platform with magnificent views of the Forth and the Bridges. The house is also available for special private evening functions throughout the year. Enquiries to Administrator's Office 031-331 2451.
Refreshments: Licensed restaurant and snack bar in Tapestry Room.

Murder, LOOTING, TREASON, ARSON, Burning, PILLAGE.

Consider an old building without any history. Dull stuff indeed.

What is it then that makes the historic buildings of Scotland so interesting? It's not just the beauty of the buildings and stones themselves but the fact that they were witness to a history crammed with heroism and betrayal, loyalty and deceit. A dastardly deed here. A conspiracy there.

And with a Historic Scotland Explorer Ticket you

Skara Brae, on Orkney, is one of the best-preserved stone-age villages in Europe and provides a wonderful illustration of life 5,000 years ago.

Fort George, eleven miles N.E. of Inverness. One of the most outstanding artillery fortifications in Europe. Visitor centre and reconstructions of period barrack rooms.

Edinburgh Castle, Scotland's most famous castle. Many attractions, including the Crown Jewels (Honours) of Scotland, the Great Hall and the famous 15th century gun Mons Meg.

Stirling Castle, without doubt, Scotland's grandest castle, both in its situation on a commanding rock outcrop and its architecture. Visitor Centre with audio-visual display.

The Border Abbeys, illustrated here is Jedburgh Abbey, founded in 1138 by David I. It is one of the four great border abbeys with Melrose, Kelso and Dryburgh. They lie within a 12 mile triangle.

New Abbey Cornmill, near Dumfries, is a fully renovated, water-powered oatmeal mill in working order which is regularly demonstrated for visitors.

can steep yourself in Scotland's turbulent past by visiting over 70 historic sites, all of which are open seven days a week from April to September. [Information on Winter opening times is easily available by telephoning 031-244 3101 (Mon-Fri 9am-5pm).]

If you have an appetite for romance and intrigue you'll find Historic Scotland has more than enough to feed your imagination.

THE PERFECT Ingredients FOR A Wonderful DAY OUT.

HISTORIC SCOTLAND

Thousands of years of history. Minutes from your door.

Historic Scotland, 20 Brandon Street, Edinburgh EH3 5RA. Tel: 031-244 3101 (Monday-Friday 9am-5pm)
Explorer Tickets give reduced cost entry for 7 or 14 days. Ask at Tourist Information Centres, Travel Agents and Historic Scotland properties.

THE GEORGIAN HOUSE

No. 7 Charlotte Square, Edinburgh map F14 ⑤
Telephone: 031-225 2160
(The National Trust for Scotland)

The north side of Charlotte Square is classed as Robert Adam's masterpiece of urban architecture. The main floors of No. 7 are open as a typical Georgian House. Audio-visual shows.

Location: In Edinburgh city centre.
Opening Times: Apr 1 to Oct 31: Mons to Sats 10–5, Suns 2–5. Adm £2.40, Chd £1.20 (under 5 free). Adult parties £1.90, school parties £1. OAPs/Students (on production of their cards) adm at half the standard adult rate.

GLADSTONE'S LAND

Edinburgh map F14
Telephone: 031-226 5856
(The National Trust for Scotland)

Built 1620 and shortly afterwards occupied by Thomas Gledstanes. Remarkable painted wooden ceilings; furnished as typical 'Old Town' house of the period. Shop.

Location: 477B Lawnmarket, Edinburgh.
Opening Times: Apr 1 to Oct 31: Mons to Sats 10–5, Suns 2–5. Adm £2.20, Chd £1.10 (under 5 free). Adult parties £1.80, school parties 90p. OAPs/Students (on production of their cards) adm at half the standard adult rate.

GOSFORD HOUSE

East Lothian map F14
Telephone: Aberlady (08757) 201
(Lord Wemyss' Trust)

Robert Adam Mansion, central block surviving; striking maritime situation. Original wings replaced 1890; South wing contains celebrated Marble Hall, fine collection of paintings etc. Part of Adam block burnt 1940, re-roofed 1987. Policies laid out with ornamental water. Grey Lag Geese and other wildfowl breeding.

Location: On A198 between Aberlady & Longniddry; NW of Haddington.
Station: Longniddry (2 m).
Opening Times: June and July – Weds, Sats & Suns 2–5. Adm £1, Chd 50p, OAPs 75p. Wemyss & March Estates, Longniddry, East Lothian EH32 0PY.
Refreshments: Hotels in Aberlady.

HARELAW FARMHOUSE

nr Longniddry
Telephone: Aberlady (08757) 201
(Lord Wemyss' Trust)

Harelaw Farmhouse. An early 19th Century 2-storey farmhouse built in the old fashioned way, as an integral part of the steading, which is also distinguished by a dovecote over the entrance arch surmounted by a windvane.

Location: Between Longniddry and Drem on the B1377.
Opening Times: Exteriors only. By appointment, Wemyss and March Estates, Estate Office, Longniddry, East Lothian EH32 0PY.

HOPETOUN HOUSE – *See page 242*

HOPETOUN HOUSE – *See page 242*

THE HOUSE OF THE BINNS

by Linlithgow map E14 △
Telephone: Philipstoun (050 683) 4255
(The National Trust for Scotland)

Historic home of the Dalyells. Fine plaster ceilings. Interesting pictures. Panoramic viewpoint.

Location: 3½ m E of Linlithgow off A904.
Opening Times: Apr 18 to Apr 20 and May 2 to Sept 30: daily Sat to Thurs 2–5 *(Closed Fris).* Parkland open 10–7. Adm £2.80, Chd £1.40 (under 5 free). Adult parties £2.20, School parties £1.10, OAPS/Students (on production of their cards) adm at half the standard adult rate. *Members of the Royal Scots Dragoon Guards (in uniform) admitted free.*

INVERESK LODGE GARDEN

Inveresk map F13
(The National Trust for Scotland)

New garden, with large selection of plants.

Location: In Inveresk village; 6 m E of Edinburgh off A1.
Opening Times: GARDEN. All year – Mons to Fris 10–4.30; Suns 2–5. *(Closed Sat).* Lodge open for temporary exhibitions only, as advertised. Adm 50p, Chd (with adult) 30p, under 5 free, OAPs/Students (on production of their cards) adm at half the standard adult rate. Honesty Box.

LAMB'S HOUSE

Leith map F13
Telephone: 031-554 3131
(The National Trust for Scotland)

Residence and warehouse of prosperous merchant of late 16th or early 17th century. Renovated 18th century and later in 1979. Now old people's day centre.

Location: In Leith.
Opening Times: Mons to Fris – Daily 9–5. *(Except Christmas/New Year.)* Visits by prior arrangement.

LAURISTON CASTLE

Edinburgh map F14 △
(City of Edinburgh District Council)

City of Edinburgh District Council, Department of Recreation.
Improving Services – Creating Jobs!

A late-16th century tower-house with extensive 19th century additions, the castle stands in attractive grounds overlooking the Firth of Forth. In the interior it is preserved as an Edwardian middle-class country house. It contains period and reproduction furniture and impressive collections of Derbyshire Blue John, Crossley wool mosaics and objets d'art. There is a free car park. Visitors are given a guided tour of about 40 minutes duration.

OPEN
April to October. Daily (except Friday) 11am-1pm, 2pm-5pm
(last tour begins at approximately 4.20pm). November to March, Saturdays and Sundays
only 2-4pm (last tour begins at approximately 3.20pm). Telephone: 031-336 2060.

ADMISSION CHARGES
Adults: £2.00 Children, O.A.P.'s, UB40's and Benefit recipients: £1.00. Admission to the grounds is free

A beautifully furnished Edwardian home, associated with John Law (1671–1729), founder of first bank in France.

Location: Cramond Road South, Davidsons Mains, 4½ m from GPO, Edinburgh.
Opening Times: Castle. All year. Apr to Oct: daily (except Fris) 11–1, 2–5. Nov to Mar: Sats and Suns only 2–4. Adm £2, Chd £1. Guided tours only (last tour 40 mins before closing time). Grounds: daily 9–dusk.

LENNOXLOVE

Haddington   map F13
Telephone: Haddington (062 082) 3720
(His Grace the Duke of Hamilton)

Lennoxlove, home of the Duke of Hamilton, is a house with a three-fold interest; its historic architecture, the association of its proprietors with the Royal House of Stewart and the famous Hamilton Palace collection of works of art, including the Casket, ring and Death Mask of Mary Queen of Scots. Formerly Lethington Tower, ancient home of the Maitlands. The Lime Avenue, known as Politician's Walk, was laid out by William Maitland, Secretary to Mary Queen of Scots.

Location: 1½ m S of Haddington on B6369; 18 m E of Edinburgh off A1.
Opening Times: Easter weekend, then May to Sept—Weds, Sats & Suns 2–5. At other times by appointment (minimum of 10 people); apply to Estate Office, Lennoxlove, Haddington. Adm £2.50, Chd £1.25. Pre-booked parties of 10 or more £1.80, Chd 75p. Price includes guided tour of House, entry to gardens and parking.

LUFFNESS

Aberlady   map F14
(Luffness Ltd)

16th century castle with 13th century keep—dry moat and old fortifications. Built on the site of a Norse raiders camp.

Location: 18 m E of Edinburgh.
Opening Times: By request during summer months.

MALLENY GARDEN 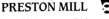

Balerno   map F13   &
(The National Trust for Scotland)

A delightfully personal garden with a particularly good collection of shrub roses. National Bonsai Collection for Scotland.

Location: In Balerno, off A70.
Opening Times: GARDEN ONLY. All the year—Daily 10–sunset. Adm £1, Chd 50p (under 5 free). OAPs/Students (on production of their cards) adm at half the standard adult rate. No dogs in garden please.

PALACE OF HOLYROODHOUSE

Edinburgh   map F14
Telephone: 031-556 7371
(The official residence of HM The Queen in Scotland)

Palace of Holyroodhouse

See entry for details

The ridge, known as the Royal Mile, that slopes downwards from Edinburgh Castle, comes to a majestic conclusion at Holyroodhouse, where Palace and Abbey stand against the spectacular backdrop of Salisbury Crag. Throughout history, Holyrood has been the scene of turbulent and extraordinary events, yet the Palace retains a modern appeal appropriate to a Royal residence still in regular use.

Location: Central Edinburgh.
Opening Times: Open all year (except when Her Majesty The Queen is in residence). Summer: Mon to Sat 9.30–5.15; Sun 10.30–4.30. Winter: Mon to Sat 9.30–3.45; Sun *Closed*. All visitors are conducted by Palace Wardens in groups leaving at about 10 minute intervals. Special group rates, and accompanied school parties are admitted free Mon to Fri; in both cases, prior application must be made. Special interest tours can sometimes be arranged, particularly during off-season. *The Palace and Abbey may sometimes be closed at short notice.*
Enquiries: Telephone (031 556) 1096.
Refreshments: Tea room outside Main Gate.

PRESTON MILL 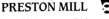

East Linton   map F14
Telephone: East Linton (0620) 860426
(The National Trust for Scotland)

The oldest mill (16th century) of its kind still working and only survivor of many on the banks of the Tyne. Popular with artists. Renovated machinery.

Location: 5½ m W of Dunbar, off A1.
Opening Times: Preston Mill and Phantassie Doo'cot: Apr 17 to Sept 30: Mons to Sats 11–1, 2–5; Suns 2–5. Oct 3 to 31: Sats 11–1, 2–4, Suns 2–4. Adm £1.20, Chd 60p (under 5 free). OAPs/Students (on production of their cards) adm at half the standard adult rate. Adult parties £1, school parties 50p.

ROYAL BOTANIC GARDEN

Edinburgh   map F14

Founded 17th century. Beautiful rock garden. Exhibition Plant Houses. Extensive programme of workshops, courses, exhibitions and children's activities throughout the year.

Location: Inverleith Row, Edinburgh.
Opening Times: All the year. Mar to Oct (during BST)—Weekdays 9–one hour before sunset, Suns 1–one hour before sunset. Remainder of year—Weekdays 9–sunset, Suns 11–sunset. *Closed Christmas Day & New Year's Day.* Planthouses and Exhibition Hall—Weekdays 10–5, Suns 11–5. Adm free.
Refreshments: Terrace cafe in the garden.

STEVENSON HOUSE

Haddington   map F13
Telephone: Haddington (062 082) 3376 Mrs. J. C. H. Dunlop
(Trustees of the Brown Dunlop Country Houses Trust)

A family home for four centuries, of charm and interest and dating from the 13th century when it belonged to the Cistercian Nunnery at Haddington, but partially destroyed on several occasions, and finally made uninhabitable in 1544. Restored about 1560 and the present house dates mainly from this period, with later additions in the 18th century. Fine furniture, pictures etc.

Location: 20 m approx from Edinburgh; 1½ m approx from A1; 2 m approx from Haddington. (See Historic House direction signs on A1 in Haddington.)
Opening Times: July to mid-Aug—Thurs, Sats & Suns 2–5. Guided tours take at least 1–1½ hours 3 pm. Other times by arrangement only. Adm £2, OAP £1.50, Chd (under 14) £1. Special arrangement parties welcome. GARDENS (House and Walled Kitchen Garden) are open daily (Apr to Oct). Entrance for these 50p only (payable into Box on House Garden entrance gate). Car parking. Suitable for wheelchairs in garden only.
Refreshments: Appointment parties morning coffee etc at Stevenson. Nearest hotels and restaurants are in Haddington, i.e. 2 m from Stevenson.

TANTALLON CASTLE

nr North Berwick   map F14
(Historic Scotland)

Famous 14th century stronghold of the Douglases occupies a magnificent situation on the rocky coast of the Firth of Forth.

Location: On the coast approx 3 m E of North Berwick.
Opening Times: Apr 1 to Sept 30: Mons to Sats 9.30–6.30, Suns 2–6.30. Oct 1 to Mar 31: Mons to Sats 9.30–4.30, Suns 2–4.30 *except Thurs pm and all day Fris and Dec 25, 26; Jan 1, 2.* Adm £1.50, Chd and OAPs 80p. Family ticket £4. Prices subject to change 1993 season.

STRATHCLYDE REGION

BACHELORS' CLUB

Tarbolton   map D13
Telephone: Tarbolton (0292) 541940
(The National Trust for Scotland)

17th century thatched house where Burns and his friends formed their club in 1780. Period furnishings.

Location: In Tarbolton village 7½ m NE of Ayr (off A758).
Opening Times: Apr 1 to Oct 25: daily 12–5, other times by appointment. Adm £1.20, Chd 60p (under 5 free), OAPs/Students (on production of their cards) adm at half the standard adult rate. Adult parties £1, school parties 50p. *Other times by appointment.*

BALLOCH CASTLE COUNTRY PARK

Balloch   map D14
Telephone: Alexandria (0389) 58216
(Dumbarton District Council)

200 acres. Situated beside Loch Lomond contains many conifers, rhododendrons and other shrubs. Walled garden. Fairy Glen. Castle Visitor Centre, site of old castle and moat. Nature trail and countryside ranger service. Guided walks in summer.

Location: Balloch, Dumbartonshire.
Station: Balloch (¾ m).
Opening Times: All the year—Daily during daylight hours. Visitor Centre: Easter to Sept: 10–6. Adm free. Car parks.

BELLAHOUSTON PARK

Glasgow   map D13
(City of Glasgow District Council)

171 acres. Sunk, wall and rock gardens. Dry ski-slope. Athletic and indoor sports centre. Charles Rennie Mackintosh Arts. Lovers' House.

Location: Paisley Road West.
Station: Dumbreck ¼ m.
Opening Times: All the year—Daily 8 to dusk. Adm free.

BENMORE YOUNGER BOTANIC GARDEN

nr Dunoon   map D14
(Royal Botanic Garden, Edinburgh)

A woodland garden on a grand scale.

Location: 7 m NW of Dunoon (off A815).
Opening Times: Daily—Mar 15 to Oct 31 10–6. Adm £1.50, Chd 50p, OAPs £1.
Refreshments: Tea at main entrance.

BLAIRQUHAN CASTLE AND GARDENS

Straiton, Maybole, Ayrshire   map D12
Telephone: Straiton (065 57) 239
(James Hunter Blair)

Magnificent Regency castellated mansion approached by a 3 m private drive beside the river Girvan. Walled gardens and pinetum. Plants for sale. Picture gallery.

Location: 14 m S of Ayr; off A77. Entrance Lodge is on B7045 ½ m S of Kirkmichael.
Opening Times: July 12 to Aug 9 *(not Mons)*. Adm £2.50, Chd £1.50, OAPs £2. Parties by arrangement at any time of year. Car parking. Wheelchairs—around gardens and principal floor of the castle.
Refreshments: Tea in castle.

BOTANIC GARDENS

Glasgow   map D13
(City of Glasgow District Council)

Covering 40 acres. Extensive botanical collections, tropical plants, herb and systematic gardens.

Location: Great Western Road.
Opening Times: All the year—Daily (incl Suns) 7—dusk. Kibble Palace 10—4.45 (winter 10—4.15). Main range of glasshouses 1—4.45 (winter 1—4.15). Suns all year 12—4.45, (winter 12—4.15). Adm free.

BOTHWELL CASTLE

Bothwell   map E13
(Historic Scotland)

The largest and finest 13th century Stone Castle in Scotland.

Location: At Bothwell but approached from Uddingston.
Opening Times: Apr 1 to Sept 30—Mon to Sat 9.30—6.30, Suns 2—6.30; Oct 1 to Mar 31—Mon to Sat 9.30—4.30. *(Closed Thurs pm and Fris in winter)*, Suns 2—4.30. *Closed Dec 25, 26; Jan 1, 2.* Adm £1, Chd & OAPs 50p. Prices subject to change 1993 season.

BRODICK CASTLE, GARDEN AND COUNTRY PARK

Isle of Arran   map C13   &
Telephone: Brodick (0770) 2202
(The National Trust for Scotland)

Historic home of the Dukes of Hamilton. The castle dates in part from the 13th century. Paintings, furniture, objet d'art. Formal and woodland gardens, noted for rhododendrons. Country park.

Location: 1½ m N of Brodick pierhead on the Isle of Arran.
Station: Ardrossan Harbour and Claonaig in Kintyre (& hence by Caledonian MacBrayne ferry).
Ferry enquiries to Caledonian MacBrayne. Tel. Gourock (0475) 33755.
Opening Times: CASTLE. Apr 1 to 17 and Oct 3 to 24 Mons, Weds, Sats 1—5. Apr 17 to Sept 30 daily 1—5. RESTAURANT: dates as Castle, Mons to Sats 10—5, Suns 12—5. SHOP AND VISITOR CENTRE: dates as Castle daily 10—5. COUNTRY PARK AND GARDEN. All the year: daily 10—sunset. Adm Castle and Gardens £3, Chd £1.50; Adult parties £2.50, School parties £1.30. Gardens only £2, Chd £1. Chd under 5 free, OAPs/Students (on production of their cards) adm at half the standard adult rate. Car park free. Shop.
Refreshments: Self-service restaurant in Castle.

BURNS COTTAGE

Alloway   map D12
(Trustees of Burns Monument)

Thatched cottage in which Robert Burns was born, 1759. Museum with Burns' relics.

Location: 1½ m SW of Ayr.
Station: Ayr (1½ m).
Opening Times: Open all year round.
Refreshments: Tea at cottage in Summer.

CULZEAN CASTLE, GARDEN AND COUNTRY PARK

Maybole   map D12   △ & ⑤
Telephone: Kirkoswald (065 56) 274
(The National Trust for Scotland)

One of the finest Adam houses in Scotland. Spacious policies and gardens. Adventure playground.

Location: 12 m SW of Ayr just off A719.
Opening Times: CASTLE, VISITOR CENTRE, LICENSED RESTAURANT AND SHOPS Apr 1 to Oct 25: daily 10.30—5.30. At other times by appointment. Adm £3, Chd £1.50 (under 5 free). Adult parties £3.50, school parties £1.90. OAPs/Students (on production of their cards) adm at half the standard adult rate.
CULZEAN COUNTRY PARK *(NTS and Kyle & Carrick; Cummock & Doon Valley District Councils & Strathclyde Region)*—open all year. Adm free to members & pedestrians. Cars £5, mini buses/caravans £7, Coaches £24, School Coaches £18, motorcycles £1.10. Apr to Oct 25 only, vehicles (except school coaches) free at other times. Open all year, daily 9—sunset. Adult parties £3.50, School parties £1.90 (includes coach entry to Country Park).

DUMBARTON CASTLE

Dumbarton   map D13
(Historic Scotland)

Sited on a volcanic rock overlooking the Firth of Clyde.

Location: At Dumbarton.
Opening Times: Apr 1 to Sept 30—Daily 9.30—6.30, Suns 2—6.30. Oct 1 to Mar 31—Daily 9.30—4.30, Suns 2—4.30. *(Closed Thurs pm and all day Fris in winter)*. *Closed Dec 25, 26; Jan 1, 2.* Adm £1, Chd & OAPs 50p. Prices subject to change 1993 season.

FINLAYSTONE HOUSE AND GARDENS   🏛

Langbank   map D13
Telephone: Langbank 285/505
(Mrs G MacMillan)

Formerly home of fifteen Earls of Glencairn; now the home of the chief of Clan MacMillan. Exhibitions of international dolls, flower books and Victoriana, and Celtic art. Beautiful Gardens, Woodlands, with picnic/play areas. Ranger service. Visitor centre. Clan Centre. Celtic Exhibition.

Location: On A8 between Langbank & Port Glasgow; 20 minutes W of Glasgow on S bank of the Clyde.
Station: Longbank (1¼ m).
Opening Times: Beautiful gardens and woods open ALL THE YEAR. Adm £1.20, Chd 80p. (House: Apr to Aug—Suns 2.30—4.30, **and** by appointment any time). Pre-booked groups welcome. Adm to House £1.20, Chd 80p.
Refreshments: Home-baked afternoon teas Sats & Suns in summer. New: Tearoom in walled garden.

GREENBANK GARDEN

Glasgow   map D13   &
Telephone: 041-639 3281
(The National Trust for Scotland)

Walled garden, woodland walk and policies. Wide range of plants, flowers and shrubs. Regular garden walks and events. Best seen Apr—Oct. Attractive series of gardens, extending to 2½ acres, surrounding Georgian house (not open to the public). Special garden and greenhouse for the disabled, together with special gardening tools.

Location: Flenders Road, near Clarkston Toll.
Station: Clarkston (1¼ m).
Opening Times: Garden. All the year: daily 9.30—sunset. Adm £1.50, Chd (accompanied by adult) 80p. Adult parties £1.20, School parties 60p. Chd under 5 free, OAPs/Students (on production of their cards) adm at half the standard adult rate.

THE HILL HOUSE

Helensburgh map D14
Telephone: (0436) 3900
(The National Trust for Scotland)

Overlooking the estuary of the River Clyde the house is considered to be the finest example of the domestic architecture of Charles Rennie Mackintosh. Commissioned in 1902 and completed in 1904 for the Glasgow publisher Walter W Blackie. Special display about Charles Rennie Mackintosh.

Location: In Upper Colquhoun Street, Helensburgh; NW of Glasgow via A814.
Opening Times: Apr 1 to Dec 29 and Dec 28 to Dec 29: daily 1–5 (last adm 4.30). Adm £2.40, Chd £1.20. Adult parties £1.90, School parties £1.

HUTCHESONS' HALL

Glasgow map DE13
Telephone: 041-552 8391
(The National Trust for Scotland)

Described as one of the most elegant buildings in Glasgow's city centre, the Hall was built in 1802–5 to a design by David Hamilton.

Location: 158 Ingram Street, nr SE corner of George Square.
Opening Times: Hall viewing subject to functions. Visitor Centre and Function Hall: open all year *(except public holidays and Jan 1 to Jan 5)*. Mons to Fris 9–5, Sats 10–4. Shop: Mons to Sats 10–4. Entry free.

INVERARAY CASTLE – *See page 249*

KELBURN COUNTRY CENTRE AND KELBURN CASTLE

Largs map D13
Telephone: Fairlie (0475) 568685
(The Home and Park of the Earls of Glasgow on the Firth of Clyde.)

Kelburn has been the home of the Earls of Glasgow since the creation of the title in 1703, but has been the seat of the Boyle family for over 800 years. The Kelburn Glen is one of the most romantic in Scotland, dropping 700 ft by way of many waterfalls and deep gorges. There is a Walled Garden full of unusual shrubs peculiar to the West Coast of Scotland, a New Zealand Garden created by the 7th Countess in 1898, a small formal Garden designed by the 3rd Earl in the 1760s for his four children, and two unique sundials. There are some very remarkable trees, including the largest Monterey Pine in Scotland, the thousand-year-old Yews, and the amazing Weeping Larch. Kelburn Castle is fully lived in, and open for only one month of the year, but it

makes an impressive background to many walks and views. The grounds and the riding school, however, are open all the year round and Kelburn Country Centre, open from Easter till mid-Oct, contains an Adventure course, Commando Assault course, pet's corner, children's stockade, pony trekking. Shop, exhibitions, craft workshop, museum, cartoon exhibition, display room.

Location: On the A78 between Largs and Fairlie in Ayrshire.
Station: Largs (2 m).
Opening Times: Kelburn Country Centre: Open with all facilities daily 10–6 from Apr 4 to mid-Oct. Adm £3, Chd (accompanied) £1.50, OAPs/UB40 £1.50; Groups (12+) £1.50 per person. Dogs admitted on leads. **Winter opening:** Grounds only mid-Oct to Mar 30. Adm £1 and 60p. **Kelburn Castle:** Open to visitors from Sat Apr 21 to Mon May 28 only. Closed at all other times, except to special parties by prior arrangement. Adm £1.50 per person excluding admission to Kelburn Country Centre.
Refreshments: Licensed cafe, lunches, snacks, home baking, ice cream parlour, picnic areas. Open from Apr 4 to mid-Oct.

LINN PARK

Glasgow map D13
(City of Glasgow District Council)

212 acres pine and deciduous woodlands with enchanting riverside walks. Nature centre, Nature trail and Children's Zoo.

Location: Clarkston Road; Netherlee Road; Simshill Road, Linnview Avenue.
Station: Muirend (³/₄ m).
Opening Times: All the year. Adm free. Car park at golf course & Netherlee Road.

PENKILL CASTLE

Girvan map D12   △
Telephone: Old Dailly (046 587) 261
(Elton A Eckstrand, JD.)

15th century Castle, impressive later additions. Fine furniture, tapestries and paintings. Favourite haunt of the Pre-Raphaelites, an inspiration to Dante Gabriel Rossetti and his sister Christina and other well known visitors.

Location: 2½ m E of Girvan on B734 Barr Road (off A77 Stranraer/Ayr Road).
Station: Girvan (2½ m). Turnberry (8 m).
Opening Times: 365 days per year by appointment. Guided tours with catering for groups. For details of other programmes contact Administrator.

POLLOK HOUSE & PARK

Glasgow map D13   &
Telephone: 041-632 0274
(City of Glasgow District Council)

INVERARAY CASTLE 🏰

Inveraray   map D14
Telephone: Inveraray (0499) 2203.
(The Trustees of the 10th Duke of Argyll)

Since the early 15th century Inveraray has been the Headquarters of the Clan Campbell. The present Castle was built in the third quarter of the 18th century by Roger Morris and Robert Mylne. The Great Hall and Armoury, the State Rooms, Tapestries, Pictures and 18th century Furniture and old kitchen are shown.

Location: ¾ m NE of Inveraray on Loch Fyne 58 m NW of Glasgow.
Opening Times: First Sat in Apr to second Sun in Oct. Apr, May, June, Sept & Oct: daily (except Fri) 10–1, 2–6. Sun 1–6. (During June, the Castle will remain open at lunch time.) July & Aug: daily 10–6, Sun 1–6. Last admission 12.30 & 5.30.. Gardens open by appointment, woodland walk open all year. Craft shop. *Enquiries:* The Factor, Dept HH, Cherry Park, Inveraray, Argyll. Telephone: (0499) 2203.
Refreshments: Tearoom.

POLLOK HOUSE & PARK – *Continued*

Built 1747–52, additions by Sir Rowand Anderson 1890–1908. Contains Stirling Maxwell collection of Spanish and other European paintings; displays of furniture, ceramics, glass and silver. Nearby in Pollok Park is the Burrell Collection. Opening times as Pollok House.

Location: 3½ m from City Centre.
Station: Pollokshaws West (1 m).
Opening Times: All the year: Mons to Sats 10–5, Suns 12–6. Adm free. *Closed Christmas Day & New Year's Day.*
Refreshments: Tea room (reservations Tel 041-649 7547).

ROSS HALL PARK

Glasgow   map D13
(City of Glasgow District Council)

33 acres. Majestic trees by River Cart. Extensive heather and rock gardens, with water features, nature trails.

Location: Crookston Road SW.
Opening Times: All the year. Adm free.

SOUTER JOHNNIE'S COTTAGE 👑

Kirkoswald   map D12
Telephone: Kirkoswald (065 56) 603
(The National Trust for Scotland)

Thatched home of the original Souter in Burns' "Tam o' Shanter", Burns' relics. Life-sized stone figures of the Souter, Tam, the Innkeeper and his wife, in restored ale house in the cottage garden.

Location: In Kirkoswald village 4 m W of Maybole on A77.
Opening Times: Apr 1 to Oct 25: daily 12–5 (or by appointment). Adm £1.20, Chd 60p. Adult parties £1, School parties 50p, (under 5 free), OAPs/Students (on production of their cards) adm at half the standard adult rate.

THE TENEMENT HOUSE 👑

Glasgow   map D13
Telephone: (041) 333 0183
(The National Trust for Scotland)

A restored first floor flat in a Victorian tenement building, built 1892, presents a picture of social significance. A second flat on the ground floor provides reception, interpretative and educational facilities.

Location: No 145 Buccleuch Street, Garnethill (N of Charing Cross).
Opening Times: Until Mar 29 1992: Sats & Suns 2–4. Apr 1 to Nov 1 daily 2–5. Nov 7 to Mar 1993: Sat & Sun 2–4. Weekday morning visits by educational & other groups (no more than 15) to be arranged by advance booking only. Adm £1.50, Chd 80p; Adult parties £1.20, School parties 60p.

TOROSAY CASTLE AND GARDENS 🏰

Craignure, Isle of Mull   map C15
Telephone: Craignure (068 02) 421
(Mr Christopher James)

Early Victorian house by David Bryce, still a family home, surrounded by 12 acres of terraced and contrasting informal gardens, all offset by dramatic West Highland scenery.

Location: 1½ m SE of Craignure by A849, by Forest Walk or by N.G. Steam Railway.
Opening Times: Castle – Easter to mid-Oct, 10.30–5.30 (last adm 5). Gardens – Summer, 9 –7. Winter – sunrise to sunset. Parties at other times to Castle by appointment only. Adm Castle £3.50, also concession rates. Garden only, £1.50, Chd (5–16), OAPs, students £1 (by honesty box when castle closed). Car park free. Dogs on lead in Gardens only. Gardens and tearoom only suitable for wheelchairs. Local Craft Shop.
Refreshments: Home baked teas in Castle.

VICTORIA PARK

Glasgow   map D13
(City of Glasgow District Council)

Fossilised tree stumps, 300 million years old, in Fossil Grove Building. 58 acres. Extensive carpet bedding depicting centennial events.

Location: Victoria Park Drive North.
Opening Times: Park: All the year. Adm free.

WEAVER'S COTTAGE 👑

Kilbarchan   map D13
(The National Trust for Scotland)

Typical cottage of 18th century handloom weaver: looms, weaving equipment, domestic utensils. (Weaving demonstrations check for times).

Location: In Kilbarchan village; 12 m SW of Glasgow off A737.
Station: Johnstone (2½ m).
Opening Times: Apr 2 to May 28, and Sept 1 to Nov 1: Tues, Thurs, Sats and Suns 2–5. May 30 to Aug 30: daily 2–5 (last tour 4.30). Adm £1.20, Chd 60p (under 5 free); Adult parties £1; Chd parties 50p, OAPs/Students (on production of their cards) adm at half the standard adult rate. Video programme.

TAYSIDE REGION

ANGUS FOLK MUSEUM

Glamis map F15
Telephone: Glamis (030 784) 288
(The National Trust for Scotland)

Row of 19th century cottages with stone-slabbed roofs, restored by the Trust. Adapted to display the Angus Folk Collection, one of the finest in the country. In agricultural annexe are farming implements and the Bothy Exhibition incl. taped recordings.

Location: In Glamis village; 12 m N of Dundee A94.
Opening Times: Apr 17 to Apr 20, and May 1 to Sept 30: daily 11–5. Adm £1.50, Chd 80p (under 5 free). Adult parties £1.20, School parties 60p. OAPs/Students (on production of their cards) adm at half the standard adult rate.

BARRIE'S BIRTHPLACE

Kirriemuir map F15
Telephone: Kirriemuir (0575) 72646
(The National Trust for Scotland)

Contains mementoes of Sir James Barrie. New exhibition features Peter Pan and other works of Barrie.

Location: No 9 Brechin Road, in Kirriemuir.
Opening Times: Apr 17 to Apr 20; May 1 to Sept 30: Mons to Sats 11–5.30, Suns 2–5.30. Adm £1.20, Chd 60p (under 5 free). OAPs/Students (on production of their cards) adm at half the standard adult rate. Adult parties £1, School parties 50p.
Refreshments: Airlie Arms Hotel.

BLAIR CASTLE – *See page 251*

BRANKLYN GARDEN

Perth map E14
Telephone: Perth (0738) 25535
(The National Trust for Scotland)

One of the finest gardens of its size in Britain (2 acres).

Location: In Perth on Dundee Road (A85).
Opening Times: Mar 1 to Oct 31: daily 9.30–sunset. Adm £1.50, Chd 80p (under 5 free) OAPs/Students (on production of their cards) adm at half the standard adult rate. Adult parties £1.20, Schools parties 60p.

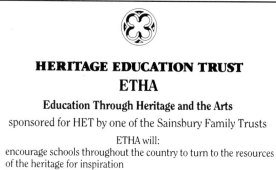
CASTLE MENZIES

Weem map E15
(Menzies Clan Society)

Magnificent example of a 16th century fortified house, seat of the Chiefs of Clan Menzies, situated in the beautiful valley of the Tay. It was involved in the turbulent history of the Central Highlands and here "Bonnie Prince Charlie" rested on his way to Culloden in 1746.

Location: 1½ m from Aberfeldy on B846.
Opening Times: Apr to mid-Oct—Weekdays 10.30–5, Suns 2–5. Adm £2, Chd 50p, OAPs £1. Reductions for parties by prior arrangement.

DRUMMOND CASTLE GARDENS

Muthill map E14
(The Grimsthorpe & Drummond Castle Trust Ltd)

The Gardens of Drummond Castle were originally laid out about 1630 by John Drummond, 2nd Earl of Perth. In about 1830, the parterre was Italianized and embellished with fine figures and statues from Italy. Probably one of the most interesting pieces of statuary is the Sundial, designed and built by John Mylne, Master Mason to King Charles I.

Location: 3 m S of Crieff, W off Crieff/Muthill Road (A822)—East Lodge.
Opening Times: May 1 to Sept 30—Daily 2–6 (last admission 5); Sept—Weds & Suns only 2–6. Adm £2, Chd/OAPs £1. Free car park. *Gardens only are open to the public, according to the Rules in force.*

EDZELL CASTLE & GARDENS

Edzell map F15
(Historic Scotland)

16th century castle. Unique renaissance garden. New Visitor Centre.

Location: 1 m W of Edzell; 6 m N of Brechin off B996.
Opening Times: Apr 1 to Sept 30: Mons to Sats 9.30–6.30, Suns 2–6.30. Oct 1 to Mar 31: Mons to Sats (*except Thurs pm and all day Fri*) 9.30–4.30, Suns 2–4.30. *Closed Dec 25 and 26; Jan 1 & 2.* Adm £1.50, Chd and OAPs 80p. Prices subject to change 1993 season.

BLAIR CASTLE

Blair Atholl map E15
Telephone: (0796) 481207
(His Grace the Duke of Atholl)

13th century home of The Duke of Atholl, Blair Castle is Scotland's most visited Historic House and has 32 rooms of infinite variety displaying beautiful furniture, fine collection of paintings, Arms and Armour, china, lace and embroidery, children's games and Jacobite relics. The Duke of Atholl has Europe's only official private army – The Atholl Highlanders.

Location: 8 m NW of Pitlochry off A9.
Station: Blair Atholl (3/4 m). Free minibus service available.
Opening Times: Open Apr 1 to Oct 30: daily 10–6. Apr, May and Oct: Suns 2–6. Last adm 5. Adm £4, Chd £2.50, OAPs £2.50, reductions for pre-booked groups, Family tickets available. Picnic areas, Deer Park, Nature trails, pony trekking, free car and coach parking. Gift shop. Children's Guide Book. Up to 2,000 visitors a day can be accommodated.
Refreshments: Self Service Restaurant. Catering for pre-booked groups of up to 200 in separate rooms with waitress service can be provided. Further details available from The Administrator, Tel: (0796) 481207. Fax: (0796) 481487.

SCONE PALACE

Perth map E15
Telephone: Perth (0738) 52300
(Rt Hon the Earl of Mansfield)

This medieval palace was Gothicised for the third Earl of Mansfield in the early 19th century. Superb collections of French furniture, china, ivories, clocks, Vernis Martin vases and objets d'art.

Location: 2 m NE of Perth on the Braemer Road (A93).
Station: Perth (2½ m).
Opening Times: Good Friday, Apr 17, 1992 to Mon, Oct 12, 1992: Mons to Sats 9.30– 5, Suns 1.30–5 (July and Aug 10–5). Adm £3.70. Special rates for booked parties. Free car park. Shops. Picnic park. Playground. Winter tours by special arrangment.
Refreshments: Coffee shop. Old Kitchen Restaurant (licensed). Home baking. State Room dinners.

GLAMIS CASTLE

Glamis   map 15
(The Earl of Strathmore and Kinghorne)

Family home of the Earls of Strathmore and Kinghorne and a royal residence since 1372. Childhood home of H.M. Queen Elizabeth The Queen Mother and birthplace of H.R.H. The Princess Margaret. Legendary setting of Shakespeare's play 'Macbeth'. Five-storey L shaped tower block dating from 15th century, remodelled 1606, containing magnificent rooms with wide range of historic pictures, furniture, porcelain etc.

Location: Glamis.
Opening Times: Apr 17 to Oct 12: daily 12–5.30 (last tour 4.45) (July/Aug from 11). Adm £3.70, reductions for Chd, OAPs and groups. Ample bus and car parking. Picnic area, Shops, Garden and Nature Trail. Further details available from The Administrator, Tel: 030784 242. Fax: 030 784 257.
Refreshments: Licensed Restaurant at the Castle.

HOUSE OF DUN

Nr Montrose   map G15
Telephone: (067481) 264
(The National Trust for Scotland)

Palladian house overlooking the Montrose Basin, built in 1730 for David Erskine, Lord Dun, to designs by William Adam. Exuberant plasterwork in the saloon.

Location: 4 m W of Montrose.
Opening Times: House, Courtyard and Tearoom: Apr 17 to Apr 20, then May 1 to Oct 18: daily 11–5.30. Garden and grounds open all year. Adm House £3, Chd £1.50, Adult parties £2.50, School parties £1.30. Garden and grounds free.

HUNTINGTOWER CASTLE

nr Perth   map E14
(Historic Scotland)

Two fine and complete towers in which are excellent painted ceilings.

Location: 2 m W of Perth.
Opening Times: Apr 1 to Sept 30: daily 9.30–6.30, Suns 2–6.30. Oct 1 to Mar 31: daily 9.30 – 4.30, Suns 2–4.30 *except Thurs pm and all day Fris and Closed Dec 25, 26; Jan 1, 2*. Adm £1, Chd & OAPs 50p. Prices subject to change 1993 season.

SCONE PALACE – *See page 251*

UNIVERSITY OF CAMBRIDGE

NOTE: Admission to *Colleges* means to the Courts, not to the staircases and students' rooms. All opening times are subject to closing for College functions, etc., on occasional days. *Halls* normally close for lunch (12–2) and many are not open during the afternoon. *Chapels* are closed during services. *Libraries* are not usually open, special arrangements are noted. *Gardens* do not usually include the Fellows' garden. *Figures* denote the date of foundation, and existing buildings are often of later date. *Daylight hours* – some Colleges may not open until 9.30 am or later and usually close before 6 pm – many as early as 4.30 pm.

All parties exceeding 10 persons wishing to tour the colleges between Easter and October are required to be escorted by a Cambridge registered Guide. All enquiries should be made to the Tourist Information Centre, Wheeler Street, Cambridge CB2 3QB.

Terms: *Lent:* Mid-January to Mid-March. *Easter:* April to June. *Michaelmas:* 2nd week October to 1st week December. Examination Period closures which differ from one college to another, now begin in early April and extend to late June. Notices are usually displayed. Important: Before entering any college, please call at the Porter's Lodge. This applies both to individual visitors and guided parties.

Address of College and Entrance Gate	*Opening Arrangements*
Christ's College (1505). St. Andrew's Street (Porter's Lodge)	The College is closed to all visitors from May 1 to mid-June. At other times it is open as follows:– *College:* Daily, all day. *Chapel:* Daily during Term. *Hall:* Weekdays 10–1. *Library:* By appointment with Librarian. *Fellows' Garden:* Mons to Fris 10.30–12.30, 2–4. (Closed Bank Hols, Easter week and weekends).
Clare College (1326). Trinity Lane CB2 1TL	*Hall:* Mons to Sats 9–12 (usually). *Chapel:* Daily during term time except Apr 17 to June 25. Otherwise by prior arrangement with the Dean. *Library:* By prior arrangement with the Librarian. *Gardens:* Mons to Fris 2–4 (usually). (Closed Bank Hols and weekends).
Corpus Christi College (1352). Trumpington Street (Porter's Lodge)	Opening times shown at Porter's Lodge.
Downing College (1800). Regent Street (Porter's Lodge)	*College & Gardens:* Daily, daylight hours. *Chapel:* Term – Daily, all day. Vacation – By appointment. *Hall:* Closed to the public. *Library:* By arrangement only.
Emmanuel College (1584). St. Andrew's Street (Porter's Lodge)	*College:* Daily 9–6. *Hall:* 2.30–5. *Chapel:* 9–6 both daily, except when in use. *Library:* Only by prior application to Librarian. *Gardens & Paddock:* Daily 9–6 or dusk if earlier. *Fellows' Garden:* Not open to visitors. (Closed for annual holidays, variable).
Gonville & Caius College (1348). Trinity Street (Porter's Lodge)	*College & Chapel:* Daily, daylight hours. *Library:* By appointment with Librarian. (Closed to all guided parties and parties of more than 6 persons) Closed during exams from early May to mid-June and for short periods each day: times shown at Porter's Lodge.
Jesus College (1496). Jesus Lane (Porter's Lodge)	*College:* Daily 9–5.30. *Chapel:* Apply Porter's Lodge. *Hall:* Closed to the public.
King's College (1441). King's Parade (Porter's Lodge)	*College:* Daily until 6. Limited access mid-Apr to end Sept. *Library:* Scholars, on application to librarian. *Chapel:* Term – Weekdays 9.30–3.45. Suns 2–3, 4.45–5.45. Summer Vacation – Weekdays 9.30–5.45. Suns 10.30–5.45 and subject to closure at other times for rehearsals etc. *Dining Hall:* Closed to the public.
Magdalene College (1542). Magdalene Street (Porters' Lodge)	*College & Chapel:* Daily 9–6.30 (except during exams). *Hall:* Daily 9.30–12.30 (except during exams). *Gardens:* Daily 1–6.30 (except during exams). *Pepys:* Jan 15 to Mar 16 1991: weekdays 2.30–3.30; Apr 23 to Aug 31 1991: weekdays (not Suns) 11.30–12.30, 2.30–3.30. Closed July and Aug during 1991 – building works.
Newnham College (1871). Sidgwick Avenue	*College & Gardens:* Daily during daylight hours. Apply Porter's Lodge. (College and gardens closed May 1–mid-June and last 2 weeks of August).
Pembroke College (1347). Trumpington Street	Opening times shown at Porter's Lodge. *Library:* By appointment with Librarian.
Peterhouse (1284). Trumpington Street (Porter's Lodge)	Guided parties of not more than 12. *Chapel:* Daily. *Hall:* Mornings only, during term. *Gardens:* Daily 10–5 (no dogs).
Queens' College (1448). Silver Street (Porter's Lodge). Visitor's entrance, Queen's Lane	Open daily 1.45–4.30 & also 10.15–12.45 during July, Aug & Sept & for guided parties of not more than 20. Adm charge.
St. Catharine's College (1473). Trumpington Street (Porter's Lodge)	*College & Chapel:* Daily, during daylight hours. (Closed May & June). *Hall:* Closed to the public.
St. John's College (1511). St. John's Street (Porter's Lodge)	*College:* Daily 10.30 until 5.30. (Closed May & June). *Chapel:* Apply Porter's Lodge. *Hall:* Closed to the public.
Sidney Sussex College (1596). Sidney Street (Porter's Lodge)	*College:* Daily, during daylight hours. *Hall & Chapel:* Apply Porter's Lodge.
Trinity College (1546). Trinity Street (Porter's Lodge)	Opening times shown at Great Gate Porter's Lodge.
Trinity Hall (1350). Trinity Lane	*College, Chapel & Gardens:* Daily, during daylight hours except during examination period (end April to mid-June). *Library:* Apply beforehand to College Librarian.

CONDUCTED TOURS IN CAMBRIDGE Qualified, badged, local guides may be obtained from: Tourist Information Centre, Wheeler Street, Cambridge CB2 3QB. Tel: (0223) 322640 or Cambridge Guide Service, 2 Montague Road, Cambridge CB4 1BX. Tel: (0223) 356735 (Principals: John Mellanby MA., and Mrs E. Garner). We normally obtain the Passes and make all negotiations regarding these with the Tourist Office, so separate application is not needed.

We have been providing guides for English, Foreign language and special interest groups since 1950. We supply couriers for coach tours of East Anglia, visiting stately homes etc. As an alternative to the 2 hour walking tour, we can now offer ½ hour panoramic tour in clients' coach (provided there is an effective public address system) followed by 1½ hours on foot or 1 hour panoramic only, special flat rate up to 55 people.

UNIVERSITY OF OXFORD

NOTE: Admission to *Colleges* means to the quadrangles, not to the staircases and students' rooms. All opening times are subject to closing for College functions, etc., on occasional days. *Halls* normally close for lunch during term (12–2). *Chapel* usually closed during services. *Libraries* are not usually open, special arrangements are noted. *Gardens* do not usually include the Fellows' garden. *Figures* denote the date of foundation, and existing buildings are often of later date.

Terms: *Hilary:* Mid-January to Mid-March. *Trinity:* 3rd week April to late June. *Michaelmas:* Mid-October to 1st week December.

Address of College and Entrance Gate	Opening Arrangements
All Souls College (1438). High Street (Porter's Lodge)	*College:* Daily 2–5. Subject to closure due to building works.
Balliol College (1263). Broad Street (Porter's Lodge)	*Hall, Chapel & Gardens:* Daily 2–5 (summer), 2–5 (winter). Parties limited to 25.
Brasenose College (1509). Radcliffe Square (Porter on duty)	*Hall, Chapel & Gardens:* Tour parties: Daily 10–5 (summer), 10–dusk (winter). Individuals 2–5. *Hall:* 11.45–2.
Christ Church (1546). St. Aldate's (Meadow Gate)	*Cathedral:* Daily 9–4.30 (winter), 9–5.30 (summer). *Hall:* Oct to Mar: Daily 9.30–12, 2–4.30. Apr to Sept: Daily 9.30–12, 2–6. Adm £1.50, Chd 50p. *Picture Gallery:* Weekdays 10.30–1, 2–4.30. Adm 50p. *Meadow:* Daily 7–dusk. Hall published hours occasionally curtailed for College or Cathedral events.
Corpus Christi College (1517). Merton Street (Porter's Lodge)	*College, Chapel & Gardens:* Terms and vacations – Daily 2–4.
Exeter College (1314). Turl Street (Porter's Lodge)	*College & Chapel, Fellows' Garden:* Term and vacations – Daily 2–5.
Hertford College (1284, 1740 & 1874). Catte Street (Porter's Lodge)	*College, Hall & Chapel:* Daily 10–6. (Closed for a week at Christmas and Easter).
Jesus College (1571). Turl Street (Gate in Turl Street)	*College, Hall & Chapel:* Daily 2.30–4.30. *Library:* Special permission of Librarian. (Closed Christmas and Easter holidays).
Keble College (1868). Parks Road (Porter's Lodge)	*College & Chapel:* Daily 10–7 (or dusk if earlier).
Lady Margaret Hall (1878). Norham Gardens. (All visitors are requested to call at the Porter's Lodge)	*College Gardens:* Daily 2–6 (or dusk if earlier).
Lincoln College (1427). Turl Street (Porter's Lodge)	*College & Hall:* Weekdays 2–5. Suns 11–5. *Wesley Room:* On application to Porter's Lodge. *All Saints Library:* Tues & Thurs 2–4.
Magdalen College (1458). High Street (Front Lodge)	*College, Chapel, Deer Park & Water Walks:* Daily 2–6.15. Parties limited to 25.
Mansfield College (1886). Mansfield Road (Porter's Lodge)	*College:* Open May, June & July, Mon to Sat 9–5. Interior of Chapel and Library may be viewed by prior appointment, please enquire at Porter's Lodge.
Merton (1264). Merton Street (Porter's Lodge)	*Chapel & Quadrangles:* Mons to Fris 2–4 (Mar 2 to Oct 31: closes at 5). Sats & Suns 10–4 (Mar 2 to Oct 31: closes at 5). *Old Library and Max Beerbohm Room:* Mons to Sats 2–4. Adm 50p. Apply Verger's Office (closed 1 week Christmas & 1 week Easter).
New College (1379). New College Lane	*College, Hall, Chapel & Gardens:* Term – Daily 2–5. Vacation – Daily 11–5.
Nuffield College (1937). New Road (Porter's Lodge)	*College only:* Daily 9–7.
Oriel College (1326). Oriel Square (Main Gate)	*College:* Daily 2–5. (Closed Christmas & Easter holidays & mid-Aug to mid-Sept).
Pembroke College (1624). St. Aldate's (Porter's Lodge)	*College, Hall, Chapel & Gardens:* Term – Daily on application to the Porter's Lodge. (Closed Christmas and Easter holidays & occasionally in Aug).
The Queen's College (1340). High Street (Porter's Lodge)	*Hall, Chapel, Quadrangles & Garden:* Daily 2–5.
St. Edmund Hall (1270). Queen's Lane (at the Lodge)	*College, Old Hall, Chapel & Garden:* Daily, daylight hours. *Crypt of St. Peter in the East:* On application to Porter.
St. John's College (1555). St. Giles' (Porter's Lodge)	*College & Garden:* Term & Vacation – Daily 1–5 (or dusk if earlier). Guided parties must obtain permission from the Lodge). *Hall & Chapel:* Summer – 2.30–4.30 (Apply Porter). (Closed during conferences & College functions).
Trinity College (1554). Broad Street (Main Gate)	*Hall, Chapel & Garden:* Daily 2–5 (summer). 2–dusk (winter). (Opening hrs may vary – visitors should check in advance.)
University College (1249). High Street (Porter's Lodge)	*College, Hall & Chapel:* Term – 2–4. Apply Porter.
Wadham College (1610). Parks Road (Porter's Lodge)	*College, Hall, Chapel & Gardens:* Daily 1–4.30. Hall: Apply Lodge.
Worcester College (1714). Worcester Street (Porter's Lodge)	*College & Gardens:* Term – Daily 2–6. Vacation – Daily 9–12, 2–6. *Hall & Chapel:* Apply Lodge.

Visitors and especially guided parties should always call at the Porter's Lodge before entering any College.

GUIDED WALKING TOURS OF THE COLLEGES AND CITY OF OXFORD Tours, conducted by the Oxford Guild of Guides Lecturers, are offered by the Oxford Information Centre, morning for much of the year, afternoon tours daily. For tour times please ring (0865) 726871.

Tours are offered for groups in English. French, German, Spanish, Russian, Japanese, Polish and Serbo-Croat. Chinese by appointment.

The most popular tour for groups, Oxford Past and Present, can be arranged at any time. The following special interest tours are available in the afternoon only: Alice in Oxford; Literary Figures in Oxford; American Roots in Oxford; Oxford Gardens; Modern Architecture in Oxford; Architecture in Oxford (medieval, 17th century and modern); Oxford in the Civil War and 17th century.

Further details are available from The Deputy Information Officer tel (0865) 726871.

Supplementary List of Properties
Open by Appointment Only

The list of Houses in England, Wales and Scotland printed here are those which are usually open 'by appointment only' with the Owner, or open infrequently during the summer months. These are in addition to the Houses and Gardens which are open regularly and are fully classified starting on page 33. Where it is necessary to write for an appointment to view, see code *(WA)*. * Indicates that these Houses are also classified and more details are shown under the respective 'County' headings.

The majority of these properties have received a grant for conservation from the Government, given on the advice of the Historic Buildings Councils. Public buildings, almshouses, tithe barns, business premises in receipt of grants are not usually included, neither are properties where the architectural features can be viewed from the street.

ENGLAND

House	Owner (with address if different from first column)
AVON	
The Refectory, The Vicarage, nr Bristol	Rev R. Salmon *Yatton* (0934) 833126
Eastwood Manor Farm, East Harptree	Mr A. J. Gay
Partis College, Bath	The Bursar *Bath* (0225) 421532
Woodspring Priory, Kewstoke	The Landmark Trust, Shottesbrooke, nr Maidenhead, Berks SL6 3SW *Open daily* (still undergoing repair)
BEDFORDSHIRE	
The Temple, Southill Park, Biggleswade	The Estate Office *(WA)*
Warden Abbey, nr Biggleswade	The Landmark Trust, Shottesbrooke, nr Maidenhead, Berks SL6 3SW *(WA)*
BERKSHIRE	
High Chimneys, Hurst, Reading	Mr & Mrs S. Cheetham Reading 345117 *(WA)*
St Gabriel's School, Sandleford Priory, Newbury	The Headmaster *Newbury* 40663
BUCKINGHAMSHIRE	
Bisham Abbey, nr Marlow	*Viewing by appointment only.* The Director, Bisham Abbey *Marlow* (062 84) 76911
Brudenell House, Quainton, Aylesbury, Bucks HP22 4AW	Dr H. Beric Wright *(WA) 1 week's notice*
Church of the Assumption, Hardmead, Newport Pagnell	Friends of Friendless Churches *For key apply to H. Tranter, Manor Cottage, Hardmead, by letter or telephone* *North Crawley* 257
Iver Grove, Shreding Green, Iver	Mr & Mrs T. Stoppard *(WA)*
Remnantz, West St. Marlow *(WA)* to	A. Wethered Esq., Brampton House, 100 High St. Marlow SL7 1AQ
Repton's Subway Facade, Digby's Walk, Gayhurst	Mr J. H. Beverly, The Bath House, Gayhurst. *(WA)* or *Stoke Goldington* 564
CAMBRIDGE	
Chantry (The), Ely	Mrs T. A. N. Bristol *(WA)*
Church of St John The Baptist, Papworth St Agnes	Friends of Friendless Churches *For key apply to Mrs P. Honeybane, Passhouse Cottage, Papworth St. Agnes, Cambs by letter or telephone* *Huntingdon* (0480) 830631
The King's School, Ely Canonry and Priory Boarding Houses, Monastic Barn	Bursar's Office, The King's School, Ely. *(WA)* (0353) 662837
Leverington Hall, Wisbech	Professor A. Barton *(WA)*
The Lynch Lodge, Alwalton, nr Peterborough	The Landmark Trust, Shottesbrooke, nr. Maidenhead, Berks SL6 3SW *(WA)*
CHESHIRE	
Bewsey Old Hall, Warrington	The Administrator *(WA)*
Charles Roe House, Chestergate, Macclesfield	McMillan Martin Ltd *(WA)*
Crown Hotel, Nantwich	Prop P. J. Martin
Shotwick Hall, Shotwick	Mr R. B. Gardner, 'Wychen', 17 St Mary's Rd, Leatherhead, Surrey *By appointment only with the tenants: Mr & Mrs G. A. T. Holland* (0244) 881717
Tudor House, Lower Bridge St, Chester	*Chester* 20095
CLEVELAND	
St Cuthbert's Church & Turner Mausoleum, Kirkleatham	Kirkleatham Parochial Church Council Mr R. S. Ramsdale (0642) 475198 Mrs D. Cook, Church Warden (0642) 485395
CORNWALL	
College (The), Week St Mary	The Landmark Trust, Shottesbrooke, nr Maidenhead, Berks SL6 3SW *(WA)*
Town Hall, Camelford	Camelford Town Trust
Trecarrel Manor, Trebullett, Launceston *(Hall & Chapel restored)*	*Telephone application only to Mr N. H. Burden* *Coads Green* 82286
CUMBRIA	
Preston Patrick Hall, Milnthorpe	Mrs J. D. Armitage *Crooklands* 200
Whitehall, Mealsgate, Carlisle	Mrs S. Parkin-Moore, 40 Woodsome Rd, London NW5 *(WA)*
DERBYSHIRE	
Elvaston Castle, nr Derby	Derbyshire County Council *prior appt only* *Derby* 571342
The Mansion, Church St, Ashbourne	*Garden, Hall and Drawing Room by appointment only with the Headmaster* (0335) 43685
10 North Street, Cromford	The Landmark Trust, Shottesbrooke, nr Maidenhead, Berks SL6 3SW *(WA)*
The Pavilion, Swarkestone, nr Ticknall	The Landmark Trust *(WA)*

House	Owner (with address if different from first column)
DEVON	
Bindon Manor, Axmouth	Sir John and Lady Loveridge *(WA)*
Bowringsleigh, Kingbridge	Mr & Mrs M. C. Manisty *(WA)*
Endsleigh House, Milton Abbot, nr Tavistock	Endsleigh Fishing Club Ltd, Apr to Sept *Milton Abbot* (082 287) 248
Hareston House, Brixton	Mrs K. M. Basset *Mons, May to Sept* *Plymouth* 880 426
Library (The), Stevenstone, nr Torrington	The Landmark Trust, Shottesbrooke, nr Maidenhead, Berks SL6 3SW *(WA)*
Sanders, Lettaford	The Landmark Trust, Shottesbrooke, nr Maidenhead, Berks SL6 3SW *(WA)*
Shell House (The), Endsleigh Milton Abbot, nr Tavistock	Endsleigh Fishing Club Ltd *April to Sept* *Milton Abbot* 248
Shute Gatehouse, Shute Barton, nr Axminster	The Landmark Trust, Shottesbrooke, nr Maidenhead, Berks SL6 3SW *(WA)*
Ugbrooke Park, Chudleigh	Captain The Lord Clifford *Chudleigh* 852179
Wortham Manor, Lifton	The Landmark Trust, Shottesbrooke, nr Maidenhead, Berks SL6 3SW *(WA)*
DORSET	
Bloxworth House, Bloxworth	Mr T. A. Dulake *(WA)*
Clenston Manor, Winterborne Clenston, Blandford Forum	Mr. Stephen Purchase (0258) 880681
Higher Melcombe, Dorchester	Mr M. C. Woodhouse *(WA)*
Moignes Court, Owermoigne	Mr A. M. Cree *(WA)*
Woodsford Castle, Woodsford	The Landmark Trust, Shottesbrooke, nr Maidenhead, Berks SL6 3SW *(WA)*
DURHAM	
The Buildings in The Square	Lady Gilbertson, 1 The Square, Greta Bridge, Barnard Castle *(WA)*
The College, Durham (on the south side of the Cathedral with access from the Bailey)	The Deanery, No. 6 The College. No. 9 The College. No. 10 The College. No. 11 The College. No. 15 The College. 28A North Bailey. The Dean and Chapter of Durham: All enquiries to the Chapter Steward, The Chapter Office, Durham DH1 3EH. Office hours Mon to Fri (091 386) 4266
Crook Hall, Sidegate, Durham DH1 5SZ.	Dr and Mrs J. Hawgood *(WA)*
ESSEX	
Blake Hall Battle of Britain Museum and Gardens, Chipping Ongar	Mr R. Capel Cure *Parties catered for. Telephone the Administrator:* *Chipping Ongar* 362502
Church of St Andrews and Monks Tithe Barn, Netteswellbury	Now the Harlow Study and Visitor Centre, weekdays 9.30–4.30 Tel: (0279) 446745
Colville Hall, White Roding, Essex	Mr C. A. Webster *(WA)*
Great Priory Farm, Panfield, Braintree	Group of 10 separately listed buildings. *(Listed Grade II 'Barn only)* Miss Lucy Tabor. anytime by telephoned appointment *Braintree* 550944
Grange Farm, Little Dunmow, Dunmow CM6 3HY 14th C Granary	Mr J. Kirby Tel: (0371) 820205
Guildhall (The), Great Waltham	Mr J. J. Tufnell
Old All Saints, Langdon Hills	Mr R. Mill *Basildon* 414146 *
Rainham Hall, Rainham	The National Trust (tenant Mr Ian Botes) (WA)
Rayne Hall, Rayne, Braintree	Mr and Mrs R. J. Pertwee *(WA)*
Round House (The), Havering-atte-Bower, Romford	Mr M. E. W. Heap *Romford* 728136
GLOUCESTERSHIRE	
Abbey Gatehouse, Tewkesbury	The Landmark Trust, Shottesbrooke, Maidenhead. Berks SL6 3SW *(WA)*
Ashleworth Court, nr Gloucester	Mr H. J. Chamberlayne *Parties only* *Hartpury* 241
Ashleworth Manor, Ashleworth	Dr and Mrs Jeremy Barnes *(WA)*
Bearland House, Gloucester	The Administrator *(WA)*
Castle Godwyn, Painswick	Mr & Mrs John Milne *(WA)*
Chaceley Hall, nr Tewkesbury	Mr W. H. Lane *Tirley* 205
Thirlestaine House, Cheltenham College (Cheltenham Boys College), Cheltenham	The Secretary to the Council, Bursar's Office, The College *Cheltenham* 513540
Cottage (The), Stanley Pontlarge, Winchcombe	Mrs S. M. Rolt *(WA)*
Daneway House, Sapperton	Sir Anthony Denny, Bt *(WA)*
East Banqueting House, Chipping Campden	The Landmark Trust, Shottesbrooke, Maidenhead, Berks SL6 35W *(WA)*
Frampton Court & Gothic Orangery, Frampton-on-Severn, Gloucester	Frampton Court Estate *Apply to Mrs Clifford* *Gloucester* (0452) 740267 home *Gloucester* (0452) 740698 office
Frampton Manor, Frampton-on-Severn, Gloucestershire	Mr & Mrs R. Clifford *(WA)* (0452) 740698
Matson House, Gloucester	The Bursar, Selwyn School *During School holidays only* *Gloucester* 305663
Minchinhampton Market House, Stroud	Mr B. E. Lucas *Brimscombe* 883241
Old Vicarage (The), Church Stanway	'Lord Weymyss' Trust; Apply to Stanway House, Stanway, Cheltenham *Stanton* 469
St Margaret's Church, London Rd, Gloucester	Gloucester Municipal Charities *Services Suns 3 pm. Other times by appointment with Warden* *Gloucester* 23316
Stroud Subscription Rooms, Stroud	Stroud District Council, Subscription Rooms Manages, Old Town Hall, The Shambles, High St, Stroud *Stroud* 764999
Tyndale Monument North Nibley	Tyndale Monument Charity, 26 Long St, Dursley P. N. Bayley *Dursley* 542357 Key available as per notice as foot of Wood Lane.

Where it is necessary to write for an appointment to view, see code *(WA)*

House	Owner (with address if different from first column)

GREATER MANCHESTER

Chetham's Hospital & Library, Manchester M3 1SB — The Feoffees of Chetham's Hospital & Library 061-834 9644
Slade Hall, Slade Lane, Manchester M13 0QP — Manchester and District Housing Assn. *(WA)*

HAMPSHIRE

Chesil Theatre (formerly St Peter Chesil Church) — Winchester Dramatic Society (0962) 867086
The Deanery, The Close, Winchester — The Cathedral Secretary, 5 The Close *Winchester* 853137
Houghton Lodge, Stockbridge — *(WA)* Captain and Mrs M. W. Busk 0264 810 502
Manor Farm House, Hambledon — Mr S. B. Mason (0705) 632433
Moyles Court, Ringwood — Headmaster, Moyles Court School *Ringwood* 472856

HEREFORD & WORCESTER

Britannia House, The Tything, Worcester — The Alice Ottley School *(WA) Apply to The Headmistress*
Church House, Evesham — The Trustees of the Walker Hall & Church House, Market Square
Grafton Manor, Bromsgrove — Mr J. W. Morris *Bromsgrove* 31525
Huddington Court, nr Droitwich — Professor Hugh D. Edmondson *(WA)*
Ley (The), Weobley — Lt Col Sir Richard Verdin, Stoke Hall, Nantwich *Wettenhall* 284
Newhouse Farm, Goodrich, Ross-on-Wye — The Administrator *(WA)*
Old Palace (The), Worcester — The Dean & Chapter of Worcester *(WA) Apply to Diocesan Secretary, Old Palace, Deansway, Worcester WR1 2JE*
Shelwick Court, nr Hereford — The Landmark Trust, Shottesbrooke, nr Maidenhead, Berks SL6 3SW *(WA)*

HERTFORDSHIRE

Homewood, Park Lane, Knebworth — Mr & Mrs Pollock-Hill (WA)
Northaw Place, Northaw — Mural can be viewed by appt only (0707) 44059
Heath Mount School, Woodhall Park, Watton-at-Stone, Hertford — The Abel Smith Trustees *Estate Office,* *Ware* 0920 830286

KENT

Barming Place, Maidstone — Mr J. Peter & Dr Rosalind Bearcroft *Maidstone* 27844
Foord Almshouses, Rochester — *(WA)* The Clerk to the Trustees Easter to Sept 30 2–5 except Mon & Thurs. Adm £1, Chd 50p
The Old Pharmacy, 6 Market Place, Faversham — Mr J. B. Kerr *(WA)*
Mersham-le-Hatch, nr Ashford — Lord Brabourne *Apply to tenant – The Directors, Caldecott Community* *Ashford (Kent)* 623954
Nurstead Court, Meopham — Mrs S. M. H. Edmeades-Stearns *Meopham* 812121
Old College of All Saints, Kent Music Centre, Maidstone — Apply to Area Director *Maidstone* 690404
Yaldham Manor, Wrotham — Mr & Mrs John Mourier Lade, Yaldham Manor, Kemsing, Sevenoaks, Kent TN15 6NN (postal address) *(WA)*

LANCASHIRE

Music Room (The), Lancaster — The Landmark Trust, Shottesbrooke, nr Maidenhead, Berks SL6 3SW *Open daily, times displayed*
Parrox Hall, Preesall, Lancashire FY6 0JU — *(WA)* Mr & Mrs H. D. H. Elletson (0253) 810245

LEICESTERSHIRE

The Forecourt, Burley on the Hill, nr Oakham, Rutland. — *Building work taking place. Not open until 1992.*
Launde Abbey, East Norton (Chapel only) — Warden: The Rev Canon Henry Evans MA. Open Easter Mon, May Bank Hol Mons, all Mons in June, July, Aug; all Sats in Aug. Other times by appointment only.
Moat House (The), Appleby Magna — Mr H. S. Hall *Measham* 70301
Old Grammar School, Market Harborough — The Market Harborough Exhibition Foundation, 12 Hillcrest Avenue, Market Harborough (0858) 463201
Staunton Harold Hall, nr. Ashby de la Zouch — Ryder-Cheshire Mission for the Relief of Suffering. Exhibition, Coffee shop and beautiful grounds open to the public. *Tours available by prior appt.* *Melbourne* 862798

LINCOLNSHIRE

Bede Houses, Tattershall — *Access for exterior viewing noon to sunset daily*
The Chateau, Gate Burton, nr Gainsborough — The Landmark Trust, Shottesbrooke, nr Maidenhead, Berks SL6 3SW *(WA)*
East Lighthouse, Sutton Bridge, Spalding PE12 9YT. Sir Peter Scott's Lighthouse Home 1933–39 — Exterior viewing of House and wildfowl ponds year round. Cdr. M. D. Joel RN. *(WA)* for interior
Fulbeck Manor, Grantham, Lincs NG32 3JN — Mr J. F. Fane *(WA)*
Harlaxton Manor, Grantham — University of Evansville *(WA)*
House of Correction, Folkingham — The Landmark Trust, Shottesbrooke, Maidenhead, Berks SL6 3SW *(WA)*
The Norman Manor House, Boothby Pagnell — Lady Netherthorpe *(WA)*
Pelham Mausoleum, Limber, Grimsby — The Earl of Yarborough, Brocklesby Park, Habrough, Lincs
Scrivelsby Court, nr Horncastle — Lt Col J. L. M. Dymoke, M.B.E., D.L. *(WA)*

LONDON

All Hallows Vicarage, Tottenham, N17 — Rev R. Pearson 01-808 2470
69 Brick Lane, E1 — *(WA)*
24 The Butts, Brentford — Mrs Sally Mills *(WA)*
192, 194, 196, 198, 202, 204–224 Cable Street, E1 — *(WA)*
11–13 Cavendish Square, W1 — Heythrop College *(WA)*
Celia and Phillip, Blairman Houses, Elder St, E1 — *(WA)*
Charlton House, Charlton, SE7 — London Borough of Greenwich *Apply to Manager* 081-856 3951
Charterhouse, Charterhouse Square, EC1 — The Governors of Sutton's Hospital in Charterhouse *(WA)* *April 1 to July 31 – every Wed 2.15 pm*
88/190 The Crescent, Hertford Rd, N9 — *(WA)*
17/27 Folgate Street, E1 — *(WA)*
36 Hanbury Street, E1 — *(WA)*
Heathgate House, 66 Crooms Hill, Greenwich, SE10 8HN — Rev Mother Prioress, Ursuline Convent 081-858 0779
House of St Barnabas-in-Soho, 1 Greek St, W1V 6NQ — The Warden of the House *(WA)* 071-437 1894
140, 142, 166, 168 Homerton High Street, E5 — *(WA)*
Kensal Green Cemetery, Harrow Rd, W10 — General Cemetery Company 081-969 0152
69/83 Paragon Road, E5 — *(WA)*
Permanent Exhibition of Judicial & Legal Costume, Law Courts, Strand, WC2 — The Administrator *Adm free Mon–Fri 10–4.30*
Red House, Red House Lane, Bexleyheath — Mr & Mrs Hollamby *(WA only, with SAE) First Sat & Sun in month 2.30–4.30 pm*
Rutland House, Park Place, St James St, SW1 1LR — Royal Over-Seas League *Open 3–5 Spring Bank Holiday and August 1–31*
Wesley's House, 47 City Rd, EC1 — The Trustees of Wesley's Chapel *Open weekdays 10 am–4 pm* 01-253 2262

MERSEYSIDE

The Turner Home, Dingle Head, Liverpool L8 9RN — *By appointment only with the Officer in Charge* Mr R. A. Waring, RGN, CGN 051-727 4177

NORFOLK

All Saints' Church, Bagthorpe — Norfolk Churches Trust – always open
All Saints' Church, Barmer — Norfolk Churches Trust Ltd – Keyholder – No 5 The Cottages on main road near the church.
All Saints' Church, Cockthorpe — Norfolk Churches Trust Ltd – Keyholder – Mrs Case at the farmhouse opposite the church.
All Saints' Church, Dunton — Norfolk Churches Trust – Always open – Key of Tower at Hall Farm
All Saints' Church, Frenze — Mrs Alston at Farmhouse opposite or adjacent cottage.
All Saints' Church, Hargham — Norfolk Churches Trust Ltd – Keyholder – Mrs Clifford Amos, Station Road, Attleborough
All Saints' Church, Moreton on the Hill — Lady Prince Smith at the Hall
All Saints' Church, Rackheath — Norfolk Churches Trust Ltd – Open
All Saints' Church, Snetterton — Norfolk Churches Trust Ltd – Keyholder – Col. R. Felton, Hall Farm next to Church.
All Saints' Church, West Binley — Key Mrs Eyre at Church Farm
All Saints' Church, West Rudham — Lord & Lady Romney, Wensum Farm or Mrs Walker; Pockthorpe Cottage
19–21 Bedford St, Norwich. — *Open times as restaurant and shops. Norwich City Council*
Billingford Mill, nr Scole — Norfolk County Council *Norwich* 222709
6 The Close, Norwich — The Dean & Chapter of Norwich Cathedral *(WA) Apply to Tenant in Residence Subud Norwich*
Erpingham Gate
3 The Close, Norwich
4 The Close, Norwich
27 The Close, Norwich
31 The Close, Norwich
32 The Close, Norwich
34 The Close, Norwich
35 The Close, Norwich
40 The Close, Norwich
41 The Close, Norwich — Cathedral Steward's Office, Messrs Percy Howes & Co, 3 The Close, Norwich *(WA)*
43 The Close, Norwich
44 The Close, Norwich
56a, b and c The Close, Norwich
67 The Close, Norwich
73 The Close, Norwich
The Deanery Norwich
Denver Mill, off A10 — Norfolk Windmills Trust, County Hall, Martineau Lane, Norwich NR1 2DH *Norwich* 6222706
Ditchingham Hall, Ditchingham, Bungay — The Rt Hon Earl Ferrers
Earlham Hall, University of East Anglia, Norwich. — *By appointment with the School of Law, University of East Anglia.* (0603) 56161
Fishermen's Hospital, Great Yarmouth — J. E. C. Lamb, FIH. Clerk to the Trustees *Great Yarmouth* 856609
Gowthorpe Manor, Swardeston — Mrs Watkinson by appointment only *Mulbarton* 70216
Hales Hall, Loddon — Mr & Mrs T. Read *(WA) Open only to parties booked by prior appointment in writing and not individuals* (050 846) 395
Hoveton House, Wroxham — Mr J. C. C. Blofeld Open only to parties booked by prior appointment in writing, and not individuals.
Lattice House, King's Lynn — Mr and Mrs T. Duckett *(WA)* *Kings Lynn* (0553) 777292
Little Cressingham Mill, Watton — Norfolk County Council *Norwich* 611122 ext 5224
Little Hautbois Hall, — Mrs Duffield (0603) 279333
Manor House (The), Great Cressingham — Mrs F. Chapman *(WA)*
Manor House (The), 54 Bracondale, Norwich — Mr P.B. Macqueen. Small parties welcome *(WA)*
Music House (The) at Wensum Lodge, King Street, Norwich — The Warden *Norwich* 666021/2
The Old Princes Inn Restaurant, 20 Princes St, Norwich — *Open times as restaurant* (0603) 621043
Old Vicarage (The), Methwold, Thetford IP26 4NR — Mr & Mrs H. C. Dance (WA)
St Andrew's Church, Frenze — Norfolk Churches Trust Ltd – Keyholder – Mrs Alston at the farmhouse opposite or ask at adjacent cottage
St Margaret's Church, Morton-on-the-Hill — Norfolk Churches Trust Ltd – Keyholder – Lady Prince-Smith at The Hall, NE of church
St Mary's Church, Bagthorpe — Norfolk Churches Trust Ltd – Open
St Mary's Church, Dunton — Norfolk Churches Trust Ltd – Open
St Peter's Church, West Rudham — Norfolk Churches Trust Ltd – Keyholder – Lord & Lady Romney, Wensum Farm or Mrs Walker, Pockthorpe Cottages, West Rudham
Stracey Arms Mill, nr Acle (A47) — Norfolk County Council *Norwich* 611122. Ext 5224

Where it is necessary to write for an appointment to view, see code *(WA)*

House	Owner (with address if different from first column)
The Strangers' Club, 22, 24 Elm Hill, Norwich	By appointment with the Steward (0603) 623814
Thoresby College, Queen Street, King's Lynn	King's Lynn Preservation Trust *(WA)*
Wilby Hall, Quidenham	Mr & Mrs C. Warner *(WA)*
Wiveton Hall, Holt	D. MacCarthy *(WA)*

NORTHAMPTONSHIRE

House	Owner
Courteenhall, Northampton	Sir Hereward Wake, Bt, M.C. *(WA)*
Drayton House, Lowick, Kettering NN14 3BG	L. G. Stopford Sackville *(WA)*
Menagerie (The), Horton, Northampton	Mr Gervase Jackson-Stops *(WA)*
Monastery (The), Shutlanger	Mr & Mrs R. G. Wigley *(WA)*
Paine's Cottage, Oundle	Mr R. O. Barber *(WA)*
Weston Hall, Towcester	Mr & Mrs Francis Sitwell *(WA)*

NORTHUMBERLAND

House	Owner
Capheaton Hall, Newcastle upon Tyne	Exterior only. Mr J. Browne-Swinburne *(WA)*
Causeway House, Bardon Mill	The Landmark Trust, Shottesbrooke, Maidenhead, Berks SL6 3SW *(WA)*
Craster Tower, Alnwick	Col J. M. Craster, Miss M. D. Cra'ster, Mr F. Sharratt *(WA)*
Elsdon Tower, Elsdon	Mr K. Maddison, Hillview Cottage, Elsdon *Otterburn* 20538
Harnham Hall, Belsay	Mr J. Wake
Morpeth Castle, Morpeth	The Landmark Trust, Shottesbrooke, Maidenhead, Berks SL6 3SW *(WA)*
Netherwitton Hall, Morpeth	Mr J. C. R. Trevelyon *(WA)*

NOTTINGHAMSHIRE

House	Owner
Flintham Hall, nr Newark	Mr M. T. Hildyard *(WA)*
Winkburn Hall, nr Southwell	Mr R. Craven-Smith-Milnes (0636) 86465
Worksop Priory Church and Gatehouse	The Vicarage *Worksop* 472180

OXFORDSHIRE

House	Owner
39/43 The Causeway, Steventon	Mr & Mrs H. C. Dance, The Old Vicarage, Methwold, Thetford, Norfolk IP26 4NR *(WA)*
26/7 Cornmarket Street, and **26 Ship Street**, Oxford	Shop on ground and first floors open during normal trading hours shop basement by written appt. Laura Ashley Ltd., 150 Bath Rd, Maidenhead, Berks SL6 4YS 2nd floor by written appt. Home Bursar, Jesus College, Oxford OX1 3DW.
Cote House, nr. Bampton	Mrs David Anderson *(WA)*
Hope House, Woodstock	Mrs J. Hageman
Manor (The), Chalgrove	Mr & Mrs Paul L. Jacques *(WA)*
Monarch's Court House, Benson	Mr R. S. Hine *(WA)*
Ripon College, Cuddesdon	The Principal *(WA)*

SHROPSHIRE

House	Owner
Clive House, College Hill, Shrewsbury	Shrewsbury and Atcham Borough Council. Open Mon to Sat (0743) 354811
Cronkhill House, nr. Crosshouses, Shrewsbury.	The National Trust. House designed c.1803 by John Nash *(WA)* Mrs L. Motley (tenant)
Guildhall, The, Dogpole, Shrewsbury	Shrewsbury & Atcham Borough Council *(WA)*
Halston, Oswestry	Mrs J. L. Harvey *(WA)*
Hatton Grange, Shifnal	Mrs P. Afia, Mon and Fri only May 1–Aug 10 *(WA)*
Moat House, The, Longnor, Shrewsbury SY5 7PP	Mr C.P. Richards (074 373) 434
Morville Hall, nr Bridgnorth	The National Trust (tenant Mrs J. K. Norbury) *(WA)*
Rowleys House and Mansion, Barker St, Shrewsbury	Shrewsbury & Atcham Borough Council *Open daily except winter Suns* (0743) 361196
Stanwardine Hall, Cockshutt, Ellesmere	P. J. Bridge (0939) 270212
St. Winifred's Well, Woolston, Oswestry	The Landmark Trust, Shottesbrooke, Maidenhead, Berks SL6 3SW *(WA)*

SOMERSET

House	Owner
Cothelstone Manor and Gatehouse, Cothelstone, Taunton	Mrs E. Warmington, Cothelstone House Estate, Cothelstone Manor, Cothelstone *(WA)*
Manor Farm, Meare, Wells	Mrs I. M. Bull (tenant Mr C. J. Look)
Old Drug Store (The), Axbridge	Mr & Mrs K. E. J. D. Schofield *(WA)*
Old Hall (The), Croscombe	The Landmark Trust, Shottesbrooke, nr Maidenhead, Berks SL6 3SW *(WA)*
Manor House (Elizabethan), Crowcombe	The Manager *(WA)*
The Priest's House, Holcombe Rogus, nr Wellington	The Landmark Trust, Shottesbrooke, nr Maidenhead, Berks SL6 3SW *(WA)*
Stogursey Castle, Stogursey, nr Bridgwater	The Landmark Trust, Shottesbrooke, nr Maidenhead, Berks SL6 3SW *(WA)*
West Coker Manor, West Coker BA22 9BJ	Mr & Mrs Derek Maclaren. Open during August. (093 586) 2646
Whitelackington Manor, Ilminster	Dillington Estate Office, Ilminster *(WA)*

STAFFORDSHIRE

House	Owner
Broughton Hall, Eccleshall	The Administrator *(WA)*
The Great Hall in Keele Hall, Keele	Registrar, University of Keele *(WA)*
Ingestre Pavilion, nr. Stafford	The Landmark Trust, Shottesbrooke, Maidenhead, Berks SL6 3SW *(WA)*
Old Hall Gatehouse (The), Mavesyn Ridware	Mr R. M. Eades *Armitage* 490312
Park Hall, Leigh	Mr E. J. Knobbs *(WA)*
Tixall Gatehouse, Tixall	The Landmark Trust, Shottesbrooke, nr Maidenhead, Berks SL6 3SW *(WA)*

SUFFOLK

House	Owner
Deanery (The), Hadleigh	The Dean of Bocking *Hadleigh* 822218
Hall (The), Great Bricett, nr Ipswich	Mr & Mrs R. B. Cooper *(WA)*
Hengrave Hall, Bury St Edmunds	The Warden, Hengrave Hall Centre, Bury St Edmunds *(WA)* *Bury St. Edmunds* 701561

House	Owner (with address if different from first column)
Martello Tower, Aldeburgh	The Landmark Trust, Shottesbrooke, Maidenhead, Berks SL6 3SW *(WA)*
Moat Hall, Parham, nr Woodbridge	Mr J. W. Gray *Wickham Market* 746317
Newbourne Hall, nr Woodbridge	John Somerville Esq *(WA)*
New Inn (The), Peasenhall	The Landmark Trust, Shottesbrooke, nr Maidenhead, Berks SL6 3SW *Great Hall open daily*
Worlingham Hall, Beccles	Viscount Colville of Culross *(WA)*

SURREY

House	Owner
Crossways Farm, Abinger Hammer	Mr C. T. Hughes (tenant) *(WA)*
St. Mary's Homes, Church Lane, Godstone	Open Oct to Mar 10–4; Apr to Sept 10–6 (0883) 742385
Sunbury Court, Sunbury-on-Thames, Middx	The Salvation Army *Sunbury* 782196

EAST SUSSEX

House	Owner
Ashdown House, nr Forest Row	The Headmaster, Ashdown House School (0342) 822574
Laughton Tower, nr Lewes	The Landmark Trust, Shottesbrooke, nr Maidenhead, Berks SL6 3SW *(WA)*

WEST SUSSEX

House	Owner
Chantry Green House, Steyning	Mr & Mrs G. H. Recknell *Steyning* 81-2239
Chapel (The), Bishop's Palace, Chichester	Church Commissioners, *(WA) only to* The Palace, Chichester *The Chaplain*
Christ's Hospital, Horsham	School buildings open by appointment with The Steward (0403) 211293

TYNE & WEAR

House	Owner
Gibside Banqueting House, nr Newcastle	The Landmark Trust, Shottesbrooke, nr Maidenhead, Berks SL6 3SW *(WA)*

WARWICKSHIRE

House	Owner
Bath House, Walton, nr Stratford-on-Avon	The Landmark Trust, Shottesbrooke, nr Maidenhead, Berks SL6 3SW *(WA)*
Binswood Hall, Binswood Ave, Leamington Spa	North Leamington School *(WA) to Head of Hall* (0926) 423686
Foxcote, Shipston-on-Stour	Mr C. B. Holman *(WA)*
Nicholas Chamberlain's Almshouses, Bedworth	The Warden (0203) 312225
Northgate, Warwick	Mr R. E. Phillips *(WA)*
St Leonard's Church, Wroxall	T. W. Alsop, Bursar, Wroxall Abbey School, Warwick CV35 7NB *(WA)*
War Memorial Town Hall, Alcester	The Secretary, Mr J. W. Roberts, 10 Haselor Close, Alcester B49 6QD *Alcester* (0789) 762101 *or* Mr J. Adams (762648)

WILTSHIRE

House	Owner
Abbey House (The), Malmesbury	Malmesbury Preservation Trust, 48 High St, Malmesbury SN16 9AT (066 82) 2212
Chinese Summerhouse, Amesbury Abbey, Amesbury	Visitors are requested to keep to the paths indicated. For open days Tel: (0980) 622957
Farley Hospital, Farley	The Warden (072 272) 231
Grove (The), Corsham	Trustees of Corsham Estate *(WA)*
Milton Manor, Pewsey	Mrs Rupert Gentle (0672) 63344
Old Bishop's Palace, 1 The Close, Salisbury	The Bursar, The Cathedral School *Salisbury* 322652
Old Manor House (The), 2 Whitehead Lane, Bradford on Avon	Mr John Teed *(WA)*
Orpins House, Church Street, Bradford-on-Avon	Mr J. Vernon Burchell *(WA)*
Porch House (The), Potterne, nr Devizes	*(WA)*

NORTH YORKSHIRE

House	Owner
Allerton Park, nr Knaresborough	Michael Farr, Administrator (0423) 330632
Beamsley Hospital, nr Skipton	The Landmark Trust, Shottesbrooke, Maidenhead, Berks SL6 3SW *(WA)*
Broughton Hall, Skipton	H. R. Tempest Esq. Open without appointment, Summer Bank Holidays and June weekdays (0756) 792267
Busby Hall, Carlton-in-Cleveland	Mr G. A. Marwood *(WA)*
Calverley Old Hall, Selby	The Landmark Trust, Shottesbrooke, nr Maidenhead, Berks SL6 3SW *(WA)*
Cawood Castle, nr Selby	The Landmark Trust, Shottesbrooke, Maidenhead, Berks SL6 3SW *(WA)*
Chapel and Coach House, Aske, Richmond	*Open daily during August 11 am–6 pm* Exterior **only**
The Church of Our Lady and Saint Everilda, Everingham	*View by appointment. Donations.* Key at Riding Cottage, Everingham (0430) 860531
Culloden Tower (The), Richmond	The Landmark Trust, Shottesbrooke, nr Maidenhead, Berks SL6 3SW *(WA)*
The Dovecote, Forcett Hall, Forcett, nr Richmond	External viewing from road through Forcett (B6274) Internal viewing – apply Mrs P. E. Heathcote, Forcett Hall, Forcett, Richmond (0325) 718226
Home Farm House, Old Scriven, Knaresborough	Mr G. T. Reece *(WA)*
Moulton Hall, nr Richmond	The National Trust (tenant the Hon. J. D. Eccles) *(WA)*
Old Rectory (The), Foston, nr York	Mrs R. F. Wormald *(WA)*
The Pigsty, Robin Hood's Bay	The Landmark Trust, Shottesbrooke, nr Maidenhead, Berks SL6 3SW *(WA)*

WEST YORKSHIRE

House	Owner
Fulneck Boys' School, Pudsey	I. D. Cleland, B.A., M.Phil., Headmaster *(WA) Open during school holidays only*
Grand Theatre & Opera House (The), Leeds	Warren Smith, General Manager (0532) 456014
Horbury Hall, Horbury, nr Wakefield	D. J. H. Michelmore Esq (0924) 277552
Old Hall (The), Calverley, nr Pudsey, Leeds	The Landmark Trust, Shottesbrooke, nr Maidenhead, Berks SL6 3SW *(WA)*
Town Hall, Leeds	Leeds City Council *Leeds* 477989
Weston Hall, nr Otley	Lt Col H. V. Dawson *(WA)*

WALES

House	Owner (with address if different from first column)

CLWYD

House	Owner (with address if different from first column)
Fferm, Pontblyddyn, Mold	Dr M. C. Jones-Mortimer *Apply to tenant*
Gatehouse at Gilar Farm, Pentrefoclas	Mr P. J. Warbourton-Lee *(WA)*
Halghton Hall, Bangor-on-Dee, Wrexham	Mr J. D. Lewis *(WA)*
Lindisfarne College, Wynnstay Hall, Ruabon	The Headmaster (0978) 810407
Nerquis Hall, Mold	Mr A. W. Furse *(WA)*
Pen Isa'r Glascoed, Bodelwyddan	Mr M. E. Harrop *St Asaph 583501*
Plas Uchaf, Llangar	The Landmark Trust, Shottesbrooke, nr Maidenhead, Berks *(WA)*

DYFED

House	Owner
French Mill, Carew	Mr Anthony Trollope-Bellew *April to Sept*
Monkton Old Hall, Pembroke	The Landmark Trust, Shottesbrooke, Maidenhead, Berks SL6 3SW *(WA)*
Old Hall (The), Monkton, Pembroke	The Landmark Trust, Shottesbrooke, nr Maidenhead, Berks SL6 3SW *(WA)*
St David's University College, Lampeter	Principal: Professor Keith Robbins *Lampeter 422-351*
Taliaris Park, Llandeilo	Mr J. H. Spencer-Williams *(WA)*
West Blockhouse, Dale, Haverfordwest	The Landmark Trust, Shottesbrooke, Maidenhead, Berks SL6 3SW *(WA)*

MID GLAMORGAN

House	Owner
Llancaiach Fawr, Nelson	Rhymney Valley District Council *Apply to Museums Officer* *Hengoed 815588 Ext 221*

GWENT

House	Owner
Blackbrook Manor	Mr A. C. de Morgan *Skenfrith 453*
Castle Hill House, Monmouth	Mr T. Baxter-Wright *(WA)*
Clytha Castle, nr Abergavenny	The Landmark Trust, Shottesbrooke, nr Maidenhead, Berks SL6 3SW *(WA)*
Cwrt Porth Hir, Llanover	Coldbrook & Llanover Estate *(WA)*
Great Cil-Lwch, Llantilio Crossenny	Mr J. F. Ingledew *(WA)*
Kemys House, Kemys Inferior, Caerleon	Mr I. S. Burge *(WA)*

House	Owner (with address if different from first column)
Overmonnow House (formerly Vicarage), Monmouth	Mr J. R. Pangbourne *(WA)*
3/4 Priory Street, Monmouth	Mr H. R. Ludwig *(WA)*
St James House, Monmouth	The Governors of Monmouth School; The Haberdashers Co *(WA)*
Treowen, Wonastow, Monmouth	Mr R. H. Wheelock *Dingestow 224*

GWYNEDD

House	Owner
Bath Tower (The), Caernarfon	The Landmark Trust, Shottesbrooke, nr Maidenhead, Berks SL6 3SW *(WA)*
Cymryd, Conwy	Miss D. E. Glynne *(WA)*
Dolaugwyn, Towyn	Mrs S. Tudor *(WA)*
Nannau, Llanfachreth, nr Dolgellau	Mr P. Vernon *(WA)*
Penmynydd, Alms Houses, Llanfairpwll	The Rector of Llanfairpwll *(Hon Secretary)* *(WA)*
Plas Coch, Llanedwen, Llanfairpwll	Mrs N. Donald *Llanfairpwll (0248) 714272*

POWYS

House	Owner
Abercamlais, Brecon	Mrs J. C. R. Ballance *(WA)*
Abercynrig, Llanfrynach	Mr W. R. Lloyd, Abercynrig, Brecon, Powys LD3 7AQ *(WA)*
1 Buckingham Place, Brecon	Mrs Meeres *(WA)*
3 Buckingham Place, Brecon	Mr & Mrs A. Whiley *(WA)*
Maesmawr Hall Hotel, Caersws	Mrs M. Pemberton, Mrs I. Hunt (0686) 688255
Newton Farm, Brecon	Mrs Ballance *(WA) to Mr D. L. Evans, tenant*
Pen-Y-Lan, Meifod	Mr S. R. J. Meade *Meifod 202*
Plasau Duon, Clatter	Mr C. Breese
Poultry House, Leighton	The Landmark Trust, Shottesbrooke, Maidenhead, Berks SL6 3SW *(WA)*
Rhydycarw, Trefeglwys, Caersws	Mr M. Breese-Davies *Trefeglwys 363*
Ydderw, Llyswen	Mr D. P. Eckley *(WA)*

SOUTH GLAMORGAN

House	Owner
Fonmon Castle, Barry	Sir Brooke Boothby, Bt *Rhoose (0446) 710206*

WEST GLAMORGAN

House	Owner
Penrice Castle, Penrice, Reynoldston, Gower, Swansea	Mr C. Methuen-Campbell *(WA)*

SCOTLAND

House	Owner (with address if different from first column)

BORDERS REGION

House	Owner
Darnick Tower, Melrose	Mrs T. H. Wilson *Melrose 2735*
Old Gala House, Galashiels	Ettrick & Lauderdale District Council *Open Apr to Oct daily. Other times by appointment* *Selkirk 20096*
Sir Walter Scott's Courtroom, Selkirk	Ettrick & Lauderdale District Council *Open weekdays 2–4 in July & Aug. Other times by appt.* *Selkirk 20096*
Wedderlie House, Gordon TD3 6NW	Mrs J. R. L. Campbell *By appointment* *Westruther 223*

CENTRAL REGION

House	Owner
Bardowie Castle, by Milngavie	Mr R. T. Allen *Balmore 366*
Castlecary Castle, by Bonnybridge, Stirlingshire	Mr Hugo B. Millar *(WA)* *Banknock 840031*
Church of the Holy Rude, Broad Street, Stirling	
Erskine Marykirk, Stirling District Council, Municipal Buildings, Stirling	Now a Youth Hostel (0786) 79000
Gargunnock House, by Stirling	Gargunnock Estate Trust *(WA)*
Guildhall, Stirling District Council, Municipal Buildings, Stirling	(0786) 79000
John Cowane's House, Stirling District Council, Municipal Buildings, Stirling	(0786) 79000
Mars Wark and Argyll Lodgings, Stirling District Council	(0786) 79000
Old Tolbooth Building, Stirling	Stirling District Council, Municipal Buildings, Corn Exchange Rd *Stirling 79000*
Pineapple (The), Dunmore, Airth	The Landmark Trust, Shottesbrooke, nr Maidenhead, Berks SL6 3SW *(WA)*
Stirling Castle, Historic Scotland	*Area Office* (0786) 50000
Touch House, by Stirling	Mr P. B. Buchanan *(WA)*

DUMFRIES & GALLOWAY REGION

House	Owner
Bonshaw Tower, Kirtlebridge, nr Annan	Dr J. B. Irving *View by appointment* *Kirtlebridge 256*
Carnsalloch House, Kirkton, nr Dumfries	The Leonard Cheshire Foundation *Dumfries 54924*
Craigdarroch House, Moniaive	Major and Mrs H. F. Stanley *Moniaive 202*
Kirkconnell House, New Abbey, nr Dumfries	Mr F. Maxwell Witham *New Abbey 276*
Tolbooth, Broad St., Stirling	Stirling District Council *Stirling 79400*

FIFE REGION

House	Owner
Bath Castle, Bogside, nr Oakley	Mr Angus Mitchell, 20 Regent Terrace, Edinburgh EH7 5BS 031-556 7671
Castle (The), Elie	Mr J. Bevan *(WA)*

GRAMPIAN REGION

House	Owner
Balbithan House, Kintore	Mr John McMurtrie *Kintore 32282*
Balfluig Castle	Mr Mark Tennant, 30 Abbey Gardens, London NW8 9AT *(WA)*
Barra Castle, Old Meldrum	Dr & Mrs Andrew Bogdan *(WA)*
Castle of Fiddes, Stonehaven	Dr M. Weir *Drumlithie 213*
Corsindae House, Sauchen	Mr Richard Fyffe *(WA)* (03303) 629
Craigston Castle, Turriff	Bruce Urquhart of Craigston *King Edward (08885) 228*
Drumminor Castle, Rhynie	Mr A. D. Forbes *(WA)*
Gordonstoun School, Elgin *(Round Square only)*	The Headmaster, Gordonstoun School, Elgin Moray IV30 2RF *(WA)*
Grandhome House, nr Aberdeen	D. R. Paton Esq *Aberdeen 722202*

House	Owner
Kintore Town House, Kintore	Gordon District Council *Inverurie 20981*
Phesdo House, Laurencekirk	Mr J. M. Thomson *(WA)*
Pluscarden Abbey, Elgin	The Abbot *Dallas 257 or 388*

HIGHLAND REGION

House	Owner
Embo House, Dornoch	Mr John G. Mackintosh *Dornoch 810260*

LOTHIAN REGION

House	Owner
Arniston House, Gorebridge	Mrs A. R. Dundas-Bekker. June to mid-Sept, each Tues & first Sun of month 2–5 for guided tours
Cakemuir, Tynehead	Mr M. M. Scott *(WA)*
Castle Gogar, Edinburgh	Lady Steel-Maitland *Corstorphine 1234*
Ford House, Ford	F. P. Tindall, O.B.E. *(WA)*
Forth Road Bridge, South Queensferry	The Bridgemaster 031-319 1699
Linnhouse, nr Livingston	Mr H. J. Spurway *(WA)*
Newbattle Abbey College, Dalkeith	The Principal 031-663 1921
Northfield House, Prestonpans	Mr W. Schomberg Scott *(WA)*
Peffermill House, Peffermill Rd, Edinburgh EH16 5UX	Nicholas Groves-Raines, Architects 031-661 7172/3
Penicuik House, Penicuik	Sir John Clerk, Bt *(WA)*
Prestonhall, Pathhead	Major J. H. Callander *(WA)*
Roseburn House, Murrayfield	Esq. M. E. Sturgeon *(WA)*
Town House, Haddington	East Lothian District Council *By arrangement with Reception Unit, Council Buildings, Haddington on Hand* 4161

SHETLAND ISLANDS AREA

House	Owner
Lodberrie (The), Lerwick	Mr Thomas Moncrieff

STRATHCLYDE REGION

House	Owner
Ascog House, Isle of Bute	The Landmark Trust, Shottesbrooke, Maidenhead, Berks SL6 3SW *(WA)*
Barcaldine Castle, Benderloch	Morton, Fraser Milligan, W. S., 19 York Place, Edinburgh EH1 3EL (Trustees of Sir A. W. D. Campbell) *(WA)*
Craufurdland Castle, Kilmarnock	J. P. Houison Craufurd Esq (056 06) 402
Duntrune Castle, Lochgilphead	Robin Malcolm of Poltalloch *(WA)*
Kelburn Castle, Fairlie	The Earl of Glasgow *(WA)*
New Lanark, Lanark	New Lanark Conservation Trust, Mill No. 3, New Lanark Mills, Lanark ML11 9DB (0555) 61345
Place of Paisley (The), Paisley	Paisley Abbey, Kirk Session *(WA) Apply to Minister* 041-889 7654
Saddell Castle, nr Campbeltown	The Landmark Trust, Shottesbrooke, nr Maidenhead, Berks SL6 3SW *(WA)*
Tangy Mill, nr Campbeltown	The Landmark Trust, Shottesbrooke, nr Maidenhead, Berks SL6 3SW *(WA)*
Tannahill's Cottage, Queen St, Paisley	Secretary, Paisley Burns Club 041-887 7500

TAYSIDE REGION

House	Owner
Ardblair Castle, Blairgowrie	Laurence P. K. Blair Oliphant *Blairgowrie 3155*
Craig House, Montrose	Charles F. R. Hoste *Montrose 72239*
Kinross House, Kinross *(Garden only)*	Sir David Montgomery, Bt *(WA)*
Michael Bruce Cottage Museum, Kinnesswood	Michael Bruce Trust
The Pavilion, Gleneagles, Auchterarder PH3 1PJ	J. Martin Haldane Esq. *(WA)*
Tulliebole Castle, Crook of Devon	The Lord Moncreiff *By appointment only* *Fossoway 236*

The Garden Specialists
in Great Britain and Ireland

A selection of nurseries specialising in rare or uncommon plants

& Denotes the major part of the property is suitable for wheelchairs

APPLE COURT

Hordle Lane, Hordle, Lymington, Hants SO41 0HU
Telephone: (0590) 642130
(Mrs Diana Grenfell)

Specialists in hostas, daylilies, ferns, grasses, unusual perennials and foliage plants for flower arrangers. Good selection of plants for a white garden, as featured in THE WHITE GARDEN, Grenfell & Grounds (Crowood Press, 1990). Wide variety of plants displayed in formal garden being created by the designer-owners within the walls of a former Victorian kitchen garden. Five National Reference Collections including small-leafed Hostas. Catalogue 3 × 1st class stamps. Mail order welcomed. Commissions for garden design accepted.

Location: 4 m equidistant Lymington and New Milton. ¼ m off A337 travelling north at Downton crossroads.
Opening Times: All year except Dec, Jan, and last two weeks in Aug. Thurs to Mon 10–1, 2–5.30. *Closed* Tues and Wed unless a prior appointment has been arranged. Parties by appointment. Car parking.

APULDRAM ROSES

Apuldram Lane, Dell Quay, Chichester, West Sussex &
Telephone: (0243) 785769
(Mrs D. R. Sawday)

Specialist Rose Nursery growing over 300 varieties of Hybrid Teas, Floribundas, Climbers, Ramblers, Ground Cover, Miniature and Patio Roses. Also a large selection of shrub roses both old and new. Mature Rose Garden to view. Field open during summer months. Suitable for disabled but no special toilet. One wheelchair available.

Location: 1 m SW of Chichester. A286 Birdham-Wittering road from Chichester. Turn right into Dell Quay Road and then right again into Apuldram Lane.
Opening Times: Every day Jan 7 to Dec 23. Mon to Sat 9–5, Suns and Bank Hols 10.30–4.30. Adm: Charity Box in Garden. Parties can be taken around by prior arrangement with guided tour of roses June to Sept. One wheelchair available. Ample car parking.

ARCHITECTURAL PLANTS

Cooks Farm, Nuthurst, Horsham, West Sussex RH13 6LH
Telephone: (0403) 891772
(Angus White)

Hardy Exotics – evergreen trees and shrubs with big, spiky and frondy leaves, including conservatory plants. Many extremely rare. Please send for free list.

Location: Behind Black Horse pub in Nuthurst, 5 m S of Horsham, West Sussex.
Opening Times: Mons to Sats 9–5.

AYLETT NURSERIES LTD

North Orbital Road (A414), St. Albans, Herts &
Telephone: (0727) 822255
(Mr R.S. Aylett)

Aylett Nurseries of St. Albans is a well known family business with a reputation of high quality plants and service. Famous for its dahlias – having been awarded a Gold Medal by the Royal Horticultural Society every year since 1961. Spacious planteria contains a profusion of trees, shrubs, herbaceous plants and many more! In the spring our greenhouses are full of geraniums, fuchsias, hanging baskets and many other types of bedding plants. Facilities also include garden shop, coffee and gift shop, houseplants, florist, garden furniture.

Location: 2 m out of St. Albans, 1 m from M10 and M1, M25 and A1.
Opening Times: Mon to Fri 8.30–5.30, Sats 8.30–5, Suns and Bank Hols 9–5. *Closed* Christmas Day and Boxing Day. Adm free. Parties with pre advice please. Suitable for disabled visitors. Five wheelchairs available.
Refreshments: Dahlia coffee shop serves light lunches, homemade cakes, creamy gateaux. Coffee, tea and soft drinks.

BLACKTHORN NURSERY

Kilmeston, Alresford, Hants SO24 0NL
Telephone: (0962) 771796
(Mr & Mrs A. R. White)

Specialist nursery growing a wide range of alpines and rock plants, with a choice selection of perennials, shrubs, climbers and ferns. Daphnes, hellebores and epimediums a speciality. 3 × 1st class stamps for catalogue.

Location: 1 m S of Cheriton just off A272 Winchester to Petersfield road. Five minutes from Hinton Ampner House & Gardens (NT).
Opening Times: Fri and Sat only from 9–5, Mar to Oct inclusive. Car parking.

BLAKENEY HOUSE NURSERIES LTD

Osier Grounds, Denton, Canterbury CT4 6NP
Telephone: Canterbury (0227) 831800, Fax: (0227) 831883

Conifer specialists, wholesalers and distributors of hardy nursery stock. As wholesalers, we can help with almost any enquiry.

Location: A260 towards Folkestone. Take first right after Jackdaw Public House then left at T junction.
Opening Times: Weekends – best to telephone first.

BODIAM NURSERY

Ockham House, Bodiam, Robertsbridge, East Sussex TN32 5RA
Telephone: Staple Cross (0580) 830811/830649
(Richard Biggs)

Set beside fine old oasthouse and Queen Anne house in unspoilt countryside. Spectacular view of Bodiam Castle just across the River Rother. Enormous selection of heathers (over 200), shrubs (over 700), climbers, conifers, alpine and herbaceous plants, many unusual, propagated and grown here. Sizes from tinies for the economy minded to specimens for 'instant gardening'. Acres of plants in pots.

Location: 11 m from Hastings, 3 m from Hurst Green which is on the A21. Follow signs for Bodiam Castle. Nursery is just across the river valley from the Castle.
Station: Etchingham (5 m).
Opening Times: Every day: 9–7 (sunset in winter).

BODNANT GARDEN NURSERY LTD

Tal Y Cafn, Nr. Colwyn Bay, Clwyd LL28 5RE &
Telephone: (0492) 650460

Bodnant Garden Nursery is famous for its rare trees and shrubs. We propagate over 800 species and varieties of flowering and foliage shrubs, including rhododendrons, azaleas, magnolias and camellias. The many thousands of plants produced in our own propagation units by experienced staff are available to purchase, either by personal selection or our efficient mail order service.

Location: 8 m S of Llandudno and Colwyn Bay on the A470, just off the A55 Coastal Expressway.
Opening Times: Daily (excl. Christmas Day) 9–5. Car parking. Ramps for disabled. Wheelchairs available.
Refreshments: Morning coffee, light lunches and afternoon teas are available from Apr to Sept.

BOSVIGO PLANTS

Bosvigo Lane, Truro, Cornwall TR1 3NH *map C1*
Telephone: Truro (0872) 75774
(Mrs Wendy Perry)

Small specialist nursery. Rare and unusual herbaceous plants. 3-acre display gardens. Catalogue available – send 4 × 2nd class stamps. N.B. No mail order.

Location: ¾ m from city centre. Take A390 towards Redruth. At Highertown turn right by Shell garage and drive 400 yds down Dobbs Lane.
Opening Times: Mar to end Oct daily 11–dusk.

J. W. BOYCE

Fordham, Ely, Cambs CB7 5JU
Telephone: (0638) 721158

Specialists in garden seeds for over 80 years. Specialising in the production of pansy seed and plants. Also over 1000 items of seed which includes a wide range of separate colours for cut flowers, bedding and drying. Also old and unusual vegetables. Seed list free on request: Telephone above number, or write to J. W. Boyce, Bush Pasture, Carter Street, Ely, Cambs CB7 5JU.

BRACKENWOOD GARDEN CENTRE

131 Nore Road, Portishead, Bristol BS20 8DU
Telephone: (0272) 843484

Five acre woodland garden in elevated scenic position overlooking the Bristol Channel. Many rare trees and shrubs. Pools, ericaceous plants.

Location: 1½ m from Portishead on Nore Road (Coast road); M5 junction 19, 4 m.
Opening Times: Apr to Sept.

BRESSINGHAM GARDENS

Bressingham, Diss, Norfolk IP22 2AB
Telephone: (037 988) 464/8133

One of Britain's leading Plant Centres with experience gained from a business with over 45 years experience of finest quality plants and service, and stocking over 4,000 varieties of hardy plants including perennials, shrubs, conifers, alpines for the discerning gardener. 5 acres of display gardens open seasonally. Professional advice. Landscaping department. Mail order catalogue £1.75 refundable with first order (min. £10).

Location: A1066 3 m from Diss on Thetford Road.
Opening Times: 10–5.30 – seven days a week.
Refreshments: Coffee shop.

BRITISH WILD FLOWER PLANTS

23 Yarmouth Road, Ormesby St. Margaret, Gt. Yarmouth, Norfolk
Telephone: (0493) 730244
(Linda Laxton)

200 plus species of British Wild Flower Plants. Nursery grown, not collected from the wild.

Location: 5 m NW of Gt. Yarmouth on main A149.

BROMAGES BONSAI CENTRE

St. Mary's Gardens, Worplesdon, Surrey GU3 3RS   &
Telephone: (0483) 232893
(D. N. Bromage)

Established 1922. Gold medalists at all major shows including Chelsea. We stock indoor bonsai from China, Israel and Hawaii and outdoor bonsai from Japan, together with pre-bonsai material. We also stock a large variety of sundries covering this fascinating art.

Location: On A322 Bagshot Road next to White Lyon.
Opening Times: Every day 10–4. Adm free. Parties welcome. Car parking. Suitable for disabled visitors. No wheelchairs available.

BURNCOOSE NURSERIES AND GARDEN

Gwennap, Redruth, Cornwall TR16 6BJ
Telephone: (0209) 861112
(C H Williams)

The Nurseries are set in the 30-acre woodland gardens of Burncoose. Some 12 acres are laid out for nursery stock production of over 2000 varieties of ornamental trees, shrubs and herbaceous plants. Specialities include camellias, azaleas, magnolias, rhododendrons and conservatory plants. The nurseries are widely known for rarities, and for unusual plants. Full mail order catalogue £1 (posted).

Location: 2 m SE of Redruth on the main A393 Redruth to Falmouth road between the villages of Lanner and Ponsanooth.
Opening Times: Mons to Sats 9–5. Suns 2–5. Adm to Nurseries free; Gardens £1. Gardens and tea rooms open all year.

THE COTTAGE GARDEN

Langham Road, Boxted, Colchester, Essex CO4 5HU   &
Telephone: (0206) 272269

Over 400 varieties of hardy perennials, alpines, herbs, trees, shrubs, conifers and hedging. All home grown. Connoiseurs' corner, climbers, conservatory plants. Garden antiques, statuary, terracotta, stone troughs, dovecotes, weather vanes.

Location: 3 m N of Colchester.
Opening Times: Thurs, Fris, Sats 8–6. Suns 9.30–6.

BRIDGEMERE GARDEN WORLD

Nr. Nantwich, Cheshire
Telephone: (09365) 381 or 239

The Greatest Gardening Day Out in Britain. Bridgemere rolls out acre upon acre of gardens, plants, glasshouses and shop with an Egon Ronay recommended coffee house. Visit the Garden Kingdom, five acres and more than 20 styles of garden – the romance of a French rose garden, the music of waterfalls and pools, the quiet charm of shade loving plants and recreated Chelsea Flower Show gold medal winning gardens, all to give you ideas for your own garden. With seasonal displays indoors and out, we are Europe's largest garden centre. We grow more plants in more varieties than anyone else, and are constantly expanding. With events all year, Bridgemere is a garden lover's paradise.

Location: Bridgemere is on A51 between Woore and Nantwich on the Cheshire/Staffordshire/Shropshire borders. Signposted from M6 junctions 15 and 16.
Opening Times: Daily until dusk – 8 summer, 5 winter (*Closed* Christmas Day and Boxing Day). Free admission, car and coach parking. Small admission charge into Garden Kingdom (£1, OAP 50p).

THE COTTAGE HERBERY

Mill House, Boraston, Nr. Tenbury Wells, Worcestershire WR15 8LZ
Telephone: (058 479) 575
(Mrs. Kim Hurst)

Large collection of herbs, aromatics, scented foliage and cottage garden plants, a mixture of old favourites and the more unusual are for sale at the garden. All plants are organically grown. Artemisias, Menthas, Rosmarinus, Salvias, Thymus. Informative catalogue available 3 × 1st class stamps.

Location: 1m E of Tenbury Wells on A456, turn for Boraston at Peacock Inn.
Opening Times: Mid Apr to end of Sept, Suns only. May Bank Hol Mon, weekdays by appointment. Adm on Suns only for National Garden Scheme. Parties by appointment only (very welcome). Car parking. Not suitable for disabled visitors.
Refreshments: Teas served on Sundays in the Garden.

CROWN POINT NURSERY

Sevenoaks Road, Ightham, Nr. Sevenoaks TN15 0HB
Telephone: Plaxtol (0732) 810694
(G. Reuthe Ltd (Mr. E. W. Reuthe))

For Rhododendrons, Evergreen and Deciduous Azaleas, Rare and Hardy Shrubs. Eight consecutive Chelsea Gold Medals including 1990. Also winner of the Rothschild Challenge Cup for Rhododendrons in 1990. Mail order a speciality. Descriptive Catalogue available.

Location: On A25 between Seal and Ightham.
Opening Times: Mon to Sat 9–4.30. During Apr and May we also open Suns and Public Hols 10–4.30.

CRUCK COTTAGE CACTI

Cliff Road, Wrelton, Pickering, North Yorkshire YO18 8PJ &
Telephone: (0751) 72042
(Ronald J. A. Wood and Dorothy Wood)

The Nursery is in a garden setting with a display area of mature cacti. On sale is an extensive selection of cacti and succulents for beginners to advanced collectors. Small to specimen plants on sale. Regret no postal service. Personal attention by owners.

Location: On A170 between Pickering and Kirbymoorside.
Opening Times: Most days including weekends 10–6. Open all Bank Hols. Parties catered for. Coach parties by arrangement. Ample parking on grass verge. Suitable for disabled visitors.

DEACONS NURSERY H.H.

Moor View, Godshill, Isle of Wight PO38 3HW
Telephone: (0983) 840750/(0983) 522243
(Grahame and Brian Deacon – Partners)

Specialist fruit tree growers. Over 220 varieties of apples on various types of rootstocks from M27 (4ft), M26 (8ft), to M25 (18ft). Plus Pears, Peaches, Nectarines, Plums, Gages, Cherry, soft fruits and an unusual selection of Family Trees. Many special offers. Catalogue always available, 30p stamp please.

Location: Godshill – a picturesque village visited by all. Deacons Nursery is in Moor View off School Crescent (behind the only school).
Opening Times: Summer – Mon to Fri 8–4; winter – Mon to Fri 8–5, Sat 8–1.

FRUIT FOR THE CONNOISSEUR

PO Box 3, Botley, Hants SO3 2EA
Telephone: (0489) 895674

A wide variety of fruit trees; also ornamental trees and old roses. Trained fruit tree specialists. Free mail order catalogues (and nursery location) from Family Trees, PO Box 3, Botley, Hampshire SO3 2EA.

HADSPEN GARDEN

Hadspen House, Castle Cary BA7 7NG
Telephone: (0963) 50939
(Nori and Sandra Pope)

An eight acre Edwardian Garden in a sheltered situation with a unique walled garden of colourist borders, ponds and a woodland area including an ancient meadow. The many unusual plants that grow and have been developed in the garden are available in the nursery.

Location: Castle Cary
Opening Times: Mar 1 to Oct 1, Thurs, Fri, Sat, Sun and Bank Hol Mons 9–6.

THE HAMPSHIRE HYDROPONICUM

Houghton Lodge, Stockbridge, Hampshire SO20 6LQ
Telephone: (0264) 810177

A Garden of the Future in a Garden of the Past. A living exhibition of horticulture without soil. No digging, no weeding, no soil borne pests. Learn about the many applications of hydroponic gardening from window sill to space capsule. Plants, produce, publications and equipment for sale.

Location: 1½ m S of Stockbridge on minor road to Houghton.
Opening Times: Mar to Sept inclusive, Sats and Suns 10–4. Mon, Tues, and Fri 2–5, and by appointment.

HEALE GARDEN'S PLANT CENTRE AND SHOP

Middle Woodford, Salisbury, Wilts
Telephone: (0722) 73504
(Maureen Taylor)

Drive through the sheep grazed park to the Plant Centre and Gardens. Wide range of old fashioned and specie roses, and the less usual herbaceous and cottage garden plants, trees, shrubs and climbers, many of which can be seen in the garden. The garden shop sells basketware, cards, stationery, pictures, iron plant supports and garden trugs.

Location: 4 m from Salisbury, Wilton, and Stonehenge, on the Avon Valley road between A360 and A345.

THE HERB AND HEATHER CENTRE

West Haddlesey, Nr Selby YO8 8QA
Telephone: (0757) 228279

The nursery has herb, heather and conifer display gardens, and specialises in herbs and heathers. Dried herbs for flower arranging. Pick your own soft fruit, everything organically grown. Herb shop and tea room. New garden centre shop. Parking, WC.

Location: 6 m S of Selby off A19.
Opening Times: Daily (except Weds) 10–6.

JUNGLE GIANTS BAMBOO NURSERY

Plough Farm, Wigmore, Nr. Leominster, Herefordshire HR6 9UW &
Telephone: (0568) 86708
(Michael John Brisbane)

Specialising in Bamboo plants.

Location: 8 m NW of Leominster, 8 m SW of Ludlow.
Opening Times: Every day 10–10. Visitors by appointment please. Adm free. Suitable for disabled visitors. No wheelchairs available.

KAYES GARDEN NURSERY

1700 Melton Rd, Rearsby, Leicester, Leics LE7 8YR
Telephone: (0664) 424578
(Mrs Hazel Kaye)

Hardy herbaceous perennials and good selection of climbers and shrubs. The garden and nursery are in Rearsby, in the Wreake-Valley countryside of Leicestershire. Once an orchard, the one acre garden houses an extensive selection of hardy herbaceous plants. Mixed borders and a fine pergola provide year-round interest, while the nursery offers an excellent range of interesting plants.

Location: Just inside Rearsby village, N of Leicester on A607, on left-hand side approaching from Leicester.
Opening Times: Mar to Oct inclusive: Weds to Sats 10–5.30, Suns 10–12. Nov to Feb inclusive: Fris and Sats 10–5.30. *Closed* Dec 22 to Jan 31 inclusive.

KELWAYS NURSERIES LTD

Langport, Somerset TA10 9SL
Telephone: (0458) 250521

The Royal Nurseries of Langport, established in 1851, have been growers and breeders of Paeonies, Irises, Bulb and Hardy Herbaceous plants for 140 years.

Location: On Somerton Road from Langport (B31530 just 200 yards from A372).
Opening Times: Daily 10–4 and special open fields in May and June during our Paeony Festival.

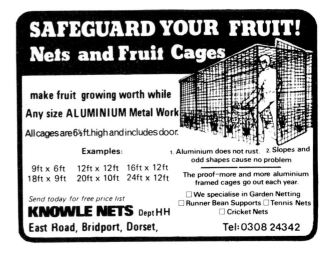

LANGLEY BOXWOOD NURSERY

Rake, Liss, Hants GU33 7JL
Telephone: Liss (0730) 894467 Fax: (0730) 894703
(Mrs. E. Braimbridge)

This small nursery in a beautiful setting specialises in box-growing, offering a chance to see together a unique range of old and new varieties, hedging, topiary, specimens and rarities. Some taxus also. Descriptive list available (5 × 1st class stamps).

Location: On A3, 3 m S of Liphook.
Opening Times: Notify by telephone first.

LEA GARDENS

Lea, Matlock, Derbyshire DE4 5GH   ♿

Telephone: (0629 534) 380 or 260

(Mr & Mrs J. Tye)

We specialise in, and grow, a wide variety of Rhododendrons, Azaleas and Kalmias. Approximately 60 varieties of Dwarf Rhodos, 120 varieties of larger growing Rhodos, 20 varieties of Yak Hybrid Rhodos, 12 varieties of Kalmias, 15 varieties of Decid Azaleas, 30 varieties of Evergreen Azaleas. These are grown outside at 600ft in Derbyshire, so are hardy and relatively compact. During our garden season we also have a large collection of Lewisias for sale.

Location: 3 m SE of Matlock between A6 and A615.

Opening Times: Mar 20 to July 31, daily 10–7; Oct, Nov: Wed, Thurs and Sun, 2–5. Also always available for plant sales by appointment. No adm charge for nursery. Car parking immediately by nursery. Suitable for disabled visitors. No wheelchairs available.

Refreshments: During spring season.

MACPENNYS OF BRANSGORE

154 Burley Road, Bransgore, Nr. Christchurch, Dorset BH23 8DB

Telephone: (0425) 72348

(T. Lowndes)

A four-acre mature woodland garden created from gravel pits in the 1950s to explore at leisure. Admission free but donations to the National Gardens Scheme welcomed. Also a large traditional nursery where many of the plants seen growing in the woodland gardens may be purchased. Many unusual plants, large herbaceous selection, camellias, rhododendrons, azaleas, heathers, conifers and general shrubs.

Location: Halfway between Christchurch and Burley on the Burley road at Bransgore. (Off A35 at Cat and Fiddle pub signed Bransgore. Turn right at Crown pub crossroads.

Opening Times: Open all year Mons to Sats 9–5, Sun 2–5. *Closed* Christmas and New Year holidays.

MEADS END BONSAI

Forewood Lane, Crowhurst, Battle, East Sussex TN33 9AB

Telephone: (0424) 83388

(Cordelia Silva)

We stock a wide variety of Bonsai trees ranging from pre-Bonsai material to mature specimens. The trees are either home-grown or imported from Japan. We also stock pots, tools, books and accessories. A 'Holiday Caring' service is offered. Kent County Show Gold Medal award winners.

Location: 1¾ m S of Battle on A2100, turn into Telham Lane. Nursery is 1.3 m from A2100 turn off.

Opening Times: 10–5 daily. *Closed* Tues. Open weekends only during Jan.

MEARE CLOSE NURSERIES LTD

Tadworth Street, Tadworth, Surrey KT20 5RQ

Telephone: (0737) 812449

(Mr D B Easton)

Herbaceous perennials including hemerocallis selections (speciality), alpines, water lilies and aquatics (speciality), shrubs, conifers, fruit trees, roses, climbing plants. Established under same ownership 1938.

Location: ¼ m from A217 at Tadworth.

Opening Times: Mons to Sats 9–5. *Closed* 1–2.15 (lunch break). Suns & Bank Holidays 10.30–1.

MILLAIS NURSERIES

Crosswater Lane, Churt, Farnham, Surrey GU10 2JN

Telephone: Frensham (025 125) 2698

(David Millais)

MILLAIS NURSERIES

RHODODENDRONS
AZALEAS

CROSSWATER LANE, CHURT, FARNHAM, SURREY GU10 2JN
FRENSHAM (025 125) 2698

Growers of one of the finest ranges of Rhododendrons and Azaleas in the country, including many rare species from the Himalayas, and a good selection of new American hybrids. Specialist advice. Mail Order Catalogue available £1. Display garden also open (see Crosswater Farm).

Location: Farnham/Haslemere 6 m. From A287 turn E into Jumps Road ½ m N of Churt village centre. After ¼ m, turn into Crosswater Lane, and follow Nursery signs.

Opening Times: Tues to Sats 10–1, 2–5. Also daily in May and early June.

PERHILL NURSERIES

Worcester Road, Great Witley, Worcestershire WR6 6JT   ♿

Telephone: (0299) 896329

(Baker Straw Partnership)

Specialist growers of 1,700 varieties of alpines, herbs and border perennials. Many rare and unusual. Specialities include penstemons, salvias, osteospermums, dianthus, alpine phlox, alliums, campanulas, thymes, helianthemums, diascias and lavenders.

Location: 10 m NW of Worcester on main Tenbury Wells Road (A443).

Opening Times: Every day except Christmas and Boxing Day and New Year's Day, Mon to Sat 9–6, Sun 9–5. Car parking. Suitable for disabled visitors.

PERRYHILL NURSERIES

Hartfield, Sussex TN7 4JP

Telephone: (0892) 770377. Fax: (0892) 770929

(Mrs S M Gemmell)

The Plant Centre for the discerning gardener, with the widest range of plants in the South East of England. Old fashioned and shrub roses a speciality, also herbaceous plants. Trees, shrubs, rhododendrons, alpines, fruit trees and bushes, bedding plants in season. No mail order. Catalogues £1.40 inc. postage.

Location: 1 m N of Hartfield on B2026.

Opening Times: Mar to Oct: 9–5. Nov to Feb: 9–4.30. Seven days a week.

PERRY'S PLANTS, RIVER GARDENS

Sleights, Nr. Whitby

Beautiful riverside tea gardens where all the plants for sale can be seen growing. Specialising in lavatera, malvacea, anthemis, euphorbias, osteospermum, uncommon hardy and conservatory plants.

Location: 2 m W of Whitby on the B1410 just off the A169.

Opening Times: Easter to end of Oct: Daily 10–5.

Refreshments: Licensed cafe.

PLANTS FROM A COUNTRY GARDEN

Wotton Road, Ludgershall, Aylesbury, Buckinghamshire

Telephone: (0844) 237415

(Mr and Mrs D. A. Tolman)

A pleasantly secluded nursery situated in unspoilt countryside and offering one of the widest ranges of traditional cottage garden plants in the country. Over 1,200 different varieties including a huge range of old fashioned pinks and violets, rare geraniums, asters, foxgloves, native wildflowers and herbs and many other uncommon hardy perennials and shrubs. Plants can be seen growing in display beds. The owners' nearby enchanting cottage garden is open several times a year – see Garden entry for The Thatched Cottage, Duck Lane, Ludgershall, Bucks. A descriptive catalogue is available from this address for £1 or 4 × 1st class stamps.

Location: 2 m S of A41 between Bicester and Aylesbury, leaving A41 at Kingswood or ¾ m from Ludgershall in the direction of Wotton.

Opening Times: Mar 1 to Oct 31, Wed to Sun inclusive 10–6. Also open 10–6 on Bank Hols. Car parking at nursery. Partially suitable for disabled visitors.

Refreshments: Teas are available on days when the Garden at the Thatched Cottage, Duck Lane, Ludgershall is open.

THE ROGER PLANT CENTRE

Malton Road, Pickering, North Yorkshire

A wide range of hardy garden plants, shrubs, fruit and ornamental trees grown on own farm. Six acres of roses in bloom from July to October. Co-holders of the National Erodium Collection. 60 page descriptive mail order catalogue 75p.

Location: Malton Road A169.

Opening Times: Mons to Sats 9–5. Suns 1–5. Bank Holidays 10.30–5. *Closed* Christmas Day to Jan 2. Ample parking.

RYTON GARDENS

National Centre for Organic Gardening, Ryton on Dunsmore, Coventry CV8 3LG
Telephone: (0203) 303517, Fax: (0203) 639229

Demonstration gardens cultivated naturally, without the use of pesticides and artificial fertilisers. Speciality vegetables, fruit, herbs, flowers, shrubs, trees, lake, wildlife, bees, play area, picnic benches. Home of Channel 4's "All Muck and Magic?".

Location: We are on the B4029 which leads north from the A45 to Wolston, 5 m SE of Coventry. Look for the brown signposts to Ryton Gardens.

SAMARÈS HERBS-A-PLENTY

Samarès Manor, St. Clement, Jersey JE2 6QW
Telephone: (0534) 70551
(Richard Adams, Lyn Le Boutillier)

Specialist Herb and Hardy Perennial Nursery situated in the grounds of Samarès Manor. Extensive range of culinary, fragrant and medicinal herbs including many variegated and ornamental forms. Specialist range of hardy perennials including plants for shade, ground cover and wet conditions. Availability list on request. Herb shop, craft centre, farm animals, herb gardens, tours of Manor.

Location: 2 m E of St. Helier on the St. Clements Inner Road.
Opening Times: Daily 10–5 Apr to Oct. Adm £2.50, Chld £1, OAPs £1.75. Special group rates.
Refreshments: Tea garden and restaurant specialising in the vegetarian and traditional Jersey cooking.

SEAFORDE NURSERY AND BUTTERFLY HOUSE

Seaforde, Downpatrick, Down
Telephone: Seaforde (039687) 225
(Patrick Forde)

Over 600 trees and shrubs, container grown. Many Camellias and Rhododendrons. National collections of E. ucryphius. Tropical Butterfly House with hundreds of free flying butterflies.

Location: On A24 Ballynahinch to Belfast Road.
Opening Times: Easter to end Sept: Mon to Sat 10–5; Sun 2–6. Nursery only: Sept to Easter, 10–5.
Refreshments: Tea rooms.

SPINNERS

Boldre, Lymington, Hants SO41 5QE
Telephone: (0590) 673347
(P. Chappell)

As wide a selection here (excluding conifers, heathers and roses) of rare and less common hardy plants, trees and shrubs for immediate sale as anywhere in the U.K. Just one example: 90 different Magnolias.

Location: 1½ m N of Lymington, 1 m off A337.
Opening Times: Nursery: All year daily 9–dusk except Christmas Day and Boxing Day. Gardens: Mid Apr to Sept 1, 10–6. Adm to Gardens: £1.

STAPELEY WATER GARDENS LTD

London Road, Stapeley, Nantwich, Cheshire CW5 7LH
Telephone: Gdn Centre (0270) 623868; The Palms (0270) 628628
(Barbara Dobbins)

World's largest water garden centre, wide range of garden sundries, pot plants, trees & shrubs, UK's largest number of varieties of acers, conifers and primulas for sale. Holder of the National Collection of Waterlilies (Nymphaea), 140 varieties of Tropical and Hardy Waterlilies as well as widest range of Aquatic and Moisture loving plants. Display gardens and pools. Free entry and parking. Also visit the Palms Tropical Oasis for a small fee. 1⅓ acre tropical and Mediterranean garden extravaganza, with rare & exotic 30ft palms and flowering plants, sharks, piranhas, pythons, sting rays, fountains & waterfalls. Full disabled facilities. No dogs. Groups catered for.

Location: Signposted – 10 mins off the M6 at Junction 16. 1 m S of Nantwich on the A51 to Stone.
Opening Times: *Garden Centre* Winter: weekdays 9–5; Sat/Sun, Bank Hols 10–6. Summer: weekdays 9–6; Sat/Sun, Bank Hols 10–7. *The Palms Tropical Oasis* Winter: weekdays 10–5; Sat/Sun, Bank Hols 10–6. Summer: weekdays 10–6; Sat/Sun, Bank Hols 10–7.
Refreshments: Restaurant and Cafes.

TREHANE CAMELLIA NURSERY

Stapehill Road, Hampreston, Nr. Wimborne, Dorset BH21 7NE
Telephone: (0202) 873490
(Miss Jennifer Trehane)

Britain's leading Specialists. Scented Sasanquas, rare Species from China and Japan, huge Reticulatas, extra hardy Williamsii varieties, specially selected free-flowering Japonicas. Also Evergreen Azaleas, Pieris, Magnolias, Blueberries. All sizes. Visitors most welcome. Mail Order and Export. Catalogue/Handbook £2.

Opening Times: All year: weekdays 9–4 and weekends in spring.

WEBBS OF WYCHBOLD

Wychbold, Droitwich WR9 0DG
Telephone: (0527) 861777, Fax: (0527) 861284

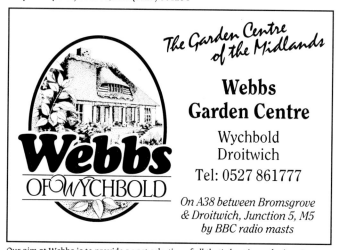

Our aim at Webbs is to provide a vast selection of all that's best in gardening. Browse at your leisure amongst thousands of plants from Azaleas to Yucca's grown in our 50-acre nursery, then perhaps relax in the popular Thatch Restaurant that specialises in good, wholesome, appetising food. Houseplants, Seeds, Bulbs, Aquatics, Garden Furniture, Books, Cards, Gifts, Greenhouses, Conservatories, Fencing, Paving and Sundries galore, it's all here for dedicated and occasional gardeners alike. Winners of the first ever Garden Centre Association award for "Overall Excellence" in 1990 and runners-up as "Garden Centre of 1991" by the magazine Retail Horticulture. Customers matter at Webbs where our emphasis is on quality and friendly service and where expert advice is always available.

Location: On A38 between Bromsgrove and Droitwich, 1 m from junction 5 of the M5 motorway and opposite the well-known landmark of the BBC radio masts.
Opening Times: Mar to Nov, Mon to Sat 9–5.45; Dec to Feb, Mon to Sat 9–5. Mar to Nov, Wed 9.30–5.45; Dec to Feb, Wed 9.30–5. Mar to Nov, Sun 10–5; Dec to Feb, Sun 10–5. Bank Hols 10–5. Late night opening from late Mar until early autumn until 8 on Weds, Thurs and Fris. Parking for 400 cars, play area and disabled facilities.

WILD SEEDS

Branas, Llandderfel, Gwynedd LL23 7RF
(Mike Thorne)

Wildflower seeds, plants and bulbs. Free Catalogue.

WYCHWOOD CARP FARM

Farnham Road, Odiham, Basingstoke, Hampshire RG25 1HS
Telephone: (0256) 702800
(Reg, Ann and Clair Henley)

The specialist producers of naturally grown water lilies, water iris, marginal plants, marsh plants, bog primulas and ensata irises. The only commercial producers of hardy water lily seed plus holders of a National Collection of Hardy Water Lilies. Free Mail Order Catalogue available on request with s.a.e.

Location: 3 m from M3 intersection 5 or 4 m from A30. 1½ m E of Odiham Village on A287.
Opening Times: Every day 10–6, open Bank Hols. *Closed* Thursdays. Adm free. Car parking available on premises. Unsuitable for disabled.

Index to Houses, Castles and Gardens

NOTES

NOTES

Page Index

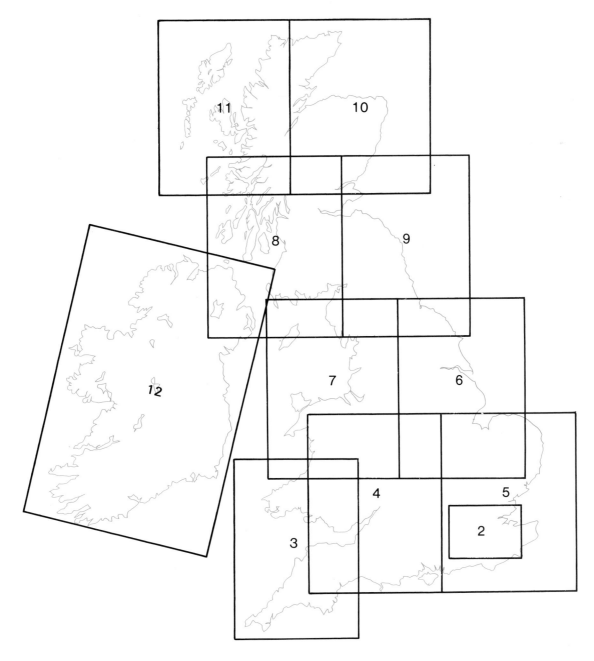

Legend

═══	Motorway	🏠	**House with or without garden**
⬥	Motorway Intersections	🏰	**Castle with or without garden**
──	Primary route	❋	**Garden**
──	Major Roads	⊞	**Property in the care of English Heritage** *(see supplement)*
			Property in the care of the National Trust

20	10	0	20	40	60	km

	10	0	10	20	30	miles

1

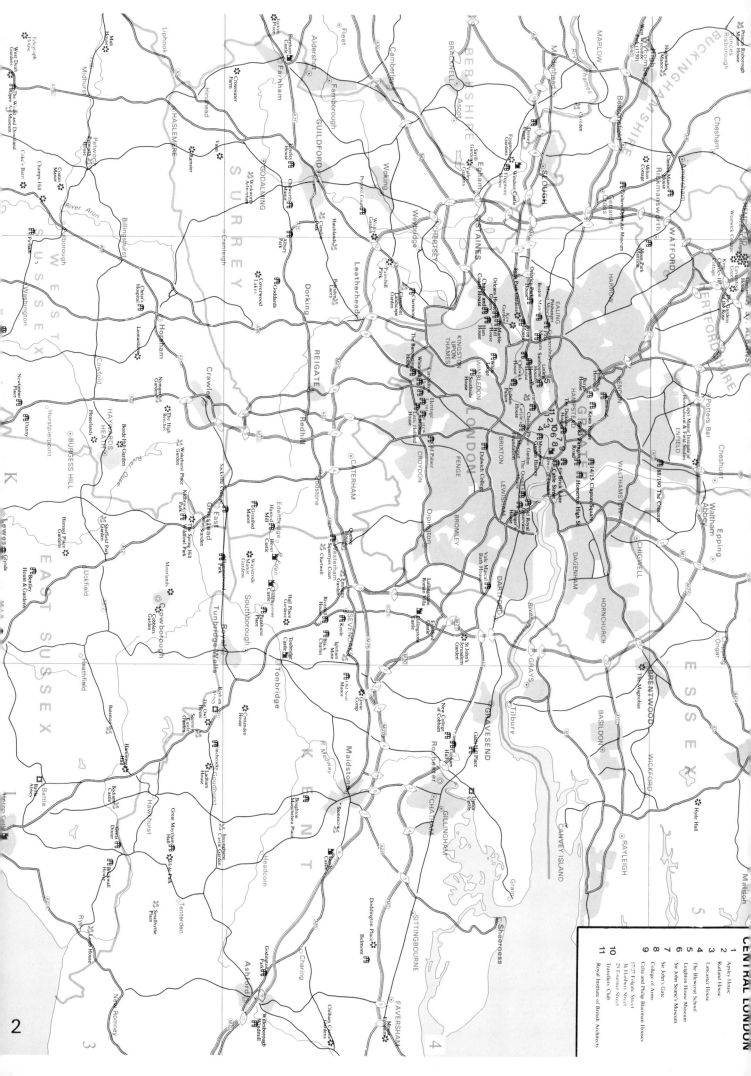

See Inset
on Page 5

See Inset on Page 2

BRISTOL AND BATH

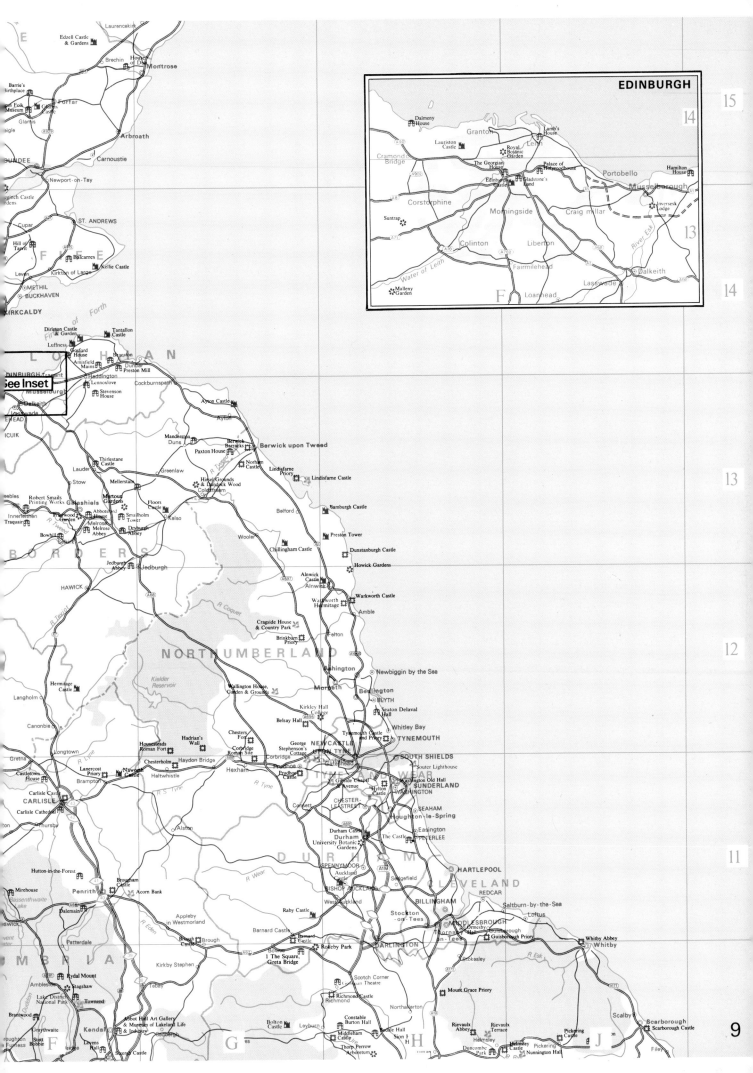

EDINBURGH

9

Durness
Eriboll
Port of Ness
Carloway
Stornoway   Portnaguran
Loch Langavat   Balallan
Loch Erisol
Lochinver   Inchnadamph
Loch Shin
R Cassley
Tarbert
Ullapool
THE MINCH   R Carron
Rodel
Inverewe
Poolewe
Gairloch   Loch Maree
HIGHLAND
Tigharry   Lochmaddy
Staffin
Uig   Kinlochewe   Achnasheen
R Meig
Contin
Creagorry
Shieldaig   R Orrin
Dunvegan Castle
Dunvegan   R Farrar
Portree
Bracadale   Cannich
Sligachan   Kyle of Lochalsh   Urquhart Castle
Eilean Donan
Castle
Broadford
Lochboisdale
SEA
Ardvasar   Invermor
Invergarry
Mallaig
Loch Arkaig   Loch Lochy
OF
Arisaig
Glenfinnan   Spean Bridge
THE
Loch Shiel   Loch Lochy
Corpach   Fort William
HEBRIDES
Acharacle
Corran   Kinlochleven
Loch Sunart   Glencoe
Tobermory   Loch Linnhe
Ardtornish   Portnacroish
Lochaline
Salen   Bridge of Orchy
Torosay Castle   Connel
Craignure   and Gardens   Oban   Tyndrum
Taynuilt
Fionnphort   Crianlarich
Bunessan
KilninveK   R Awe

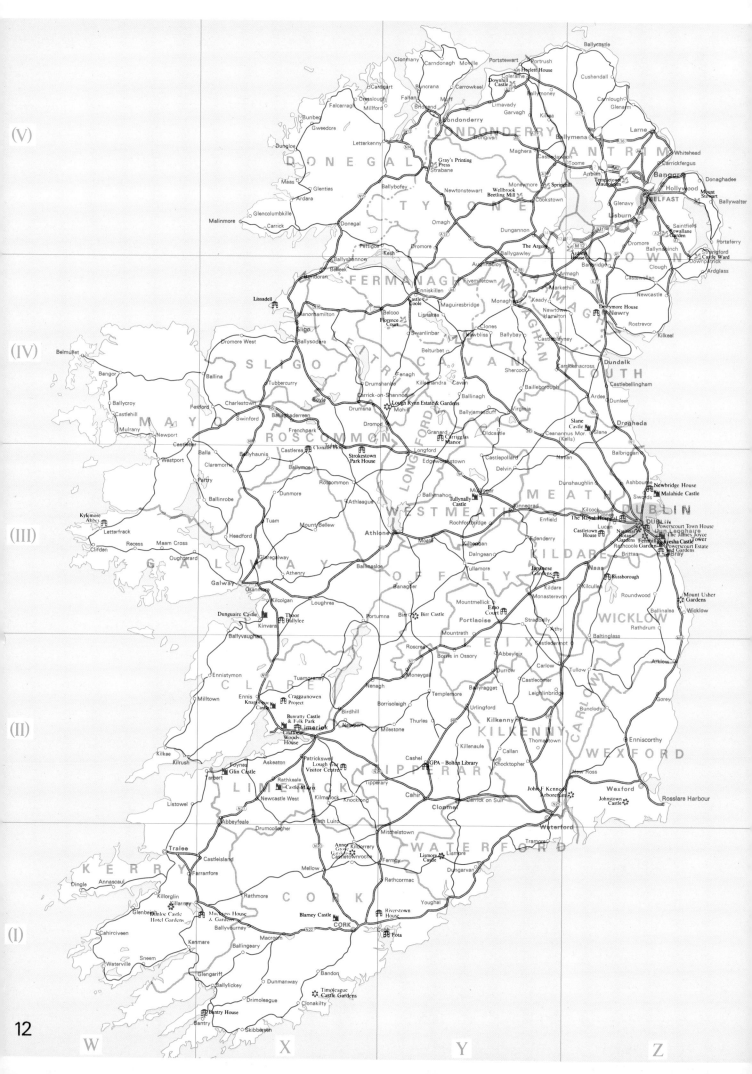

NOTES

NOTES

NOTES

NOTES

Phototypeset by Composing Operations Limited, Tunbridge Wells, Kent. Printed by Boekhoven Bosch, Utrecht, Holland